THE PRINCIPALSHIP

NEW ROLES IN A PROFESSIONAL LEARNING COMMUNITY

THE PRINCIPALSHIP

NEW ROLES IN A PROFESSIONAL LEARNING COMMUNITY

L. Joseph Matthews
Brigham Young University

Gary M. Crow
Indiana University

Allyn & Bacon
Boston Columbus Indianapolis New York San Francisco Upper Saddle River
Amsterdam Cape Town Dubai London Madrid Milan Munich Paris Montreal Toronto
Delhi Mexico City Sao Paulo Sydney Hong Kong Seoul Singapore Taipei Tokyo

Editor in Chief: Jeffery W. Johnston
Executive Editor and Publisher: Stephen D. Dragin
Editorial Assistant: Anne Whittaker
Director of Marketing: Quinn Perkson
Project Manager: Holly Shufeldt
Art Director: Jayne Conte
Cover Designer: Bruce Kenselaar
Cover Photo: Getty, Inc.
Full-Service Project Management: Aparna Yellai, GGS Higher Education Resources, PMG
Printer/Binder: Hamilton Printing Co.
Cover Printer: Lehigh-Phoenix Color
Text Font: Palatino

Credits and acknowledgments borrowed from other sources and reproduced, with permission, in this textbook appear on appropriate pages within text.

Many of the designations by manufacturers and seller to distinguish their products are claimed as trademarks. Where those designations appear in this book, and the publisher was aware of a trademark claim, the designations have been printed in initial caps or all caps.

Library of Congress Cataloging-in-Publication Data

Matthews, L. Joseph
   The principalship : new roles in a professional learning community / L. Joseph Matthews, Gary M. Crow. — 1st ed.
     p. cm.
   Includes bibliographical references and index.
   ISBN-13: 978-0-205-54567-4
   ISBN-10: 0-205-54567-X
  1. School principals—United States. 2. Educational leadership—United States. I. Crow, Gary Monroe, 1947- II. Title.
   LB2831.92.M38 2010
   371.2'012—dc22

                                                            2009027693

10 9 8 7 6 5 4

Allyn & Bacon
is an imprint of

www.pearsonhighered.com

ISBN 10: 0-205-54567-X
ISBN 13: 978-0-205-54567-4

Dedication

This book is dedicated to Aislyn, Zion, Keaka, Lani, and Jason, our grandchildren and all the other grandchildren—may you always find school to be a caring community that stimulates your inquiry and creativity, that invigorates your learning, and that engages your contributions to society.

CONTENTS

Preface   xvii

Acknowledgment   xix

About the Authors   xxi

Chapter 1   New Conceptions of the Principalship in a Professional Learning Community   1

Introduction   2

   Role Conceptions   3

Principalship and Leadership   5

   The Definition of Leadership   5

Professional Learning Community   8

Principals and Professional Learning Community in a Global, Knowledge Society   10

Learning About Leadership   11

   Principal Leadership in Practice   12

Eight Role Conceptions for the Principalship   13

   Principal as Learner   14

   Principal as Culture Builder   14

   Principal as Advocate   14

   Principal as Leader   15

   Principal as Mentor   15

   Principal as Supervisor   15

   Principal as Manager   16

   Principal as Politician   16

      Conclusion   16   •   Activities   17   •   Self-Reflection Activities   17   •   Peer Reflection Activities   17   •   Course Activities   17   •   Websites   17

Chapter 2   Historical View of the Principal's Role   18

Introduction   19

Origin of the Principalship   20

Origin of the Assistant Principal Role   21

Women and Minorities in the Principalship   22

   Interacting Elements That Have Influenced the Principal's Role   26

   Changing Social Demographics of Cities and Schools   26

   Academic Study and State Licensure Requirements   27

Professional Associations   28

Practice of School Leaders   29

Conceptual Frameworks Influencing the Principalship Role   30

Moral and Ethical Leadership   30

Social and Community Leadership   32

Instructional Leadership   34

School Reform and Implications to the Role of School Principals   35

Contemporary Conditions and Implications   37

*Conclusion   39   •   Activities   40   •   Self-Reflection
Activities   40   •   Peer Reflection Activities   40   •
Course Activities   40   •   Websites   40*

Chapter 3   Professional Learning Communities as School Reform   41

Introduction   43

Educational Reform and Professional Learning Communities   43

Understanding Community   45

Various Models of a Professional Learning Community   46

Elements in a Professional Learning Community   46

The Case for Professional Learning Communities   48

Barriers to the Development of Professional Learning
Communities   50

The Principal's Role in Developing a Professional Learning
Community in a School   51

The Principal's Focus on Student Learning   53

Principal and Assistant Principal Functions in Developing and
Facilitating Professional Learning Communities   54

*Conclusion   55   •   Activities   56   •   Self-Reflection
Activities   56   •   Peer Reflection Activities   56   •
Course Activities   56   •   Websites   56*

Chapter 4   The Principal as Learner   57

Introduction   59

Learning: Transmission Versus Construction   60

The Traditional Conception of Learning   60

The Constructivist Conception of Learning   61

Adult Learning   63

Principal as Learner   65

Importance of Learning in a Knowledge Society   65

Four Components of Principal as Learner   67

Principal as Facilitator: Supporting a Professional Learning Community
to Enhance Learning Capacity   74

Schools as Learning Organizations   75

Principal's Role in Facilitating Learning Organizations   78

The Roles of the Assistant Principal and Teacher Leaders for Building and Cultivating Learning Capacity   80

Principal's Role with Teacher Leaders   82

Conclusion   83   •   Activities   83   •   Self-Reflection Activities   83   •   Peer Reflection Activities   83   •   Course Activities   84   •   Websites   84

Chapter 5   Principal as Culture Builder   85

Introduction   86

A Cultural Perspective for Learning in Community   87

Defining School Culture   87

Understanding a School's Existing Culture   89

Toxic Cultures   90

Outcomes of Strong School Cultures   91

Principal Leadership in Creating, Maintaining, and Changing Culture Creating School Culture   92

Maintaining School Culture   93

Changing School Culture   94

The Principal Facilitating Others in Understanding and Developing Culture   97

Facilitating Internal Veterans in Understanding and Developing Culture   98

Facilitating Newcomers in Understanding and Developing Culture   100

Facilitating External Constituents in Understanding and Developing Culture   101

Facilitating a Culture Change   101

Leadership Teams as Culture-Builders   102

Conclusion   103   •   Activities   103   •   Self-Reflection Activities   103   •   Peer Reflection Activities   103   •   Course Activities   103   •   Websites   103

Chapter 6   Principal as Advocate   104

Introduction   106

Social Justice as a Basis for Advocacy   108

Components of Social Justice   109

Social Justice in a PLC   110

Leadership as Transformative   110

Definition and Elements of Advocacy   111

The Moral Criterion for Advocacy   111

The Legal Criterion for Advocacy   113

The Thoughtfulness Criterion for Advocacy   114

Principals and Social Justice   115

Your Own Identity Within a Social Justice Context   115

Barriers to the Role Within a Social Justice Context   116

Priorities Within a Social Justice Context   116

Principal as Advocate   117

Advocate for the Whole Child and for All Students   117

Racial, Ethnic, and Cultural Diversity   120

Religious Diversity   122

Language Diversity   122

Poverty and Social Class   124

Gender   125

Sexual Orientation   125

Students with Special Needs   126

Gifted and Talented Students   127

Students Placed At-Risk   128

Being an Advocate for the School   129

Multicultural Education Programs   129

Bilingual Education   130

Special Education   131

Gifted and Talented Programs   133

Title I   134

Alternative Education Programs   135

Advocate for the Community   136

Principal as Facilitator of Others' Advocacy   137

*Conclusion   139   •   Activities   139   •   Self-Reflection
Activities   139   •   Peer Reflection Activities   139   •
Course Activities   140   •   Websites   140*

**Chapter 7   Becoming a Leader in a Professional Learning
Community   141**

Introduction   143

The Nature of Principal Leadership   143

Leadership from External Sources   143

Leadership from Internal Sources   145

Principal Leadership   146

Leadership Literature   146

Popular Literature   146

Professional Literature   147

Scholarly Literature   147

Research on Leadership   149

Trait Approaches   149

Behavior Approaches   150

Contingency Approaches   152

Leadership as a Relationship   153

Leadership as an Organizational Feature   153

Moral Leadership   154

How Useful Is Research on Leadership?   155

The Purpose of Principal Leadership   156

Defining Significant School Change and Reform   156

Creating a Collective Vision   158

Principal Leadership in Vision Building   158

The Principal's Roles as Visionary Leader   160

The Dark Side of Visions   161

Challenges of Vision Building   162

Communicating the Vision   162

Principal as Facilitator of Leadership in Others   164

Teacher Empowerment   164

Facilitating Others in Vision Building   165

Facilitating Others in Collaboration   167

Approaches to Collaborative Decision Making   168

Collaborative Teaming   170

Mediating Conflict   171

Problems with Collaboration   173

Conclusion   174   •   Activities   175   •   Self-Reflection
Activities   175   •   Peer Reflection Activities   175   •
Course Activities   175   •   Websites   175

Chapter 8   The Principal as Mentor   176

Introduction   177

Introduction to Mentoring   178

The Nature of Mentoring   178

Mentoring Roles and Functions   180

Participants of Mentoring   181

Content of Mentoring   182

Processes of Mentoring   183

Benefits and Pitfalls of Mentoring   184

Benefits of Mentoring   184

Pitfalls of Mentoring   184

The Principal's Role in Mentoring   185

Mentoring New Teachers   185

Mentoring New Teachers in Professional Development   186

Reflective Mentoring   190

Mentoring New Teachers in Psychosocial Development   192

Mentoring New Teachers in Career Development   194

The Principal as Facilitator of Mentoring for New Teachers   196

Selecting and Matching Teachers to Be Mentors:
Two Perspectives   198

Mentor Training   199

Providing Support for Peer Mentoring   200

Mentoring Veteran Teachers   201

Mentoring Teacher Teams   203

The Principal as Facilitator of Mentoring of Veteran Teachers   204

The Principal as Mentor of Students   205

Conclusion   206   •   Activities   207   •   Self-Reflection
Activities   207   •   Peer Reflection Activities   207   •
Course Activities   207   •   Websites   207

Chapter 9   Principal as Supervisor   208

Introduction   209

Traditional Role of Principal as Supervisor   210

Historical Overview of the Supervisor's Role   211

Elements of the Traditional Role of Principal as Supervisor   211

Traditional Supervisory Role of the Assistant Principal   213

The Principal's Role in Direct Supervision: An Innovative
Conception   214

Overview of the Innovative Role of Supervisor   214

Establishing a System of Accountability   215

Recruiting, Selecting, and Retaining Capable and Committed
Educators   216

Recruiting and Selecting Teachers   216

Retaining Qualified Teachers   219

Promoting Educator Growth   220

Fostering Teacher Practical Knowledge   220

Reflection   220

Inquiry   221

Establishing Trust   226

Evaluating Educational Results   227

The Regular Collection and Analysis of Student
Performance Data   231

The Principal's Role as Facilitator of Supervision   232

Why Supervision Should Be Shared   233

Elements of the Principal's Role as Facilitator of Supervision   234

Establishing a System of Accountability   234

Recruiting, Selecting, and Retaining Capable and Committed
Educators   234

Promoting Educator Growth   236

Building Trust with the Leadership Team   236

Evaluating Educational Results   237

*Conclusion   238   •   Activities   239   •   Self-Reflection
Activities   239   •   Peer Reflection Activities   239   •
Course Activities   239   •   Websites   239*

Chapter 10   Principal as Manager   240

Introduction   241

The Principalship and Management Roots   242

Managing the Unexpected in a PLC   244

Principal's Direct Role in Managing the Unexpected   246

Supporting   246

Information   250

Direct Role in Implementing the PLC   252

Planning   252

Taking Action   253

Evaluating and Assessing   254

Managing through Technology   255

The Principal as Facilitator of Others in Management of a PLC   256

Facilitating Support   257

Facilitating Others in Planning and Taking Action   261

Facilitating Others in Evaluating and Assessing   262

Institutionalizing a PLC   263

*Conclusion   264   •   Activities   264   •   Self-Reflection
Activities   264   •   Peer Reflection Activities   264   •
Course Activities   264   •   Websites   264*

Chapter 11   Principal as Politician   265

Introduction   267

Thinking Politically   268

Principal as Politician In the Society   270

Schools as Political Systems   271

Schools as Civil Societies   272

Schools as Democratic Institutions   272

Role of Principal as Politician in Society   274

Principal as Politician in the Community   276

Views of School-Community Relationships   277

Role of Principal as Politician in the Community   278

Principal as Politician In the District   280

Role of Principal as Politician in the District   281

Principal as Politician In the School   282

Role of Principal as Politician in the School   282

Assistant Principals as Politicians   285

The Principal as Facilitator of Others as Politicians   286

In the Society   286

In the Community   287

In the District   288

In the School   288

Building Social Capital in Professional Learning Communities   289

Students   290

Teachers   290

*Conclusion   291   •   Activities   291   •   Self-Reflection
Activities   291   •   Peer Reflection Activities   291   •
Course Activities   291   •   Websites   291*

**Chapter 12   Becoming an Innovative Principal in a Professional
Learning Community   292**

Introduction   293

Socialization: Learning a New Role   294

Nature of Socialization   295

Sources of Socialization   297

Stages of Socialization   299

Methods of Socialization   301

Individual Influences   303

Outcomes of Socialization   304

Focus of Socialization Outcomes   304

Types of Outcomes   305

Becoming a New Assistant Principal   306

Distinctive Features of the Socialization of Assistant Principals   307

Becoming a New Principal   314

Content of Socialization   314

Sources of Socialization   315

Stages of Socialization   318

Methods of Socialization   321

Outcomes of Socialization   323

Becoming an Innovative Midcareer Principal   324

Unique Features of Midcareer Socialization   325

Learning to Be an Innovative Principal at Midcareer   326

*Conclusion   328   •   Activities   328   •   Self-Reflection
Activities   328   •   Peer Reflection Activities   329   •
Course Activities   329   •   Websites   329*

Chapter 13   Looking to the Future as a Principal   330

Introduction   331

Societal Trends   332

Future Scenarios for the Principalship and Schools   334

*Conclusion   336   •   Activities   337   •   Self-Reflection
Activities   337   •   Peer Reflection Activities   337   •
Course Activities   337   •   Websites   337*

References   339
Index   369

PREFACE

Changing student populations, rapidly expanding knowledge, increasing accountability requirements, federal and state policy demands, competition from other educational entities, and escalating expectations that schools provide more services are the new conditions facing principals and assistant principals. This book will help aspiring school and practicing leaders to bridge the gap from traditional notions of the principal's role to innovative conceptions that respond to these changing conditions and demands through the reform strategy of professional learning communities.

Learning is a major topic of this book—the learning of principals, the learning of other professionals in the school, and especially the learning of all students in the school. School improvement to increase student learning requires principals and assistant principals to reconceptualize their roles.

Instead of viewing your role as a principal or assistant principal as a cluster of skills and competencies, we will encourage you to see your role as a series of images or conceptions. Instead of viewing the principal's role as that of a technician who has a toolkit to fix problems, we view the principal's role as that of a professional who responds to messy issues and situations; who has to have good judgment, imagination, and creativity to respond to students' needs; and who has to have passion and commitment to ensure that all students learn and develop. You are preparing for a dynamic, professional role that will require your intellect, your commitment, your emotions, your interpersonal abilities, and your creativity.

To encourage you to think of yourself as a professional, we identify eight role conceptions—learner, culture builder, advocate, leader, mentor, supervisor, manager, and politician. In each case, we will help you see the principal's role not only in a direct way but also in a facilitative way. Being proactive toward learning for all students and doing this in the context of a complex, changing knowledge society means that you cannot be the only source of leadership for learning. You will play an important role in creating a professional learning community in which assistant principals, teachers, students, parents, and community members all serve leadership functions in the school. In doing so, you will expand the learning and leadership capacities of a school.

This book will provide the theory, research, and practical suggestions to help you visualize yourself as a principal in these various ways. We open each chapter with a realistic vignette based on real school situations and principal actions to ground your reading in the complexities of daily life in schools. Professional dilemmas are presented to encourage you to think outside the box and realize that your imagination and creativity are critical in responding to the issues of contemporary schools. We present the latest thinking on these roles and how you can enact them in ways that support learning and the creation of a professional learning community. We end each chapter with activities for you to do alone, with a colleague, and in the course. These activities will not only help you to bridge your readings with the everyday activities of principals, but encourage you to reflect on yours and others' practices. To be an innovative principal you will need to constantly reflect on your actions.

We welcome you to this journey toward the principalship—toward becoming a professional who is knowledgeable, skillful, imaginative, and innovative for the benefit of all students and all members of the professional learning community. You will find it an exciting journey, and we hope this book with assist you on the journey.

ACKNOWLEDGMENTS

We wish to acknowledge several people who have been helpful in bringing this book to publication. We first want to thank our faculty colleagues at Brigham Young University (BYU), University of Utah, Florida State University, and Indiana University for their support and helpful suggestions that have contributed in many ways to ideas found in this book. Especially are we indebted to our colleague Ellen Williams, BYU, for her friendship, inspiration, and vision in creating learning communities and her understanding of how children develop and learn. Other colleagues have also been inspiring and motivating: Merrell Hansen, Cliff Mayes, Buddy Richards, and Sterling Hilton (BYU).

Two graduate assistants were especially helpful. Courtney Stewart (BYU) who became known as the "gopher" and "cabana boy" because of his untiring service in running, messaging, and managing the research. Colleen Chestnut (IU) for her work in locating lost references and identifying valuable Web sites in the final stages of editing the book. Their work was always timely, accurate, and creative! Other graduate assistants were also very helpful: Kim Berry and Jian Gao located references and databases in the development of the book. We appreciate all of our graduate students in our courses and in the profession of education who have posed stimulating questions, responded to course activities, and influenced our thinking about the principalship. We wish you the best in your new careers.

We appreciate the work of several Pearson (Allyn & Bacon) staff members, including Arnis Burvikovs, our first editor who helped us develop the ideas for this book; Anne Whittaker, editorial assistant; and Steve Dragin, our final editor who kept us on task and contributed to the quality of the book. We would also like to thank the reviewers who provided comments: John C. Daresh, University of Texas at El Paso; Mary Harris-John, Marshall University; James E. Lyons, University of North Carolina at Charlotte; Richard A. Simon, (SUNY) Stony Brook University; Bill Thornton, University of Nevada; Mary Lou Yeatts, Murray State University; and Judith Zimmerman, Bowling Green State University.

Our wives, as always, have been extremely supportive of our work, helping us focus but pulling us away when we most needed a break. Thanks Sue and Judy for your love and devotion.

ABOUT THE AUTHORS

Joseph Matthews is Associate Professor in the Department of Educational Leadership and Foundations at Brigham Young University. Dr. Matthews has taught for two decades in principalship courses. His writing has appeared in many publications as well as in three books in which he coauthored: *Being and Becoming a Principal: Role Conceptions for Contemporary Principals and Assistant Principals* (2003, Allyn & Bacon); *Leadership: A Relevant and Realistic Role for Principals* (1996, Eye on Education); and *Finding Ones Way: How Mentoring Can Lead to Dynamic Leadership* (1998, Corwin Press). He has served as a high school teacher and principal in three different states. He also served on the faculty at the University of Utah.

Gary M. Crow is Professor in the Department of Educational Leadership and Policy Studies at Indiana University (USA). Previously he held faculty and department chair positions at Florida State University and University of Utah, and as a faculty member at Louisiana State University and Bank Street College of Education (NYC). He also was a visiting faculty member at the University of Reading (UK). His research interests include work socialization of school site leaders, school leadership and school reform. Crow is currently conducting research on successful school principals and professional identity of school leaders in reform contexts. His most recent book is *Being and Becoming a Principal: Role Conceptions of Contemporary Principals and Assistant Principals* (with Matthews, 2003, Allyn & Bacon). In addition, he and J. Matthews have coauthored *Finding One's Way: How Mentoring Can Lead to Dynamic Leadership* (1998, Corwin Press) and *Leadership: A Relevant and Realistic Role for Principals* (1996, Eye on Education). He is also a coeditor of the *International Handbook on the Preparation and Development of School Leaders* (2008) and the *Handbook of Research on Leadership Education* (in press). Articles authored by Crow have appeared in *Educational Administration Quarterly, Educational Management, Administration and Leadership, Journal of Educational Administration, and American Educational Research Journal.* Crow is a past president of the University Council for Educational Administration and founding editor of the *UCEA Journal of Cases in Educational Leadership.*

CHAPTER 1

New Conceptions of the Principalship in a Professional Learning Community

Vignette

Tomorrow is the first day for teachers at Morning Heights Junior High School and the first formal introduction of Monica Brown, the new principal. As Monica sat in her office preparing for the meeting and upcoming year, all the advice she had been given over the years flooded into her mind. She remembered her university advisor who reminded her that the principalship is a great opportunity to be an innovative leader, guiding the school's vision toward learning for all students. She also thought back to her internship experience and her mentor who cautioned about trying to accomplish too much in the first one hundred days and the importance of building political coalitions with teachers and parents. More recently, some of the parents had visited her and, while warmly welcoming her to the school, made sure she knew that what got the last principal in trouble was trying those "hair-brained" university ideas about reform when he just needed to be a good manager, running the school efficiently. The words of her superintendent, when he called to inform her of her appointment, also rang out that he wanted to see student test scores improve and he assumed she would spend as much time as possible in the classroom as an instructional supervisor.

Although she acknowledged the importance of these role expectations that others were emphasizing, she also had her own ideas of how she wanted to be viewed and the practices she wanted to emphasize. Most of Monica's experience as a teacher had taken place in a middle school where the principal and teachers had developed a professional learning community. The group believed that schools were places for learning for everyone—teachers, administrators, parents, as well as students. Over the years the group had created an exciting environment where study groups and other types of job-embedded professional learning were frequent and focused, where action research was on-going and directed toward solving the learning challenges of all students, where teachers openly and frequently discussed teaching and learning, where observations of classroom practice were a regular part of the school day, and where there was a strong sense of trust among administrators, teachers, students, and parents. It was hard for her to leave this school, but her advisor, her principal, and several friends had said she had the skills and dispositions to support professional learning communities in other schools.

Although she was determined to create this kind of rich learning community at Morning Heights, she knew she would also have to respond to others' expectations. Not only would she have to facilitate the leadership of others in the school but she would also have to demonstrate direct leadership to encourage a vision of learning for all students. She would have to build coalitions among teachers and parents to support these learning community actions. She would have to make sure that the buses ran on time, the schedules were completed, funds were fairly and efficiently spent, and planning was completed. And she knew that not only the superintendent but also everyone expected that she would support the learning of all students.

As she put the final touches on her introductory remarks to the teachers, she knew that the teachers would bring their own images of her role as principal. Perhaps they would imagine her performing the same duties, having the same expectations, and paying attention to the same things as her predecessor in the school. Perhaps they were anxious that she might have different expectations than her predecessor; some might see these expectations as a welcome reenergizing of the school; others might seem them as worrisome, difficult expectations that they were unable or unwilling to meet. Whatever their expectations were, Monica wanted to make sure that she sensitively but forcefully communicated to these teachers that she would provide the kind of direct leadership to ensure that all students were learning and that she would facilitate their own leadership efforts to educate all students.

INTRODUCTION

Most likely, you, like Monica, have developed some idea of the role of a principal. After all, since you were a student in school, you have seen and known principals as the people in the school with power and authority, who often dished out discipline. As a teacher, you probably developed mixed perceptions of your principals that may have encompassed both respect and resentment. Perhaps you were even confused as to what your principal did all day. You may have dreaded the principal's observations of your classroom or the conversations about your students' test scores and how they affected the school's adequate yearly progress (AYP). Perhaps you are a parent who has dealt with your own children's principals. You may have had to call your child's principal when a problem arose, or maybe you sat in the principal's office with your child. Perhaps you called the principal to "fix something," such as requesting a particular teacher or class for your child. You may have disagreed with some of the decisions of principals you have known. One of the authors decided to go into school administration at a time when, as a teacher, he was disappointed with a principal's decision making and decided that he should pursue school administration so that he would have a broader and more positive impact on young people's education.

Similar to the opening vignette, many players inside and outside of the school have different perceptions of and influences on the role. A new person coming into the principalship can be confused as to what is expected, what is needed, and what should be done. Considerable evidence indicates that the role has changed significantly over the past few decades (Archer, 2004; Crow, Hausman, & Scribner, 2002; Grubb & Flessa,

2006; Institute for Educational Leadership, 2000; Pounder & Merrill, 2001; Valentine, Clark, Hackmann, & Petzko, 2003). Grubb and Flessa (2006) noted,

> The job of the school principal has become increasingly complex. He or she is responsible for hiring and perhaps firing teachers, coordinating bus schedules, mollifying angry parents, disciplining children, overseeing the cafeteria, supervising special education and other categorical programs, and responding to all the stuff that walks in the door. (p. 519)

In fact, the principal's role that you have witnessed in the past might not be the one that you will eventually accept. Furthermore, much of the current debate on school reform and restructuring emphasizes that reform necessitates further reconceptualizing the principal's role (Crow, Hausman, & Scribner, 2002). The bottom line is this: the principalship has emerged as a vibrant and dynamic role, in many ways unique in its influence on students' education, but inherently important in establishing *social justice*—the value that focuses on helping members of a community who have been disadvantaged by personal, social, and environmental forces and changes and inequities. One major example of the change is the emphasis on learning for *all* children.

Role Conceptions

When you begin your career as a principal or assistant principal, several factors will affect how you will practice the role. You bring with you experiences, knowledge, and basic assumptions that factor into your practicing the role. For example, Monica, in the opening vignette, brought her experiences as a teacher in a professional learning community. Other people in the school also will affect your work. Teachers will influence how you will perform the role. The district office, also, will outline policies and expectations. All of these factors play into the role conception of the principal and assistant principal.

Sociologists often describe role conception by using two perspectives; individual and social. As you begin your administrative position, as either a principal or an assistant principal, you carry with you to that position a certain amount of baggage, both good and bad. Individual baggage items include your personality, personal characteristics, experiences, education, training, and so forth. For example, your experiences as a teacher will play heavily in the way you will take on an administrative role.

From the social perspective, role conception has been defined as an image or a set of images of the profession held by members of the organization (Caplow, 1954; Van Mannen & Barley, 1984). In a school, these images usually are defined by teachers, students, parents, and community members and are identified as important for that person in that role. Although a concept of the principalship role exists in most people's minds, school communities and cultures define the role differently. For example, in some communities you will be strongly expected to be part of community organizations such as Kiwanis or Rotary clubs. Another example, in some schools you will be expected to be highly involved with the school activities programs. And, in some school districts, others will expect you to be a visible leader in promoting the district's goals, such as bond elections and districtwide reform efforts.

ROLE TAKING   Roles are also constructed in the context in which they are performed. Principals have to act within these specific contexts. When you accept an appointment as a principal, you likely will accept a role that predates you. The role was established long before you signed the contract. Although you may come to the school with a certain role in mind, it is very likely that this role will be altered around the context that exists at the school. The process in which a principal accepts the role at a school that has been established within that context is referred to as role taking (Hart, 1993). Hall (1987) stated, "To function effectively in a new role, a person must develop a way of viewing himself or herself in that role—a subidentity" (p. 302). This concept of subidentity is needed in role taking.

ROLE MAKING   This does not rule out entirely principals developing their own concept of the role; for example, Monica's desire to promote a professional learning community. Over time and depending on the context, you can have influence as to what the role is or becomes. When as a new principal or assistant principal, you apply knowledge, skills, and behaviors to the school and act in ways not previously expected of the role, then you assert a new role. This process is referred to as role making (Hart, 1993).

Both role taking and role making can occur when a principal comes to a new school. Seldom do principals have opportunities to create their roles without consideration of the expectations by people in other roles in the school, district, and community. However, one principal can enter a school that has experienced previous problems and may have more influence on role making than another principal who comes to a successfully led school. The contexts of both the school and the individual determine how much role taking and role making take place.

WHO HELPS DEFINE THE ROLE OF THE PRINCIPAL?   A distinctive feature about the principalship role is that it has multiple influences, both internal and external. Internal sources of influence are teachers, students, secretaries, custodians, coaches, hall monitors, librarians, and anyone else who works in the building. Some have been in the building for most of their careers and can have an especially strong influence on shaping the role. Most principals have encountered the statement, "This is not the way we've done things before." Such statements from those who have been around for some time help shape and influence the role and the expectations of the principal. Others, for example, new teachers, may have limited influence.

External sources of influence may include the superintendent, the school board as a whole and its members individually, other administrators and coordinators in the district office, principals in other schools, parents of students, community members, state and national policymakers, and the media. Another distinctive aspect of the principalship role is its familiarity to so many. Virtually everyone has had some experience with the role of the principal, either as a student or as a parent. Although many external sources of influence do not fully understand the role, they definitely help shape the role. This influence can be a source of role conflict.

ROLE CONFLICT   Role conflict exists if coexisting expectations conflict or if simultaneous demands cannot be met. For example, teachers may expect the principal to help with classroom instructional activities, whereas parents may expect the principal to be available in the office during school time. In the opening vignette, Monica might find that the superintendent's expectations that she spend time observing and conferencing with teachers about instruction may conflict with some of the parents' views that she focus on the managerial side of the principalship. These coexisting expectations cause conflict because the principal is hard-pressed to be in both places to satisfy both groups. Further, role conflict could exist within the principal if he or she wants to help teachers with instruction and wants to be available to the parents and the public.

Understanding role conception is important in understanding principalship. Several researchers and theorists contend that role conception plays an important part in the way individuals successfully enact a particular role. Researchers found that the meaning principals attach to their actions differs between those who are effective and those who are ineffective. Effective administrators have a broader vision of their actions and tasks, which includes values and beliefs that prioritize tasks, an understanding of how these actions and tasks fit into the school, and a determination of the ultimate purpose of their role—the promotion of student learning (Dwyer, Barnett, & Lee, 1987; Elmore, 2003; Lambert, 2003; Murphy, 2002; Reeves, 2006; Scheurich & Skrla, 2003). For example, principals can view disciplining a misbehaving student as either enforcing a punishment or educating the student as to natural consequences based on the student's actions.

In this book, we emphasize broader role conceptions of principals and assistant principals rather than specific technical functions. In the past, principal preparation programs and textbooks often have emphasized learning certain functions or skills of the role. Some publications have finitely numerated these skills, such as twenty-one domains of the principalship or the top ten skills needed to be an effective principal. These functions and skills, such as decision making, communication, and student management as a few examples, are important aspects of the job, but they are also contingent on the context of the school culture. By emphasizing role conceptions, we hope to provide a stronger and broader link between the role and how it is practiced in the particular context of a school. In order to do this, however, we must first discuss leadership and how it applies to the principalship.

PRINCIPALSHIP AND LEADERSHIP

A major assumption in this book is that the principalship involves the leadership of learning. Such an assumption does not mean that all principal behaviors are leader behaviors or that all principals by virtue of their position are leaders. It also does not mean that we view the principal as a technician or bureaucrat—hired, for example, to purchase supplies and complete reports. Instead, we view the principal as a critical player in giving direction and focus to the school to bring about learning for *all* students.

The Definition of Leadership

The term *leadership* has literally hundreds of definitions. Although commonalities exist, there is not a universally accepted definition. In fact, there are several controversies around various definitions. For example, definitions of leadership in the military usually are quite different from those in religious organizations. Some politicians view leadership as maintaining the status quo, whereas other politicians view leadership as change. Before we discuss a definition for educational leadership, we need to explore some of the misconceptions that presently exist and how these misconceptions affect the principal's role.

The first misconception is that leadership is management. We are not suggesting that management is less important or is less desirable than leadership; in fact, in Chapter 10 we discuss the vital importance of management for creating a learning environment. What we suggest is that leadership and management have common elements but are also quite different. Although management is very necessary, we believe that leaders do more than just manage. They help establish a shared vision and influence a school's culture to focus on learning for *all* students. Leaders probably will use management activities to influence others, such as scheduling the preparation period of a middle school team of teachers at the same time so that they can meet and plan together. Although scheduling is a management activity, it has leadership implications. Clearly, good leadership requires good management, yet management can exist without evidence of any real leadership. For example, if the principal schedules faculty meetings without any vision or goal in mind, then the activity is only a management task and involves no leadership. On the other hand, if the faculty meetings are organized around the vision of developing a positive learning environment for *all* students, then leadership is more apparent.

On occasion, policymakers such as school board members and state legislators expect more management activities from a principal or assistant principal than leadership activities. For instance, some districts have outlined discipline codes with zero-tolerance policies for certain student misbehaviors. A zero-tolerance policy not only outlines the infraction but also will often state the punishment or consequence of a violation that is applied in every case. Often such policies inhibit the leadership of the principal and the assistant principal by limiting judgment, which in turn limits the leadership capacity in the school.

A second common misconception held by many people is that leadership resides only in a particular person or position. Perhaps this misconception began with the reign of kings and queens passing on the crown to their sons and daughters. When the prince or princess received the crown, he or she became the leader. However, holding such a position only gives authority and power but not necessarily leadership. Leadership consists of far more than the activities of one person or position, and it exists among many people in the organization. A formal position does not necessitate that leadership exists in any greater degree than it does with any other subordinate position. For example, leadership in a school is more likely to change and adapt because of the interrelationships among the administrators, faculty, and staff than because of the inspiration of one individual. In this book, we emphasize distributed leadership in which leadership is "a product of the joint interactions of school leaders, followers and aspects of their situations such as tools and routines" (Spillane, 2006, p. 3). In order to emphasize that leadership is not only something principals do, we organize the discussions of the various role conceptions around the principal and other leaders; for example, assistant principals and teacher leaders. This broader leadership approach allows us to avoid the misconception of one person, or role, performing all the leadership in a school and to encourage the development of greater leadership capacity in a school, which has been found to be associated with improved schools and student learning (Lambert, 2003).

A third misconception about leadership is that it comes naturally and is something that a person has rather than develops. Many people believe that leadership is not learned. This misconception is associated with the so-called *great man theory*—certain individuals have qualities and traits that will produce good leaders. People who adhere to this misconception look at the qualities and traits of leaders such as Winston Churchill, Mahatma Gandhi, Mother Teresa, or Martin Luther King Jr. and try to emulate their traits so that they too can be great leaders. Seldom do they recognize that these individuals became great leaders through their own experiences. They did not just arrive at a leadership position as effective leaders. Likewise, this misconception implies that great leaders can survive and thrive under any environment. For example, this belief would hold that Winston Churchill would have been a great leader even if Great Britain were not involved in World War II. History, however, indicates that Churchill struggled as prime minister when the war was over. In fact, Churchill lost his office shortly after World War II ended. Leaders succeed in some environments but are unsuccessful in others. Perhaps you are aware of a principal or superintendent who was effective and popular in one setting and then moved to another setting and experienced difficulty.

Another slant on this misconception occurs when a new principal tries to emulate another principal's traits. A beginning principal may think that successful leadership traits can be imitated. Emulating another principal's traits, however, is seldom effective because of environmental factors, such as faculty, community, and district goals. This is especially true in emulating a noneducational leader. Leaders in corporate and military organizations usually are involved in different environments than school environments, and, therefore, the leadership strategies might not be emulated effectively.

ROST'S DEFINITION   With these misconceptions in mind, we extend a definition of leadership that supersedes these misunderstandings and attempts to focus on essential elements of the leadership process. Rost (1991), after studying various definitions of leadership, finally created his own definition: "Leadership is an influence relationship among leaders and followers who intend real changes that reflect their shared purposes" (p. 102). We emphasize four key elements within Rost's definition:

1. Leadership involves influence.
2. It occurs among leaders and followers.
3. These people intend significant changes.
4. These changes reflect shared purposes toward creating a learning environment for *all* students.

Influence designates a relationship among people that is not passive or coercive. Western culture often has depicted leadership as something that someone does to someone else. However, in an influence relationship, leadership is reciprocal; that is, principals influence teachers, and teachers influence principals. Those participating in a leadership relationship use a variety of power resources to influence others. These power resources could include rewards, coercion, prestige, position, authority, and many others. We discuss these power resources and the implications that they have on the relationships among participants in Chapter 11.

According to Rost (1991), the people involved in leadership want significant changes. Leadership involves creating change, not necessarily maintaining the status quo, unless a good reason exists to do so. The changes are enduring, essential, and improve key elements of the purpose of the school, including democratic schooling, school improvement, and social justice. In addition, leaders do not dictate the changes, but the changes reflect purposes shared by both leaders and followers. Daft (2007) suggested that these changes are working toward an outcome that leaders and followers want, a desired future or shared purpose that motivates them toward this more preferable outcome, "thus leadership involves the influence of people to bring about change toward a desirable future" (p. 5). Rost (1991) used the term *intend real change* (p. 113), suggesting that people are actively involved in the pursuit of change toward a desired future. Each individual takes a personal responsibility to achieve the intended change. In schools, leadership should not focus on any change but rather on change that is learner centered.

Rost (1991) also suggested that leadership inherently involves followers. "Followers can become leaders and leaders can become followers in any one leadership relationship" (p. 109). Followers may be leaders for a while, especially when they have a certain expertise that is needed by the group. For instance, a principal may need the assistance of a teacher to help a newcomer implement cooperative learning as an instructional method. However, Rost pointed out that followers do not do followership; they do leadership. Both leaders and followers form one relationship that is leadership. They are in the leadership relationship together and the more these leadership relationships develop, the greater the leadership capacity of the school.

Rost's (1991) definition suggests the need to conceive of leadership as the direct influence that an individual has on others and the facilitating of others' influence. In this book, we discuss the role conceptions of the principalship in terms of the context in which principals exert direct leadership and facilitate the leadership capacity of the school specifically through the work of other leaders, especially assistant principals and teachers. In her introductory remarks to the faculty, Monica wanted to ensure that she focused on both direct and facilitative leadership roles of the principal. Obviously there are others in the school in addition to the principal, assistant principal, and teachers who exert influence and leadership. In Chapter 7, we will discuss this larger sphere of leadership capacity in the school. However, we have chosen to focus on these three positions due to the increasing attention on and potential of these positions for exerting leadership for student learning through professional learning communities.

PROFESSIONAL LEARNING COMMUNITY

Although John Dewey began the process of establishing schools as social communities, the more current view is that Peter Senge established learning organizations as the new contemporary metaphor for improving organizational productivity. Senge's (1990) work reestablished systems thinking as a metaphor in understanding organizations. A decade after his first book, he carried his work into the educational arena (Senge, et al., 2000). Other writers (Wenger, 1999; Wenger, McDermott, & Snyder, 2002) likewise have suggested that organizations should study their processes and procedures within the system in order for that organization to learn together to implement reform and change. Sergiovanni (1994) utilized the metaphors of organization and community to examine schools. He clarified the term *community* as a way to think about schools. He used the organization metaphor to emphasize management structures and procedures. Frequently, schools are described in terms of department or grade levels, job descriptions, and curriculum plans. A major part of the school leader's role in this way of thinking about schools is control and, therefore, school leaders try to convince others that they are in control by using rules and regulations. In contrast, using the community metaphor, Sergiovanni emphasized commitment rather than control.

> Communities are socially organized around relationships and the felt inter-dependencies that nurture them. Instead of being tied together and tied to purposes by bartering arrangements, this social structure bonds people together in special ways and binds them to concepts, images, and values that comprise a shared idea structure. This bonding and binding are the defining characteristics of schools as communities. (Sergiovanni, 1994, p. 217)

The school that operates as a professional learning community (DuFour, DuFour, Eaker, & Many, 2006; Hord, & Sommers, 2008; McLaughlin & Talbert, 2006) recognizes that its members must engage in the ongoing study and constant practice that characterize an organization committed to continuous improvement. Individuals in such schools, such as the one in which Monica was a teacher, collaborate formally and informally to learn with, and, from one another to help all students succeed in school.

To understand the concept of community, Westheimer (1999) identified five characteristics of community found in the literature. First, communities can be identified by the shared beliefs held by their members. Second, communities are known by the high level of interaction and participation among members— Identity and commitment result from this high level of interaction. Third, members of communities exhibit a great deal of interdependence that results in reciprocity and mutual need. Fourth, in addition to this interdependence there is a concern for individual and minority views. Finally, meaningful relationships that are based on common purpose are developed in community. Although variations in these characteristics may be found in any actual community, these components are critical to the existence and maintenance of community.

When we apply the concept of a learning community to schools, several characteristics can be noted. A number of researchers have identified these components, but we use those found in the research of Bryk, Camburn, and Louis (1999) because they capture the essential elements and ethos of learning communities. These authors defined professional learning communities as referring to schools where "interaction among teachers is frequent and teachers' actions are governed by shared norms focused on the practice and improvement of teaching and learning" (p. 753).

Bryk and his colleagues (1999) identified three major core practices of professional community. First, teachers in these communities engage in reflective dialogue with their colleagues about their instructional practices and student learning. This reflective dialogue occurs frequently and in various places in the school, including the cafeteria, the hall, and the teachers' lounge. Second, these communities are recognized by the deprivatization of practice. Instead of teaching practices being confined behind the classroom door, teachers regularly observe one another's practices. This interaction also involves joint problem solving as a typical rather than exceptional activity. Teachers act as advisors, mentors, and specialists to one another. Third, professional communities are known for their peer collaboration in which teachers engage in actual shared work in schoolwide problem solving and decision making.

These three practices—reflective dialogue, deprivatization of practice, and peer collaboration—are supported by two other components, according to Bryk and his co-authors (1999). Teachers and school leaders in these learning communities share norms that are focused on student learning. Thus, the dialogue, practice, and collaboration are focused specifically on student learning and are reflected in shared norms. In addition, these learning community practices are supported by socialization structures that reinforce the shared norms around student learning, especially for new teachers.

Bryk and his associates (1999) described the importance of principal leadership for building learning communities. Principals play a key role, according to these authors, in creating a normative climate that reinforces the practices of learning communities. The results of Bryk's, Camburn's, and Louis' Chicago study found:

> The elements of professional community are supported by principals who are in regular contact with their faculty, even to the extent of visiting teachers' classrooms on a regular basis. The elements of professional community were also more prevalent when principals were viewed as having more inclusive facilitative styles. These results suggest that principals' regular involvement with faculty members is important, but that involvement that goes beyond regular contact, that encourages teachers to be involved, to innovate, and to take risks, may be particularly supportive of professional community. (p. 768)

In Chapter 3, we will expand the discussion of professional learning community as a school reform movement and the principal's importance for building and maintaining this type of community.

PRINCIPALS AND PROFESSIONAL LEARNING COMMUNITY IN A GLOBAL, KNOWLEDGE SOCIETY

One reason why professional learning communities are important and why we have chosen to use this idea as a central feature of a book on principals' role conceptions is the nature of the global, knowledge-based context in which contemporary principals enact their roles. This context is very different from that in which many current and past principals learned their role.

Currently, several labels are in fashion for describing the society and the societal changes we are currently experiencing: information era, knowledge society, post-industrial society, technology era, information age, digital age. Each of these points to a series of contextual factors that contrast with a previous societal era. Primarily, these factors relate to the move from an industrial economy to a service, knowledge-work society. This change involves a trend away from making things to knowing and serving. The economy, instead of being based on manufacturing, is now based on knowledge and serving other people. The types of jobs that are expected to increase in the next few years will require post–high school training and education far more than jobs in the previous century. In addition, the knowledge that is required is not based on a fixed, concrete set of facts learned in school, but rather a fluid and dynamic type of knowledge. We will return to the implications of this type of knowledge for learning in Chapter 4.

The context of the knowledge society is global, requiring workers to interact with individuals across regional, national borders. Understanding global contexts and cultural sensitivities has become critical for more jobs. Finally, demographic diversity will increasingly become part of the workplace and influence the conditions of learning.

Hage and Powers (1992) suggested that work, itself, is changing in response to this knowledge society. First, instead of the type of scripted responses appropriate to an industrial society where managers were expected to enact their roles by following company policies, more customized responses are necessary to meet the rapidly changing demands of individuals. Second, work in a knowledge society is more substantively complex, involving greater discretion and judgment, in order to meet these rapidly changing demands. Third, work involves greater interaction with more and different roles. Instead of a division of labor that involves the individual performing his or her own role in isolation from others, a knowledge society requires more interdisciplinary, multiple-role work. Finally, instead of evaluation being focused on individual efficiencies, the work will increasingly be evaluated in terms of group effectiveness and creativity.

These conditions of the knowledge society influence principals as well as other professionals (Crow, 2005). The role conceptions of principals in a professional learning community must involve the ability to collect and use information rapidly to diagnose needs and develop customized responses. These conceptions must recognize and value the substantively complex work of principals and other educators and facilitate the development of skills to do this kind of work by other educators in the school. Furthermore, this knowledge society requires principals and other school leaders to interact increasingly with multiple and diverse agencies and roles, for example, social service and health professionals and governmental policymakers, in meeting the individual and unique needs of students. Principals and other leaders will increasingly be evaluated on whether they can develop creative solutions and environments for learning that enable all students to learn.

The role conceptions we will be discussing in this book are all part of what principals can and must do in a changing knowledge society in which professional learning communities become the vehicle for student learning. Reform, instead of being something that can be described in waves, is increasingly becoming a dynamic and constant process. As a principal or assistant principal, you will play a pivotal role in creating and responding to these reforms.

LEARNING ABOUT LEADERSHIP

Learning how to be an effective leader in a professional learning community involves a complex set of factors. Many people and organizations have marketed a variety of materials on becoming a successful leader. Bookstores have a number of publications proclaiming how to be an effective leader. Leadership seminars, centers, consultants, and programs are available everywhere. If you want to learn the "how to" of leadership, you do not have to go far. The problem arises as to how you are going to determine the type of training that is effective and appropriate for public-sector organizations such as schools. If we adhere to Rost's (1991) definition of leadership, we must recognize that learning about leadership is quite complex and will involve most of our careers. In fact, most principals who are near the end of their careers will tell you that what they once thought important in leadership turned out to be less important.

Daft (1999) organized four stages of acquiring leadership competence. Most people start in the first stage: unconscious incompetence. In this stage, individuals do not have any competence in leadership, and they are unaware that they lack competence, probably because they have never tried to be a leader. They discover their incompetence and find that they need help to move ahead. By reading, observing, listening, and studying, they become conscious of what is required, moving into the second stage. In this stage, individuals become conscious of what they are required to do but are still personally incompetent. Daft likens this to swinging a golf club for the first time. You are trying to keep ten things in your mind as you attempt to hit the ball straight down the fairway—and as most golfers know, this seldom happens in the beginning.

In the third stage, the individual's conscious awareness of the correct things to do gradually transforms into leadership competence. The person learns to visualize a desired future, influence others to engage in that future, and has the courage to take on real change for student learning. This is the stage when individuals receive positive feedback so that they are aware of how well they are doing. This competence sets up the transition into the fourth stage, where the leadership skills and behaviors become a part of the individual. These skills and behaviors occur naturally, and as Daft (1999) indicated, "You no longer have to consciously think about creating a vision; it emerges intuitively" (p. 24).

Principal Leadership in Practice

Principals do not develop their conceptions of leadership in a vacuum. The general society, the larger educational community, other principals, the schools in which they work, and their own experiences influence the ways principals and assistant principals understand and develop their roles as leaders.

Society, in particular, plays an important role. We see leaders everywhere. We watch C-SPAN and see our political leaders debating and speaking on issues. We go to the movies and see a "take charge" general leading his troops into battle. We listen to our neighbor who is a chief executive officer (CEO) talk about the trends in her business. It is easy to see parallels between leaders in society and the types of leaders that we think are needed in our schools. Consequently, many people believe that leaders in other organizations in our society have answers to leadership problems in our schools.

We certainly can learn about leadership in, for example, the corporate world, but is it the type of leadership that we want to use in schools? Will it be an influence relationship among leaders and followers who intend real change? The answer seems to be both yes and no. There is no doubt that school principals can learn leadership from other elements in society, but we have to be cautious and realize that schools are quite different types of organizations requiring a different kind of leadership—leadership for learning.

The larger educational community, composed of federal, state, and district policy-makers and communities, also will influence your conception of leadership. Schools and their leaders are receiving a great deal of attention and scrutiny regarding how well the school enables all students to reach achievement test goals. Along with this attention comes a variety of conceptions of how principals should act in order to ensure student learning. Some of these conceptions assume a narrow range of activities and perspectives that attempt to standardize principal behavior. The assumption is that if all principals act in similar ways it will be easier to implement federal and state policies to ensure increases in student achievement scores. Other conceptions, which we promote, urge broader, diverse, and innovative perspectives on the principal's role that ensure student learning for a broader goal than only raising test scores. The influence of this larger educational community is intense and the stakes in some states and districts are high. You will have to develop a variety of skills and dispositions related to the role conceptions identified in this book to decide which perspectives and approaches make sense not only for you but also for all the students and educators you serve.

Principals also learn about leadership from other principals. You have spent count-less hours observing other principals since you began kindergarten many years ago. You continued your observation as a student, then as a teacher, and perhaps as a parent. You will begin your career as a school administrator with a significant number and variety of leadership images. It is certainly a much longer exposure period than exists for most other professions. Thus, it is not surprising that Greenfield (1977) found that veteran principals were the most significant influence on the socialization of new principals. This can be good and bad. For instance, veteran principals might contribute to the filtering process of what a newcomer will learn as a leader. The veteran might filter out more innovative and even radical images of what a principal should be in a modern setting, an area we discuss in Chapter 12. However, veteran principals also add wisdom. They have experiences that transcend generational gaps.

The school in which a principal and an assistant principal work also influences the kinds of leadership that can be learned and practiced. In the past when principals entered a new school, it was believed that they brought with them a toolbox of leadership traits and behaviors that could be applied to the new setting. However, research (Hart, 1993) suggested otherwise. Schools and the people in them act as socializing agents for both newcomers and veteran principals. Teachers, parents, and students express and reward the types of leadership qualities and images that fit the context and are acceptable.

PERSON AND SYSTEM VIEWS OF LEADERSHIP   Our specific view of leadership can be described in terms of two sources of leadership: person and system. If we think of the source of leadership as a person, we usually (but not always) think in terms of an individual in a position of authority. Individuals use various resources such as rewards, punishments, expertise, tradition, loyalty, and charisma to achieve the goals of the organization. Others, who we call followers, look to and rely on this individual for guidance, direction, and interpretation. This view of leadership is the most common notion of the source of leadership found in both research and the practical literature. By far the largest attention to the principal's role uses this view of the principal as the school's leader responsible for developing a vision and persuading others to accept that vision.

Another way to think of the source of leadership is systemic (Ogawa & Bossert, 1995). In this view, leadership is the network of individuals and groups within an organization— a professional learning community. These networks also use various resources such as expertise, rewards, and punishments. Instead of leadership flowing from one individual, the leader, it flows within the organization from various sources. This view of the source of leadership has been used only recently in discussing the principal's role. In this view, the principal is one among many individuals who are involved in the leadership process. The network of relationships among principals, teachers, students, staff, parents, community members, district supervisors, and governmental entities is the source of vision, inspiration, direction, and persuasion. As we mentioned previously, we have chosen to focus on the role conceptions of principals within the professional learning community and specifically include the leadership of the principal, assistant principal, and teachers.

EIGHT ROLE CONCEPTIONS FOR THE PRINCIPALSHIP

In discussing the principalship as an evolving role and as a leadership role for improving instruction, we will organize our discussion in terms of eight role conceptions that we believe most clearly and comprehensively define the roles of an assistant principal and principal. We begin with three role conceptions—learner, culture builder, and advocate—that we believe are foundational to the principal's primary role conception of leader in a professional learning community. We follow with a discussion of five other role conceptions that contribute to the improvement of teaching and learning in a professional learning community: leader, mentor, supervisor, manager, and politician. We then discuss each of these role conceptions in terms of principals' and assistant principals' direct and facilitative responsibilities.

Principal as Learner

Fundamental to the conceptions of the principal's role that we identify and discuss in this book is the centrality of learning. The principal as learner is necessary and pivotal for an innovative understanding of the role. As we discuss in Chapter 4, as a leader in a school organization, you should hold learning as central because schools are above all else professional learning communities. As Barth (1990) suggested, principals should be neither head managers nor head teachers but rather head learners in the school. Within the current context of administering schools in a period of governmental, community, and media scrutiny; student achievement; and school improvement, you must be a constant and rigorous learner using various capacities and methods. The principal as learner involves being connected to the wider community of education, schooling, and leadership. The school leader needs to seek and create knowledge—a requirement that is more critical in a global, knowledge society. This conception of learner provides the skills and dispositions to both influence school constituents and interpret the rapidly changing and complex school context for constituents. The principal as learner involves self-awareness, reflectivity, inquiry, and complexity that are essential for school leadership in a global, knowledge-based society.

Principals not only must engage themselves in lifelong quests for knowledge but also need to model and instill this behavior in others. Principals, assistant principals, and teacher leaders play an important role in facilitating opportunities for the continued growth of faculty and staff through individual and professional development. Reform movements involving empowering teachers and developing teacher leadership encourage a systemic view of leadership in which leaders have an important role.

Principal as Culture Builder

The principal as learner does not occur in a vacuum and the context for learning emphasizes the role conception for principals as culture builders. Schools are not just collections of people conducting some activity, but rather they include norms and values that undergird the professional learning community of the school. Deal and Peterson (1999) have demonstrated the critical role that principals play in creating school cultures that promote student learning. In Chapter 5, we will focus on what school culture means, how to analyze school cultures, and the types of leadership necessary for shaping, maintaining, and changing school cultures. The principal alone cannot do all the work of culture building and so this chapter discusses how the principal facilitates the leadership of others, including assistant principals and teacher leaders.

Principal as Advocate

Learning also involves advocacy. Foundational to the leadership of principals, is the moral imperative of being an advocate for all students, for the whole student, for the school, and for the community. As we mentioned before, school populations have become increasingly diverse, and learning goals affect all students, not only the average or gifted students. Driven by social justice; access to knowledge; statutory regulations; and legal decisions; the professional learning community must recognize, value, and enhance racial, ethnic, gender, sexuality, disability, linguistic, and socioeconomic diversity. As we will note in Chapter 6, demographic changes have led to the creation of new programs to serve special populations. Likewise, some changes have been received with increased tension and stress by some teachers, students, and parents. The principal needs to serve as advocate for all students by helping other educators perform their roles equitably and by promoting social justice and access to positive educational outcomes for all students.

Principal as Leader

Based on these three foundational roles, the primary role of principals is leadership. Leadership is intimately tied to learning in an innovative conception of the principal's role. Principals are not only learners themselves; they are also leaders of learning. This role, as we describe in Chapter 7, necessitates examining the learning environment and influencing reform that brings about school improvement in learning for *all* students. Leadership is also the vehicle for creating change and reform in schools. Principals and assistant principals build a shared school vision; solve problems; and develop collaborative and teaming strategies.

Principal as Mentor

The principal and other leaders in the school cannot and should not be the only learners in the school. Principals are primarily responsible for the professional learning community within the school. The two conceptions of principals as mentors and supervisors emphasize the responsibility that is focused on learning. As a mentor, the principal takes a central role in helping others, namely, teachers and students, to learn. The role of mentor is closely associated with the role of teacher and coach. The traditional concept of the principal separates the role of principal and the role of teacher. However, in Chapter 8, we emphasize a newly conceptualized role that renews an understanding that historically placed the role as a principal teacher. In addition, an important role is to instill the concept of mentoring in others, especially teachers as they collaborate with one another and work to improve teaching and learning.

Principal as Supervisor

Inherent in the role of principal has been the task of supervision. The traditional conceptualization of this role often has placed the principal and assistant principal as middle managers. Teachers often perceive their administrators as evaluators of their teaching performance by coming into their classroom to observe two or three times a year, completing a personnel evaluation report, and forwarding it to the superintendent and school board. In Chapter 9, we emphasize a newly conceptualized role that requires more of the principal than this. Principals are expected to become instructional leaders who plan, develop, supervise, and assess student learning, instructional capacity, and curriculum programs. These tasks involve both influencing faculty to improve their instruction and helping them make sense of external demands on school improvement such as No Child Left Behind (NCLB) Act of 2001 and internal school cultures that promote learning for all students. The principal also empowers teacher leaders and assistant principals to be instructional leaders. In this way, principals expand the instructional leadership capacity of the school.

Principal as Manager

Traditional roles of principals emphasized the role of scientific management and often excluded the role of leadership. In contrast to these earlier conceptions of the principal's role, our framework, presented in Chapter 10, views management as serving leadership and learning conceptions. Principals play an important managerial role in school reform especially as they deal with finance, facilities, programs, and activities. In many of these areas, the principal helps faculty and staff understand the connections among programs, activities, buildings, finances, and so on. The principal also enables others to manage efficiently. In a context of school reform and professional learning communities, the development of systems thinking and the acquisition of various managerial skills are critical for school leaders. Management decisions of innovative principals focus on how to enable internal and external school constituents to contribute to a professional learning community where all students and adults learn.

Principal as Politician

Principals span the boundary between the school and the larger community by being politicians. In spanning this boundary, learning is fundamental and leadership is critical. For many decades, school leadership and politics were artificially separated. However, as we will discuss in Chapter 11, politics is a necessary concept of the new role of the principal. Helping external constituents understand the school's mission and helping internal school constituents understand the external demands are important. Equally important to the role of principal as politician is the role that the principal plays as a facilitator and mediator of others to be politically astute through their involvement in parental and community arenas. Building community, mediating conflict, and fostering meaningful collaboration are important political roles of the principal that lead to improving student learning. In an age of governmental, community, and media scrutiny, being able to communicate the school's progress in meeting student learning goals has become even more critical than before.

After identifying and discussing these eight role conceptions, in Chapter 12 we examine how you learn to be an assistant principal and principal, and how this learning contributes to leadership in a professional learning community. Understanding your own learning processes will assist you in developing the types of role conceptions that make a difference for all students.

Conclusion

As you read this book and engage in conversations with your professors, colleagues, and principals, reflect on how your own conception of the principalship is evolving. Your awareness of your own growth and development is important in becoming an innovative principal and assistant principal. Your learning is also fundamental in helping to make contemporary schools inviting and stimulating learning environments for both students and adults.

Activities

SELF-REFLECTION ACTIVITIES

1. Reflect on your own image of the principalship. What is the content of that image, and what sources influence that image?
2. Peruse the titles of leadership books in your local bookstore. What different conceptions of leadership did you find?
3. Interview a veteran principal in terms of how accountability and reform demands such as NCLB have influenced his or her perspective and enactment of the role.
4. Assume you are Monica in the opening vignette. Plan your introductory remarks for tomorrow's meeting with the teachers at Morning Heights Junior High School.

PEER REFLECTION ACTIVITIES

1. Discuss with a colleague the principals you have both known. How did each principal balance leadership and management?
2. Choose two classic movies that you have seen. Compare and contrast the conceptions of leadership found in these two movies.

3. Consider the opening vignette. Discuss the conflicting role conceptions of leadership that Monica faced.

COURSE ACTIVITIES

1. Invite a second- or third-year principal and a veteran principal (someone who has had several principalships) to class. Interview the principals regarding changes they made when they first entered their current schools. Afterwards, discuss the degree of role taking and role making in each principal's experience.
2. Have class members ask their principal the following question: the principalship is like _____? Analyze the types of metaphors and what they suggest about different role conceptions.
3. Use a case such as "Changes at Honey Grove High" found in the *UCEA Journal of Cases of Educational Leadership* and discuss the different roles conceptions that the groups within the community have for the principal or the assistant principal.

Website

Interstate School Leaders Licensure Consortium (ISLLC) Standards for School Leaders
   www.ccsso.org/content/pdfs/isllcstd.pdf

CHAPTER 2

Historical View
of the Principal's Role

Vignette

Principal Ronald Montgomery's retirement open house attracted hundreds of people. It was to be expected, however, because anyone who had served as a principal for twenty-two years in the same building naturally would create a wide network of acquaintances. Besides, Principal Montgomery was well liked by the community. For most of his twenty-two years at Valleyview High School, it was the only school in the community. The community rallied around its high school, and Principal Montgomery became an icon in the community. As the valley grew, so did the need for another high school. Two years before his retirement, a new school was built, drawing on the new suburban housing developments for its population. Valleyview High School changed. Only half the size it used to be and serving part of the community that mostly housed lower-income families—Valleyview's demographics had changed rapidly. During the last two years, the high school lost most of its football and basketball games, could not field a marching band, and the once-popular annual school musical was dismally attended by the community. The state's standardized testing indicated, for the first time in school history, that average scores were below the fiftieth percentile. Although Principal Montgomery was given the choice to go to the new school, he chose instead to stay at Valleyview. However, not even he had predicted the changes that occurred in such a short time.

The "Blame Game" became part of the school culture. Those teachers remaining at Valleyview High blamed the school board for creating unbalanced attendance area boundaries. Some of the teachers also were upset that they had not been given the opportunity to transfer whereas other teachers had been "chosen" as the new faculty. The new school had fully equipped science labs, computers in every classroom, and athletic facilities that rivaled that of a small college. Parents blamed the newcomers for manipulating the board into building a showcase for their part of the community but leaving the old for the old.

Principal Montgomery had realized finally that new leadership was needed at Valleyview High. He recognized that education had changed, that the community had changed, and that he and many others at Valleyview had not changed. The last two years had been extremely hard on his health, and the more he thought about what was needed at the school, the more he realized that his fire had long since been extinguished. It was time for new blood.

The retirement open house was a huge success—the only event that had tied the two communities together in the past two years. Coming through the reception line were present and former teachers, students, and parents. Civic dignitaries such as the mayor and several city council members were present. Also, standing in the line was Consuelos Gonzales, who had flown into town to attend the open house. She was the new blood—recently appointed as the principal of Valleyview High School. From out of town and out of state and a Latina, she knew that she had an uphill battle to gain community support. The open house would be a good start. Besides, she respected Mr. Montgomery for the many years of service he had given to the school and community. It was only right for her to be at his retirement open house. She knew she needed his support and help in the coming years. She also had been given a charge from the board to jump-start things at Valleyview High—and the sooner the better.

Consuelos had been a principal for the past five years in a rural setting in a neighboring state. She had been recognized by the state affiliate of the Association for Supervision and Curriculum Development (ASCD) as the state's outstanding instructional leader for her innovative and comprehensive teacher development programs at her school. She understood the board's directive to give Valleyview a jump start, and she had great ideas especially in developing a professional learning community. She also knew that the faculty and community were not as anxious or ready for these curricular and instructional changes. They were quite satisfied to continue with the same kind of leadership methods that Principal Montgomery used.

INTRODUCTION

As a new principal, you will assume a historically important education role. The imprint of professional history is a powerful influence on your role, responsibilities, and practice as a principal or assistant principal. In this chapter, we describe the various historical conceptions of the principal and assistant principal roles. This discussion is designed to demonstrate how administrators are in part influenced by the previous emphases of the role and how society has influenced the values and assumptions of the role. We identify and discuss contemporary demands, expectations, and challenges that influence how the roles of the principal and assistant principal are viewed.

American schools during the seventeenth and eighteenth centuries were mostly private or church institutions. Around 1800, the demand for public education in America began to grow. Thomas Jefferson was among the first to propose a system of free public elementary schools. Jefferson's theory of education grew out of his political ideals: "If a nation expects to be ignorant and free in a state of civilization, it expects what never was and never will be." Establishing and maintaining a system of public instruction at the state's expense was not the popular and accepted belief that it is today. Jefferson's proposal encountered the opposition of wealthy taxpayers who protested at being taxed to educate other people's children. Consequently, Jefferson's proposal was never adopted, but the seeds were sown. A few decades later, largely as a result of the work of Horace Mann in Massachusetts and Henry Barnard in Connecticut, the public school movement in America was launched, usually referred to as the *common school movement.* The common school movement became one of the most significant social crusades in American history. Tyack and Hansot (1982) suggested that it takes some effort of historical imagination to reconstruct the context within which Americans of the mid-nineteenth century embarked on the ambitious and successful social movement to create a common school system:

> It is easy to forget that mid-nineteenth century America was four-fifths rural, had a minuscule government, possessed only a rudimentary industrial system composed mostly of small firms, and had only begun the bureaucratization that would later make a mature corporate society. . . . Yet, this social movement produced by the end of the century more schooling for more people than in any other nation and resulted in patterns of education that were remarkably uniform in purpose, structure, and curriculum, despite the reality of local control in hundreds of thousands of separate communities. (p. 17)

ORIGIN OF THE PRINCIPALSHIP

It has been said that the principalship was conceived in a halo of chalk dust because of its roots in religion and management. However, the precise origins of the principalship are not clearly recorded. We do know that the word *principal* appeared in Horace Mann's (1842) report to the Massachusetts School Board in 1841. We also know from such early writers as Pierce (1935) and Cubberley (1916) and more recent writers such as Campbell, Fleming, Newell, and Bennion (1987) and Beck and Murphy (1993) that the role of the principal emerged from the teaching ranks and that it was connected with teaching for several decades before it became a separate role. Campbell and his colleagues reported that the administration of schools was hardly differentiated from teaching. Teachers in one-room schools throughout America simply performed the necessary administrative, clerical, and janitorial tasks associated with schooling. As schools grew, however, the complexity of these tasks increased, requiring a single person to assume responsibility for them. The person designated as the *principal teacher* continued to function in the classroom but also served as the head of the school (Pierce, 1935).

The Common School Teachers' Association addressed an inquiry to the Board of Education in Cincinnati in 1839 to determine the relative duties of principal teachers (Pierce, 1935). The committee outlined what it deemed the chief responsibilities of the principal teacher, namely,

1. to function as the head of the school charged to his care;
2. to regulate the classes and course of instruction of all the pupils, whether they occupied his room or the rooms of other teachers;
3. to discover any defects in the school and apply remedies;
4. to make defects known to the visitor or trustee of ward or district if he were unable to remedy conditions;
5. to give necessary instruction to his assistants;
6. to classify pupils;
7. to safeguard school houses and furniture;
8. to keep the school clean;

9. to refrain from impairing the standing of assistants, especially in the eyes of their pupils;
10. to require the cooperation of his assistants.

When exactly the word *principal* changed from being an adjective to a noun is not clearly known. Pierce (1935) reported that the modern public school principalship had its beginnings in America's early high schools. These high schools were patterned after the private academies of the late eighteenth and early nineteenth centuries, which were designed after English and other western European schools. Some of the earliest descriptions of the work of school administrators can be found in the writing of the German Johann Sturm (1507–1589). In 1537, the magistrates of Strasburg, Germany, needed a rector to organize a local gymnasium, a secondary school for boys. They hired Johann Sturm, a classically trained renaissance scholar, to organize a curriculum, develop teaching methods, and hire and supervise teachers for approximately six hundred male secondary school students. With this specific charge in mind, in 1538 Sturm published *The Best Mode for Opening Institutions of Learning.* In this particular work and in numerous other books, essays, and treatises published over the next forty-five years, we find such modern problems discussed as principles of education, school organization, educational values, teachers' salaries, relation of parent and school, entrance requirements, discipline and conduct of pupils, how to bring education within the reach of poor boys, class instruction against individual instruction, responsibility of the teacher, and the like (Ensign, 1923).

Johann Sturm was singular. Many of his ideas for organizing schools and the curricula were not adopted to any significant degree across Europe until several centuries later.

In the English public schools, we also find antecedents of the modern-day principalship. By the eighteenth century, the term *headmaster* was in common use, and the roles and responsibilities for these headmasters were focused primarily on discipline and supervision of student life of boys attending school away from home (Ensign, 1923). Hart and Bredeson (1996) speculated that this early role responsibility provides at least a partial explanation for the importance of discipline in the evolving role of principals codified in the legal principle of in loco parentis, which means "in place of the parent."

The early American school principal had responsibilities very similar to those of the headmaster of the English academies. He (the principal was invariably male) had a small number of teachers to supervise and only simple administrative duties to perform. A large share of his time was spent in teaching.

ORIGIN OF THE ASSISTANT PRINCIPAL ROLE

The history of the assistant principal is also quite vague. Glanz (1994) suggested that the role might have emerged from two teacher supervisory roles. During the 1920s in larger school settings, the principal selected a special supervisor from among the teaching faculty to help less experienced teachers in subject matter mastery. Some of the larger schools, for example, had special supervisors in each of the major subject areas. Because this role came from the ranks of teachers, the special supervisor was most often female. These special supervisors had little independent authority and did not serve in an evaluative capacity. Another role emerged that Glanz referred to as a *general supervisor*. Male teachers more often filled this role to assist the principal in logistical operations of the school. Glanz believed that the general supervisor became the primary assistant to the principal. Because of the amount of authority given to the general supervisor, the special supervisor role disappeared in most schools in the 1930s. By the 1940s and 1950s, the literature more accurately reflected the relationship between the principal and the general supervisor by using the title *assistant principal.*

Kelly (1987) suggested that the assistant principal's role was developed originally to aid principals in meeting the increasing demands of the job. The role was not intended to change the structure of the principal's job but was meant to give the principal more time for instructional leadership by sharing the load. The assistant principal's part of the load was attending to administrative and management details—those activities that were essential but could be carried out by someone other than the principal.

In the 1970s, the literature began reflecting the assistant principal role as being a significant position in educational administration. The literature since the 1970s has used such metaphors describing the assistant principal as "subordinate to the principal," "parallel with the principal," "henchman," and "specialist." The more recent literature suggests an expanded and significant instructional role for principals, one that we acknowledge in this book (Hartzell, Williams, & Nelson, 1995).

We maintain that the assistant principalship holds a critical position in educational organizations. Marshall & Hooley, 2006 offered two major reasons for the role's increasing importance in school administration. First, the assistant principal role is a frequent entry-level position for school administrative careers. A majority of principals expect to move upward in administration. For this reason, assistant principalships often provide opportunities for observing and interacting with supervisors and learning the behaviors necessary for professional advancement. Second, assistant principals maintain the norms and rules of the school culture. They are usually the first ones to handle the most difficult disciplinary problems. Social issues such as poverty, racism, and family disruption help define the world in which assistant principals find themselves. For these reasons, our purpose in this book is to describe the assistant principal's role as a mirror image of the principal's role in that both should function in a parallel fashion.

WOMEN AND MINORITIES IN THE PRINCIPALSHIP

It is obvious to any observer that women and minorities are underrepresented in school administration and have been for most of history (Shakeshaft, 1999). Although both groups have occupied the classroom, fewer women and minorities have occupied the principal's office as compared with white males. Ortiz and Marshall (1988) reported that "women, especially minority women, but even minority men, continue to occupy the lowest positions in the administrative hierarchy, white males the higher and the more powerful positions" (p. 127). The National Center for Education Statistics (NCES) periodically studies the demographics of school principals in public and private schools. The results of the 1988–1989, 1990–1991, 1993–1994, and 2003–2004 studies are given in Tables 2.1 and 2.2. Although the percentages of female and most minority principals have increased since 1988, the growth has been small. To understand the phenomenon behind the under-representation of women and minorities in educational administration, we look again at history.

TABLE 2.1 Percentage of Public School Principals by Sex within School Level: 1987–1991, and 1993–1994

	Overall		Elementary		Secondary	
Year	Male	Female	Male	Female	Male	Female
1987–1988	75.4	24.5	69.9	30.1	90.6	9.4
1990–1991	70.0	30.0	63.5	36.5	89.0	11.0
1993–1994	65.4	34.5	58.9	41.1	86.2	13.8

Source: National Center for Education Statistics (1992, 1994, 1998).

TABLE 2.2 Percentage of Minorities as Principals in Public Schools: 1988–1989, 1990–1991, and 1993–1994

Year	White	Black	Hispanic	Asian or Pacific Islander	American Indian or Alaskan Native
1987–1988	88.6	8.6	3.19	0.557	1.050
1990–1991	85.9	8.6	3.93	0.671	0.887
1993–1994	84.2	10.1	4.11	0.779	0.792

Source: National Center for Education Statistics (1992, 1994, 1998).

An early woman pioneer in school leadership was Ella Flagg Young. A principal of two elementary schools in Chicago, she became superintendent of Chicago schools and later was elected as the first female president of the National Education Association (NEA). In 1909, she confidently predicted that women were destined to rule the schools in every city. Her comments reflected movements during the early part of the twentieth century that had been gaining momentum among women teachers in New York, Chicago, and other major cities. The women were protesting the domination of top administration and professional associations by males and the higher pay for male teachers. These early movements by women such as Ella Flagg Young (see Text Box 2.1) accounted for some gains in the first decades of the twentieth century, but as schools became even larger and more bureaucratic, women "lost even their tenuous toehold on good jobs" in education (Tyack & Hansot, 1982, p. 181).

Kalvelage (1978) researched the early gains of women in educational administration and the subsequent demographic changes that occurred in mid-century. She reported that in 1928, 55 percent of elementary school principals were women (the highest year ever recorded). However, by the 1970s, the number of women as elementary school principals had declined drastically to about 20 percent. During the 1980s and 1990s, women slowly regained some principalship positions. By 1994, women comprised 41 percent of elementary school principalships but only 13.8 percent of secondary school principalships (National Center for Education Statistics, 1998).

What caused the decline of female elementary principals in mid-twentieth century? Kalvelage (1978) offered several suggestions. First, she proposed that since the early elementary principalship was both a teaching and an administrative position (principal

BOX 2.1

ELLA FLAGG YOUNG

Born in Buffalo, New York, but reaching fame in Chicago, Ella Flagg Young was one of America's earliest female principals, Chicago's first woman superintendent and the first in a large city in America, and the National Education Association's first female president. She began her teaching career in Chicago at the tender age of seventeen in a classroom full of young roughneck students called "the cowboys"—young men who herded cattle on the out-skirts of the city. After her husband died early in her marriage, she devoted the rest of her life to education, and the children of Chicago became her adopted family. She expected other educators to have the same devotion. As principal and superintendent, she frequently visited classrooms and observed teaching. On one particular occasion she was observing a fourth-grade class when a student came in tardy. The teacher told the young girl to stand in a cor-ner and then asked Ella Flagg Young, "What would you do with a little girl that came in tardy?" "Well," said Mrs. Young crisply, "I do not see that she has lost much" (Fenner & Fishburn, 1944).

For six years Mrs. Young was a professor in the Department of Pedagogy at the University of Chicago. As a colleague of John Dewey, her experience in education and his phi-losophy resulted in their coauthoring six monographs. She helped John Dewey translate his philosophical ideas into educational practice. Dewey said of her that she was the inspiration of many of his thoughts and conceptions about education. Dewey once wrote, "I would come to her with these abstract ideas of mine, and she would tell me what they meant."

teacher), females related to that role more than to the nonteaching principal role that became more prominent as the schools increased in size. Second, she suggested that as male-dominated school boards gained more authority, a more corporate model for schools prevailed, limiting the role of women in leadership positions—similar to the cor-porate world. Third, Kalvelage proposed that as the role became more specialized and university training became more of a requirement, the transition from being a teacher to being an administrator became more difficult for women because a university education was more accessible to men than to women. Tyack and Hansot (1982) also mentioned this problem for early women educators. They claimed that in graduate work in educa-tional administration the professors were almost all men and they recruited and spon-sored males. Finally, Kalvelage also suggested that as court cases and legislation sought for equity, women "had lost even the dubious asset of being cheaper than men" (p. 18). All these factors combined to cause a gradual decline in the number of female elemen-tary school principals that would not see a reversal until the late twentieth century.

Estler (1975) identified another reason that women were not well represented in school leadership. She claimed that women lacked role models in educational adminis-tration and, therefore, were less inclined to enter into school leadership. Obviously, few women were in school leadership positions, but her studies also indicated that women faculty members in teaching colleges were concentrated in elementary education and least represented in the field of educational administration. In fact, she reported that only 0.9 percent of the faculty in educational administration were women in 1969–1970. Her conclusion was that women needed more encouragement from role models to enter into the field of educational administration and few of those role models existed in the public schools or in institutions of higher education.

Tyack and Hansot (1982) offered some additional insight into the cultural reasons that many women did not pursue or were not appointed to school leadership positions. According to these authors, women who wished to climb the normal ladder to become top administrators faced both external and internal barriers. The early advocates of employing women as teachers assumed that they would leave their work when married and that marriage was the goal of all proper women. In fact, in 1900, only 10 percent of female teachers were married, and in 1940, only 22 percent were. As Tyack and Hanson reported, "Not only did most women internalize these cultural norms, but official policies also barred married women from educational employment. . . . The situation grew worse during the depression, as thousands of districts passed new bans" (p. 191).

More recent history of women in school administration is encouraging. According to several reports (e.g., Bell & Chase, 1993; Tingley, 1996), women have made up at least half of educational administration program enrollments since the mid-1980s.

Compared with research on women, there is even less historical information available about minorities entering school-leadership positions. With some ethnic groups, the rise and fall of numbers in school administration almost parallel those of women. For example, African Americans held more school leadership positions in the first half of the twentieth century than they did in the second half. One explanation given for this in the literature is the elimination of segregated schools during the 1950s, 1960s, and 1970s that resulted in fewer African Americans in the leadership hierarchy. Almost all segregated schools had African American administrators. When schools were integrated, few African Americans were appointed to leadership positions. African American female school leaders were even more affected. Loder (2005) reported that the unique race, gender, and generational statuses of these principals made them especially vulnerable to the impact of governance reforms that rearranged long-standing authority relationships between African American principals and parents.

The first African American school administrators mentioned in history were those in the Quaker-sponsored institutions. At the turn of the twentieth century, Quaker Anna T. Jeanes endowed $1 million toward maintaining and assisting rural, community, and county schools for southern African Americans. The Jeanes supervisors, about 80 percent of whom were black women, concentrated on bringing the school and community together and raising the general standard of living. They trained teachers, developed curricula, demonstrated teaching methods, and conducted professional development activities in child growth and development, in other words, duties that principals were doing in schools across America. Most of the Jeanes' supervisors were in rural schools with small populations. As schools grew and more principals were hired, the Jeans' program became less important. Nevertheless, the program established black leadership in black schools in many areas of the south.

Representation of Latino/as and Native Americans in school leadership appears to be affected by cultural issues. Both groups historically have resented attempts by public schools to acculturate them to white Anglo-Saxon values and beliefs. DeJong (1990) reported that Native Americans are not adverse to Western education, but they see it as a way to acculturate rather than educate. Negative perceptions ingrained in culture have affected the career choices of many Latino/as and Native Americans.

Repeatedly, studies focusing on women and minorities in school administration raise the issue of sponsorship. Sponsorship is a major mechanism for recruiting and selecting school administrators. Veteran administrators sponsor potential candidates by encouraging them to enroll in university preparation programs and by providing visibility opportunities to promote their careers. Both women and people of color, historically, have been less likely than white males to be sponsored by other administrators to enter school leadership (Shakeshaft, 1987). As Ortiz (1982) noted, problems created by a lack of sponsorship are compounded by blockages to socialization. In this respect, both women and minorities who aspire to school leadership have not had a mentor in a position to sponsor them and therefore find it difficult to gain entry. In a previous work, we (Crow & Matthews, 1998) examined the importance of mentors and socialization in succeeding in school leadership. The sponsorship by those already in the career level has been a contributing factor for career advancement for newcomers. As you reflect on your choice to go into school leadership, most likely you also can identify someone in a leadership position who has formally or informally influenced your career decision.

INTERACTING ELEMENTS THAT HAVE INFLUENCED THE PRINCIPAL'S ROLE

The principal's role emerged from the teacher's role over time and over various geographic areas. The present role in which you are most familiar is a product influenced by various interacting elements. In the following section, we discuss four of these elements and how each has helped the principal's role emerge to its present concept.

Changing Social Demographics of Cities and Schools

An important factor in the early development of the principalship was the growth of cities, which caused school enrollment to grow rapidly, resulting in an increase in the number and size of schools. The early American high schools and elementary schools were relatively small. For example, Pierce (1935) reported the enrollment of the St. Louis High School in its first year (1853) as seventy-two pupils and the enrollment of the Chicago High School in its fourth year (1859) as 286 pupils. In the larger metropolitan centers, both elementary and secondary schools grew to considerable size, and their organization became more complex. The most rapid development of the principalship resulted from conditions and problems connected with urban schools. Between the American Civil War and the end of the nineteenth century, the growth of cities resulted in larger and more diverse school-age populations enrolled in larger and more complex schools. In 1890, approximately 2,500 high schools were serving over two hundred thousand students. By 1910, over ten thousand high schools were serving over nine hundred thousand American students (National Center for Education Statistics, 1992).

Not only did population growth lead to more and larger schools, but also in urban areas higher concentrations of population encouraged the creation of school districts and the separation of elementary and high schools. These conditions lead to the practice of designating one of the instructors as the principal teacher, someone who had some authority over other faculty. In urban secondary schools with diverse student populations, principal teachers increasingly spent more time carrying out administrative responsibilities.

Coinciding with the changes in the cities, the character of the school population also changed dramatically, particularly at the high school level. Early in the twentieth century, a minority of the high school age group went to high school. By the end of the twentieth century, due in part to compulsory education laws, nearly all youth of high school age enrolled in high school, resulting in a much more diverse school population. The issue became more critical as many central cities deteriorated and impoverished people became concentrated within the inner cities. Changes in the school population required more work than any one principal teacher could handle adequately. Despite the desire to retain a role combining both teaching and administrative responsibilities, the sheer numbers of students and teachers and the time required for principal teachers to complete major organizational and administrative reporting tasks in larger schools resulted in school boards relieving principal teachers of classroom teaching responsibilities.

Historically, larger school systems possessed several characteristics not commonly found in rural schools, and these assets gave urban schools some educational advantages. Larger student enrollments permitted greater specialization in instruction and more diversified curriculum. Social and cultural conditions of cities resulted in more emphasis on education, and a greater concentration of economic and cultural resources provided more material support for program development. Callahan (1962) reported that school districts in the largest cities, such as Boston, New York, and Chicago, became lighthouses for public education. Superintendents in these urban systems emerged as prototypes for educational management, and their behaviors were admired and adopted by many principals and superintendents throughout the United States. In a sense, these early occupants of the superintendent's office established an exemplary role not only for superintendents but also for principals throughout the country.

Academic Study and State Licensure Requirements

Data concerning the academic qualifications of early principals are meager. Some of the early school leaders, notably in the eastern cities, were either ministers or men trained in theology. Little professional development for individuals in the principalship or for those who desired to go into the principalship took place before the twentieth century. Likewise, little formal training took place for teachers, except for those who were geographically connected with *normal schools,* and educational institutions which focused on teacher training. Those who occupied school principal posts relied on their common sense, innate abilities, and teaching experience to perform largely management-related tasks.

Tyack and Hansot (1982) reported that an 1890 survey of educational departments in twenty leading universities uncovered only two courses in educational administration. Starting in 1914, pressures to utilize management techniques to broaden the education of school executives forced Teachers College of Columbia to give more attention to business methods, finance, and efficiency techniques. By 1917, offerings in educational administration at Columbia increased from two to eight courses (Callahan, 1962). Culbertson (1988) noted that the 1950s saw a "leap toward an administrative science" (p. 14) in education. Culbertson also noted the high value placed on the development of professional preparation programs that emphasized "theory development and . . . the building of a 'science of administration' " (p. 16). This trend, referred to as the *theory movement,* applied theories and concepts from the social and behavioral sciences to problems of educational administration (Crowson & McPherson, 1987).

As the levels of academic and professional training of principals increased, so did the states' requirements in certifying principals. In fact, state requirements often stimulated the growth of university preparation programs. At first, certification of principals was not necessary because the only prerequisite was a teaching certificate. However, as university programs grew to include more administrative preparation, states followed with more requirements for administrative certification (Tyack & Hansot, 1982).

Kowalski and Reitzug (1993) reported that during the 1920s, certification of school administrators was advocated primarily for two reasons: (1) many superintendents of that period had not taken a single college course in school administration, and (2) certification was perceived as one avenue for achieving professionalization of the role of principals. Callahan (1962) stated that by 1932, nearly half the states had adopted certification standards for administrators. In the 1950s, all states required some form of administrative certificate, although the requirements for each state varied as to both university course work and teaching experience. Currently, certification (often called licensure now) requirements still vary among the states, although a majority use the Interstate School Leaders Licensure Consortium Standards (*www.ccsso.org*) you prepare to become a principal or an assistant principal, you should check your state's certification/licensure requirements and determine if your preparation program meets those requirements (*www.ecs.org/clearinghouse/50/85/5085.htm*).

Professional Associations

Another large event in the emergence of the modern principalship occurred when the NEA established the Department of Secondary School Principals in 1916, followed by the Department of Elementary School Principals in 1921. During this time, the NEA was an umbrella association for many groups of educators, including superintendents, teachers, professors, and educational researchers. The creation of the school administrative departments signaled official recognition of the position of principal by a national body of professional educators. The influence these departments had on shaping the role of the contemporary principal cannot be overestimated. By establishing these departments, more scientific research was conducted in the work, problems, and role of the principal. The departments stimulated the professional interests not only of individual principals but also of other principals' associations throughout the country. Research studies on the principal's role regarding significant aspects of the work appeared in professional and scholarly journals and conferences.

During the 1960s and early 1970s, the NEA went through several stages of reorganization. The specialty divisions of the NEA, including those serving school administrators, disaffiliated themselves from the national organization. Several researchers (e.g., Kowalski & Reitzug, 1993; Tyack & Hansot, 1982) have claimed that the increased popularity of collective bargaining developed tensions among the specialty divisions. This dissatisfaction resulted in the formation of independent national organizations to serve the needs and interests of school administrators. Although many of these groups maintain a close working relationship with one another, they often compete for members. Superintendents tend to belong to the American Association of School Administrators (AASA, *www.aasa.org*), high school principals and assistant principals to the National Association of Secondary School Principals (NASSP, *www.nassp.org*), and elementary school principals and assistants to the National Association of Elementary School Principals (NAESP, *www.naesp.org*). Middle level administrators often choose either NASSP or NAESP or belong to both. Two other associations that principals often choose are the Association for Supervision and Curriculum Development (ASCD, *www.ascd.org*), which generally focuses on curriculum and instruction, and the National Staff Development Council (NSDC, *www.nsdc.org*), which concentrates on professional development of educators.

Since breaking away from NEA, both NAESP and NASSP have worked to improve the status and profession of the principalship. Both associations provide legal protection for members, conduct research, publish journals and newsletters, and provide development opportunities such as workshops and national conventions. These association activities and their state affiliates' activities have helped in establishing the principal's and assistant principal's role.

Practice of School Leaders

An important factor in the emergence of the principalship is the development of the practice of school administration over a period time. Two interconnected areas, namely, management and supervision, helped establish the role of the principal as a separate and distinct responsibility from its roots in teaching. In the early history of the principalship, management and supervision were often associated. It was not until the mid-twentieth century that the two areas became distinct.

The growth of cities and schools was a contributing factor in the transfer of management and supervision from the superintendent to the principal. One of the main functions of early superintendents was to evaluate the schools. Pierce (1935) claimed that the problems in administration caused by increased population put so many demands on superintendents' time that they were unable to give personal attention to the management and supervision of local schools. The logical step was to turn local management of schools over to the principals.

An initial approach to educational administration was grounded in the scientific management and industrial efficiency tenets of Frederick W. Taylor (1911). During the early years of the twentieth century, schools were under considerable pressure to produce results. America was becoming an industrial nation. It was perhaps inevitable that Taylor's philosophy of scientific industrial management would now be applied to the schools. The *scientific management* approach asserted that educational organizations, like commercial establishments, could be made businesslike and efficient. Tasks and responsibilities could be defined carefully and planned fully to lead to maximum organizational productivity. Many people believed that educational administration could best be improved by the scientific application of managerial expertise. This included carefully planned schedules for work, the instructions for doing it, and the expected standards of performance (Morris, Crowson, Porter-Gehrie, & Hurwitz, 1984).

Industrial scientific management was a movement that perfectly reflected its time because it emphasized the critical importance of managerial officialdom. Ellwood P. Cubberley (1916) wrote a highly influential textbook for school leaders in which he emphasized the school administrator as organizer, executive, and supervisor of work. In fact, Cubberley suggested that the educational leader should exercise large powers, apply broad knowledge and larger insight to educational needs, and plan all policies even though "the details might be best kept to himself" (p. 15). The importance of the school administrator was not diminished by Cubberley's added advice to be honest and square, clean and temperate, honorable, and "able to look men straight in the eye"

(p. 15). To Cubberley, so important was the role of the principal that he later wrote in 1923, "We are not likely to overestimate the importance of the office of school principal" (Cubberley, 1923, p. 28). He further summarized his belief with his often-quoted statement: "As is the principal, so is the school" (p. 15).

Another important factor in the emergence of the principalship was the freeing of principals from teaching duties so that they could supervise other classroom teachers. In dealing with the supervisory functions of the principal, the definition of the term *supervision* becomes important. A common definition is that supervision is the technique for improving teaching. However, distinguishing between supervisory and managerial activities of principals is usually quite difficult. A common distinction is that a principal manages things and supervises people. Although this statement is too simplistic, it does draw attention to the two functions. For purposes of studying the emergence of the principalship, however, it is important to note that supervision may have related more to the early principal's management role of "inspector" than to the role of "mentor" as it should be more commonly used today.

Pierce (1935) reported that supervisory activities were first exercised in public schools by visiting committees of laymen, usually consisting of the learned men of the town, namely, ministers and physicians. These committees visited the schools and determined the efficiency of instruction by examining the teachers. After boards of education were established, schools were inspected, pupils examined, and teacher's methods directed by official school committees. As the complexity of school organization increased, many of the supervisory functions developed by these committees were delegated to the principal.

CONCEPTUAL FRAMEWORKS INFLUENCING THE PRINCIPALSHIP ROLE

As the principalship emerged, a distinct and important role in American education was created. Certain conceptual frameworks influenced how the role was played out. In this section we will discuss three of these frameworks,—moral and ethical leadership, social and community leadership, and instructional leadership—and how, in particular, these frameworks have influenced the eight roles that we discuss later in this book.

Moral and Ethical Leadership

Many of the first principals of schools were directly associated with the ministry, and many others were heavily influenced by the Christian (mostly Protestant) ideal. Cubberley (1923) noted "the great spiritual importance" (p. 561) of the principal's work and likened the principal to "the priest in the parish" (p. 26). Cubberley's own career story gives interesting insight to the influence of religion in education. Tyack and Hansot (1982) reported

> When Ellwood P. Cubberley applied for the superintendency of schools in San Diego in 1896, the chairman of the school board was worried about his qualifications for the job. Cubberley had never had a course in education, but that was not the problem. He did not have a graduate degree, but that was not the problem either. The sticking point for the chairman was the question of Cubberley's piety, his religious orthodoxy, for he was a scientist who had written about geology and was known to be a believer in evolution. What was his view of religion, the chairman wanted to know, and what were

the guarantees of his good character? Cubberley replied to the inquiry with a strong testimonial from his Indiana minister and his own affirmation that "I believe firmly in God and the principles of the Christian religion." He continued, "I am in the strongest sense a harmonizer of Religion and Science, there is no conflict in my mind between the two." (pp. 114–115)

The people in public school leadership in the early years of the twentieth century usually were individuals who worked hard, were thrifty, and maintained high moral values—influenced by strong Protestant principles. Many either had been clergymen or had intended to enter the ministry. In fact, many not only were leaders in the schools during the week but also took on teacher and leader roles on Sunday. Religion provided an important criterion for selection to school leadership. Being Protestant and an active church member were important requirements for selection as a leader in the public school system.

During the middle to late nineteenth century, the Catholic Church opposed the common school movement because of its reliance on Protestant teachings, its use of the King James Bible, and the refusal to use public tax monies for Catholic schools (Tyack & Hansen, 1982). Because of these issues, many Catholic parents chose not to send their children to public schools. Many parishes developed their own schools, leading to the largest private educational system in America. Initially, these Catholic schools were mostly administered and staffed by the religious orders of sisters and brothers, as well as the priests of the congregations. The Second Vatican Council of the early 1960s changed the school personnel regulations. Although Catholic schools employed few laypersons in administration before the 1960s, since then, laypersons are the majority of Catholic principals, especially in elementary schools. The transition to laypersons in high school administration is also the trend but has proceeded much more slowly (Michaletz, 1984). Brubacher (1966) suggested that although well meaning and sympathetic to education, few priests were professionally trained and, therefore, lacked the pedagogical insight to supervise instruction and curriculum. Thus, the transition to laypersons was important in the Catholic system to have schools staffed and administered by professional educators.

Public school principals and parochial school principals are more similar than different. Both emerged as efficiency-minded, thrifty, and highly moral school leaders. Beck and Murphy (1993) submitted that these character images combined to create "a picture of the principal as one whose role is linked to timeless truths and values" (p. 15). Cubberley (1923) also suggested that values are linked to the community:

> The principal must remember that he holds a particularly responsible position as a model in his community. He must, in his dress, his manner, his speech, and his bearing, so conduct himself that he will easily win and hold the respect of teachers, pupils, and the community. (p. 26)

The nature of the moral and ethical leadership provided by the principal has changed since the early part of the twentieth century, but many of the standards still exist. Each year principals are terminated for failure to assume their leadership obligations or for breach of ethics or for immoral activities. Because of these kinds of ethical breaches and the principal as an ethical role in the community, preparation programs are typically required to teach and assess candidate dispositions such as fairness and integrity (e.g., *www.ncate.org*). Additionally, the Interstate School Leaders Licensure Consortium

(ISLCC) standard five states, "An education leader promotes the success of every student by acting with integrity, fairness, and in an ethical manner" (ISLCC, p. 15).

In the last decades of the twentieth century, several writers revisited the moral and ethical aspects of leadership. Greenleaf (1970) proposed a powerful conceptual framework in suggesting that the leader begins by being a servant leader. Greenleaf maintained that "conscious choice brings one to aspire to lead" (p. 7). Burns (1978) differentiated between transactional and transformational leadership by suggesting that most leaders are transactional—exchanging one thing for another thing with followers. "Transforming leadership is a relationship of mutual stimulation and elevation that converts followers into leaders and leaders into moral agents" (p. 4). According to Burns, leadership is a process of morality because leaders and followers have shared motives and goals. Covey (1989) presented a conception of leadership that is centered on ethical principles. For Covey, principle-centered leadership is based on the reality that we cannot violate natural laws with impunity. Sergiovanni (1992) advocated that principals need to learn skills that approach moral leadership. He maintained that followers would be more receptive to leadership if the leader showed them that certain changes are the right thing to do.

Social and Community Leadership

In addition to being ethical leaders, present day principals are also expected to be social and community leaders. Cubberley (1923), writing on the principal, noted, "No other person in the community can so immediately mould [*sic*] its life and shape its ideals" (p. 36). He further commented that the principal "must remember to carry himself at all times as a gentleman of the world should and would" (p. 26).

Other early twentieth-century writers on the principalship advised school leaders to develop positive community relationships. For example, Douglas (1932) recommended that the principal study the community as accurately as possible to determine its key people and organizations. "In every community there are men, women, and organizations that are outstandingly influential in determining community actions, attitudes, and actions. The principal must not neglect to know these people and to gain their confidence and their interest in his educational program" (p. 498). Cubberley (1923) claimed that community relations are one of the most important aspects of the work and that the community is, indeed, an asset to the school. A school leader "should know his community and be able to feel its pulse and express its wants, and the community should know him and believe in his integrity and honesty of purpose" (p. 153).

Concerns with community leadership of one type or another was present in the literature in every decade of the twentieth century. During World War II, Gregg (1943) reported the need for the principal to be a leader in the community for the war effort. Gregg claimed that every leader "has not only the professional, but also the patriotic responsibility of an all out effort to make his school function in such a way that the nation and youth of his community will be served in the most effective way" (p. 7). Postwar America saw communities trying to rebuild themselves, often around their schools. Campbell and his colleagues (1987) noted that the principal had an increased concern with community relations during this time that meant more involvement with parents and other community members. In 1973, Burden and Whitt (1973) suggested that principals relate not only to those within the school but also to persons in the community.

Arguing that changing social situations force principals to extend the scope of leadership activities, they wrote,

> Community power is a coming reality. The previous view that the local school could remain aloof and isolated from those it was purported to serve is no longer a viable one. The changing concept of democracy that means all people are to be involved, not just those in power, places new responsibilities on the building administrator. (p. xiii)

The last two decades of the twentieth century and the beginning of the twenty-first century saw school leadership turn its attention to educating all children, no matter what their socioeconomic background or academic abilities were. The principal is part of the social reconstruction of communities in which every person deserves an education with dignity and respect. At times, this social leadership role puts the principal at odds with certain fundamentally conservative subcultures of the community. Consequently, being a strong social leader also requires the principal to be a strong moral leader in the community and to take a position of what is right rather than what is popular or what has been done in the past. As Beck and Murphy (1993) suggested, "there [are] serious efforts developing to transform the principalship into an instrument of social justice" (p. 194).

To a modern observer, the community relations role of the principal might be associated with "playing politics." However, in the first half of the twentieth century, most educational leaders accepted the doctrine that politics should be separated from education. Playing politics often was associated with selfish and self-aggrandizing politicians and was meant to be more allied with policymaking than with social and community leadership. Kimbrough and Burkett (1990) speculated that politics in the early twentieth century took on a sleaziness that many political reformers wanted to keep out of government operations such as the public school system. As they put it, "No self-respecting educational leader would admit to engaging in . . . [politics]" (p. 90). However, during the last half of the twentieth century, politicians and educators collaborated on many issues of policymaking, and it would be difficult today for any school leader to claim that he or she is not engaged in some form of politics. Likewise, it would be difficult for any modern politician to have no agenda in education.

Not only did politics change but also communities did likewise, and with them so did the schools. These changes have made it difficult for school leaders to remain as close and responsive to their communities as they once were. Several modern reformers have suggested that community building and economic development are essential responsibilities for school principals and schools (Crowson, 2001). Proposals such as those offered by Theobold and Nachtigal (1995) aimed to "redesign education for the purpose of recreating community—community that is ecologically sustainable" (p. 35). Sergiovanni (1996) saw community members responding to the substance of ideas, which implied that leadership builds a "shared followership . . . not on who to follow, but on what to follow" (p. 83). A school community, then, is a group of people who share common ideas about schooling and learning. The implications for school leaders are clear. Persons within the community need to be part of a group working toward the common good and sharing a set of values within the school. The school, as a community entity, needs to be part of a larger group that also has mutual values and goals (Drake & Roe, 1999). The continuing emphasis on social and community leadership is evident in a recent proposal for reforming the profession of educational leadership (Murphy, 2002). Two of the three pillars on which educational leadership should be based, according to Murphy, are democratic schooling and social justice.

Instructional Leadership

Instruction has always been a part of the role of the principal. Since its inception as a role separate from teaching, some responsibility has been assigned to the principal to influence teaching and learning in a school. At times and with some persons, the role of instructional leadership was submerged because other roles were more prominent, such as cleric, manager, and bureaucrat. Nevertheless, one of the reasons to free principals from their teaching assignments was to give them more time for instructional supervision. As good as the intentions of the normal schools were, many teachers never had the opportunity to attend them or did so only briefly. Consequently, much training occurred after the teachers entered into active service. In addition to helping teachers be better instructors, another condition evolved—the addition of new subjects in the curriculum. The dominant assumption was that the principal was in the best position to be the instructional leader and should be directly involved with teachers in improving instruction, creating a learning climate in the school, and facilitating development of the curriculum.

During the educational reform movements of the 1980s, the term used most to describe the principal's responsibilities with instruction and curriculum was *instructional leadership*. Greenfield (1987) noted that this term was used often as a slogan guiding the efforts of educational reformers. DeBevoise (1984) defined instructional leadership as "those actions that a principal takes, or delegates to others, to promote growth in student learning" (p. 15). Hallinger and Murphy (1987) noted that research on effective schools led to the expectation that principals in the 1980s were to play a more active role in instructional leadership. Their suggestion, however, was that instructional leadership was context dependent rather than uniform in nature. Principals were to first understand the school environment, including teachers and students, and then diagnose what was appropriate instructional leadership.

This type of instructional leadership left out an important component—the role that teachers need to play as instructional leaders. As it became more apparent that principals could not correctly diagnose teaching and learning needs of teachers and students and that teachers, who were most involved in the learning process, understood their own and their student's needs, instructional leadership shifted from the principal as the sole leader to include teachers as instructional leaders. This shift then returned the principal's role to what it was originally as the principal teacher—that of being an educator of educators, a leader of leaders. Furthermore, Barth (1990) recommended that principals not only be leaders of instructional leaders but also leaders of learning. Not only are principals to be well educated, but also they are expected to model and exemplify learning themselves. The focus on learner-centered leadership has been reignited by societal pressures of accountability and equity that emphasize learning for all students. This focus can be seen in Public Law 107-110, titled No Child Left Behind Act of 2001 (NCLB), professional association programs such as those sponsored by NASSP, NAESP ASCD, and NSDC; and university preparation programs. Likewise, this emphasis on learner-centered leadership is the third pillar of Murphy's (2002) proposal for educational leadership reform.

The current movement known as professional learning communities (PLC) is a framework to improve student learning by empowering teachers as instructional leaders and collaborators, which this book emphasizes as the best method for current school reform. A PLC has at its core the centralized ideas of standards and accountability, the decentralized notions of shared leadership with attention to individual students and their learning, and the notion of collaboration of teachers to improve instruction, assessment, and ultimately student learning. Many researchers and theorists (DuFour, 2004; Hord & Sommers, 2008; Louis, Marks, & Kruse (1996); Matthews & Crow, 2003) have reported on the benefits of schools developing into PLCs. We will discuss the history and concepts of the PLC movement in more depth in Chapter 3. The main purpose in this book is to introduce you to the framework of a PLC and the eight role implications for principals and assistant principals in a PLC.

SCHOOL REFORM AND IMPLICATIONS TO THE ROLE OF SCHOOL PRINCIPALS

A casual observer could be forgiven for saying that, as far as educational reform for public schools is concerned, nothing has changed in over one hundred years. On April 20, 1893, the *Chicago Tribune* announced a meeting of "all citizens who have at heart the interest and welfare of the public schools" and then on April 26, 1893, reported that the people of Chicago needed to "inquire minutely into the workings of the public school system, because if the criticisms referred to are true there is grave cause for mortification and alarm" (McCaul, 1959, p. 269). How similar that report of the state of schools is to several more modern reports such as the 1983 National Commission of Excellence in Education's (NCEE) report titled *A Nation at Risk: The Imperative for Educational Reform* that stated that American schools were falling behind those of other countries and that "We have, in effect, been committing an act of unthinking, unilateral educational disarmament" (NCEE, 1983, p. 5). Further, the report defines itself as, "An Act to close the achievement gap with accountability, flexibility, and choice, so that no child is left behind" (p. 1).

These proposals for school reform have swayed between centralization and decentralization. Moves for centralization are those that promote national academic standards and national criteria for teacher and principal certification/licensure. Efforts that advance decentralization focus on student-centered instruction and local control of curriculum. Obviously, these two are reform efforts that have had an impact on the roles that principals would play. In the section that follows, we offer a short discussion of the history of reform efforts and how these efforts have affected the principalship.

The Committee of Ten report in 1893, *A Nation at Risk* report in 1983, and the NCLB Act of 2001 are similar in that they call for centralization in the form of more formal control of standards, teacher quality, and more time spent learning selected standards. In 1896, William Rainey Harper, the president of the University of Chicago, held conferences for teachers because of a "deep interest in pedagogical theory and practice and serious concern for the improvement of the public schools" (McCaul, 1959, p. 261). The emphasis was to standardize the curriculum and teacher preparation as a means of improvement. This concern to standardize what students are learning has a long and contested history.

John Dewey, as a faculty member at the University of Chicago, was another strong supporter of improving education and teacher quality. However, Dewey favored a child-centered approach that would more likely be described as decentralization because the needs of the individual child were the focus of instruction. His ideas permeated the educational movements up through the 1950s until there was a new cry for national standards because of the cold war. The launching of Sputnik in 1957 by the USSR (Union of Soviet Socialist Republics) brought a movement for centralization in American schools. The fear of being outperformed by the Soviets resulted in raising standards and funding in science and mathematics through several federal and state legislated acts.

As the reforms toward national standards moved into the 1960s, a new push for decentralization began in response to an increasing gap in achievement among low-income and minority students. The question arose in civil rights arenas as to whether centralized school boards could make appropriate decisions for local schools with different populations. In 1990, Cuban observed that "values of participation and equity lay at the core of the impulse to decentralize authority to govern schools" (p. 5).

The Civil Rights Act of 1964 directed the U.S. Commissioner of Education to study equal opportunity for poor and minority students and was encompassed in the Elementary and Secondary Education Act of 1965, which had as a primary tenet to serve the individual needs of low-income and minority students. The study was presented in what was known as the Coleman report in 1966 and stated that the achievement gap was greater within schools than between schools when controlling for student background and the availability of resources (Coleman, et al., 1966).

The controversy that ensued over the Coleman report spurred research in the 1970s and 1980s to discover what constituted effective schools. The effective schools movement culminated with the *Nation at Risk* report in 1983 and its primarily centralized notions of improving schools through legislation. The suggested legislation from these reports was that standards should be raised for high school graduation and that teachers must be held accountable for academic success (Orlich, 2000). An additional centralized proposal for the professionalization of teaching came from the Carnegie Forum's report (*A nation prepared: Teachers for the 21st century*, 1986) recommending that there be tougher certification requirements based on national standards.

However, it was not long before there was an acknowledgment "that state-driven reforms were not penetrating individual schools" (Cuban, 1990, p. 5) and a decentralized movement toward school improvement began with results such as school-site councils and school-based management (Kearns, 1988; Rowan, 1995). As site decisions gained popularity, a new movement toward centralization in the form of standards and curriculum alignment resurfaced. The standards movement aimed to improve education for all by articulating academic and achievement standards for students and providing school sanctions and incentives based on student achievement. One of the foremost proponents of the standards-based reform was Marshall Smith, the Undersecretary of Education during the Bill Clinton presidency. He ensured that the standard-based reform was included in the reauthorization of the Elementary and Secondary Education Act in 1994.

Interestingly, in the 1990s and 2000s, there were movements toward centralization and decentralization occurring at the same time. The Obey-Porter Comprehensive Reform Demonstration Program of 1997 (US Congress 1997 and the elementary and secondary education act, Public Law 105-78, 105th Congress, Sec 249) was a centralized government-reform measure requiring decentralized implementation of individual school plans. The national plan outlined specific requirements, but at the same time mandated that each individual site define innovative strategies, assessment components, and a community involvement plan in order to receive government funds.

The notion of centralized legislation with decentralized requirements is embodied in the George W. Bush plan of No Child Left Behind Act of 2001 with goals that are to raise the academic achievement level of all children in reading, math, and science to a proficient level, regardless of economic status or background. The act, signed into law in 2002 by President Bush, is an aggregation of earlier laws—the Elementary and Secondary Education Act (ESEA) of 1965 and the Improving America's School Act (IASA) of 1994, designed to enhance educational opportunity and to diminish the discrepancy of performance between subgroups of students. The identified subgroups were students who were economically disadvantaged, who had limited English proficiency, who belonged to racial and/or ethnic minorities, or who had disabilities.

NCLB contains centralized elements of national standards and accountability as well as teacher quality components. The law provides that, among other penalties, schools that fail to make adequate progress toward national goals will have federal funds withheld. Concurrently, the law requires that schools be held accountable for the separate achievement of all sub-groups and it contains school-choice components for parents and mandates parental involvement in forming school plans, all of which are provisions more closely aligned with ideas of decentralization.

With these swings of the pendulum from centralized to decentralized, the roles of the principal and assistant principal have likewise swung back and forth. During centralized reform efforts, principals' roles were considered more as middle management. They were to implement the decisions of those who were directing educational efforts. During decentralized reform efforts, the principal's role became more involved with distributed leadership. The principal was to lead others into a shared leadership model. Consequently, these reform efforts have developed the principalship into a complex role—far more complex than it was originally conceived.

CONTEMPORARY CONDITIONS AND IMPLICATIONS

Historically, the principal and assistant principal roles have been shaped by numerous social and cultural forces, and these roles continue to change as schools and society reshape them. Currently, there is an urgent and widespread demand to improve student performance and to reform schools. The push for standards-based reform—and the pressure on schools to deliver in terms of academic performance—has raised the demands and pressures on principals, assistant principals, and teachers and brought an unprecedented level of public scrutiny to their job performance (see Professional Dilemma 2.1).

The management functions traditionally associated with school leadership have not gone away—if anything, they have become more demanding. Charter schools, school choice, vouchers, decentralized governance, standardized testing, accountability, and youth social issues have provoked new pressures that no principal could have anticipated a decade ago when many entered the profession. In addition, other societal changes, including shifting demographics, the speed of communication, and the explosion of knowledge, are rapidly changing the look of and the demands on schools (Marx, 2000). Indeed, many worthy veterans have become disenchanted with the rapid changes and have considered or acted on early retirement. Whitaker (1995) interviewed

---

Professional Dilemma 2.1

In Cesar Chavez Elementary School, Principal Mary Evans has been working for several years with the faculty in developing a professional learning community. The teachers have put in extra time, attended numerous professional development sessions, and demonstrated a strong commitment in making their school a learning community. Recently, the Cesar Chavez Elementary School did not meet adequate yearly progress (AYP) under the No Child Left Behind Act. The local media announced the AYP report for all schools in the district indicating that Cesar Chavez was the only school that did not meet AYP. The teachers at the school were demoralized and complained that they had put in a lot of extra hours for nothing. If you were Principal Evans, what would you be saying to your teachers?

---

principals to examine emotional exhaustion and depersonalization in their jobs. Four themes emerged that were related to these issues and that the respondents indicated might prompt them to leave the principalship:

1. *Increasing demands of the principalship*   Respondents cited accountability pressures, increased paperwork, time-management issues, and tensions related to restructuring.
2. *Lack of role clarity*   Respondents expressed frustration over the lack of clarity in new roles related to school-based management and shared decision making.
3. *Lack of recognition*   Principals perceived a need for more intrinsic and extrinsic rewards and recognition, especially from the district office.
4. *Decreasing autonomy*   Principals perceived that autonomy was slipping away because of collaborative decision making. Making decisions with staff, parents, and community members left principals feeling somewhat powerless and vulnerable. (Whitaker, 1995, pp. 290–291)

Another study by the Education Research Service (2000) revealed an increasing shortage of administrative candidates for leadership positions in schools. The shortage was most acute at the secondary level and in urban settings. Although researchers (e.g., Bridgman, 1986) have reported shortages of school principals previously, the present shortage has caught many school officials without qualified candidates for administrative positions.

These reported shortages and the concern with recruiting sufficient numbers of qualified candidates have led to a focus on the attractions of the job. Pounder and Merrill (2001) found that potential candidates to the secondary school principalship identified two major attractions of the job: the desire to influence or improve education and the position's salary and benefits as compared to teachers' salaries and benefits. However, these potential candidates identified time demands as the most unattractive aspect of the job, followed by the problems and dilemmas that come with the job.

The outlook for you as an aspiring school leader to get a position is somewhat positive. According to the U.S. Department of Labor, school leader positions should grow about 9–17 percent by the year 2014. With education taking on greater importance in everyone's lives, the need for people to administer education programs will grow. And, a large proportion of current educational leaders are expected to retire over the

TABLE 2.3 Average Salaries in Dollars of School Administrators in the United States as of 2004

Principals	Average Salary in Dollars
Senior high school	82,225
Junior high/middle school	78,160
Elementary school	74,062
Assistant Principals	
Senior high school	68,945
Junior high/middle school	66,319
Elementary school	63,398

Source: Education Testing Service (2005).

next ten years. However, opportunities may vary by geographical area, as enrollments are expected to increase the fastest in the West and South, where the population is growing, and to decline or remain stable in the Northeast and the Midwest. School leaders also are in greater demand in rural and urban areas, where salaries are often lower than in the suburbs (U.S. Bureau of Census, 2006).

Likewise, salaries and benefits for school leaders will probably remain pretty good. In May 2004, elementary and secondary school administrators had median annual earnings of $74,190. Salaries of education administrators depend on several factors, including the location and enrollment level in the school or school district. According to a survey of public schools, conducted by the Educational Research Service, average salaries for principals and assistant principals in the 2004–2005 school year were as indicated in Table 2.3.

Benefits for school leaders are considered good by most standards. Many principals and assistant principals get four or five weeks of vacation every year and have generous health and pension packages.

Nevertheless, the fact that school administration has been, and continues to be, a white male–dominated profession also obviously affects the way many potential principals and assistant principals perceive the roles. As might be expected, as students of color in the public schools become the majority, a higher demand will exist for principals of color.

Conclusion

In this chapter, we have introduced the role of the principal and assistant principal and discussed how history has influenced the way you will practice those roles. While many school leaders feel the sand shifting under their feet, the men and women who become principals and assistant principals do so because they believe they can make a difference for children and youth. Although ever-changing, these positions have proven their worth in the educational arena and in addressing various social needs. In this book, we emphasize the professional learning community as a vehicle in which principals and assistant principals can continue to make a difference for children and youth. Chapter 3 explores the PLC concept in more depth.

Activities

SELF REFLECTION ACTIVITIES

1. Consider the reform efforts that you have seen in your career or in that of a colleague's. Determine if those efforts were centralized, decentralized, or both.
2. If you were Consuelos in the vignette, what conceptual framework would you emphasize during your first few weeks as principal of Valleyview High School?

PEER REFLECTION ACTIVITIES

1. Shadow an assistant principal for a day, and discuss with a colleague the kinds of tasks performed. Compare and contrast the tasks with those of Consuelos' and speculate on what conceptual framework seems to be emphasized by these two administrators.

2. Consider Consuelos' first faculty meeting at Valleyview High School in the opening vignette. Considering the facts of the vignette, what should she emphasize at that faculty meeting?

COURSE ACTIVITIES

1. Interview a veteran principal who is near retirement. In what ways does this principal believe the role of principal has changed? Discuss with your classmates the specific purpose of the role as well as the tasks.
2. What are the strengths and weaknesses of leadership styles such as those of Principal Montgomery in the vignette?
3. Research the demographic changes in your school community in the last decade. How have these changes affected the principal's role in promoting learning for all students?

Websites

National Association of Elementary School Principals (NAESP)
www.naesp.org

National Association of Secondary School Principals (NASSP)
www.nassp.org

American Association of School Administrators
www.aasa.org

Association of Supervision and Curriculum Development (ASCD)
http://ascd.org

National Staff Development Council (NSDC)
www.nsdc.org

The Oral History of the Principalship (Project from Virginia Tech, online database of interviews from public school principals, all retired)
http://scholar.lib.vt.edu/faculty_archives/principalship/

National Center for Education Statistics (NCES)
www.nces.ed.gov/

National Education Association (NEA)
www.nea.org/

No Child Left Behind (NCLB) Act—p. 67
www.ed.gov/nclb/landing.jhtml

CHAPTER 3

Professional Learning Communities as School Reform

Vignette

The spiral reform movement has been evident in the Highland County School District for twenty years. Through the professional development activities available to educators, school-based decision making and action research were mixed with districtwide standards of instruction and assessment. Several reform efforts had been tried by the district and some from the school level. One mandate from the district in the 1980s required all schools to embrace the Madeline Hunter teaching effectiveness model wherein teachers learned the principles of effective teaching. In the 1990s, two other efforts emerged: the district moved the sixth grade into the junior high and changed the name to middle school, and the high schools moved into an eight-block schedule. To coordinate the state core and testing in 2003, teacher teams were established at each level. These teams met once a month to align the curriculum with the state criterion-referenced test.

Besides the district reform efforts, several schools also embraced change efforts. One elementary school adopted student education planning conferences with every child. Highland High School started the writing across the curriculum movement and instituted the international baccalaureate curriculum. Overall, schools in Highland County School District had seen a lot of reform efforts but, unfortunately, not a great deal of improved learning, at least as measured on the end of level student achievement tests.

After several years of reform, the test results were the same as they were when the reforms began. The superintendent and principals, although well-meaning, had not seen the results that they had hoped to obtain with the new reforms. In fact, the superintendent retired because of the frustrations he was facing with all of the reforms. Toward the end of his tenure, even his supporters were tired of all the reform efforts.

Most teachers were also tired of the endless reforms and had taken a "this too shall pass" attitude. A few teachers even had filed grievances with their teaching association, claiming that the reforms were causing them stress and requiring more time at work. The teachers who could, took early retirement. Many teachers left the district for other "safer" and less stressful positions elsewhere.

A different kind of movement started emerging at Highland High School, a school that had failed adequate yearly progress. In the summer of 2004, Principal Paul Swatt took one assistant principal and ten teachers to Lincolnshire, Illinois, to learn more about Adlai Stevenson High School's movement into a professional learning community (PLC). They learned how this large suburban high school had established collaborative teams that had developed common standards and assessments for each curricular area. They also learned about preventions and interventions for students who were not achieving the standards. Afterwards, the team came back enthusiastic and energized with the concept of PLCs.

In August 2004, several of the teachers gave a presentation about PLCs to the faculty at their opening institute. Their enthusiasm about PLCs was contagious with some teachers who wanted to immediately implement the PLC. Most teachers, however, only nodded politely as they thought, "Here we go again. Another bandwagon we are going to get on." Nevertheless, Principal Swatt and the team were not easily detoured from their vision. As the year progressed, the team distributed reading materials about PLCs and conducted small voluntary workshops. The seeds were planted. Two math teachers started collaborating with each other and developed common standards and assessment in their Algebra I classes. Soon thereafter, they began to see fewer students fail Algebra I. All of the English teachers except one collaborated on a common grading rubric for essays. They also noticed that compositions were now more complete and thoughtful.

By the end of that year, the PLC team, with the help of others in the faculty, won the hearts of about half of the faculty. Those involved in the culture shifts to a PLC anxiously awaited the results from the criterion referenced tests (CRT). During the early summer, the principal shared the results with the team. Only small gains were registered. The team was disappointed, but Principal Swatt insisted that the vision was right and encouraged the faculty to stay the course.

When the faculty met for opening institute in August of the following year, Principal Swatt remained undaunted with his vision and shared the results with enthusiasm and celebration. He helped the faculty understand that change such as the PLC culture shift had to be sustained over time to be effective. He encouraged more reading of the literature on PLCs and organized more voluntary workshops. Other teachers, who had not attended the summer conference, went to another PLC conference in a neighboring city. They also caught the vision.

As the year progressed, Principal Swatt and his assistant principals sat with as many collaborative teams as they could and helped mentor those who needed help with collaboration, common standards, assessments, preventions, and interventions. In midyear, Principal Swatt invited a principal of a nearby elementary school who had experience with PLCs to visit with the faculty and to show her school's student achievement data. Slowly, as teams of teachers started focusing on results of student learning, more of the faculty came on board with PLCs. There were still dissenters, but their voice was muted as enthusiastic teachers celebrated their success.

The CRTs for that year had significant gains and the school passed adequate yearly progress (AYP). It was becoming apparent to everyone that those teachers who were embracing the PLC cultural shift, focusing on students' results, and collaborating with one another on assessments, interventions, and preventions were seeing the most gains in student learning and the increased CRT scores. As the third year of the implementation began, other schools in the district started taking notice. The new superintendent became more involved with PLCs and started encouraging other schools to look into them.

Finally, after five years of implementation at Highland High School, all schools in the school district had adopted the PLC model. Not all teachers were on board, but those who had were more enthusiastic about teaching and learning than they had ever been in their careers. The patrons saw the positive culture shifts and were thrilled with their children's learning. A lot of work still needed to be done, but the district was definitely headed in the right direction.

INTRODUCTION

The many years of educational reform have left many educators, parents, and researchers skeptical as to what the next reform movement might be. As was the situation in Highland County School District, many of these reform efforts did not produce the desired results that many educators had hoped. Part of the problem was the focus on structural or technical changes rather than on student learning. In fact, the Madeline Hunter teaching effectiveness model had its important points, but its focus on teaching did not always improve student learning. Likewise, other reform efforts such as the middle school movement, writing across the curriculum, and several literacy programs looked more at what teachers did than what students learned. In addition, many of these efforts were not given the time to become effective. Thus, educators and patrons have become discouraged at most school reform efforts.

The No Child Left Behind Act (NCLB) of 2001 called for some of the most radical and sweeping changes in American education since 1965, when the Elementary and Secondary Education Act (ESEA) was first implemented. However, while the scope of the changes required by NCLB was unprecedented, the American education system has for centuries been subject to frequent waves of school reform initiatives. This almost constant demand for reform has produced a variety of solutions and approaches. A different approach is the establishment of PLCs in schools. The PLC movement should not be considered as a program approach or a single effort reform. Instead, the PLC effort should be considered as a cultural shift. This PLC cultural shift provides an environment for ongoing assessment and exchange of ideas so that teaching and learning will be improved constantly, and the need for sweeping reform obviated.

Several educators, researchers, and patrons advocate the PLC cultural shift. DuFour and Eaker (1998) asserted that "the most promising strategy for sustained, substantive school improvement is developing the ability of school personnel to function as professional learning communities" (p. xi). Hord (2004) underscored this view, "The question of how to transform low-performing or underperforming schools into high-achieving schools is not easily answered. But . . . professional learning communities can play a major role in turning troubled schools around" (p. 5). Hord (2004) further pointed out that "through their participation in a professional learning community, teachers become the first learners, continuous learners, and more effective teachers. In turn, student outcomes increase" (p. 5). Huffman and Hipp (2003) noted that "professional learning communities are increasingly identified as critical to the success of school reform efforts" (p. 4). These and many practicing educators have seen substantial results in schools as they make this PLC cultural shift. We endorse this movement as a way that educators can indeed improve instructional practices that will improve student learning. Before we go into the details of a PLC, we offer a short history of educational reform and PLCs.

EDUCATIONAL REFORM AND PROFESSIONAL LEARNING COMMUNITIES

Since Horace Mann introduced the notion of common schools in the middle of the nineteenth century, reform has been a central and sometimes unrelenting theme in the American education system. Because reform of American schools has been viewed as important to reforming society, during the last several decades, the call for educational reform has come increasingly from the political arena, with the result that reforms have been initiated at the school, district, state, and national levels with various frequency and foci.

As was the situation with the Highland County School District in the opening vignette, despite the district administrators' good intentions for improving student learning by fixing educational problems, many reform efforts enjoy only partial success or fail altogether. Elmore (2004) suggested one reason for this failure is that the "capacity to initiate and sustain reform has exceeded, to a considerable degree, our capacity to solve the problems that undermine the effects of reforms" (p. 3). Indeed, teachers often become overwhelmed with reform because they continue to teach their students while simultaneously grappling with reform initiatives from several sources, each with its own particular focus. Cuban (1984), however, reported an even deeper reason for the failure of educational reforms. He noted that teachers tend to teach in the same way even in the presence of reform efforts and that the teaching culture "breeds conservatism and resistance to change in instructional practice" (p. 243).

A further problem with educational reform lies in the complex and multidimensional nature of educational systems. Weick (1982) identified this problem over two decades ago. He claimed that schools were unique organizations, quite different from organizations that exist elsewhere in the society, and he further claimed that schools could not be governed by conventional management theory. Weick described schools as *loosely coupled systems*, observing that loosely coupled systems often are organizations with coordination that is often lacking, regulations that are often absent, and networks that are highly connected but with very slow feedback. While these characteristics appear negative, Weick claimed that they actually might help organizations such as schools because they can persist through rapid environmental fluctuations, can allow local adaptations and creative solutions to develop, can allow subsystem breakdown without damaging the entire organization, and can allow more self-determination by the stakeholders involved. In general, Weick concluded that loosely coupled systems probably are cheaper to coordinate; however, they are much more difficult to change systematically.

Putting all of this together creates a challenge for you as a principal or assistant principal who wants to implement reform efforts. Perhaps the important part for you to understand is that the process of reform needs to be both fluid and flexible. Reform efforts that intend real change need to be fluid enough to be adaptable to individual school cultures, and these efforts need to be flexible so that various voices in the school community can be heard and accommodated. In fact, we hope to show you that PLCs are both fluid and flexible if the process is implemented successfully.

Furthermore, while reform efforts need to be directed at the various levels of educational systems, each level engenders its own, sometimes unique problems. Local reform initiatives, for instance, are often volatile and superficial (Elmore, 2004). At this level, schools often do as Highland County School District in the opening vignette in that they move quickly from one reform idea to the next in a short period and tend to choose reforms that have only a shallow impact on the problems they need to address. On the other hand, reforms mandated at the federal level, such as NCLB, require such sweeping changes that they might lead to uproar and chaos.

Perhaps a better way at looking at reform would be as culture shifting. A PLC is a system of culture shifting, meaning that the way teaching and learning occurred in the past does not work as well now and a shift in the culture is needed. Consequently, a shift in school culture needs to occur so that teaching and learning will improve.

Culture shifts under a PLC will occur when such things as teacher isolation shifts to teacher collaboration, assessment *of* learning shifts to assessment *for* learning, fixed time for learning shifts to variable time for learning, and remediation shifts to systems of prevention and intervention (DuFour, DuFour, Eaker, & Many, 2007). Such cultural shifts in school have given positive results in improving student learning.

Let us now discuss what a PLC looks like. We begin by looking at the concept of community.

UNDERSTANDING COMMUNITY

Before we explore the various models of PLCs, we begin with a discussion of the concept of *community*. In Chapter 1, we discussed the characteristics of community. The term *community* is used in different ways in the literature, but common to most of these definitions is the concept of belongingness (Soloman, Watson, Battistich, Schaps, & Delucchi, 1996). While there are differences in opinion on specific characteristics of organizations that constitute communities, as Furman (1998) explained, community is not present until members experience feelings of belongingness, trust in others, and safety.

Trust is worth mentioning, in more detail, in constituting a community. When trust exists, communities tend to feel a more sense of belongingness and safety. Hord and Sommers (2008) claimed that trust is a social lubricant that makes an organization run. Bryk and Schneider (2002) studied more than 250 elementary schools in Chicago after the district implemented school-based management in some schools. They looked at three different relationships regarding trust: trust between administrators and teachers, trust between teachers and teachers, and trust between parents and teachers. They found all of those relationships were significant in establishing trust in a school. From your own experience in schools, you also have seen that when teachers trust each other, they share more, they help one another more, and they are more supportive of one another. Likewise, when teachers trust their administrators, they feel less threatened and more likely to take risks in creating learning opportunities. With trust, building communities will more likely occur.

McMillan and Chavis (1986) maintained that the term *community* has two uses. The first refers to a territorial or geographic unity; the second is relational and describes the quality or character of human relationships. Operationally, McMillan and Chavis proposed that community consists of four elements: membership, influence, integration and fulfillment of needs, and a shared emotional connection. A community exists when its members experience a sense of belonging. In a community, the members feel that the group is important to them and that they are important to the group. Members of a community feel that the group will satisfy their needs; they will be protected, nurtured, watched over, and supported. Finally, the community has a shared and emotional sense of connection to each other (Osterman, 2000).

The significance of community is reflected in the work of Dewey (1900, 1958). Dewey viewed education as a social rather than an individualistic process. The quality of education, Dewey argued, "is realized in the degree in which individuals form a group" (Dewey, 1958, p. 58). It is the school's responsibility to encourage the development of this sense of community, and it is through collaboration that learning occurs. In this sense, Dewey described community in schools primarily as consisting of students and teachers caring for each other. In a PLC, the term *community* embraces that sense of belongingness; that sense of caring for each other; and that the group will be supportive of each of its members, which includes everyone at the school, especially principals, teachers, and students. Keep in mind this concept of community, as we explore the elements that constitute a PLC.

VARIOUS MODELS OF A PROFESSIONAL LEARNING COMMUNITY

Many researchers, theorists, and practitioners have defined different models of PLCs, yet few attempts have been made in combining existing thoughts into a unified idea (e.g, Blanstein, 2004; DuFour, DuFour, Eaker, & Many, 2006; Hord, 1997; Louis & Marks, 1998; Senge, 1990, 2000). In the following sections, we explore some of these PLC models and then attempt to establish a unified definition.

One author who we will discuss again in Chapter 4 is Peter Senge (1990) who described five different elements of a learning organization: shared vision, mental models, system thinking, personal mastery, and team learning. In a later work, Senge and his colleagues (2000) connected and described how these elements functioned in a school setting in his work *Schools That Learn*. Around the same time as Senge's work, two educational researchers arrived at similar ideas in what they termed *professional communities*. Kruse and Seashore-Louis (1995) provided an introductory view of what they considered a learning community model. Their elements were made up of two integral areas: internal structures and organizational factors. Internal structures essential to professional communities consisted of reflective dialogue, deprivatized practice, collaboration or shared work, normative control, and socialization of new professional members. Kruse and Seashore-Louis described the organizational factors as school size, principal leadership, and trust. In all, Kruse and Seashore-Louis suggested nine elements in their description of a professional community.

Hord (1997) also developed a model for PLCs. Hord presented five elements that she found to make up learning communities in schools, namely shared values and vision, supportive shared leadership, shared personal practice, supportive conditions (which included physical conditions and people capacities), and collective creativity. Although some elements were similar to the Kruse and Seashore-Louis model, Hord's model added supportive conditions in which she considered not only building leader support but also district leader support.

Probably the most known model among practitioners is the Richard DuFour and Robert Eaker (1998) model that has been widely published. They presented six elements: shared mission, vision, and values; collective inquiry; collaborative teams; action orientation and experimentation; continuous improvement; and results orientation. Unique to DuFour and Eaker at the time was that their elements began to focus specifically on student learning. Blankstein (2004) also contributed a PLC model with many of the other elements in other models but also adding important elements to his model. Blankstein was the first to specifically mention the systems of prevention and intervention.

ELEMENTS IN A PROFESSIONAL LEARNING COMMUNITY

Because several models for PLCs exist, Mathews, Williams, and Stewart (2007) searched the literature and studied schools and then developed ten cultural elements that existed as common in most successful PLCs. Their work identified the following elements.

Principal Leadership That Is Focused on Student Learning.   The reality of principal work has not always focused on student learning. As we discussed in Chapter 2, the rise of the scientific management movement in America in the twentieth century influenced the work of principals because the efficiency management of the school became more important than did effective teaching and learning. In Chapter 5, we discuss the role of a principal in a PLC as someone who creates conditions that help adults in the school continually improve their ability to ensure students gain knowledge and skills that are essential to their success.

Common Mission, Vision, Values, and Goals That Are Focused on Teaching and Learning.   It is important to note that we use mission and vision as two different elements in a PLC. A mission provides the foundation for creating a vision by defining the school's core values and creating goals in accomplishing the vision (Matthews & Crow, 2003). Further, we use the Bolman and Deal (2003) definition of a vision as a "persuasive and hopeful image of the future" (p. 315). We believe that the principal's work with the faculty, staff, and community in developing a common mission and vision will be important in establishing the values and goals that will propel the school's culture into a PLC.

Participative Leadership That Focuses on Teaching and Learning.   In Chapter 1, we discussed the definition by Rost (1991) of leadership as an influence relationship among leaders and followers. In a PLC, principals must share leadership with others. The terms *democratic leadership, teacher leadership, distributed leadership, school leadership, collective leadership*, and *teacher empowerment* are often used to describe the practice of involving others especially teachers in the decision-making process within a school.

High-Trust Embedded in School Culture.   Trust is considered a critical factor in any school improvement effort especially in a PLC. When distrust is present in the school's culture, it is likely that the improvement efforts will not be effective. As we discuss trust in more detail in Chapter 4, trust will be a pivotal factor in your leadership in facilitating a PLC.

Interdependent Culture That Sustains Continuous Improvement in Teaching and Learning.   In a PLC, teachers specifically focus on learning and they do that through sharing personal classroom practices with other teachers. This interdependency allows for a review of instructional behaviors that help foster and create a community of learners. As teachers leave behind their isolated practices, they work together to accomplish higher learning for all students.

Teaming That Is Collaborative.   Although interdependence among teachers is important in establishing a learning community, it is through collaborative teams that instruction improves and student learning increases. In fact, without teacher collaborative teams, it is doubtful that a PLC exists. We will discuss the collaborative teams in more detail in Chapter 7.

Decision Making Based on Data and Research.   In a PLC, the process in which principals and teachers function to improve student learning is by using data and research to inform practice. The benefits from this focus help identify both low-achieving students before they fail and high-achieving students so they can receive enrichment activities. Using research and data-based decision making is crucial in facilitating collaboration, providing participative leadership, and guiding instructional decisions.

Use of Continuous Assessment to Improve Learning. Even before it was legislated in NCLB, educators were using assessment as a tool to monitor student learning. In a PLC, continuous assessment is that of an ongoing cycle of checking and acting on the results from student data that drives continuous improvement.

Academic Success for All Students with Systems of Prevention and Intervention. In PLCs, principals and teachers continually provide strategies for prevention and intervention of students who are at risk for failure. In such schools, there is no blame handed out toward families, cultural differences, social conditions, or ability, instead PLC educators use strategies to prevent failure and interventions to help students who are failing.

Professional Development That Is Teacher Driven and Embedded in Daily Work. A different approach with professional development emerges in PLCs that is a different method than in the past. The "one-shot" workshops that failed to provide knowledge and skills to improving teaching and learning are now replaced with professional development that is job-embedded in the real work of teaching.

However daunting these elements seem to be, it is nevertheless what all educators should want for all schools everywhere. Although we have experienced such schools, we know that the process in which they got there was long, at times hard, and always worth it. You need to keep the big picture in mind as you proceed ahead in establishing your role as principal or assistant principal and your quest in developing a PLC.

One further note, while you should not view PLCs as a panacea to solve all school problems, the PLC process does offer you options and opportunities for growth and learning with your colleagues in a way that previous reform initiatives have not. In addition, PLCs are flexible enough to accommodate changes required by future needs. As Highland High School realized, you should keep in mind and recognize that the creation of a PLC is not an end in itself. It is, rather, a cultural shift that will take years to develop and will probably never be fully realized because there will always be more to do.

THE CASE FOR PROFESSIONAL LEARNING COMMUNITIES

Although there has not been a lot of research on PLCs, some researchers have found positive effects on students' success in schools that were characterized with the PLC elements mentioned earlier. The following are a few examples from various empirical research studies that show the positive effects of using the PLC elements and their effect on student achievement.

- High school students in PLCs demonstrated higher levels of achievement in math, reading, science, and history (Lee, Smith, & Croninger, 1995).
- Elementary students achieved higher reading proficiency (Tighe, Wang, & Foley, 2002).
- Hispanic students demonstrated higher levels of academic achievement when their schools began functioning as PLCs (Reyes, Scribner, & Paredes-Scribner, 1999).

- Students achieved higher levels of authentic learning where teachers worked inter-dependently and used authentic pedagogical and assessment practices (Louis & Marks, 1998).
- Elementary students were three times more likely to improve in math and reading with schools that had established high trust communities (Bryk & Schneider, 2002).
- Students were absent less often and were less likely to drop out of school before graduating from high school (Hord, 1997).

As researchers continue to study PLCs in schools, more results will be reported in academic and professional journals. You might be well advised to look for these research studies as they emerge to give you added support in establishing a PLC in your school.

Not only did students fare well in the PLC research studies, but teachers also bene-fited (Shellard, 2003). When teachers engaged in ongoing professional conversations with other teachers, their knowledge increased with subject matter and teaching skills, and their morale increased significantly. In addition, teachers reported feeling ener-gized and renewed (Louis & Marks, 1998). These problem-based dialogues increased the levels of trust, which provided a necessary foundation to build student-focused col-lective action among teachers (Bryk & Schneider, 2002). In another study, faculty who were involved in a PLC provided higher intellectual learning tasks for their students because they were engaged in more collaborative learning, which was more powerful than independent learning (Hord & Sommers, 2008).

A pressing concern on many school leaders in the present decade has been the strong emergence of policies from federal and state governments for school reform. School leaders and teachers have had to scramble to find ways of meeting the require-ments that these policies have imposed. Most of these policies have been linked to showing strong evidence of student achievement. Several researchers and theorists (e.g., DuFour & Eaker, 1998; Hord, 1997; Rosenholtz, 1989; Senge, 1990) have suggested learning communities as a way to meet the school improvement directives that have emerged from such federal and state policies. Louis and Marks (1998) conducted a three-year study of twenty-four schools to determine to what extent a professional com-munity influenced the classroom. They concluded that when schools were organized to support collaboration and maintained a culture where teachers could collaborate, the collaboration led to greater teacher effectiveness, which in turn translated to increased student success. They warned that simply meeting to achieve an administrative man-date or to fulfill a government policy did not lead to true collaboration. They showed effective collaboration that led to student success occurred when team members

1. shared a sense of purpose,
2. participated in collaborative activities,
3. focused on student learning,
4. deprivatized their teaching practices, and
5. engaged in reflective dialogue.

Other research has also demonstrated that consistent and meaningful interaction with professional peers is important to teacher success in the classroom (Darling-Hammond, 1996). The more teachers are involved with district personnel, principals, and other

Professional Dilemma 3.1

As a principal, you have encouraged the teachers on an instructional team to observe each others' teaching and afterwards engage in reflective dialogue. One of the teachers on a team comes to you with information regarding another teacher's intimidating behavior toward Latino/a students. How do you encourage the reflective dialogue to continue within the team and assure that all students are being treated fairly?

teachers, the more likely they will persist and succeed in the face of successive waves of educational reform. The U.S. Department of Education (2000) noted that because teachers can provide a holistic and coherent approach to reform, learning communities offered a potentially more sustainable approach than many more narrowly based reform initiatives.

An important element in PLCs is the collaborative teaming among teachers who are discussing teaching and learning. In research on effective collaboration, Crow and Pounder's (2000) study of teacher teams examined a junior high school that was in its second year of using teacher work group enhancement with their grade-level teams. The goal of the teams was to improve student learning. Crow and Pounder found that all of the teams they studied reported positive student intervention because of their collaboration, but only when the collaboration focused on student learning. While all the teams reported frustration with the time and scheduling collaboration entailed, they agreed that "the benefit from increased information and effectiveness with students outweighs the cost of collaborating" (p. 246). Teachers felt that the teaming efforts were worth the extra time and effort when they saw students respond with higher levels of learning.

The evidence, therefore, is quite strong. The research and the practice indicate that schools making the PLC cultural shift will improve the learning in schools and teachers will be more likely to feel a part of the school and want to continue to improve their practices. However, moving into a PLC is not without challenges, as we indicate in the next section.

BARRIERS TO THE DEVELOPMENT OF PROFESSIONAL LEARNING COMMUNITIES

Numerous barriers to the development of PLCs can emerge in schools. DuFour and Eaker (1998) listed several barriers to the successful implementation of PLCs in schools, including the complexity of the task, a misplaced focus with ineffective strategies, a lack of clarity of outcomes, the failure of many PLCs to persist, and a lack of understanding of the change process. Perhaps the most significant of these is encouraging both educators and the public to understand and value professional development, a topic we will discuss further in Chapter 9.

Resistance to change poses another significant obstacle to establishing PLCs in schools. Because the predictable human response to change is resistance (Duffy, 2003), anyone promoting significant change should anticipate opposition. Duffy reminded us that "one of the most powerful ways to respond to all kinds of resistance is through involvement" (p. 217). Rather than relying on a few department heads and administrators to spearhead development of a PLC, the principal needs to involve the school community in the process, much like what occurred in the opening scenario at Highland High School.

It is always important to remember that change is difficult. In an age of constant change and reform, teachers and administrators, as was the case in Highland County School District, grow weary and wary of new ideas and models for school improvement. Even the process of building individual elements of PLCs, such as teams, takes a huge volume of work. Effective change is difficult, complex, and time-consuming.

The isolation experienced by many teachers is another impediment to PLCs. In traditional teaching models, teachers seldom have opportunities for working collaboratively with their peers. As anyone who has ever walked into a school has noticed, the isolation of teachers is apparent. This isolation poses a formidable barrier to effective school improvement (DuFour & Eaker, 1992, p. 73). As Little (2002) pointed out:

> For teachers to engage seriously in professional communication with their colleagues, they must be able to initiate open and critical discussions of instruction. Mentoring and advising must constitute an accepted and valued aspect of school life. Staff must be able to put forward new ideas and critically evaluate ideas as they are tried out in practice, but also live with one another through the messiness of discovery. (p. 51)

Teachers who rarely work collaboratively with other teachers will likely be reluctant to do so when the opportunity presents itself, and even if they are willing, they lack the experience to make collaboration an effective and ongoing process. Therefore, principal leadership is vitally important for a school to function successfully as a PLC.

We hope to show in subsequent chapters presented in this book that most of these obstacles can be overcome. It will take a strong commitment on your part to develop such a culture so that a PLC will thrive. You can be assured that obstacles will, at times, impede your progress, but the goal must always be kept in focus.

THE PRINCIPAL'S ROLE IN DEVELOPING A PROFESSIONAL LEARNING COMMUNITY IN A SCHOOL

The principal's leadership that is both supportive and shared is critical for implementing a PLC and achieving school improvement. Likewise, the principal's importance in developing a strong culture that will support the PLC concept supports Barth's (1990) assertion that "the principal is a central figure in determining the quality of a school" (p. 81), and Heller and Firestone's (1995) claim that the principal is key to school change.

Principal Centrality

The importance of the principal's involvement in establishing effective PLCs is often referred to as *centrality*. The importance of centrality was explained by Brass (1984): "Persons who are centrally located in the communication network are hypothesized to have potential access to and control of relevant information and thus have potential power" (p. 524). The role of the principal allows for centrality, control of information, and power because the principal has the opportunity to observe and hold discussions with every teacher. Further, most teachers seek out the principal for feedback and advice, and the principal has the authority to form teams, therefore connecting teachers to one another.

The concept of principal centrality can be seen with elementary school grade-level teams and secondary school department teams. Teachers on grade-level teams and departments might have the opportunity to interact with one another, but across grade levels and across departments becomes more difficult. The principal or the assistant principal is a central link across the school as "persons who are more than two steps removed from each other in a network are unlikely to be aware of each other's current work" (Friedkin, 1983, p. 70). To illustrate this, a particular situation occurred in a junior high school wherein the history department was using the popular and Newberry Award–winning novel *Johnny Tremain* by Esther Forbes as supplemental reading in the study of the Revolutionary War in the eighth grade. Interestingly enough, the English department had also been using the book but in the seventh grade and had been doing so for several years. When the students entered their eighth-grade history classes, they had already read the book, and the teachers were not aware of it. This scenario went on for three years before an assistant principal recognized it when she was ordering new books for the English and history departments. At first, the assistant principal thought it was a mistake, so she visited with the history chairperson to see if the order was correct. She soon found out that both departments had no idea that they were both using the same book. Subsequently, the two departments finally got together and coordinated their use of the book. The English department gladly moved *Johnny Tremain* to its eighth-grade reading list so it coordinated with the time that the history department was teaching the Revolutionary War. Furthermore, the two departments actually designed a unit together around the book.

As this illustration shows, the principal's network centrality allows him or her to help organizational structures that facilitate collaboration. The history and English departments had gone on for three years without realizing the conflict in using the same book. The two departments could have gone on for even more years before the assistant principal's network centrality was able to get the two departments together. When the assistant principal noticed the situation, it was then only a matter of fostering collaborative teaming and providing time for teachers to meet and work out a coordinated unit of study in using the book. Friedkin and Slater (1994) found teacher networks that developed into PLCs, which were associated with student success, were also associated with principal centrality.

Being central in the teacher network allows a principal to model professional involvement and be personally engaged in reflective inquiry. When teachers judged the principal's instructional behavior to be innovative and geared toward student achievement, they were willing to commit to innovative actions and schoolwide learning as well (Hallinger et al., 1996; Marks & Printy, 2003). In Friedkin's and Slater's (1994) study, the principal's centrality was measured by the extent to which teachers in the network selected the principal as a prominent discussion partner. They found that there was a positive association between principal network centrality and school performance, and that there was an association with teacher networks and performance, but it was a by-product of the principal's influence. The number of teacher interactions dealing with instructional practices was a result of principal centrality in the network. In addition to being central, they concluded that the principal needs to be accessible and attentive to teacher concerns.

Another interesting point is illustrated by a Louis and Mark (1998) study that found that the organization and culture of the school, because of principal centrality, led to greater teacher effectiveness, which also led to increased student success. They found that when professional communities were present, the support for achievement in the classroom increased significantly. They reported that the stronger the professional community, the greater the support for achievement and the better the quality of pedagogy. An even more significant finding was that where strong professional community existed, student achievement rose. Effective principals led from the center of the school organization rather than from the top of a hierarchy.

This centrality image of the principal might be quite different from that which you have experienced in schools in your career. Many veteran principals were socialized into their roles as managers and caretakers. As an example, contrasting leadership practices in an elementary school illustrate the differences between two principals. One veteran elementary school principal was viewed by the teachers as a fatherlike figure. He dispensed the supplies and the budget as rewards for teachers whom he considered worthy. No one really understood the criteria he used, but most teachers were satisfied that if they did their jobs, he would give them what they needed. He often sheltered teachers from ugly situations involving parents and community members. However, student achievement at the school was below average in the state and the school was notified that it had not met the adequate yearly progress that was expected under the NCLB policy. The principal was able to retire and leave the school, and as the new principal became involved in making necessary reform efforts to improve student achievement, the retired principal became a folk hero among the faculty. The new principal, however, pushed for collaborative teams of teachers to look at their instructional practices and to focus on student learning. The extra time and energy that the teachers took in these collaborative teams was at first controversial. Many teachers wanted their old principal back so they could revert to their old ways of isolationism and freedom. However, as test results started improving and the school passed AYP, these same teachers started realizing the importance of the centrality of the principal in their teaching networks.

THE PRINCIPAL'S FOCUS ON STUDENT LEARNING

The principal's focus on student learning is a critical component of a PLC. Principals must help teachers understand that their efforts in teaching all students centers on student learning. In the past, much has been written on good teaching methods without regard to whether students learn from those methods. Likewise, many structural and technical changes such as class schedules and school organization have been implemented without learning as the focus. A PLC focuses on learning—learning for adults and learning for students.

A model used to identify this learning focus was introduced by DuFour in 1998 and later revised in 2006. He proposed four questions for all educators to ask and answer:

- What should each student learn?
- How will we know students have learned it?
- How will we respond to students who do not learn it?
- How will we respond to students who have already learned it?

Activities based on answering these four questions will keep the focus on the student learning. It is not enough to have a vision of these four questions; principals and teachers must focus their work and attention in answering all four questions for each child. Little (1990) stated that joint work with a focus on explicit goals (student learning) led to improved instructional solutions, greater teacher confidence, and higher achievement gains for students. When principals and teachers work together to determine what a learning standard is and then identify what students would be able to do to show proficiency toward the standard, clarity of expectations developed leading to greater student learning.

Likewise, principals and teachers who examined data rather than relying on gut feelings about student performance were able to reveal the strengths and weaknesses of teaching programs that could otherwise have gone undetected. Principals need to help teachers know how to evaluate the data from student work and then know how to adapt their teaching to get better results. Cooperating in these efforts leads to modification of instruction and better interventions for struggling students. Thus, such cooperation between principals and teachers in a PLC not only supports teachers in their instruction but also aids students in their learning.

PRINCIPAL AND ASSISTANT PRINCIPAL FUNCTIONS IN DEVELOPING AND FACILITATING PROFESSIONAL LEARNING COMMUNITIES

Principals play a key role in creating a climate that reinforces the practices of PLCs. The results of a study in Chicago elementary schools by Bryk, Camburn, and Louis (1999) found that the elements of professional community are supported by principals who are in regular contact with their faculty, even to the extent of visiting teachers' classrooms on a regular basis. The elements of professional community were also more prevalent when principals were viewed as having more inclusive facilitative styles. These results suggested that principals' regular involvement with faculty members is important, but involvement that goes beyond regular contact, that encourages teachers to be involved, to innovate, and to take risks, might be particularly supportive of professional community.

Scribner and his colleagues' (1999) study of three rural schools identified principal leadership practices that fostered or impeded the development and maintenance of professional learning communities. At the Northridge School, one of the schools in the study, the principal's leadership focused on building trust among the school's faculty and staff and in so doing helped create a sense of common purpose. This leadership was reflected in the principal's trust in the faculty's ability to lead, and in turn, the faculty's trust in the principal grew out of the principal's commitment to both teachers and students.

The principal of the Cedarbrook School, another school in the study, took a more hands-off approach that negatively affected the PLC. The principal approached school improvement by abdicating responsibility to a group of teacher leaders. In refusing to use his position as a "bully pulpit" to engender support for improvement, this principal impeded the development of professional community.

In the third school in the study, Westwood School, the principal's espoused values failed to match his practice. Although cordial and professional in his treatment of faculty and staff, this principal tended to choose the same leadership group for all improvement efforts and thus weakened the chances of the faculty as a whole for developing decision-making expertise. Limiting the wider opportunities for shared leadership impeded the development of a PLC at Westwood.

Both of these studies (Bryk, Camburn, & Louis, 1999; Scribner et al., 1999) emphasized that the principal's facilitative role in creating a sense of social trust among faculty was critical for developing PLCs. Trusting faculty enough to share leadership was a potent resource for encouraging reflective dialogue, deprivatization of practice, and collaboration.

Recent research (e.g., Mitchell & Sackney, 2006; Mulford & Sillins, 2003) maintained that the principal played an active role—both in terms of position and in terms of facilitating distributed leadership—in cultivating learning communities. "We have discovered that, without the school principal's focused and continued attention, efforts to build a learning community among staff flounder and attempts to extend the learning community beyond the professional cadre fail to get off the ground" (Mitchell & Sackney, 2006, p. 631). Mitchell and Sackney identified four functions of principals in supporting learning communities:

1. center,
2. holder of the vision,
3. builder, and
4. role model.

First, the center function means that the principal was "at the hub of school operations and activities" (p. 631). The principal at the center knows what is happening throughout the school. The authors identified several strategies principals used in performing this center function, including an open-door policy (either in the office or walking around the school), supporting the constant flow of information (traditionally and electronically), and taking a systemic perspective by connecting people together to meet learning needs.

In the second function the principal was the "holder of the vision," so that the learning community did not become distracted or lose sight of its vision. "We saw very few vision statements on the walls; instead, we saw principals saying things like "How does this help teaching and learning? How does this help the children?" (p. 634).

The third function, "builder," meant that the principal was responsible for creating structures in the school, such as grade-level teams or databases, that facilitated and "focused professional discourse, practice, and learning on pedagogic and student issues" (pp. 635–636).

Finally, Mitchell and Sackney (2006) described the principal as "the role model." "Those who were most successful in creating a learning community were those who served as role models with respect to good teaching strategies, effective collegial processes, respectful treatment of students, and systemic approaches to practice" (p. 636).

Your role as a principal is an active rather than passive role. Research findings continue to emphasize that the principal plays a powerful role in facilitating both learning organizations and PLCs.

Conclusion

As a principal you want to improve student learning. Therefore, you need to intentionally foster conditions that result in teachers working together toward student learning. The process of becoming a PLC is a cultural shift that is both fluid and flexible: fluid enough to be adaptable to individual school cultures, and flexible so that various voices in the school community can be heard and accommodated. The chapters that follow attempt to guide your practice by illuminating the deliberate actions principals take to develop PLCs and improve student learning.

Activities

SELF-REFLECTION ACTIVITIES

1. Reflect on your own experiences with working on teams. How effective were those teams? How could they have been more effective?
2. As you participated on teams with other teachers, what experiences did you have that focused on the learning for underachieving students?
3. As a teacher, what influenced you to share teaching practices with others? What inhibited you from sharing with other teachers?

PEER REFLECTION ACTIVITIES

1. Reflect with a peer on which of the ten elements of a PLC exist in your school.
2. Share student assessment data from your class with a peer. Reflect together as to how you could improve your teaching practice to improve learning for the most underachieving students.

COURSE ACTIVITIES

1. Refer to www.allthingsplc.info. Locate a school in your area and arrange for a class field trip to observe the school. Reflect on the ten elements that were present in the school.
2. Compare the reform activities in the Highland County School District in the opening vignette that were centralized to those activities that were decentralized. What reform efforts were decentralized in purpose but implemented in a centralized process?
3. Reflect on the reform efforts in the Highland County School District in the vignette. Name possible reasons why test scores did not improve with the original reform efforts? Name possible reasons why test scores improved with the PLC movement?

Websites

The Center for Comprehensive School Reform and Improvement—includes resources on PLCs and other school reform initiatives, information about conferences, publications, and additional organizations
www.centerforcsri.org/

All Things PLC—site built and maintained by Solution Tree, no advertisements, includes blogs, journal articles, and research on professional learning communities, and networking tools.
www.allthingsplc.info/

National Staff Development Council (NSDC)—includes links to conferences and standards for PLCs
www.nsdc.org/index.cfm

CHAPTER 4

The Principal as Learner

Vignette

Nancy Lowenstein became the principal of East Jersey Elementary School during a changing time. Not only had the previous principal retired after twenty-five years in the school, but also the district recently had redrawn the school boundaries to include a part of the community that was predominately African American, and a new superintendent, Marcia Downing, had been hired last year. When Dr. Downing and Nancy had their first meeting after the board appointed Nancy, Dr. Downing made it clear that she wanted some changes at East Jersey.

Until that year, East Jersey Elementary School had been the center for a homogeneous segment of the district that primarily included Caucasian parents from evangelical Protestant backgrounds. The parents trusted the former principal and the largely veteran teacher group to maintain their values, nurture their children, and keep controversy out of the schools. The former principal, Don Martin, had grown up in the community and was revered as a father figure not only by the community but also by the teachers. The teachers appreciated the way Don buffered them from distractions and left them alone in their classrooms. Over time, Don had developed the practice of making all schoolwide decisions, which he claimed protected the teachers' instructional time. The teachers did not seem to mind this practice and developed a dependency on Don to tell them what they absolutely needed to know and trusted Don to make the big decisions.

In their first meeting, Dr. Downing and Nancy discussed the upcoming school boundary changes that would be made at the beginning of Nancy's first year as principal of East Jersey. They also discussed Dr. Downing's vision of creating learning communities within the schools so that teachers, parents, students, administrators, and other community members would all contribute toward a shared vision of student learning. Nancy was excited about working with the East Jersey school community in creating their own learning community. In her administrative internship in a different district, Nancy had worked with a mentor principal who had been successful in helping his school to think of itself as a professional community where there was collaboration among teachers, where teaching practices were open to parents and other teachers, and where the focus was on developing shared values concerning student learning.

As she began her new job, Nancy made a point of meeting individually with the teachers and finding out something about their learning styles. The teachers for the most part were warm and inviting to Nancy. She also held an open house for all parents and teachers, expressing her openness to the entire school community and inviting everyone to discuss any concerns with her. The year began with few problems, and Nancy was amazed at how easily the students from the new part of the community adjusted to the school.

Early in the school year, Nancy met with the faculty to discuss the idea of developing a learning community. She distributed readings from Peter Senge and others and encouraged teachers to discuss with one another how they might include parents and others in developing a learning organization at East Jersey and specifically how to focus on the particular needs of the new students.

At the next meeting, which Nancy had set aside to focus on the learning organization idea, teachers were quiet. When Nancy asked them what they thought of the ideas in the readings and how they might apply to East Jersey, one veteran teacher replied that this would take too much time away from their classrooms and preparing students for the upcoming state achievement tests. Nancy countered that she believed a learning organization would benefit each classroom's learning environment and provided some examples from her own administrative internship experience. A few of the newer teachers were familiar with the concept of a learning organization and said they were interested in talking more about how to implement such an idea at the school. The veteran teachers, however, for the most part were either silent or politely opposed to the idea. The meeting ended with Nancy setting up a discussion group for all those interested in the idea to read more material and discuss ways to implement a learning organization at East Jersey.

As the year progressed, the small discussion group became more and more excited about creating a learning organization at East Jersey. The group met regularly, attended conferences, and developed a partnership with a local university to conduct action research in their classrooms. Many of the action research projects focused on how to respond to specific learning needs of the new students who had been transferred to the school. Nancy found resources for the group, including money for travel to conferences and substitutes to facilitate meetings and observations. Most veteran teachers, however, remained skeptical of the idea.

By midyear, several of the veteran teachers were coming to Nancy frequently with discipline problems, primarily with the new students. They said the new students could not keep up with other students and were disruptive in class; they also said that the parents were unresponsive when the teachers called them to discuss student problems. When Nancy observed these teachers' classrooms, she frequently found they were mostly using direct instruction with few individualized approaches. In some cases, the teachers expressed resentment of the new students. When Nancy conferred with the teachers, she found their typical response was to blame the students and their parents. She also heard rumors that these veteran teachers resented the attention being paid to the newer teachers who were in the discussion group focused on learning organizations. Some of the rumors reflected feelings of mistrust toward Nancy, suggesting that she was giving more resources to these teachers and perhaps even placing more students with behavior problems in the veteran teachers' classes.

Toward the end of the year, a group of veteran teachers asked to meet with Nancy. Although polite, they expressed deep frustration in what they perceived "these new children and their parents have done to our school." Nancy tried to be sensitive to their frustrations. When she suggested that they look at the students' previous school experience, test scores, and learning styles and reflect on what the teachers could do, one teacher's frustration boiled over. "It's the principal's job to get these kids out of our rooms so we can teach. They're going to bring down our test scores. Are you going to help us or not?" Nancy became more and more frustrated as each teacher pushed her to remove the disruptive students from their classrooms. She ended the meeting without expressing her frustration.

That evening as she discussed the meeting with her good friend and mentor, Sue Bennett, she finally expressed her frustration that the teachers were unwilling to consider their own behavior and how that might be contributing to student disruptions. After giving Nancy time to vent, Sue encouraged her to do what she wanted the teachers to do, reflect on her own behavior as a learner. Sue asked her what information she had about the teachers' styles and experiences, and she encouraged Nancy to consider what kinds of professional development resources she might find for these teachers.

INTRODUCTION

Nancy Lowenstein's experience as a new principal illustrates a primary way to view the principalship—the principal as learner. It may seem surprising to you that in an organization that focuses on learning, the role conception of principal as learner has received attention only recently. As we discussed in Chapter 2, the scientific management focus on school administration, until recently, has received the greatest attention. However, as Nancy and countless other new principals have discovered, the managerial focus of the principalship provides a limited conception of the role.

We begin with the principal as learner because it sets the stage for all the other role conceptions you will read about in this book. Understanding the principal's and assistant principal's roles as culture builder, advocate, leader, mentor, supervisor, manager, and politician is based on the primary role of these leaders as learners and as facilitators of the school's learning capacity. As we will do in subsequent chapters, we examine this role conception by beginning with the principal as learner and then as facilitator of others' learning. As Nancy hopefully realized, if she wants teachers to be learners, she must practice learning techniques herself.

The principal as learner is the basis for understanding the rest of the roles primarily because of the nature of what schools do and what school environments should be. First, the central tasks and techniques (core technology) of schools are teaching and learning. Nothing distinguishes schools from other organizations more than teaching and learning. The "bottom line" for schools is not generating money or products. This unique quality of schools has created numerous debates and conflicts among educators and others in society, especially those in business. Although good business practices have a place in school operations, they are secondary to the primary purpose of schools as contributing to the learning of students, their families, and other adults.

Emphasizing the primacy of learning leads to understanding schools as learning organizations and communities. If the core technology of an organization is to generate a product, then the organization can be seen more as a factory than as a community. As we will discuss later, learning is not an individual event but occurs within a social context—within a community. Although it may be possible to generate a product with individuals performing separate and isolated activities, the very nature of learning involves community. Research on learner-centered leadership has demonstrated that "schools organized as communities (rather than bureaucracies) are more likely to exhibit academic success" (Goldring, Porter, Murphy, & Elliott, 2007, p. 3).

In this chapter we organize our discussion of the principal's role as learner in five ways. First, we will briefly discuss the meaning of learning, examining the traditional model of learning and more recent conceptual and empirical understandings of the meaning of learning, especially for adults. Second, we describe the principal as learner. In this section we will discuss the importance of continual learning for work roles in the twenty-first century and various components of the principal's role as learner, including self-awareness, inquiry, reflectivity, and complexity. As we discuss these components, we will identify practical ways you can develop skills in these areas. In the third section of the chapter we focus on the principal as facilitator of learning. Here we view schools as learning organizations and identify how you as a principal are key in building the school's learning capacity. Since in a professional learning community (PLC) the principal is not the only lead learner, in the last section we focus on the roles of assistant principals and teacher leaders as part of the PLC for building and cultivating learning capacity in the school.

LEARNING: TRANSMISSION VERSUS CONSTRUCTION

The Traditional Conception of Learning

The traditional understanding of learning is tied to the industrial-age notion of organizations and schools. If we see schools as machines, we tend to see learning as machine-like, emphasizing worksheets and drills. Although recent developments in cognitive science suggest a different way to define learning (which we will discuss later in this section), schools have typically reflected a more traditional conception of learning. This traditional conception involves the purpose, direction, and nature of learning.

The traditional image focuses on the purpose of learning as transmission of skills, facts, knowledge, truth, and culture. The assumption, held over from the industrial age, is that learning involves transmitting the storehouse of facts and knowledge. Such an assumption ignores the dynamic nature of knowledge as constantly changing, which we described in Chapter 1. This traditional view holds that it is the responsibility of schools to transmit the previous generation's values, knowledge, and cultural norms to the next generation. Schools have a valid role in transmitting values and norms to the new generation. However, to a certain extent, each generation negotiates and constructs its own values, norms, and knowledge.

Second, the traditional view assumes that learning occurs in one direction—from the teacher to the student. Peter Senge and his colleagues (2000) suggested that this traditional conception of learning is based on the assumptions that children are defective and that the school's job is to fix them. "The deficit perspective assumes that something is broken and needs to be fixed. It is a reasonable way to think about machines, because machines cannot fix themselves. But it is a poor fit for living systems like children, which grow and evolve of their own accord" (p. 37). Senge and his colleagues also suggested two other assumptions about learning that seem to flow from this unidirectional notion of learning. First, this view assumes that learning takes place only in the classroom, not in the world. If the direction of learning is one way, then learning originates only with teachers in classrooms. Obviously, however, students and adults learn outside the school in their daily routines, conversations, and experiences. Second, Senge and his colleagues argued that the industrial-age notion of learning has led us to view the school as being run by specialists whose chief aim is to maintain control. If a child is inherently defective, then control becomes a major issue. As Senge and his colleagues suggested, there is nothing wrong with control, but the issue is the agent of control. In the industrial model, machines are controlled by their operators, but living systems learn to control themselves.

The third component of the traditional view of learning is that the nature of learning is individualistic, is uniform, occurs in the head, and is based on knowledge as fragmented. One of the major views of learning is that it occurs individualistically. Senge and his colleagues (2000) used the two basic actions of walking and talking, which seem totally individualistic, as examples of the limitations of this view. Young children hear others talking and watch others walking, running, and skipping. Their learning to walk and talk is actually learning to join the community of walkers and talkers. In this way, learning is collective rather than individualistic. Individuals also do not learn in the same way. Howard Gardner's (1983, 2006) work on multiple intelligences has emphasized that the linguistic and mathematical ways of knowing, which are emphasized in schools, are by no means the only ways of knowing. Research on learning styles suggests that individuals learn in different ways.

The nature of learning embedded in the traditional view also considers learning as occurring only in the head. Senge and his colleagues (2000) suggested that the prevailing Western understanding divorces reason from perception, motion, or emotion. However, recent studies suggest otherwise. Senge and his coauthors gave examples, such as riding a bike or recalling a telephone number by the action of dialing it, and suggested that these illustrate how much of what we know is involved not just in our heads but in our bodies.

The traditional conception of learning is based on a view of knowledge as fragmented. Schools teach subjects in discrete units, for example, American literature, language arts, world history, biology, and algebra. Yet the majority of learning that is necessary to live, work, and solve problems involves the integration of knowledge.

The traditional view of learning emphasizes the transmission of separate facts, values, and norms; the sole reliance on the teacher (or some other "expert") and the classroom as the source of learning; and an individualistic, uniform, mental, and discrete perspective on learning. As we have noted, many of these assumptions are not supported by recent cognitive research and fit only in an industrial-age model of schooling.

The Constructivist Conception of Learning

The conception of learning that we emphasize in this book is referred to in the literature as *constructivist*. We do not assume that this is the only valid perspective on learning (Delpit, 1996; Bailey & Pransky, 2005), but we believe that it fits the notion of learning that occurs in a PLC that we want to emphasize in our discussion of the principal as learner.

In your preparation program, you will probably take or would have already taken courses in curriculum and instruction that elaborate, in more detail than this chapter can cover, on how learning occurs and other theories of learning, such as behavioral, cognitive, social cognitive, and humanist. The following section, however, will provide a brief overview to ground our discussion of the principal's role as learner.

A constructivist approach to learning "maintains that learning is a process of constructing meaning; it is how people make sense of their experience" (Merriam, Caffarella, & Baumgartner, 2007, p. 291). Constructivist conceptions of learning (there are multiple) have a notable history that includes such distinguished writers and educators as Dewey, Piaget, Bruner, and Vygotsky. Each of these authors contributed important ideas to the development of constructivism. According to Walker and Lambert (1995), Dewey set the stage for constructivism by emphasizing that students need to make meaning of their own learning based on individual and collective experiences. Piaget emphasized that knowledge is an ongoing process of continual construction and reorganization rather than some static operation. Bruner emphasized the learner as a constructor of knowledge and prior experience as deepening the learning experience. Vygotsky emphasized context as critical to understanding learning and the process of building on prior knowledge to create knowledge (scaffolding). In this case, knowledge and intelligence are socially constructed, rather than personally (Piaget), which is the other form of constructivism. Activity theory, or situated cognition, brings the personal and social approaches together (Wilson, 2005). We will return to activity theory when we discuss adult learning.

The constructivist approaches to learning can have a significant impact on how you understand teachers teaching, and schools becoming PLCs. "Teachers who understand, in a deep and profound way, a powerful idea behind much of the current discourse on learning and teaching—the notion that children literally construct their own knowledge, drawing on whatever resources, past or present, are available—not only think differently about student learning, but also view teaching and even disciplinary knowledge in a new light" (Prawat & Peterson, 1999, p. 220). This notion of groups constructing their own knowledge is a powerful way to think about school-level learning as well as classroom learning. At a school level, this model of constructivism moves away from restructuring to "reculturing" (Fullan, 1993, 2001), for example, teachers changing the way they think about teaching and learning as part of a professional community of learners.

Three major components of constructivism are emphasized in the literature and in our understanding of learning used in this book. We have chosen to refer to them as the three Cs: capacity, community, and criticality. First, learning involves the capacity of the learner to draw on prior experience, which contradicts the traditional deficit model of learning. Instead of assuming that students at the classroom level and teachers at the school level are deficit in their knowledge, we assume the opposite. Both students and teachers bring with them knowledge based on prior learning and experience. They actively use this experience to construct new knowledge. The traditional deficit view has so contaminated our instructional approaches as educators that we forget not only that others bring capacity to the learning process but also that new learning occurs by building on this prior knowledge. In this sense, learning "reshapes classroom interaction from student as passive listener and teacher as source of knowledge, to learning as an interactive process entered into by both students and teachers" (Walker & Lambert, 1995, p. 15). As new administrators, your own learning works in the same way. You bring previous experience as a student, teacher, and learner that provides the scaffolding to construct new learning as an administrator (Vygotsky, 1986). Reflecting on your previous experience can help you understand your own processes of learning.

The second component of constructivism is community. As we have noted, Vygotsky's (1986) major contribution to the development of constructivism was his emphasis on the collective nature of learning. Thus, the cultural and historical communities that students bring with them to school are part of the context in which learning occurs and must be recognized and valued by teachers and principals. Rather than the individualistic quality of learning emphasized in the traditional view, social constructivism assumes a community of learners. One of your primary roles as a new administrator is to facilitate this PLC. As teachers come together to make meaning of their collective experiences as learners and teachers, new learning develops. In the vignette that began this chapter, Nancy's proposal to develop a learning community can be seen not only as an innovative tool but also as a necessity for enabling the school and its constituents to grow professionally.

Third, social constructivism emphasizes critical reflection. In contemporary social contexts, such as schools, students, teachers, administrators, and parents encounter an avalanche of information—a knowledge explosion. Often this information comes with no interpretative tools or evaluation. In the business field, some writers have estimated that the duration of innovations has shortened from a decade to less than a year (Micklethwhait & Wooldridge, 1996). Much like business, the tendency in education is to cycle through fads. Such an uncritical acceptance of new ideas produces headaches for teachers in finding time for yet another new idea, for administrators in encouraging teachers to be innovative, and for the public in viewing the school's innovations as credible. "Christmas tree schools" (Bryk, Sebring, Kerbow, Rollow, & Easton, 1998) seem to compete to try to have the most innovations. As a new principal, part of your role is to help teachers and parents as members of a PLC critically reflect on new ideas in such a way that learning is not mere assimilation of these ideas but the construction of meaning that acknowledges the tensions and contradictions of collective life in a community.

The definition of learning that we use in this book is based on constructivism and emphasizes the active capacity of all learners to construct new knowledge, the necessity of a community for the development of learning, and the importance of critical reflection in this learning process. In our discussion of learning, it should be obvious that these three components apply to the learning of teachers and administrators as well as students. In the next brief section we identify some of the major elements that are specific to adult learning.

ADULT LEARNING

"All individuals have the potential to continually learn and grow. Adults, like children, bring their prior experiences, beliefs, and perceptions to their work with new experiences to construct knowledge and meaning" (Walker & Lambert, 1995, p. 26). Until a few years ago, this understanding of adult learning was not accepted or understood by the general public or psychologists. Many people assumed that once an individual completed puberty, no more development was possible or necessary. This assumption, fortunately, has been debunked. Now we know that, except in the case of those with certain rare diseases, there are no organic reasons why all adults cannot continue to learn. (See Oja & Reiman, 1998, for an excellent summary of adult conceptual development theories as they apply to teacher development and supervision.)

Although the components of constructivism that we identified in the previous section apply to all learning, there are some elements that differentiate adult from childhood learning, including "the accumulation of experience, the nature of that experience, the developmental issues adults address, how the notions of development and experience relate to learning, and how aging affects our memory and the more general neurological basis for learning" (Merriam et al., 2007, p. 426). One major difference that is especially relevant to your understanding of adult learning in schools is that adults are able to combine reflection and action, what Freire (1970) called *praxis*. They are able to consider the assumptions and values behind their actions and evaluate those actions. This quality is critical for building PLCs, such as schools, in which teachers and administrators reflect on their practice in ways to improve it (Osterman & Kottkamp, 2004).

Earlier in this chapter, we identified activity theory or situated cognition as blending the personal and social approaches to constructivism. Situated cognition is a useful way of understanding adult learning and has special significance for you as a principal in creating and maintaining PLCs. Situated cognition brings learning and the situation together; in fact this approach argues that learning occurs only within a context. "The proponents of the situated view of learning argue that learning for everyday living (which includes our practice as professionals) happens only when people interact with the community (including its history and cultural values and assumptions), 'the tools at hand' (such as technology, language, and images), and the activity at hand" (Fenwick, 2003, as cited in Merriam et al, 2007, p. 178).

For you as a principal, helping teachers learn means acknowledging and valuing what teachers bring with them from their cultural and historical communities, and also how the PLC of the school influences learning. For teachers, then, learning does not occur in some unrelated workshop unconnected to the particular learning situation in which the teacher works. Building a professional community means taking seriously that learning for teachers occurs in the school, in the context of learning, and focusing on the particular learning needs and contributions of teachers in this situation. It also means that learners (e.g., new teachers) are participants in the learning practices of the community. "Learners inevitably participate in communities of practitioners and . . . the mastery of knowledge and skill requires newcomers to move toward full participation in the socio-cultural practices of a community" (Lave & Wenger, 1991, p. 29).

However, adult learning, and especially the learning in a school community, has a purpose. Transformational learning theory helps (Mezirow & Associates, 2000). Transformational, or transformative, learning focuses on the change that occurs in a belief or in our entire perspective or orientation. As Mezirow and his associates (2000) admitted, not all learning is transformative; it could simply be additive. Teachers can simply add more skills to their repertoire—the proverbial bag of tricks. To be transformative, teachers are learning in ways that change the way they see students, learning, and even the world. Critical reflection on experience is essential to transformative learning. PLCs in schools certainly can and should help teachers develop new skills to teach math and science. But to be truly creative, the PLCs you lead as a principal should support teachers' critical reflection on their practices, which may include questioning long-held assumptions about student behavior and learning and assumptions about their role as teachers.

Brookfield (1986) identified six principles that are critical to facilitating adult learning:

1. Participation in learning is voluntary; intimidation or coercion has no place in motivating adult participation.
2. Effective practice is characterized by respect among participants for one another's self-worth.
3. Facilitation is collaborative, with learners and facilitators sharing responsibility for setting objectives and evaluating learning.

4. Praxis is at the heart of effective facilitation, with learners and facilitators involved in a continual cycle of collaborative activity and reflection on activity.

5. Facilitation aims to foster in adults a spirit of critical reflection. Educational encounters should assist adults to question many aspects of their personal, occupational, and political lives.

6. The aim of facilitation is the nurturing of self-directed, empowered adults who will function as proactive individuals.

PRINCIPAL AS LEARNER

As Chapter 2 emphasized, the principal's role has had a checkered history in terms of instruction. With beginnings as "principal teachers," principals moved quickly into a scientific management role that all but ignored teaching and learning, except as they affected efficiency. More recently, the literature on the principalship as key to effective school reform has emphasized an instructional leadership role, in which principals are expected to focus on teaching and learning and facilitate the learning community of the school. However, few writers have emphasized the principal as a learner.

The traditional role of principal seems to view teaching and learning as something that other professionals do, with the principal only facilitating resources for these professionals. In order for you to be an instructional leader and facilitator of learning communities, you first must be an active learner yourself.

In this section, we will identify and discuss several components of the principal's role as a learner. However, before moving to this discussion, we begin with a discussion of the importance of learning for work in contemporary society and for schools that must address the issues of this contemporary society.

Importance of Learning in a Knowledge Society

In Chapter 1, we noted that schools and their educators exist in a new era—a postindustrial society (Bell, 1973), where knowledge is critical. Merriam et al. (2007) identified three elements of this postindustrial society that affect learning: changing demographics, globalization, and technology. In addition, we have added a fourth element that is central to postindustrial society—the knowledge explosion. These four elements affect you as a learner and your role in facilitating others' learning.

CHANGING DEMOGRAPHICS   "For the first time in our society, adults outnumber youth, there are more older adults, the population is better educated than ever before, and there is more cultural and ethnic diversity" (Merriam et al., 2007; p. 7). The aging of the population affects all societal institutions but especially education and work (Bills, 2004). As a principal, you will face this aging population through community struggles over funding for schools, as more and more community members no longer have students in the schools. You might also confront these changing demographics by the need to provide lifelong education through the schools. The increasing educational level, although good news, comes at the same time as an increasing number of high school dropouts. Because of the growing importance of education, those who dropout risk becoming an educational underclass. This increases the pressure on principals and other educators to meet the needs of these students. The greater cultural and ethnic diversity of the population affects schools before any other societal institution. The age of the minority population is significantly lower than that of the majority population (27.7 years for Hispanics versus 41.8 years for the white (non-Hispanic) population, U.S. Bureau of the Census, 2006). By the year 2050, what have been called *minority children* will be closer to the majority. In many communities, a highly diverse student body is already a reality. In addition, the particular needs of an increasing population of children of immigration will become an everyday reality in schools. "Today's immigrant population reflects a pattern of demographics that reveals deep polarization between the most educated and wealthiest and the least educated and poorest" (Alfred, 2004, p. 14). As a principal, it is highly likely that your school will be culturally and ethnically diverse as well as include children of immigration. These factors necessitate your ability to learn new cultural and ethnic sensitivities and to facilitate the learning of the teachers and other administrators in your school to these realities.

GLOBALIZATION   Although globalization is a contested issue, most descriptions of it involve economic and communication elements among others. Economically, globalization involves the transfer of low-skilled and low-wage jobs to less developed countries. In the United States, globalization has resulted in fewer of these jobs available for high school graduates. In terms of communication, national and political boundaries are flattening (Friedman, 2005) in ways that facilitate and increase communication across borders. No educator will deny the increased use and expertise by students—both elementary and secondary—of Internet and other forms of communication. Not only does this dramatically change the forms of educational and information sources, but it changes the learning of both children and adults. But, these globalization elements are not equally available to students. Not only poor students in developing countries but also poor students in developed countries are without the resources for learning. Globalization has increased the inequities that schools and their leaders encounter. As a principal in many types of schools, you will be responsible for the learning of students who do not have the types of economic and communication resources necessary in a knowledge society. The digital divide severely restricts the learning of many of your students.

TECHNOLOGY   The communication changes we talked about before as well as the knowledge explosion we identified in Chapter 1 are facilitated by the rapid increase in technology. The use of computers and other audio and video equipment increases the ability of students and educators to access information quickly to meet the learning demands of the postindustrial era. Again, however, these resources are not equally available to all the students and families in schools.

KNOWLEDGE EXPLOSION   "The proportion of occupational categories that are knowledge intensive is expanding rapidly, while the number of less knowledge-intensive occupational categories is on the decline" (Hage & Powers, 1992, p. 38). This knowledge explosion confronts schools with the need to change outdated forms of teaching that were developed during the industrial age and to prepare students for postindustrial, knowledge-intensive work and life. Economic realities, as well as Internet capabilities, make students global citizens in a context where information and knowledge have no national borders.

Hage and Powers (1992) claimed that one of the most important characteristics of work in postindustrial society is the continuing need for workers to redefine their roles.

Instead of a job description that clearly and permanently defines a position, current and future jobs will be dynamic, and individuals will hold a variety of roles in their jobs. This book assumes that as a new principal or assistant principal, you will encounter some or all of these postindustrial realities. Instead of viewing the principal's role as only, for example, the instructional leader, you will need to be able to view your role from multiple standpoints and acknowledge that the nature of society and schools will require the ongoing ability to redefine your role. Such ability necessitates your continual learning and the learning of the teachers, students, and parents for whom you facilitate learning.

As a principal in a society where knowledge forms the basis of the economy, you must be a learner and must facilitate others' learning. In the rest of this section, we will identify four components of the principal as learner that reflect postindustrial reality: self-awareness, inquiry, reflectivity, and complexity.

Four Components of Principal as Learner

SELF-AWARENESS   The scientific management and industrial-age conception of administration emphasized technical skills and intellectual capacity. Although these continue to be important, another set of skills is necessary for contemporary leaders. Daniel Goleman (2005) popularized the notion of emotional intelligence (as well as social intelligence) and emphasized its importance for leaders. While Goleman's ideas are not universally accepted (Waterhouse, 2006), his fundamental notion of the importance of self-awareness is useful for your understanding of the principal as learner. Goleman defined *emotional intelligence* as

> a different way of being smart. It includes knowing what your feelings are and using your feelings to make good decisions in life. It's being able to manage distressing moods well and control impulses. It's being motivated and remaining hopeful and optimistic when you have setbacks in working towards goals. It's empathy; knowing what the people around you are feeling. And it's social skill—getting along well with other people, managing emotions in relationships, being able to persuade or lead others. (as cited in O'Neil, 1996, p. 6)

Educators have long realized that interpersonal skills can make or break a principal (Davis, 1998). Schools in postindustrial society—with multiple roles, diverse populations, and the need for rapid, customized responses—are likely to be places where conflict is present (Hage & Powers, 1992). As a principal or assistant principal, you will need good interpersonal skills in general and self-awareness in particular to respond to these highly conflictual situations. (See Chapter 7 for more discussion on conflict management.)

Self-awareness involves "having a deep understanding of one's emotions, strengths, weaknesses, needs, and drives" (Goleman, 1998, pp. 95–96). Goleman told the story of a Wall Street executive who intimidated his employees. The executive was interested in improving his empathy. He was amazed to find that not only his coworkers but also his family felt intimidated by him and often hesitated to deliver bad news for fear of his wrath. The executive hired a coach to help him become more aware of his behavior and took a trip to a foreign country where he did not speak the language to understand his reactions to the unfamiliar. Over time, with feedback from his colleagues and coach, he

Johari Window	Known to Self	Unknown to Self
Known to Others	Public (Open)	Blind
Unknown to Others	Private (Hidden)	Unknown

FIGURE 4.1   Johari Window.

was able to improve his understanding of himself and eventually of how people perceived him.

According to Goleman (1998, 2005), emotional intelligence components such as self-awareness can be improved. Instead of the traditional assumption that principals' interpersonal skills are set before they enter the occupation, Goleman argued that these critical skills could be developed. As principals in a postindustrial society, you must focus on your own self-management skills, such as self-awareness, to lead schools to become PLCs.

One way to consider your own self-awareness is with a device known as a Johari window (Luft, 1970). Imagine a window with four panes (Figure 4.1). The first pane, referred to as the *public self*, involves your behaviors known by you and others. The second pane, the *blind self*, includes your behaviors that are known by others but unknown by you. For example, you may unintentionally behave in an aloof fashion, which is apparent to teachers but not to you as the principal or assistant principal. The third pane, known as the *private self*, involves your behaviors that are known by you but unknown by others. For example, the principal who in new situations "masks his or her unsureness by being extroverted in greeting others. Only the supervisor knows that this behavior is covering up insecurity" (Glickman, Gordon, & Ross-Gordon, 2007, p. 121). The fourth pane, the *unknown self*, includes your behaviors that are unknown by both you and others. The Johari window device emphasizes the need to be aware of your private and public behaviors as much as possible and to understand how they affect others. Sensitivity to how others perceive you provides a basis for understanding and developing your own self-awareness.

INQUIRY   A second component of the principal as learner involves developing skills as an inquirer. Again, if you want to lead others to learn, you must be a learner yourself. The ability to be an inquirer has become essential for principals and assistant principals in understanding the school, making sense of such data as test scores, and using information to make decisions. Copland (2003) in a study of the Bay Area School Reform Collaborative found that "where reform processes are most mature, the principal's role shifts to focus more narrowly on key personnel issues, framing questions and supporting inquiry processes" (p. 375).

Data-driven decision making has become part of the vocabulary of principals and district administrators and involves the intentional collection and use of information to guide decision making. (See Chapter 7 for more information on the principal's role as decision maker.) With recent accountability trends, principals can no longer depend on others to analyze data and interpret them to school faculty and the community. Frequently, principals discover that interest groups with a particular axe to grind misuse data in ways that reflect poorly on the school. Understanding data and being able to interpret them are critical skills for you as a principal or assistant principal.

There are at least four components to the principal as inquirer worth emphasizing. First, principals and assistant principals, to be good inquirers, must be able to define the problem. Sometimes administrators focus on problem solving without first understanding the real problem (problem finding) (McPherson, Crowson, & Pitner, 1986). Are there not enough problems without finding more? Problem finding is the inquiry skill of being able to identify the problem that needs to be solved rather than the problem as assumed or presented by others. Most veteran principals can tell you stories of solving what they presumed to be the problem, for example, a playground conflict or an "unmotivated" teacher, only to realize that this was not the real problem. In addition to a waste of time and energy, identifying the wrong problem can create new problems. Research on expert problem solvers recognizes that experts view problems in ways that make problem solving more efficient, they use methods specific to particular types of problems, and they are able to store and retrieve information in more efficient ways (Anderson, 2005). Leithwood and Stager's (1989) research on principals who are expert problem solvers found that the experts were more likely than the novices to see abstract patterns across problems and to be more efficient in responding to "messy or ill-defined problems"—the type of problems found in complex situations. Identifying credible sources of information, looking for patterns, and understanding history are among the many skills that principals and assistant principals need in problem finding.

Once a problem is identified, principals need skills in collecting information. There are two broad types of methods for collecting information as an inquirer: quantitative and qualitative. Quantitative methods, for example, surveys or checklists, focus on finding out the frequency of occurrence of an event or problem, such as how many times a teacher is absent or how often a student gets into trouble or how well students with different demographic characteristics are doing on achievement tests and other learning measures. Qualitative methods, for example, interviews or observations, answer the question of why something happened or explain the meaning of a conversation. For example, what does a teacher mean when he says that a student is lazy? What does a student mean when he or she refuses a teacher's directive? Both types of methods are important for collecting information, but they have different purposes and will provide different information. Knowing how often something occurs will tell you whether it is an exception or a pattern, but it probably will not help you know why it occurs. On the other hand, knowing that a student refuses to obey a directive because of a home disruption gives you insight about the reasons for this behavior but not whether it is typical.

Principals most often use two specific inquiry tools: talking to others and observing events. Talking to others is the most common administrative practice. The work of principals and assistant principals is essentially *talk* (Gronn, 1983). Principals collect information by talking to teachers, secretaries, custodians, students, cafeteria workers, parents, community members, and other administrators. The value of this talk for inquiry is related to several factors, including developing trust and rapport with these individuals, knowing what questions to ask, and listening actively to what others are saying.

The second most common method for inquiry is observing events. Knowing what to observe, when to observe, and how often to observe is critical to an inquirer. A useful set of observation skills has been developed in various classroom walk-through models (Downey, English, Frase, Poston, & Steffy, 2004). In Chapter 9, we will discuss observation as a key element in the role of principal as supervisor, but observation also occurs in other areas of decision making, for example, resolving conflicts and identifying school-improvement strategies. Principals as learners develop an acuity that permits them to quickly and accurately size up situations without jumping to unwarranted conclusions. Malcolm Gladwell (2005), in his best seller, *Blink: The Power of Thinking Without Thinking*, acknowledges the value of intuition for everyday experience and the tools for avoiding painful and sometime dangerous reliance on immature intuition.

Collecting information, through talking, observing, or any other means, is only part of inquiry. Principals must know how to make sense of their communications, observations, or of other forms of data such as test scores. Information does not appear already interpreted. Placing this information in the school context, identifying possible explanations and consequences, connecting the data to other forms of information (e.g., relating test scores to teacher assessments), acknowledging the limitations and assumptions of the information, and considering plans of action are all part of the inquiry process. Frequently, principals are faced with community groups that have taken uninterpreted data, such as test scores, and have drawn faulty interpretations. Knowing how to interpret data for yourself is a critical role for you as a learner and as a facilitator of others' learning.

Finally, inquiry must not remain in the head of the observer or listener. It must be reported to the appropriate stakeholders. It may mean reporting to teachers, district administrators, and parents who need the information to make decisions. If the information stays in the head of the principal, it cannot provide the needed input for school improvement and data-driven decision making.

REFLECTIVITY   The third component of the principal as learner involves the practice of reflectivity. Reflection is not a new idea; John Dewey discussed it as an integral part of the educational process. Donald Schon (1983) acknowledged its importance to practitioners. Peter Senge and his colleagues (2000) described reflection as part of the cycle of change. "People learn in cycles, moving naturally between action and reflection, between activity and repose. These cycles represent the way we improve what we do" (p. 93). York-Barr, Sommers, Ghere, and Montie (2001) related several aspects of reflective practice to student learning.

Reflective practice is a deliberate pause to assume an open perspective, to allow for higher-level thinking processes. Practitioners use these processes for examining beliefs, goals, and practices, to gain new or deeper understandings that lead to actions that improve student learning. Actions may involve changes in behaviors, skills, attitudes, or perspectives within an individual, partner, small group, or school. (p. 6)

In discussing reflection, Argyris and Schon (1974) distinguished between single-loop learning and double-loop learning. This distinction is useful in understanding how you can be more effective in your reflection. Single-loop learning is "observing our previous action, reflecting on what we have done, using that observation to decide how to change our next action, and applying that decision to another action" (Senge et al., 2000, p. 93). Single-loop learning is the typical way to use reflection, that is, simply thinking about whether your previous action worked. Obviously, this type of reflection is more effective than not reflecting at all on your actions. However, a more effective form of reflection is found in Argyris and Schon's concept of double-loop learning. In this type of learning, as a principal, you extend the reflection to include time to consider why you made certain choices, that is, your assumptions and values. "You reconsider the tasks you've set for yourself and you try to understand the ways that your own choices (both conscious and unconscious choices) may contribute to the frustration you feel or the effectiveness of your organization" (Senge et al., 2000, p. 95).

Senge and his colleagues (2000) identified a cycle of learning that includes the double-loop use of reflection.

1. **Observing.** Here the principal asks: "How well did it go? What were we thinking? When we made a mistake, what assumptions or attitudes might have helped lead us there?"
2. **Reflecting.** In this type of reflection, the principal contemplates the implications of what is observed and draws conclusions from them.
3. **Deciding.** The principal ponders the next action.
4. **Doing.** The principal "performs a task with as much experimental frame of mind as possible" (p. 95).

According to Senge and his colleagues, what makes this process double-loop learning is what happens during the reflecting stage. They argued that three processes take place in this type of reflection that are different from the simple single-loop reflection.

1. We reconsider our assumptions that got us to this place.
2. We reconnect by using new approaches and perspectives that are different from our usual sources of information.
3. We reframe or use new guiding ideas and consider whether they will stretch our capabilities.

This type of reflection is more effective because it forces us to look deeper—by examining our assumptions—and look broader—by venturing outside our usual sources of information.

The double-loop method is not the most common approach to administrative learning. More typically, administrators tend to stay within the box, never questioning their assumptions nor venturing beyond the "tried-and-true" sources of information. Senge and colleagues (2000) described a school district that decided that student tracking was not working effectively. The faculty observed that students in some tracks were not achieving minimal standards; they reflected on the fact that the bright kids got the most effective teachers and the other kids got the rest of the teachers. However, because they had always tracked, they never considered eliminating tracking. The faculty of the district did not question their assumptions about tracking itself. This example illustrates the nature and limitations of single-loop learning.

Dress codes and school uniform policies as methods for fighting gang activity are other examples of single-loop learning. These policies often are the result of reflections on and responses to gang activities in the school that never question assumptions about the reason for gangs. Typically, creating dress codes that outlaw certain types of clothing that are associated with gangs often results in the gangs changing their clothing patterns.

Another way to improve your reflective skills is to use the distinction made by Argyris and Schon (1974) between espoused theories and theories in use. These authors identified the importance that theories play in our thinking and learning. These theories are not the abstract type typically discussed in graduate classes but rather are the assumptions that lie behind our everyday practices. Espoused theories involve the conscious and easily changeable assumptions that we make about our actions. Theories in use, on the other hand, are deeper, are frequently difficult to articulate, and are more difficult to change. Osterman and Kottkamp (1993) illustrated the discrepancies between espoused theories and theories in use:

> A school administrator may espouse the concept of collaborative manage-ment and not recognize autocratic aspects of his or her own behavior. A teacher may read the effective schools research and agree wholeheartedly on the importance of high expectations for all students and not see the inconsis-tency in having very high expectations for students perceived to be bright and having "adjusted" expectations for students with learning or behavioral problems. (p. 12)

Osterman and Kottkamp argued that these discrepancies could only be addressed when individuals reflect on their habitual behavioral patterns, their assumptions, and the impact of what they do.

Responding to the demands of a postindustrial society will require you to be a learner that reflects in such a way that your assumptions are questioned and informa-tion is used from a wide variety of new sources. This reflectivity is not a luxury of professors but a necessity for administrators.

COMPLEXITY   In our discussion in Chapter 1 of the nature of work in postindustrial society, we noted that the primary feature is its emphasis on complexity. As a principal or assistant principal who is a learner, you must develop skills that allow you and others to respond to complexity in the school context and environment.

Karl Weick (1978), an organizational psychologist, proposed a somewhat surprising suggestion that leaders need to be docile. Counterintuitive to the typical prescription that leaders should be directive and firm, Weick's proposal is built on the idea that lead-ers who are more flexible are more capable of reflecting and addressing complex envi-ronments. Weick used the example of the contour gauge, which allows one to trace an outline of an object, to illustrate this flexibility. The more teeth in the contour gauge, the more specific the tracing will be. A contour gauge with fewer and larger teeth will pro-vide only a very rough estimate of the object, whereas a contour gauge with more and smaller teeth—thus providing more flexibility in tracing the object—will provide more detail of the object. Principals who have the flexibility (willingness and versatility) to use multiple sources of information to understand what is happening in their schools and communities are more effective in responding to complex situations than principals who rigidly hold to one "reliable" source of information.

Weick (1995) provided useful guidelines for principals in dealing with complexity. Based on his research on how firefighters deal with the complexity of dangerous situations, Weick made connections between educational administration and fighting fires (not a far-fetched connection). He identified five suggestions that can facilitate principals being learners who respond to complexity. Effective firefighting (principaling) occurs when people

1. appreciate the complexity of small events and mobilize complex systems to make sense of and manage them,
2. know what they do not know and simultaneously trust and mistrust their past experience,
3. have a model for the origin of rogue events,
4. strive to manage issues rather than to solve problems, and
5. improvise after first putting into place a system of lookouts, communication, escape routes, and safety zones.

These suggestions are different from the standard operating procedures and administrative folklore of the past era in which routinization was emphasized. In a postindustrial age, the ability to learn in a complex environment is essential for you as a principal.

In addition to Weick's suggestions for the principal as learner in a complex setting, Bolman and Deal (2003) offered useful ways to consider this component of learning (see Table 4.1). They identified four frames for understanding organizations that can be useful to you as a principal and learner in using multiple perspectives to increase your ability to deal with complexity. Bolman and Deal's four frames are

- structural,
- human resource,
- political, and
- symbolic.

The structural frame focuses on goals, roles, and structures. The human resource frame emphasizes the individuals who inhabit organizations—their feelings, needs, and motivations. The political frame draws attention to power in organizations and how individuals and groups struggle for power. Finally, the symbolic frame views organizations as cultures with stories, heroes, and myths. No single frame provides a complete picture of the school. Instead, Bolman and Deal encouraged the development of multiple frames that enable us to see and act on the complexity of the school. "Frames are windows on the world of leadership and management. A good frame makes it easier to know what you are up against and what you can do about it. . . . Like maps, frames are both windows on a territory and tools for navigation" (2003, pp. 12–13). Ignoring the complexity of schools and assuming that there is one way of looking at schools is similar to "managers who master the hammer and expect all problems to be nails" (p. 13). However, learning to use multiple perspectives that enhance the view of the school's complexity enables you to be a learner who is more effective not only in your own learning but also in facilitating and improving others' learning.

TABLE 4.1 Four Frameworks for Leadership: The Bolman and Deal Mode

Four Frameworks for Leadership: The Bolman and Deal Model

1. The Structural Framework

The structural principal tries to design and implement a process or structure appropriate to the problem and the circumstances. This could include the principal trying to

- clarify school goals
- manage the external environment
- develop a clear structure appropriate to the task and the environment
- clarify lines of authority
- focus on task, facts, logic, not personality and emotions.

This approach is useful when goals and information are clear; when cause-effect relations are well understood; when technologies are strong; and when there is little conflict, low ambiguity, low uncertainty, and a stable legitimate authority.

2. The Human Resource Framework

The human resource principal views people as the heart of the school and attempts to be responsive to needs and goals to gain commitment and loyalty. The emphasis is on support and empowerment. The HR principal listens well and communicates personal warmth and openness. This principal empowers people through participation and attempts to gain the resources people need to do a job well. HR principals confront when appropriate but try to do so in a supportive climate.

This approach is appropriate when teacher productivity is high and improving or when teacher morale is low or declining. In this approach, resources should be relatively abundant; there should be relatively low conflict and low diversity.

3. The Political Framework

The political principal understands the political reality of schools and districts and can deal with it. He or she understands how important interest groups are, each with a separate agenda. This principal understands conflict and limited resources. This principal recognizes major constituencies and develops ties to their leadership. Conflict is managed as this principal builds power bases and uses power carefully. The principal creates arenas for negotiating differences and coming up with reasonable compromises. This principal also works at articulating what different groups have in common and helps to identify external "enemies" for groups to fight together.

This approach is appropriate where resources are scarce or declining, where there is goal and value conflict, and where diversity is high.

4. The Symbolic Framework

This principal views vision and inspiration as critical; people need something to believe in. People will be loyal to a school that has a unique identity and makes them feel that what they do is really important. Symbolism is important as is ceremony and ritual to communicate a sense of organizational mission. These leaders tend to be very visible and energetic and do a lot of walking around. Often these principals rely heavily on organizational traditions and values as a base for building a common vision and culture that provides cohesiveness and meaning.

This approach seems to work best when goals and information are unclear and ambiguous, where cause-effect relations are poorly understood, and where there is high cultural diversity.

Source: Bolman, L. G., & Deal, T. E. (2008). *Reframing organizations,* (4th ed.). San Francisco: Jossey Bass.

PRINCIPAL AS FACILITATOR: SUPPORTING A PROFESSIONAL LEARNING COMMUNITY TO ENHANCE LEARNING CAPACITY

Research on school leadership effects on student learning and school effectiveness has found that while principals do not ordinarily have a direct effect on student learning, they have a significant indirect effect (Hallinger & Heck, 1998). That indirect effect occurs primarily through school leaders' (broader than principals') influence on work setting, motivation, and capacity (Leithwood & Jantzi, 2006). Gurr, Drysdale, and Mulford (2006) elaborated on school capacity building to support the type of teaching and learning that leads to student outcomes by identifying four components. The four components include

- *personal capacity* (the principal's own knowledge, skills, attitudes, knowledge creation/construction, and professional networks),
- *professional capacity* (team building, schoolwide pedagogy, teachers as leaders, and professional infrastructure),
- *organizational capacity* (shared leadership, organizational learning, organizational structures, and building a safe environment), and
- *community capacity* (social capital, parent–school relationships, community networks/alliances, and relationship building. (p. 386)

In the earlier section of this chapter, we focused on many of the elements of personal capacity as we discussed the principal as learner. In Chapter 11, as well as other chapters, we will discuss elements of community capacity. In the remainder of this chapter, we will discuss components of professional and organizational capacity.

In the vignette that began this chapter, Nancy Lowenstein attempted to make learning an organization wide effort and priority. Nancy's emphasis reflects one of the most discussed areas of reform in both the educational and business literatures. Instead of focusing on the principal as instructional leader working alone, this emphasis views the entire school and its community as learners. The principal's role becomes one of developing and cultivating a community, which enhances the professional and organizational learning capacity of the school. Capacity building is important not only because student achievement and school effectiveness are too complex for one person to achieve. Capacity building is also important because student learning and school effectiveness need "the motivation, skill, resources, resilience, and conditions to more readily engage in and sustain the continuous learning necessary for improvement" (Stoll & Bolam, 2005, p. 51). Instead of temporary student learning gains or school improvement that lasts only while the principal remains in the school, capacity building permits "sustainable leadership (in order to) . . . create lasting, meaningful improvement in learning" (Hargreaves & Fink, 2004, p. 9).

In this section, we will examine a perspective on schools using the learning theme: learning organizations. After describing this perspective and the principal's role, we will discuss how assistant principals and teacher leaders contribute to building the school's learning capacity.

Schools as Learning Organizations

Many of the concepts we discussed earlier in this chapter regarding the nature of learning have been applied to organizations as well as individuals. Schools where organizational learning is an integral part of the practice are referred to as *learning organizations*. Frequently these terms, *organizational learning* and *learning organization*, are used interchangeably. "Organizational learning is a concept used to describe certain types of activity that take place in an organization, while the learning organization refers to a particular type of organization in and of itself. . . . A learning organization is one which is good at organizational learning" (Tsang, 1997, p. 74). Learning organizations are also called adaptive, resilient, and innovative organizations (Marsick & Watkins, 2005).

CORE IDEAS OF ORGANIZATIONAL LEARNING   Senge and his colleagues (2000) popularized the notion of organizational learning, a concept first credited to Karl Weick (1969). Senge and colleagues identified three core ideas that are foundational for our understanding of schools as learning organizations. First, "every organization is a product of how its members think and interact" (p. 19). The kinds of difficulties that schools, like all organizations, face are rooted in the way people in schools think and work together. This usually means the assumptions and values underneath our actions that influence and sometimes limit the way we think about what is possible. The second core idea is that "learning is connection" (p. 20). This idea reflects our earlier discussion of the nature of learning as a social process. The third core idea is that "learning is driven by vision" (p. 21). There must be some relevant purpose for learning. Senge and colleagues used the example of bike riding, which children learn to do because they want to play with their friends. Learning that results in school change is also guided by purpose. These three core ideas create a way of thinking about schools as learning organizations.

SENGE'S FIVE DISCIPLINES   These three core ideas about learning in organizations create the foundation for the five disciplines identified by Senge and his colleagues (2000) (see Table 4.2). First, personal mastery involves "the practice of articulating a coherent image of your personal vision—the results you most want to create in your life—alongside a realistic assessment of the current reality of your life today" (p. 7). Although this discipline is what individuals do, they can be supported by their schools, "where people have time to reflect on their vision, by establishing an organizational commitment to the truth wherever possible, and by avoiding taking a position (explicit or implicit) about what other people (including children) should want or how they should view the world" (p. 60).

Shared vision, Senge and colleagues' (2000) second discipline, involves "the set of tools and techniques for bringing all of these disparate aspirations into alignment around the things people have in common—in this case, their connection to the school" (p. 72). Once individuals have identified their visions for the future and the current reality, organizations bring those visions together toward some common purpose. Frequently, teachers such as those at East Jersey Elementary School expect the principal's vision to be the vision of the school. Yet, if organizational learning is to occur, there must be a collective purpose.

Third, organizational learning involves surfacing the mental models that we use to understand and learn. Mental models are typically below the surface, off our radar screens, in terms of our understanding of what we know and how we know it. Senge and his coauthors (2000) pointed out that these mental models are the reason why two

---

TABLE 4.2 Senge's Five Disciplines

Senge's Five Disciplines

Personal mastery
Mental models
Building shared vision
Team learning
Systems thinking—The Fifth Discipline that integrates the other four

Source: Senge, P. (1990). *The fifth discipline: the art and practice of the learning organization.* New York: Doubleday.

people can look at the same event and interpret it differently. Frequently, our mental models are built on our feelings that "our beliefs are the truth; the truth is obvious; our beliefs are based on real data; the data we select are the real data" (p. 68).

Ruff and Shoho (2005), in their study of the mental models of three elementary principals, found that career stage as well as expertise led to differences in how these principals defined instructional leadership. The novice principal's focus was, "What is the right set of programs for this school?" (p. 571). The experienced, typical principal's focus was, "How should I be involved?" (p. 572). The experienced, recognized principal's focus was, "How can expectations be promoted?" (p. 573). These differences led to filtering information in different ways, for example, assessing by accountability expectations, assessing on what is best for the child, and assessing by determining what optimizes the situation for the child. Another way to think of mental models is the idea of role conception, on which the various roles identified in this text are based (Crow, 1993).

The fourth discipline, according to Senge and his colleagues (2000), is team learning. This discipline is reflected in current attempts, most notably in PLCs, to develop teacher teams that involve individuals coming together to combine their ideas and energies toward some common purpose. "Team learning is based on the concept of alignment— as distinct from agreement . . . [and] has the connotation of arranging a group of scattered elements so they function as a whole, by orienting them all to a common awareness of each other, their purpose, and their current reality" (p. 74). Team learning occurs primarily through dialogue—team members exchanging ideas. "In the process of dialogue, we pay attention not only to the words but also to the spaces between the words; not only to the result of an action but also to its timing; not only to the things people say but also to the timbre and tones of their voices" (p. 75). We will return to this idea of team learning later in this chapter as we discuss teacher leaders as part of the PLC.

The final discipline of organizational learning is systems thinking, in which "people learn to better understand interdependency and change and thereby are able to deal more effectively with the forces that shape the consequences of their actions" (Senge et al., 2000, p. 8). Instead of seeing events in the school as isolated occurrences, individuals consider the ways other parts of the school interact to influence the events, for example, how reward systems and communication systems at East Jersey Elementary School may discourage teachers from trying innovative ideas. Weick's (1978) description of complexity, discussed earlier in this chapter, is an example of systemic thinking.

CHARACTERISTICS OF A LEARNING ORGANIZATION   More recently, Marsick and Watkins (2005) identified the characteristics of a learning organization as including,

1. openness across boundaries, including an emphasis on environmental scanning, collaboration, and competitor benchmarking;
2. resilience or the adaptability of people and systems to respond to change;
3. knowledge/expertise creation and sharing; and
4. a culture, system and structures that capture learning and reward innovation" (p. 357).

Fullan (2002) acknowledged that knowledge sharing and building are not typical in schools, but where they are found there are the following five core components of leadership: "moral purpose, understanding change, relationship building, knowledge creation and sharing, and coherence making" (p. 414).

This critical component of knowledge creation/sharing requires a conversation among individuals in the school that creates collective meaning. Dixon (1997) labeled this type of conversation as *hallway learning* and identifies the following elements:

1. reliance on discussion, not speeches;
2. egalitarian participation;
3. encouragement of multiple perspectives;
4. nonexpert-based dialogue;
5. use of a participant-generated database;
6. the creating of shared experiences; and
7. the creation of unpredictable outcomes. (As cited in Merriam et al., 2007, p. 46)

Hargreaves (1995) acknowledged that organizational learning could benefit schools by being a source of learning.

It helps people see problems as things to be solved, not as occasions for blame; to value the different and even dissident voices of more marginal members of the organization; and to sort out the wheat from the chaff of policy demands. Collaborative cultures turn individual learning into shared learning (p. 19).

Principal's Role in Facilitating Learning Organizations

The learning organization image of schools is a powerful one for contemporary schools that want to reform learning and teaching. According to research, organizational learning affects student learning and other outcomes. The Leadership for Organizational Learning and Student Outcomes (LOLSO) study was conducted in Australia to examine these student outcomes (Mulford & Silins, 2003; Silins, Mulford, & Zarins 2002). These authors found, as did other researchers, that leadership is indirectly related to student outcomes, but its relationship is through organizational learning. Leadership contributes to organizational learning, which, in turn, influences what happens in the core business of schools—teaching and learning. Leadership influences the way teachers organize and conduct their instructions, their interactions with students, and the challenges and expectations teachers place on their students (Mulford & Silins, 2005). "Organizational learning is more likely to occur in schools where staff are looking out for opportunities to increase knowledge and improve skills and are provided with sufficient resources and time to develop professionally" (Silins, Mulford & Zarins, 2002, p. 634). These authors also found that both direct transformational leadership from the principal and distributed leadership from leadership teams led to organizational learning. The specific balance of direct, positional leadership and distributed leadership depends on a variety of factors. For example, Southworth (2004), in his study of English headteachers in different contexts, found that school size influenced the leadership approach that heads took in leading learning. He developed a leadership cube model to understand these differences. The three dimensions of the cube are school size, leadership effects (direct, mediated/indirect, and reciprocal), and leadership patterns (personal, shared and distributed). Although all these effects and patterns can be found in small-, medium-, and large-sized schools, heads in small schools are more likely to take a direct, personal approach, whereas heads in larger schools are more likely to take an indirect approach that includes personal, shared, and distributed leadership patterns.

Southworth found that school leaders, taking both direct and indirect approaches primarily use three tactics: modeling, mentoring, and professional dialogue/discussion.

Roberts (in Senge et al., 2000) identified four major competencies for the principal's role based on learning organization principles: engagement, systems thinking, leading learning, and self-awareness. Engagement involves the capability to recognize "messy" issues. Heifetz (1994) suggested that the principal ask questions in order to step back and diagnose the nature of the crisis and the attitudes of people involved; reflect on the levels of tension, stress, and learning in the community; and identify the places to intervene. Systems thinking involves helping the faculty "recognize the hidden dynamics of complex systems and to find leverage" (Senge et al., 2000, p. 415). The principal also models learning. Instead of an authority-centered approach to all problems, the principal models a learner-centered approach, which means that the principal is willing to accept uncertainty. "Leaders expect themselves and others to be uncertain, inquiring, expectant of surprise, and perhaps a bit joyful about confronting the unknown" (Senge et al., 2000, p. 417).

Roberts (as cited in Senge et al., 2000) also advised that principals need self-awareness, a competency we identified earlier. This self-awareness requires taking time away to reflect and to engage others in helping this awareness to develop. For the same reason that principals need time for their own self-awareness, they need to facilitate the self-awareness of others in the learning organization.

HART AND BREDESON'S LEADERSHIP ROLES   Hart and Bredeson (1996) applied three leadership roles identified by Senge and colleagues to the principalship: designer, teacher, and steward. The principal as designer is in contrast to the typical engineer or director conception of the role. As a designer, you facilitate the learning organization by helping to formulate and nurture the mutual purposes of the school, develop policies and structures that translate this vision into reality, and institutionalize self-renewing learning processes so that they are norms and not surprises. As a teacher, the principal acts as a coach or facilitator to

> help students, teachers, and other staff understand the mental models and basic assumptions about teaching and learning in particular schools and communities. . . . Principals bring attention to the realities of school life at three distinct levels—individual events, patterns of individual behavior, and systemic structures—and help others understand the relationships among the three. (Hart & Bredeson, 1996, p. 137)

"Principals as 'servant leaders' are stewards for the people they lead and for the larger purposes and mission of the school" (p. 138). As a principal, you remind teachers and other school constituents of the mission of the school and strive constantly for what is best for the children and their families.

Your role as a principal in facilitating the school as a learning organization occurs at all three levels: classroom, school, and community. In later chapters, we will focus on the principal's role in facilitating learning in the classroom as a mentor and supervisor. As a facilitator of the school as a learning organization, you will play both internal and external roles. The internal role requires you to model the learner-centered approaches to teachers and students, helping them to understand their own visions, develop shared visions, acknowledge their mental models, develop their skills in team learning, and think systemically (Senge et al., 2000). As a new principal or assistant principal, as you "get involved in organizational learning at your school, you become even more of a fulcrum point—not just a supervisor of teachers, but a 'lead teacher and lead learner,' and steward of the learning process as a whole" (Senge et al., 2000, p. 15).

The external role is no less significant. Schools are not isolated learning organizations but exist within a larger learning community that includes parents and extended families, the district office, community institutions, the media, and government entities. Understanding the systemic quality of learning organizations and communicating that to school constituents are vital and profound responsibilities for you as a new principal or assistant principal.

The learning organization image of schools is a necessary one for contemporary schools in a knowledge society. Fullan (2002) described the role of principal in a knowledge society as being one of knowledge management, "the principal of the future has to be much more attuned to the big picture, and much more sophisticated at conceptual thinking, and transforming the organization through people and teams" (2002, p. 414).

The Roles of the Assistant Principal and Teacher Leaders for Building and Cultivating Learning Capacity

One thing that should be clear is that building and cultivating learning capacity in the school—either in terms of learning organizations or in terms of PLCs—is too big a job for one person. More importantly, this learning capacity will only develop as others are brought into the leadership for learning practice. We encourage the use of leadership teams made up of both assistant principals and teachers. Certainly, others including parents, community members, and students are appropriate leadership team members, but we focus on school staff because of their responsibility. In this final section, we identify the types of roles that assistant principals and teachers can play in building and cultivating learning capacity in the school.

ASSISTANT PRINCIPAL ROLE   The traditional role of assistant principal has tended to ignore instructional leadership and focus, sometimes entirely, on student management. A more innovative conception of the role of assistant principal as learner and facilitator of learning broadens the role to emphasize instructional leadership. The assistant principal can join with the principal in providing instructional focus and a concern with learning throughout the organization. Many of the principal's roles we identified in earlier sections are easily shared with the assistant principal.

The assistant principal can make a distinctive contribution to the school as a PLC. Assistant principals, because of their potentially extensive understanding of individual students in the school, can provide a sensitive and profound advocacy role for students as learners. Assistant principals often see students in a more holistic way than some teachers do. They see how learning is related to physical, emotional, and social aspects of the students' lives and how creating a learning community must take these elements into consideration. This sensitivity can help other educators avoid the illusion that learning occurs only in the classroom. In this way, the assistant principal becomes a major resource for teachers in understanding the learning process and building capacity in the school to increase the school's resources around learning.

Assistant principals can also facilitate the school as a learning community through their familiarity with outside school agencies, such as social services, mental health, and other community organizations that can be resources in enriching the school's learning capacity. In addition to promoting and improving learning beyond the classroom, assistant principals can help other educators think systemically about how learning occurs.

Assistant principals can also serve in a professional development role to help teachers understand how to use data to understand and respond to student learning needs. As important as data-driven instructional decision making has become, it is not inappropriate to assign this role to an assistant principal. Interfacing with instructional technology staff at school and district levels, ensuring that teachers have data on a timely basis, helping teachers develop the skills to use and interpret data, and being a role model for the use of data to facilitate student learning and teacher practice are all critical leadership roles that assistant principals can play.

Assistant principals can also be a resource to aid the principal in building learning capacity in the school (Mitchell & Sackney, 2006). For example, the assistant principal, because of his or her movement around the school, can be a valuable source of information for the principal in staying in touch with what is happening in the school. While this does not relieve the principal of this function, it complements the principal's ability to effectively perform this function.

Finally, the assistant principal can be a strong sounding board and loyal critic for the principal. A learning community needs individuals who can remind others of the school's purpose and caution others when they become distracted from external pressures or fads that are out of line with the school's vision. If encouraged by a thoughtful and learning-centered principal, assistant principals can serve this vital function.

TEACHER LEADER ROLE   Teacher leaders are also part of the leadership team that can work with administrators in building and cultivating the learning capacity of the school. Linda Lambert (2002) provided a telling statement of the need for teachers to become learners in a learning community,

> For decades, educators have understood that we are all responsible for student learning. More recently, educators have come to realize that we are responsible for our own learning as well. But we usually do not move our eyes around the room—across the table—and say to ourselves, "I am also responsible for the learning of my colleagues." (pp. 37–38)

Creating a sense of responsibility and ownership among teacher leaders of their role in building and cultivating learning capacity is a critical and highly effective role for principals.

Teacher leadership has become an innovative and increasingly used element of schools. York-Barr and Duke (2004), in a extensive review of the literature on teacher leadership, identified seven dimensions of teacher leadership practice: coordination/management (e.g., administrative meetings), school or district curriculum work, professional development of colleagues, participation in school change/improvement, parent and community involvement, contribution to the profession (e.g., officers in professional organizations), and preservice teacher education (p. 266). These functions contribute to enriching the learning capacity of the school, as well as the district.

Chrispeels and Martin (2002) extensively studied four teacher leadership teams and found these teams played four roles over time and to varying degrees: communicators, staff developers, problem solvers, and leaders of change. The degree to which these teams played these roles and how they played the roles depended on a variety of factors including organizational structures and political factors: "reporting relationships, flow of information, committee structure, and environmental, and relational factors" (p. 356).

Teacher leaders can build and cultivate the learning capacity of the school in several specific ways. Each of these needs the support of principals, through providing resources, professional development, and encouragement. Lambert (2002) found examples of the following: study groups, action research teams, and vertical learning communities ("multiple grades are linked together in a common community" [p. 39]).

An especially powerful way that teacher leaders can build and cultivate the learning capacity of the school by encouraging teachers and others to become learners involves action research. In the vignette that began this chapter, the small discussion group that Nancy established to examine learning organizations conducted action research to investigate how to improve the learning of the new students in the school.

ACTION RESEARCH Action research is a technique or a collection of techniques that focuses inquiry on some problem of practice or attempts to make change. Although it uses many of the techniques of academic research, action research is more narrowly focused on practice and is conducted by educators working alone or in groups with other educators, including professors within the context of the school. The process typically involves the steps of identifying a problem area, collecting and organizing data, interpreting data, acting based on the data, and reflecting. Action research can focus on a single classroom issue, a collective of classrooms with a common issue, a school-wide issue, or a districtwide issue (Ferrance, 2000).

Some school reform strategies use action research as a central component of their approach. For example, in the accelerated learning model (Levin, 1987), administrators, teachers, and parents develop processes of inquiry to investigate solutions to common problems and ways to implement change. The leadership team not only can facilitate action research on the part of other teachers but also can be an active participant in the process in ways that benefit the leadership and learning of administrators and teachers.

Principal's Role with Teacher Leaders

The principal plays an important role in facilitating the success of teacher leadership teams. Understanding that the influence relationship between principals and teachers is reciprocal is important as you work with leadership teams. Anderson (2004) identified three models of leadership reciprocity that may occur in the principal–teacher leader relationship.

1. The Buffered Model was used by some principals as a way to buffer them from the other teachers. In this model, teacher leaders isolate the principal from external influences. According to Anderson, this model "can impede more collegial forms of teacher leadership especially from informal leaders" (p. 108).
2. The Interactive Model is a more transformational leadership model where the principal interacts and extensively involves all teachers.

3. The Contested Model positions the principal against teacher leaders who attempt to usurp authority from the principal.

Anderson's study suggested that not all teacher leadership models are effective. Certainly, for building and cultivating learning capacity in the school, an interactive model would be more effective. Pankake and Moller (2007) made eight recommendations for principals in supporting teacher leaders in taking on learning coaching responsibilities:

1. collaboratively build and monitor an action plan,
2. negotiate the relationship,
3. be available,
4. provide access to human and fiscal resources,
5. maintain the focus on instructional leadership,
6. help maintain balance to avoid overload,
7. protect the coach's relationship with peers, and
8. provide leadership development opportunities.

Although these are specific to instructional coaches, they apply to the support that principals can give to other roles that teacher leaders play in the school.

Conclusion

Nancy Lowenstein, in the opening vignette, attempted as a new principal to create a learning community at East Jersey Elementary School. The faculty met Nancy's attempt with both excitement and reluctance. Her focus on learning is illustrative of what we believe is the fundamental role conception for principals who are moving beyond the traditional managerial role to an innovative leadership for learning role. Principals as learners have a profound role to play in their own learning and in facilitating the learning of others. We have identified specific ways you, as a new principal or assistant principal, can enrich your own learning as you respond to the complexity of schools in a knowledge society. We have also described how you can facilitate a PLC committed to teaching and learning for all students.

The emphasis on the principal as learner in this chapter is foundational, along with culture builder and advocate, to the other role conceptions we believe characterize innovative principals and assistant principals for contemporary schools.

Activities

SELF-REFLECTION ACTIVITIES

1. If you were Nancy's mentor in the opening vignette, what other suggestions would you provide to help Nancy respond to the veteran teachers' reluctance to be part of a learning organization?
2. Reflect on how your previous experience provides "scaffolding" for your current preparation to be a school leader.
3. Identify examples of school policies that are responses to single-loop learning and double-loop learning.
4. Using the five disciplines of Senge and colleagues, assess the organizational learning of a recent reform effort in your school.

PEER REFLECTION ACTIVITIES

1. Compare the traditional and constructivist views of learning in terms of your and your peers' experiences as students in high school classes.
2. With a valued and sensitive peer, try the Johari window activity explained in this chapter. Identify, as much as possible, behaviors that fit into each pane.

3. Identify and interview one or two assistant principals who are reputed to have developed an instructional leadership image of their role. What do these assistant principals do to facilitate the learning of others in the school?

4. Discuss with a peer your experiences as a member of a school team. What were the positive and negative outcomes of this experience? How could the teaming experience be improved, and how could the principal support this improvement?

COURSE ACTIVITIES

1. Select one of the cases in the online *UCEA Journal of Cases in Educational Leadership* (www.ucea.org). Reflect on the inquiry skills used in the class to analyze this case. For example, what different methods do class members use to define the problem or collect information to address the case?

2. Using Bolman and Deal's (1991) frames, analyze the opening vignette. What strengths and weaknesses do you find for each frame?

Websites

Society for Organizational Learning (SOL)—Web site has information about conferences, courses, consulting, and publications (formerly the Center for Organizational Learning at MIT)
http://www.solonline.org/

Teacher Leaders Network (TLN)—initiative from Center for Teaching Quality—includes networking resources, publications, recent news, and blogs
http://www.teacherleaders.org/

Data-Driven Instructional Systems
http://ddis.wceruw.org/

CHAPTER 5

Principal as Culture Builder

Vignette

Mark Taylor arrived at Dockside High School five years ago. He had been principal at a suburban middle school and high school, but this was the first time he had entered the world of an inner city high school. His first year was eye-opening and he experienced a sharp learning curve. Dockside was not a "school in trouble" but was large enough to have its own challenges. After his first year, Mark felt better about his ability to lead in an inner city high school environment. He had established structures to solve some of the safety and security problems, he had reenergized the school improvement council, and he had secured resources to clean up and repair the school.

In spite of these successes, the student achievement at Dockside had continued to drop. The state's accountability plan, in response to No Child Left Behind (NCLB), used letter grades to evaluate schools, and Dockside had gone from being a C school to being a D school for the past two years. The state and district had poured lots of money into Dockside and, although there were improvements in some areas, overall student achievement was continuing to fall.

The teachers and parents on the school improvement council were getting demoralized. They had worked hard, but things had not changed. Mark realized that he, too, was discouraged. Although he had had support from the district, he realized that if things did not change the district might decide to bring in a younger principal with more charisma. Mark did not want to leave Dockside feeling like a failure. However, more importantly, he had grown to love this community and its students and to be committed to their learning.

As Mark prepared for the school improvement council meeting at the end of the school year, he started to consider his own assumptions about the school, its community, and student learning. He realized that at times he had assumed that because of the numerous challenges these students had at home and in their personal lives, they probably were not going to be more than average at best. He did not like this thought; yet he realized he had it frequently.

Mark wondered if perhaps this assumption was coming through in his behavior. In particular, perhaps his expectations of teachers and students were gradually lowering.

When he thought about the teachers at Dockside, he realized they were all well intentioned and loved their students. A few teachers had grown disenchanted and were taking their frustrations out on the students. But most teachers still tried hard to make the students feel at home at Dockside. However, he realized that they, too, had lower learning expectations for their students.

When he talked to parents, most were pleased with the disciplinary changes that had occurred at Dockside that resulted in it being a safer school. Most parents seemed to feel comfortable with this success and not be too concerned with the D grade. In fact, teachers and parents tended to view the D grade as a feature of the controversial state accountability system rather than an indicator of what was not working at Dockside.

As Mark assessed his own assumptions, he realized that Dockside faculty, students, administrators, and parents needed to rethink their assumptions about student learning. He decided to use an idea that he had read in an *Educational Leadership* article by Michael Fullan (2002) about reculturing. Perhaps Dockside needed a reculturing in which faculty, administrators, students, and parents began to think of the school in a new way—a learning community.

As he prepared for the school improvement council meeting, he called his mentor and former university faculty member. Craig Allen had first introduced Mark to the idea of school culture and its importance for student learning. Craig suggested that they meet for breakfast on Saturday and perhaps invite three of Mark's classmates from his principal preparation program days who had been involved in reculturing programs toward a professional learning community (PLC).

When the group met, Mark described the situation at Dockside and his realization of his own assumptions about learning for inner city kids. The group helped Mark uncover the implications of his assumptions and identified several ideas for helping the reculturing effort. For example, they described how the school improvement council could undertake a culture audit of the school to identify other assumptions, values, and behaviors—some of which were working against student learning and others that could be used to support it. They also discussed various aspects of the school's current culture—its athletic program, its connection to the arts community, and its impressive array of former students who were now in important political and entertainment positions—and how these could be used in the reculturing effort.

Mark left the breakfast meeting feeling overwhelmed but excited. Clearly, this would take work, but it provided some new energy for him. As he drove home, he began to think about how he would share this excitement and get others in the school improvement council to feel this energy.

INTRODUCTION

In Chapter 4, we focused on the critical and foundational role of the principal as learner in which the principal serves as an instructional leader. Without diminishing the importance of this role conception, the principal as culture builder is also foundational to the other principal role conceptions. Michael Fullan (2002) maintained that instructional leadership is not sufficient by itself; schools need community/culture building in order to be successful for student learning. To realize the school as a PLC, you as a principal will certainly have to be a learner, but you also will have to help build, maintain, or change the school's culture. As indicated in the Interstate School Leadership Consortium Council (ISLLC) standards (Council of Chief State School Officers, 2008) Standard 2, "An education leader promotes the success of every student by advocating

⚞ nurturing, and sustaining a school culture and instructional program conducive to student learning and staff professional growth" (p. 14). As Mark found part of reforming schools and increasing student learning is to build a culture that reinforces learning values throughout the school and community.

If learning is a social construction as we argued in Chapter 4, it is critical to link it with a culture perspective that constructs and reinforces learning. Just as learning is a social effort for students, it is a social (cultural) effort for the school as a learning organization and PLC.

This chapter will describe the principal's role as a culture builder. We use a cultural perspective as a way to understand the principal's direct and facilitative role. In this section, we begin by defining school culture—discussing ways to understand the school's culture, to identify the elements of a toxic culture, and to discuss the impact of culture on student learning. Next, we move to a discussion of the principal's direct and facilitative role in creating, maintaining, and changing school culture. In the final section, we examine leadership teams as culture builders.

A CULTURAL PERSPECTIVE FOR LEARNING IN COMMUNITY

Defining School Culture

Before recent reform efforts, school *culture* had not been an area that had been considered in school reform. Studying culture in schools is relatively new and somewhat ambiguous. Suggesting that the field of education lacked a clear and consistent definition of school culture, Stolp (1994) reported that the term came to education from the corporate world with the idea that it would provide direction for a more efficient and stable learning environment. Deal and Peterson (1999) noted, "Of the many different conceptions of culture, none is universally accepted as the one best definition" (p. 3). Several writers have suggested definitions of culture such as the way we do things around here (Bower, 1996), the shared beliefs and values that closely knit a community together (Deal & Kennedy, 1982), a pattern of basic assumptions (Schein, 1992, 2004), and a complex web of traditions and rituals (Deal & Peterson, 1999).

Schein's Cultural Elements.   Based on Schein's (1992, 2004) work, we believe that ⟫ culture is best defined as a blend of several elements:

- Historical and current artifacts (including behavior norms, traditions, and myths)
- Commonly held values and beliefs among internal and external participants in the organization
- Basic assumptions that provide the underlying basis for actions, values, and beliefs by the participants

Some educators have simplified the understanding of culture by referring to certain isolated aspects as school culture. For example, some educators mistakenly use such terms as school environment, climate, community, or school spirit as synonymous with culture. In this book, we use culture as one perspective in thinking about how principals build a PLC, but culture and community are not the same. In addition, school culture has been referred to as the history of the school or the traditions that have been established. School culture consists of much more than any one of those elements. It is a combination of many aspects that teachers, principals, students, parents, and community members construct to make sense of the school's organization and features. Veteran teachers, staff members, community members, and administrators translate and interpret the school's culture to newcomers as the way to do things in the school. They pass along the culture to newcomers in various ways, both formally and informally. Beginning-of-the-year orientations, faculty meetings, and professional development are examples of more formal approaches to passing along school culture. Hallway conversations, faculty lounge discussions, and veteran storytelling are examples of informal approaches.

Historical and current artifacts.   Artifacts are characteristics of an organization's activities. School cultural artifacts include such things as celebrations, rituals, stories, heroes, and language. Artifacts also include jargon and metaphors that help describe the school. For example, a historical artifact of an old three-storied elementary school is that it grows and nurtures community leaders. On a hallway wall in the school is a "Hall of Fame" with pictures of prominent alumni who have served as leaders. The school has many alumni who have become civic leaders, including a governor, senator, three mayors, a lunar mission astronaut, and several collegiate and professional athletes. The metaphor of growing and nurturing leaders is displayed prominently and communicated in and out of school. Artifacts can be a part of history that is no longer used, or they can be myths that serve to explain a practice or a belief. Many myths have no historical foundation but are passed along and often embellished.

Commonly held values and beliefs.   Values and beliefs that are commonly held by most members of the school community also add to its culture. *Values* and *beliefs* provide reasons why people behave as they do. "Values are the conscious expressions of what an organization stands for." "Beliefs are how we comprehend and deal with the world around us." (Deal & Peterson, 1999, p. 26). These values and beliefs are commonly reflected in the school's mission and purpose. "At the heart of a school's culture are its mission and purpose—the focus of what people do. Although not easy to define, mission and purpose instill the intangible forces that motivate teachers to teach, school leaders to lead, children to learn, and parents and the community to have confidence in their school" (pp. 23–24). Successful school improvement will depend a great deal on how well leaders understand the values and beliefs of those involved in the school. Because the beliefs and values of people in the school shape that school's culture, the effect of school culture on school improvement is significant. Many well-intentioned innovations are not implemented because they conflict with deeply held beliefs and values of school constituents.

Basic assumptions.   Likewise, basic assumptions provide the underlying basis for people's actions, beliefs, and values. For example, some teachers might assume that students from high socioeconomic backgrounds can learn quickly whereas students from other backgrounds cannot. They then act on those assumptions by their teaching methods with those students. These assumptions can permeate the entire school and affect its culture. In the vignette that opened this chapter, the principal, Mark Taylor, realized that he carried certain assumptions about the inability of students from difficult home contexts to learn. Daft (2006) claimed that most assumptions generally start as expressed values but that over time, they become more deeply embedded and less open to question. Members take these assumptions for granted and often are not even aware that they guide their behavior, language, and patterns of social interaction.

Culture levels of understanding.   Some theorists (Daft, 2006; Schein, 1992, 2004) have suggested that culture consists of different levels of understanding. The first level consists of visible elements such as a manner of dress, office organization, or ceremonies. These elements are things that people easily see, hear, and observe by being around members of the school.

At a deeper level of culture are the expressed values and beliefs that are not necessarily observable but can be discerned by how people explain and justify what they do. These are values that members of the school hold at a conscious level. Some elements of culture are so deeply embedded that members might not be consciously aware of them. These basic underlying assumptions are the deepest essence of the school's culture. At Dockside High School, these assumptions might include teachers' lowered expectations of students' learning.

UNDERSTANDING A SCHOOL'S EXISTING CULTURE

One of the challenges you will face as a new school leader is to view the school's organization in a holistic way. Traditionally, teachers view the school through a lens that often is confined to their own classrooms. The challenge for school leaders is to open that lens to a broader view of the whole organization. This wide-angle view helps create an understanding of the school's culture and how that culture affects the values, beliefs, and attitudes that exist. This perspective is not only important for you as principal but also for the larger school community in general and leadership teams of teacher leaders and assistant principals in particular.

Principals who are interested in school reform and improvement need first to understand the existing culture. How do principals read and understand the school's culture? Deal and Peterson (1999) suggested that principals and assistant principals should be both historians and anthropological sleuths in understanding their school's culture. In fulfilling these roles, they recommended several questions that would give principals a way to understand school culture:

1. How long has the school existed?
2. Why was it built, and who were the first inhabitants?
3. Who had a major influence on the school's direction?
4. What critical incidents occurred in the past, and how were they resolved, if at all?
5. What were the preceding principals, teachers, and students like?
6. What does the school's architecture convey? How is space arranged and used?
7. What subcultures exist inside and outside the school?
8. Who are the recognized (and unrecognized) heroes and villains of the school?
9. What do people say (and think) when asked what the school stands for? What would they miss if they left?
10. What events are assigned special importance?
11. How is conflict typically defined? How is it handled?
12. What are the key ceremonies and stories of the school?
13. What do people wish for? Are there patterns to their individual dreams? (pp. 31; 86–87)

We suggest that you use all or part of these questions as you enter a new school so that you can understand the culture that exists there. We also believe that any school leader should consider these questions and reflect upon them periodically.

Wagner (2006) identified three cultural elements that relate specifically to the overall culture of learning in the school:

- professional collaboration,
- affiliative and collegial relationships, and
- efficacy or self-determination.

In addition to the questions identified by Deal and Peterson, your audit of the school culture should include an investigation of these three cultural elements that support a PLC.

Perhaps nothing is more important as you enter a school as a principal or assistant principal for the first time than to take the time to understand the school's culture. All other efforts will be contingent on your understanding of what already exists. In addition to the questions from Deal and Peterson, you also might consider the following questions to link the understanding of the school's culture with your role as a leader:

- What do students, staff, and community members say (and think) when asked what the school stands for? What would they miss if they left?
- How do the key people in the school use personal pronouns in describing the school? For example, how do they answer these questions: How is this school doing? What do you like about this school? What does this school need?
- Do they use pronouns such as "we" or "our"?
- Do they use pronouns such as "I" or "my"?
- Do they use pronouns such as "they" or "them"?
- What other language do key people use that distinguishes the school culture?

Toxic Cultures

As part of understanding a school's culture, you will need to be on the lookout for elements of a toxic culture. In spite of your best intentions and those of effective teachers, a toxic school culture can subvert strong visions and the efforts of committed collaborators in creating and maintaining a PLC. Although an entire school culture can be toxic— obviously an unpleasant and ineffective educational and work environment—more often specific parts of the school culture can be toxic. For example, a particular department could reinforce a negative approach to reform. Teachers could enjoy one another's company outside school, but ignore their responsibilities to address student learning needs.

CHARACTERISTICS OF A TOXIC CULTURE   Deal and Peterson (1999) identified four characteristics of toxic cultures. Such cultures become

1. focused on negative values;
2. fragmented—meaning is derived from subculture membership, antistudent sentiments, or life outside work;
3. almost exclusively destructive;
4. spiritually fractured.

The negative values can be those values that take away the focus of learning for all students and focus instead on "unimportant (football championships), too low (basic skills), or undemocratic" outcomes (p. 118). Fragmentation also leads to toxicity in the school culture when loyalty is to the subculture, for example, department or grade level. In a famous educational leadership case study entitled, *The Robert F. Kennedy High School,* (Gabarro, 1974), teachers and some administrators formed strong attachments and loyalties to individual houses (schools within the larger school) rather than to the entire school, creating adversarial relationships and even security issues for the school. The destructive behaviors in toxic school cultures can be seen when teachers, in an attempt to share innovative ideas, are put down and ridiculed for "trying to impress the principal." Finally, spiritual fracturing is reflected in people's sense of hopelessness and focus on their own needs rather than the needs of students and other teachers.

NEGATIVE ROLES   These characteristics of a toxic culture are carried by individuals in the school who perform negative roles:

- saboteurs,
- pessimistic storytellers,
- keepers of the nightmare,
- negaholics,
- prima donnas,
- space cadets,
- martyrs, and
- deadwood (Deal & Peterson, 2009).

A more destructive role can be seen in faculty, administrators, or students who exhibit bullying behavior especially toward newer or more vulnerable staff or students (Blase & Blase, 2002; Dupper & Meyer-Adams, 2002). Such conduct is unethical, frequently illegal, and certainly not part of a positive school culture. Left to their own devices, individuals who perform toxic roles can severely and negatively influence a PLC. As a principal, you have a responsibility to identify and diminish the effect of these roles. Later in this chapter, we will examine some ways you can address this toxicity.

OUTCOMES OF STRONG SCHOOL CULTURES

Several researchers have compiled some impressive evidence on the outcomes of school culture. Certain school cultures, in particular those that emphasize a PLC, correlate strongly with increased student achievement (Louis & Kruse, 1995; Strahan, 2003; Hawley, 2007). Fullan's (1999) studies on school change efforts identified the school culture as critical to the successful improvement of teaching and learning. In addition, a five-year study by Newmann and associates (1996) concluded that to have success, both new structures and professional culture are needed. The researchers found that school success thrived in cultures with a focus on student learning, high expectations, and support for innovation. Trust among faculty, which is a critical part of PLCs, has also been found to be a major factor in successful schools that significantly improve student learning (Bryk & Schneider, 2002). In a three-year study of three elementary schools that have all significantly increased low-income and minority student achievement, Strahan (2003) found that "developing supportive cultures that enabled participants to coordinate efforts to improve instruction and strengthen professional learning communities" (p. 127) was key to student achievement increases. He found that one of the most critical factors was data-directed dialogue, in which educators in the school discussed collective and individual student achievement data. These educators would then implement preventions and interventions to improve student learning.

Deal and Peterson (1999) maintained that a school's culture encouraged "learning and progress by fostering a climate of purposeful change and support for risk taking and experimentation" (p. 8). Markman (2002) found that school cultures that emphasize morality and self-esteem also affected adolescents' prosocial motivations. School culture also correlated with teachers' attitudes toward their work. Cheng (1993) found that stronger school cultures had more motivated teachers. Lortie's (1975) classic study of teachers also found that culture helped teachers overcome the uncertainty of their work. Thus, there is ample evidence that your work in building, maintaining, and changing school culture can have immense payoffs for school improvement and student learning. But these collaborative cultures and PLCs must intentionally focus on student learning and student-adult interactions. This is why culture building is only one of the foundational roles of the principalship. The learner role must be combined with culture building.

School culture also has a certain staying power. This stability can promote school change, or it can inhibit it. The tenacity of school culture is often seen with principals who make a difference while they are at a school, but their vision is more their own than the organization's. Therefore, soon after the principal leaves, the school reverts to its old culture. Essentially, the vision dies with the leader. Commitment is short term, and the culture is not altered significantly. If this trend continues with other principals, teachers often will become tenacious in their reluctance to change. But culture can be a strong factor of continuous school renewal, where a PLC helps to break down resistance and sustain learning and improvement beyond one principal (Hawley, 2007).

PRINCIPAL LEADERSHIP IN CREATING, MAINTAINING, AND CHANGING CULTURE CREATING SCHOOL CULTURE

Only a few principals have the opportunity to create a new school culture. More than likely, you will inherit a culture that has developed over several years. However, you still can play a major role in maintaining and changing a school's culture. With the new models that are emerging in education, such as charter, magnet, and alternative schools, you may even be part of creating a school's culture. In these cases, the types of teachers and students recruited, the particular features of school life to which you pay attention, and the ways you react to crises help to create an organizational culture.

Schein (2004) identified two sets of mechanisms that leaders use to embed culture. The first set, primary embedding mechanisms, included the following:

1. What leaders pay attention to, measure, and control on a regular basis,
2. How leaders react to critical incidents and organizational crises,
3. Observed criteria by which leaders allocate scarce resources,
4. Deliberate role modeling, teaching, and coaching,
5. Observed criteria by which leaders allocate rewards and status, and
6. Observed criteria by which leaders recruit, select, promote, retire, and excommunicate organizational members.

One example of the importance of these mechanisms is Mark's focus in the opening vignette on the unacknowledged assumptions about underachieving students, which demonstrated his commitment to the norms of success for all students.

Principals in new schools, such as charter schools or redesigned schools, create culture by the activities and behavior to which they attend. If resources are distributed in ways that emphasize one subject or grade level over another, these actions and their underlying values become part of the culture.

As the culture of new organizations begins to develop, a second set of mechanisms acts as culture reinforcers:

1. organizational design and structure;
2. organizational systems and procedures;
3. organizational rites and rituals;
4. design of physical space, facades, and buildings;
5. stories, legends, and myths about people and events; and
6. formal statements of organizational philosophy, values, and creed. (Schein, 2004)

In creating school culture, principals can use artifacts to embed and transmit the values, beliefs, and basic underlying assumptions. For example, the dress code, the physical layout of the school, the language used to describe school activities, and the behavioral expectations of teachers and students create and reinforce values and beliefs about how things are done at the school.

MAINTAINING SCHOOL CULTURE

Often teachers, students, and parents expect the principal to maintain the existing school culture, especially if it has been perceived as successful in solving the school's internal and external problems. If the school's culture effectively emphasizes and enacts a PLC that includes the elements we identified in Chapter 3, your job is to maintain and enrich that culture. The role of maintaining culture involves three audiences: internal veterans, internal newcomers, and external constituents.

Internal veterans.   As principal, you would hope to influence veteran teachers and staff members to "keep the faith," that is, to abide by the norms of the school's culture, for example, inquiry, innovation, and learning for all students. Principals often do this by using ceremonies, stories, and rituals that reinforce the values, beliefs, and basic assumptions of the culture.

Internal newcomers.   Internal newcomers to the school present a special challenge for leaders in maintaining culture. Newcomers may bring with them new ideas and different backgrounds. Often new teachers are recent graduates of university programs and hold to more idealistic philosophies. Because of these different values, beliefs, and assumptions, they can be either a positive or a negative threat to the existing culture. As principal or assistant principal, your role is to help recruit and hire new teachers and staff members who already possess some of the school's values and beliefs and then provide a socializing process to the newcomers about the prevailing norms, values, beliefs, and assumptions of the school's culture. A major complaint of new teachers is their difficulty in uncovering the secrets of how things are done in the school (Crow, Matthews, & McCleary, 1996).

Even in the midst of helping new teachers learn to survive, principals can socialize newcomers by what principals attend to, how they deal with crises, what kinds of behavior they reward, and how they respond to failure. Peters and Waterman (1982; 2004) argued that the leader's response to failure is as important as his or her response to success in building an innovative culture. If new teachers see attempts at innovation punished if they are unsuccessful, these new teachers are less likely to be innovative (Crow et al., 1996).

External constituents.   The third audience to which leaders must attend in maintaining the culture is external constituents—those individuals outside the organization who are connected to it. Your role is to communicate the norms, values, beliefs, and assumptions of the school culture to these individuals and groups. You will want to ensure their understanding of the school's culture and to enlist their support in the school's mission and vision toward a PLC. At the same time, you will have to be sensitive to the concerns of the external constituents. School cultures cannot remain vibrant if they only emphasize the values and beliefs of faculty and staff members and ignore the concerns of the community. Because of this, principals must be actively involved in their communities, being sensitive to the ways communities are changing and to the views that external constituents have about the school's values and how well schools are doing in student learning and engagement. Parents and community members enhance the school culture by engaging and motivating students to learn (Lee et al., 1993) and enhancing the teachers' work with students (Ingersoll, 2001). Leithwood (2007) identified these partnerships with parents and the wider community as one of the major organizational conditions that enhance teaching and learning.

To illustrate the importance of the principal's sensitivity to the needs of the community, consider this unpleasant incident. Several years ago, a hazing incident occurred among high school students in a small rural community. This particular hazing incident was only one in a long chain of similar incidents at the high school over several years. In fact, it could be considered part of the school's culture because it had become a ritual, even though the school's administrators and faculty did not support the ritual. One high school boy was particularly offended by the incident and attempted to protest to the principal. Unable to gain an audience with the principal, the boy and his parents wrote a letter to the editor of the local newspaper. Other news media from a larger nearby city became interested in the story and sought an interview with the principal. The principal, for whatever reason, turned down the opportunity for an interview, and the media published the story without hearing both sides of the issue. Many observers of this situation thought that if the principal had responded in a timely and sensitive manner to the student, parents, and the media, he could have saved the school from embarrassment. Because school board policy already existed, the school board soon addressed the hazing incident with the school administrators. The principal soon thereafter sought to take out early retirement because of the public outcry.

Changing School Culture

At times, principal leadership also involves changing culture. The two major reasons for changing a school's culture reflect the two primary organizational problems, namely, external adaptation and internal integration (Parson, 1951). When environmental demands on the school change and the school's culture is out of step with these demands, cultural change is necessary. The external environment that confronts many schools today provides good examples. This environment has undergone fundamental changes. First, diversity and changing demographics of student populations have created challenges and opportunities for schools in redefining their mission to focus on the changing needs of students. Second, technology and the knowledge explosion have troubling consequences for traditional curriculum-based programs. Third, new school structures and organizations such as charter schools and increased choice have made schools more competitive than they have ever been. Fourth, the accountability movement by policymakers and other public entities has placed greater scrutiny and focus on school improvement efforts. All these external environmental factors, and others that you will no doubt experience, place a challenge on a school's culture. As a school leader, you will need to help coordinate change in the school's culture to reflect these external environmental forces.

Oakdale Elementary School is a good example of external adaptation problems that require cultural change. The school at one time served the children of professors and other professionals in a suburban college town. The private college in the town was built around the turn of the twentieth century, and the buildings were in disrepair. The governing board of the college did not have the finances to upgrade the facilities and was forced to close the college and sell the campus to a medical instrument manufacturing firm. As the professionals moved out of Oakdale Elementary School boundaries, blue-collar workers moved in. The school's population went through a dramatic change. Rather than changing to meet the educational needs of the new community, the teachers and principal stood on their past accomplishments and blamed the students' lack of achievement on their families. The once-positive culture of the school soon became very negative.

Changing school culture also becomes necessary when internal integration breaks down, such as when faculty morale becomes low or teachers are resistant to meeting students' learning needs (Crow et al., 1996). At times, groups within a school can hold differing and opposing values and beliefs. This type of situation can occur when a group of newcomers enters a school where a group of veterans has remained close. The two groups might hold different instructional and curricular beliefs and thus lack a sense of community or shared vision. In an instance such as this, the principal must use influence to reinforce the current set of values that are working and support cultural change where it is needed.

Another stimulus for culture change is when the culture of the school has become toxic, as we described earlier in this chapter. In this case, you as a principal will have to take decisive action to change the culture. Deal and Peterson (1999, 2009) identified seven steps in responding to toxic cultures:

1. Confront the negativity head on; give people a chance to vent their venom in a public forum;
2. Shield and support positive cultural elements and staff;
3. Focus energy on the recruitment, selection, and retention of effective, positive staff;
4. Rabidly celebrate the positive and the possible;
5. Consciously and directly focus on eradicating the negative and rebuilding around positive norms and beliefs;
6. Develop new stories of success, renewal, and accomplishment;

7. Help those who might succeed and thrive in a new district make the move to a new school. (pp. 127–128)

In the section dealing with facilitating others in understanding and developing culture, we will further explore actions that principals can take that will help make change of culture possible.

The school's culture plays an important role in school improvement efforts by creating a PLC. Although no school culture is totally free of some toxicity, and likewise, no school culture is totally toxic, school improvement efforts start with understanding the culture that exists and then reinforcing the valuable aspects, revitalizing the aspects that have slipped away, and changing the toxic aspects that need it. We suggest that as a principal or assistant principal you carefully consider the school's existing culture before embarking on any reform efforts. After you understand the culture, you may then want to decide what parts of the culture need to change and what parts need to be enhanced. In some instances, the culture is so toxic that a radical shift in culture needs to occur. More often, the type of culture change you will encounter will be more incremental and gradual.

Fullan and Hargreaves (1996), however, identified another type of culture change—reculturing. In this case, the school shifts from a culture that emphasizes isolation, balkanization, and contrived collegiality—conditions that are found in traditional schools—to a culture that emphasizes authentic collaboration aimed at student learning. Reculturing is the type of cultural change that focuses on developing norms, beliefs, and practices that support a PLC. This type of reculturing was also identified by Dufour, Dufour, Eaker, and Many (2006) as cultural shifts. We identified some of these cultural shifts in Table 5.1.

TABLE 5.1 Cultural Shifts in a PLC (DuFour et al., 2007)

From a culture of independence	To a culture of interdependence
From focus on teaching	To a focus on learning
From an emphasis on what was taught	To a fixation on what students learned
From providing individual teachers with curriculum documents such as state standards and curriculum guides	To engage collaborative teams in building shared knowledge regarding essential curriculum
From infrequent summative assessments	To frequent common formative assessments
From assessments to determine which students failed to learn by the deadline	To assessments to identify students who need additional time and support
From each teacher determining the criteria to be used in assessing student work	To collaborative teams clarifying the criteria and ensuring consistency among team members when assessing student work
From focusing on average scores	To monitoring each student's proficiency in every essential skill
From remediation	To intervention
From isolation	To collaboration
From privatization of practice	To open sharing of practice
From an assumption that these are "my kids, those are your kids"	To an assumption that these are our kids
From external teacher training (workshops)	To job embedded learning

THE PRINCIPAL FACILITATING OTHERS IN UNDERSTANDING AND DEVELOPING CULTURE

Earlier we discussed two of Deal and Peterson's (1999, 2009) suggested leader roles in understanding a school's culture: historian and anthropological sleuth. Deal and Peterson used six other roles that are connected to the principal's responsibility in helping others understand and develop school culture:

1. *Visionary.*   Works with other leaders and the community to define a deeply value-focused picture of the future for the school and has a constantly evolving vision.
2. *Symbol.*   Affirms values through dress, behavior, attention, and routines.
3. *Potter.*   Shapes and is shaped by the school's heroes, rituals, traditions, ceremonies, and symbols and brings in staff who share core values.
4. *Poet.*   Uses language to reinforce values and sustains the school's best image of itself.
5. *Actor.*   Improvises in the school's inevitable dramas, comedies, and tragedies.
6. *Healer.*   Oversees transitions and change in the life of the school and heals the wounds of conflict and loss. (pp. 87–88)

The two roles of *symbol* and *potter* warrant further discussion in understanding how principals facilitate others in shaping the school culture.

Principals as symbols reflect what they do, attend to, and seem to appreciate. Teachers and community members constantly watch these interests and actions, for they signal the values the principal holds. As Deal and Peterson (2000, 2009) suggested, seemingly innocuous actions send signals as to what leaders value. These authors suggested five possibilities that symbolize what principals and assistant principals can do.

1. symbolize core values in the way offices and classrooms are arranged;
2. model values through the leader's demeanor and actions;
3. use time to communicate what is important, what should be attended to;
4. realize that what is appreciated, recognized, and honored signals the key values of what is admirable and achievable;
5. recognize that official correspondence is a visible measure of values and reinforces the importance of what is being disseminated. (pp. 207–208)

These five aspects of a principal's behavior exemplify the public persona that carries considerable meaning.

Principals as potters symbolize the way they shape elements in the school culture. Deal and Peterson (2000, 2009) suggested that principals help shape the culture in four ways:

1. They infuse shared values and beliefs into every aspect of the culture.
2. They anoint heroes and heroines, anointing and recognizing the best role models in the school.
3. They observe rituals as a means of building and maintaining *esprit de corps*.
4. They perpetuate meaningful, value-laden traditions and ceremonies.

In addition to these roles, principals are responsible for developing supporting conditions that will facilitate others in understanding, developing, and changing school cultures. Little (2007) emphasized three of these conditions: shared interests and purposes, opportunity, and resources.

Shared interests and purposes.   You, as a principal, facilitate the culture building of others by helping teachers and administrators identify their common interests—shared problems, goals, and values. But as Supovitz (2002) found, PLCs, to be instructionally effective, must be engaged in instructional improvement. Thus, the common interests around student learning and teaching improvement must be emphasized.

Opportunities.   You also play a major role in facilitating opportunities for teachers and administrators to share their interests and work on instructional challenges. These opportunities include time and space at multiple levels—schoolwide; grade, department or team level; informal meetings; and outside school arrangements (Little, 2007, Stokes, 2001; Louis & Kruse, 1995).

Resources.   In terms of resources, you have the responsibility and opportunity to facilitate a culture of inquiry and collaboration by providing or encouraging teachers to find and develop resources to enhance their problem-solving skills, understanding, and instructional improvement. In this technological age, material resources, networks, and experts are more easily available. Little argued that collaboration is more fruitful when it is informed by three types of knowledge resources: "*substantive* knowledge that improves the quality of ideas, plans, and solutions; *process* knowledge, skill, and norms that make a group effective as a group; and *political* and contextual knowledge that makes the group effective in its larger environment" (p. 59).

We believe that the eight roles and the supporting conditions contribute to positive actions that principals can perform that will bind faculty, staff, students, parents, and other community members and facilitate their efforts as culture builders. There are some differences, however, in how these constituents will help in shaping a school's culture. In the next subsection, we address the needs of three audiences: internal veterans, internal newcomers, and external constituents.

Facilitating Internal Veterans in Understanding and Developing Culture

As mentioned earlier in this chapter, one of the challenges you face as a new school leader is to view the school through a wider lens than you have previously. However, another equal challenge is for you to help assistant principals and teachers do the same. Since the historic one-room schoolhouses, teachers often have been kept isolated and remote from the total school organization. In fact, they were socialized to view their classroom as the only location where they performed their role. Thus, many veteran teachers have had limited responsibility outside the classroom and seldom have become formally involved with the school organization. A common misperception among some veteran teachers is that the role of the principal and assistant principal is to take care of the school and that the role of the teacher is to take care of the classroom.

Veteran teachers serve an important role in the cultural leadership of a school. They reinforce the values, beliefs, and behavioral norms of the school's culture to one another and to newcomers. They also check the principal's own susceptibility to being trapped by the culture (Crow et al., 1996). Often they can be the loyal opposition, reminding and prodding the principal and assistant principals to be critical of certain cultural elements. For example, teachers can be helpful to the school's instructional culture by encouraging fewer classroom interruptions that can be distracting and reminding administrators of the problems of too many simultaneous reforms introduced uncritically (Fullan, 1999, 2005).

A major part of veteran teacher involvement in the school's culture is through subcultures. All schools have subcultures because functional differences single out special aspects of the school environment (Deal & Kennedy, 1982). Veteran teachers often form these subcultures around functional areas such as departments, grade levels, extracurricular activities, car pools, and certain causes, for example, the middle school concept. Subcultures also can develop around socioeconomic and educational backgrounds, educational interests, gender, and out-of-school interests, for example, golf teams, bridge clubs, and religious groups. Each of these subcultures has its own values and beliefs, basic assumptions, and behavioral norms. Subcultures can shape beliefs and determine behaviors of others outside the subculture and can influence the culture as a whole. At times, these subcultures bump into one another and create conflict, which can be both healthy and troubling. These subcultures also can develop into toxic cultures and spread the toxicity into the larger school culture. However, in a healthy school culture, subcultures do not cause serious problems because the overall values and beliefs are strong enough to overcome the subculture's influence. In addition, the differences created by subcultures actually can add to the strength of the entire culture if diversity is welcomed and appreciated (Deal & Kennedy, 1982).

To help veterans understand culture and subcultures and the implications that these subcultures have for the total organization, Deal and Kennedy (1982) offered the following suggestions that we have adapted to fit school cultures:

1. *Encourage each subculture to enrich and understand its own cultural life.*   Rather than be afraid of subcultures, a principal can encourage the positive aspects of the group. For instance, a principal can embrace the English Department's literary student publications and celebrations.
2. *Help subcultures understand the problems and needs of other subcultures.*   Principals can encourage members from various groups to participate on school-wide teams. Often such participation will help others understand different viewpoints.
3. *Help teachers understand that the overall culture is richer because of the strength of subcultures.*   Once the learning and sharing of problems of the subcultures are complete, you can help veteran teachers understand how each subculture brings unique strengths and values to the overall culture. Thus subculture conflict can be shown to add to the overall culture of the school.

Another way that principals facilitate veteran teachers in understanding and developing school culture is through routine activities. Saphier and King (1985) suggested that cultures are built through the daily business of school life. "Culture building occurs through the way people use educational, human, and technical skills in handling daily events or establishing regular practices" (p. 72). Deal and Kennedy (1982) also suggested that what people do is determined by what they value. The daily activities that are present in a school are good indicators for veteran teachers to understand what is important in that school. Principals can help teachers reflect on these activities and how they affect the school's culture.

A new principal decided that there would be no traditional Halloween carnival. His decision was based on a belief that the carnival caused the students to be more hyperactive and created unhealthy competition among students as they competed for the best costume awards. He assumed that although students would be disappointed, teachers and parents would understand the rationale behind his action. Surprisingly, the most vocal opponents to his decision were teachers and parents, who argued that the carnival was a long-standing school tradition. There was so much opposition to his decision that he ended up agreeing to retain the carnival. This principal learned the hard way that activities take on symbolic importance for the school culture. In this instance, the importance that teachers and parents gave to this activity made an important statement about what they valued. Perhaps, the lesson to learn from this incident is that some rituals are best left alone while you go about working on more important matters.

Facilitating Newcomers in Understanding and Developing Culture

The other group of teachers who principals, assistant principals, and teacher leaders need to address in facilitating cultural leadership is newcomers who arrive on the scene after the culture is well established. New teachers often are forgotten or overlooked as to how they contribute to the school's culture. New teachers can be valuable sources of culture building, especially in reculturing.

Newcomers as part of the learning process point out the strengths and weaknesses in a school culture. The assumptions that lie hidden for veterans frequently are brought to the surface by newcomers. This process of exposing the cultural assumptions lays bare both the functional and dysfunctional elements of the culture. The principal can facilitate cultural leadership by recognizing newcomers' perspectives and encouraging leadership teams to listen to their viewpoints.

The principal's role as it relates to newcomers also involves the attention devoted to induction (Youngs, 2007). This is the most powerful time for helping newcomers understand the culture and for using their perspectives to assess and possibly change the school's culture. Ignoring the importance of intentional induction experiences for newcomers is a sure recipe for diminishing the strength of a strong, instructional culture. In contrast, intentionally organizing and reinforcing the induction process and involving veteran teachers in it is one of the strongest ways to reculture in ways that reinforce and support a PLC.

Professional Dilemma 5.1

As a new principal in rural Sunset View Elementary School, Mary Stewart found after a cultural audit of the school that the annual Christmas Pageant was the most popular school tradition, supported by a majority of the community and the teachers. A small group of veteran teachers were responsible for the pageant and put in countless hours of class time for rehearsals and scenery construction. After her first year's experience with the pageant, a group of younger teachers approached Mary with the concern that the pageant took away from instructional time that they felt was needed for student learning. Because Mary wanted to develop the school into a PLC, she could see the dilemma in respecting the traditions of the school and community and building norms of student learning.

Facilitating External Constituents in Understanding and Developing Culture

External constituents to the school are also a part of cultural leadership. The principal and the larger leadership team must encourage a dialogue with these constituents regarding the school's values and beliefs. In this regard, communication is not a one-way process in which administrators or teacher leaders transmit the values and beliefs of the school to parents and the community. Rather, communication needs to flow both ways so that there is an opportunity to listen to, be sensitive to, and address their concerns. School cultures cannot remain vibrant if they only emphasize the values and beliefs of faculty and staff members in the school and ignore the concerns of the community. "Principals must be actively involved in their communities, being sensitive to the ways communities are changing and to the views that external constituents have about what and how well schools are doing" (Crow et al., 1996, p. 66).

FACILITATING A CULTURE CHANGE

Eventually, it becomes necessary to facilitate cultural changes. Once it is determined that reculturing is needed, you can take several actions that will help make the change possible. First, you need to start with yourself. You must become aware of your own assumptions, values, and beliefs. As Schein (1992) suggested, "If [leaders] cannot learn new assumptions themselves, they will not be able to perceive what is possible in their organization" (p. 380). As a school leader, you need to develop the ability to reflect on your own practice and the practice of others. We suggest a simple model: reflect on what you have done in the past, analyze its impact, reflect on what you could or should have done, and then analyze what you need to do to bridge the gap. In other words, demonstrate double-loop learning (Argyris & Schon, 1974).

Second, as a school leader, you need to exhibit the emotional strength and sensitivity to manage your own and others' anxieties with change. Change creates anxiety. Deal and Peterson (1990) labeled this function of the leader as "healer." The principal as "healer recognizes the pain of transition and arranges events that make the transition a collective experience. Drawing people together to mourn loss and to renew hope is a significant part of the principal's culture-shaping role" (p. 30). Related to this idea is the role that mentors play within schools, as we will discuss in Chapter 8. Mentors should be able to help you and others in understanding the anxieties that exist. New teachers especially should receive mentoring to help with the changes that come on top of their own newcomer anxieties.

Third, you can help the reculturing process by involving others, especially the leadership team, in understanding the social realities of the environment. Teachers and others might not recognize the changing demographics in the community. Likewise, many people might not have had the opportunity to diagnose the culture, or they have only a limited knowledge of the culture.

A fourth way of being involved in reculturing is using subcultures to change basic assumptions, values, beliefs, and behaviors. Subcultures can provide a psychological safety net that is often needed to allow teachers, students, and parents to deal with change. Subcultures also can provide the alternative assumptions that may need to be brought to light for the school to consider change. Rather than getting everyone to conform to the same set of assumptions, principals can take advantage of subcultures. These subcultures can help in changing cultural assumptions in the school. Related to the use of subcultures is the use of the loyal opposition. Block (1987) and Sergiovanni (1994) suggested that a *loyal opposition* could help leaders understand the reality and practicality of certain changes. As a principal or assistant principal, you will want to embrace those in your school who will offer challenging criticism because they often will help build the stronger ideas. The criticisms and questions of these individuals are critical components of a PLC.

LEADERSHIP TEAMS AS CULTURE-BUILDERS

We do not want to leave the impression that culture-building or reculturing is done by the principal acting alone. School culture is too important and too complex to be left to one person. Newmann (2007) argued that building and sustaining a school culture that supports student achievement "requires strong leadership by the principal and by teacher leaders to focus staff energy on instruction, reflective teacher dialogue, trust, and internal accountability within the school" (p. 34).

Peterson (2002) identified the three areas of reading the culture, assessing the culture, and shaping the culture. All three are areas for the work of leadership teams. These teams can provide rich sources for understanding the culture of a school, through its history, symbols, and rituals. As a new principal you will need to depend on the leadership team to help you understand these artifacts of the school that will reflect the culture.

Leadership teams can also be critical for assessing the school culture. Teacher leaders, as well as assistant principals, can work with the principal in determining: "What aspects of the culture are positive and should be reinforced? What aspects of the culture are negative and harmful and should be changed?" (Peterson, 2002, p. 14). One of the most important ways leadership teams can help in assessing is to identify negativity in the school culture. DuFour and Burnette (2002) identified four elements of negativity that create bad or toxic cultures: "we are not responsible for student learning, we prefer to work by ourselves; we must protect our territory; and we focus on activity rather than results" (pp. 28–29). Teacher leaders and assistant principals may be in a better position than the principal to hear these types of negative comments.

Finally, leadership teams can work with the principal in shaping a positive, school culture of PLC. Peterson (2002) gave three examples of ways teacher leaders can work with principals in reinforcing positive aspects of culture:

- celebrate successes in staff meetings and ceremonies;
- tell stories of accomplishment and collaboration whenever they have the opportunity; and
- use clear, shared language created during professional development to foster commitment to staff and student learning. (p. 14)

Teacher leaders are in a critical position to build colleague support for inquiry and student learning. As they meet with colleagues, teacher leaders reinforce the norms and values of a PLC.

Conclusion

Culture building is the second of the foundational roles we discuss for the principal. Creating, sustaining, and changing culture will be one of the most fundamental parts of your job and your success in other aspects of your role will depend on whether there is a positive PLC culture that supports learning for all students in the school. But you are not alone in this culture-building role; your leadership team shares this responsibility and provides valuable insights, support, and actions to help create this PLC. In Chapter 6, we move to the final foundational role of the principal—advocacy.

Activities

SELF-REFLECTION ACTIVITIES

1. How is conflict handled in your school? How has this affected your school's culture?
2. Consider how your school improvement council has created, changed, or maintained cultural elements in your school. What cultural elements have been ignored?

PEER REFLECTION ACTIVITIES

1. With a peer, consider the toxic cultural elements in each of your schools using Deal and Peterson's four characteristics of toxic cultures.
2. With a peer, if you were Mark Taylor, how would you raise teacher and parent awareness of the lower expectations for underachieving students in the school?

COURSE ACTIVITIES

1. Have each student conduct a culture audit of his or her current school using the Deal and Peterson questions for understanding school culture presented earlier in this chapter. Discuss the results of the audit in terms of similarities and differences.
2. Consider the opening vignette and Mark's excitement at the conclusion of the meeting he had with his former colleagues. How does Mark communicate this excitement with the school improvement council and encourage their involvement in changing the school culture?

Websites

ISLLC—Interstate School Leaders Licensure Consortium Standards
  www.ccsso.org/content/pdfs/isllcstd.pdf

Alliance for the Study of School Climate—organization from Cal State, Los Angeles
  www.calstatela.edu/centers/schoolclimate/

Ethics Resource Center (ERC)—website with research on ethical culture building in organizations
  www.ethics.org/erc-publications/EthicalCulture.asp

CHAPTER 6

Principal as Advocate

Vignette

As the only assistant principal at Salt Creek High School, Curtis Erickson was facing more challenges than he ever had before becoming an administrator. Curtis had grown up and attended schools in this rural Rocky Mountain valley. After his graduation from Salt Creek High School, Curtis went to a Christian church–sponsored college in the Midwest. There he met and married a woman from Nebraska. He and his wife were offered teaching positions in his hometown, and after teaching for five years, Curtis took extension courses in administration from the state land grant university. He was the first assistant principal at the high school since its opening seventy-five years ago. The school had been small and only needed one administrator. However, in the twelve years since Curtis's own graduation, Salt Creek High School had grown considerably. Another small high school on the other end of the valley had been consolidated into Salt Creek, with students either being bused or driven into town. The Bureau of Indian Affairs had closed a nearby reservation school, and the Native American students were now being bused into Salt Creek High School. A large California electrical power company constructed and opened a new plant nearby. The mountain coal mines surrounding the valley had expanded and increased production to supply the power plant. Larger ranching firms were buying out the small ranches. These changes had increased the population of the entire valley, and the new families moving in were quite different from the families that had settled the valley originally.

Curtis's own family had moved to the valley in the late 1890s and had started a cattle ranch. All six of his brothers and sisters continued to live in the valley, and an older brother worked the ranch, although it had long lost its profitability. Most of Curtis's friends from school also were still hanging around the valley, working at various jobs, and supporting fairly large families. Curtis was known throughout the valley and his family was well respected; his father and his grandfather had served in various leadership positions, including the local school board.

Now, Curtis was looking out over the assembly of high school students. It was almost as if he were noticing for the first time how different they were from his own high school student body. The students represented several ethnic groups besides the Anglo whites. The next largest population was Latino, most of whom had migrated to the valley from southwestern states. Some had emigrated from Mexico. A few were in the United States as undocumented immigrants. The Native Americans mostly were indigenous to the area, and most lived on the reservation. Other groups, such as Pacific Islanders, Asian Americans, and a few African Americans had migrated to Salt Creek Valley for employment reasons. The valley ranches and grain farms attracted some seasonal migrant families who mostly came from Central and South America. There also was some religious diversity among the newcomers. In addition to large Protestant and Catholic groups that settled in earlier times, the newcomers were also Hindu, Muslim, and Buddhists and many Native Americans practiced a traditional worship.

The assembly today was the annual Winter Music and Drama Festival. The school choir, band, orchestra, and drama departments had put the assembly together for the student body and then for the community in the evening. In the past, the assembly was known as the Christmas Pageant. This year, however, Curtis convinced the student council to rename the assembly because of pressure from some individuals who did not think it appropriate to call it a Christmas Pageant.

Changing the name was not as easy as he had anticipated. The student council was receptive and immediately voted to change the name. A few days later, however, three parents and a minister entered his office demanding to know the reasons for taking Christ out of the school. The three parents were long-time members of the community who had strongly influenced the valley and school politics. They expressed concern about changing the assembly name. One parent commented that it was bad enough not to be able to have prayer in school, but now even Christ had been kicked out. She told Curtis that his father and grandfather would have been appalled at the change. The group demanded that the school administration immediately change the name back to Christmas Pageant. Curtis had a hard time responding and knew that he was unprepared to defend the change adequately.

The name change was only part of the controversy. The day before the festival, the choir teacher approached Curtis and told him that one of her students was protesting the singing of traditional Christmas carols. She told Curtis that she had never even thought about the music being offensive to anyone, and it was definitely too late to change the songs for the next day's festival. Curtis later met with the student and found out that her family was Jewish. He had no idea that the community or the high school had any Jewish members. He did not know what to do about the situation and added it to the long list of items he needed to talk to the principal about.

However, the meeting never occurred that day. After school, a fight broke out in the bus pickup area between two groups of students. One group was known as the "Cowboys" because they often came from the ranch families and wore cowboy boots and other western regalia. The other group was a Latino group. Evidently, the Latino group of students had been waiting for the bus to go home. A few members of the Cowboy group had lobbed snowballs over the crowd and hit several of the Latino students. In the beginning it was only a snowball fight, but tempers flared and soon several students were in fisticuffs. Fortunately, Curtis was not far away and was able to get to the scene before anyone was seriously hurt. However, he had to take the main instigators into his office and suspend them. By the time he had finished, it was after 6:00 P.M. and he was exhausted. The principal was supervising the basketball games in the gymnasium. Curtis left his office and walked down to the game.

On his way to the gym, Curtis saw some members of the Latino group huddling in the corner. When they saw him, one of them came up to him and asked him why they had been suspended when they had not started the fight. Curtis reminded them that the "Safe School Policy" strictly prohibited fighting of any kind. He then told them that they had been suspended from school and needed to leave the building. One of the group members told him that they would be back to settle the matter.

By the next afternoon, Curtis and the principal still had not had time to discuss these pressing issues, and the assembly was underway. Curtis was tense during the entire program. He was concerned about the decisions he had made recently. He found it hard to concentrate on the assembly because of all the issues surrounding the school. He knew that if he was to remain in school administration, he had a lot more learning to do. He had felt confident when he was appointed to be the new assistant principal. Now, however, he was not so sure. He was uncertain about his own values and beliefs concerning the changes in the school and community. He recognized his own weaknesses in handling differences among the students. He wondered if Salt Creek would ever be the community it was when he was growing up. As his thoughts swirled with inadequacies, the principal came and sat next to him. His words brought some comfort when he whispered to Curtis, "I can tell you're troubled. Remember, we are here for *all* the kids. After the assembly, let's go to my office and talk about some of these issues."

INTRODUCTION

Similar to Salt Creek High, school populations everywhere have become increasingly heterogeneous, and the principal's role has become increasingly complex in responding to these demographic changes. Driven by social justice, access to knowledge, statutory regulations, and legal decisions, school communities have had to adapt to the diversity of race and ethnicity, disabilities, language acquisition, gender, sexuality, religion, immigration, and socioeconomic status. Some of these types of diversity have resulted in the creation of new programs that have to be administered. Some issues have caused increased tensions and stresses on principals, teachers, students, and parents. As a principal or assistant principal, you will be expected to serve as an advocate for all children and to help other educators perform advocacy roles. You will be expected to act equitably and promote social justice and access to education for all children.

This chapter describes the third foundational role, which follows the learner and culture-builder roles that are the basis for the leadership role that will be discussed in Chapter 7. There are four major reasons why we believe the principal's role as advocate is foundational. First, the demographic changes, which we mentioned in earlier chapters, are a significant change for many principals and present a necessary condition for leadership. This is not the first time principals have confronted demographic changes. As Chapter 2 pointed out, the common school movement itself can be seen as a response to demographic changes as public schools were established to assimilate students into social institutions (Riehl, 2000). However, the size, changing composition,

Professional Dilemma 6.1

In a school district that recently changed its boundaries and added neighborhoods with lower socioeconomic families, several veteran teachers were troubled with the makeup of their classes. Not having had much experience with the populations they were now teaching, many of the best teachers were asking for transfers. The principal knew that if the veteran teachers left, the best of the faculty would be gone. At the same time, the principal wanted to honor their requests for transfers because of their loyalty in the past. What should the principal do?

and orientation to diversity have changed more recently. Various projections suggest that the white school-age population will decrease to a degree that these students will no longer be a majority. In fact, several states including Texas, California, New York, Florida, and Illinois have already become minority-majority states in which students of color are the majority. One projection is that by the year 2020, 49 percent of students will be white, 26 percent will be living in homes with incomes below the poverty line, and 8 percent will speak a primary language other than English (Scheurich & Skrla, 2003; Riehl, 2000; Natriella, et al., 1990).

Race is but one factor contributing to this diversity. Ethnicity, immigration, language, and poverty also affect the diversity for which principals must serve as advocates. In addition, issues of disability, sexual orientation, and gender enrich the diversity of schools and confront the principal with advocacy roles that we will address later in this chapter. Lest you think this diversity only occurs in urban settings, remember that child poverty is greater in rural areas than in urban. "Rural America is home to 2.5 million children locked in deep poverty. Of 200 counties persistently poor, 195 are rural, with child poverty rates often exceeding 35 percent" (Lyman & Villani, 2004, p. 13).

The changing demographics are being presented in a different way than in previous times. In earlier periods, diversity frequently was treated in deficit terms with assimilation being the preferred outcome for leaders (Riehl, 2000). Such an approach, rather than valuing diversity, sought ways to create more homogenous attitudes, frequently for satisfying economic and employment goals. "The idea that all students should be acculturated to a single way of knowing or behaving is contested and the concept of cultural pluralism is receiving serious attention as a social and educational ideal" (Riehl, 2000, p. 57). The changing demographics of U.S. schools—the size, composition, and orientation—create a critical piece of the fabric of leadership and the principal's role. To discuss the principal's roles devoid of special attention to advocacy for diversity and social justice is incomplete at best and distorted at worst.

The second reason we have included advocacy as a foundational role is the increasing demands of accountability. Whether you agree or not with a particular policy such as No Child Left Behind (NCLB), it is no longer possible to treat learning in schools as directed toward the average student and to ignore large segments of the school-age population. Accountability is not a party affiliated Democratic or Republican agenda; it has become an accepted expectation of schools, whether they are urban, suburban, rural, or characterized in other ways. As a principal, your major task is to ensure that all children not only have the resources to learn but also actually learn. Advocacy for all students is foundational to your role as leader in the school and to your facilitating the leadership of others.

Third, advocating for all students is simply the right thing to do. It might be possible to talk about learning and culture building without including the ethics of care and advocacy (although that would be seriously flawed), but it is impossible to talk about leadership in schools without talking about the ethical behavior and orientation of principals as advocates.

As early as 1923, Cubberley suggested in describing the principal's responsibility: "No other person in the community can so immediately mould [sic] its life and shape its ideals" (p. 36). Indeed, being an advocate for children is not a new role for principals, but educators and policy makers have emphasized advocacy more as school populations have become more diversified, accountability trends and demands have increased, and the moral role of the principal has gained attention.

The last two decades of the twentieth century saw school leaders turn more attention toward educating all children, no matter their socioeconomic status or their academic abilities. Principals are part of a social reconstruction of communities, where every person deserves an education with dignity and respect. At times, this type of leadership has put principals at odds with fundamentally conservative subcultures of their communities. Consequently, being a strong school leader also requires the principal to be a strong moral leader in the community and to take positions that are morally right rather than those that are popular or have been taken in the past. As Beck and Murphy (1993) suggested, in the 1990s, "there . . . [were] serious efforts developing to transform the principalship into an instrument of social justice" (p. 194).

As we discussed in earlier chapters, emphasizing learning for *all* children leads to the view of schools as professional learning communities (PLCs). When we discuss the principal as advocate, we do so with the understanding that this role conception is focused on advocating for individual students as learners and each student's right to learn within the school organized as a PLC. Advocating in a PLC does not mean simply abiding by the requirements of the law, for example, Individuals with Disabilities Education Improvement Act (IDEIA), although you certainly have the responsibility to do that. Some principals believe their advocacy role stops at implementing the law. But such a role conception ignores the advocacy role of principals in which creating a PLC includes developing a rich environment in which the education of all students is more than abiding by the letter of the law. Being an advocate in a PLC also does not mean that the role may be viewed as fixing what is wrong with students or assimilating students into a melting pot of homogeneity. Ensuring that all students learn and that the school is a PLC that supports learning means that diversity is valued as a learning resource. As we will discuss later in this chapter, this goes far beyond holding Black History month events. Instead, it involves advocating for the rich contribution that all students make toward their own learning and one another's learning as well as that of the educators in the school. A PLC does not mean everyone holds the same view or that students are "moulded" (Cubberley, 1923) into a uniform, conforming product. Rather, being an advocate in a PLC means the principal uses diversity as a valued part of the community and works toward social justice for all students and educators.

In this chapter, we organize the discussion of the principal's role as advocate in three ways. First, we discuss social justice as a basis for advocacy, which helps us identify what advocacy means, who is involved, and why it is important. Second, we describe the principal as advocate and identify practical ways you as a principal or assistant principal can develop your own advocacy in a PLC. In this section, we discuss being an advocate for all students, the school, and the community. In the third major section of this chapter, we focus on the principal as facilitator of advocacy, helping create advocacy among others.

SOCIAL JUSTICE AS A BASIS FOR ADVOCACY

Social justice is a contested term. That means not only do people disagree on its meaning but also some people actively reject it as an important value. In your school community, you might find an individual who says, "Why focus on social justice, why not just individual justice?" or "If I had to make my own way, why shouldn't everyone else?" There have been active efforts as well in some communities, states, and the nation to seek out and eliminate requirements or programs focusing on social justice. Although you will need to be aware of these community groups and efforts, as an advocate you should not shy away from social justice. After all, the marginalized students that you are hired to serve as well as the majority students deserve your social justice advocacy.

Components of Social Justice

Social justice has at least three components. First, although it surely does not ignore the rights and needs of individual students, these are seen primarily in the context of larger social, institutional forces that impact the learning of all students. "Social justice theorists and activists focus their inquiry on how institutionalized theories, norms, and practices in schools and society lead to social, political, economic, and educational inequities" (Dantley & Tillman, 2006, p. 17; Tillman, 2002). These forces differentially influence different groups of students. Some students are benefited or privileged by these forces; others are marginalized, disadvantaged, and even oppressed by these forces. For example, think of the students in your school who are impacted by poverty, racial injustices, or social views of what is normal regarding ability or sexuality. These social conditions may not and often do not originate inside the school, but the school must respond to these conditions in ways that enable students regardless of the impact of these forces on them to learn. As an advocate, you will need to look at the ways students are impacted by these forces. Also, as an advocate you will have to make sure that the school itself does not contribute to or reproduce the oppression and marginalization of these students. For example, you must seek out and eliminate practices such as when teachers belittle students who are impacted by poverty; curriculum that normalizes certain sexual behavior and de-humanizes other behavior; and school structures, such as tracking, that disadvantage some groups of students.

The second component of social justice is that it is change oriented or activist oriented. As Foster (1986) emphasized, "Leadership must be critically educative; it can not only look at the conditions in which we live, but it also must decide how to change them" (p. 185). Foster claimed that social justice advocacy goes from a simple awareness of how students in schools are oppressed or marginalized (although this is critical) to focusing attention on doing something about it. This activism involves working both to eliminate the oppression created by the school and to educate students to eliminate this oppression in the society that they inherit. Starratt (1994) identified three ethics that could be seen as specifying the activism of social justice: ethics of care, justice, and critique. A principal as advocate means that you are actively involved in eliminating oppression and marginalization that prevent all students from learning and from participating actively in a PLC.

The third component is that advocacy based on social justice is intentional, deliberate, and conscious. This means that principals as advocates do not leave learning, equity, social justice, and transformation to chance. As an advocate, you are directly and actively responsible to see that the institutional forces that prevent all students from benefiting from school are eliminated. You may not always be successful in these efforts, but this is no excuse for leaving it to chance.

Social Justice in a PLC

Like the other roles we have and will discuss in this book, we see the principal as advocate within the context of a PLC. Social justice as a basis for advocacy fits well into this idea because it is not only the job of principals but everyone within the learning community. The three components of social justice discussed above also relate to a PLC. First, all members of the PLC must recognize the institutional forces—both inside and outside the school—that marginalize students and prevent them from learning. The historical foundations of teaching have tended to emphasize a classroom orientation to the teacher's role, that is, to only focus on what occurs inside the walls of the classroom. But any effective teacher knows that what happens to students inside the walls of the classroom is significantly impacted by outside forces, for example, poverty, hunger, racial injustice. Members of a PLC must recognize the oppressive forces that influence student learning. This recognition is frequently difficult and controversial because as members of the PLC inquire regarding these institutional forces, they might discover that school practices are themselves contributing to the marginalization. The principal as advocate has a primary responsibility in helping teachers and others recognize and respond to these difficult and controversial discoveries.

Second, members of the PLC must be activists for social justice. It is not enough to recognize these oppressive forces. PLCs are change oriented; they seek to solve the problems of learning—be they individual or social.

Third, social justice as an intentional, deliberate, and conscious set of activities relates to the actions of members of the PLC. Thus far, much of the deliberate actions of many schools especially since NCLB have been based on reversing test scores without looking at the causes of learning problems. All educators in a PLC must be intentional and deliberate about responding to the institutional forces that marginalize students if they are to be advocates for social justice.

LEADERSHIP AS TRANSFORMATIVE

Before discussing the specific roles of principals as advocates, we identify an orientation to the advocacy role. Advocacy is inherently transformative. Dantley and Tillman (2006) identified moral transformative leadership as an essential component of social justice. "Leadership for social justice interrogates the policies and procedures that shape schools and at the same time perpetuate social inequalities and marginalization due to race, class, gender, and other markers of otherness" (p. 19). This takes your role as principal beyond being merely a technician or enforcer of policies or laws and provides a significant, moral element. Dantley and Tillman identified three components of transformative leadership.

1. Moral transformative leadership focuses on the use and abuse of power in school settings,
2. Transformative leadership seeks "to unearth how leadership practices generate and perpetuate inequities and the marginalization of members of the learning community who are outside the dominant culture" (p. 19),
3. Principals as transformative leaders "help to create activists to bring about the democratic reconstruction of society" (p. 19).

DEFINITION AND ELEMENTS OF ADVOCACY

In this chapter, we use the term *advocacy* in the sense of supporting, maintaining, and defending moral, legal, and thoughtful educational principles and practices for children and youth. In supporting moral, legal, and thoughtful principles and practices, the principal actively promotes these principles and practices through specific behaviors such as speech, nonverbal messages, behaviors, and activities. For example, principals can support inclusion of students with disabilities in regular education classes by talking to interested teachers and sharing the philosophy of inclusion, providing resources for their attendance at inclusion workshops, and allowing the teachers to visit other inclusive classrooms. In this way, principals support a moral educational practice such as inclusion by supporting teachers to become involved in the practice. The three criteria for advocacy are moral and legal advocacy and thoughtfulness.

The Moral Criterion for Advocacy

The first criterion for being an advocate is maintaining what is morally right. The principal is an advocate by sustaining and upholding the principles and practices that have proven successful and that are needed for their continuance. For example, maintaining a safe school is necessary for all children to learn.

An advocate defends moral causes when internal or external forces threaten those causes. Internal forces such as a teacher subculture can be destructive to good causes. For example, a principal may need to defend a girls' soccer team's right to have the same access to the playing field as the boys' soccer team. External forces, such as the parents and minister in the opening vignette, also threaten moral causes: in that case, the attempt by Curtis to create a more sensitive name for the winter assembly. In some communities, fundamentalist religious groups and individuals have sought to ban the Harry Potter and Goosebumps books because these books are perceived to promote the occult and mystical powers. Although the principal has to be sensitive to these concerns, allowing subgroups in a society to censure reading materials can be quite dangerous.

If principals are to be advocates for moral, legal, and thoughtful causes, then it is important to understand what constitutes a moral cause. We advance the concept that education is inherently a moral enterprise. Because parents entrust their children to the school, educators have a moral responsibility to protect and educate all those children. In addition, schools act as a major source of moral instruction for the young to be socialized into the larger society. Youth learn citizenship, language, respect, laws and mores, and the inherent responsibilities that are needed to live in and contribute to a community.

Sirotnik (1990) identified five moral responsibilities of educators:

1. inquiry;
2. knowledge;
3. competence;
4. caring; and
5. freedom, well-being, and social justice.

In the following subsections, we will discuss each of these moral responsibilities.

INQUIRY Sirotnik (1990) suggested that the first principle of moral commitment, and its ethical root, is inquiry. A matter of increasing concern to many is what appears to be a decline in three areas: thoughtfulness, reflective habit, and value placed on inquiry itself—especially in a culture that is amusing itself to death. As Sirotnik put it, "Too often we have heard educators say something to the effect, 'Well, that's interesting, but it's just philosophical; let's get back to what we can do in the real world.' Thinking appears to have become increasingly alienated from 'doing' " (p. 299).

As principal or assistant principal, you need to acknowledge explicitly the moral commitment to inquiry. As we discussed in Chapter 4, the demands of a postindustrial society will require you to be a learner who reflects in such a way that your assumptions are questioned and information from a wide variety of new sources is used. This reflectivity is not a luxury of professors but a necessity for practitioners. In the opening vignette, Curtis realized that he had to learn more about the students in the school and their differences. He reflected on his own learning and realized that he had a lot more learning to do. Similarly, you also need to be constantly reflecting on your own learning and on ways to continue your learning, especially regarding those social justice issues that are critical in your school.

As you practice inquiry, you also must promote inquiry and reflectivity among teachers and students. At times, practicing and promoting inquiry may put you at odds with policymakers and others who may champion standardized measurements without understanding their limitations. As Arendt (1958) said over fifty years ago, "The highest and perhaps purest activity of which men are capable is the activity of thinking" (p. 5). Unfortunately, many policymakers and educators do not always understand or practice the concept of thinking.

KNOWLEDGE Sirotnik (1990) suggested that inquiry without knowledge is fraudulent and that knowledge without inquiry is impossible. The question has to be asked, however: What kind of knowledge is a moral commitment? Is knowledge being viewed as bits and pieces of information that can be deposited and withdrawn as a series of facts in a bank? Knowledge is far more encompassing and dynamic than a body of accumulated information. As Sirotnik argued, as important as the facts are, taken separately or together they do not constitute knowledge. Knowledge is what we make of the facts and what we learn through explanation, interpretation, and understanding. In short, knowledge is what we gain through inquiry; moreover, inquiry is stimulated and sustained by what we know. This process is accomplished through active and intellectual engagement with information in the context of being human.

COMPETENCE In describing competence and incompetence, Sirotnik (1990) suggested that competence is a natural aspiration for humans. He suggested that we as humans aim to reward success and not failure. We also reward excellence and not mediocrity. Because we are more interested in success and excellence, being competent is something that humans aspire to. An "ethic of competence," or a moral commitment to doing and learning to do things well, seems to be an important moral ingredient in working in a society and a community. As Sirotnik suggested, when we focus on justice and human interrelationships, we do so under the assumption that people will serve one another well, not poorly.

CARING The fourth moral principle outlined by Sirotnik (1990) is based on the premise that the relationships among people are basic to the human condition. He used caring to refer to "deep relationships among people based on mutuality, respect, relatedness, receptivity, and trust" (p. 302). In Noddings' (1984) words:

> Apprehending the other's reality, feeling what he feels as nearly as possible, is the essential part of caring from the view of the one caring. For if I take on the other's reality as possibility and begin to feel its reality, I feel, also, that I must act accordingly; that is, I am impelled to act as though in my own behalf, but in behalf of the other. (p. 16)

Because we care about each other and ourselves, we need to watch out for each other. However, we would argue that we must be somewhat prudent and wise in our caregiving. Educators can and do burnout because of the caretaking of others. We suggest that you first take care of your own basic needs, such as nutrition, exercise, and other good health habits. We then suggest that you take care of your family and loved ones. If you do not care for your own and your loved ones' needs, you may find that your energy for caring for others will be greatly diminished and you may approach burnout.

FREEDOM, WELL-BEING, AND SOCIAL JUSTICE   Madison (1788) observed, "If men were angels, no government would be necessary" (p. 262). Freedom and well-being are essential features of the human condition, and we are duty-bound to preserve and protect these features. When preserving and protecting freedom and well-being cannot be adequately accomplished by individuals, then society, usually through government, has to become involved. Americans have placed a great deal of faith in the nation's schools (most of which are an arm of the government) to socialize and acculturate youth into the society. However, socializing our youth does not mean accepting the way things are but helping youth to be willing to change things to the way they ought to be. It is here that schools can be more than a mechanism for transmitting social values but also a way of reconstructing values for a just society.

The Legal Criterion for Advocacy

You also should consider the second criterion for advancing educational principles and practices—of being legal. Everyone should receive equal access under the law. If a government provides a school system, everyone should have equal access to the educational system and the curricular and extracurricular programs.

The Fourteenth Amendment to the U.S. Constitution provides for equality under the law by stating: "No State shall . . . deny to any person within its jurisdiction the equal protection of the laws." Although, by today's standards, "equal protection of the laws" is interpreted as everyone having equal access, in 1895, the U.S. Supreme Court stated that equality under the law also could mean "separate but equal." One of the results of the *Plessy v. Ferguson* ruling was that segregated education based on race could be legal under the Fourteenth Amendment. This ruling, of course, was overturned in 1954 when the Supreme Court ruled in *Brown v. Board of Education of Topeka* that segregated education was inherently unequal. This ruling meant that if school facilities, teachers, equipment, and all other physical conditions were equal among racially segregated schools, the schools would still be unequal because of racial segregation.

The Thoughtfulness Criterion for Advocacy

The third criterion for defining educational principles and practices to advocate is thoughtfulness. Perhaps one of the problems today is the demand for instant decisions and comments. For example, no sooner does the president of the United States give a press conference than newscasters are following with commentaries. When a critical incident occurs at a school, principals find microphones in their faces asking for an immediate decision or comment. There is little tolerance for uncertainty and doubt. However, in advocating the moral and legal principles and practices, we also must be thoughtful as to the consequences of the principles and practices. For example, suspending a first-grade boy for kissing a playmate on the cheek because it is a violation of sexual harassment rules may be following a policy, but it also is a mindless act. As a principal or assistant principal, you must learn not to be afraid of withholding judgment, of challenging the assertions of others, and of having your own ideas challenged in return. Thoughtfulness often takes time, and it flourishes as more questions are asked. In the opening vignette, perhaps Curtis could have taken more time to solve some of the problems more thoughtfully by asking questions and having others ask questions.

Some people have argued that government has no place in socialization efforts for moral, ethical, and thoughtful principles and practices. They have argued that family, churches, businesses, and other private organizations, such as scouting, can be better socialization agents for youth than can government organizations such as schools. Perhaps they can, or at least perhaps they have the potential. However, if we relied on these organizations entirely, then some of our children and youth who do not have access to family, church, or scouting would be left out of the socialization process. Schools are the only available means that have the potential of reaching all youth and instilling accepted moral commitments.

As a principal and assistant principal, you become a major player in this charge. Any practice that perpetuates social and economic inequities should be targets of your advocacy efforts. Schooling in America has a long history of attempting to balance equity and excellence, and at times, schools have excluded populations in an attempt to achieve excellence. It is important to understand that equity and excellence do not have to be mutually exclusive in schools. Sirotnik (1994) offered definitions for equity and excellence, indicating that both could be attainable:

> Excellence is indicated by conditions, practices, and outcomes in schools that are associated with high levels of learning for students in all valued goal areas of the common curriculum. Equity is indicated when there are not systematic differences in distributions of these conditions, practices and outcomes based upon race, ethnicity, sex, economic status, or any other irrelevant group characteristic. (p. 168)

In the past, the debate over equity or excellence tended to polarize educators and policymakers. It often came down to either having one or the other. As a principal, however, you can go beyond this rhetoric and choose to advance both equity and excellence. In fact, Sirotnik (1994) claimed that there could be no educational excellence without educational equity.

As an advocate, you can be a leader of a school that not only serves the best interests of all students but also provides a valuable educational lesson by modeling the *just* society. Kerr (1987) summarized the purpose of moral commitments of schooling:

> This cultural conception of education is fundamental to social justice, to cultural community, to democracy, and to our ability to interpret what we see—to structure experience. It is this broad and basic conception of education that justifies the institution of schooling generally. . . . The central task of schooling is education as an initiation into the ways of understanding and inquiring. Education so conceived cannot be improved by courses in critical thinking, for it is itself an initiation into the disciplines of critical thinking. It cannot be passed over in favor of "basic education," for there is no education that is more basic. (p. 25)

Throughout this book, we have proposed the concept of learning as being part of community. In the larger sense of community, consider America as a collection of multiple communities defined by different interests, races, ethnicities, regions, economic stratifications, religions, and so on. Celebrating these differences is part of what makes the nation great (Sirotnik, 1990).

PRINCIPALS AND SOCIAL JUSTICE

Although we have already provided much of the conceptual justification for advocacy based on social justice, before moving to more specific elements of the principal's advocacy role we want to position the principal's role within a social justice context. To do this, we will focus on three elements: your own identity, barriers to the role, and priorities.

Your Own Identity Within a Social Justice Context

A critical need in your becoming an advocate is to understand how your own identity, race, ability, gender, sexual orientation, language, national origin, and religion influence your role as advocate. Although we do not have space in this chapter to delve deeply into this, we want to stress the importance of your acknowledging your own position, privilege, and marginalization. Characteristics such as race, gender, sexual orientation, religion, and language are not value-neutral elements. By virtue of the way power and privilege in a society and a school is determined, these characteristics carry with them power and privilege. Well-intentioned individuals often say, "Why don't we just act as if race doesn't matter and treat each other equally." This view, known as color blindness, may sound like it promotes equity and social justice. But in fact, color blindness can reproduce power differences and marginalization. If you and I start out, because of our race or national origin, with different privileges and power resources, holding everything constant (i.e., not considering the effects of race) merely continues the same power differences. As a principal, these characteristics of your identity should not make you feel guilty, but rather should be acknowledged as influencing the lens with which you look at the world—your role, your school, your PLC. Lenses, as Bolman and Deal (2003) reminded us, help us focus but they also limit our focus. Understanding how your own characteristics, history, and role help you focus but also how they limit your focus is a critical part of learning to be an advocate. Understanding how your own identity affects your practice as an advocate for social justice also involves understanding how other administrators with different characteristics may provide insights to your practice (Riehl, 2000). Being a learner involves more than simply finding out how to do a budget or which law pertains to certain problems that arise. It also involves reflecting critically on your own identity and how your position influences your practice as an advocate for social justice in your school.

Barriers to the Role Within a Social Justice Context

As an advocate, you will also face several barriers to social justice. One barrier is the controversial nature of some issues regarding social justice, for example, programs for gays, lesbians, bisexuals, and transgender individuals (GLBT). In some communities, actions by administrators to actively support the learning and school experiences of these students are seen as promoting a political agenda or an alternative lifestyle. If community members see activities or programs that they perceive as diminishing their exclusive power and privilege, for example, supporting the learning of students who do not speak English, they may actively resist and protest against these programs. Another barrier is the nature of many educators. For example, some teachers reject practices that are more inclusionary for students with disabilities because they claim it impacts their classroom routines and practices. A third barrier is the intensity of the role of educator. Some teachers and administrators reject professional development on social justice issues, not necessarily because they are opposed to all students learning, but because of the mammoth amount of mandates, programs, and demands placed upon them (Marshall & Ward, 2004). As an advocate, you must be aware of these and other barriers to social justice and develop approaches to respond to them.

Priorities Within a Social Justice Context

Before moving to a more specific discussion of the principal's direct role as an advocate, we want to identify general tasks and priorities for the principal as advocate in the context of social justice. Riehl (2000) identified three broad categories of tasks that are necessary for principals in responding to diversity that is part of social justice.

The first category of tasks for principals includes fostering new meanings about diversity. Although creating structures and programs such as those we will discuss later in the chapter are important, even more important is the principal's role in working with individuals both inside and outside the school in developing shared meanings regarding diversity and social justice. In Chapter 5 on the principal as culture builder, we laid the foundation for this important work. Riehl identified three strategies that principals use to influence meaning-making: "through the day-to-day management of meanings among organizational stakeholders, through the mediation of conflict when open contention arises, and through the cognitive task of resolving contradictions with their (principal's) own ideological perspectives" (p. 60). Specific actions, such as developing official ceremonies, public relations events, and meetings provide the opportunities to help individuals develop these shared meanings about diversity and social justice.

The second category of tasks, which Riehl (2000) identified, for the principal is "promoting inclusive practices within the school" (p. 62). She maintained that this occurs through "promoting forms of teaching and learning that enable diverse students to succeed and molding school cultures that embrace and support diversity" (p. 62). Louis and Kruse (1995) found that administrators in PLCs play an important role "through their attention to individual teacher development and by creating and sustaining networks of conversation in their schools around issues of teaching and learning" (Riehl, 2000, p. 63).

Riehl's (2000) third category of tasks for principals in promoting diversity and social justice is "building connections between schools and communities" (p. 66). In the same way that teachers have to look beyond their classrooms, principals must look beyond the school and connect with the community to find resources that enhance diversity and social justice, to shield students from the negative community influences, and to provide services that enhance the community as well as students (Riehl).

As a further elaboration on the tasks and priorities of your role as an advocate for social justice, Walker and Dimmock (2005) identified six priorities for principals in multiethnic schools, but which have relevance for principals in any school.

1. demanding that staff members' values cohere with principles of social justice and equality
2. insisting that staff members demonstrate a willingness to understand the cultures and background realities of their students and school community
3. recruiting and retaining staff members with cultural and ethnic backgrounds similar to those present in the school community
4. positioning the school firmly within the immediate and broader societal context
5. improving learning and teaching to address disadvantage
6. constructing and nurturing an inclusive school culture. (pp. 294–298)

These priorities do not result in a one-way to lead or one-size-fits all leadership. Rather, they mean that as an advocate for social justice, you will look critically at your school and its context and determine what types of learning, culture building, mentoring, supervision, management, and political action, and leadership is necessary to build a PLC that enhances diversity and promotes social justice. But fundamentally, as an advocate for social justice you will be committed to a moral purpose. As Scheurich and Skrla (2003) stated:

> The most important characteristics of a leader who is creating or who is going to create an equitable and excellent school is that this person has developed a strong ethical or moral core focused on equity and excellence as the only right choice for schools in a democracy. For this person, this is an indomitable belief, an indomitable commitment. (p. 100)

In the next section, we examine more specifically the role of principal as advocate and as developing other advocates. We will discuss areas and programs in which you will be an advocate for the whole child and for all students, an advocate for the school, and an advocate for the community.

PRINCIPAL AS ADVOCATE

Advocate for the Whole Child and for All Students

We begin our discussion of the principal as advocate by first exploring the nature of differences that exist within society and schools that are important for you to understand in being an advocate for the whole child and for all students. We then discuss nine factors that can affect education and schooling and thus your role as an advocate for students: race, ethnicity, and culture; religious diversity; language diversity; poverty and social class; gender; sexual orientation; students with special needs; gifted and talented students; and at-risk students.

Because our culture is so much a part of what we are and what we do, we often view other cultures as being inferior. Ethnocentrism, the belief in the superiority of our own culture, can lead us to judge others in terms of our culture and to conclude that those who do not conform to the norms of our culture are in some ways inferior or irresponsible. When the dominant group in a society adopts the posture that its own set of values constitutes the only idealized norm in that society, the practices or traits of minority cultures are likely to be seen as deficient and must be corrected either by education or coercion. As Pai and Adler (2001) put it, the dominant culture tends to treat minority cultures as sick forms of the normal culture and to define differences as deficits. Earlier in this chapter we introduced the concept of deficit *view*, which assumes that something is wrong and needs to be fixed. This deficit view can target many groups and behaviors in the schools, such as racial and ethnic groups, language usage, students with disabilities, gender, sexual orientation, students from other countries, and those living in poverty. Too many times in America's history, educators and policy-makers have segregated groups of students because of their differences from main-stream students. As a principal or assistant principal, your role as advocate should be to oppose the deficit view among teachers, staff members, students, policymakers, and community members.

The notion that a difference is not a deficit is also useful in exposing ethnocentric assumptions underlying various school curricular and extracurricular programs. Access to all school programs has not been available to all groups. For instance, some schools have ability groups and tracking programs to differentiate among student interests and abilities. Poor, minority students and students from immigrant or migrant families often have been left at the bottom of the system (Burnett, 1995). Ability grouping is still common in schools because teachers often believe that it is eas-ier to teach a group of students with similar abilities. Groupings usually are based on reading and math levels, but the grouping designations often transfer into other sub-ject areas, especially if standardized testing is used to determine the groupings. Ability grouping usually begins in elementary school and continues through high school as students are tracked into curricular paths. For example, the college-preparatory track has had fewer representatives from poor and minority students than from majority students. Unfortunately, too often placement in school programs correlates directly with the child's background, language usage, appearance, and socioeconomic vari-ables (Oaks, 1986). Because teachers and counselors often recommend students for placement into programs, some of these educators may hold a deficit view of various students. Even more troubling is the fact that these placements tend to be fairly stable over time. Students placed in low-ability groups find it more difficult to catch up with high-ability groups over the years.

In an early classic study, Rosenthal and Jacobsen (1968) tested the effects of teacher expectations on interactions, achievement levels, and student intelligence. Their conclu-sion that once a child is labeled by the teacher and others, a "self-fulfilling prophecy" operates. The teacher expects certain behaviors from the child, and the child responds to the expectations. More recent studies (e.g., Banks, 1999) have shown that teacher expectations play a significant role in determining how much and how well students learn. Teacher expectations are influenced by various factors, including records of a student's previous work and test scores; the student's dress, name, physical appearance, attractiveness, race, gender, language, and accent; the parents' occupations; single-parent and motherhood status; and the way the student responds to the teacher.

Ethnocentric assumptions also can affect extracurricular programs. For instance, certain athletic programs have become known as "country club" sports because of the nature of those who participate. To compete with others and qualify to participate in certain sports, students have had to have considerable experience in playing in year-round sport clubs or access to expensive golf courses, tennis clubs, and ski resorts. Because of these high-cost activities, many students and their families simply cannot afford to participate and thus are viewed as being deficient because their talents are not as visible as those who can participate. Likewise, instrumental music also can pose a barrier to participation for students who cannot afford to rent or purchase musical instruments. Often schools have to charge extra fees for the musical and athletic activities, preventing some students from access to the programs. Eliminating ethnocentric assumptions that lead to discriminatory practices is a target of the principal's advocacy role.

Your role as an advocate for social justice within the context of a PLC means that you not only value differences among individual students, but you help to establish an understanding among culturally different groups. We propose that your advocacy role in terms of difference involves helping to create a "culturally proficient" school. Lindsey and colleagues (2005) identified a cultural proficiency continuum that involves the following:

- *Cultural destructiveness:* negating, disparaging, or purging cultures that are different from your own
- *Cultural incapacity:* elevating the superiority of your own cultural values and beliefs and suppressing cultures that are different from your own
- *Cultural blindness:* acting as if differences among cultures do not exist and refusing to recognize any differences
- *Cultural precompetence:* recognizing that lack of knowledge, experience, and understanding of other cultures limits your ability to effectively interact with them
- *Cultural competence:* interacting with other cultural groups in ways that recognize and value their differences, motivate you to assess your own skills, expand your knowledge and resources, and ultimately cause you to adapt your relational behavior
- *Cultural proficiency:* honoring the differences among cultures, viewing diversity as a benefit, and interacting knowledgeably and respectfully among a variety of cultural groups. (pp. xvii–xviii)

Cultural proficiency within the context of a PLC means that cultural differences, insights, values, and interactions become a necessary and valuable part of the community. Cultural proficiency must be part of the learning goals and processes of the community and your role as an advocate in a PLC is critical.

Another important issue regarding differences relates to advocating for the whole student. Some current accountability trends have emphasized one aspect of student development, namely math and reading achievement, and have essentially ignored other forms of achievement, as well as social and emotional development and civic engagement. You as an advocate must emphasize educating the whole student so that he or she not only becomes a worker but also becomes a citizen, a partner, a contributing member to society, and an activist for moral causes. As you develop your conception of yourself as an advocate, remember this more holistic view of student needs and development and develop ways to respond to these significant areas of need.

In the next subsection, we discuss several types of differences that are important in schools and for the advocacy role of principals. Developing your role in these areas will help you become an advocate for the whole child and for all students.

Racial, Ethnic, and Cultural Diversity

The late nineteenth and early twentieth centuries were a time of massive immigration to the United States. However, the immigrants who reached American shores after 1870 were different from their predecessors (Pai and Adler, 2001). The new immigrants came from southern and eastern Europe, Asia, and South America and did not have the Anglo-Saxon heritage. Thus, they had more difficulty adjusting to the English language and the Protestant orthodoxy that dominated the public schools. Rather than establishing schools as a multicultural microcosm of society, educators reaffirmed their belief that being an American meant conforming to the Anglo-Saxon, Protestant view. The educational historian, Cubberley (1909) remarked:

> Our task is to break up these groups or settlements, to assimilate and amalgamate these people as a part of our American race, and to implant in their children, so far as can be done, the Anglo-Saxon conception of righteousness, law and order, and popular government, and to awaken in them a reverence for our democratic institutions and for those things in our national life which we as a people hold to be abiding worth. (pp. 15–16)

It soon became apparent to native-born Americans and the new immigrants that simple Anglo conformity was not reasonable. Hence, what emerged was the idea of a melting-pot ideal. Pai and Adler (2001) reported that according to this view, ethnic differences that were melted into a single pot would produce a synthesis—a new homogeneous culture that was not Anglo-Saxon, Jewish, Italian, or Asian. However, the melting-pot ideal never materialized. "In reality, what happened in the melting pot . . . was that all varieties of ethnicities were melted into one pot, but the brew turned out to be Anglo-Saxon again. The ingredients of this melting pot were, in fact, to be assimilated to an idealized Anglo-Saxon model" (p. 63). Most people realize now that using the melting pot metaphor to describe the United States was never accurate.

BANKS' FOUR APPROACHES   In the 1960s, many educators and minority leaders pointed out that America's schools were ethnocentric in curriculum and instructional practices despite the 1954 *Brown v. Board of Education* ruling that pronounced "separate is not equal" in schools. They proposed that schools failed to provide equal educational opportunity to poor and minority children. What followed was a confusion of meanings for multicultural education. Several kinds of curricular and instructional practices came under the guise of being multicultural, although they did little in promoting better understanding of cultural differences. Banks (1999) suggested four approaches or levels in developing multicultural curriculum:

1. the contribution approach,
2. the additive approach,
3. the transformative approach, and
4. the social action approach.

The first two levels, the contribution approach and the additive approach, are most common. Using the contribution approach, the curriculum includes content about holidays and celebrations of various ethnic groups. Because of this approach, educators started celebrating Black History Month, Cinco de Mayo, and Pacific Islanders Week. The second level, additive approach, uses the curriculum to add content about minorities without changing the basic goals and structure of the curriculum. An example of the additive approach would be including Langston Hughes' writings in a literature course.

Banks (1999) advocated that schools should move to the levels of the transformative and the social action approaches. The transformative approach changes the basic assumptions of the curriculum and enables students to view concepts, issues, themes, and problems from different perspectives. Curriculum is aimed at helping students understand events from the perspective of different ethnic groups. For example, Columbus's discovery of America is seen differently from the Anglo-Saxon perspective than it is from the Native American perspective. Students would be expected to study events and institutions from various points of view and to reach their own conclusions based on their study. This is a type of constructivist learning as discussed in Chapter 3.

The social action approach suggests that once students have studied an issue and drawn their own conclusions, they should be able to take personal, social, or civic action. For example, a class of students could investigate literature anthologies as to the reasons publishers do not include more pieces by people of color. The students then could create their own anthology or write to publishing companies urging a more balanced approach.

As Beyer, Engelking, and Boshee (1997) reported, in the United States, an individual's race and ethnicity are socially, not scientifically defined. On most government forms, including those used by schools, people are asked to identify their race. In some countries, a person's ethnicity is defined by an individual's ancestry. In other countries, religion or language distinguish the major ethnic groups. For example, race and ethnic definitions overlap because Latino/as may be of any race. The overlap confuses many Latino/as who do not identify with any of the race categories that are often on government forms. Furthermore, individuals of mixed racial parentage are also confused as to the category to which they belong. For example, professional golfer Tiger Woods has a mixed racial parentage. Because race is self-reported, individuals are free to choose the racial category with which they most closely identify.

As an advocate for moral, legal, and thoughtful principles and practices, you have a responsibility to protect all students from discrimination and feelings of isolation. One helpful hint may be to evaluate activities in the school as to their intended purpose. If the purpose is not to promote knowledge or reflection of other cultures, then the activity may exist only because of tradition and could alienate some students and parents.

Religious Diversity

Cultural differences also apply to religious diversity. It is important to note that religious diversity does not relate solely to children from immigrant or ethnic minority backgrounds. Catholic and Jewish families who have been in America for generations often have felt discrimination in the public school system.

Some school and classroom practices have conflicted with religious beliefs. For example, consider the following situations:

1. Muslim students having to go to the cafeteria during lunch even though they were fasting during Ramadan,
2. Sikh children assigned to play angels in the Christmas pageant,
3. Hindu children having to participate in Easter egg painting and hunting,
4. Seventh-Day Adventist students scheduled to play athletic events on Saturdays,
5. Evangelical Christian students asked to participate in the Halloween costume parade.

Although most educators understand the concept of separation of church and state, especially regarding prayer and Bible study, the issues are more confusing when it comes to other classroom practices such as those listed above. A holiday party might be considered an example of how a school as a state agency does not always remain neutral in some of its practices. Although some of these activities may be longtime traditions in the school, what is frequently absent is recognition that some children are isolated by the activities. Often these children are left to decide if they will participate or remove themselves from the activity and their peers, which further emphasizes their differences and alienates them from other students.

In 1963, the Supreme Court ruled in *School District of Abington Township v. Schempp* and *Murry v. Curlett*, with regard to support of religion, the "State is firmly committed to a position of neutrality." This ruling, however, does not prevent educators from including religious thought and practices in the curriculum to reflect a multicultural society. Indeed, to completely remove religion from the curriculum is to limit student understanding in such areas as history, music, and literature in other cultures. Often culture is manifested through religious practices.

Misunderstanding of the court rulings also has led to wrongful practices. Consider the following:

1. A teacher confiscates a Bible from a student during free reading time and states, "This is against the law!"
2. Students were told that they could no longer assemble for a morning prayer circle in the common area.
3. A student is told not to offer a silent prayer before eating lunch.
4. A teacher was told by her principal to remove classroom posters that had sayings by Moses, Jesus, Buddha, Mohammed, and Gandhi.

Language Diversity

One area of concern for educators that is often linked to racial and cultural diversity is language differences. The challenges with language diversity are usually with immigrants and native-born students who are raised in a non-English-speaking environment.

An increase in school enrollments because of immigration and rising birth rates started in 1977. The anticipated growth of students for whom English is a second language poses a challenge for teachers and principals.

Native-born students also can experience language barriers. Most notably is the use of what is considered nonstandard English among African Americans (often called *Ebonics*), Native Americans, and Latino/as. Many principals and teachers regard Standard English as the only form of English and treat other language patterns as broken English. Often these children's language diversity is viewed as a serious learning obstacle to their cognitive development and classroom success. We do not suggest that children from ethnic communities not be taught to use Standard English. However, as Pai and Adler (2001) suggested, "Standard English should be learned as a second language similarly as non-English-speaking students learn English as a second language." Generally, these students want and need to learn Standard English to be successful in the American culture, but their native language usage should not be viewed as a deficit. As principal or assistant principal, your respect and advocacy for students and their language diversity will indicate to others the importance you place on their ethnicity and culture. When a school community is likely to have a community of language diversity for a period, then you also might consider acquiring that language. You can provide professional development programs for teachers to acquire the language basics. Such programs have been successful in areas such as the America Southwest with educators in Latino and Native American communities.

Another challenge regarding limited English proficiency (LEP) students involves their parents, who may not be as involved with their children's school because of the language barrier. The school building may be an uncomfortable place for parents who cannot speak English fluently. Likewise, written school communications that are sent home, for example, notices of parent meetings and conferences, may not be understood. Each school will have its own community culture that will require special consideration in bridging communication gaps.

Zepeda and Langenbach (1999) offered three personal qualities that social workers and psychologists have used in building relationships with those who speak a language different from the mainstream culture. These three qualities are warmth, empathy, and genuineness.

WARMTH   Warmth can be communicated to students and parents both verbally and nonverbally. Warmth promotes a sense of comfort and well-being and can put students and parents at ease.

EMPATHY   Empathy involves being in tune with how the students and parents feel. Empathy requires the educator to convey that the student's and parents' situations are understood. In the context of LEP student relationships, the teacher may convey in both verbal and nonverbal ways an understanding of how the student and parents may feel torn between what is being taught in school and what is taught at home. As Zepeda and Lagenbach suggested, empathy is a skill that involves visualizing how it must be to walk in that person's shoes.

GENUINENESS   The third quality is genuineness, or the ability to be authentic or real. Genuineness involves the sharing of self by relating in a natural, sincere, spontaneous, and open manner.

In the context of a PLC, language diversity can become a tool rather than a challenge. This diversity can become an important learning resource for all students and educators by enriching the learning opportunities and encouraging students to see themselves as citizens of a larger, language-plural world. Parents, community members, and older students whose primary language is different from English can be invited to work with teachers and administrators in enriching the learning environment not only for students whose native language is different from English, but also for students whose native language is English.

Poverty and Social Class

Educational researchers have indicated for several years that a statistically significant relationship exists between poverty and academic achievement. For example, one of the earliest studies by Wolf (1977) reported that a poor child is almost twice as likely to be a low academic achiever as a child who is not living in poverty. However, the factors that explain the variation in student achievement are not necessarily linked to the parental income levels or socioeconomic status. Rather, measures of home atmosphere such as parental aspirations for their children, the amount of reading material in the home, and family attitudes toward education are more indicative of student achievement. Two conditions of poverty affect student achievement. Some children are from families that are impoverished temporarily because of such things as illness, job loss, marital breakup, or unexpected expenses. Other children may be living in families in later-term poverty that is due to a lack of occupational skills, disabilities, or living in a high-impact unemployment area. A student's home atmosphere and expected academic performance differ among children residing in households experiencing different types of poverty (Orland, 1994).

Another research finding by Wolf (1977) showed a statistical relationship between poverty and achievement at the school-building level. From this study, researchers and educators have been able to predict with considerable accuracy a school's academic performance by knowing its overall rate of poverty. In fact, the school's rate of poverty has been a stronger predictor of student achievement than an individual student's poverty level. A nonpoor student in a poor school is actually more likely to be a low achiever than is a poor student in a wealthier school. There appear to be several factors of the school environment that may contribute to student achievement. Examples of such factors include the influence of peers, the resources available, the quality of the teachers, the presence of school characteristics such as a shared vision, the expectations of teachers for student performance, and parent involvement (Orland, 1994).

There is also an association between the length of time students are poor and the likelihood that they will be behind their expected grade level. For each age cohort and among each ethnic group, the proportion of students behind grade level increases with the number of years in poverty. The length of time a child is likely to be poor is related to several demographic conditions, the most important of which is probably race. For example, among black sixteen-year-olds, about one in six is behind the expected grade level. This likelihood doubles to about one in three for those who have spent eight or more years living in poverty (Orland, 1994).

These findings should not be construed to suggest that increased time in poverty causes lower student achievement. Other factors in combination with the length of time in poverty play into children falling behind in school. For example, more boys are behind than girls. Also, a mother's education level increases the likelihood of her children's lower achievement. More than likely, the length of time in poverty is strongly associated with many other features of the home and school environment (Orland, 1994).

Poor children and children attending a school with high poverty concentrations have a greater likelihood of performing poorly in school. We suggest that as a school leader, your efforts in school reform will be more effective in serving these students than in blaming the students' or the community's impoverished conditions. As a principal, you can be an advocate by reducing some of the barriers at the building level that prevent high student achievement. As suggested in Chapter 8, principals can use school-community initiatives such as interagency collaborations to attack the effects of poverty.

Gender

Gender differences and issues in education are not new. Most early European and American schools discouraged girls from attending. Evidence indicates that both subtle and blatant differences in the treatment of girls and boys still occur at all levels of the school system. However, factors other than education play into gender differences. Parental support and involvement also influence attitudes among girls and boys in their curricular choices (Tocci & Engelhard, 1991). Parents with higher socioeconomic status are more likely to be active in their daughters' course selections (Muller, 1998). Societal factors also influence gender differences. Boys tend to receive more toys that are science-related, such as chemistry sets, doctor kits, telescopes, and microscopes (Richmond-Abbott, 1992). Popular video games, television shows, and movies also often portray gender-role stereotypes.

In some subjects in school, girls are doing better than boys, and this has caused disagreement among researchers and educators as to which gender is actually doing better. In her book, *The War Against Boys*, Sommers (2000) cited research that showed boys, not girls, on the weak side of an educational gender gap. Her reports indicated that boys, on average, are a year and a half behind girls in reading and writing; they are less committed to school and less likely to go to college; girls get better grades; girls have higher educational aspirations; and girls follow a more rigorous academic program and participate more in advanced placement (AP) courses. Sommers concluded, however, that "none of that has affected the 'official' view that our schools are 'failing at fairness' to girls" (p. 14).

Many young people experience other forms of sexual discrimination in school. Both boys and girls often experience some form of sexual harassment, with sexual jokes, gestures, and comments being most common followed by touching or grabbing in a sexual way. Most of the harassment comes from the students' own peers.

The implication for you as the principal or assistant principal is in developing your own awareness as to how gender affects student learning and how you advocate for improving learning for all students as you mentor and supervise all students. In addition, as advocate, you must develop a nonthreatening culture where sexual jokes, gestures, and other forms of harassment have no place.

Sexual Orientation

Another form of discrimination exists with sexual orientation among students and among their parents. Sexual orientation has become one of the most controversial areas of difference in our society and in schools. Physical violence, verbal insults, and other inappropriate behaviors have been leveled against Gay Lesbian Bi-sexual Trans-gender (GLBT) individuals. Being sexually different in a society of sexual sameness can create a heavy psychological toll on students. Struggling to cope with their sexual identity, these students are more likely than other youth to attempt suicide, to abuse drugs or alcohol, and to experience academic problems (Zera, 1992). The American School Health Association issued a policy statement regarding gay and lesbian youth in schools that stated:

> School personnel should discourage any sexually oriented, deprecating, harassing, and prejudicial statements injurious to students' self-esteem. Every school district should provide access to professional counseling, by specially trained personnel for students who may be concerned about sexual orientation.

Students with Special Needs

From the beginning of American education, the needs of students with disabilities often were neglected. The political movement for legislation to aid students with special needs followed a path similar to other civil rights movements. After efforts to change local and state governments regarding the education of students with disabilities, organized parent groups turned to the federal government. In 1975, Congress passed Public Law 94-142, the Education for All Handicapped Children Act (EAHC), requiring that all handicapped children between the ages of three and twenty-one have access to a free, appropriate public education in the least restrictive environment (LRE). The law also required public agencies to ensure that children with disabilities are educated with children without disabilities to the maximum extent possible. The law was renamed in 1990 as the Individuals with Disabilities Education Act (IDEA). IDEA changed terminology from *handicapped children* to *children with disabilities,* shifting emphasis from the handicap or disability to the child. Under these laws, each student classified with a disability has to have an individual education plan (IEP). The law requires that the local education agency (LEA)—the school—and the child's parents or guardians jointly develop the IEP. Thus, the law gives parents the right to negotiate with the school the type of services to be delivered. IDEA went through another change in 2004. Individuals with Disabilities Education Improvement Act (IDEIA) maintains the basic principles of the original law, a free appropriate public education for all students with disabilities in the least restrictive environment (LRE); however, there are many changes and modifications to the IEP process and other aspects of the identification and evaluation of students with disabilities. One element of the new legislation is response to intervention (RTI), which

> integrates assessment and intervention within a multi-level prevention system to maximize student achievement and to reduce behavior problems. With RTI, schools identify students at risk for poor learning outcomes, monitor student progress, provide evidence-based interventions and adjust the intensity and nature of those interventions depending on a student's responsiveness, and identify students with learning disabilities. (www.rti4success.org)

The number of children identified with disabilities has risen since 1977. Currently, approximately 13 percent of all children from birth to twenty-one years of age qualify for special-education services. Of these students, the largest number has learning disabilities followed by speech and language impairments, mental retardation, and serious emotional disturbances. If student disabilities are a new area for you, take time to become familiar with all types of disabilities and the programs that will benefit children with such disabilities.

A major concern regarding the education of children with special needs has been their isolation from other students and the lack of access to the educational opportunities of a regular classroom. Under the original act, Public Law 94-142, the requirement of LRE resulted in the practice of mainstreaming. The basic idea of mainstreaming was that students with disabilities should spend part of the day in regular classrooms. However, many parents and educators felt that mainstreaming did not go far enough to provide a LRE. The concept of full inclusion was introduced that allowed special-needs students to spend all or most of their time in a regular classroom. The isolation of children with special needs often deprived them of contact with other students and denied them access to facilities and equipment found in regular classrooms. However, all educators and parents of children with disabilities do not support the idea of inclusion. Some believe that separate education classrooms have provided benefits for children that inclusion would not have provided. Further, some surveys find that most teachers object to including students with special needs in their classrooms (Spring, 2002). This does not mean that inclusion does not work. As an advocate of children and those practices that help children, you need to help others understand the concept of inclusion and how best to serve all children regardless of their disabilities. Your advocacy role also involves removing the structures and obstacles that discourage teachers from creating inclusive classroom environments.

Gifted and Talented Students

The U.S. Department of Education estimates that about 2–3 percent of students are considered gifted. In one of the earliest studies, Marland (1972) identified gifted children as those who generally exhibit high performance or capability in one or more of the following ability areas, singly or in combination:

1. General education ability
2. Specific academic aptitude
3. Creative or productive thinking
4. Leadership ability
5. Visual and performing arts
6. Psychomotor ability

Gifted and talented (GT) education has been a hotly debated topic. Those who promote gifted programs claim that gifted children need instruction at a level, pace, and conceptual complexity commensurate with their levels of ability and achievement. Those who oppose GT programs claim that they are a neoconservative reaction to the funding for special-education students or that they are a subtle way to avoid integration. GT program opponents often indicate that privileged backgrounds contribute to the classification of being gifted and talented. They also claim that by creating GT programs, the schools create an elitist group among students.

Regardless of how you feel about GT programs, the fact is that some students do have characteristics that may be defined as gifted. Again, as an advocate for *all* children, you will want to provide the best educational programs for those who have exceptional abilities. Whether you promote a pullout program or an in-class enhancement program, a GT program should be something you consider.

Students Placed At-Risk

The term *at-risk* has been used in various ways in education. Some people have used the term to describe students who are placed at-risk because of conditions out of their control, such as disabilities, ethnicity, language, and poverty. The term has been used to describe behaviors that students engage in that affect their education, such as alcohol and drug abuse, sexual experimentation, or suicidal tendencies. The term also has been used to describe students who are at-risk of dropping out of school or being expelled from school. For the purposes of this chapter, we use the term *students placed at-risk* to describe students who, for one reason or another, are not succeeding academically and are unlikely to finish their schooling unless interventions occur. Regardless of the reasons or conditions, students placed at-risk should be of major concern to principals and assistant principals.

Several researchers (e.g., Beyer et al., 1997; Sagor, 1993) have outlined behaviors that identify students placed at-risk:

1. Students at-risk usually exhibit low self-esteem, a lack of self-confidence in themselves and their work, and a lack of self-worth. They regard themselves as being in a state of helplessness and feel powerless in most situations.
2. Students placed at-risk often avoid school, and they avoid contact or confrontation with other students and adults. They find it easier and often more enjoyable to skip classes rather than to face the reality that they are behind and do not know what is going on. School is seen as threatening to them because it is not responsive to their needs.
3. Usually, students placed at-risk distrust adults and the adult world in general. They often view adults as the cause of the unfairness they are experiencing. Adults are deemed unresponsive to their needs and are even seen as being abusive by some students.
4. Students placed at-risk tend to live in the present and have a very limited view of what the future will bring them. They are responsive to their own short-term successes but do not do well with long-term projects or planning. The future to them does not hold a positive place in their lives. Because of their viewpoint, they experience a detachment from the school setting.
5. Students placed at-risk often feel that the adults they know in general have given up on them by the time they reach their teen years. They are usually behind academically by this time because they lack skills in reading, writing, and math and think that others view them as being dumb rather than unskilled. This leads them to feel hopeless about their situation at school and implants the idea that they cannot learn.
6. Students placed at-risk generally do not do very well in regular classroom settings, where the norm is a routine with long periods of sitting and listening with little variety. They are usually impatient with this type of environment and often are viewed as being disruptive because of their impatience.
7. Students placed at-risk often can apply what is being taught in a very practical manner if this type of behavior is encouraged or even allowed. They do well with

experiential-type learning situations and usually can verbalize what takes place better than they can write about it.

8. Students placed at-risk have a hard time forming a link between the effort something takes and the achievement gained. Instead, they view success as just luck, or they talk about how easy the task was to begin with. They see everything as happening to them, and they believe that they have little control over what goes on in their lives. When a task is not done or when it is done poorly, it is because the task was too hard to begin with, or they could not get the help they needed to complete the task. At-risk students generally do not assume personal responsibility and seldom learn anything from the mistakes they make.

As an advocate for all students and for the whole student, as well as for moral, legal, and thoughtful educational principles and practices, you will need to further your knowledge and understanding of these areas of difference that can affect students, their access to education, and their success in schooling.

BEING AN ADVOCATE FOR THE SCHOOL

In addition to your role as an advocate for the whole student and for all students, as principal you are an advocate for the school and for its programs that enhance diversity and promote social justice. Special programs have been designed and developed to meet the academic and social needs of students, especially in preventing at-risk behaviors and conditions. No one program can in and of itself be either preventive or compensatory. The total schooling experience that involves educators, parents, and community has to be considered for *all* children. In the following sections we discuss a few of the more common programs and their implications for your role as an advocate for the school.

Multicultural Education Programs

Multicultural programs have developed over a period of time. To understand the development of multicultural education programs, Banks (1999) identified four phases: mono-ethnic courses, multiethnic studies courses, multiethnic education, and multicultural education.

MONO-ETHNIC COURSES   Originally, multicultural education was linked to concerns about racism in schools and the lack of representatives in nonwhite cultures in school curricula such as history, music, and literature. In phase one, mono-ethnic courses focused on ethnic courses for a particular race and culture. For example, black studies were needed for African American students and Native American studies for Native American students.

MULTIETHNIC STUDIES COURSES   Phase two, multiethnic studies courses broadened curricula offerings to be more inclusive of the whole school. Phase two focused on several ethnic histories and cultures often from a comparative point of view. School curricula offered such courses as multiethnic history, minority literature, and ethnic music. Banks (1999) concluded that phase two did not bring about educational reform toward equality. In phase three, multiethnic education developed an educational reform that included the entire school environment.

MULTIETHNIC EDUCATION   Phase three developed a pluralistic approach that tried to address all racial and ethnic minority groups. However, it excluded numerous subcultures within mainstream culture. For example, Native American tribes usually were considered as one group, Appalachian whites were not considered as a culture, and certain religious groups were included only within ethnic groups. Because of these omissions, a broader reform movement began that attempted to focus on a wider range of groups.

MULTICULTURAL EDUCATION   Currently, phase four refers to education that relates to race, ethnicity, religion, and social class. However, multicultural education also considers gender, disabilities, and regions and how these factors interrelate. For example, we often now refer to black women, young and impoverished Latino/as, and second-generation Asian Americans (Banks, 1994).

The current view of multicultural education considers more of a process or philosophy than a program. It is a movement built on the ideals of freedom, justice, equality, and equity. Multicultural education involves all academic disciplines and extracurricular programs. Its intent is to help all students develop positive self-concepts and understand the strength of human diversity. Multicultural education involves curriculum and instruction that includes the contributions, perspectives, and experiences of various groups that are a part of society. As Banks (1992) suggested:

> Rather than excluding Western civilization from the curriculum, multiculturalists want a more truthful, complex, and diverse version of the West taught in the schools. They want the curriculum to describe the ways in which African, Asian, and indigenous American cultures have influenced and interacted with Western civilization. They also want schools to discuss not only the diversity and democratic ideals of Western civilization, but also its failures, tensions, dilemmas, and the struggles by various groups in Western societies to realize their dreams against great odds. (p. 34)

Bilingual Education

Schools across America are enrolling greater numbers of children who have LEP (sometimes referred to as English as a Second Language [ESL] or English Language Learners [ELL]). The Bilingual Education Act was first legislated by Congress in 1968. The act is also known as Title VII of the Elementary and Secondary Education Act. The optional programs under this act called for instruction for LEP students that was well organized and encompassed part of the regular school curriculum. Due to slow program implementation, stronger legislation was required, and the act was again amended in 1974, making bilingual education mandatory in all schools receiving federal funds. The purpose of the act was to educate LEP children and youth to meet the same rigorous standards for academic performance expected of all children and youth. The act was amended again in 1978, 1988, 1994, and noted in NCLB in 2002 clarifying that the goal was to help develop the English-language skills of students who were deficient in these skills while simultaneously providing instruction in their native language. However, most existing bilingual education programs are designed to be "transitional" as opposed to "maintenance." The goal is for children to learn English and move into regular classrooms as soon as possible (Zepeda & Langenbach, 1999).

English as a second language (ESL) programs emerged as a way to teach LEP students in the secondary schools. ESL programs typically are pullout programs that teach English based on the principles of foreign-language teaching. Literacy in the first language is necessary for learning a second language. Usually in ESL programs, students receive English instruction one or two periods per day and continue to participate in the regular classroom for the rest of the time.

Discussions about the effectiveness of bilingual education have continued since the first congressional act in 1968. The controversy often has focused on identifying the types of programs that work best in helping LEP students. The debate is frequently around which approach is better: teaching children in their native language or teaching them in English. The research on these methods of instruction has not proven conclusive.

As an advocate for LEP children, you should provide the direction and administration of bilingual programs. The following recommendations are adapted from Beyer and colleagues (1997). As a principal or assistant principal, you should

1. implement family education programs and parent outreach and training activities designed to assist parents to become active participants in the education of their children;
2. improve the instructional program for LEP students by identifying, acquiring, and upgrading curriculum, instructional materials, educational software, and assessment procedures and, if appropriate, applying educational technology;
3. compensate personnel, including teacher aides who have been specifically trained or are being trained to provide services to children and youth of LEP; and
4. enrich instruction and other related activities, such as counseling and academic and career guidance.

Special Education

The development of special-education programs for students with disabilities has been long, hard, and problematic for parents, students, teachers, and administrators. This subsection offers an overview of special education; however, it should not replace your own investigation and personal study.

With the enactment of Public Law 94-142 in 1975 and the subsequent legislation since then, most notably IDEA, special and regular educators began developing programs that would better help meet the needs of special-needs students. The first programs and services were pullout programs. Typically, students who were identified as having a special need were pulled out of the regular classroom to receive services. Depending on the degree of the disability, some students were excluded from the regular classroom and placed in, what is still referred to as, a self-contained classroom. Pullout programs were and still are questioned as to their effectiveness. More inclusive services began to emerge in the form of mainstreaming and inclusion. However, with inclusion came tension between regular education and special-education teachers, parents and teachers, and teachers and administrators and among students.

Approximately one in ten students in public education qualifies for and receives services under special education (Terman, Larner, Stevenson, & Behrman, 1996). Administering the correct educational programs is one of the biggest challenges for special educators and principals. However, this is an area in which no one person in the school can or should make all the decisions. Special education teachers, regular-education teachers, district office personnel (if necessary), parents, and sometimes the students themselves help determine what services are needed and provided by the school.

The Individuals with Disabilities Education Act mandates that students with disabilities receive their education with nondisabled peers to the maximum extent appropriate. To meet this requirement, federal regulations require schools to develop a continuum of placements ranging from general classrooms with support services to homebound and hospital programs. Determining the LRE will be the challenge. The intent of each individual's plan would be to transition to the next environment. For example, if the student is presently in a self-contained classroom, the challenge will be to develop a plan to transition the child to only a partial self-contained classroom and partial resource room or a regular classroom.

As principal, a major challenge that you will face in special education is hiring the right people. Selecting qualified special-education teachers has always been a challenge because special-education teacher candidates have been among the scarcest of all teaching candidates. Some districts have collaborated successfully with universities to provide certification and masters' programs for existing teachers. These programs often are paid for in part or in full by the district if the teacher is willing to become a special-education teacher in that district.

However, selecting special-education teachers is only part of the challenge. As principal, you also want to select regular-education teachers who are willing and able to work with special-needs students in the regular classroom. In your selection process, it is important for you to determine their beliefs, interest, and qualifications in such areas as inclusion, knowledge of disabilities, learning styles, and teaching methods.

As principal, you also will want to coordinate professional development activities for existing teachers in working with special-needs students. Regular-education teachers hardly can be expected to perform well in inclusive classrooms without training in teaching students with disabilities. Usually, teachers will have to consider changing their instructional methods to provide for children with special needs. This may include both a philosophical and an instructional change. You also will need to allow time for shared planning and collaboration among special-education teachers and regular-education teachers so that they can coordinate their services and provide the best education.

In addition to the hiring and professional development roles, you serve another advocacy role, protecting students from over diagnosis. This is especially important for students of color and students from poor backgrounds, who are more likely to be labeled special education. When special education services are legitimately needed, you should be the first to emphasize them. But when labeling is occurring for the most marginalized students, you must be the first to warn against and protect from inappropriate labeling.

Your challenge is to rise above the rhetoric that surrounds special-education issues and provide the services, programs, and opportunities that are needed for students with disabilities. If inclusion in regular classes of students with special needs is in their best interests, then you can help reduce the barriers that prevent inclusion and work toward its implementation. Students are most likely to achieve their potential by learning in the company of their peers.

Gifted and Talented Programs

Although controversial, GT programs are a reality in many schools. Your knowledge and leadership will be expected. The program options for GT students vary from limited to extensive adaptations of the regular instructional programs. The following types of GT programs are listed from the least to the most adaptation:

ENRICHMENT IN THE REGULAR CLASSROOM Enrichment in the classroom means accommodating the wide range of abilities and interests that are present in any group of students. Enrichment in the regular classroom is the easiest to provide from the administrative point of view because there is no need for special teachers, extra classrooms, or special scheduling. It may be the most challenging for teachers because of the extra preparation in creating instructional activities for the individuals identified as gifted and talented. The critics of GT programs often contend that enrichment activities are the most fair for all students (Zepeda & Langenbach, 1999).

ENRICHMENT PULLOUT PROGRAMS Pullout programs necessitate GT students leaving the regular classroom for part of the day or week. Pullout programs are more common at the elementary school level. In secondary schools, GT students more likely would be assigned to honors or AP classes.

ACCELERATION Acceleration at the elementary school level could mean an early entry into school, for example, beginning first grade at age 5. It also could mean skipping grades along the way. Acceleration may make sense when GT students are seen as being more like older students than their age-mates. Acceleration at the secondary school level usually takes the form of advanced classes or AP classes for college credit. Many high schools have adopted early-graduation policies, where students may accelerate their studies by taking more credits or testing out of some classes and may graduate a year or a semester earlier than their classmates.

CURRICULUM COMPACTING Curriculum compacting is a means by which GT students can pass through the content without spending as much time as is usually allocated for it. It is different from enrichment in that it is not horizontal exploration of content but rather vertical progression through the curriculum in an accelerated manner (Zepeda & Langenbach, 1999).

EXTRA-SCHOOL ACTIVITIES After school, Saturday, or summer programs can be opportunities to offer educational experiences that may not be available during the school day and year. Special courses or activities are offered for GT students that extend beyond the regular curriculum. Some of these programs are offered by universities that sponsor summer programs in math, sciences, technology, and the arts (Zepeda & Langenbach, 1999).

MAGNET SCHOOLS Magnet schools specialize in a field such as math and science or performing arts. Parents and students elect to apply for admission to a magnet school

> ## Professional Dilemma 6.2
>
> Many college preparatory and advanced placement courses in high schools have high admissions criteria based on testing, teacher interviews, and previous experience. Often these criteria eliminate many students of color and those of diverse cultural backgrounds. Should these honors courses be open to any student who wishes to take the course if they are committed to do the work, or should the courses be restricted by admissions criteria?

where typically there are high admission criteria. For example, students may have to audition, provide a portfolio of previous work, or have high marks on a test in the fields the school emphasizes. Some magnet schools are housed in regular schools, making them "schools within a school" (Zepeda & Langenbach, 1999).

Regardless of the program that your school uses or the ones you want to develop, as an administrator and leader, you need to be aware of the following:

- Use various instruments in the selection process rather than rely on one measure (for example teacher recommendation) (Zepeda & Langenbach, 1999).
- Be aware that performance on intelligence and achievement tests is often influenced by the child's socioeconomic status, racial and cultural background, and previous educational experience (Sapon-Shevin, 1994).
- Increase learning opportunities for disadvantaged and minority children with outstanding talents.
- Emphasize teacher development. Teachers must receive better training in how to teach high-level curricula (Beyer et al., 1997).
- Work with parents and community members in providing opportunities for students with special talents.

Title I

As part of President Lyndon Johnson's Great Society and War on Poverty, he encouraged Congress to enact the Elementary and Secondary Education Act (ESEA) in 1965. Title I of this act provided for supplementary academic assistance and compensatory services for economically disadvantaged children. These services were meant for all children of poverty, including children from Native American families living on or near reservations, migrant families, homeless families, and urban and rural families. The purpose of Title I was to provide supplementary services in the basic skill areas of reading and mathematics. In 1994, Congress reauthorized the ESEA and renamed the Title I section "Helping Disadvantaged Children Meet High Standards." Part of Title I addressed prevention and intervention programs for children and youth who are neglected, delinquent, or at risk of dropping out. The most recent addition to Title I, as amended by the No Child Left Behind (NCLB) Act, requires a participating LEA to provide eligible children attending private elementary and secondary schools, their teachers, and their families with Title I services or other benefits that are equitable to those provided to eligible public school children, their teachers, and their families. These services must be developed in consultation with officials of the private schools. The Title I services provided by the LEA for private school participants are designed to meet their educational needs and supplement the educational services provided by the private school.

Not all schools or districts qualify to receive Title I funding. School districts may identify as eligible any school in which at least 35 percent of the children are from low-income families. The following criteria are used by districts as a measure of poverty to determine student eligibility for Title I services:

1. the number of children ages five to seventeen in poverty as counted in the most recent census data
2. the number of children eligible to receive free or reduced-priced lunches
3. the number of children in families receiving assistance under Aid to Families with Dependent Children
4. the number of children eligible to receive medical assistance under the Medicaid program
   (ESEA was reauthorized in January 2002. Check Web site for up-to-date criteria. www.ed.gov/offices/OESE/esea).

These criteria are important to the school principal because it is at the individual school level that total student count must be determined. The number of students in the school eligible for "free and reduced-priced lunches" is often used as a baseline for low-income student count. The accuracy of this student head count may mean the difference between a school receiving Title I funds or not.

Originally, Title I was a pullout program in which identified students were taken out of their regularly assigned classrooms to receive supplemental instruction in reading and mathematics. Subsequently, send-in programs were implemented, in which services were provided within students' own classrooms. Other programs have used extended-day services, where students meet before or after school.

Professional development is an important element of Title I programs. The legislation requires the schools or districts to describe the strategy they will use to provide professional development. Because of this opportunity, principals can help teachers and aides in collaborative planning, integrated instruction, and teaming.

Your role as principal is critical in administering Title I programs. If economically disadvantaged students are to be served, your role as advocate is to become familiar with the program requirements and new legislation that affects Title I. You also need to be aware of the funding opportunities and the formula that your district or state uses for eligibility.

Alternative Education Programs

Most alternative programs are established to help at-risk students to achieve academic success in a smaller, more personable environment that will lead to their graduation with a high school diploma. Some contemporary alternative programs are not designed solely for at-risk students. For example, earlier in this section we discussed magnet schools for GT students. Magnet schools are a type of alternative program. However, most alternative programs are meant to serve adolescents who do not fit in traditional school settings. Kelly (1993) reported that these kinds of alternative schools represent a dual response to (a) students' need for flexibility and personalization and (b) conventional high schools' need for mechanisms to isolate students who pose discipline and other problems.

Alternative programs are housed in both traditional schools as "schools within schools" and in separate school buildings. Both kinds of schools usually provide a structure in which students can be mentored by adults who care about their personal, academic, and social success. Alternative school programs were created, in part, to face the emergence of large and impersonalized school systems in which high numbers of students were dropping out. A typical school within a school has a small group of teachers and counselors that provides individual assistance to students. Testerman's (1996) study of alternative schools indicated positive effects for students, such as improved grades, better attendance, increased studying, and more dedication to school-work. As Zepeda and Langenbach (1999) reported, changing the structure of the day and encouraging more meaningful interactions between students and teachers can yield positive results.

Raywid (1994) suggested that features that made alternative educational programs effective were their small size, their being designed by those who were going to operate them, and their relative freedom from district interference. Kellmayer (1995) believed that as much as possible, participation in the alternative program should be voluntary for both students and teachers. Teachers should volunteer for the program rather than being assigned by an administrator to teach in the program. If they are interested in working with these youth, usually they will have more success if they have the training and experience in working with at-risk behaviors and are willing to accept the challenges of developing caring relationships with their students.

Although these educational programs were created to attend to the special needs of children and youth, as a principal, you should not limit your advocacy to only these formal programs. Some students still are left out. Some programs are ineffective. Some students need more service than a program offers. Your advocacy means more than just administering educational programs. It means a total awareness of the needs of all students all the time.

One of the features of declining schools (Duke, 2008) is the use of one program as a catch-all or panacea for meeting all student needs. As an advocate, you will need to identify new programs that meet unique needs and also critically evaluate all programs to make sure they respond to the needs of the whole student.

ADVOCATE FOR THE COMMUNITY

In addition to being an advocate for all students and the whole child and an advocate for the school, as principal you are an advocate for the community. Later chapters will add more detail to your roles with the community, for example, politician. But at this point, we want to emphasize three roles you play as an advocate for the community: valuing, educating, and leveraging.

VALUING   Being an advocate for the whole student means being an advocate for the community in which the student lives. Teachers, principals, and schools that try to divorce what happens to students at school from what happens in the community are doomed to frustration and failure. Being an advocate for the community means that you value and respect the community. Our earlier mention of the idea of "culturally proficient" school (Lindsey et al., 2005) involves the importance of valuing the diversity, traditions, values, and norms within the community. School leaders that espouse valuing students but devalue their communities send very loud and contradictory messages to students and their parents. Using community resources, celebrating community history and events, including community members in the curriculum, and, especially, being sensitive to community language, norms and values, for example, sending correspondence to parents in the parents' language sends a strong message of valuing the community. Frequently, this involves acknowledging and honoring the diversity within communities.

EDUCATING   Being an advocate for the community involves educating the community. This may involve providing resources for parents and community members to develop job, parenting, and life skills that enrich community capacity and student learning. It also involves educating the community regarding school programs and expectations.

LEVERAGING   Being an advocate for the community also involves leveraging the community for the good of students. Hargreaves and Fink (2004) told the story of a courageous principal who built alliances with community groups that provided support for his struggle against standardization of the curriculum by the district office. Forging alliances with media, government, business, and charitable organizations and individuals connects the community to the school's mission and values.

PRINCIPAL AS FACILITATOR OF OTHERS' ADVOCACY

You not only play a direct advocacy role as a principal, but, in a PLC, you also must facilitate others to be advocates. To be effective, advocacy needs to be both a personal and a collaborative effort. As an individual, you can and should advocate for children and for moral, lawful, and thoughtful principles and practices that help to serve *all* students and the whole student. However, alone this can be a daunting task. As an advocate for children, the school, and the community, you must help others be advocates as well. For example, to be an inclusive school requires the efforts of nearly all members of the PLC.

Facilitating advocacy among others is a foundational role to all the subsequent roles that we will discuss in this book. In this section, we will discuss how each of the roles that will be identified is part of facilitating the advocacy role.

In the leader role, one way that you can perform advocacy is by developing your own personal vision in ways that value differences in a PLC. Only then can you lead others to a collective vision in which differences are treated as rich resources for the school.

Mentoring is an act of advocacy. You have the opportunity to mentor new and veteran teachers, parents, and other community members. In particular, the support and development of a new teacher are highly moral acts of leadership that you need to take seriously. Unfortunately, principals too often neglect or abdicate these responsibilities. The reality is that new teachers do not emerge from their preparation program as fully developed professionals. They vary widely in the skills and life experiences that they bring to the classroom. Many have had no or only limited experience with teaching children of color or children with disabilities. New teachers need administrative support and help with these types of assignments. Likewise, carefully and thoughtfully assigning a supporting peer mentor to a new teacher also can promote advocacy. However, peer mentoring runs the risk of perpetuating the status quo. If peer mentors have not developed their own moral, legal, and thoughtful practices or have not advocated for social justice in the school and community, then it is unlikely that they will advocate such attributes. Never forget that as a leader and facilitator of advocacy, you are the most important part of the new teacher's induction.

Mentoring veteran teachers as advocates can be a daunting task. Some veteran teachers have fallen into the endurance game, wherein they are simply trying to outlast the latest education reform, and they are not interested in changing the curriculum or their practice to respond to changing student characteristics. Some have remained in the same school for most of their careers and have found a sense of pride in being part of the school history and culture. A few of these teachers find it difficult to change their teaching styles and want schools and students to remain the way they think they were in the past. This is especially difficult when the demographics of a school have changed and the community is experiencing new populations with different cultures. Many veteran teachers have not been trained or have not had any experience working with students with disabilities, students with LEP, or students with disadvantages. As a facilitator of advocacy, your task in mentoring veteran teachers to become advocates for all children requires considerable patience and understanding. However daunting, your advocacy and your mentoring of teachers in advocacy for all children and youth are the right things to be doing.

Facilitating advocacy also involves the role of supervision, especially in building instructional capacity in the school. The main component of your supervisory role is the learning that occurs with *all* teachers and *all* students. Recruiting and selecting capable and committed teachers who are diverse and are passionate about diversity enriches the learning capacity in schools. Providing professional development that enables teachers to understand differences, to value those differences, and to recognize those differences as part of the richness of a PLC is a critical part of your role in facilitating others' as advocates.

In the manager role, four major areas of management are especially important for advocacy: supporting, planning, taking action, and evaluating. For example, your support in money, time, and other resources will greatly improve the chances that teachers will be advocates of multicultural education. Likewise, your help in planning the implementation of inclusion will greatly improve the chances for inclusion to work. Taking action and implementing the changes that are proposed also help teachers understand that there is something that emerges from the rhetoric. And finally, managing the evaluation and assessment of the effort will allow others the opportunity for critical input.

Perhaps one of the most important roles that you can take as facilitator of advocacy is the political role. A traditional political role of the principalship has been one that often buffered the school from parents and community. Although at times the principal needs to buffer teachers from interruptions and inappropriate pressures, if buffering becomes the primary political role of the principal, the school loses the rich contributions of diverse constituencies. Bridging is a more appropriate political role for contemporary principals than buffering. Bridging involves developing a shared vision with the community so that community organizations and individuals understand and work toward creating a PLC for all students.

In Chapter 11, we will discuss the principal's role as politician based on two views of school-community relationships (Driscoll & Kerchner, 1999). The first perspective views schools as beneficiaries of community support. This perspective could help in advocacy by identifying the human and financial resources that community members could supply. For example, parents from diverse cultures and languages can bring their valuable perspectives to the learning environment by leading and supporting multicultural activities. The second perspective views schools as agents of social capital. Education in a democracy is important because schools can help create a public good from which the whole society benefits. Instead of schools only being recipients of what the community offers, this perspective suggests that schools need to stress what they contribute to the community, including the diversity in the community.

One of the most thoughtful political actions you can take as you help others become advocates of children and children's causes is to help them examine existing inequities and to help them understand how the school can act as a civil community. Children learn to be civil to one another by watching the civility of their teachers and parents. You can help teachers and parents to see that schools can and should become civil societies that support individual and social growth in and for community. Likewise, you can facilitate advocacy by helping teachers, students, and parents to model democracy in the school, by recognizing and eliminating oppression and marginalization in the community. Schools under your leadership can be change agents to make local communities ethically and socially just environments for all.

Conclusion

In the opening vignette, Curtis is an assistant principal in a school that has seen dramatic changes in its community. Because of some of these changes, Curtis has had to learn to be an advocate to promote learning for all students. Advocacy involves supporting, maintaining, and defending moral, legal, and thoughtful educational principles and practices. In contemporary school settings, being an advocate and facilitating advocacy of others involve understanding racial, ethnic, and cultural diversity; language diversity; religious diversity; poverty and social class; gender; sexual orientation; gifted students; and students with special needs. The principal's advocacy role is the third foundational role on which the other roles of the principal are based. We move next to the critical role of leader.

Activities

SELF-REFLECTION ACTIVITIES

1. Using the definition of advocacy as social justice, think of ways that you have supported, maintained, and defended educational principles and practices for children in the schools in which you have served.
2. Think of an example when principals and assistant principals were not familiar with federal, state, and local policies regarding special-needs children. Reflect on the implications.

PEER REFLECTION ACTIVITIES

1. Reflect on Salt Creek High School. What ways have schools in your area changed because of demographic changes?

2. Brainstorm ways that schools can involve more parents in the programs offered for special-needs children.

COURSE ACTIVITIES

1. Invite special-education, at-risk, and gifted and talented directors to present to the class the scope of their roles and the services they provide for principals and schools.
2. As a class, discuss ways that could have prevented the incidents at Salt Creek High School.

Discuss how the principal could have helped Curtis.

3. Investigate schools in your area. How has inclusion been implemented? What constraints exist in these schools to be inclusive?
4. Visit an alternative school in the area. Reflect on the school's successes and failures.
5. Invite a local community activist to talk about the needs of groups within the community and how schools can be involved in social justice activities.

Websites

Teaching Tolerance—A Project of the Southern Poverty Law Center
www.tolerance.org/

NAACP—Education Advocacy website
www.naacp.org/advocacy/education/

Gender.org—website for gender education and advocacy
www.gender.org/

IDEA 2004 website
http://idea.ed.gov/

The Federation for Children with Special Needs
http://fcsn.org/index.php

National Association for Bilingual Education (NABE)
www.nabe.org/

National Association for Gifted Children
www.nagc.org/

ESEA (now NCLB)
www.ed.gov/nclb/landing.jhtml?src=mr

CHAPTER 7

Becoming a Leader in a Professional Learning Community

Vignette

"I love teaching in this school," stated Louise as she visited with her principal in his office. "I think we are doing some great things. We have some wonderful students who are achieving great things. But, I worry about all of our students. It almost seems as if we do not do enough for our lower achieving students. I know that I have said this before, but I want to say it again. We are too much like a mini-high school. In fact, the high school drives our curricula. The teachers are similar to private contractors, working hard but very independent of each other."

Robert sat listening to Louise as he had done with the entire faculty during the end of the school year goal reviews. He had established these informal chats with the teachers and staff at the end of each school year since he became principal five years ago. Louise was his last teacher, and school was ending in two weeks. No teacher had expressed any great concern about Franklin D. Roosevelt Junior High School, in fact, everyone had expressed positive comments. Robert knew that he had a stable and dedicated faculty.

Louise continued with her conversation, "I recently visited Lakeside Middle School over in Vernon. Several years ago, they changed their junior high into a professional learning community (PLC) in a middle school. They have done some interesting things, and they have increased their student achievement scores. Maybe we should consider some of their ideas." Robert pondered this for a few moments and then responded, "You know, I would be interested in that. Perhaps, we could get a team of teachers together, go over there, and see what they are doing."

Louise left the meeting feeling positive. It was refreshing, indeed, for her to be able to talk to her principal so informally. She appreciated how he listened to her ideas and had not wanted to implant his own philosophies on her. When she had visited Lakeside Middle School, her intention was not to understand a PLC in a middle school, but it was to attend a meeting of the local Phi Delta Kappa (PDK) chapter. The speaker for the breakfast meeting was a university professor who addressed the issue of the needs of early adolescents. She was followed by Lakeside's principal who talked about how the school faculty had used the PLC concept to shift into a middle school model. He showed data that indicated a substantial gain in student achievement.

Louise had left the PDK meeting impressed but had been too busy to think about a PLC in a middle school, and she had always wanted to learn more about the concepts but had never had the opportunity. Now with the invitation from her principal to investigate the ideas further, she started reflecting on changing the culture at Roosevelt Junior High School.

A month later, school out of session and her summer vacation going quite well, Louise happened to meet Robert at a movie theater. After some casual conversation, Robert suggested that they get together before the summer ends and explore establishing a PLC in a middle school. Robert asked her to think of others who might be interested. Louise had no idea who else might be interested but did think of four teachers who were innovative and open to new thinking. The next day, she e-mailed a message to Robert with her suggestions. In the meantime, Robert decided to do some investigating on the Internet and searched for some Web sites on PLCs in middle schools. He was surprised to find so much information. He explored several Web sites and was delighted to find some useful information. He printed several research summaries and made copies for Louise and other interested teachers.

Robert and Louise invited the four teachers to a luncheon to explore the idea of developing a PLC in a middle school. As they met, one teacher asked if Roosevelt Junior High School was going to adopt a middle school model. His brother had told him about the school where he was teaching that had changed to a middle school. His brother's experience was that the faculty felt that the curriculum was watered down and that the students were just meant to feel good and not learn anything. The teacher reminded Robert that Roosevelt Junior High School had emphasized high academic standards for a long time and that he was not interested in changing that. Robert acknowledged the teacher's comments and confirmed his own allegiance to high standards. But, Robert emphasized that all students in the school need to have the best learning opportunities available to them, and not just the high-achieving groups. Robert also suggested that the team not think about adoption quite yet until they had done some studying and reflecting. He then suggested that they arrange a visit to Lakeside Middle School and see what they have done with PLCs. They could also read some materials he and Louise had put together and meet again. They all thought that was a good idea and arranged to meet in two weeks at Lakeside Middle School.

After the school visit, Robert kept the team reading new materials. As the summer ended, the team had put together an impressive portfolio of information regarding PLCs in middle schools. They decided to organize a retreat in August before school began and share their information with the faculty. They would then explore the faculty's interest in pursuing a PLC and changing to a middle school. The team's plan was to develop five important components of PLCs and suggest that the faculty adopt one for the next school year. A new team could be developed to study the components and suggest the order of implementation if, indeed, the faculty chose to pursue it.

Louise had not been as excited for school to begin since her first year of teaching. She continued to explore the various components of PLCs in middle schools and was convinced that this was a positive move for Roosevelt. She hoped other teachers would feel the same.

In August, Robert talked to his area superintendent and the district curriculum director. They gave their approval to continue exploring the idea. Robert then went to the newly elected parent representatives and suggested some readings for them. He was encouraged at the reception of the district office and the parent committee. Although the concepts were still far from being implemented, he knew that some major hurdles had already been crossed.

INTRODUCTION

The three previous roles—learner, culture-builder, and advocate—provide the foundation for the next role of the principal. In this chapter we explore the concept of leadership—an obvious role for the twenty-first-century principal who is trying to implement a PLC in a school. The roles of learner, culture-builder, and advocate make it possible for you as a principal or assistant principal to be a leader of a PLC, where active, engaging learning within a rich, learning culture is committed to the learning of all students. Interestingly, the leadership role is a rather new role conception in the history of principals. Robert, Louise, and other teachers showed leadership by planning and implementing a change at Roosevelt Junior High School. Although they went about the changes in a systematic and systemic manner, not all school reform movements will ever go this smoothly. Our reason to introduce this chapter with a positive vignette is to attempt to show that change can happen, improvement in teaching and learning can take place, and reform is an expected part of the principal's leadership role. In fact, by the definition we use, *leadership* means change, and if a principal is not looking at instructional improvement efforts, then the role of leader is not taking place. We have yet to see a school that has successfully implemented a PLC without the strong leadership of the principal.

Leadership is a broad area and cannot be covered adequately in one chapter. Our attempt in this chapter is to discuss some leadership concepts and in particular the principal's and assistant principal's roles as leaders and facilitators of leadership. We first explore the nature of leadership and its purposes. This is followed by a brief exploration of research on leadership. Then we discuss the purpose of principal leadership in developing PLCs in schools. The final section discusses the principal's role in facilitating leadership of others.

THE NATURE OF PRINCIPAL LEADERSHIP

As we discussed in Chapter 2, the origin of the principalship and its practice have not always emphasized a leadership role. The early responsibilities of principals had little to do with leadership and more to do with managing the daily routines such as unlocking the doors and getting the school cleaned. Indeed, the managerial function of the principalship rather than any leadership qualities has received most of the attention (Beck & Murphy, 1993). Principals were assumed to be more like business executives, using good management and social science research to run schools effectively and efficiently. The topic of leadership has grown in importance for contemporary principals and assistant principals because of three sources of leadership: external sources, internal sources, and the principal as his or her own source of leadership (Crow, Matthews, & McCleary, 1996). In the following sections, we discuss these three sources of leadership.

Leadership from External Sources

As a new principal or assistant principal, you will quickly discover that many individuals and groups outside the school practice leadership. In the opening vignette, Robert recognized the importance of district office administrators and the Parent-Teacher

Association (PTA) as sources of external leadership that influenced Roosevelt Junior High School. Likewise, as a principal, you will need to recognize those external sources that influence your school. To help you understand these external sources, we have categorized them into three areas: other administrators, policymakers, and constituents.

OTHER ADMINISTRATORS' INFLUENCE ON SCHOOL LEADERSHIP   Other administrators in the district, in particular the superintendent, personnel director, curriculum directors, and other school principals, exercise leadership by influencing the district vision, rewarding and sometimes suppressing particular administrative practices, and setting the direction for policies and procedures. "Schools are nested in districts and therefore are both nurtured and constrained by them" (Crow et al., 1996, p. 3). In the opening vignette, Robert's attempt to investigate PLCs in middle schools was influenced by the willingness of his district administrators and by the other school administrators who had converted to a middle school model. For example, the Lakeside Middle School principal and faculty served as the catalyst for Robert and the Roosevelt Junior High School faculty to implement the middle school concept.

POLICYMAKERS' INFLUENCE ON SCHOOL LEADERSHIP   Policymakers, such as school boards, also offer leadership that can affect the school and your role as a school leader. In particular, school boards and state legislatures establish policies that guide schools in what they can and cannot do. In the late 1980s, state governments took a stronger leadership role in education (Odden, 1995). These policymakers focused public attention on particular features of school effectiveness by directing the financial resources for specific areas, such as statewide testing. The ways schools respond to national accountability mandates, such as NCLB, is significantly influenced by the leadership of state policymakers, who set the benchmarks, design the type of testing, and develop rewards and sanctions. Likewise, policymakers such as school boards and state legislatures receive widespread media attention. When the media reports on the proceedings from these groups, they also increase the attention of the public to the issues. The publication of school report cards and other accountability reports in the media also influences what happens in schools.

Similar to government policymakers are high school state activities associations. Although schools voluntarily join these associations, they can greatly influence the schools' activity and academic programs. For example, a high school's alignment with an athletic conference will determine the school's travel for competitions. These travel arrangements can affect the academic programs if they require students to be out of class to participate. This is especially an issue in rural school settings where traveling long distances is necessary to have an interscholastic activity program.

CONSTITUENTS' INFLUENCE ON SCHOOL LEADERSHIP   The school's constituencies also exercise leadership that affects your leadership in the school. School constituencies consist of such individuals and groups as parents, business people, religious groups, media personnel, and community agencies. For example, parents influence schools in such areas as curricular offerings, teacher and principal selection, library books, and textbooks. Parents now, more than ever, have greater opportunity to choose the schools their children attend and the teachers they will have. These decisions affect the leadership of the principal. For example, in considering the opening vignette, what if several parents protested Roosevelt Junior High School's move to a middle school concept? Or, what if many parents chose to take their children out of the school and enroll them elsewhere? The principal and faculty would have to consider these parental decisions, which would affect the planning and implementation of a PLC in a middle school. Chances are that if many parents were against the concept, the plan would have to be abandoned until the school personnel could educate and help the parents understand the concepts better.

As a principal or assistant principal, you will work within a context in which leadership is exercised by various external sources. These sources are often strong enough and vocal enough to make it clear that you are not the only leader in the school. You need to recognize these external leadership sources, listen to them, and when needed, attempt to influence them for the benefit of student learning. A principal juggling different balls in the air illustrates external sources of leadership—it only takes a glance away from the juggling act to miss catching one of the balls.

Leadership from Internal Sources

Within a school, several individuals and groups play leadership roles. Many reform efforts such as school-based management and shared decision making have emphasized stronger leadership roles for teachers and others in the school. Likewise, PLCs are systems of democratic leadership with shared decision making. Instead of being threatened by such power and influence from teachers, you should learn to embrace it because from it you will have a stronger and more viable learning community. As in the opening vignette when Louise was the catalyst in getting the middle school concept introduced at Roosevelt, teachers can be a positive influence in exerting leadership for improved student learning. Likewise, the teacher team that the principal organized also was influential in influencing others to consider the cultural shifts necessary to implement a PLC and a middle school approach.

Two other roles within the school deserve mentioning as strong influences on leadership, namely, secretaries and custodians. In subtle but powerful ways, these two roles can affect your decision making as a school leader. For example, a secretary often screens the communication that goes into and out of the principal's office. A school secretary can also be a keeper of the cultural history of the school, often knowing more about the school and its community than many others in the building. Similarly, school custodians influence leadership by their contact and visibility with teachers, students, and visitors in the building. Not only are custodians and secretaries often the first to meet parents and visitors to the school, but also their influence on leadership is seen in how they communicate the school's vision to others. As a principal, you should not overlook their valuable input.

Although students always have influenced leadership in the school, their presence in leadership roles is greater now than ever. Many school boards have student representation. Most site councils include student participation. Student councils are no longer limited to secondary schools but are integral parts of elementary schools. Student groups other than the elected student councils are also influential. For example, some student groups have become more visible and influential in their demands, such as those promoting social issues, for example, religious, political, gay and lesbian, ethnic, feminist, and environmentalist groups. Other student groups have promoted curricular and extracurricular issues, for instance, International Baccalaureate curriculum, Amnesty International clubs, and athletic teams such as hockey and soccer. For an interesting case study on a gay and straight club's influence on a high school, see McCreary (2001).

Principals must acknowledge and work with these internal groups to carry forward the vision of a PLC in the school. Otherwise, principal leadership will be ineffective as an influence in any substantial improvement efforts. You will be a more potent source for improvement efforts if you recognize, develop, and empower the leadership of others.

Principal Leadership

Your leadership as a principal or an assistant principal is influenced not only by external and internal sources but also by your own leadership practice, style, and development. Knowing how to influence and develop leadership capacity in others is a significant and important endeavor. For example, Robert at Roosevelt Junior High School recognized the limitations of his formal position of principal and instead used his influence to develop leadership capacity in Louise and other teachers. By distributing leadership among others, he was able to gain faculty ownership of the middle school concept.

As we have discussed throughout this book, the assistant principal plays a significant role in schools. Although we believe that this role should be reconceptualized in many school settings, assistant principals in any school do more than just student management and campus supervision. The principal's leadership is incomplete without the assistant principal's participation. As a team member, contributor, counselor, advisor, mentor, and soul mate, assistant principals significantly influence the leadership in the school. In addition, the leadership team of administrators and teacher leaders also influence and enrich the leadership capacity of the school.

As you go through your preparation program and as you read about, discuss, and observe leadership, you will develop new ways of seeing your role as a leader. By reflecting on your own style and on the influences and constraints that affect your leadership capacity, you will begin to develop a relevant and realistic role for school leadership.

LEADERSHIP LITERATURE

When you walk into a bookstore, you probably notice the volumes of leadership and management books on the shelves. Many of these books are meant to be self-help and motivational books. Often these popular books take on a cookbook style of sharing recipes that have worked for the author. With the vast amount of literature that exists on leadership, it is important to determine what will be of most help to you as you begin your career as a principal or assistant principal. In this subsection, we have created three categories in which to organize leadership literature in an attempt to help you understand the kinds of literature that are available.

Popular Literature

The first category of leadership literature we call the *popular literature,* or what often can be found easily in bookstores. This category of literature can include books and popular magazines that occasionally print leadership-related articles. Popular magazines are often written by staff members such as reporters and are not peer reviewed before publication. The publisher's purpose is most often to market and sell the magazines and books. Be careful with these kinds of publications in developing your own ideas and theories. You should critically evaluate these resources in terms of their basis in research and their value in supporting a PLC that emphasizes learning for all students.

Professional Literature

The second category includes literature from professional associations. This type of literature is usually available through educational leadership associations. We recommend journals in Table 7.1. These publications are available in most libraries, especially university-associated libraries, but these books and journals often are not peer reviewed but are selected by an editorial board or staff based on the topic's relevance and applicability. You may have to have membership in the association to receive its literature, but most associations will offer their literature to nonmembers.

Scholarly Literature

The third category includes research-based, scholarly works. This type of literature is available in most university and college libraries and is becoming increasingly available on the Internet. Most of this literature is found in scholarly journals and books that are reviewed by peers. A peer review indicates that the editors sent the manuscript to scholars in the field to review the author's research and findings for relevance, reliability, credibility, and timeliness. Because of the peer review, authors are especially careful with their research design and data interpretation so that errors are not published unwittingly. However, just because it is reviewed by peers does not make the literature accurate, only that it is more likely to have been closely reviewed for research and theoretical errors. In Table 7.2, we offer our recommendations for strong scholarly journals that pertain to school leadership.

These three categories are not absolutes, and some works will have characteristics in more than one category; for example, professional associations publish research studies that are relevant to practitioners. Remember that there is a considerable amount of leadership literature, and you need to be aware of the kinds of literature that exist and the

TABLE 7.1 Sample of Professional Journals in School Leadership

Journal	Association	Web site
Educational Leadership	Association of Supervision and Curriculum Development (ASCD)	*www.ascd.org*
The Kappan	Phi Delta Kappa (PDK)	*www.pdkintl.org*
Principal	National Association of Elementary School Principals (NAESP)	*www.naesp.org*
Principal Leadership (both a high school version and a middle school version)	National Association of Secondary School Principals (NAASP)	*www.nassp.org*
The School Administrator	American Association of School Administrators (AASA)	*www.aasa.org*
American School Board Journal	National School Board Association (NSBA)	*www.nsba.org*

TABLE 7.2 Sample of Scholarly Journals in School Leadership

Journal	Association or Publisher and Web site (if applicable)
Education Administration Quarterly	University Council of Educational Administration (UCEA) (*www.ucea.org*)
Journal of School Leadership	Rowan & Littlefield Publisher (*www.rowmaneducation.com/Journals/JSL*)
Journal of Education Policy	Taylor & Francis Publisher (*http://www.tandf.co.uk/journals/TF/02680939.html*)
NASSP Bulletin	National Association of Secondary School Principals (*www.nassp.org*)
The Canadian Journal of Educational Administration and Policy	The University of Manitoba (*www.umanitoba.ca/publications/cjeap*)

TABLE 7.3 Rubric for Evaluating Literature for Reading and Researching

Relevance:

• Does the publication help answer your questions?

Reliability/Credibility:

• Is the information presented accurately?
• Has the information been peer reviewed?
• Are the author(s) and publisher reputable?
• Do the authors cite their credentials accurately?
• Is there sufficient documentation to help you determine whether the publication is reliable? In other words, are there citations, references, or credits?

Perspective:

• If research is used, does it come from a primary source (presenting the author's own research and ideas) or a secondary source (summarizing and discussing the research and ideas of others)?
• How objectively is information presented?
• Is a bias evident (in other words, does the author or publisher profit from the article)?
• Is the author attempting to sway your opinion?

Timeliness:

• How recently was the information published?
• Have there been developments in the field that may have been inappropriately represented because of the publication timeframe?

relevance of the work in schools. Effective leadership does not involve quick fixes, so be cautious as you read popular literature that involves an easy solution. Likewise, some leadership literature offers a "how to" approach that may be effective in some organizations or with some circumstances but not in others. It is especially important for you to realize that many leadership books and articles are written from perspectives other than for public-sector organizations such as schools. This type of leadership literature might be more effective for business or corporate organizations. Regardless of the source or the type of literature, you should critically evaluate the literature. In Table 7.3, we offer a rubric for evaluating literature for your reading and research. One way to evaluate the literature is to use research that has been conducted on leadership, as we explain in the next subsection.

RESEARCH ON LEADERSHIP

Just as many authors have written about leadership, many researchers have studied it, especially in the last sixty years. In this section, our attempt is not to provide an exhaustive review of the leadership literature but to offer a description of how this research relates to the leadership role of principals and assistant principals. We organize the discussion around six major approaches in the literature: trait, behavior, contingency (situational), relationship, leadership as an organizational quality, and moral leadership.

Trait Approaches

Early efforts to understand leader effectiveness focused on personal traits. Research in the twentieth century examined leaders (almost always male) who had achieved a level of greatness and hence became known as the *great man theory*. Fundamental to this theory was the idea that some people were born with qualities and traits that made them natural leaders. The research sought to identify those traits that leaders possessed that distinguished them from people who were not leaders. However, these attempts to identify and measure leadership traits were unsuccessful primarily because of the lack of any evidence that such qualities guaranteed effectiveness. Many critics of this approach such as Yukl (2005) found only a weak relationship between personal traits and leader success. Blackmore (1991) labeled the great man theory as the search for the "fantasy figure or philosopher-king" (p. 101) and critiqued its over reliance on masculine imagery and valorization of hierarchical and elitist relationships. Watkins (1986) believed that trait theories ignore the relationship between leaders and followers and separate the world into leaders and nonleaders.

Regardless of the lack of evidence for trait theories, many people, including educators, still use the approach. For example, many who hire school principals do so based on certain personal qualities that they have witnessed that made other principals effective, for example, decisiveness, self-assurance, and persuasiveness. Likewise, many principals hire teachers based on certain qualities that they possess.

In the 1990s, interest in personal qualities of leaders was resurrected as psychologists and social scientists continued to study leadership in social settings. Research conducted by Kirkpatrick and Locke (1991) indicated that some traits were essential to effective leadership if practiced in combination with other factors. Three of the traits deemed essential were self-confidence, honesty, and drive. These leadership traits were hard to argue against, especially in the context of social settings such as schools. However, there are examples of people deemed as good leaders who did not possess these personal traits. Consider Abraham Lincoln, who many claimed did not have high self-confidence, or Adolf Hitler, who was anything but an honest leader. Nevertheless, traits such as self-confidence, honesty, and drive have great value for school leaders, especially in combination with other behavioral and situational factors.

Professional Dilemma 7.1

One assistant principal candidate had tried for several years to attain a position. The problem: He was a big man and did not fit the usual high school assistant principal mold. Weighing in at 340 pounds, he was a highly successful and popular teacher but could not get beyond an interview for an administrative position. Most of the principals who had interviewed him were concerned that the position was too taxing for an obese man. Should obesity be considered as a criterion for an assistant principal who has responsibilities to supervise high school campuses? Although this candidate was a successful teacher, does his physical appearance and physical abilities determine how effective he will be as an assistant principal?

Behavior Approaches

Behavior theories appeared after the early trait theories proved inadequate. Instead of looking at what leaders are, social scientists began looking at what they do, especially because behaviors can be learned more readily than traits, enabling leadership to be accessible to more people.

The first studies on leadership behaviors were conducted at Iowa State University (Lewin & Lippet, 1938). These experiments indicated that individuals reacted differently to an autocratic leadership style than to a democratic leadership style. The groups with autocratic leaders performed effectively as long as the leader was present to supervise them. However, feelings of hostility arose frequently. Participative techniques used by the democratic leaders helped groups perform well even when the leader was not present. Daft (2006) suggested that these characteristics of democratic leadership might explain in part why empowerment is a popular trend in organizations today.

Another set of studies on leader behavior was conducted at Ohio State University. Narrowing a list of nearly 2,000 leader behaviors into a written instrument, researchers developed the Leader Behavior Description Questionnaire (LBDQ). Hundreds of employees, including many educators, responded to behavior examples according to the degree to which their leaders engaged in the various behaviors. The analysis of ratings resulted in two categories of leader behavior types named *consideration (person orientation)* and *initiating structure (task orientation)*. Thousands of research articles and dissertations, many of them concerning the principalship, have used the LBDQ.

Although many leadership behaviors fall along a continuum comprising person and task orientation, these behavior categories are independent of one another. A leader can display a degree of both behaviors. For example, a principal can be high in task orientation and low in people consideration or high in both areas. In the opening vignette, Robert could be described as high in both task orientation and people skills. He developed strong relationships with the faculty, but at the same time he had high expectations of them. For example, he asked teachers to establish goals at the beginning of the year and then conducted goal review sessions near the end of the year. His personal regard for each of the teachers and their ideas was also evident.

Simultaneous studies at the University of Michigan (Katz, Maccoby, & Morse, 1950; Likert, 1961) took a different approach by analyzing the behaviors of effective and ineffective leaders. The effectiveness of leaders was determined by the productivity of their groups. Similar to the Ohio State study, the Michigan study identified two types of leadership behavior: job-centered and employee-centered. Unlike the consideration and task structure defined by the Ohio State studies, Michigan researchers considered job-centered and employee-centered to be distinct styles in opposition to each other. In addition to the job- and employee-centered types of leadership, the Michigan researchers also went beyond the Ohio State studies in identifying a third type of effective leadership behavior—participative—in which the leader focused on the effectiveness of the group, not just the individual.

At the University of Texas, Blake and Mouton (1978) plotted leadership on a grid with concern for people on a vertical scale and concern for production on a horizontal scale. Blake and Mouton offered some interesting titles to the leadership styles when the two criteria were plotted on this grid. For example, high concern for people and low concern for production were labeled "country-club management." "Impoverished management" was the absence of concern both for people and for production. Blake and Mouton considered the most effective style as "team management," where both people and production were regarded highly. This style fits well within the PLC approach.

Daft (2006) suggested that the research into behavior approaches raises certain questions for students of leadership. The first question is whether the two dimensions (people orientation or task orientation) are the most important leadership behaviors. Daft suggested that these two behaviors are important because the findings are based on empirical research; that is, researchers went into the field to study leaders across a variety of settings. While these are not the only important behaviors, they certainly require attention.

Daft's (2006) second question concerns whether people orientation and task orientation exist together in the same leader and, if so, how. Blake and Mouton's (1978) study argued that both were present when people work with or through others to accomplish an activity. Some researchers have argued that "high-high" leaders alternate the type of behavior from one to the other, showing concern one time and task initiation another time. Another approach claimed that effective "high-high" leaders encompass both behaviors simultaneously in a fundamentally different way than people who behave in one way or the other (Fleishman & Harris, 1962). A high task-oriented and low relationship-oriented principal might set difficult goals and pressure teachers to improve student achievement without concern for morale. A high relationship-oriented and low task-oriented principal might deemphasize test scores and seek improvement by building positive relationships with teachers. In contrast, the "high-high" leaders seem to have a knack for displaying concern for both people and production, by keeping the focus on student learning but recognizing the importance of building strong relationships within a PLC.

A third question suggested by Daft (2006), and one that leads into the next leadership research approach, is whether "high-high" leadership styles are situational; that is, does the behavior tend to be effective in every situation? Likewise, does it mean that the behavior succeeds only in certain situations? Daft reported that leadership with concern for people tended to be related to higher employee satisfaction and fewer personnel problems across a wide variety of situations. Likewise, task-oriented behavior was associated with higher productivity across a large number of situations.

The last question raised by Daft (2006) concerns whether people actually can change themselves into leaders high on people and/or task orientation. The original behavior studies at Ohio State, Michigan, and Texas assumed that leadership behaviors could be learned. This does not mean that it will always be practiced effectively. Consequently, studies emerged as to what leader behaviors should be used in certain situations. These studies form a group of research investigations known as situational or contingency theories.

The behavior approaches in school leadership can be of some help to school leaders as they consider establishing PLCs. A good study of trust, Bryk and Schneider (2003) drew upon research of elementary schools in Chicago. They established four considerations for school leaders in building trust, namely, respect, competence, personal regard for others, and integrity. Their premise was that these four behaviors should be considered as foundational to trust building, an important element in a PLC.

Contingency Approaches

While leader behaviors were still studied, the central focus of contingency research was the situations or contingencies in which leadership occurred. Daft (2006) suggested that contingency means that one thing depends on other things, and for a leader to be effective, there must be an appropriate fit between the leader's behavior and the conditions in the situation. A leadership style that works in one situation might not work in another situation. Daft suggested that there is not one best way of leadership.

Consider the opening vignette to this chapter. Several situational features such as task, school structure, teachers' commitment and abilities, resources, and external factors such as the district office and parental commitment contributed to the successful implementation of a middle school PLC. In particular, the maturity and cohesiveness of the teachers and the principal played an extremely important role.

Contingency theories try to match the various styles of leadership to the appropriate situations. Among the various studies were House's (1974) path-goal theory, Fiedler's (1967) contingency model, Vroom and Jago's (1988) contingency model, and Hersey and Blanchard's (1977) situational leadership model. In Chapter 8, we introduce the Glickman, Gordon, and Ross-Gordon (2001) supervision model. This model would fit under this category of situational leadership theories because it helps principals understand that they should consider the development level of teachers as they determine the appropriate supervisory approach for instructional improvement efforts.

The movement from the leader's personal traits and behaviors to situations or contingencies acknowledged two important factors in the leadership research. First, situational leadership models recognized that others in the organization (we will use the term *followers*) matter. Follower characteristics, primarily those inherent in the organizational or group context (e.g., experience, training, and effort), influence leadership effectiveness. An example of this is the opening vignette to this chapter in which Louise aptly and successfully influenced the leadership of the school. Without Louise's influence, the question has to be asked, would Roosevelt Junior High School be as successful in implementing change? The second contribution made by the contingency theories was that leadership could be developed (and thus be more effective) by understanding the situation. Again, in the opening vignette, because Robert allowed and developed leadership among teachers, they became the leaders of change. Both of these contributions added to the understanding of leadership and influenced more research, especially on the interactions that developed among the participants in the leadership relationship.

Leadership as a Relationship

Theorists who emphasized leadership as a relationship believed that trait, behavior, and contingency theories oversimplified the relationship between leaders and followers. Leadership as a relationship approach studied the influence that followers have on leaders and why leaders have more influence over some followers than others. These theorists argued that leaders do not uniformly broadcast a trait such as self-confidence and have it received equally by each person in the organization.

Leadership as a relationship grew out of social science literature that emphasized power and influence. The approach identified the types of power that leaders used to influence followers. For example, French and Raven (1959) identified five sources of power: reward, coercive, legitimate, expert, and referent (personal). Later they added a sixth source of power similar to expert, namely, information power, which involves controlling the information that individuals need to reach goals. We discuss sources of power and influence further in Chapter 11. Although informative as these sources of power and influence are on leadership, this literature ignored the reciprocal nature of the relationship among leaders and followers.

Leadership as a relationship is often presented as a dyadic approach. The development of the dyadic approach is based on four stages. The first stage is the awareness of a relationship between a leader and each subordinate rather than between a leader and a group of subordinates. The second stage examines specific attributes of the exchange between leader and subordinate. The third stage explores whether leaders could intentionally develop partnerships with each subordinate, and the fourth stage expanded the view of dyads to include larger systems and networks (Daft, 2006). A good example of research that used a reciprocal understanding of the leader–follower relationship is Blase's (1991) work on the tactics used by teachers to influence principals. These tactics varied depending on whether principals were open or closed in their approach to teachers. Currently, the dyadic approach has not received a lot of research to substantiate the theory. Nevertheless, the theory suggests an important leadership concept, especially for PLCs. As a principal or assistant principal, you will need to build fourth stage dyads or networks that encourage a large number of people to influence one another. This relationship approach brought attention to yet another level of research and theorizing, that of leadership as an organizational feature.

Leadership as an Organizational Feature

Moving beyond defining leadership as particular positions or roles, leadership as an organizational quality focused on the social interaction among roles in the organization. This perspective had roots in the work of several organizational theorists, including Barnard (1948), Katz and Kahn 1978), Tannenbaum (1962), and Thompson (1967). However, Ogawa and Bossert (1995) described leadership as an organizational quality in schools from an institutional theory view. Instead of the traditional emphasis on leadership to accomplish organizational goals, their approach focused on leadership to make the organization legitimate and credible in the eyes of its constituents. Their argument extends beyond the obvious by suggesting that leadership flows through the networks of roles that comprise organizations. The currency of leadership lies in personal resources of people, an important element of PLCs. In the opening vignette, you might describe leadership in terms of the different ways the expertise and charisma of

Robert and Louise helped increase the influence and leadership across and among the roles in the school. Leadership shapes the system that produces patterns of interaction and the meanings that other participants attach to organizational events, such as school improvement efforts, successes, and celebrations.

This perspective is particularly useful in understanding the principal's role by broadening the understanding of leadership beyond one role or position and acknowledging the interaction among roles (Crow et al., 1996). Ogawa and Bossert (1995) also suggested that principal leadership roles are changing because of reforms that emphasize empowering teachers and others associated with the organization. Similarly, discussions on the development of PLCs and the shared responsibility that characterize these communities reflect the change in principal leadership.

Distributed leadership (Spillane, 2006) is a more recent understanding of leadership as an organizational feature. This theory moves beyond the heroic idea of the leadership of the principal and the idea of shared leadership to understand leadership practice occurring as "a product of the joint interactions of school *leaders, followers,* and aspects of their *situation,* such as tools and routines" (p. 3). Not only has this theory helped move us away from focusing solely on the dramatic actions of the official leader but also to understand how leadership involves the actions of leaders and followers and various features of the school context.

Moral Leadership

The leadership approaches we have examined so far in this chapter are nonevaluative; that is, the perspectives could be used to describe both effective and ineffective leaders in good and poor organizations. Many theorists have developed a leadership approach that is based on moral authority. For example, many authors (e.g., Covey, 2004; Johnson,1990; Sergiovanni, 2009) wrote that morally based leadership is meaningful because it taps what is important to people and what motivates them.

Most of the literature on moral leadership implies the development of followers into leaders, thereby developing their potential rather than using the leadership position to control others. This type of moral leadership began with Burns's (1978) concept of *transformational leadership,* in which "leaders and followers raise one another to higher levels of morality and motivation" (p. 20). Burns contrasted transformational leadership with transactional leadership. *Transactional leadership* involves an exchange process between leaders and followers. The leader recognizes specific follower desires and provides resources that meet those desires in exchange for the follower's loyalty and goal attainment. Leadership is a series of transactions to achieve specific goals. Because transactional leadership involves commitment to follow the rules, transactional leaders often maintain stability within the organization rather than promote change (Daft, 2006). On the other hand, transformational leadership is based on personal values, beliefs, and qualities of the leader rather than on an exchange process.

Another moral leadership approach that supports the belief that leaders are to empower others is stewardship theory. Block (1993) argued that traditional views of leadership were based on patriarchy and self-interest and maintained by command and control—hence breeding dependency. Stewardship is grounded in service and is supported by commitment and empowerment. Block suggested that stewardship is the belief that leaders are accountable to others as well as to the organization. He provided four principles in a stewardship framework:

1. *Reorient toward a partnership assumption.*   Leaders and followers are jointly accountable for outcomes.
2. *Localize decisions and power to those closest to the work and the customer.* Decision making should be at the point where the work gets done.
3. *Recognize and reward the value of labor.*   The reward system ties everyone to the success of the organization.
4. *Expect core work teams to build the organization.*   Teams define goals, create a nurturing environment, and respond to a changing environment.

These principles work well as the types of leadership practices important for implementing, developing, and supporting PLCs.

Sergiovanni (2009) believed that the concept of stewardship was attractive to principals. He suggested that stewardship embraced all internal and external members of the school as community and argued against the premise that good leaders are those who get their subordinates to do something. Sergiovanni suggested that shifting emphasis from leader behavior to establishing meaning can help schools recapture leadership as a powerful force for school improvement.

Servant leadership takes stewardship one step further. Servant leadership transcends self-interest to serve the needs of others, helps others grow and develop, and provides opportunity for others. The fulfillment of others is the servant leader's principal aim. Greenleaf (1970) proposed that leaders can operate from the basic precepts of servant leadership, such as the principal encouraging teachers to participate in a master's degree program or engaging the faculty in a shared vision.

Moral leadership also produces an interest in the cultural side of leadership, as outlined by Schein (2004) and presented in Chapter 5. Whereas most leadership has focused on the technical side, be it task-oriented or person-oriented, this approach focuses on the values, beliefs, and assumptions of work—how values and beliefs are formed, how they affect the quality of life and work in schools, and how they are modified. Leadership from this perspective examines what principals do to build and maintain a school culture that reinforces the values, norms, and beliefs and to add meaning to the educational work that goes beyond mere accomplishment of task (Crow et al., 1996; Heifetz & Laurie, 1996).

How Useful Is Research on Leadership?

Scholars and practitioners have argued for decades about the practical uses of leadership research. Many studies involved groups that were not representative of leaders in certain fields or categories. For example, the early studies were conducted with mostly male subjects who had usually had military experience in World War II or the Korean War. Obviously, the results from these studies might not have been the same as findings from an occupation with many female participants such as nursing or teaching. Also, some studies reported results only from American business organizations that often were going through declining budgets, layoffs, and union threats. Leadership in the public sector is likely to be different from that in the private sector. Some people argue that leading an organization of professionals such as teachers is quite different from leading a factory of union workers. Likewise, some studies looked only at certain kinds of success, such as a financial profit or followers' satisfaction.

Some researchers (e.g., Pfeffer, 1978) also claimed that other researchers were only seeing leadership because they expected to see it. Proponents of *attribution theory* argued that if, for example, researchers observed a business turnaround and there was no other obvious cause, the turnaround was attributed to leadership. Alternatively, if the researchers were looking for certain traits or behaviors, they would find them although the traits and behaviors might not have contributed to the leadership outcome.

Regardless of the various critics of leadership study, the research has contributed to a greater understanding of leadership and the literature base. Because of the scholarly research on leadership, we know more about what has proven effective in certain environments. However, there is still considerable understanding about leadership that we do not possess.

THE PURPOSE OF PRINCIPAL LEADERSHIP

Could schools operate efficiently without principals? If a head teacher managed the resources and other incidentals, would not that be enough for schools? To argue for the value of principal leadership requires adding a purpose to the role of principal as leader. In this section we discuss that purpose and present a model that depicts the ingredients of principal leadership.

In Chapter 1, we proposed a definition of leadership presented by Rost (1991) who, after studying many definitions, defined leadership as "an influence relationship among leaders and followers who intend real changes that reflect their mutual purposes" (p. 102). With this definition serving as our foundation, we suggest that the purpose of principal leadership involves the intention to significantly change schools in substantive ways to improve teaching and learning for *all* students. Of course, the vehicle in which we suggest that this type of leadership occurs is through PLCs. Under the concept of a PLC, all participants in the school are constantly learning how to do things better whether or not their test scores are considered high. Therefore, principals—even those in high-performing schools—must constantly lead their schools to improve teaching and learning for *all* students. The nature of the knowledge society, the dynamic changes in communities, and the evolving needs of students in a global society require all schools to be open to change.

Defining Significant School Change and Reform

Three important points about the purpose of leadership are evident from Rost's (1991) definition. First, leaders and followers intend real change, and they see change as a continuing process rather than a one-time reform effort. These changes involve not only the leader's goals for change but also the goals of both leaders and followers. Indeed, if this purpose is only the leader's, no leadership exists. In a PLC, both leaders and followers must acknowledge the need for improvement in teaching and learning for *all* students.

Second, real change in schools is change that is substantial. Cuban (1988) suggested labeling the difference between superficial and substantial change as *first-order* and *second-order changes*. First-order changes only seek to make current practices more effective. No new practices are adopted. Teachers and students perform their duties in much the same way as they have done in the past. Examples of first-order changes may be a new attendance policy where the expectation is still held that students are to be in school, but the consequences of nonattendance are stiffer.

Second-order changes entail a cultural shift in values, beliefs, and practices. Underlying assumptions are challenged. School goals, mission, vision, and roles shift. Teachers become leaders and take responsibility in the school's decision-making process, in analyzing data, and in their own learning. Likewise, students are not just recipients of learning, but they take an active role in constructing their learning. Teachers and principals are not satisfied with some or even most students learning but are committed to *all* students learning. And the learning goes beyond simply raising test scores to develop higher-order, critical-thinking skills, civic engagement, and other areas of social and emotional development. Second-order changes are significant and have a lasting impact on the school's culture. Leadership for school improvement involves changing the school culture so that leaders and followers are willing to consider substantive second-order changes (see Table 7.4). The type of change Robert and Louise in the opening vignette encouraged is an example of second-order change, because it involved a substantive change of values, beliefs, and practices.

The third element of Rost's definition of leadership is that change focuses on the mutual purposes of leaders and followers. Rost (1991) maintained that this mutuality is forged in the noncoercive influence relationship. As principals, teachers, students, and parents work together in a learning community, they forge shared purposes about changes that will positively affect teaching and learning. The content of mutual purposes should reflect what many reformers (including Barth, 1990; DuFour, DuFour, & Eaker, 2008; Louis & Murphy, 1994; Sergiovanni, 2009) repeat as the main theme in school reform: teaching and learning is at the heart of school change. The mutual purposes of leaders and followers should be located in classroom instruction and learning. Teachers, principals, parents, and students come together to forge a shared purpose for improving classroom instruction and enhancing student and adult learning. As principal or assistant principal, the most critical purpose of your leadership will be to shift the school culture so that adults and children grow together in developing a learning community that shares a mutual purpose to improve student learning.

TABLE 7.4 Examples of First- and Second-Order Changes in a Professional Learning Community

First-Order Changes	Second-Order Changes
Providing teachers with district curricular documents and state standards	Engaging collaborative teams in building shared knowledge regarding the essential curriculum
Improving the types of assessments of student learning	Developing common assessments by teams of teachers that identify students who need preventions and interventions
Improving individual teacher's ability to determine an appropriate response to lack of a student's achievement	Developing a collaborative response from a team of teachers that support
Improving professional development	Improving team-based action research

CREATING A COLLECTIVE VISION

A major ingredient of leadership involves developing a vision for the school. *Vision* works in a number of important ways. An effective vision provides a link between the present and the future, serves to energize and motivate people, provides meaning for their work, and sets a standard of excellence in the organization (DuFour et al., 2006). Vision is also misunderstood in leadership. It was not too long ago when leaders, including principals, were encouraged to develop a strategic vision and then sell it to others in the organization. However, as we will discuss in this section, vision in a PLC involves a collective process.

A school's vision is not just a dream—it is an ambitious view of the future that principals, assistant principals, teachers, staff members, and parents can believe in, one that can be realistically attained and offers a future for the school that is better in instruction, curriculum, programs, and activities than what presently exists. In the opening vignette, the vision that Louise had developed of a PLC in a middle school is a good example. After being introduced to the idea of a PLC in a middle school, she started putting it together in light of her own school. Soon she was able to develop a vision of what Roosevelt Junior High School should be doing. As such, the vision she developed presented an ambitious view of the future that required her to communicate and persuade others to accept and become part of the vision.

Daft (1999) identified five characteristics of an effective vision:

- *Vision has broad appeal* The vision cannot be the property of the leader alone.
- *Vision deals with change* The vision is about action and challenges people to make important changes toward a better future.
- *Vision encourages faith and hope* A vision helps people believe that they can be effective—that there is a better future they can move to through their commitment and actions.
- *Vision reflects high ideals* A good vision has power to inspire and energize people only when it points toward an uplifting future.
- *Vision defines the destination and the journey* A good vision for the future includes specific outcomes that the school wants to achieve.

Many people use the terms *vision* and *mission* interchangeably, but mission is not the same thing as vision. A school's mission is its broad purpose and reason for existence. It often defines the school's core values and reason for being. A mission provides a basis for creating the vision. Likewise, goal statements differ from vision statements. Goals are detailed, specific statements directed at accomplishing the mission and are guided by the vision. Goal statements include the more specific objectives. As we defined it earlier, vision is an ambitious desire for the future, whereas mission is what the school stands for at the present. (See Table 7.5 for an example of each.)

Many schools have mission statements that define what they stand for, including their core values and core purpose. Some schools also include the specific vision as a part of their mission statements. It is important to remember that the vision continually grows and changes, whereas the mission endures longer with fewer changes.

Principal Leadership in Vision Building

Principal leadership in vision building involves two levels: the principal's personal vision and the school's collective vision. The effective principal as leader should have a

TABLE 7.5 Sample Mission and Vision Statements

Example of Mission Statements	Examples of Vision Statements
West Lake Middle School is a learning community that strives for excellence in its classroom teaching; intellectual growth in its students; and commitment to the arts, athletics, and service to others.	We want Suncrest Elementary School to become a school where all students gain the confidence to become positive learners who know how to read, compute, and think.
By providing quality education, Suncrest Elementary School empowers students to become caring, competent, responsible citizens who value education as a lifelong process.	

personal vision as to the direction the school should be going, especially for improving teaching and learning for *all* students. This vision concentrates the principal's attention, provides the passion for one activity over another, and inspires others to respond to the vision and develop a collective vision. As Starratt (1993) claimed,

> The leader's vision is what motivates him or her to be a genuine player in the drama and is a call to greatness as well. The leader's vision is also what enables him or her to articulate the major themes of the drama in the role of director. The vision enables the leader/director to see the unity within the various scenes and subplots of the drama, and to call the various actors to express, in their parts, those overarching themes. (p. 145)

This perspective involves the principal's own purpose and understanding of the school's mission and provides the passion that motivates the principal's work.

Just as the principal can have a personal vision, likewise other members of the organization, such as assistant principals and teachers, also have personal visions. In fact, at times, someone else's personal vision is the catalyst for the principal's vision. This event was played out in the opening vignette when Louise shared her personal vision with Robert. Obviously, Louise's vision was congruent with Robert's, and thus they were able to pursue a schoolwide collective vision.

A school's collective vision is what leaders, teachers, staff members, and others in the school community construct regarding the school's future. A school's collective vision is multileveled. *Programmatic vision* refers to specific kinds of teaching and learning activities, such as a particular reading program (e.g., Reading Recovery). Systemic vision focuses on broader organizational directions. A school's reform efforts that reconceptualize roles, relationships, and responsibilities are part of a systemic vision. Roosevelt Junior High School's change into a PLC in a middle school would be an example of a systemic vision because it affects almost all aspects of the school's organization. As Senge and his colleagues (1990) put it, a collective vision changes people's relationship with the organization. It can create a common identity for all participants, connecting them personally and emotionally in the organization. The vision of a middle school PLC at Roosevelt Junior High School became the common thread by connecting the principal, teachers, staff members, and parents.

To develop a collective vision, principals share their personal visions with others and encourage others to express their personal visions. This openness requires that the principal, teachers, and others have both strong communication skills and courage to connect on an emotional level. Good principals give up the idea that vision emanates from only the top and that their personal vision is the only one that can become a collective vision. As Nanus (1992) said, "Often some of the best ideas for new directions float up from the depths of the organization, but only if they are sought and welcomed when they arrive" (p. 38). As a principal, your ultimate responsibility is to be in touch with the visions that others in the school community have and find common ground that binds these personal visions into a collective vision for the school.

The Principal's Roles as Visionary Leader

Nanus (1992) suggested four roles that visionary leaders play based on the dimensions of time and environment. These roles are useful in understanding the principal's responsibility beyond a sole authorship function.

- *Direction-setter.* This role focuses on the future and the external environment. The leader selects and articulates the target in the future external environment toward which the organization should direct its energies.
- *Change agent.* This role emphasizes the future and focuses on the internal environment. The leader is responsible for stimulating changes to make the vision achievable. At times, this role means providing disconfirming data that demonstrates the ineffective ways the school is meeting the needs of students and families.
- *Spokesperson.* This role directs attention to the present and external environment. The leader is both a skilled speaker and a concerned listener. The leader advocates and negotiates the organization's vision with outside constituencies. This role is becoming increasingly important as schools become more competitive and schools of choice become more widespread.
- *Coach.* This is a present function within the internal environment. The leader lives the vision, thereby serving as a mentor and example for others. Principals cheer the school on toward vision achievement. This coaching and cheering function occurs by what the principal pays attention to, rewards, and celebrates.

It is important to understand that as a principal or assistant principal, you play a visionary leadership role in both external and internal spheres. To ignore one in favor of the other is to abdicate leadership responsibility. Although others in the school may function in these roles at certain times, you, as a school leader, have the critical responsibility to ensure that these roles are enacted effectively.

Further, with the demands of a knowledge society, the changing demographics of students, the explosion in technologies, the rise of accountability movements, and consistent emphasis on school reform by policymakers, you will face a more difficult job in keeping the purpose of schooling clearly in the minds of school constituents. The school's vision cannot remain stagnant. It will need to be reexamined and revised in the exciting and dynamic environment that now exists for schools.

Sadly, many reform and instructional improvement efforts have ignored the consideration of the school's vision. Such efforts can leave the school's organization in disarray and place unpleasant burdens on teachers and staff members. As principal or assistant principal, you need to provide direction to the vision process and content. This is not to suggest that others have no role in constructing the vision but rather that you, as a leader, have a primary responsibility for providing the direction to the process. Likewise, as a school leader, you provide the energy for persisting with the process, although it may become uncomfortable and threatening to some in the school. Your commitment, passion, and inspiration for the vision process are critical in finding a direction that enriches students' educational experiences and teachers' work lives.

The Dark Side of Visions

Visions can have a dark side. Similar to the dark side of culture, visions can blind leaders and others and cause confusion and chaos in the organization. Fullan (2005) suggested three ways that visions blind school leaders and others in the school. First, the leader who is committed to a particular innovation may pursue that innovation in such a narrow and self-defeating way that teachers resist the idea. Numerous stories from schools tell of principals who became so enamored with their own personal visions with an innovative program that they created confusion and resentment among the faculty and staff. In these situations, it is unlikely that a collective vision was developed, and the personal vision of the principal eventually caused chaos within the organization. For example, in a new high school that was built to overcome crowding in two nearby high schools, the new principal wanted to establish activities and ceremonies that would be new traditions and rituals that were different from the other two schools. In establishing these activities, she failed to incorporate the suggestions and comments from others, especially the high school students. Thus, most of the ideas that she established failed because others in the school did not share her vision.

A second way visions can blind is when the leader successfully involves others to use an innovation but does not engage them in other basic changes and alternatives. The dynamic nature of schools requires an ongoing visioning process rather than a fixation on one innovation. This is one of the reasons why we encourage a more systemic and dynamic, cultural approach—professional learning communities. In PLCs, visioning is part of an ongoing, learning process rather than a series of the latest programmatic fads.

Third, visions can blind school leaders and faculties in the case of a charismatic leader where so much depends on personal strength or pressure but innovation is short-lived (Fullan, 2005). The superhuman image that is used by some principals is not realistic and is not valuable in creating a collective vision. Again, stories from schools abound with charismatic leaders who are able to implement an innovation in a school only to have it die after the leader leaves or moves to another cause. As an example, an elementary school had one principal for fifteen years before he decided to retire. During his tenure at the school, the school had to establish a year-round schedule to accommodate rapid growth in the attendance area. After another elementary school was built to accommodate the increased numbers of students, the year-round school could have gone back to a traditional schedule. However, through the efforts of this longtime principal, he convinced the faculty and community that the year-round schedule was superior to student learning (although he had no solid evidence to prove it). The school continued with a modified year-round schedule when he was the principal, because he was its main supporter and cheerleader. The year-round schedule lasted only two years after he retired because the faculty and community no longer had someone to advocate for it.

Challenges of Vision Building

Hoyle (1995) described two challenges for principals in developing a school vision. First, many school leaders give up on the school's vision too soon. Too often school leaders cave in to the opposition. This kind of opposition might come from the external environment, such as community activists, or internally, such as a resistant, veteran teaching force. Principals hear horror stories from colleagues who fell from grace in their communities because of their resistance to some innovative ideas such as new mathematics or reading programs. Hoyle suggested that a practical way to keep the vision alive is to invite everyone to contribute to the visioning process. As a leader in the school and the community, you should constantly measure the pulse of the external and internal environments and be sure that constituents from both environments have opportunities to voice their opinions. Your challenge is to show enough respect to those who may resist your vision that they will in turn show enough respect for your opinions.

A second challenge that Hoyle (1995) suggested in transforming the vision into reality is the allocation of resources, especially money. "If the foundation to the vision is to be built, the money must be there somewhere" (p. 36). Hoyle's observations of various schools indicated that faculties and communities soon tired of the visioning process if their visions could not be implemented because of finances. Likewise, vision building requires time to plan and reflect. Vision-building teams become frustrated easily when they do not have time built into their schedules to accommodate the visioning process. Likewise, to be effective, most visions must be developed over time so that all members can reflect on the vision consider how it will work in the school. If, as the principal, you desire to transform a school's team vision into reality, then time and reflection are needed to facilitate careful planning and team building.

Some principals might complain that there is no need to change the school's vision. Perhaps they are right, but consider the number of businesses, for example, the U.S. automobile industry that held onto past success only to find that they have not kept up with the new trends and are on the brink of bankruptcy. Schools can be in similar situations. Often school people become blinded by their own perceived successes. As a strong leader committed to improving teaching and learning in your school, you will want to carefully analyze the school's vision and explore possible future developments with the faculty. Roosevelt Junior High School moved ahead with establishing a PLC in a middle school because the principal and the faculty realized that although things were going well at Roosevelt, there was always room for improvement. They wanted to offer the best learning possible for all of their students, not just the ones who were already successful.

Although developing a vision is critical, it is insufficient for making the vision a reality. Many school visions have never been fully implemented beyond the paper that they were written upon. In the next subsection, we discuss how you as the school leader need to communicate the vision to others so that it can be put into action.

Communicating the Vision

Communication is the process by which information and understanding are transmitted from a sender to a receiver. Feedback occurs when the receiver sends a message back to the sender that then enables the sender to determine if the message was interpreted correctly. Errors occur when background, attitudes, and knowledge act as filters and create noise. The processes of sending, receiving, providing feedback, and reducing noise underlie school leadership.

In order to be precise and to help others understand the vision, your first means of communicating is preparing a written vision statement. Written vision statements serve two important purposes. First, being able to write a vision statement on paper helps make commitment possible. Without a written statement, many participants might misinterpret or misunderstand the school's vision. Likewise, newcomers, who were not involved in the initial development of the vision, have a written version to read and understand. Second, an organization's ability to write down a vision is an indication of its commitment and understanding of the vision. Visions must be understood to be achieved.

Beyond writing a statement, visions need to be communicated by the actions of those in the school. The principal has a primary leadership role in expressing the school's vision. We suggest five ways that the principal communicates the vision:

1. Communicating the vision personally to faculty, staff, and community members,
2. Focusing attention on specific elements of the vision when appropriate,
3. Being trustworthy (i.e., say what you mean and mean what you say) and showing trust in others,
4. Using the vision in making decision and solving problems, and
5. Communicating the vision constantly to everyone involved.

As a final, but critical, thought, you must remember that the focus of any vision should always be on students and their learning. As Hord and Sommers (2008) emphasized, communicating the vision means that throughout the school and its community and across the school year, reminders will be communicated of what quality student achievement and successful student learning looks like. Only when you as the principal or assistant principal express the vision in your daily activities by what you say and do will you be able to influence others in the school to believe in and commit to the vision to improve student learning.

Using communication as a strategy also involves active listening. Active listening is necessary as a daily, ongoing part of a principal's communication. When principals and assistant principals do not listen, it sends a clear message that others in the school are not important, thus decreasing their commitment and motivation toward fulfilling the school's vision, which, in turn, affects the school's culture. The connection between personal satisfaction and being listened to applies to everyone in the school. Teachers want to voice opinions and goals, parents want to offer suggestions, and students want to express ideas. Snowden and Gorton (2001) offered an important suggestion for school administrators in listening. They maintained that many administrators' sources of information are limited either because of their position in the organizational hierarchy or because of other people's perception of their lack of availability or receptivity to communication. Although school administrators often proclaim an open-door policy, everyone may not perceive these administrators as open, especially those who disagree with the administrator's message. Consequently, an administrator's contacts may be restricted to only certain kinds of individuals bearing information that is regarded as nonthreatening. Snowden and Gorton suggested that school leaders must be careful to avoid receiving their information only from a select group of people who tend to see things in a similar way. School leaders in a PLC need diversity rather than similarity of opinion. They need to identify and secure ideas and opinions from those students, teachers, parents, and other professional or community members who may hold contrasting sets of values or objectives. It will only be through listening to various opinions that a vision becomes acceptable and collective effort can be implemented.

Dialogue is what you get when active listening spreads throughout the school. As suggested in Chapter 3, a learning community develops among teachers when they can openly speak with one another about their teaching practices and student learning. In a profession that has been shrouded in isolation, teacher and principal dialogue is a welcome and important step toward improving the instructional climate in schools.

As a principal, you also must communicate the school's vision with the people outside the school (external constituents). Again, instead of thinking of communication as a one-way process where principals sell the vision to other members of the school community, you should see it as a two-way process. Principals need to listen and be sensitive to the concerns of external constituents. A vision cannot be vibrant and dynamic if it only expresses the desires of the faculty and staff. As a principal or assistant principal in contemporary schools, it is imperative that you become involved in the community, be sensitive to the changes in the community, and be aware of the views that the external constituents have about what and how well schools are doing. In the opening vignette, Robert maintained open communication with teachers by inviting them to express their ideas at the end of every school year. Consequently, an open culture existed so that Louise talked freely to him about middle schools. His verbal response and nonverbal symbols acted as feedback to her to continue pursuing her idea. The entire school community felt similarly as the middle school concept was presented in a nonthreatening and open manner. Further, Robert facilitated leadership so that faculty members took on much of the leadership that was needed.

PRINCIPAL AS FACILITATOR OF LEADERSHIP IN OTHERS

Although principals are important, their mere presence does not automatically result in the leadership that is needed for school improvement efforts. Effective leadership cannot be centered around one person or one role. Leadership involves an entire organization of leaders and followers who often switch roles. As a principal or assistant principal, leadership will come not only from you but also from those around you, such as teachers, staff, students, and parents. This practice has been referred to as *distributive leadership*, meaning that the leadership does not rest with an individual but is distributed throughout the organization. It is important to understand that you, as the principal, do not become irrelevant by distributing leadership in a PLC (Hord & Sommers, 2008) but, indeed, you facilitate leadership in others, thereby increasing the school's leadership capacity.

Teacher Empowerment

A term used with expanding leadership is *empowerment*, which became a motto of educational reforms in the 1980s and 1990s and continues to be used as a means of getting others in an organization to become more involved in the management and leadership of the organization. Short and Greer (1997) identified two versions of empowerment. The first version draws on the labor-management tradition where power is conceived as a finite commodity within an organization. For example, in a school, teachers become empowered if the principal gives some power to them. School-based councils that control the school's budget would be an illustration of this version of power. However, a second version of empowerment is a process with a different view in which power becomes an infinite commodity that is available to everyone and continually produced by many in the organization. To expand the amount of power, the principal involves others in the basic decisions of the school and attends to the leadership influence provided by others. To illustrate this version of empowerment, Short and Greer used the statement, "The principal gains power by giving it away" (p. 13). Obviously, this version of empowerment is more closely associated with the kind of leadership a principal needs to help others become leaders. However, empowerment does not always come easily, and it usually initiates a learning process on the part of all involved. Learning how to empower and how to be empowered are important elements in leadership. In the opening vignette, Robert exemplified the principal's role in empowering others. He valued Louise's leadership, encouraged her ideas, expanded the number of individuals involved in the ideas, and maintained the focus on teaching and learning.

Certainly, the school above other organizations should develop leadership capacity among its members. Compared with other organizations, most notably in the private sector, the majority of the participants in school organizations are educated, ethical, and well-meaning individuals who generally think and act as professionals. As Short and Greer (1997) stated, "They have a wealth of insight into the nature of the learning process and are able to apply such understandings to the problems of the school" (p. 14). Facilitating leadership in others provides principals with the avenue to share these understandings and, in so doing, helps the school expand its resources for teaching and learning and, thereby, increase the learning capacity of the school.

In this section we discuss the principal's and assistant principal's role in facilitating leadership in others. We will begin by discussing the area of facilitating leadership in vision building, and then we will turn our attention to facilitating leadership through the tool of collaboration.

Facilitating Others in Vision Building

The principal as leader needs to attend to the two areas of process and content in facilitating a collective vision. Typically the content of vision is emphasized, giving the direction toward which the school is heading. Vision, however, also involves a process by which those in the school create the vision. Creating a vision "involves sharing ideas, clarifying and understanding the various points of view reflected in the community as well as the beliefs and assumptions underneath those points of view, negotiating differences and building a consensus" (Starratt, 1996, p. 50). The result of this process should be what Sergiovanni (2009) called bonding, in which those in the school community become committed to the vision. If no bonding occurs (i.e., no agreement is achieved on the direction the school should take), then the result is a vision that has no commitment and will more than likely die. Many schools and school districts have had experience with visions that have died when they became involved in strategic planning movements. These strategic plans usually had good intentions, but the faculty and principal's commitment often was missing in the process, and consequently, the vision soon died.

As we noted earlier in this chapter, the principal's personal vision may serve as a preliminary conception from which the collective vision is developed. Principals "may not possess the total content of the vision—no one does—but they should be willing to lay out a first attempt at articulating the content of a vision" (Starratt, 1996, p. 50). The principal's personal vision, or anyone's, must not become the final version. Preliminary visions may serve as guides to immediate action and places to begin a dialogue, but they should never serve as a sole direction for the future.

Teacher, Student, and Parent Roles in Vision Building. Other members of the school community, that is, teachers, staff members, parents, students, and community members, can play at least three roles in developing visionary leadership: source of vision, sustainer of vision, and critic of vision (Crow et al., 1996). As a source of vision, others actually might provide the image or picture of the future. "Often some of the best ideas for new directions float up from the depths of the organization, but only if they are sought and welcomed when they arrive" (Nanus, 1992, p. 38). Teachers play an important role in vision building because they are in the position to do so as they perform in the trenches. A principal should never ignore teachers' suggestions as to the direction of the school because they are so close to the work of teaching and learning. Fortunately for Roosevelt Junior High School, Robert paid attention to Louise's ideas for the school's direction. Likewise, parents and students also can play an important role because of their proximity to the learning process. Parents often can see the strengths and weaknesses of the school's instructional approach and should be encouraged to offer constructive comments. No principal in today's schools should ever ignore the constructive comments that parents can give regarding the school's instructional programs.

Teachers also play an important vision-building role as sustainers of the vision. Because teachers must be committed to the achievement of the vision, their role as sustainers of the collective vision is vital. Principal commitment is not enough to sustain a vision if teachers are not equally as committed. Their belief that a particular vision will work for the school at a particular time is critical to the vision process.

Teachers, students, and parents are also important as critics of visions. Teachers provide leadership by assessing the vision and suggesting ways that it can be redirected. From start to finish in vision building and implementing, principals need to listen carefully and sensitively to what others are saying about the significance and saliency of the school's vision. Listening to a respected teacher's criticism regarding the vision, often, will stave off serious criticism later and will help in building a stronger commitment to the vision.

Certainly, there are individuals who use their critic role in a negative rather than constructive way and thereby create toxic, dysfunctional cultures. This potential, however, is not a valid reason for silencing critics of the vision. In fact, as the principal values a critical perspective about the vision, he or she sends an important message to others that constructive criticism of the vision will make it better and more likely to be implemented.

FACILITATING TEACHERS IN VISION BUILDING   Earlier in this chapter, we identified Nanus' (1992) four roles in vision building. Just as principals and assistant principals take on those four roles, they also encourage teachers, students, and parents to be direction setters, change agents, spokespersons, and coaches. These roles are too critical and too large to be performed by one person in the school. Beyond these four roles, you need to acknowledge the powerful personal visions that teachers bring to the school.

Often these personal visions are overlooked as contributions to the school. Because they perform in the trenches, teachers have sensitivity to what works and does not work. Your role as a facilitator is to encourage teachers to develop personal visions and then to express those visions to others. Robert's example in the opening vignette suggests that his encouragement over a period of years allowed teachers to develop strong personal visions. Robert's conferences with individual teachers prompted their personal vision building and expression. Teachers came to expect that their personal visions counted for something and that they had an opportunity to express their ideas for a school vision. It is not atypical for many teachers to have had ideas about school vision only to have the ideas thwarted by the school's bureaucracy.

Facilitating Others in Collaboration

We established earlier that leadership should come from a variety of sources in the school community, thereby increasing and enriching the school's leadership capacity. It would be wonderful if all teachers were to develop into leaders. For this to occur, however, a greater emphasis on leadership development needs to take place. Although schools differ, many exist as isolated workplaces where teachers work mostly alone in their classrooms and interact with one another in faculty rooms. In these schools, teachers feel separated from one another and seldom engage in professional dialogue, reflection, or sharing about teaching practices and student learning. In other schools, teachers engage in professional dialogue with colleagues; share ideas, knowledge, and methods; and participate in decision making and problem solving around teaching and learning issues. We propose that in collaborative schools, collegiality is valued and reinforced, and leadership emerges. As a principal or assistant principal, you can facilitate leadership among others through a collaborative culture. Our discussion will focus on five aspects of facilitating a collaborative culture: deciding to collaborate, developing collaboration, developing collaborative teaming, mediating conflict, and understanding and solving problems that can arise in collaboration.

DECIDING TO COLLABORATE   In the current rhetoric of school reform, principals and assistant principals could come away with the view that collaboration is the panacea to cure all school ills. However, collaboration has its costs (Pounder, 1998), some of which we will address later in this chapter. Here, however, it is important to discuss when collaboration is appropriate for building PLCs and promoting success for all students. Based on their review of literature, Hoy and Miskel (2000) identified three tests for determining when to share decision making: relevance, expertise, and commitment. We suggest one other criterion for collaboration, time.

RELEVANCE   The test of relevance applied to teachers asks whether they have a personal stake in the decisions or the outcomes of the collaboration. For example, collaborating on decisions regarding resurfacing the parking lot is not likely to engender a great deal of enthusiasm for collaboration. Collaborating on student learning problems and finding solutions for those problems are areas on which teachers should be engaged in collaborating. A general rule would be that teachers are most engaged in collaborating with one another when the topics of discussion are dealing with decisions and problems that are embedded in their classrooms or school-level issues that directly affect their classroom practices. These types of collaborative endeavors are a major component of PLCs because it is through these activities that teachers improve their practice and students learn more at deeper levels.

EXPERTISE The test of expertise asks whether teachers have the expertise to collaborate on the issues at hand. For example, adoptions and innovations in foreign-language curricula would not necessarily include all teachers. However, the test of expertise must be applied carefully. A principal might decide that teachers do not have expertise in an area in which they have a personal stake, but the principal has a responsibility if the other tests apply to determine whether professional development to provide the expertise is warranted. We draw your attention back to the opening scenario in this chapter. Teachers at Roosevelt did not have expertise in PLCs or in middle schools, but through the efforts of the principal and the initial teacher team, teachers gained expertise. Frequently, principals must provide not only the expertise in some content issue, for example, a reading program, but also the expertise in the processes of collaboration itself. We will return to this role later in this chapter.

COMMITMENT The test of commitment asks if teachers are committed to the vision of the school such that their decisions will be in the best interests of the school. Again, this becomes a major judgment for a principal. If personal interests are likely to outweigh organizational ones, the principal might decide that collaboration in a particular area is not in the best interest of the school. However, this decision should be based on ample evidence from multiple sources to ensure that the lack of commitment exists and is not being used by the principal to avoid opposing views. Furthermore, the principal should help build commitment through providing professional development, creating an enriched culture, and being an advocate for student learning.

TIME Besides the three factors listed earlier, one other factor should also be considered in deciding if collaboration is appropriate to make a decision or solve a particular problem. You need to consider the time that is available before a decision needs to be made or a problem solved. If time is short, then collaboration probably is not the best decision-making approach. However, you must be sure that the decision needs to be made rapidly. Many decisions are made "off the cuff" when they could have been given more deliberation. Decisions that are made in crises, especially those that affect the safety of students, obviously require immediate action.

Collaboration is not a panacea, but when used sensitively and appropriately to enrich the learning community and enhance learning for all students, it is a powerful tool. If the decision is made not to collaborate due to time constraints, the principal should plan for future collaboration in which teachers are prepared to take on major leadership and decision-making roles.

Approaches to Collaborative Decision Making

Moving toward collaborative problem solving and decision making needs to be developed deliberately over time and in consideration of the school's culture. Moving too fast can produce disappointing and wrong decisions. As you consider developing collaboration, several approaches should be considered. Figure 7.1 shows seven kinds of decision-making approaches. We discuss each of the approaches here.

Seventh Approach: In this full-collaboration approach, the principal places trust in the team by enabling the team to find and determine the problem and collaborate as to the best decision. This approach can only be used with advanced collaborative teams.

Sixth Approach: The principal offers the problem to the team and then steps back and allows the team to collaborate.

Fifth Approach: The principal is part of the collaborative team and participates in problem identification and problem solution. The principal is an equal member on the team.

Fourth Approach: Principal shares the problem with the team and the team offers a recommended solution. The principal is part of the process and offers help with team collaboration. The principal accepts the recommended solution or helps the team come to a better solution.

Third Approach: This approach is often termed *advisory*. This first attempt as a decision-making team gives members the opportunity to recommend suggestions for decisions and solutions for problems.

Second Approach: The principal consults with individuals, gathers information, and decides the best solution to the problem.

First Approach: This approach involves unilateral decision making. The principal makes the decision without any input from others.

FIGURE 7.1   Decision-Making Approaches.

1. The first approach involves unilateral decision making. The principal can make the decision without input from others. In some emergency or urgent situations, this approach would be most appropriate. Obviously, the time factor is one of the determinants to use this unilateral approach.

2. The second approach is consulting. The principal consults with individuals, gathers the needed information, and decides based on the information received. This approach might be needed if teacher commitment and expertise is low or there is not enough time for teaming to occur.

3. The third approach is advisory. This is the first approach that involves a team. The principal seeks input and suggestions from the entire team, and the principal makes the decision, which may or may not reflect the team's suggestions. Because some teams are only beginning the collaborative process, advisory might be a necessary first step in the teaming process. However, this approach carries with it a warning. A principal who overuses advisory teams might find that advisory teams soon become discouraged and often quit the process.

4. With the fourth approach, the principal shares the problem with the team, and the team offers a recommended decision. The principal mentors the team in the collaborative process that leads to the decision. The committed team recognizes that it lacks total expertise and wants to learn the collaborative process. Of course, the important element in this approach is that the principal has the expertise to conduct the mentoring.

5. The fifth approach involves a collaborative team effort with the principal as an equal team member. Consensus is desirable for the final decision, but majority vote may be acceptable. The principal might offer some mentoring but mostly allows the team to collaborate and learn from the process. Mentoring might occur more after the decision has been made than during the collaborative process.

6. The sixth approach involves the principal offering the problem to the team (e.g., mediocre test scores) and then stepping back and allowing the team to collaborate and reach consensus or vote. The principal is now off the team and the team is more or less acting independently with the principal's full trust. Mentoring occurs after the decision has been made.

7. The seventh approach is placing trust in the team by enabling it to find and determine the problem and then collaborate as to the best decision. This approach shares the governance with the team, and the team actually makes authoritative decisions. Obviously, this approach to decision making works only with a team that has expertise and commitment, considers the issues as being relevant, and has time during the regular school day for teaming. The principal would offer mentoring only after the decision is made unless asked to do so before.

Collaborative Teaming

An important aspect of collaborative cultures and PLCs involves professionals working together on teams. The work of teams is not a simple matter. Teams can become complicated groups that lack focus and direction, and they sometimes become so powerful that they create a dark culture. Your responsibility as a principal is not only to create teams and encourage collaborative teaming but also to mentor good collaborative processes among team members. The research on teamwork by Maeroff (1993) suggested that teams need skills and knowledge in the following areas:

- group roles,
- stages of group development,
- leadership in small groups,
- effective communication,
- trust building,
- problem solving, planning, and decision making,
- effective ways to conduct meetings,
- conflict resolution, and
- group process evaluation.

Without developing team process skills, many teams with great intentions fail to reach conclusive results. Because many school leaders and teachers have had few successful opportunities to collaborate in team settings, it is important that development be offered. One of the authors was a team member in a school where several veteran teachers refused to commit time and energy to school teams because of some past team efforts. They had previously committed time to teams that ended in disagreement with no team consensus. It is hard to blame these teachers' reluctance in pursuing new team efforts when their experience had been so negative. In other situations, teams are given initial training, but ongoing professional development is frequently ignored. Research emphasizes that the professional development needs of teams are different at different stages in the teaming process (Crow & Pounder, 2000). As principal or assistant principal, you need to help these teachers with group process skill development that will alleviate some of the team problems.

It is not enough, however, just to have good processing skills as team members. Collaborative schools devote considerable time to working in teams on improving teaching and learning. For example, teams are used for establishing curriculum standards, course standards, instructional activities, summative assessments, formative assessments, and student learning concerns and problems. Teams also should be analyzing student data to improve teaching methods and student learning, and considering ways for teacher development.

The important element in PLCs centers around *what* are teams doing when they meet. Teams in a PLC do not just meet for administrative and managerial needs of the school such as organizing the next field trip or the high school prom. Teacher teams in a PLC meet to reflect and discuss teaching practices to improve learning for all students. They do this by analyzing student data from various kinds of assessments and then reflecting on how their teaching practices contribute to or hinder student learning. The bottom line for teacher teams in a PLC is always to improve student learning and increase student engagement.

Mediating Conflict

Because interaction among people is high in collaborative teams and with school improvement efforts, conflict is inevitable. As we emphasized in Chapter 2, newly defined work roles in contemporary schools are also likely to involve conflict because of greater interaction among roles. *Conflict* refers to the thwarting of goal attainment between and among people. Conflict is not necessarily a sign of weaknesses or destructiveness. However, too much conflict or conflict that is not resolved can interfere with an organization's effectiveness and eventually can cause toxicity in the culture. Although conflict occurs, it may go hidden in some schools for long periods of time. As a principal or assistant principal, one of your greatest responsibilities will be both to identify and to mediate conflict effectively.

Identifying the specific sources of conflict in school settings is a complex matter. Organizational variables, interpersonal issues, and personality characteristics influence the conflicts that are experienced by principals, teachers, and others in the school. For example, organizational variables such as leadership styles, communication norms, and decision-making practices can trigger conflict among the various stakeholders in the school. Interpersonal factors also contribute to conflict in various ways. Interpersonal conflict can originate from the different expectations that people have toward roles in the school, especially the expectations that teachers might have toward the principal's or assistant principal's role. Finally, personality characteristics such as highly aggressive and competitive behaviors can create conflict among individuals in groups. For example, you might have experienced being on a committee or team in which one particular person dominates the discussion. At times that person is so aggressive in getting his or her ideas out on the table that other good or even better ideas are suppressed. You might have left the meeting feeling frustrated and disenchanted with the process, especially if no one tried to alleviate the conflict.

Although various writers have speculated as to methods and models for conflict mediation, there does not seem to be one generally accepted method. In fact, leaders dealing with conflict successfully have used various strategies. It also might be necessary for some conflict to go to arbitration. A third party who is not emotionally involved with the situation may give insight into solving the conflict.

Friend and Cook (1992) identified five conflict-management strategies that vary along the dimensions of cooperativeness and assertiveness, two elements that were first introduced by Thomas (1976):

1. competitive,
2. avoidance,
3. accommodation,
4. compromise, and
5. collaboration.

Each conflict-management strategy has its strengths and weaknesses. Persons who use a competitive strategy are assertive and opt less to cooperate with others. Winning becomes the most important endeavor regardless of whether their ideas are good or bad. On the other hand, avoidance strategies of conflict management are characterized as uncooperative and unassertive. People who use these strategies tend to withdraw in the face of conflict, perceiving both their own goals and relationships as low in importance. In schools or in teams that comprise avoiders, conflict continues because no one is willing to address and resolve it. A person with an accommodating style believes that relationships are more important than personal goals and thus demonstrates cooperativeness but little assertiveness.

Two strategies use a balance of cooperativeness and assertiveness. A compromising style uses both cooperativeness and assertiveness but at a moderate degree. Compromisers sacrifice some of their own ideas and solutions and bargain with others to do the same. The outcome is usually a common ground where issues are addressed and a political solution is chosen so that both conflicting parties make some gains. The collaborative strategy tends to be both highly assertive and highly cooperative. These people may see the conflict as an opportunity to seek out better solutions and achieve a better outcome. Both sides of the conflict collaborate by using problem-solving approaches in an attempt to achieve the best solution to the conflict. The importance of this strategy is that task and relationship goals remain very important. A positive culture will remain while the conflict is solved.

None of these strategies are completely good or completely bad, but rather dependent on the situation. The use of any one particular strategy might be more effective in some situations than in others. For example, faced with an emergency, you may have to employ a competitive style and aggressively tell people to evacuate the building with little concern about how people feel about it. Another example could be that as an assistant principal you avoid a conflict with a teacher regarding his or her designated parking space because there are other more important and pressing needs at the time.

Problems with Collaboration

Fullan and Hargreaves (1996) argued that some kinds of collaboration are best avoided and some are a waste of time. They identified three forms of collaboration that could pose problems in the school:

1. balkanization,
2. comfortable collaboration, and
3. contrived collegiality.

BALKANIZATION In some schools, teachers associate more closely with some of their colleagues' in-group behaviors at the expense of the school as a whole. Fullan and Hargreaves (1996) identified these kinds of schools as having a balkanized teacher culture—"a culture made up of separate and sometimes competing groups, jockeying for position and supremacy like loosely connected, independent states" (p. 52). They also suggested that balkanized cultures are a familiar feature of junior and senior high schools because of the subject and department structures on which these schools are based. However, elementary schools also can feature balkanization, primarily when teachers separate into various divisions such as early grades or upper grades or within certain wings of the school building. Fullan and Hargreaves also cautioned that "innovation-oriented subgroups such as those found in team teaching or peer coaching" (p. 54) may develop into balkanized groups and actually impede the collaborative culture of the school as a whole.

COMFORTABLE COLLABORATION Collaborative teams can become bounded in the sense that they do not reach down into the principles or ethics of practice. In so doing, they become stuck with the more comfortable business of advice giving, trick trading, and material sharing. Fullan and Hargreaves (1996) suggested that such collaboration does not extend beyond particular units of work or subjects to the wider purpose of what is taught and how it is taught. "It is collaboration that focuses on the immediate, the short-term, and the practical to the exclusion of longer-term planning concerns" (pp. 55–56). As they suggested, collegiality should not stop at congeniality. It is too easy to avoid searching discussions and joint work that might expose disagreements and conflict. "This kind of collaboration is too cozy" (p. 57).

CONTRIVED COLLEGIALITY Because collaborative cultures do not evolve quickly, they can be unattractive to educators who want quick implementation. Collaborative teams are also unpredictable, which can be disconcerting to school principals. What collaborative teams develop may not correspond with the principal's preferred purposes or fit into current school board priorities. The unpredictability of collaborative teams can lead administrators toward forms of collegiality that they can control. These more controlled approaches toward collaboration are what Hargreaves and Dawe (1990) called *contrived collegiality*, which is characterized by a set of formal, specific bureaucratic procedures to increase the attention being given to various forms of collaboration, such as peer coaching, mentoring, and school-based management. These sorts of initiatives are administrative contrivances designed to get collegiality going in schools where little has existed before. They are meant to encourage greater association among teachers and to foster more sharing, learning, and improvement of skills and expertise. So where does the problem lie? Contrived collegiality is double-edged. Fullan and Hargreaves (1996) suggested that, at best, contrived collegiality could be a useful preliminary phase in setting up more enduring collaborative relationships among teachers. In fact, some contrivance is necessary in the establishment of virtually all collaborative cultures. Scheduling joint preparation times, releasing teachers to plan together, arranging teacher visits to other classrooms, and allowing a team of teachers to attend a workshop—all these situations can be contrived to create conditions for collaboration.

At its worst, however, contrived collegiality can be reduced to a quick and slick administrative substitute for collaborative teacher cultures. Colleagueships are imposed administratively. For example, a peer-coaching relationship that mandates teachers to work together on improving classroom instruction is an imposed collegiality. It may meet certain administrative ambitions but probably makes no lasting cultural changes. As Fullan and Hargreaves (1996) suggested, "Collaborative cultures do not mandate collegial support and partnership: they foster and facilitate it" (p. 59) and "over managing collegiality is something to avoid" (p. 60). When it is used in a facilitative, not a controlling, way, contrived collegiality can provide a starting point for collaborative cultures. However, a strong collaborative culture takes time.

Conclusion

In this chapter we identified the importance of the leadership role for the principal and assistant principal. After a discussion of what leadership is and does, we identified important areas on which you need to focus your energies: vision, communication, and collaboration. As in the other roles, we also discussed ways that principals and assistant principals facilitate others' leadership.

The opening vignette illustrated how a collaborative culture builds leadership and helps develop a learning environment in a school. As the principal, Robert was not the only leader in Roosevelt Junior High School. Many teachers were as committed as he and showed their commitment by their dedication to the school, their teaching, and the students. They were much more valuable in implementing a change such as the middle school concept because of their commitment.

In Chapter 8, we will discuss the important, and sometimes forgotten, role of principal as mentor. We will explore the ways that principals and assistant principals should be involved in improving teaching and learning in the direct role of mentoring.

Activities

SELF-REFLECTION ACTIVITIES

1. In the opening vignette, Louise commented that she was concerned about all students in the school and not just the high-achieving ones. How common is it for school leaders to be concerned about *all* students? In your experience, what have you seen done to improve the learning of all students, especially low-achieving students? What has your principal or other leaders done to improve learning for all students?
2. Talk to the custodian and secretary in your school. What are their perceptions of the instructional program in the school? How do they influence leadership in the school?
3. Reflect critically on your own leadership as a teacher. How would you characterize your style and behavior as a leader?
4. What is the vision of your current school? What is its mission? How do they differ?

PEER REFLECTION ACTIVITIES

1. With your colleagues, discuss principals with whom you have worked. Analyze their leadership in terms of the proportion of task versus person orientation. How well do these two orientations describe your principals' leadership?
2. Compare and contrast the vision and mission of your schools. To what degree is the mission or vision a collective one or only the principal's personal vision?
3. From your experiences, how do principals facilitate the leadership of parents and community members in their schools?

COURSE ACTIVITIES

1. Role-play and discuss a meeting between the principal at Roosevelt Junior High School in the opening vignette and a group of parents. What kinds of issues might parents raise regarding the middle school concept.
2. Discuss Rost's definition of leadership presented in this chapter and in Chapter 1. What are its strengths and weaknesses for defining school leadership?
3. Assign biographies of various well-known leaders, for example, Gandhi, Eleanor Roosevelt, Martin Luther King Jr., or Mother Teresa. In addition to discussing their traits, discuss what aspects of leadership are not included in the biographies.

Websites

North Central Regional Educational Laboratory (NCREL)—site on critical leadership issues, including additional research and resources
http://www.ncrel.org/sdrs/areas/le0cont.htm

Free Management Library—online resource for nonprofits and forprofits. Includes many online resources related to leadership (broad definition, could relate to business or education)
http://managementhelp.org/ldrship/ldrship.htm

E-lead: Leadership for Student Success, A Partnership of the Laboratory for Student Success and the Institute for Educational Leadership
http://www.e-lead.org/

Leadership Learning Community—online community with links to resources on leadership around specific issues and networking opportunities
http://www.leadershiplearning.org/

CHAPTER 8

The Principal as Mentor

Vignette

Felicia Martinez had been the assistant principal of I.S. 254, in a large metropolitan district, for the past two years. She and her principal, Latonya Jefferson, began their careers at the school at the same time. Both knew each other from the time Latonya had been assistant principal at the school where Felicia taught. When Felicia was selected as assistant principal, Latonya had made it clear that she wanted the assistant principal to be a partner in the leadership team and an instructional leader. Some bumpy roads had emerged during the past two years, especially in convincing the faculty that the assistant principal's role involved more than student management. Some of the teachers worried that if the assistant principal spent time on instruction she would not pay enough attention to the discipline problems they relied on her to solve. Additionally, Felicia's age was a factor of contention. Some teachers felt that, at twenty-six years old, Felicia did not have sufficient teaching experience to help them with curricular and instructional issues.

Last year, Felicia and Latonya worked with the faculty in developing a schoolwide mentoring program where volunteer veteran teachers and the two administrators were matched with new teachers. Since the school had experienced a large influx of new teachers because of several retirements and transfers to suburban schools, the program was definitely needed and most veteran teachers had cooperated in the plan by offering to be mentors. Felicia was matched with Gloria Ayres, a forty-five-year-old new teacher who had come to teaching after staying home until her children were in junior high school. Gloria had grown up in the school neighborhood and knew many of the parents.

Felicia and Gloria had met once to discuss the mentoring arrangement. They agreed to meet every two weeks to discuss any issues with which Gloria felt she needed help. Their first two meetings went fine, with Felicia mostly giving Gloria information about school procedures, for example, requisition forms, testing dates, and student fee procedures. After the second meeting, Felicia made a routine observation in Gloria's room. She expected to find some classroom management concerns, as she had found during the early weeks with other new teachers. What she found surprised her. Gloria's sixth grade classroom was extremely orderly and quiet. In fact, students made no sounds—no questions, no comments, no responses. Gloria did all the talking. As she watched she noticed that these new intermediate school students seemed afraid to make a sound. Gloria's style was extremely stern and teacher-directed. She made no attempt to engage the students in conversations and discussions. Students who did speak asked only for directions and expectations. The slightest misbehavior was dealt with immediately and severely.

At their third mentoring meeting, Felicia discussed her observation with Gloria and asked her about her teaching style. Gloria responded that she knew what adolescent students in an urban setting were like because she was a parent and that they needed strict discipline. She said other teachers also had told her to begin firm and then lighten up. She also maintained that many of these students came from homes with little parental supervision and that if these students were going to perform well on the state achievement tests, they would first have to be taught to respect their teachers and follow directions.

Felicia could tell that when they began to discuss Gloria's teaching style, Gloria became more guarded in her comments and seemed to dismiss Felicia's suggestions for creating an open environment for learning. Felicia had the distinct feeling that while Gloria appreciated Felicia's help on procedural matters, she was more suspicious of her help with matters of instruction and classroom management. Felicia felt the age difference and realized that the mentoring program was more complicated than she first imagined.

INTRODUCTION

The traditional model of school administration includes roles that differ from paternalistic guidance to autocratic direction to laissez-faire indifference. Some administrators attempt to support teachers and others by smothering them with guidance. This approach frequently creates dependency relationships in which the teacher, for example, is dependent on the administrator for resources, ideas, and support. Although this approach in the short run reduces the teacher's isolation and frustration, such paternalistic dependence reduces the teacher's long-term professional growth and learning. Autocratic direction may give the new teacher strategies to reduce survival anxiety, but it also decreases the teacher's opportunities for professional growth. The laissez-faire approach leaves the guidance of new and veteran teachers to chance, hoping that someone else will come along to mentor and support the teacher. These traditional approaches are ineffective because they ignore either the importance of professional growth or the way that learning occurs in new and veteran teachers in the context of professional learning communities.

Innovative school administrators—both principals and assistant principals—play a critical role for teachers and for school reform. This role does not involve telling teachers what to do or ignoring their needs but rather creating a professional learning community where mentoring is encouraged and supported. In addition, mentoring provides the innovative principal with a strategy for school improvement that involves creating the kind of learning community that we discussed in Chapters 3 and 5. In the vignette, Felicia's experience illustrates a more innovative conception of principals as mentors. It also, however, illustrates some of the difficulties inherent in this role conception. In this chapter, we discuss the research, theory, and practice of mentoring and identify how the principal's and assistant principal's roles can include a mentoring conception. Mentoring has received considerable attention in the current literature, but much of that literature assumes that principals have only an indirect role to play. We believe that principals and assistant principals have a direct and significant role in mentoring that deserves special attention, especially as a way to create a professional learning community that contributes to improving student learning in a complex and turbulent environment (Gross, 2006).

Our treatment of the principal's role as mentor begins with an introduction to the literature on mentoring, focusing on the expanding nature of mentoring; the roles, participants, content, and processes of mentoring; and the benefits and pitfalls of mentoring. In the second part of this chapter, we focus on the principal's direct role in mentoring new and veteran teachers and students. In the third part, we discuss how principals contribute to systemic mentoring by facilitating a professional learning community that encourages mentoring relationships to improve student learning.

INTRODUCTION TO MENTORING

In Homer's *Odyssey*, Odysseus requests a friend, named Mentor, to guide his son, Telemachus, while Odysseus is away on a twenty-year-long trip. Thus began the use of the word mentor to identify the process of guiding one person by another. Although the idea of mentoring has been around for years, more recently it has gained attention in the business and education literatures. Businesses have created formal mentoring programs to guide and support newcomers to facilitate their successful entry and performance. In education, mentoring has become a popular strategy for supporting the entry of new teachers. Frequently, educators assume that mentoring is always an effective strategy for inducting new teachers or the only induction strategy and thus ignore its pitfalls.

The Nature of Mentoring

In the traditional view, mentoring has been understood as an expert guiding a novice in what is typically a one-to-one relationship.

> A mentor acts as a coach, much like in athletics, advising and teaching the political nuts and bolts, giving feedback, and rehearsing strategies. He or she provides you with exposure, visibility, and sponsorship, helping to open doors to promotions and seeing that you get assignments that will get you noticed. And mentors take the blame for your mistakes, acting as protectors until you're established enough to shoulder criticism on your own. (McPartland, 1985, p. 8)

This traditional definition of mentoring assumes that the mentor has all the knowledge, skills, and attitudes needed by the new teacher and that the transfer of this knowledge is one-way communication from the mentor to the novice.

Some writers have expanded the understanding of both the nature and sphere of mentoring. Gehrke (1988), for example, argued that the traditional definition of mentoring focuses on the transfer of knowledge and sponsorship. Instead of the market economy view of mentoring, where knowledge and skills are exchanged, she proposed an understanding of mentoring, at its most personal level, as "gift giving." She also suggested that what is given is an awakening. The mentor as "door opener, information giver, supporter [is] no doubt important. . . . The greatest gift the mentor offers is a new and whole way of seeing things. . . . It is a way of thinking and living that is given" (p. 192). Gehrke's understanding of mentoring moves us beyond the concept of a principal as mentor simply giving the technical secrets of the teaching role to the new teacher to that of imparting a new way of conceiving the role of teacher. Such an awakening reduces the typical shortcoming of mentoring as perpetuating the status quo and opens up possibilities for learning and innovation in the community. However, as Felicia discovered in the opening vignette, moving beyond the technical procedural aspects to imparting a new way to conceive of teaching may not be accepted readily by the teacher.

CO-MENTORING MODEL   Literature on mentoring also involves expanding who mentors are and the nature of their relationship with protégés. Mullen and Cox (1997) and Mullen and Kealy (1999) proposed a co-mentoring model:

> The best way to teach a new skill is to create a collaborative whose members share a common purpose yet bring different abilities and levels of understanding to the group. Co-mentoring names a process of supportive assistance that is provided by several connected individuals who reconstruct traditional mentoring relationships in nonhierarchical ways. (Mullen & Kealy, 1999, pp. 38–39)

This approach highlights mentoring as an evolving relationship between mentors and protégés. Co-mentoring also is very relevant to a professional learning community where one goal is to support the learning of all individuals in the school. In this approach, mentoring becomes a collaborative effort, not a hierarchical one.

This change in the understanding of mentoring also suggests that individuals can have multiple mentors. Higgins and Kram (2001), leading researchers and theorists in the mentoring field, discussed the relationship constellation (or developmental network) in which mentoring exists. Individuals find support from a number of groups, including family, peers, superiors, and subordinates. As they develop, teachers' needs change, and the place where they find support to meet those needs is likely to change as well. Understanding the relationship constellation would enable organizations to "create avenues for employers to build such relationships through job design and various human resource management practices. Then as individuals feel unsupported or exposed to considerable stress, they could consider how their relationship constellations could be modified to provide critical developmental functions" (Kram, 1986, p. 173).

Mendez-Morse (2004), in her study of role models and mentors of Latina educational leaders, found that these women experienced an absence of the formal, traditional mentoring relationships, but mitigated the effect of this absence by using mentors from nonprofessional contexts of their lives, in particular their mothers. Furthermore, these women leaders "constructed a mentor from varied sources that collectively met their specific needs and priorities" (p. 561). Mendez-Morse's findings suggested that as a principal you will need to be aware and supportive of the dynamic process of creating mentoring relationships, in which new teachers may be using a variety of sources to construct mentoring that meets their unique needs.

EXPANDED NATURE OF MENTORING   The nature of mentoring that is reflected in recent literature is one that occurs with a variety of individuals, throughout life, and need not be unidirectional. This expanded nature of mentoring offers principals a more dynamic mentoring model that can enrich a professional learning community. Instead of being the parent figure, smothering the new teacher with directives on how to perform the job, the principal and assistant principal mentor and facilitate an environment that supports mentoring so that individuals at all career stages are mentors and are mentored. Such an understanding of mentoring has the possibility of creating communities for professional learning that are not dependency-based but are lifelong and systemic. Likewise, this expanded understanding offers the principal and assistant principal an effective strategy for supporting organizational learning that focuses on teaching and learning.

MENTORING AND COACHING   At this point, it is important to distinguish mentoring from another popular resource used in professional learning communities, namely, coaching. Although coaching can be a tool of mentoring, it is not the same as mentoring. Mertz (2004) distinguished mentoring from other supportive work relationships based on intent and involvement. Intent refers to three types of relationships: modeling, advising, and brokering. Involvement refers to the amount of time and effort required in the relationship. Coaching is closer to the modeling end of the intent continuum, whereas mentoring is closer to the brokering end. Also, mentoring requires greater involvement than coaching. Coaching, as in the example of using literacy coaches (Marsh et al., 2008), may be one of the tools you use and encourage others to use in their mentoring relationships. However, mentoring is more than coaching. "The heart of mentoring, however, goes beyond any specific form of direct assistance to the ongoing relationship of a mentor and beginner" (Glickman, Gordon, Ross-Gordon, 2009, p. 238).

Mentoring Roles and Functions

Odell (1990b) characterized the roles that mentors play as trusted guide teacher (Levinson et al., 1978), sponsor (Schein, 1978), challenger (Daloz, 1983), and confidant (Gehrke & Kay, 1984). Gardiner, Grogan, and Enomoto (2000) identified nine metaphors that describe the types of interactions mentors have with protégés:

- Boss or superior
- Advisor
- Teacher
- Guide
- Parent
- Spiritual or philosophical guru
- Gatekeeper
- Public role model
- Friend or peer

These metaphors suggest the wide variety of roles and relationships that are possible in mentoring. Some are more likely than others to occur in school settings and in principal-teacher relationships.

THREE FUNCTIONS OF MENTORING   Although these roles have different qualities, there are three functions that are included in these different roles: professional, psychosocial, and career. Career development functions refer to "those aspects of a relationship that enhance learning the ropes and preparing for advancement in an organization" (Kram, 1985, p. 161). Kram included in this category sponsorship, coaching, protection, exposure, and challenging work (p. 162). Psychosocial development functions refer to "those aspects of a relationship that enhance a sense of competence, clarity of identity, and effectiveness in a professional role" (pp. 161–162). These functions include role modeling, counseling acceptance and confirmation, and friendship.

Although Kram (1986) included both career development and professional development in the career development function category, we believe that career development in education is different from that in business and other occupations and should be separated from the more technical aspects of learning the role (Crow & Matthews, 1998). Thus we identify three roles that administrators as mentors play in schools. First, the professional development role of mentors refers to helping teachers learn the knowledge, skills, behaviors, and values inherent in their role, for example, how to motivate students whose view of school emphasizes failure. Second, the psychosocial development role of administrators as mentors focuses on personal and emotional well-being, as well as role expectation, conflict, and clarification, for example, how to balance personal and professional time demands. Finally, the career development function of mentors includes issues of career satisfaction, career awareness, and career advancement, for example, the types of instructional committee work that enrich the role and provide visibility.

PRIMARY AND SECONDARY MENTORS   As principal or assistant principal, you will not necessarily mentor individuals in the school in all three areas. Mentoring literature suggests two types of mentors: primary mentors and secondary mentors (Phillips-Jones, 1982). Primary mentors have characteristics such as altruism, unselfishness, and caring and are less common than secondary mentors. They also tend to play more of the three roles identified earlier. Secondary mentors play a more limited role and are likely to be part of an exchange relationship in which mentoring benefits both mentor and protégé. Principals and assistant principals may be primary or secondary mentors, or they may contribute to mentoring by facilitating the development of professional learning communities where others become the primary and secondary mentors.

Participants of Mentoring

In a traditional model of school administration, principals are the mentors, and teachers are the protégés. Or perhaps veteran teachers are the mentors, and new teachers are the protégés. The expanded notions of mentoring described earlier suggest a broader and more inclusive set of participants.

In the co-mentoring view (Mullen & Cox, 1997; Mullen & Kealy, 1999), mentors are likely to be a diverse group who play different roles in the professional learning community. Principals and assistant principals, such as Felicia in the opening vignette, of course, should be mentors. But they also can be mentored. As a new principal or a principal new to a particular school, you may participate in a mentoring relationship with veteran teachers or staff members who help you learn the role and discover how to fit into the organizational culture and context.

Teachers, both new and veteran, can and should act as mentors and protégés. Although it might seem unusual to think of a new, barely surviving teacher as a mentor, this individual does not come to the school with a blank slate. New teachers come with skills, knowledge, insights, and beliefs that can be beneficial to the learning environment of a school. Although veteran teachers are frequently seen as mentors, they also need the professional, psychosocial, and career support that mentoring can provide.

In addition to experience and position, gender and race are relevant considerations in mentoring. In both business and education, research has demonstrated the tendency for men to be more likely to have mentors than women (Rowe, 1981; Nicholson, 1996). Although this may be changing, it is extremely important for principals and assistant principals to recognize that both men and women need mentoring and are potential mentors and to facilitate a school environment in which mentoring is a resource for all. Gardiner and colleagues (2000) found that race was a factor in the effectiveness of the mentoring process and selection. Thomas (2001) identified several inherent difficulties in mentoring across race, including difficulty in forming, developing, and maturing relationships, negative stereotypes, skepticism about intimacy, and others. However, there can be benefits to both mentors and teachers. In addition to broadening experiences and perspectives, the African women protégés in Gardiner and colleagues' (2000) study "argued that their white mentors provided crucial access to the system and insights to assist their rise as educational administrators" (p. 145). Lomotey (1993) and others found that African American principals have a strong commitment to the local school neighborhood and community, which could be a needed aspect of mentoring for white teachers without experience in these communities.

In a school environment where all individuals—new and veteran, teacher and administrator—are seen as both mentors and mentored, collegiality and innovation are more likely. This expanded understanding makes mentoring a significant and effective strategy for creating professional learning communities.

Content of Mentoring

The content of mentoring is reflected in the three functions we identified earlier: professional, psychosocial, and career development. Mentoring in the professional development area includes knowledge, skills, and values. For example, new teachers need mentoring in such areas as knowledge of learner differences, school procedures, and curriculum sequencing. They also need mentoring in such skill areas as classroom management, instructional decisions, and student motivation. In the opening vignette, Felicia's mentoring of Gloria reflects a focus on professional development. However, mentoring also involves helping new teachers develop values and professional identities that are central to the school's vision, such as innovation and collaboration. For veteran teachers, one of the most important components of mentoring content is helping these teachers develop new ways to conceive of their roles (Gehrke, 1988).

Personal and professional roles overlap and individuals' self-esteem affects their professional abilities. Kohn and Schooler's (1978) and Schooler's (1989) research on the reciprocal relationship between intellectual flexibility and job complexity demonstrated that personal characteristics interact with job and role characteristics. In addition, the psychological and social qualities of teaching and other roles in the school demand attention to psychosocial development. Role conflict and role ambiguity are common challenges for teachers in a knowledge society. For example, urban teachers find themselves in a conflict between their role as advocates for children in poverty and agents of the school and district where accountability mandates emphasize test scores. These issues have psychosocial implications for mentoring.

The career development function of mentoring includes such content as networking, career awareness, and procedures for advancement. Obviously, career mentoring will vary depending on the needs and career stage of the teacher. Principals frequently view the teacher's career within the confines of a classroom or even the school. However, career development requires expanding this notion to recognize the teacher as a professional whose growth includes awareness of career opportunities and networking possibilities.

Another view of the content of mentoring is in terms of two types of learning: technical and cultural (Greenfield, 1985b). Technical aspects include learning "how things are done," that is, the instrumental knowledge and skills necessary to perform the job. Cultural aspects include learning "how things are done around here," that is, the expressive norms, values, and beliefs of a school culture. (Crow & Matthews, 1998, p. 13)

Learning "how things are done" without learning "how they are done around here" can be problematic for new faculty members and ineffective for instructional improvement in a professional learning community. For example, new teachers who come from different racial, ethnic, cultural, and geographic areas may experience different norms regarding what is considered appropriate disciplinary methods and instructional strategies. Thus, mentoring must include both technical and cultural learning.

Processes of Mentoring

McIntyre and Hagger (1996), in their research on mentoring in British schools, suggested three types of processes involved in mentoring: personal relationship, active guidance, and systemic mentoring.

The first and most basic level of mentoring is a personal relationship "where a relative novice is supported by a more experienced peer in coming to terms with a new role" (p. 147). The second process is "active guidance, teaching, and challenging of the protégé by the mentor, who accordingly needs to claim some expertise, wisdom and authority" (p. 147). The final process is more organizational and involves "management and implementation of a planned curriculum tailored, of course, to the needs of the individual, and including collaboration with other contributors in one's own and other institutions" (p.147). Whether or not you agree with these authors' view of the nature of mentoring, the three processes of relationship-building, active guidance, and provision of systemic resources are common to most formal mentoring arrangements.

The personal relationship and active guidance are fundamental to the process of mentoring in schools. Dembele (1996) argued that intentionality is a critical component of what mentors do. He referred to the mentor as an "educational companion" who is constantly asking what the teacher needs in this context at this time to meet these demands. The specific content of mentoring, whether it be professional, psychosocial, or career development, must be viewed with the intention of how it will help meet the needs of this teacher within a learning and reforming context.

The third process identified by McIntyre and Hagger (1996) ascribed an organizational or systemic quality to mentoring. Instead of understanding the processes of mentoring strictly as a one-on-one interaction, mentoring should be seen systemically. Whether one refers to this as "circles and chains of relationships" (Mullen & Cox, 1997; Mullen & Kealy, 1999), "relationship constellations" (Kram, 1986), or "development networks" (Higgins & Kram, 2001), mentoring processes take on a more communal spirit. Principals and assistant principals play a significant role in facilitating a professional learning community that supports these mentoring processes and encourages the use of mentoring to improve teaching and learning for all.

BENEFITS AND PITFALLS OF MENTORING

Principals who are considering mentoring as an instructional improvement strategy should recognize that it has both benefits and pitfalls. In this section we will examine the benefits for protégés, mentors, and others, as well as the pitfalls of mentoring.

Benefits of Mentoring

Mentoring has advantages for both new teachers and mentors. Hansford and Ehrich (2006), in their meta-analysis of 159 studies of mentoring in education, identified four major positive outcomes for new teachers: support and empathy, assistance in classroom teaching, contact with others and discussion, and feedback via positive reinforcement or constructive criticism.

Daresh and Playko (1993) found that mentoring also helps renew the enthusiasm of the mentor. Megginson and Clutterbuck (1995) suggested that mentoring can provide new insights to veterans. Mentors also can benefit by becoming more reflective and critical of their own intuitive processes and by developing networks for ideas and opportunities for promotion. The mentoring relationship can also develop into long-lasting and meaningful friendships. Some mentors find that mentoring allows them to regain the satisfaction they felt in becoming a teacher (Crow & Matthews, 1998). An additional benefit of mentoring lies in its role in fostering leadership development for the mentor teachers (Ganser, Marchione, & Fleischmann, 1999).

Although mentoring has obvious benefits for individual teachers—both novices and mentors—the primary reason for mentoring in schools is to improve teaching and student learning. In Hansford and Ehrich's (2006) meta-analysis, they found studies that demonstrated the positive effect of mentoring on student grades, attendance, and behavior. Daresh and Playko (1993) argued that mentoring could energize school leaders and encourage a community of learning within the school. Mentoring can contribute to a school culture that emphasizes collegiality and innovation, features found in effective schools (Fullan, 1999; Little, 1982) and professional learning communities.

Pitfalls of Mentoring

Mentoring has potential pitfalls to which you, as the principal, must be sensitive. Mentoring can simply perpetuate the status quo and discourage innovation (Crow & Matthews, 1998; Hart, 1991, 1993). Hay (1995) noted that mentoring could encourage cloning, where mentors attempt to replicate themselves in the conduct of new teachers.

Sometimes mentors have personal agendas that are dysfunctional for the teacher (Muse, Wasden, & Thomas, 1988). For example, mentors may use the honor of being a mentor to gain visibility for themselves or may create a dependency relationship in which the newcomer is forced to rely on the mentor for answers (Daresh & Playko, 1993). Moreover, a major pitfall that principals and assistant principals must acknowledge and avoid is the potential for using mentoring in a power-abusive way. Manipulating and coercing teachers to support the principal's agenda is a dangerous and unethical use of mentoring. For example, Felicia, in the opening vignette, needs to be sensitive to Gloria's potential feeling of being coerced into changing her classroom management philosophy.

Mentoring also runs the risk of restricting decision making, classroom management, or problem-solving perspectives. In so doing, new teachers and administrators may come to believe that there is only one way to establish discipline, one type of instructional approach, or one way to work with parents. This, obviously, does not support or enrich the inquiry of a professional learning community.

Hansford and Ehrich (2006) found two major problematic outcomes from the perspectives of both mentors and new teachers. These were lack of time available from both mentors and teachers and mismatches related to professional expertise and/or personality. These two problems are critical for you as a principal to attend to in overcoming the pitfalls of mentoring. Providing sufficient time for mentors and new teachers to meet and carefully matching them will go a long way in making mentoring effective for both mentors and new teachers.

As a principal or assistant principal using mentoring as a reform strategy and as a way to facilitate a professional learning community, you must be aware not only of the benefits but also of the pitfalls. Such awareness permits you and the community of learners in the school to create an environment that diminishes the restrictive, dysfunctional, and conservative elements of mentoring and increases the expanding, innovative, and functional benefits of mentoring.

Having this understanding of mentoring, we now turn to how principals and assistant principals can include mentoring as a reform strategy to improve teaching and learning. This section discusses the principal's direct involvement as a mentor and as a facilitator of mentoring in a school-wide professional learning community. The principal's role in mentoring and facilitating mentoring focuses on three categories: new teachers, veteran teachers, and students.

THE PRINCIPAL'S ROLE IN MENTORING

Mentoring New Teachers

The support and development of a new teacher are highly moral acts of leadership that every administrator must take seriously (Tillman, 2005). The principal's role in a beginning teacher's life and career is a substantial responsibility. Although hiring and placement of new teachers are extremely important, the leadership role in supporting and developing new teachers is even more important, especially for retaining them (Guarino, Santibanez, & Daley, 2006). Unfortunately, this responsibility is too often neglected or abdicated by principals. Susan Moore Johnson (2004) found in her study of new teachers that most newcomers felt their principals failed to meet their expectations for support. In fact, "a surprising number were, in these teachers' views, ineffective, demoralizing, or even destructive" (p. 99). In the same study, those teachers who left the profession identified several factors that influenced their decision to leave, including "principals who were arbitrary, abusive, or neglectful, and they spoke with disappointment about the isolation and lack of support they experienced" (p. 113). Marvel and colleagues (2006) found that 37 percent of public school teachers and 27 percent of private school teachers identified dissatisfaction with support from administrators at their previous school as a very important or extremely important reason for moving to a new school.

The prevailing thought concerning new teachers is that if they come from a reputable teacher education program, they have the needed skills and behaviors for teaching. In reality, new teachers do not emerge from their college or university preparation as fully developed professionals. They vary greatly in the skills and life experiences that they bring to the classroom. Newly prepared teachers need administrative support and help with the types of assignments, the nature of the school's norms and values, and their development in terms of making the transition from novice to experienced professional. Mentoring needs to be seen as part of a larger induction process for new teachers (Gross, 2006). Thus, although mentoring is not the only responsibility you will have for new teacher induction, it is a critical one. Such support and development fall heavily on principals, who must be both mentors themselves and facilitators of mentoring by others.

The principal's and assistant principal's roles in mentoring new teachers are far more complex than when most administrators were mentored when they were beginning teachers. Because most administrators began teaching with limited mentoring from their administrators, they often do not know exactly what mentoring is or how to mentor or they simply abdicate the role of mentoring to others. Traditional mentoring programs often relegate the principal to organizing the program and ignore responsibility for directly mentoring teachers.

Although new teachers may feel more comfortable with peer mentors than with their administrators, principals cannot relinquish this important role. Peer mentor programs are an important part of the new teacher's induction, but principals should be directly and personally involved in all aspects of the induction and mentoring process—much more than just assigning a good peer mentor to coach and assist a new teacher. In the beginning, newcomers seek feedback and observe both supervisors and experienced peers. As they progress in their jobs, they are more likely to seek feedback from supervisors, since they understand that supervisors control most organizational rewards (Callister, Kramer, & Turban, 1999). In the following subsections, we discuss the process and content of the principal's role in mentoring and facilitating mentoring for new teachers in the three areas of professional development, psychosocial development, and career development.

Mentoring New Teachers in Professional Development

As a new teacher, one of the authors remembers the first time he turned his lesson plans in to the principal, a weekly task asked of all new teachers. No instructions or lesson designs were added to the directive other than to have the lesson plan book into the principal's office before leaving on Friday afternoons. He was taught in college to have a lesson plan that included objectives, anticipatory sets, learning activities, and student assessment. He began working on the lesson plans for each of his six classes late on Friday afternoon. Well into the evening, he was still not finished. Furthermore, he could not figure out how to write his whole lesson plan outline into the small squares of the plan book that was to be turned in. Frustrated and tired, he finally stapled his completed lesson plans to the plan book and put them in the principal's box. The next Monday morning he received his lesson plans back with an attached note from the principal that simply stated, "These plans are very complete, but all I am interested in is what you are doing in each of your classes and when you are doing it. Please abbreviate and turn back into me."

More frustrated than ever, he finally went to his department chair and asked for help. She kindly explained what the principal expected and what he needed to do. It became obvious that the detailed lesson plans he had learned in his college class were not an expected norm in this school. Although he continued to put considerable time into lesson planning, the Friday afternoon plan book exercise was a lot simpler and quicker after that first week's experience.

Many new teachers have similar experiences that can be frustrating, time-consuming, and even embarrassing. Although principals and peer mentors cannot be expected to mentor new teachers in every aspect of their job, they need to be aware of the needs and anxieties of beginning teachers and of their professional development. We identify two goals of mentoring new teachers in professional development. The first goal is to improve performance in all aspects of teaching, including the classroom environment, instructional practices, planning and preparation, student assessment, and professional responsibilities. The objective with this goal is, of course, to improve student learning. The second goal in mentoring new teachers in professional development is to transmit the culture of the district, school, and community. Both are critical for integrating new teachers into a professional learning community. Too often, beginning teachers are not aware of the cultural aspects of the school and the district. New teachers rarely learn the history, lore, or values of a particular school or district. If anything, they are oriented to policies, procedures, and plan books rather than to philosophy and pedagogy. Typically, a new teacher learns the ropes in isolation through trial and error. As discussed earlier in this chapter, cultural aspects include learning "how things are done around here, that is, the expressive norms, values, and beliefs of a particular school culture" (Crow & Matthews, 1998, p. 13).

Mentoring new teachers in professional development involves at least three roles for you to play: change agent, listener, and questioner (Marquardt & Loan, 2006). Mentoring is ultimately about enabling new teachers to support the learning of all students. To accomplish this, new teachers need a mentor who is an insightful, open-minded, and creative change agent committed to the learning of all students. As a mentor, you will need to have expert listening skills that enable you to sensitively understand the developmental and learning needs of new teachers, including their anxieties and weaknesses as well as strengths. Finally, as a mentor in a professional learning community, you must be able to ask insightful, even challenging, questions that encourage dialogue, exploration, and change focused on student learning. Tillman (2005) found in a case study of the mentoring of a first-year, African-American teacher that the principal used mentoring in three ways: "as a means for enhancing professional and personal competence, as a means of transmitting the culture of the educational environment, and as a catalyst for transformational leadership." (p. 609). Tillman's themes provide a critical and substantive mentoring role for the principal in a professional learning community and remind principals of the importance of this role, especially for teachers of color.

CONTENT Compared with other professional organizations, the importance of bringing new people into valued practices of a school is too often left to chance. Consequently, teachers often fumble their way through their first years. As Susan Moore Johnson (2004) found, many teachers, including those that leave teaching, find the school context isolating. New teachers are not drawn into a shared system of meaning. Whatever meaning they construct is often done alone and with students in an individual classroom. New teachers bring their previous experience into this process of constructing meaning. In the vignette at the beginning of this chapter, Gloria's parenting experience influenced her perception of how early adolescents should behave and how she should respond to them. Glickman (2009) contended, "Teaching has been a career in which the greatest challenge and most difficult responsibilities are faced by those with the least experience—a strange state of affairs indeed" (p. 20).

In most professions, the challenge of the job increases over time as one acquires experience and expertise. In teaching, we have had it reversed. Typically, the most challenging situation a teacher experienced was in his or her first year" (p. vii). This process of inverse beginner responsibilities is expanded in Glickman's (1985) work, "The Supervisor's Challenge":

> Administrators often place the most difficult and lowest achieving students with the new teacher. . . . The message to beginning teachers is, "Welcome to teaching. Let's see if you can make it." . . . If new teachers do make it, they pass their initiation rites onto the next group of beginners. (pp. 38–39)

Usually, the problems about which new teachers complain and the discouragement that they express have little to do with their command of the subjects they teach. Most of them have been successful in their college course work and their teacher training experiences, so they are more than ready to handle the subject matter requirements of the job. However, all this knowledge is of little use if new teachers have not yet learned how to establish instructional techniques for their classrooms.

Although the problems confronted by new teachers, for example, student behavior and learner differences, may be similar to those problems of teachers twenty years ago, new teachers today confront a level of uncertainty created by a knowledge society with increased diversity and complexity. This uncertainty is especially evident for new teachers working in urban schools, where poverty, demographic differences, and other student and school characteristics are more pronounced. The new teachers in Johnson's (2004) study identified four types of uncertainty: what to expect from students, student engagement and discipline, student skills and preparedness, and the limits of teacher responsibility (pp. 73–78). In addition, these new teachers had concerns that dealt with factors related to how the school was organized for learning. These included the principal's influence, stability/instability among administrators, positive personal relationship with the principal, instructional leadership, appropriate teaching assignments, sufficient supplies and equipment, a comprehensive and flexible school infrastructure, using teacher time well, establishing schoolwide standards for student behavior, providing coordinated student support services, and building bridges with parents (pp. 98–112).

Beginning teachers have substantial needs in understanding important aspects of pedagogy, relationships, and school culture. School leaders cannot assume that these aspects should be left for new teachers to learn as they go. On the other hand, the principal and assistant principal's responsibility also extends to how this content is best given to the new teacher.

PROCESS   Anne Sullivan mentored Helen Keller in important content areas such as communication skills, but it was through Anne Sullivan's process of mentoring that Helen Keller became a nationally recognized spokesperson for those with disabilities. Likewise, famous artists, musicians, writers, athletes, and performers have learned certain important skills, but it is through mentoring and coaching that they learned to excel. Even Olympic champions, who can outperform their own coaches, have a constant mentor who guides, directs, and motivates them. Given the importance of teaching, it is only logical that teachers also need mentoring and coaching in their professional development—especially from their leaders.

Your mentoring role with new teachers will occur in several stages: preparation, negotiation, enabling, and closure (Zachary, 2000). During preparation, you as a mentor will assess your own commitment to the mentoring relationship, your own strengths as well as the new teacher's strengths and areas to work on. Essentially you and the teacher are assessing the "viability of the prospective relationship" (Marquardt & Loan, 2006, p. 63). During the negotiation stage, you and the new teacher establish the ground rules—goals, content, and processes of the relationship. Marquardt and Loan also suggest that issues such as confidentiality, boundaries, and limits should be addressed at this stage. The enabling stage is the actual implementation of the mentoring. A variety of processes occur at this stage, but ultimately feedback and reflection are the most essential processes for improvement.

Remember that a few weeks or months earlier, the new teachers were probably students in college, fulfilling roles quite different from the ones they now fulfill. Although new teachers do not come to their first year without any knowledge or expertise, mentors, especially early in the beginning teacher's career, may have to tell the new teacher what things need to be done, how those things are done, and how those things are done in a particular school. Caution should be given, however, in that the learning style of most adults does not fit well with being told what to do, especially in a culture that encourages learning by doing. When information giving is necessary, a show-and-tell approach is usually more beneficial.

Tomlinson (1995) recommended that the mentor consider suggesting specific possibilities to the new teacher. Beyond directly telling the new teacher how to do something, a principal may additionally offer suggestions. For example, the principal may inform the new teacher about reporting student progress to parents and then suggest various approaches to communicating with parents that have been effective with parents in that particular community. The principal and the new teacher can later discuss the approaches and reflect on what worked best.

An important aspect of a teacher's induction is solving and resolving problems and conflicts. Tomlinson (1995) suggested that when mentors perceive problems in some aspect of a new teacher's work or teaching style, they should "alert, explain, and challenge" (p. 187) the new teacher. The mentor alerts the teacher to the perceived problem, explains the problem, and then challenges the teacher to try new approaches. Likewise, a principal coaches new teachers to handle potentially damaging situations and conflicts that may occur in the future. Together, the principal and teacher consider problems that may occur and reflect on possible ways for the new teacher to either solve the problem or seek help to solve the problem.

At times, the principal may protect the new teacher from certain situations because the newcomer may not yet have the necessary skills. An example may be the principal who shields the beginning teacher in responding to an angry and irrational parent. Shielding novices may be essential, but Kram (1985) warned that a mentor's decision to intervene and to provide protection is critical in that it enhances or interferes with the new teacher's learning experience. Although a beginning teacher can learn a great deal from problematic situations, certain incidents can be devastating to a beginner's morale and may even interfere with future job security and career advancement. Likewise, a new teacher may need to experience problematic situations to gain insightful solutions for future encounters. Herein lies an important decision for the principal: to shield and protect the beginner or to allow the natural course of events to unfold. In either situation, principals need to be close at hand, mentoring and coaching the new teacher so that problem-solving skills are learned.

Reflective Mentoring

One method for helping new teachers become better problem solvers and decision makers is using the process of reflective mentoring. Reflective mentoring is a method in which the mentor guides the protégé through a mindful analysis of present, past, and future decision making and problem solving. Schön (1983) identified this process as mentoring "in-action, on-action, and for-action." Because teaching is a matter of decision making, reflective mentoring is a method of improving decision making. Mentors facilitate reflection by conferencing with the teacher in an active, open-minded exploration of the teacher's perspectives.

CONFERENCING Conferencing is an important reflective mentoring activity. Sitting with the new teacher in a conference, the principal may ask about certain aspects of the teacher's instructional approach, discipline methods, or pedagogical philosophies. The post-observation conference is one type of conference between the principal and the teacher (discussed in Chapter 9). However, conferences with new teachers should not be limited to formal conferences following a classroom observation. Establishing both formal and informal times for conferencing can bring rewarding, and sometimes

Professional Dilemma 8.1

Should the principal inform the new teacher about all parental criticism? Parents will often call the principal to complain about a new teacher's approach to instruction and discipline. Should a principal relay all complaints to the new teacher, or should certain complaints be put aside until the new teacher is better adjusted to teaching and the school culture? Likewise, should criticism that is not constructive or helpful ever be shared with teachers?

surprising, results. As an illustration, Ava, an assistant principal, was informally meeting with Bryan, a young, new teacher, reflecting on his first days in the school. It became apparent to Ava that Bryan did not know that she was the assistant principal. Although the two had been introduced and had been together at the orientation, Bryan was over-whelmed with meeting so many people that he had confused Ava with another teacher. When Bryan realized who Ava was, he was surprised that she had come by his class-room to talk with him regarding his students. Ava created a mentoring moment by her availability to visit Bryan and engage in an informal conference. Consequently, they were able to reflect on other issues regarding Bryan's assimilation into the school.

Reflective mentoring does not just occur. The following guidelines should help you to make the reflective conference more effective:

1. *Engage in active listening.*   Use good verbal and nonverbal cues that show good listening, such as leaning forward, making eye contact, and paraphrasing.
2. *Refrain from judgment and offering too much advice.*   Allow the new teacher to reflect on options rather than simply suggesting your own opinions.
3. *Ask insightful questions.*   Consider the circumstances and then frame questions around those conditions. These circumstances may change in another situation or setting. Ask the teacher to consider those other situations.
4. *Brainstorm alternative approaches.*   (Crow & Matthews, 1998, pp. 63–64)

Reflective mentoring also helps to avoid the potential mentoring pitfall of restrict-ing perspectives. By asking the new teacher insightful questions that help him or her to understand what happened in the classroom, the mentoring helps broaden the alterna-tive approaches that new teachers are able to consider.

STORIES   Part of the adventure in a new setting is listening to stories from the past. Stories play a significant role in integrating a newcomer into a professional learning community. They are useful tools for mentors to use to share important events, rites, and legends. However, to be most effective, storytelling should be combined with reflection. Leaving the new teacher with the story without reflection can lead to misun-derstanding and confusion. Stories provide an excellent means for engaging in a reflec-tive conference on the meaning of roles, norms, beliefs, values, and basic assumptions in the school culture.

Helping new teachers develop professionally involves planning, commitment, and time. Although socializing new teachers involves many methods, mentoring is one method that cannot be replaced adequately by any other process. Mentoring new teachers involves improving the beginning teacher's performance and understanding roles in all aspects of the school, including the school and classroom environment, instructional practices, planning and preparation, and professional responsibilities. The objectives are always to increase student learning and success in school and to increase teacher professional learning.

CLOSURE   The final stage of the mentoring process, according to Zachary (2000), is clo-sure, which is often neglected. Especially in formal mentoring relationships, closure should be planned. Successes need to be celebrated and benefits to both parties need to be acknowledged. A more informal relationship may be continued, but this needs to be more explicit for both mentor and new teacher.

Mentoring New Teachers in Psychosocial Development

Most aspiring principals have either taught or been associated with teaching and can identify easily with the feelings of loneliness, frustration, fear, and bewilderment that new teachers face. Several researchers have suggested that a lack of self-esteem is strongly related to burnout, which has a direct causal relationship with the teacher attrition rate. Hargreaves (2003) reminds us that teaching is not only a cognitive practice but "always an emotional practice of engagement with learning, relationships with students and adults, and attachment to the purposes and work that teaching achieves" (p. 117). He and his colleagues, in their study of U.S. and Canadian secondary teachers, identified much evidence for the emotional side of teaching, including health consequences, stress, loss of purpose, loss of job and passion, and alienation.

New teachers bring with them the developmental needs that any adult has. Frequently, these needs affect the resources that new teachers have available in responding to the self-esteem and confidence issues in the early months of teaching. In Chapter 4 we identified the important adult development considerations that principals and assistant principals must understand in their roles as learner and facilitator of learning. Nowhere is this understanding more important than in mentoring new teachers.

The mentoring goal in psychosocial development involves offering assistance, support, and perhaps counseling for new teachers to enable them to understand their role in the district, in the school, and in balancing their private and professional lives. Brighton (1999) highlighted the need for psychosocial development when he reported that a gap emerges between new teachers' expectations and the realities of the job.

Novice teachers are optimists, certain that they can change the world and the children in their charge. Many young people enter the field of education for the same reasons that others join the Peace Corps or other service organizations. New teachers in urban schools especially feel the dissonance between expectations and realities. They see their mission as shaping the lives and minds of children. Once these idealistic teachers enter their classrooms, they often are discouraged that the work is so challenging, the children so needy, and the expectations so high. New teachers do not leave because of the difficulty but feel disheartened that the reality is so different from their expectations (Brighton, 1999). Mentoring provides a resource for helping new teachers maintain the passion, commitment, and enthusiasm for student learning and well-being while recognizing and responding to the realities of the job. Principals in urban schools must acknowledge the dissonance these teachers feel and pay special attention to their psychosocial needs.

CONTENT. The preservice training experience for new teachers does not seem to contain many elements of psychosocial development. Although most new teachers have had some type of student teaching practicum, these experiences vary greatly from one institution to another. As Brighton (1999) reported, student teaching experience is sometimes misleading because the cooperating teacher and the student teacher share job responsibilities, which do not usually occur in real teaching situations. Additionally, the student teaching experience typically begins after the cooperating teacher has established classroom climate, rapport with parents, and behavior and work expectations. The cooperating teacher supervises closely so that he or she is able to rescue the student teacher from lessons gone awry. Brighton concluded that student teachers are easily lulled into believing that these elements will be the same in their future classrooms.

Therefore, when new teachers realize that their real jobs differ from their student teaching experiences, they feel anxiety and frustration.

From whatever sources, anxieties and frustrations can emerge easily for beginning teachers and can contribute to their psychosocial development. The current literature provides several themes that principals should consider in the mentoring content of new teachers. Beginning teachers reported some degree of stress or anxiety with the following:

1. Conflict with administrative policies and practices (Rosenholtz, 1985). This is an area that may not be limited to new teachers.
2. Student misbehavior (Johnson, 2004; Rosenholtz, 1985). This is a fairly common problem with new teachers.
3. High stakes testing and accountability expectations (Hargreaves, 2003). Teachers may feel they are on their own and are expected to have complete control over student achievement test scores.
4. Overwhelming workload with insufficient preparation time or preparation time that is not coordinated with other teachers that teach the same subject or students (Johnson, 2004; Rosenholtz, 1985). This is often linked with too many preparations and out-of-class responsibilities.
5. Changes in administrators (Johnson, 2004). These usually affect teachers after they have been hired by one administrator but teach with yet another administrator.
6. Grade-level changes (Bowers & Eberhart, 1988). These affect new teachers and second- and third-year teachers who have taught at one grade level and then are assigned to a new grade level.
7. Lack of parental support (Brighton, 1999). Some parents communicate reticence about dealing with new teachers, fearing that they are largely unorganized, inexperienced, and unable to control student behavior.
8. The expectations and scope of the job (Brighton, 1999; Johnson, 2004). A disparity exists between new teacher's original perceptions and the realities of the job, especially in regard to the amount and nature of the teaching assignment.
9. Feelings of isolation in their classrooms (Brighton, 1999; Darling-Hammond, 1983; Hargreaves, 2003). Teachers are usually the only adult in a room full of children during the instructional day, a cultural norm rooted in the one-room school era.
10. Complexity of urban contexts. Many of these previous stresses and anxieties converge in urban settings (Noguera, 2003).

A significant factor that appears in the literature dealing with new teachers' psychosocial development is the cultural context of the school and the community. Schools with diverse populations pose differing factors in the psychosocial development of new teachers. As we noted in Chapter 1, teachers perform their jobs in an increasingly diverse context. Many teachers are not prepared to teach diverse learners and need the support of their administrators to develop the knowledge, skills, and dispositions for teaching in this context. Providing a quality education for all children in such an environment can be difficult even for experienced teachers, so the task can often be overwhelming for novices. Ingersoll and Alsalam (1997) indicated that teacher turnover rates are higher in public schools where half or more of the students receive free or reduced-price lunches. Teachers in these schools often perceive a lack of respect from parents in part due to the parents' own negative childhood experiences within the schools. Studies in both California and New York City cite school poverty and race characteristics as factors in teacher turnover (Boyd et al., 2007; Futernick, 2007).

PROCESS A strong mentoring program is an essential element in the socialization of new teachers adjusting to their roles. Certain elements in the mentoring process should be considered for purposes of psychosocial development. Brighton (1999) suggested that administrators should provide teachers with tiered expectations—a gradual induction into the profession—for responsibilities involving class assignments, outside duties, and committee work. Within each tier, principals and assistant principals should offer guidance and support. New teachers are often shocked to realize that they have more duties, more challenging classes, and more committee expectations than their more experienced peers. The added expectations beyond regular teaching duties are often the straws that break the backs of new teachers. Gradually assigning responsibilities and duties can be a gentle way of inducting new teachers. They will be more prepared, and subsequently more successful, if they are presented with new challenges in small, incremental steps.

Storytelling is a favorite activity for educators and an important mentoring tool. When mentors tell stories, they share information about how they handled similar situations in their teaching experience. New teachers may feel that they are the first to experience the role conflicts that emerge and that other teachers have been immune to such conflicts. It is through listening and reflecting on stories from mentors that new teachers develop a sense of meaning and understanding of their role (Crow & Matthews, 1998).

One of the most stressful factors for new teachers (and for that matter, veterans) is the expectations from high stakes accountability and NCLB in particular. The principal as mentor can play a valuable role in listening to new teachers' anxieties, reassuring teachers that they are not alone and that student learning is the responsibility of the entire professional learning community, and in providing resources, such as coaching, to increase new teachers' sense of self-efficacy.

Mentoring New Teachers in Career Development

Thirty-three percent of teachers leave the profession in the first three years and 46 percent leave within five years; the exodus is even greater in low performing and urban school districts (Fulton, Yoon, and Lee, 2005; Guarino et al., 2006). Research also indicates that the most talented new educators are often the most likely to leave (Boyd, Lankford, Loeb, & Wyckoff, 2005; Guarino et al., 2006; Podgursky, Monroe, & Watson, 2004). In addition, the teaching career is unique among professions in that it is unstaged in its reward system (Lortie, 1975). Thus, most of the rewards that come with teaching arrive at the beginning of the career rather than later. Although various writers have identified career development stages, such as concern, survival, mastery, and impact (Fuller, 1969), these stages do not reflect the reward system. Although most school systems have a salary structure based on experience and education, additional responsibility or merit promotion are not routinely considered for career development. However, some states and districts, such as Georgia, Kentucky, Iowa, Denver, Cincinnati, and Minneapolis, have considered or actually tried performance-based salary systems. New teachers typically enter with the same responsibilities as veteran teachers and do not expect promotions. In addition, contextual differences, such as teaching in high-poverty or high-need urban schools, typically makes no difference in salary or other rewards.

This presents a significant issue for the principal and assistant principal in mentoring the new teacher in career development.

The mentoring goals in career development are both systemic and individual. A system goal would be to increase the retention of promising new teachers and to help them establish lifelong, productive careers in education. An individual goal would be to mentor new teachers in establishing a positive role conception for a satisfying and promising career.

CONTENT   The content in career development involves mentoring new teachers as to the responsibilities and opportunities of teaching as a career and profession. Most states have instituted professional development requirements that are necessary for relicensure. Although a new teacher may have trouble seeing this as relevant, the principal is responsible for making sure that all teachers see the need for and experience the advantage of continuing learning that supports career development.

Perhaps one of the toughest realizations for both teachers and principals is the fact that not all individuals are suited for teaching. Teaching may not be the glamorous position that many think it is. In fact, some new teachers soon realize that unmotivated learners, disruptive students, and burned-out colleagues replace the dream they once held.

Furthermore, marginality cannot be accepted in teaching. Accountability is more than a catchword in present-day schools. Teacher accountability is the focus of many reform efforts both inside the education community and among policymakers on the outside. Because marginality in veteran teachers is a major concern for administrators, mentoring beginning teachers becomes even more important. New teachers need to be mentored by their principal in helping them understand tenure laws, orderly dismissal policies, evaluation systems, accountability initiatives, and classroom supervision techniques.

PROCESS   The principal's role in mentoring new teachers for career development involves three processes. The first process is establishing career goals, that is, creating a vision of what the new teacher wants to become. Too often new teachers are overwhelmed by so much of the newness that exists around them that they can easily forget their own goals and vision. Their engagement in surviving the present does not allow a vision for the future. The principal should support beginning teachers through conferencing and modeling to help them establish realistic goals and to challenge them to work toward fulfilling their vision.

The second process is celebrating the new teacher's accomplishments. Celebrations can be an important mentoring opportunity for career development. Too often new teachers are not recognized for their performance or achievement when they reach certain milestones in their careers. Isolation among educators probably contributes to this lack of celebration. Through celebrations, principals provide meaningful mentoring in career development that enhances role identity by giving new teachers assurance, validity, and recognition—which also enhances their psychosocial development. Celebrations promote continued positive behavior in instructional methods. If beginning teachers receive recognition for their behaviors through celebrations, they are likely to repeat those behaviors.

Celebrations involve both private and public activities. Private celebrations could be the administrative team having lunch with the new teacher or stopping by the teacher's classroom to give a simple gift. A private celebration can be a validating gesture for the new teacher. Public celebrations could involve an announcement at a faculty meeting or an article in the school newsletter. The emphasis we have placed in this book on professional learning community in no way invalidates recognition of individual accomplishments. In a supportive learning community there is room for individual as well as group recognition and celebration.

The third important mentoring process in career development involves counseling new teachers to continue in their development or, perhaps, to leave teaching. Although great care always should be given before counseling a person out of his or her chosen career, it is imperative that an unhappy teacher or a person unsuited for the profession be given guidance in finding the right career.

Counseling new teachers who show promise involves challenging them to attend workshops and conferences, to read professional journals and books, to participate in teacher associations, and to attend faculty and staff socials and activities. New teachers are socialized into the profession as they participate in these types of activities. They also develop networks of relationships with others who may be valuable assets to their professional career growth.

Networking can be an important mentoring tool for the retention of teachers. Through relationship building, a person can find personal satisfaction and reduced isolation in a job. The principal needs to introduce the new teacher, formally or informally, to the school community. Networking is an especially valuable tool in the context of mentoring in a professional learning community.

THE PRINCIPAL AS FACILITATOR OF MENTORING FOR NEW TEACHERS

Although principals and assistant principals serve as mentors for new teachers, the induction process would be woefully incomplete if it did not include mentoring by other teachers. Peer mentors are veteran teachers who serve as primary and secondary mentors for beginning teachers. In response to the needs of beginning teachers, peer mentoring programs have become increasingly common. These programs are sponsored by a variety of organizations, including individual schools and school districts, consortia of schools, state departments of education, and colleges and universities (Gold, 1996).

Many states and districts have written policies outlining a mentoring program for beginning teachers. Policies such as these, however, may not always receive the results that policymakers intended. In one study (Withers, 2003), 48 percent of provisional teachers had not received any formal mentoring. The current movement in peer mentoring began in the mid-1980s. Feiman-Nemser and colleagues (1999) reported that before 1980 only one state had mandated a beginning teacher mentoring program. It is reasonable to presume that most American districts and schools either have or will have new teacher mentoring programs.

Beyond its part in providing beginning teachers with a more humane and professionally sound induction into teaching, peer mentoring makes a desirable professional activity for veteran teachers and reflects the expanded nature of mentoring recommended in the co-mentoring models (Mullen & Kealy, 1999). Experienced teachers gain insight into their own teaching by sharing and reflecting as they mentor novices. Mentoring encourages them to be reflective about their own beliefs about teaching, students, learning, and their careers. Ganser (1996) found in his studies that veteran teachers frequently characterized working closely with beginning teachers as a source of fresh, new, cutting-edge ideas about curriculum and teaching. Mentors often characterized what they learned from new teachers as more immediately accessible and more useful in their work than much of what they learned through graduate courses or traditional inservice activities and workshops. Ganser found several cases where a mentor and a beginning teacher simultaneously implemented innovative strategies in both their classes. This experience provides a valuable opportunity for both to reflect on a common instructional problem and to provide a valuable model for others in the professional learning community.

The principal's role and responsibility with peer mentoring programs have not always been clearly defined. In some districts, the peer mentoring program exists outside the principal's responsibilities, a system that appears to be incongruent with strong principal instructional leadership. The principal's role should be that of primary facilitator in developing the peer mentoring program. The principal's responsibility in developing the mentoring program involves selecting, matching, training, and supporting: selecting veteran teachers to serve as peer mentors, matching them with the new teachers, training them to be mentors, and supporting them with resources to enable effective mentoring relationships.

Before discussing these roles, it is important to identify the various ways principals can relate to the peer mentor and the new teacher. Barkley (2005) identified four models for this interaction:

Model 1: Two-way Communication. In this model the principal and the mentor communicate with the new teacher, but not with each other. This assures the new teacher that the discussion with the mentor is confidential.

Model 2: The Silent Mentor. In this model, the principal meets with the mentor to share concerns or questions, but the mentor does not share anything from the mentoring relationship with the principal. This, again, assures confidentiality, but informs the mentor of issues from the principal's perspective.

Model 3: Positive Reinforcement. This model is similar to Model 2 but the mentor shares only positive comments regarding the new teacher with the principal.

Model 4: Full Communication. In this model all three individuals have two-way communication with each other. (pp. 28–32).

Barkley recommended the fourth model as most effective for teacher growth and success. However, there may be times when you as the principal decide that another model will be more productive and more acceptable to the new teacher. The important point is to make sure that the new teacher, the mentor and you understand and agree on which model to use.

Professional Dilemma 8.2

Should any good veteran teacher be selected as a mentor? Some veteran teachers might be great teachers with children but lack the relationship skills to be a good mentor with adults. As principal, should you pursue helping the outstanding veteran teacher become a good mentor or just move on to other teachers who show more promise as mentors?

Selecting and Matching Teachers to Be Mentors: Two Perspectives

FIRST PERSPECTIVE: COLLEGIAL AND SUPPORTIVE ENVIRONMENT Principals should consider two perspectives in selecting teachers as mentors and then matching those mentors with beginning teachers. The first perspective is the approach in which the principal helps establish and maintain a collegial and supportive environment that promotes peer mentoring and in which beginning teachers have several mentors, both primary and secondary. This approach reflects the expanded nature of mentoring proposed by the co-mentoring model (Mullen & Kealy, 1999) and the presence of a relationship constellation in which individuals can rely on a variety of mentors in the school (Kram, 1986). In this approach, the principal is the facilitative leader who brings together new and veteran teachers to help create a professional learning community within the faculty. Informal, but intentional, suggestions that connect teachers is one of the ways principals can facilitate this type of mentoring. As you observe and meet with teachers, you can make them aware of these connections with others who are trying similar innovations or confronting similar challenges. The entire faculty helps novices as they encounter the newness of the school's culture and classroom challenges. This is a type of learning community that this book encourages, and as each year passes, the culture becomes stronger in its professional collegiality. A professional learning community of this nature takes time to develop and requires constant and consistent nurturing. It can be time-consuming, disappointing, and frustrating. However, the results can be immense, as we suggest throughout this book. As this type of community is in transition, the principal should consider a more formal approach that a second perspective can offer. Research (Scandura & Williams, 2002) has shown that this type of informal, peer mentoring is more effective than the second perspective which involves mentoring as a formal programmatic approach. However, the formal approach is better than no mentoring.

SECOND PERSPECTIVE: FORMAL MENTORS With the second perspective, the principal formally selects veteran teachers who are willing and qualified to mentor and then matches them with novice teachers for at least a year—perhaps longer. This approach is more programmatic and can usually be established sooner than that put forth by the first perspective, depending on the existing culture of the school. Not surprisingly, achieving this kind of mentoring program does not happen by magic. It requires planning and special effort by the school principal. As described earlier in this chapter, mentoring is a specialized and complex role. To assume that all veteran teachers can be effective mentors, even if they are outstanding teachers, is not realistic. Furthermore, many veteran teachers may not want to be mentors because mentoring requires a considerable amount of time and energy. Those teachers whom principals may want to serve as mentors are usually very active professionally, and the demands of mentoring may require them to be freed from other activities.

The first step for principals in the mentor selection process is to consider those teachers in the faculty who would be qualified, available, and willing to serve as mentors. Principals should consider several issues in mentor selection. The first consideration was recommended by Odell (1990a) who suggested that, when possible, the mentor and the new teacher should teach the same grade level or academic area so that the new teacher can get help with specific questions about curriculum, instruction, and student assessment. Johnson (2004) found that mentoring was perceived as most helpful to new teachers when "their mentors taught the same subject as they did, had common planning times, and had a classroom close by" (p. 196). These mentoring characteristics also seem to vary for teachers in different types of schools, for example, new teachers in high-income schools were more likely than teachers in low-income schools to have mentors and to have them from the same school, the same grade level, and the same subject (Johnson, S. M. et al., 2004).

A second consideration is how much teaching experience a mentor should have. Doyle (1988) reported that it takes at least five years for a novice to master the demands of teaching. Likewise, it takes several years for an individual to fully understand the school and community culture. A third consideration is the quality of teaching and the quality of the individual as a contributing member and team player within the professional learning community. Fourth, the principal has to determine if personalities are compatible and relationships can be established between the veteran teacher and the beginner. Finally, consideration needs to be given as to the mentor and beginning teacher's gender, age, race, ethnicity, personality, and other factors that contribute to the relationship. In the opening vignette, Felicia's age was problematic for some teachers in her school. Although this does not mean that newer teachers or administrators cannot mentor more experienced educators effectively, age may influence the mentoring relationship and should be considered carefully in mentor selection. Race also is an important consideration. In Gardiner, Grogan, and Enomoto's (2000) study of African American and Latin American women who were participating in a mentoring program, they found that these women of color reported that race was more of an obstacle than gender in receiving adequate mentoring.

The West Des Moines Community School District established qualifications, knowledge areas, and skills that mentor teachers should have. These are shown in Figure 8.1.

Mentor Training

You should not assume that good or even outstanding teachers will be successful mentors without any special training and support. Several studies (Feiman-Nemser, et al., 1999; Ganser, 1996; Marquardt & Loan, 2006) supported the unique role of mentoring, a practice that warrants special preparation. These studies indicated that the unique training for prospective mentors includes knowledge, values, and skills. Training in the knowledge of mentoring includes four parts:

1. Information about teacher career development and the predictable problems of beginning teachers
2. An understanding of the profession of teaching itself, including the induction of beginning teachers and schools as work places with site-specific cultures
3. Information about adult development and adult learning
4. Information about mentoring beginning teachers, including typical mentoring roles and activities

Although training may not be the appropriate way to develop all values related to mentoring, the following values (Marquardt & Loan, 2006) should be encouraged: service, trust, empowerment, humility, openness, curiosity, courage, integrity, sensitivity, and balance in life.

Qualifications:

__Ability to model effective teaching strategies
__Ability to work in a collaborative manner
__Ability to maintain confidentiality
__Ability to manage time effectively

Knowledge:

__Knowledge of research-based effective teaching strategies
__Knowledge of instructional effectiveness

Demonstrated skills:

__Professional competence
__Effective verbal and nonverbal communication
__Interpersonal skills of caring, kindness, and understanding

Experience:

__Subject and/or grade-level experience
__Three or more years of successful teaching experience

Responsibilities:

__Attend training as required
__Provide expertise and ongoing support
__Visit new teachers' classrooms and provide feedback

FIGURE 8.1   West Des Moines Community School District Job Description for a Mentor Teacher.
Job summary: Provide expertise and ongoing support and professional growth opportunities to enhance the skills and effectiveness of beginning teachers.

Mentor training for specific skill building includes

1. Listening
2. Questioning
3. Reflective conferencing and storytelling
4. Devising problem-solving strategies (e.g., defining a problem, collecting information, determining and implementing a strategy, and assessing the outcomes)
5. Helping teachers formulate short- and long-term professional goals
6. Methods of observing teaching and conducting a reflective conference
7. Managing differences
8. Building relationships
9. Creating an understanding of and commitment to learning
10. Facilitation
11. Advocacy

Providing Support for Peer Mentoring

At the heart of effective mentoring is the time that beginning teachers and their mentors spend together. Ganser (1996) reported that new teachers were generally less interested in extrinsic rewards than in being provided with at least some time released from other obligations to engage in mentoring activities. Peer mentors and beginning teachers need time to reflect on and discuss experiences and to engage in collaborative problem solving and goal setting. Observing a beginning teacher and then conferencing with that teacher as a reflective activity require time for both the mentor and the protégé.

What peer mentoring reasonably can be expected to accomplish is related to the amount of time available for mentoring. The principal and assistant principal may overload teachers in the number of preparations, types of courses, schedules, duty assignments, and "floating" or "carting" among several classrooms. Principals have to consider these elements in assigning a new teacher responsibilities so that the mentoring process can be positive. Lightening the load of new teachers allows them the time and the energy to be effective recipients of mentoring.

Feiman-Nemser and colleagues (1999) claimed that if administrators took new teachers seriously as learners, they would not expect them to do the same job or have the same skills as experienced teachers. Rather, they would adjust their expectations for success and effectiveness to fit the teachers' stage and structure assignments to allow time for observation, collaborative problem solving, and reflection. A high school in the San Francisco Bay Area developed an induction program for new teachers that reduced the new teacher's load considerably and allowed for mentoring to take place. New teachers are assigned only half the normal teaching load. They have one subject preparation and repeat the courses they teach. During the other half of the day, new teachers receive mentoring from both an assigned peer mentor and the principal or assistant principal. They have opportunities to visit experienced teachers' classes, visit other schools, attend workshops and conferences, and consult with district personnel. The administrators and faculty of this school are committed to the development of beginning teachers. Although the challenges faced by first-year teachers make the case for such an induction program, the sad reality is that in most schools new teachers are assigned similar workloads as veterans and are expected to perform at par with experienced teachers.

Schlechty (1984) recommended another supportive strategy for principals to use: afford the beginning teacher the opportunity to develop a sense of being a member of an important group that shares an ordeal and understands that others are experiencing the same stressful period. Cohort groups of beginning teachers might reduce isolation among novice teachers and foster their professional growth. Carter and Richardson (1989) suggested that networking among beginning teachers should allow them to develop understandings of teaching and that in some instances it may be necessary to include beginning teachers from several schools to achieve a functional cohort group.

Mentoring Veteran Teachers

The mid-career stage of teaching varies for each teacher. Many veteran teachers have fallen into a survival mode. Others may be less concerned with survival but continue to seek recognition in their work and lives. Often teachers have changed grade levels or have been assigned other subjects to teach to rejuvenate their careers. Some veteran teachers have remained in the same school for most of their careers and have found a sense of pride in being part of the school history and culture. A few of these teachers find it difficult to change their teaching styles and want schools and students to remain the way they think they were in the past. Some teachers may find the high stakes accountability environment as threatening their expertise and even job security. These teachers need support and mentoring in responding to threatening and stressful accountability mandates in ways that help them focus their efforts on authentic student learning.

Not all veterans will be enthusiastic about the development and maintenance of a professional learning community. The isolation that new teachers complain about has become for some veterans a comfortable element of their teaching practice. Your mentoring will need to be sensitive to their anxieties and resistance to deprivatizing their practices, collaborating with others, and engaging in ongoing inquiry. Arranging observations of other teachers and visits to other schools as well as opportunities to discuss their practices in nonthreatening contexts will be essential in your role as mentor.

Kram (1986) reported that many individuals in mid-career are no longer establishing competence and defining an occupational identity. Instead, they are adjusting self-images and realizing they are no longer novices. They question their own competence in relation to peers and new teachers. For those who are satisfied with their accomplishments, it may be a time of shifting creative energies away from advancement concerns toward interests about leisure time and family commitments. Alternately, for those who are dissatisfied with their accomplishments, it may be a time of self-doubt and a sense of urgency as they realize that life is half over and their careers have been determined (Crow & Matthews, 1998). For these different types of veteran teachers, mentoring as an "awakening" to a new way of seeing things can be a powerful learning resource for improving their teaching (Gehrke, 1988).

A typical assumption by many educators—including administrators—is that most veteran teachers have been involved in teaching for a number of years and do not need mentors. Effective principals recognize the importance of continued mentoring of teachers in mid-career. Research clearly links student achievement with teacher quality (Hanushek, Kain, O'Brien, & Rivkin, 2005). Although many reform efforts have failed to recognize the importance of teachers, effective principals have not. In fact, several studies have indicated that effective schools have principals who emphasize quality teaching in those schools (e.g., Edmunds, 1979).

Many strategies for mentoring teachers in mid-career are similar to those used in mentoring new teachers. For example, veteran teachers have continued needs in professional, psychosocial, and career development. One important strategy in mentoring veteran teachers involves principal visibility. As a principal's visibility increases, so do mentoring opportunities. Principals in isolation seldom have the opportunity to be active mentors of veteran teachers. Studies have indicated that strong positive relationships exist between principals' visibility and teacher commitment (Sheppard, 1996) and teacher motivation (Blase & Blase, 1998). Teachers and students notice when principals are actively involved in instructional improvement. Relationships are developed more easily, and mentoring opportunities occur more often.

Several studies (e.g., Blase & Blase, 1994) have indicated that veteran teachers respond well to individual praise and compliments. Criticism, although sometimes needed, often results in a negative effect on the mentoring process. Criticism seldom promotes positive behaviors in others, whereas individual praise actually can cause positive behaviors to be repeated. A study by Blase and Kirby (2000) indicated that praise is most effective when it deals with professional performance (such as a specific teaching strategy) rather than with appearances (dress or hairstyle).

Perhaps one of the most challenging aspects of being a principal is dealing with marginal veteran teachers. Marginal teachers are those who exhibit a range of problems, including limited teaching skills, ineffective communication, unproductive student achievement, and neglect of or indifference to professional responsibilities. The challenge for school administrators is to work with these teachers in ways that will return them to the ranks of effective educators. Principals are responsible for helping marginal teachers make the improvements that are needed for the benefit of the children and for the success of the professional learning community. Supervising marginal teachers is discussed in Chapter 9; however, mentoring should be the first strategy in helping these teachers become better educators. The literature on helping marginal teachers offers several suggestions for principals:

1. Modeling. The principal should model effective leadership skills and professionalism and demonstrate by word and action that maintaining productive learning opportunities for students is a top priority (Blank, Kershaw, and Sparks, 1999).
2. Information giving. Principals need to have a working knowledge and be able to advise others as to state tenure laws and district policies and procedures that relate to teacher performance and employment.
3. Conferencing. Principals need to help the teacher become aware of the problem early. Helping a teacher correct small problems is easier than resolving crises.
4. Supporting. The psychosocial problems of teachers can affect their professional roles. Principals can support teachers who need assistance with personal problems by offering suggestions as to resources, remediation, and counseling.

In a professional learning community, principals have an important role to play in addition to mentoring individual teachers, that is, mentoring teams. Teams are a vital part of the professional learning community. However, often schools have established teams and administrators have told teachers to collaborate. The teachers had little training and had no idea what they were supposed to collaborate on. In the following subsection, we discuss a plan in which principals and assistant principals mentor teacher teams in collaboration.

Mentoring Teacher Teams

As we discussed in Chapter 7, schools that are professional learning communities have a shared vision that is centered on learning. When schools create a vision that is results-oriented, they can use the vision to make decisions about what is important for students to know and be able to do. Written, shared vision statements become the foundation for the work of the school when they are centered on curriculum, assessment, and instruction. It is this vision that directs the mentoring for teacher teams. Principals and assistant principals use the vision to ensure alignment between the school's needs and the team's collaboration topics. Especially at the beginning of teaming and because teachers are not used to collaboration, they often need principals to guide them into what the important topics are on which they are to collaborate. For example, a new elementary teacher team used its collaboration time to discuss field trips and holiday parties, topics that might be important but not part of the school's vision for improving student learning. The principal then spent several sessions with the team in developing the right agendas that were more aligned with the school's vision.

To ensure that they mentor their teacher teams in the appropriate direction, effective principals use data to develop a focus area. Schools already have considerable data such as standardized tests, district made tests, student work samples, portfolios, and classroom assessments. From these sources of data, the principal mentors the team in deciding what data is going to be the most important to improve student learning. As a team, a focus area is then determined in which the team will begin collaborating. For example, the principal shares data with a fifth grade team that their writing assessment scores indicated that many students did not write paragraphs that were unified around a topic sentence. The principal then mentors the team on developing strategies that the teachers could use to improve paragraph development.

The principal can then help the teacher team identify other learning needs related to curriculum, instruction, and assessment. Often, the principal mentors the team to understand that they need other assessment data to help with determining the right instructional strategies. For example, a high school world history team analyzed the sample questions that were given to students taking the SAT and ACT tests. The principal helped the team to understand that they did not know how their students were doing on Middle Eastern affairs. The team then developed formative assessments that they used when they taught that unit, analyzed the data from those assessments, and developed strategies together as a team to improve their instruction, which ultimately improved student achievement.

This process of collaborative teaming sets the stage for the use of an inquiry process to examine current teaching practice and to evaluate current achievement results. Thus, the principal might also mentor the team in professional development needs that emerge from the teaming process. Martin (2008) suggested, "As teachers engage in challenging dialogue regarding classroom practices and student achievement, they begin to see the value of professional development in supporting their own growth and responding to their individual and collective educational needs" (p. 148).

Principals can also model using data to improve practice by collecting and interpreting data on their own leadership. Huff (2008) wrote how she asked teachers, staff, colleagues, and district supervisors to complete a survey on her leadership. She modeled what she was asking teachers to do: collect and analyze data to see how they could improve. As Huff reported it, "Digging deep into data is risky; it forces us to confront our current reality, which may cause discomfort" (p. 213). By modeling her own data collection, she was mentoring how she wanted teachers in the school to collect and analyze data.

Principals cannot expect instructional teams to begin collaboration that will have meaningful results until those teams have been instructed and mentored in the content and the process of teaming. The principal takes on an important role in this process, and developing the strategies to do this is often challenging.

THE PRINCIPAL AS FACILITATOR OF MENTORING OF VETERAN TEACHERS

Much of the discussion of the principal as facilitator of mentoring new teachers can be applied to the principal's and assistant principal's roles in creating a professional learning community that supports mentoring for veteran teachers. For example, the importance of time to meet and the significance of training are pertinent to system-wide mentoring for all teachers. In fact, it is highly unlikely that a professional learning community that supports mentoring of new teachers will exist separately from the larger school context that supports mentoring of veteran teachers.

One of the most important things that principals do to facilitate mentoring for veteran teachers is to emphasize its relevance to the school by paying attention to mentoring. Principals who talk about mentoring, encourage mentoring for instructional improvement, and acknowledge the role of mentoring in their own development send a strong message about its importance for all teachers in the school.

Another important contribution that principals and assistant principals make to facilitating mentoring of veteran teachers is to develop and support relationship constellations (Kram, 1986) in which teachers can find mentors to help with different aspects of their professional, psychosocial, and career development. Sometimes the principal's and assistant principal's actions are as simple as making teachers aware of what other teachers are doing—their innovations, experiments, and successes. This awareness encourages teachers to talk frequently with each other about instructional improvement—a significant component of professional learning communities (Bryk, Camburn, & Louis, 1999). This awareness of what other teachers are doing also facilitates peer mentor pairing. The more teachers know what other teachers are doing in their classes, the more information they have for choosing a mentor and developing a peer mentor relationship.

In Chapter 4, we discussed various components of the principal's role as learner and facilitator of learning. Certainly these components apply to facilitating an environment for mentoring all teachers. One component, however, stands out in its importance for facilitating mentoring. As principals and assistant principals, you should recognize your own mentoring needs, participate in peer mentoring, and communicate the importance of mentoring as a central feature of the school's professional learning community.

THE PRINCIPAL AS MENTOR OF STUDENTS

Although the principal's greatest responsibility in mentoring is with teachers and improving the instructional and educational environment, principals are also teachers and thus interact with and influence students. Principals and assistant principals find many opportunities to mentor students, such as correcting behavior problems, encouraging them to use their talents, achieving better academic results, and fulfilling leadership roles. Including students in the mentoring process is inherent in a professional learning community that includes everyone in the school.

Research has indicated that leadership development starts early in a child's life. Gardner (1987) concluded that the skills critical for effective leadership, including the capacity to understand and interact with others, develop early. In another study, Garrod (1988) found that these skills begin to form before five years of age. He also found few differences between those adolescents identified as student leaders and those not identified as such. Garrod concluded that it is not possible to predict exceptional leadership performance in adolescents. Van Linden and Fertman (1998) supported this assertion and concluded that all teenagers have the potential to lead.

Employers are more interested in adolescents who are leaders. For many employers, this initially equates with being at work on time, doing the job, and not causing problems. Over time, though, employers assess youths' leadership in the workplace in the form of taking on more responsibility and showing concern about the quality of the work being done. Van Linden and Fertman (1998) warned that leadership in the workplace could be confused with the concepts of management and supervision. "These can be particularly overwhelming notions for adolescents, and their fear of 'bossing' can keep them from exploring their leadership potential" (p. 7). It makes sense that teenagers may be reluctant to lead or to take on formal leadership positions if they believe it is associated with "bossing." However, the basic premise of student leadership is a set of skills and attitudes that can be learned and practiced and developed by all students (Van Linden & Fertman, 1998).

School is the place where students begin to learn how to behave in groups outside their family and to see leadership in action. Students learn a lot about leadership from their teachers and principals. Most students associate teachers and principals with authority and leadership. In many cases, unfortunately, the principal is someone a student wants to avoid, perceiving principals only as people who make decisions about the school and the students. If principals are going to serve as mentors for students, these young people must get to know them and not shy away from them.

The principal's opportunity to mentor students to develop leadership skills can occur in many settings and situations. Principals and especially assistant principals often have opportunities to mentor students in understanding correct social behaviors, which may include skills in decision making, communication, and relationship building. Mentoring leadership behavior in students is usually much easier in positive situations than in negative ones. When students excel or do something extraordinary, it is easy to encourage and support their efforts. If their effort to use leadership skills has a less than positive outcome, it is difficult for school leaders to see the benefit. However, it might be in those settings and situations that the principal provides the most beneficial mentoring.

Perhaps the most important message you can give to students of any age is that you believe that they can be valuable leaders and can influence what happens inside and outside their school. This message about their value as leader is reinforced by your willingness to take the time to mentor them.

Conclusion

In the opening vignette, Felicia and Latonya attempted to develop a schoolwide mentoring program for new teachers using themselves and veteran teachers as mentors. Although difficulties arose, persistence in creating such an environment will help develop the professional learning community that they desire. Your understanding of mentoring is an important aspect in developing a learning community and in improving student learning. However, mentoring does not happen without careful planning, preparation, training, and organization. Your understanding of both the process and the content of mentoring is important in developing a mentoring program in a school. Furthermore, your own participation in mentoring will indicate to others the importance you place on it.

Activities

SELF-REFLECTION ACTIVITIES

1. Describe a primary mentor and a secondary mentor in your career. What were the differences between your primary and secondary mentors?
2. Do you know of new teachers who quit? How might a mentoring program have helped them?
3. Who are the teacher mentors in your school? What are their characteristics? What are the characteristics of effective teacher mentors?
4. ISLLC Standard 4 states, "An education leader promotes the success of every student by collaborating with faculty and community members, responding to diverse community interests and needs, and mobilizing community resources" (p. 21). Develop a plan for mentoring experiences that will help you in meeting the intent of this standard.

PEER REFLECTION ACTIVITIES

1. With a colleague, identify the different professional, psychological, and career functions that your own mentors have played. Were there times or settings in which different functions were more important for you?

2. Compare your mentoring experiences as new teachers in terms of the benefits and pitfalls.
3. Discuss with your colleague the two professional dilemmas in this chapter regarding whether the principal should inform the new teacher about all parental criticisms and whether a good veteran teacher should be a mentor.

COURSE ACTIVITIES

1. Have each class member identify the characteristics of her or his mentor. What are the similarities and differences between men and women mentors, mentors of different races, and mentors at different career stages?
2. As a class, develop a formal mentoring plan for a specific school. Be sure to include purpose, participants, content, and processes and to cover the three functions of mentoring.
3. Use the opening vignette as the basis for a class role play of a mentoring conference between Felicia and Gloria. Reflect on how age may affect the mentoring relationship. Also identify possible approaches Felicia might take to make the mentoring relationship more effective and nurturing.

Websites

International Mentoring Association
http://www.mentoring-association.org/

NEA Foundation—this Web site lists resources and suggestions for creating a teacher mentoring program
http://www.neafoundation.org/publications/mentoring.htm

CHAPTER 9

Principal as Supervisor

Vignette

Bill Payne sat in his office at the end of the day before the December holiday reflecting on his first semester as a new principal. He was appointed principal of Mt. Ares Elementary School fresh out of graduate school. Bill had been a fourth-grade teacher who was well known in the district for his innovative teaching style and his mentoring of new teachers. He was excited about his appointment not only because of his desire to be a principal but also because Mt. Ares was known as one of the district's best schools. The teachers at Mt. Ares were considered among the most innovative in the district, and because the state had an open choice policy, many out-of-area parents hounded district administrators to get their children into the school.

Last year several of the veteran teachers retired, and Bill was faced with more new teachers than the school had had since it opened twenty-five years ago. He looked forward to working with these new teachers but knew that with his new administrative responsibilities this would be a hectic year.

After his appointment, Bill developed a plan for working with the new teachers that involved two approaches. First, he wanted to conference with each of the new teachers and make appointments to observe them in the classroom. Second, he knew that he needed help from the veteran teachers in order to provide effective mentoring and supervision for these new teachers, so he needed to establish a team of teachers who were willing to supervise and mentor.

Soon after the school year began, Bill approached Frances Kilgore, one of the most respected teachers in the school, and one who had students with consistently high test scores, to discuss his plan for professional development of the new teachers. He talked to Frances about the need for the new teachers to have veteran peers who would observe them in their classrooms, coach them with establishing instructional methods to help them with student learning, and mentor them in establishing good assessments for learning. Bill also wanted the new teachers to observe the veterans. He promised that he would get substitutes for the teachers and even offered to substitute himself whenever possible so that these activities could occur.

The reaction from Frances was shocking to Bill. Essentially, she said that the reason the veteran teachers at Mt. Ares were respected by the community was that they limited their "extracurricular activities" and focused on the children and their own classrooms. She said that she also believed that new teachers needed to spend some time struggling and working out their own style. When Bill pointed out the statistics that one-third of new teachers leave teaching by their third year, Frances replied, "Well, maybe that's the way to weed out the bad teachers." Frances also told Bill that she could see no incentive for herself in spending all that time working with new teachers. "How will that benefit me or my students?"

When Bill left the conversation with Frances, he thought maybe Frances was the exception. In the next few weeks, however, as he spoke with other veteran teachers at Mt. Ares, it became clear that Frances' views were the norm, not the exception.

As he sat in his office pondering the past few months, Bill felt good about most things that had happened. He had made a good impression on the parents and teachers, and the district office felt that he had made a nice transition to administration. However, Bill was not satisfied with what was happening with new teachers. As much as he tried to spend time in their classrooms and conference with them, he simply could not provide the kind of supervisory support that most of these new teachers needed.

INTRODUCTION

Bill Payne's concerns call attention to a role for principals and assistant principals that results from the roles we have discussed in Chapters 4, 5, 6, 7, and 8: learner, culture builder, advocate, leader, and mentor. These roles come together in the role of supervisor. Although not as much attention has focused on the principal as learner and mentor, a great deal of literature, both popular and academic, has discussed supervision. However, most of the literature has discussed the principal as supervisor for improving teaching. Although important, the more current view, and the one we support in creating a professional learning community (PLC), is the role of supervisor to improve learning, especially through collecting data and analyzing results (Joyce, 2004).

The educational administration literature has a love–hate relationship with the word *supervision*. On one hand, the instructional leadership literature emphasizes the principal's role as supervisor by observing and working with teachers to improve instruction. On the other hand, educators have criticized the word *supervision*, referring to it at times as *snoopervision*. Some have even suggested that principals and assistant principals, because of their hierarchical positions, cannot effectively supervise for instructional improvement because of their role as evaluator.

School administrators have had a similarly contradictory perception of supervision. Principals claim that instructional leadership activities such as supervision are extremely important and should receive high priority in their practice (Doud & Keller, 1998). Yet studies repeatedly demonstrate that principals and assistant principals spend less time on supervision than on managerial concerns. Goldring, Huff, May, and Camburn (2008) found that principals allocate the highest amount of time to student affairs (about 10 hrs/week), next was instructional leadership (about 8 hrs/week), then personnel (about 5 hrs/week).

In this chapter, we discuss a conception of the principal's and assistant principal's role as supervisor that attempts to refocus attention on the importance of supervision within a PLC that not only improves teaching but more importantly improves student learning. We begin with a discussion of the traditional role of principal as supervisor before moving on to our discussion of a new conception. As in the previous chapters, the discussion in this chapter of the principal as supervisor includes both the direct ways principals and assistant principals act as supervisors and the more indirect but critical way principals and assistant principals can facilitate a culture of supervision within the school. This chapter is not intended to replace a course or textbook on the foundations and techniques of supervision. Rather, we hope this chapter introduces you, as a new and aspiring assistant principal or principal, to a new way to think about how you can contribute to the PLC of the school. Thus, our focus is not on techniques but on conceptions of the role.

Before beginning our examination of the more traditional conception of the supervisor role, two points need to be clarified. First, as we noted previously, the term *supervision* typically connotes inspection. The word suggests hierarchical and perhaps autocratic techniques. We struggled with whether we should use a different word to label this principal role. However, supervision is part of the administrative vocabulary. We have decided to use the word rather than replace it because of its common use in the profession. However, we will apply the word *supervision* in a more contemporary usage than what you might have seen it in the past. As we discuss the traditional role and the innovative conception of the role, this contemporary usage will become clearer.

The second clarification we need to make is to point out that supervision and evaluation frequently are used synonymously in practice. We maintain, however, that there needs to be a separation between the formal and typically summative process of evaluation and the more formative process of supervision. However, unlike some writers, we argue that both these functions can be performed by principals and assistant principals and, in fact, should complement one another. Although we spend the majority of space in this chapter on the formative process of working with teachers to improve practice, we believe that much of this material is useful for the summative process of evaluating teachers.

TRADITIONAL ROLE OF PRINCIPAL AS SUPERVISOR

The traditional conception of the role of supervisor is chiseled into the minds of most new administrators. Because most principals and assistant principals were teachers and remember principal "visits" to their classrooms, new administrators come to the principalship with a traditional view of supervision. However, this conception did not appear overnight. There is a history to the role of principal as supervisor. As Murphy (2002) suggested, "The educational roots of the profession of school administration atrophied over the course of the 20th century as the field gravitated toward conceptions of leadership based on scientific images of business management and social science research" (p. 76).

Historical Overview of the Supervisor's Role

We noted in Chapter 2 that the principal's role began as a teacher and moved to a hierarchical position in part responsible for monitoring the behavior of both students and teachers. Luehe (1989) described this early role as an inspection role in which the principal's responsibility as supervisor was to weed out weak teachers and assure school boards that standards were being upheld. With the advent of the scientific management movement, the role took on additional elements. Luehe emphasized the attention to added administrative and managerial tasks involving checking to make sure that the teacher's behavior contributed to improved student performance. Monitoring test results became a function of supervision. According to Luehe, a third shift in the role came as a result of a human relations focus. The early human relations advocates, although still interested in increasing productivity, focused on faculty and staff morale. This more contemporary approach advocates supervision as building collegial relationships among teachers to support student learning. This contemporary supervisory role involves exchanging ideas, collaborating with teachers to identify instructional problems and their solutions, serving as a resource person, and assisting in bringing about change where appropriate.

Beach and Reinhartz (2000) charted similar changes in the way supervision has been conceived. They began with the colonial period, when the focus was on inspection, and subsequent expansion and growth periods of the late 1800s, when state and local authorities monitored curriculum and instruction. The early 1900s saw the scientific and professionalization periods, when supervisors became efficiency experts or educational specialists. During the progressive period, supervision became less focused on monitoring than on providing assistance to teachers to improve instruction. During the late 1950s and 1960s, more attention was paid to curriculum development. These authors argued that during the 1970s the focus was more clinical, helping teachers to diagnose teaching and learning problems. Finally, the 1980s and 1990s brought the instructional leadership era, when supervisors were responsible for coaching teachers in the context of reform. Table 9.1 charts these changes in supervisory practice. Although Beach and Reinhartz's chronicle ends with the 1990s, we could suggest that the period of the 2000s is focusing on supervision in the context of accountability. In this case, supervision becomes closely connected with evaluating student learning outcomes.

Blase and Blase (1998) argued that although there has been considerable disagreement on the appropriate approaches to supervision over the last 140 years, there has been little change in practice. "The practice of supervision has often been one of inspection, oversight, and judgment" (p. 8).

Elements of the Traditional Role of Principal as Supervisor

Blase and Blase's (1998) criticism of the practice of supervision suggested that the traditional role of supervision needs examination and change. In the following description of the traditional role of principal as supervisor, we have relied on Reitzug's (1997) discussion of the various components of the conception of principal as supervisor. He based his discussion on a careful examination of ten of the most frequently used supervisory texts. The discussion identified elements based on the views of the principal, the teacher, teaching, and the process of supervision.

TABLE 9.1 Charting the Changes in Supervisory Practice

Time Period	Theme	Supervisory Role	Supervisory Focus
1600–1865	The Colonial period—early beginnings	Authoritarian and autocratic committees	Inspecting to maintain conformity to lay standards
1865–1910	The state and national period—expansion and growth	State and local administrators and managers of schools, students, and curriculum	Overseeing of state and local curriculum and instruction
1910–1920	The scientific and organizational period—science applied to learning and organizations	Efficiency experts and scientific managers	Implementing standardization and regimentation of curriculum and instruction
1920–1935	The professionalization and bureaucratic period—becoming a profession	Career managers and educational specialists (bureaucrats)	Monitoring progress of teachers and students toward educational goals
1935–1955	The progressive and cooperative period—changing the way schools are viewed	Facilitators and counselors	Providing direct assistance to teachers in improving instruction
1955–1970	The curriculum development and change-oriented period	Curriculum specialists and writers	Assisting teachers in developing curriculum and implementing instructional change
1970–1980	The clinical and accountable period—dealing with differences	Clinicians and analytical observers	Helping individual teachers be more effective and accountable by analyzing the teaching—learning process
1980–1995	The entrepreneurial and reform period—the reform influence from business	Instructional leaders and managers	Coaching teachers in the fine points of effective instruction while reconfiguring the school organization
Present and the future	The student learning accountability period	All teachers as instructional leaders and collaborative partners	Creating schools as PLCs

Source: Adapted from Beach & Reinhartz (2000). *Supervisor Leadership: Focus on Instruction*. Boston: Allyn & Bacon

According to Reitzug (1997), texts "primarily portrayed the principal as expert and superior, the teacher as deficient and voiceless, teaching as fixed technology, and supervision as a discrete intervention" (p. 326). In this traditional view, principals, because of their hierarchical position, are assumed to be the experts in student learning and instruction. Reitzug argued that this image weakens the role of both teachers and principals. First, it devalues the practical knowledge that teachers have developed in their work. Second, it burdens the principal with having to possess all knowledge in regard to student learning and instruction. Third, it reduces the value of collaborative inquiry.

This traditional view of the principal as supervisor often assumes that the teacher is deficient. Instead of focusing on teaching and learning as a continuing process of improvement, the images found by Reitzug (1997) focused on finding and correcting errors. The images assume "that it is the supervisor/principal's judgment that counts; that the teacher may have an opinion is barely recognized. Finally, the images imply that the principal is the agent of improved instruction, not the teacher" (p. 333).

This traditional conception also assumes that teaching is a "fixed technology," a view that is incongruent with contemporary research on the nature of teaching. Several researchers on teaching (e.g., Darling-Hammond & Bransford, 2005; Darling-Hammond, Wise & Klein, 1995; Stodolsky, 1988) and on supervision (e.g., Nelson & Sassi, 2000) have pointed to the finding that good teaching techniques can vary with the situation or the subject. For example, direct instruction, which is sometimes used as the major form of teaching for all subjects, is only appropriate less than half of the teaching time (Darling-Hammond & Bransford).

Finally, the traditional role assumes that supervision consists of a discrete intervention, for example, an observation or evaluative conference. Such an image ignores the value and need for continuing learning and a school-wide culture of learning. Reitzug (1997) pointed out that this traditional conception includes only the teacher as needing growth. Instead of a conception of the school as a PLC (Bryk, Cambron, & Louis, 1999; DuFour, DuFour, & Eaker, 2008; DuFour, Eaker, & DuFour, 2005; Joyce, 2004) or as a community of inquiry (Copland, 2003; Smyth, 1997), this traditional image focuses attention only on teachers as learners.

The traditional image also assumes that the principal's role consists solely of directly supervising teachers rather than facilitating supervision through others. In the traditional conception, everything flows from the principal. However, this limits the instructional capacity of the school and thwarts the development of a PLC.

Traditional Supervisory Role of the Assistant Principal

In addition to the previously identified components of a traditional role of the supervisor, assistant principals encounter other factors that are part of a traditional role. First, the assistant principal's role has often come to reflect a noninstructional orientation that primarily emphasizes student management, defined as crowd control or policing disruptive students. Some assistant principals are hired specifically for these functions and are expected to take on this role rather than to make or mold a more innovative role. They find that the informal expectations for them to handle the student management function are so strong that little time is left for any instructional leadership role and that the student management role is usually not seen as a component of instructional leadership. Although job descriptions may include instructional leadership elements, the actual practice of many assistant principals tends to de-emphasize any instructional supervisory contribution.

Second, when assistant principals are expected to take a supervisory role, it frequently emphasizes the inspection function we discussed previously. In this traditional role, the assistant principal becomes essentially an informant who extends the inspection arm of the principal to check up on teachers. Clearly, such an inspection/informant role decreases the assistant principal's credibility with teachers to be a resource for instructional reflection and improvement and a collaborative partner in a community of learners.

In the next two sections, we focus on what we believe is a conception of the principal's and assistant principal's roles that takes seriously the role of supervisor but redefines that role in a more effective and facilitative way—the type of role Bill Payne tried to implement in the opening vignette. In the following, section we focus on what principals can do and be in a direct way as supervisors. In the subsequent section, we focus on how principals can facilitate supervision throughout the PLC of the school.

THE PRINCIPAL'S ROLE IN DIRECT SUPERVISION: AN INNOVATIVE CONCEPTION

In Chapter 4, we discussed the critical role of principal as learner and facilitator of the learning capacity of the school. In Chapter 5, we discussed the principal as culture builder. The principal's contemporary supervisory role, which we will describe in the remainder of this chapter, fits within the context of a community of learners. The contrast we make with the traditional inspection role of the principal emphasizes supervision as a learning process rather than as a monitoring process. In this chapter, we focus on the principal's role in improving learning by focusing on classroom practices. In the following section, we begin with a brief overview of this innovative role conception and then move to a discussion of five major functions of the principal's role, namely, establishing a system of accountability; recruiting, selecting, and retaining capable educators; promoting educator growth; building trust; and evaluating educational results.

Overview of the Innovative Role of Supervisor

If supervision is a learning process rather than a monitoring process, what does this mean for your role as a principal? In Reitzug's (1997) terms, it means that principals are partners in collaborative inquiry around teaching and learning. Frequently, however, the argument for collaborative inquiry fails to specify what the principal's direct role is in addition to a facilitative role. We argue that principals have a direct role to play in supervision in addition to facilitating a school-wide culture of collaborative inquiry among teachers.

This direct role involves building instructional capacity, the capability of schools to enhance student learning based on internal and external resources. If, as we have emphasized in Chapter 2, principals and assistant principals are responsible for helping the school become a PLC, one component of that role is the learning that occurs with teachers and students. The central focus of schools is teaching and learning. One of the most important ways principals and assistant principals contribute to this focus is to ensure that the school has the capability for teaching and learning to take place. Although instructional capacity involves a variety of concerns including fiscal and physical management, community support, and resources, one of the central features of instructional capacity is what happens when students and teachers come together.

We identify five major functions of the principal's role in building instructional capacity:

1. establishing a system of accountability,
2. recruiting, selecting, and retaining capable educators,
3. promoting educators' professional growth,
4. building trust,
5. evaluating educational results.

All five of these functions are direct and vital roles that principals and assistant principals play in building instructional capacity.

Establishing a System of Accountability

With the current advance of accountability in school settings, one of its manifestations has been the emphasis on teacher accountability that is connected to student achievement. School-building leaders need to develop the skills and knowledge to be able to know "when" and "how" to take the steps to raise student achievement (Wong and Nicotera, 2007). Most obvious of these measures to improve student achievement will be through improving the instructional capabilities of teachers.

One of the key provisions in the No Child Left Behind (NCLB) Act is accountability. Schools must meet adequate yearly progress (AYP) by developing objectives for all students. Schools not only meet AYP for the total aggregate of students, but must meet AYP for specific groups: economically disadvantaged, major ethnic and racial groups, students with disabilities, and students with limited English proficiency (LEP). The AYP objectives must be set with the goal that all students are proficient or better by the 2013–2014 school year. Schools that fail to meet their AYP objectives for two years will be identified for improvement. The students in these failing schools can transfer. If the school's scores do not improve after three years, the school is held accountable in two areas: the school curriculum and the school faculty, which can be replaced.

Thus far in the implementation of NCLB, the results are mixed. Some schools have improved because of accountability. Other schools have become demoralized. The fact is, accountability is part of our schooling system whether NCLB is fully enforced or not. Because of accountability, your role as a supervisor has increased substantially in the past decade. Most signs indicate that in the foreseeable future, this role will not soon dissipate.

Nevertheless, there are ways in which you as a principal or an assistant principal can develop positive and functional systems of accountability that will improve student learning. In a study with school principals in San Diego, California, Schnur and Gerson (2005) observed five core beliefs underlying the new responsibilities of principals to improve student learning.

1. Actions taken by adults (i.e., teachers and principals) are a primary determinant of student achievement.
2. The quality of classroom instruction is the single greatest determinant of student achievement.
3. A specific instructional and pedagogical agenda should be carried out in every public school classroom.

4. School leaders must provide teachers necessary skills and knowledge through professional development and coaching, and hold teachers accountable to using new strategies to change practice.

5. These instructional leadership practices can only be carried out effectively if principals have the knowledge and skills to play this role, especially to know about what good instruction looks like and how adults learn to improve their instructional methods.

RECRUITING, SELECTING, AND RETAINING CAPABLE AND COMMITTED EDUCATORS

Among the most important roles that you will play as a principal is securing capable and committed teachers for the school. There is no way to build instructional capacity without finding teachers who are able, effective educators for students. Although most new principals do not have the opportunity to recruit and select all teachers for a school, the appointment of each teacher sends an important message to students, parents, district administrators, and other teachers of your view of a capable and committed educator. Selecting teachers also gives you the opportunity to show others of your commitment in developing a PLC.

Recruiting and Selecting Teachers

Districts vary in terms of the role that principals can play in recruiting and selecting teachers. Most districts involve the principal significantly in this process, even to the point of allowing the principal or a school committee to make the final recommendation to the school board. Some districts have a school-based management process in which this final recommendation ultimately is left to a school committee composed of principal, teachers, parents, and occasionally students. A few districts make teacher selection decisions at a centralized level, essentially leaving out school-level input. This approach ignores the fact that the selection process significantly influences an educator's credibility. If administrators, fellow teachers, parents, and community members are left out of the recruitment and selection process, the teacher often will be seen as an outsider and will face an uphill battle for acceptance. Being an effective teacher involves supportive relationships with other educators, parents, and students.

Recruiting teachers is as important as selecting teachers and often is overlooked. Except in times of critical teacher shortages, the typical practice of some principals is to "wait and see" who the district office sends to be interviewed or who applies. This approach seldom results in finding the cream of the crop. A more proactive recruitment approach involves the principal keeping in close and continuing contact with university teacher educators, professional association representatives, and administrative colleagues to know who and where the best teachers are. Word travels fast about the best, conducive environments for teaching and the schools with the greatest instructional capacity, for example, PLC. Word also travels quickly about which schools lack the instructional capacity to foster teacher growth and student learning.

Although recruiting a teacher who is presently teaching in another school is sometimes seen as unprofessional, principals can employ certain recruiting tactics that are not offensive. For example, one high school principal recruited a band instructor simply by announcing the open position at a state music festival. An elementary school principal told the Parent Teacher Association (PTA) about openings for the next year, which resulted in one parent telling a neighbor, a teacher, who became interested in the opening. Further, many schools and districts are crossing state and national lines to recruit teachers. For example, recently more than twenty-five residents of the Philippines committed to teach in Nevada's Clark County School District.

A critical factor that has emerged in education has been the shortage of teachers. Using data collected from the National Education Association, Susan Moore Johnson (2004) indicated that the career longevity of teachers who were hired in the late 1960s and 1970s has had a significant effect on the distribution of teachers. As a group, the current retiring cohort has moved like a bubble through the teaching workforce. From 1971 to 1983, the largest proportion of the teaching force was under the age of thirty-five. This same cohort of teachers constituted the largest group, at ages thirty-five to forty-five, between 1983 and 1991. That cohort of teachers is retiring from the schools, which leads to a drastic need for principals and school district officials to increase their recruiting efforts.

The present teaching force also poses another implication for school leaders. The U-shaped distribution of new teachers on one end and veteran teachers on the other end of the career stage has developed into a generation gap. For many years, the teachers who approach retirement had no formal responsibility for the induction of new colleagues. As Johnson (2004) reported and the opening vignette illustrated, these veteran teachers have become accustomed to working alone and have tacitly endorsed the isolation that has typified classroom teaching for the last twenty-five years. We discussed this as a mentoring challenge in Chapter 6.

Selecting teachers is a critical part of your role as a principal, even if the final selection is not yours. We offer three major criteria that are critical in the selection process:

- fit
- expertise
- diversity

FIT Selecting teachers who *fit* the school's culture is critical. Although fit is a traditional concern of teacher selection, a more innovative supervisory role for principals involves recruiting and selecting teachers who have similar values and norms that contribute specifically to a PLC. These norms and values involve elements of a professional community that we discussed in Chapter 2, namely collaboration, de-privatized practice, shared values, and reflection. Selecting teachers who are willing to collaborate, reflect, open up their teaching to other educators, and share similar values of teaching and learning is a critical role for principals in building instructional capacity. No doubt there are other considerations of fit, for example, teaching philosophy, but these are usually less critical if the teacher is collaborative, reflective, open to critique, and if the teacher values learning.

EXPERTISE When considering expertise, criteria become more difficult to identify succinctly. There has been considerable research on effective teaching. However, the clear finding is that what is effective must be defined in terms of the goals (Glickman, Gordon, & Ross-Gordon, 2007). Effective teaching in a school where the goals are the development of a learning community is different from effective teaching in a school where higher achievement test scores are the only goal. Sergiovanni and Starratt (2007) identified characteristics of teachers who would be recruited in a learning community. These teachers

- are committed to the principle that all children can succeed at learning and will do all in their power to bring that about,
- are convinced that significant learning is achieved only by the active engagement of the learner in the production or performance of multiple expressions of authentic understanding,
- are committed to collaborating with other teachers in the school to build a flexible, responsive, and dynamic learning environment that engages every student,
- know the content of the academic disciplines they are teaching as well as the methodologies of inquiry of these disciplines,
- know the components of the meta-curriculum—the aspects of higher-order thinking and the major conceptual frameworks, models, and methodologies of the disciplines—and can recognize productions and performances that authenticate learners' reflective proficiency in the meta-curriculum,
- have executive control of a wide variety of instructional protocols and strategies for opening up the curriculum for youngsters,
- can design a variety of learning activities for individuals as well as groups that will maximize autonomous, active involvement with the material,
- continually monitor students' work through dialogue and action research so as to assess whether an individual student is experiencing difficulties, to discover what the source of those difficulties are, and to respond in ways that will facilitate mastery of the learning tasks,
- are committed to working with parents as partners in supporting the learning tasks in which their children are engaged,
- can evaluate, in both formative and summative procedures, a variety of assessment performances and portfolios,
- can construct, in collaboration with parents, administrators, and the school board, the school's learning environment whenever necessary. (pp. 103–104)

DIVERSITY The third criterion that principals must address in recruiting and selecting capable educators is diversity. In light of the changing demographics of contemporary schools and the increased heterogeneity projected for the future, school faculty and staff members need to reflect the ethnic diversity of the students. For example, in 2003, nearly 40 percent of U.S. public school children were members of minority groups, compared to less than 10 percent of teachers (Snyder & Hoffman, 2003). Although school boards may differ in terms of controversial issues such as using quotas to diversify the faculty, there should be no disagreement that students, both majority and minority, need the opportunities inherent in an ethnically diverse teaching force.

In addition to recruiting ethnically diverse faculty, principals must recruit and select educators who represent different points of view. Here lies a dilemma for the principal. As we have noted previously, teachers need to share the values with the school's culture. However, if everyone thinks the same, shares the same philosophy of teaching, and graduates from the same university teaching program, innovation is likely to be thwarted. The fundamental values of reflection, collaboration, and shared values do not mean that there is one best way to teach or interact with students. Contrived collegiality (Hargreaves, 1990) and groupthink, in which everyone uses the same process for reaching the same decisions, are not conducive to the development of a PLC. Principals need to actively recruit and select educators who value openness, collaboration, reflection, and inquiry and who are not afraid to disagree with other educators, including the principal.

Although recruiting and selecting may have been a responsibility of the principal, an innovative conception of the role means that principals and assistant principals will perform these functions in a new way. Primarily, this innovative conception of the role of principal means that principals and assistant principals will be proactive in their recruitment, will consider characteristics that contribute to the school as a PLC, will focus on teaching and learning within this context of collaborative inquiry, and will encourage diversity.

RETAINING QUALIFIED TEACHERS

As important as recruiting and selecting teachers is, the retaining of qualified teachers in the profession is also critical. In the traditional role, a supervisor will often not renew a struggling teacher's contract by claiming that hiring a new teacher would be better. However, that choice is not only unavailable in times of a teacher shortage, but it is also unethical. The newly conceptualized supervisor knows that the best way to develop a strong teaching faculty is through professional development and mentoring. Likewise, teachers must want to remain in the profession and in your school. Many teachers chose to leave schools in which they were currently teaching. For example, of the 3,214,900 public school teachers who were teaching during the 2003–2004 school year, 84 percent remained at the same school (stayers), 8 percent moved to a different school (movers), and 8 percent left the profession (leavers) during the following year. Among private school teachers, 81 percent were stayers, 6 percent were movers, and 14 percent were leavers (Marvel, Lyter, Peltola, Strizek, & Mortan 2006).

Why do movers and leavers choose to depart from their schools? Thirty-eight percent of public and 33 percent of private school movers rated the opportunity for a better teaching assignment as very important or extremely important in their decision to change schools. Another 25 percent of public and 30 percent of private school leavers rated pursuing a position other than that of a K–12 teacher as very important or extremely important in their decision to leave K–12 teaching. According to Marvel and colleagues' (2006) study, 63 percent of public school teachers who left a school in 2003–2004 did so to find another place of employment. Obviously, these teachers who were not retained in their schools were a lost resource to that school's learning community. As they left, they also took with them the professional development, experience, and expertise that might not have been replaced with the hiring of new teachers.

As Johnson (2004) claimed, from the perspective of the school, the departure of an experienced, effective teacher reduces that school's capacity to do its work. Whether the departing teacher leaves for another career or moves to the school across town because it offers a better workplace, that individual takes away an acquired expertise and accumulated knowledge about the students, their families, the curriculum, and the school's practices. Such turnover compromises the chance that all students will be taught by effective teachers. Johnson also claimed that losses of teachers impose

Professional Dilemma 9.1

Recruiting and selecting teachers is usually a difficult task. Do you recruit and select a teacher who matches the school's culture or one who contributes to the diversity of points of view? What situational factors contribute to the decision?

substantial financial and organizational costs on school districts—estimates can range from $5000 to $10,000 per teacher who leaves.

In many ways, your position as a principal or assistant principal will determine the retention rates of teachers in your school. Recruiting qualified teachers is important but retaining qualified teachers and developing their abilities is probably even more important. In the next subsection, we discuss how educator growth is an important element in building instructional capacity.

PROMOTING EDUCATOR GROWTH

The third function in building instructional capacity involves the role of the principal and assistant principal in promoting educator growth. In this role, we discuss three components:

- fostering teacher practical knowledge,
- encouraging reflection,
- offering expertise in a climate of mutual inquiry.

These three components represent an innovative role for you as a principal or assistant principal in contributing to teacher growth and student learning within a PLC.

Fostering Teacher Practical Knowledge

First, the principal fosters teachers' practical knowledge (Darling-Hammond & Bransford, 2005; Sternberg & Wagner, 1986). Teachers are not blank tablets waiting for principals to write strategies for improvement. They have more potential understanding of classroom culture, student learning styles, and in most cases, curricula than the principal. The principal's role is to value this practical knowledge and help teachers articulate it and use it to solve instructional problems and create more responsive learning environments. Obviously, the degree of practical knowledge will vary depending on the teacher's career stage, experience, and ability.

Reflection

Second, the principal encourages reflection. The purpose of supervisory practices such as post-observation conferences is not simply to list the teacher's strengths and weaknesses. Rather, fundamentally, the conference is to provide an opportunity for reflection within an accepting context, which enhances teachers' own learning. In addition, the principal's role is to encourage reflection on teaching and learning throughout the school and throughout the teacher's career. Reflection is an ongoing process, not a once-a-year event.

Professional Dilemma 9.2

Who should help in the teacher selection process? In a middle school social studies department, a teaching opening created a difference of opinion between the school's principal and
the department chair. The social studies department in the school was well known as being the
most social group in the school. The teachers had their own Friday afternoon parties and
frequent out-of-school activities, and they often went to the local NBA games together. The
department chair wanted to select a teacher who fit the department's social circle. The principal wanted someone who believed in the middle school philosophy and had experience in
teaching early adolescents. Although the principal wanted input from the department, it was
obvious that department members were looking for different attributes than the administration. To solve the problem, the principal asked other teachers from the school to help with the
selection. This proved to be quite successful in that other teachers looked for more of a school
culture fit than a department clone.

Reflection also involves teachers working with other teachers in a collaborative
way to improve and experiment with instructional practices. Reeves (2004) commented:

> Reflection, therefore, requires not only the analytical task of reviewing one's
> own observations but also the more challenging task of listening to
> colleagues and comparing notes. The reflective process is at the very heart of
> accountability. It is through reflection that we distinguish between the popu-
> larity of teaching techniques and their effectiveness. The question is not "Did
> I like it?" but "Was it effective?" (p. 52)

Inquiry

The third component in promoting educator growth is for the principal to offer
expertise in a climate of inquiry. Being an expert and sharing expertise are positive characteristics, unless the principal and teachers assume that only the principal possesses
expertise. Opening the principal's own practice to inquiry and critique not only encourages teachers to do likewise but also sends a powerful message to the school that inquiry is valued by all. The principal also shares expertise by identifying and using alternative perspectives for the critique of practice.

In the following subsection we will continue the examination of the role of principal
as supervisor in promoting educator growth by organizing our discussion around
Reitzug's (1997) elements: conception of teacher, view of teaching, conception of the
supervisor, and conception of supervision.

CONCEPTION OF THE TEACHER   The first element of an innovative role of the principal
in promoting educator growth is a view of the teacher as a professional with practical
knowledge or the potential for developing this knowledge. As Reitzug (1997) pointed
out, research has demonstrated the presence of widespread knowledge acquired by
teachers through their daily involvement in defining and shaping the problems of practice (Lieberman & Miller, 1991). Viewing the teacher as a learning professional means
that the teacher may have more understanding of the classroom culture, more knowledge of the curricula, and greater sensitivity to student needs and learning styles than

the principal or assistant principal. Admittedly, new teachers and some veteran teachers may not yet have developed these characteristics or are incompetent (Bridges, 1986; Roberts, 2000), but the existence of incompetence or inexperience in a few teachers does not necessitate viewing teachers generally as incompetent or inexperienced. Discovering doctors who are callous or lack knowledge regarding particular diseases should not result in a view that all doctors are quacks. Why should teachers be considered otherwise?

Part of being a professional is being a self-directed learner. The teacher is responsible for reflecting on and improving teaching and learning in the classroom. In a PLC, this learning is also collaborative. The principal promotes educator growth by having confidence in and encouraging the learning capacity of the teacher.

The principal's understanding of the teacher's role also acknowledges teacher differences and development. Glickman and colleagues' (2007) developmental approach to supervision is based on the recognition that teachers differ, and the need for supervisory approaches varies depending on these differences. A number of models of adult and teacher development identify teacher differences with regard to concerns (Fuller, F., 1969), conceptual level (Hammerness, Darling-Hammond, & Bransford, 2005; Hunt, 1966), moral development (Gilligan, 1982; Kohlberg & Armon, 1984), and life-cycle development (Erikson, 1963). For example, Fuller's concerns model identified the stages of concern that teachers face in their careers: survival, mastery of tasks, and impact. This model suggests that not only are teachers professionals but also that, like all adults, they vary in terms of their development. As Tracy (1998) pointed out, this variation in development means that the supervisory focus is not predetermined; the teacher rather than the supervisor or some external criteria decides on the focus.

VIEW OF TEACHING Reitzug (1997) argued that the traditional view of supervision holds that teaching is a fixed technology. In fact, research demonstrates that teaching is a highly complex, context-specific, interactive activity (e.g., Cochran-Smith & Lytle, 1992). Instead of viewing teaching as a set of generic principles that occurs similarly in all contexts regardless of demographics, goals, values, and so on, a principal should view teaching as a dynamic, complex process.

Regardless of whether teaching is seen as art (Darling-Hammond & Bransford, 2005; Eisner, 1985), science (Hunter, 1984), or some combination of both, it needs to be viewed as a complex and dynamic activity. It is complex because it involves discretion and judgment rather than routines and scripts. It is dynamic because it necessitates responses to students who are constantly changing in their maturity, development, interests, and commitment and knowledge that is fluid and co-constructed.

As pointed out in Chapter 4, work roles in the twenty-first century will move from an emphasis on rationality to an emphasis on complexity (Hage & Powers, 1992; Johnson, S. M., 2004). Work defined by routines and standardization of practice will give way to work that emphasizes human agency and the continuing process of information search. This type of work also will emphasize customization and innovation rather than efficiency and volume of work. After decades of trying to "teacher-proof" the curriculum, administrators and teachers must look at teaching as a complex and dynamic process.

Teaching is also complex because of the increasing demand that teachers interact with multiple agencies and professionals (Crowson, 2001; Forbes, & Watson, in press).

Instead of isolated classroom activities with occasional interactions with parents, many teachers interact daily with professionals, such as counselors, special educators, mental health and social service agency personnel, and law enforcement officers. In order to provide more comprehensive responses to the needs of students, teaching has become more complex in the variety and number of professionals who are interacting. Encouraging the professional growth of teachers, then, requires acknowledging this more complex form.

CONCEPTION OF THE SUPERVISOR   The third element of Reitzug's (1997) view of supervision is a new conception of the supervisor. Instead of the principal being the sole repository of expertise and the author of change, the teacher becomes the agent of improved instruction. The supervisor's role becomes one of facilitating the teacher's agency within a context of mutual, collaborative inquiry.

Revising the role of supervisor means considering anew the notion of professional authority and control. Instead of the principal having supervisory authority by virtue of position and having absolute control of the supervisory process, an innovative role of supervisor acknowledges a more functional authority and variation in control of the supervisory process. Tracy (1998) presented categories of supervisory approaches that reflect different notions of authority. In the case of clinical supervision, principals have functional authority based on experience and insight rather than expertise. In this case, they partner with teachers to identify goals, problems, and alternative courses of action. In collegial supervision, the role of the supervisor is to provide resources and help for teachers. In self-directed supervision, professional authority resides with the teachers who work alone on their professional development. Informal supervision includes encounters that are more casual and authority that is more functional. Finally, in the inquiry model, instructional problems are coresearched.

In their developmental supervision approach, Glickman, Gordon, and Ross-Gordon (2004) argued that authority and control depend on the developmental level of the teacher. In a directive approach, where the teacher's development is at a low, more conceptually concrete level, the principal as supervisor takes more control. The authority resides with the principal. In a nondirective approach, where the teacher's development is at a high, more conceptually abstract level, the teacher takes the control and possesses the authority. In a collaborative approach, principal and teacher share authority and control.

In addition to issues of authority and control, the role of the supervisor raises concerns about the relationship between teachers and principals. This relationship is critical in the everyday work life of schools. Principals frequently are concerned that supervisory activities can threaten this relationship. Several research studies have examined this relationship in the context of supervisory practice. Bulach, Bothe, and Michael (1999) surveyed over two hundred graduate students to examine their view as teachers of their principals' supervisory behaviors. Two interesting findings resulted. Teachers with more experience were more likely to rate their principal's supervisory behavior as lower in terms of trust behavior. These authors suggested that one possible explanation for this is that "principals could be using the same authoritarian leadership style with experienced and better prepared teachers as well as beginning and bachelor degree teachers" (p. 10). These authors also found that elementary school teachers were more likely to rate their principals' supervisory behavior as more caring and trustworthy than were secondary school teachers. Elementary school teachers also were more likely to see their principals as more capable in curricular and instructional areas.

Some principals assume that teachers do not want them involved in supervision. However, Gordon, Stockard, and Williford (1992) found that teachers want their principals knowledgeable of and involved with the instructional program. Other principals may not believe that their supervision is effective. Sheppard (1996) found a strong and positive relationship between principals' instructional leadership behaviors and teacher commitment, professional involvement, and innovation. The kinds of principal behaviors related to these teacher practices included supervising and evaluating instruction, providing incentives, and maintaining high visibility. The most influential behavior for both elementary and secondary school teachers was the principal's behavior in promoting professional development.

Probably the most important characteristic of the role of principal and assistant principal as supervisor relates to mutual inquiry. The conception of supervisor that we encourage is one in which principals and assistant principals are participants in the community of learners. In this regard, they open their own practice to critique and inquiry.

Part of acknowledging the principal and assistant principal as participants in the community of inquirers is an acknowledgement that principals, like teachers, continue to develop in their roles. Crehan and Grimmett (1989) examined the relationship between teachers' conceptual level and principals' conceptual level and concluded that although a teacher's conceptual level may be critical to the success of the supervisory conference, the principal's conceptual level may be key to its failure. When the principal's conceptual level was low, there was a tendency for the focus of the conference to get deflected to other issues. These findings suggest that the principal's own conceptual growth is an important component of supervisory practice. Very little research has been conducted on principals' conceptual development, yet it seems critical to the success of supervisory practice.

Although it should be obvious by this point, we believe that assistant principals have an important role to play as supervisors. The traditional role of assistant principal has tended to ignore the instructional leadership role and force the assistant principal into a role-taking orientation. However, a more innovative role places a strong emphasis on the assistant principal as an instructional leader with a supervisory function. Glickman and his colleagues (2004) and Peters (1989) maintained that good supervision requires time, and thus the assistant principal needs to be involved in observing and conferencing with teachers. This innovative role conception encourages assistant principals to focus on role making, in which they mold the role to a more instructional leadership orientation.

CONCEPTION OF SUPERVISION   Reitzug (1997) argued that the traditional conception of supervision involves a discrete intervention, usually an observation and a conference. However, innovative conception views supervision as a sustained, integrated, and ongoing process in which professional development is seen as involving all educators, including the principal, and continuing throughout the career. Based on Smyth's (1997) notion of communities of inquiry, Reitzug viewed supervision as providing an environment in which it is safe to make mistakes, try new ideas, and risk failure. This learning environment also involves greater autonomy, opportunities for professional conversation, and alternative frameworks for thinking about teaching and learning.

Tracy (1998) identified a set of assumptions of future models of supervision that seem especially relevant to an innovative conception of supervision. These assumptions included the following.

1. The school is a community of life-long learners.
2. Persons are capable of taking responsibility for their own growth, of being self-directed and self-supervising, when the proper resources and support mechanisms are available.
3. Adult learners have their own unique needs that are distinct from those of children.
4. To improve the performance of any one individual, supervisors must consider the total organizational environment in which that person works.
5. People learn best and are motivated by collaborating with others. (p. 105)

This conception of supervision that encourages a community of learning and inquiry also involves a broader and more varied view of supervisory activities. Claudet and Ellett (1999) suggested that supervision involves both micro- and macro-level events. Traditionally, supervision has included only "isolated micro-events," where the principal observed the teacher and conducted a conference. However, supervision activities in schools should be much broader.

Supervisory activities engaged in by school personnel can include, but are not limited to, such things as involvement of teachers and administrators on instructional and curricular improvement teams and committees, supervision and mentoring of intern and beginning teachers by veteran teachers, formal and informal peer or colleague supervisory and mentoring activities, and individual and group (collaborative) planning of professional development activities.

In addition, activities that are more casual, such as informal hall conversations or ongoing memos around instructional issues, are supervisory in nature. We will return to these larger macro-level supervisory events in the last section of this chapter. However, it is useful to realize that the conception of supervision recommended in this chapter involves the principal, assistant principal, and teachers in a broad and varied set of activities that go beyond the discrete interventions of observing and conferencing.

Another way to conceive of supervision has been introduced by Blase and Blase (2004). In their study of what good instructional leaders do, these authors proposed that the conception of supervision of good principals involves three major components, which they refer to as the *TiGeR model*. First, good principals talk with teachers. This involves activities such as observing, conferring, building trust, and maintaining visibility. Second, good principals promote teacher growth by providing resources and time, giving feedback, providing professional development, and supporting practice of new skills, risk taking, and innovation. Third, good principals foster teacher reflection. In order to do this, these principals engage in such activities as developing teachers' reflection skills; modeling and developing teachers' critical study (action research) skills; becoming inquiry-oriented; using data to question, evaluate, and critique teaching and learning; and extending autonomy to teachers. Their conception of supervision is based on findings regarding the differences between effective and ineffective principals. Effective principals are visible but do not interrupt or abandon teachers. Effective principals praise rather than criticize. And effective principals extend autonomy rather than maintain control.

An innovative conception of supervision involves more sustained professional development and a broader assortment of activities than the traditional conception. Principals and assistant principals who mold their roles in this more innovative way will see supervision as an ongoing process rather than a once-a-year event. They will be actively engaged in activities that keep teaching and learning at the forefront of attention in a PLC. And they will be involved in mutual inquiry, which means that they will model by subjecting their own practice to scrutiny. These practices build on the relationship of trust among all educators, the subject we discuss in the next subsection.

Establishing Trust

The fourth function of principals in establishing instructional capacity involves creating a culture of social trust. Simply put, principals and assistant principals who have the trust of faculty, staff, and parents are more likely to be successful in creating PLCs. Although the majority of principals and assistant principals mean well, often their practices are such that social trust is destroyed by these practices. For example, a principal avoiding confronting an incompetent teacher because the principal does not like to deal with conflict is actually exhibiting a trust-defeating type of behavior. Others in the school know of the teacher's incompetence and know it is the responsibility of the principal to handle the problem. When the principal fails to confront the issue, trust diminishes.

Trust has paradoxically been viewed as both a glue and a lubricant. As glue, trust binds organizational participants to one another, but without it, things fall apart. To be a productive learning community and to accomplish goals, a school faculty needs cohesive and cooperative relationships. Trust is essential to fostering these relationships. As a lubricant, trust greases the machinery of the school organization. Trust lubricates communication and contributes to greater efficiency when people can have confidence in others' words and deeds (Tschannen-Moran, 2004)

What exactly is trust? After studying various definitions of trust, Tschannen-Moran (2004) developed her own definition: Trust is one's willingness to be vulnerable to another based on the confidence that the other is benevolent, honest, open, reliable, and competent. The problem with a definition such as this is that it is a difficult quality to put into practice. The context of the situation often dictates how a person reacts to others. Although knowing what trust is important, it is not always something that can be easily established.

In a study of Chicago elementary schools, Bryk and Schneider (2003) established four considerations for establishing relational trust with others: respect, competence, personal regard for others, and integrity. We next discuss each of these components with implications for principals and assistant principals in their supervision roles.

RESPECT In the context of schooling, respect involves recognition of the important role each person plays in a child's education. Bryk and Schneider (2003) reported that the key in this regard is how conversation takes place within a school community. "A genuine sense of listening to what each person has to say marks the basis for meaningful social interaction" (p. 23). In their observations, Bryk and Schneider found that the communication among individuals in meetings was often regulated through formal parliamentary procedures. They claim that these procedures might grant someone a right to speak but do not necessarily mean that anyone actually attends to what is said.

"Such exchanges are quite different from those where individuals intently listen toeach other and in some fashion take others' perspectives into account in further action. Genuine conversation of this sort signals that each person's ideas have value and that the education of children requires that we work together cooperatively. (Bryk & Schneider, 2002, p. 23)"

These types of conversations are important in establishing a culture of trust. Teachers need to be able to voice their concerns and feel that the principal will consider their concerns. Likewise, principals in turn need to feel that teachers share their efforts for the effective supervision of personnel in the school. In each case, genuine listening fosters a sense of respect.

COMPETENCE Competence is defined by Bryk and Schneider (2002) as the execution of an individual's formal role responsibilities in such a way as to achieve desired results. A principal's incompetence could be displayed by the disorganized nature of observations and the conferences that follow. Such incompetence will soon undermine the efforts of the relational trust with teachers and the ability of the principal to improve the instructional process.

PERSONAL REGARD FOR OTHERS In general, relational trust deepens as people perceive that others care about them and are willing to extend themselves beyond what their role might formally require. For example, a principal might understand a young mother's tardiness at school because of childcare problems. The principal could arrange for the class to be covered in such emergencies until the teacher can get the childcare situation resolved. A small act such as this shows a personal regard for the teacher and her classroom. As Bryk and Schneider (2002) commented, "When school community members sense being cared about, they experience a social affiliation of personal meaning and value. Such actions invite reciprocation from others" (p. 25).

INTEGRITY Most people credit individuals with integrity if there is consistency between what they say and what they do. However, in a deeper sense, integrity also implies that an ethical perspective guides a person's work. A school community consists of many individuals with various goals. Conflicts arise when someone's goals are threatened at being or actually are thwarted. The school culture must be of such that conflicts can be resolved around the primary mission and vision of the school. The adults in the school might have to park their personal egos outside of school while students' welfare and well-being are considered.

Principals can demonstrate integrity when they do what they say they are going to do. For example, if a principal tells teachers that an after school faculty meeting will only take 30 minutes, then the principal must cut the meeting off at the half hour mark or face the consequences of being disingenuous with what is said to teachers.

We see relational trust as a resource for developing a PLC. Without it, the cultural shift into a PLC will certainly be impeded and the supervisor role of the principal and assistant principal will be diminished.

Evaluating Educational Results

The fifth function of an innovative role for the principal as supervisor involves evaluating educational results. In this subsection, we focus on evaluating educational results in the classroom by discussing two aspects: evaluating instructional capacity in the classroom and the regular collection and analysis of student performance data.

In general, the focus for school leaders has been on procedural and programmatic compliance rather than results driven leadership. The bureaucratic structure of the education system created divisions in the roles of educators that often manifested itself in teacher isolation and principal overseeing. In general, principals and teachers have always cared about students and their learning, but their roles were defined in such narrow ways that the opportunities for them to interact with others to improve student learning were limited; principals were not as interested as perhaps they should have been with results as with teacher compliance, and they fell into what Wong and Nicotera (2007) described as "managing by rules" rather than what Schlechty (2002) called "leading by results."

EVALUATING INSTRUCTIONAL CAPACITY   Too often teacher evaluation means the rating, grading, and classifying of teachers using some locally standardized instrument as a yardstick. Often the instrument lists traits of teachers assumed to be important, such as "The teacher has a pleasant voice," and certain tasks of teaching considered critical, such as "The teacher plans well."

The traditional conception of evaluating teachers usually includes an annual observation followed by a conference with the teacher. In some districts, new teachers are evaluated more often during their probation period, and veteran teachers are evaluated less often and sometimes rarely. State and local policies and procedures usually prescribe the evaluation process.

This evaluation process is typically held to two types of standards Webb, L. D., Montello, P. A., & Norton, M. S. (2004). Technical standards involve validity, reliability, and utility. Legal standards involve substantive due process concerns that relate to the objectivity of criteria, standards, evidence, and results and procedural due process issues that relate to the fairness of the process.

The typical evaluation process involves summative evaluations rather than formative ones. This process may involve comparison of the teacher with others (norm referenced) or with some established standard (criterion referenced).

This traditional conception of evaluation relies on several assumptions that Sergiovanni and Starratt (2007) called into question and issued a caution to supervisors. The first assumption is that there is a clear set of criteria or standards understood and accepted by all with which a teacher's performance can be evaluated. As we pointed out earlier in this chapter, the research suggests that there is no one set of teacher behaviors that is appropriate in every context.

The second assumption is that sporadic, unannounced classroom visits, with no prior conversations and no subsequent discussion, are a legitimate and acceptable way to assess teacher performance. Some principals believe that if they and the teacher plan the classroom visit, the teacher may be able to "stage" an atypical lesson. In addition to a conception of the role that emphasizes inspection, this belief assumes that what the principal observes in an unannounced visit is a fair sample and that the principal knows what the teacher intended by the lesson.

The third assumption identified by Sergiovanni and Starratt (2007) is that student achievement of course objectives is the only way to evaluate teacher performance. Two difficulties inherent in this assumption are that we know how to measure student achievement in a holistic sense and that student achievement is totally controlled by what the teacher does. This assumption is currently in vogue in several state and district evaluation policies. Without devaluing the teacher's responsibility for student achievement, it is nevertheless important to acknowledge the complexity of student learning.

Finally, the fourth assumption that Sergiovanni and Starratt (2007) argued was that the summative evaluation frequently assumes that the "evaluation of teacher performance should deal only with observable classroom behaviors" (p. 304). If the principal assumes that counting, for example, the types of questions the teacher asks or how many times the teacher calls on boys versus girls, is the only measure of teacher performance, this ignores the content that the teacher teaches.

These assumptions do not mean that evaluation is unimportant nor impossible for the principal. Rather, they suggest that if the principal evaluates teaching with these assumptions in mind and assumes that the evaluation is a completely objective assessment of the teacher, the result may be an incomplete picture of the classroom instruction and perhaps a legally indefensible position.

We propose that evaluation can be an important role for principals in assessing the instructional capacity of the school. An innovative conception of evaluation involves creating an environment that helps teachers and other staff in the school, including principals and assistant principals, to assess the instructional strengths and needs of the classroom. This conception of evaluation begins with the recognition that the teacher is a partner in evaluation. Instead of evaluation targeting the teacher's deficiencies, the purpose becomes one of assessing the classroom's instructional capacity, which includes not only what the teacher does but also what students do, what the principal provides, what resources parents and others provide, and so on.

TYPES OF EVALUATION   In developing this innovative conception, it may be helpful to distinguish types of evaluation and to understand the difference between evaluation and supervision. Sergiovanni and Starratt (1998) identified three types of evaluation: supervisory formative evaluation, supervisory summative evaluation, and administrative evaluation.

Supervisory formative evaluation is designed to provide ongoing reflective professional growth and is the process we discussed in the preceding subsection. We would in fact label this as formative supervision and the other two as summative evaluation and administrative evaluation. The point of supervisory formative evaluation, from our perspective, is not evaluation in the usual sense of the term but rather professional growth. No attempt is being made to provide a summative judgment of the teaching or the teacher.

Supervisory summative evaluation, on the other hand, is designed to provide an assessment of performance. Although the typical gatherer of this information is the administrator in the context of some district or state requirement, we believe that teachers should be partners both in its process and in its product.

The typical tool used in this type of evaluation is an observation checklist completed by the principal to rate the teacher. However, numerous other tools provide multiple sources of information and thus perspectives on classroom instruction, for example, portfolios, client surveys, student performance data, self-evaluations, and peer evaluations.

These last two tools are used rarely but offer valuable sources that could enrich the information provided on instructional capacity in the classroom and could encourage teachers to become collaborative partners in the evaluation process. If the purpose is to move beyond simply giving a judgment of the teacher's deficiencies to providing a richer assessment of the classroom's instructional capacity, these multiple sources could be very useful.

One principal described how he and the teachers redesigned the evaluation process to make it more useful to teachers. The process included a peer evaluation model in which teachers observed each other's classrooms and conducted post-observation conferences with the principal present, which satisfied the district's conferencing requirement. However, the principal's role was nonevaluative during the conference. Instead, the principal asked questions of the teachers to help them reflect on and assess the classroom learning. The final annual conference continued to be between the principal and the teacher, but the potency of that conference was strengthened by the previous peer evaluations.

The third type of evaluation is administrative evaluation. This type must be clearly distinguished from the other two in purpose. Administrative evaluation occurs when there is some quality control issue or problem, for example, an incompetent teacher. It is also used to make tenure, promotion, or dismissal decisions. The process is formal and must be consistently administered in legally defensible ways.

This type of evaluation, obviously, is not the most comfortable for administrators. However, the principal often is legally responsible for making recommendations in this type of evaluation. Bridges (1986), in a classic study on incompetent teachers, identified four responses of principals: to avoid, to compromise, to confront, and to tolerate. Further research by Roberts (2000) found that principals were most likely to say that they confronted incompetent teachers and were next likely to say that they compromised. She also found that there were a variety of factors including union pressure, contracts, and time that principals said influenced the response they made to incompetent teachers.

We note here that some educators have argued that the principal cannot both supervise and evaluate because the two processes are contradictory; one is for professional growth, and one is for quality control. We believe, however, that it is important for the principal and assistant principal to do both because to limit the principal's role to evaluation removes the principal from a substantive instructional leadership role. There are, undoubtedly, problems inherent in the principal performing both supervision and evaluation, for example, diminished rapport with teachers who realize that the person encouraging their professional growth is also the one who will provide the summative assessment. In order for the principal and assistant principal to do both supervision and evaluation, you as the principal and the teachers within the school must clearly distinguish these roles and when they are being performed. The different purposes and processes of supervision and evaluation must be clearly articulated and acknowledged. The principal and teachers must understand why and how administrative evaluation is conducted and distinguish it from supervision and summative evaluation. The issue of being both an evaluator and a supervisor can be reduced if you as the principal establish a culture of trust and collaboration that has a vision for school improvement and increased student learning. Within this culture, a PLC will thrive.

The Regular Collection and Analysis of Student Performance Data

Lortie (1975) wrote more than three decades ago that "the monitoring of effective instruction is the heart of effective instruction" (p. 141). A good example of using Lortie's advice can be witnessed at one elementary school. The school's principal and teachers decided to systematically raise overall achievement because they were tired of being last in the district. A crucial component of their effort was collecting data on a regular basis from student work. Teachers were then able to base instructional decisions on solid data rather than on assumptions and isolated anecdotal evidence. With the help of their principal, teachers made regular adjustments early on in a teaching unit before students had a chance to begin the downward spiral of failure. Through a system of preventions and interventions, the student achievement scores rose steadily and after three years surpassed even the highest elementary school in the district. (For further information regarding this school and its progress, see Huff, 2008).

What kind of results and data is needed to make improvements such as this example in student achievement? Our view is that a more balanced and pragmatic understanding of data is needed. Schools have historically been collecting data from such sources as standardized test scores, drop out rates, attendance percentages, and the number of student failures in certain courses. What has happened, however, is that this kind of data is either not used for learning or often misused for other purposes. Schools also have not collected the right kind of data. Test scores and letter grades do not give much help for improving student achievement. What is needed is a more balanced system of creating and using data to improve student learning.

What we propose is redefining what is meant by results. The current assessment atmosphere pervading the school culture makes a new definition possible. As Schmoker (2006) suggested, results should take us beyond the exclusive use of annual indicators such as standardized test scores. If educators want standardized tests to improve, then it is necessary to focus on short-term results that indicate progress toward instructional goals. Short-term results give more timely information that teachers can use to adjust their instructional methods along the way before the standardized test. These short-term results are produced from teacher generated assessments. These assessments must line up with the instructional goals that are measured by the annual standardized tests.

Likewise, Schmoker (2006) advised that all accountability should focus primarily on improvement. The information that is collected and analyzed needs to help teachers to understand and improve instructional processes that help get better results. If we as educators do not supplement standardized tests with more meaningful alternatives, then we invite parents and policy makers to use only the standardized test scores to hold us accountable.

We do not want to suggest that standardized tests are unnecessary or that they are meaningless. In fact, such tests can be helpful in the instructional process. Too often, however, teachers do not use standardized test results for improving instruction. The results of the tests are either not shared with teachers or they arrive too late for teachers to do anything with the results. Furthermore, the problem as Wiggins (1994) pointed out is not standardized tests but the failure of teachers to be results focused and to use the results as a part of their wider array of assessments. Standardized tests, indeed, reveal progress and areas that are in need of improvement. They provide a level of analysis for the principal and teachers who are trying to improve their school. By analyzing and disaggregating the test results, you and teachers can see what instructional areas are in the most need for initial improvement. However, as principal, you need to go beyond the standardized tests to improve teaching and instructional methods. It is here that we suggest that as a supervisor wanting to improve student learning that you help teachers establish such strategies as action research, common assessments, rubrics, and authentic assessments.

Good examples of regular collection and analysis of student performance data already exists in the schools. You need to look no further than what special education teachers have been doing for years. They have used collection and analysis of student performance quite successfully for improving reading and math scores. Likewise, other examples of good collection and analysis can be found in music and athletic programs. These directors and coaches are constantly assessing and analyzing student performance. They then adjust their teaching and coaching from the results to help their student improve their performance. As principal, you need to establish similar models of collection and analysis of data to help all teachers improve all student learning.

Tucker and Stronge (2005) suggested several steps in using student learning results in the supervision and evaluation of teachers.

1. Use student learning results as only one component of a teacher assessment system that is based on multiple data sources.
2. Always consider the context in which teaching and learning exist. For example, student mobility, absenteeism, and other variables beyond the control of the teacher can be real impediments to student learning.
3. Compare learning gains from one point in time to another point in time for the same students, not different groups of students.
4. Select student assessment measures that are most closely aligned with existing curricula.

In this section we have identified a direct role as supervisor for the principal and the assistant principal. We have defined this role in terms of five areas: establishing systems of accountability; recruiting, selecting and retaining capable educators; promoting educator professional growth; building trust; and evaluating educational results. All five of these areas contribute to building instructional capacity in the classroom. In the next section we focus our understanding of the principal's role in facilitating the leadership in supervision.

THE PRINCIPAL'S ROLE AS FACILITATOR OF SUPERVISION

As principal or assistant principal, you can extend the instructional capacity of the classroom by facilitating the involvement of leadership teams in the supervisory process. In the opening vignette, this facilitative role is what Bill attempted to implement with the veteran teachers providing supervisory help to new teachers. As Bill's experience pointed out, this facilitative role is not always welcomed but is, nevertheless, a critical, innovative role for principals and assistant principals to play. This facilitative supervision role fits into the previously discussed role of the principal as learner in facilitating the PLC. It also fits with Chapter 8 as the principal facilitates other educators in mentoring. In this section, we will discuss why the facilitative role in supervision is critical. We will develop a conception of the role of principal as facilitator of supervision with others.

Why Supervision Should Be Shared

Facilitating others in supervision in a PLC is critical both to your own work as principal and to the work of the faculty. First, the increased complexity of the principal's role (Crow, 2006b) and the resulting time demands necessitate that building instructional capacity in the school must be the responsibility of others in addition to the principal. Various writers in the supervision literature (e.g., Glickman et al., 2007) pointed out that the specific requirements of conducting intensive supervision defined as professional growth requires significant time. These authors, in fact, estimated that an average principal could directly supervise (based on the developmental supervision model) approximately ten teachers per year. Because most supervisory assignments are larger than this, it is obvious that others in addition to the principal and assistant principal must be involved in supervision.

The second reason for sharing supervision is reflected in the innovative role we proposed in the preceding section. The principal should not be considered the sole expert on supervisory knowledge or skills. If we assume that there are multiple experts, the principal may not always be the appropriate person to work with a particular teacher. Other educators may have more appropriate expertise because of their experience, perspective, subject matter, or training. For example, because teaching expertise is related to content (subject matter) as well as pedagogy, a teacher may be the most relevant supervisor (Nelson & Sassi, 2000).

Third, sharing supervision with others in the school communicates the important message that professional growth is valued in the school community. When the principal or assistant principal does all the direct supervision in the school, other faculty members find it easy to assume that this is not a value of the school's culture but an administrative preference. Professional growth needs to be viewed as a school-wide responsibility, not an administrative duty.

In addition to promoting professional growth as a value in the school community, sharing supervision can contribute to other features of the school culture. Ebmeier (1999) found that collaborative supervision by peers contributed to increased teacher desire for collaboration and commitment to teaching. Ebmeier also established that sharing supervision made teachers more involved in decision making about their classroom activities, supported classroom innovation, supported collaboration among teachers, increased the clarity of school goals, provided feedback on classroom performance, and provided opportunities to observe the practice of other teachers. All these behaviors are elements of a PLC.

Finally, sharing supervision contributes not only to the teachers who are the focus of problem solving or professional growth but also to the veteran teachers and administrators who work with them. Sharing supervision contributes to the professional growth of all faculty members who are involved in the process, thus enriching the instructional capacity of the school.

ELEMENTS OF THE PRINCIPAL'S ROLE AS FACILITATOR OF SUPERVISION

In this subsection, we will identify several elements that constitute an innovative role for the principal as facilitator of others in supervision. We do not assume that these constitute all the activities you will engage in and responsibilities you will have as a principal or assistant principal in facilitating others in supervision, but we provide these activities as examples to stimulate your conversation and development of the innovative supervisory role. In the preceding section on the principal's direct role in supervision, we identified five major areas. We return to these five areas and discuss how others can be involved in supervision.

Establishing a System of Accountability

As a leader in the school, principals might have a different perspective on accountability than do the teachers in the school. Jones and Egley (2006) found that many administrators and teachers indicated that they thought high-stakes testing as a form of accountability had negative effects on public schools. In their study, Jones and Egley found that administrators, however, had more positive and fewer negative views than did teachers. The authors suggested that administrators thought the tests were useful to them because the tests provided student and teacher data.

Because some teachers are concerned about the effects of some testing programs, they do not see the connection between the test results and student learning. This problem has historical roots in that many teachers never had access to these standardized tests in the past, and the tests were usually norm referenced rather than criterion referenced so that useful data to improve student learning was limited. Also, because of the closed practice of teaching that has existed in the system for many years, teachers often continue to be reluctant in wanting others to view their practice and results.

Jones and Egley's (2006) findings are important for you as a principal in communicating the benefits of an accountability system to the teachers for improvement of learning and that high-stakes testing is not the only method in the accountability system. Developing a system of accountability in a PLC has to go beyond high-stakes testing. The administrators and teachers must look at the total package of accountability and help others in the school understand how openness with assessments can improve student learning.

Recruiting, Selecting, and Retaining Capable and Committed Educators

Although the traditional role often involves the principal alone in recruitment and selection processes, we suggest that a more innovative role is one in which the principal facilitates the involvement of the entire school in this important function. This involvement can include the use of faculty and teacher leaders in helping to design the job. Teachers have a wealth of expertise in understanding what responsibilities and qualities are needed in a new appointment. Furthermore, including teachers and other school constituents in this process builds an awareness of school-wide needs. One of the traditional reasons for the principal being involved in the recruitment and selection process is that principals have a school-wide perspective that enables them to understand the gaps in faculty or staff strengths that need to be filled to build or maintain school instructional capacity. However, involving others in this process increases the aware- —Dis advantage ness of those strengths and gaps among school constituents.

Two difficulties with involving others in recruitment and selection are the schedule of the school year and teacher availability. In order to solve these problems, principals may need to work with district administrators to secure compensation for teachers to stay late or come in during the summer months to interview teacher candidates.

Facilitating the involvement of teachers and other school constituents in recruiting and selecting is also valuable in building instructional capacity and is an important element in a PLC. Taking advantage of teacher networks increases the chances of recruiting a large and rich pool of candidates. As we mentioned earlier in this chapter, taking a "wait and see" attitude is counterproductive for locating the best teachers.

More and more principals are developing strategies for including the entire school in the selection process, including teachers, support staff, parents, and in some cases students. Group interviews, role playing, observations of teaching, and other simulations, as well as screening applications can involve a wide array of school personnel and enrich the perspectives for selection. In order for this to be done appropriately, the principal must help those involved in the recruitment and selection process to be aware of good interviewing techniques, district policies, and legal parameters (Webb, Montello, & Norton, 1994). We suggest that a leadership team establish the criteria in which a new teacher will be hired. For example, if collaboration is important for a new hire, then those involved in the interviewing process need to know how to determine those candidates who are willing and able to collaborate with others.

In addition to recruiting and selecting educators, teachers in the school have a role in retaining quality teachers and the principal has a role in facilitating this process. As a principal your words and actions remind veteran teachers that the quality of working conditions in the school strongly influence the retention of quality teachers. These working conditions include such things as how newcomers are treated by veterans, how resources are shared, and how veterans support the work of these newcomers. In an especially important way, principals can facilitate others' contributions toward retention by connecting newcomers with relevant veterans, that is, facilitating relationships between teachers who have common interests, experience, and needs.

Professional Dilemma 9.3

In a small, isolated school on an Indian reservation in Arizona, a heavy turnover of teachers occurred each year. Often young teachers would begin at the school but would leave after the first year or two. The teachers who had stayed at the school had become accustomed to this turnover and were reluctant to share any of their expertise with new teachers. What had developed was a situation in which new teachers felt isolated and removed from the faculty. The principal liked hiring young new teachers because they brought energy and youthfulness to the school. However, good reforms were hard to sustain because of the constant turnover. What should the principal do to help veteran teachers include new teachers into the faculty?

Promoting Educator Growth

Various supervisory models, including peer supervision, collaborative supervision, mentoring, and cognitive coaching, take advantage of veteran teachers in the process of stimulating and promoting educator growth. In Chapter 8, we discussed the value and process of mentoring and the principal's role in facilitating others in mentoring. In this subsection we will discuss how principals facilitate others in ways that promote educator growth.

Earlier, we discussed Claudet and Ellett's (1999) distinction of micro- and macro-level supervisory events. This distinction is especially useful in understanding the kinds of activities that principals do in promoting educator growth as an organizational and an individual phenomenon. Although micro-level events such as individual principal-teacher supervisory conferences are important, macro-level events are also critical. These can include department and grade-level faculty curriculum planning projects, group planning of various professional development activities, joint participation in supervisory meetings, and planning activities. By developing these opportunities and providing the time and other resources necessary for them to be successful, principals facilitate the school-wide promotion of educator growth.

At times, the principal's facilitating role involves providing resources such as time, training, and other supports for teachers to work with each other in promoting professional growth. This includes providing time for teachers to observe each other, visit classrooms and other schools, meet in conferences, and enjoy other opportunities to promote growth. Principals secure substitutes or cover teachers' classes themselves in order to provide the opportunities for peer supervision to occur.

Another resource that principals provide and by so doing facilitate the involvement of others in promoting growth is training. Providing opportunities to attend local, regional, and national conferences not only inspires, builds supervisory skills, and encourages networking but also provides incentives for veteran teachers to take on the additional responsibilities of peer supervision.

Another element of the principal's role in facilitating supervision by promoting educator growth involves who serves as supervisor. Tracy (1998) described models of supervision that should include teams of professionals rather than the traditional supervisor-teacher dyad. Tracy explained that members of a team will have different expertise, yet they should function as equals. A single supervisor, which is common in the traditional models, will not have sufficient knowledge or skills to support this new paradigm. A variety of people will, therefore, be needed. The majority of these persons will probably be peers, preferably from the same building, rather than individuals designated with some formal supervisory title. Teacher leaders can play a critical role in leading these teams.

Yet, with this move to a broader representation of people as supervisors, the principal has a critical facilitative role to play in making sure this happens. The principal facilitates this broader view by providing training and resources to these teacher leaders who serve as new supervisors.

Building Trust with the Leadership Team

Although training and resources are important for successful school-wide involvement in promoting educator growth, even more important is the supportive relationship that leadership teams demonstrate with teachers and other staff. In order for teachers to accept the help of other teachers, for novice teachers to respect veteran teachers' views, and for veteran teachers to look to each other for help in their professional growth, there must be trust in the school. Social trust is a critical element in promoting professional growth and enriching instructional capacity in the school (Smylie & Hart, 1999). Hoy, Tarter, and Witkoskie (1992) found that a supportive relationship between principal and teachers influenced collegiality among teachers and trust in the principal, which in turn influenced a school-wide trust in colleagues. This collegial trust then can lead to school effectiveness and improved student learning.

As was discussed previously, part of growing professionally involves making teaching practices public. Doing so requires trust not only between the principal and teacher but also among teachers. Principals can go a long way toward facilitating the involvement of others in supervision by the supportive relationship that is demonstrated by respecting teachers' practical knowledge, providing needed resources, keeping confidences, and emphasizing the power of a school-wide culture of learning and growth. Also, the principal is responsible for helping teacher leaders understand the importance of and develop the skills to build relational trust with new teachers as well as veteran teachers.

Evaluating Educational Results

Within this culture, evaluating educational results should be expected. This type of evaluation means assessing the entire instructional program of the school, including curricula, student performance, teacher performance, and resources. Typically, evaluation involves only the assessment of teacher performance. There is ample evidence of teacher reluctance to engage in peer evaluations. The egalitarian norm in which teachers avoid comparisons among themselves discourages experimentation with peer evaluation. Yet one critical feature of a profession is evaluation by peers.

In most districts, principals retain the legal responsibility for evaluating teachers. We propose an argument for peer evaluation and for the principal's role in facilitating evaluation by colleagues. If we define evaluation in terms of assessing the instructional capacity of the classroom, as we did earlier in this chapter, peers play a vital role in helping each other make this assessment. Because of their expertise in the classroom and the rapport that hopefully exists in a culture that supports professional growth, teachers are in an excellent position to help their colleagues assess the various components of instructional capacity in the classroom. Teacher leaders, in particular, can play a critical and useful role in this type of peer evaluation. They have the respect of other teachers and the experience and expertise to provide valuable feedback.

Teacher leaders, along with administrators, need to develop skills in data-driven decision making. Although we discussed some of the elements of assessment in Chapter 4, for example, qualitative and quantitative methods, these tools of data-driven decision making are critical for evaluating instructional capacity in classrooms. Principals and assistant principals can help teachers understand how to use quantitative techniques not only to measure student achievement but also to assess student growth and areas for additional instructional emphasis. Enlisting district and university personnel to help teachers develop quantitative and qualitative tools to measure specific classroom instructional processes and outcomes is an important facilitative role for principals. Such a role enhances teachers' abilities to diagnose instructional problems, assess growth, and evaluate practices and contributes to an environment of mutual inquiry.

◊ Principals can facilitate peer evaluation by providing time, training, support, and trust. In the same way that these resources are necessary for promoting educator growth, they are important for facilitating peer evaluation. Teachers need time to observe and talk with each other. They need training in how to assess instructional capacity and to use a variety of information sources. They need encouragement from the principal to make the process effective and to continue when the result is not always positive. Finally, they need the respect and trust of the principal that such an evaluation results in a more effective learning environment for students and adults.

Professional learning communities establish clear and common goals about the purpose and methods of learning, as well as concentrate on student outcome results. In order to develop a clear vision on student learning, DuFour, DuFour, Eaker, and Many (2006) suggested a set of four questions that should guide the work of PLCs to increase learning capacity for all students:

1. What knowledge and skills should every student acquire as a result of this unit of instruction?
2. How will we know when each student has acquired the essential knowledge and skills?
3. How will we respond when some students do not know?
4. How will we respond when some students have clearly achieved the intended outcomes? (p. 21)

The essential issue is that you as the principal must develop a collective responsibility with teachers for student learning, which includes high expectations for all students and the belief that each teacher has the capacity to teach all students. Furthermore, as J. D. Thompson's (1995) study concluded, "The single most powerful mechanism for creating a learning environment is that the leadership of the organization be willing to model the approach to learning they want others to embrace" (p. 96). When this leadership is broadened to include others in the school, and with the support of the principal, a stronger, richer learning environment can be created, enhanced, and sustained.

Conclusion

Bill Payne, the new principal in the opening vignette, discovered what we emphasize in all the role conceptions we discuss in this book, that is, that although principals have a direct role to play in supervision, they cannot succeed alone. Supervision, like the other roles, requires the principal to facilitate supervision by others. In this chapter we have described an innovative way to think about supervision that moves beyond the inspection role, which devalues the expertise of individual teachers to a more collaborative role, all of which builds instructional capacity. This innovative role involves the five activities of establishing a system of accountability; recruiting, selecting, and retaining capable and committed educators; promoting educator growth; building trust; and evaluating educational results.

In the next chapter, we move into the important management role that principals and assistant principals play. Like the other roles, the principal as manager if focused on creating and supporting a PLC that advocates for all students.

Activities

SELF-REFLECTION ACTIVITIES

1. Interview an assistant principal in terms of his or her experience in attempting to provide supervision to teachers. What kinds of opportunities were provided by the principals so that the assistant principal could supervise? What were the reactions from the teachers?

2. Reflect on your own appointment as a new teacher. What selection processes were used? How could the process be improved?

PEER REFLECTION ACTIVITIES

1. Compare and contrast the positive and negative characteristics of the ways that you and a colleague have been supervised.

2. With your colleague, develop and critique a plan for involving teachers, parents, and students in the recruitment and selection process.

3. Brainstorm ideas for Bill Payne in the opening vignette to encourage veteran teachers to contribute their efforts toward the supervision of new teachers.

4. Reflect on your answer to the Professional Dilemma 9.1 presented earlier regarding selecting teachers who match the school culture versus opting for diversity.

COURSE ACTIVITIES

1. Invite a principal reputed to be an effective instructional leader to visit your class. Interview the principal in terms of the mechanisms used to recruit and select teachers.

2. Conduct a small research study on teachers' responses to their principals' supervisory styles. Examine the relationship between teaching experience and perceptions of supervisory style.

3. As a class, design a process for peer evaluation. What would the principal's role be in implementing this? Consider such issues as district support, legal and union considerations, and trust building.

4. As a class, develop a recruitment, selection, and induction plan for a local district or school.

Websites

National Comprehensive Center for Teacher Quality—site on teacher recruitment and retention
www.tqsource.org/topics/recruitment.php

National Association of State Boards of Education (NASBE) Leadership Database—site has links to resources and research for different topics in leadership, including recruitment, mentoring, PDprofessional development, and evaluation.
www.nasbe.org/leadership/

Education Commission of the States (ECS)—issue site on teacher quality, with links to resources on recruitment and retention, PD,professional development mentoring, evaluation, effectiveness, and so on.
ww.ecs.org/html/issue.asp?issueid=129

CHAPTER 10

Principal as Manager

Vignette

Three weeks into his administrative internship, Abe Rosenblatz was still excited each morning as he came into his small office at Martin Luther King Middle School. After fourteen years as a journalism teacher, he enjoyed the new direction in his career. Although he had enjoyed teaching, the university course work and administrative internship had rejuvenated his interest in education. He was facing his new challenges with enthusiasm and vigor. Although extremely busy with his studies, internship, and family responsibilities, he cherished these opportunities to learn and advance in his career. Abe felt the school was a great place to learn the role of principal. Located in a declining, intercity neighborhood, the school had recently been reconstituted after being closed for a year because of consistently falling test scores and demoralized staff and parents. The principal, assistant principals, and teachers were new to the school but had excellent experiences in inner-city schools. They had been very welcoming to Abe and seemed to appreciate his journalism background. In fact, the principal asked him to develop a student newspaper as one of his responsibilities.

Abe was troubled, nevertheless, by one aspect of his internship. In his evening courses on campus, he was excited to learn more about leadership, especially the principal's role in developing a professional learning community (PLC). In his internship, he was too busy with administrative matters to do much of anything in improving the school's learning community. His observations of the other three administrators in the school indicated that they too were more involved with day-to-day management activities than they were in leading the school to improve learning capacity. He had envisioned that the principal and the assistant principals would be visiting classrooms, talking with teachers, meeting with curriculum committees encouraging grade-level teams, and planning professional development. Instead, he found none of these activities in the first three weeks of his internship but was assigned to work on student discipline, bus duty, hall monitoring, and equipment inventory.

As he talked to his mentor about this dilemma, the principal only said, "Welcome to administration. I remember my classes on leadership. The reality is that we have to hold down the fort here. The teachers expect that of us, and so does the district office. If we don't, we won't be around here very long." After saying these words to Abe, the principal was prompted by his secretary to answer a telephone call, an assistant principal started asking the principal about the afternoon assembly, and a teacher was knocking on the principal's office door wanting to get a purchase order signed. The principal shrugged his shoulders, raised his eyebrows, and gave a little nod to Abe, as if saying, "See what I mean?"

After the conversation, Abe returned to his small office, picked up his daily planner, checked on his next to-do item, and went to work ordering equipment and material for the new student newspaper. He tackled each of his assigned tasks with vigor and enthusiasm. It was not that he disliked the daily tasks, but he wanted to work more with teachers and instructional programs. He silently resolved that when he became an assistant principal, he would somehow organize his schedule to allow for more impact on the school's learning capacity and community.

INTRODUCTION

As you have observed principals in action, you invariably have seen managers at work. In fact, many observers see the principal's largest and most time-consuming task as that of managing the affairs of the school. At the same time, however, many teachers, district administrators, and policymakers want more from principals and assistant principals than just managing the schools. Although from its early roots the principal's role was that of managing the building and those who work in it, in recent years the roles of manager and leader often have become conflictual—or at least this has appeared to be so. Principal candidates such as you often have learned that leadership is more important than management and especially that good principals need to be good instructional leaders. You could face the same dilemma as Abe Rosenblatz as you enter administrative practice. You may find a similar dilemma between what you learned the role is supposed to be and what the realities of the position actually are.

In this chapter, we acknowledge the important role that principals and assistant principals play in the management of schools. We heartily endorse the concept that the role of the principal as manager is key in the daily planning, organizing, operating, executing, budgeting, maintaining, and scheduling of numerous processes, activities, and tasks that permit a school to accomplish its goals as a learning community. Research on PLCs (Spillane & Louis, 2002) emphasizes that certain managerial tasks, for example, providing resources such as time, materials, and support are essential to the establishment and maintenance of a PLC. The principal's management role includes the routine behaviors and tasks that must take place daily to establish and keep a safe and secure school. However, many of these tasks are school specific and are not taught easily from a textbook or a course. This does not mean that these tasks are less important because, in fact, they are very important. For instance, safe-school issues are much more emphasized in contemporary schools than they were a few decades ago. Principals and assistant principals have the sacred responsibility of protecting children while they are coming, going, and attending school. Learning safe-school strategies is probably best done in the field, learning from your internship and mentor principals. Our attempt in this chapter is to acknowledge the importance of these tasks and to emphasize the management role in the context of building a strong PLC and establishing a shared vision that encompasses school improvement and promotes learning for *all* students.

Too often principals fall into the trap of managing without really improving. We believe that as Speck (1999) described it, effective management helps a school achieve its goals in part by making the school function well enough to allow the leadership roles of the principal, assistant principal, teachers, and others to emerge. Unlike in the opening vignette, principals and assistant principals do not have to be bogged down in the managerial tasks of the school at the expense of good leadership. Furthermore, school leaders who claim that they do not have time for improving instruction do so because they either do not know how to go about improvement efforts or choose not to take on those improvements because of the assumed risks involved. As a principal or assistant principal, you need to make sure that schedules work, textbooks are ordered, hall and classroom floors are swept, and students are safe. However, you should not be fooled into thinking that success as a principal or assistant principal ends with orderly lunchrooms, quiet hallways, or computerized student records. Furthermore, you must not forget that students should be the ultimate beneficiaries of all management actions and that your role as a school leader is to improve their learning and that of all members of the PLC.

This chapter begins with a review of the historical perspectives of the scientific management movement that has affected the principal's role. We then consider the importance and nature of the principal's role in managing a PLC, especially in a complex environment. Because we encourage and focus on PLC, we end the chapter by discussing how principals can facilitate others in building management capacity within a learning community.

THE PRINCIPALSHIP AND MANAGEMENT ROOTS

As described in Chapter 2, the role of the principal changed in the early part of the twentieth century, and a larger portion of the principal's time was allocated to general management activities. Pierce (1935) noted that by the turn of the century, the principal had become the directing manager rather than the presiding teacher of the school. An initial approach to educational administration was grounded in the scientific management and industrial efficiency tenets of Frederick W. Taylor. This movement grew out of a reform era in which the administrative functions of school districts were being centralized under strong superintendents. The scientific management approach asserted that educational organizations, like commercial establishments, should be businesslike and efficient. Tasks and responsibilities should be defined carefully and planned fully to lead to maximized organizational productivity. Organizational scholars such as Henri Fayol and Luther Gulick suggested that organizations should be structured systematically at the top with specialized divisions in a hierarchical model to cause the entire organization to pull together efficiently as a total organic unit. Close coordination and control of subordinate behavior were considered vital to overall efficiency, and an administrator should be careful not to distribute responsibilities among lower-level employees beyond the bounds of what each manager could fully supervise. One culmination of the scientific management effort was Gulick's (1937) master list of things managers do, abbreviated in the acronym POSDCoRB: planning, organizing, staffing, directing, coordinating, reporting, and budgeting.

Raymond Callahan's (1962) book, *Education and the Cult of Efficiency: A Study of the Social Forces That Have Shaped the Administration of the Public Schools*, provided a useful critique of the impact of scientific management on the field of education. From the management of classroom instruction through the school system hierarchy, educational organizations were designed for efficiency. Standardized tests, record systems and reports, and score cards for buildings provided a systematic information system for the educational administrator. Studies of cost economics and time usage, even an efficiency index of pupils' study habits, were added to the list of what should be considered in judging managerial effectiveness in education. Standards of behavior, qualifications for entry-level jobs, and detailed instructions for job performance were all incorporated into specifications for teachers and administrators.

Gross (1994) labeled the working doctrine of the scientific management era as the "gospel of efficiency" because the dedication of its adherents was of a quasi-religious intensity. Many believed that educational administration could best be improved by the scientific application of managerial expertise. This included carefully planned schedules for work, the instructions for doing it, and the expected standards of performance (Morris, Crowson, Porter-Gehrie, & Hurwitz, 1984).

Many historians believe that the scientific management movement was perfect for its time in education because it indicated the critical importance of organizational management. To the newly developing profession of educational administration, the gospel of efficiency offered a role description similar to managers in other fields, especially in the private sector. This movement added legitimacy to the role and elevated it to the level of other community leaders.

Some critics of education today argue that our schools need to be more tightly managed—a return to the earlier scientific management theories. Other critics argue that our school systems are too tightly managed and often ignore local and individual interests at the expense of the whole system. The debate over principals being managers or leaders has been ongoing for most of a century, and there is little evidence that it will discontinue in the near future. You can be assured that this debate will continue for much of your career. The important matter for you to consider as a new principal or assistant principal is not only understanding these management roots but also assessing your school and its culture as to management expectations and effectiveness in supporting a PLC. Schools and school districts have different expectations as to management levels and styles. Some schools and districts adhere more closely to the scientific management routines, with a bureaucratic organization in the district. Other schools are experiencing a movement to decentralize, having decision making be more school based. This movement, often called *school-based management*, places more responsibility and management on the school level rather than on the district level. The school-based management movement does not mean, however, that the principal has more autonomy. Rather, *shared decision making* and *collaborative problem solving* usually refer to the expectations that community members, teachers, and administrators will work together to solve the school's problems and establish a collective vision. As we have noted, a PLC makes use of these processes within a culture of inquiry and support for student learning. Understanding your district's and school's management style is critical for your understanding of the role you will be expected to take and for the boundaries of role making within a PLC.

In the opening vignette, Abe faced a dilemma that many beginning school leaders encounter. At times, it is difficult to be an instructional leader when maintaining an orderly school because managing the school is often so time consuming. However, many principals and assistant principals needlessly get sucked into the drain of maintaining without ever attempting real improvement efforts. Crow (2007) found that new headteachers in England experienced major managerial responsibilities, in some instances at the beginning of their appointments. These new leaders had excellent instructional leadership experience, but they, nevertheless, had to learn how to manage fiscal, personnel, community, and building processes and controversies.

Perhaps, the best way to distinguish between managerial and leadership functions is to think of the two not as separate tasks but rather as a combined, conceptualized role of the principal. Surely certain tasks will tend to be more managerial than leadership, but the principal's role should be conceptualized as one in which both leadership and management are important for creating and enriching a PLC.

Managing the Unexpected in a PLC

Throughout this book, we have distinguished ways for principals to provide leadership for a PLC, namely, through culture, advocacy, leadership, mentoring, and supervising. This leadership is critical in a complex, knowledge society in which the unexpected is frequently the rule. We begin this section, by considering what management of the unexpected looks like in a PLC. We then discuss more specific ways in which principals and assistant principals manage PLCs: supporting, planning, taking action, and evaluating. We also emphasize a more recent management role for principals in PLCs, namely, managing with technology.

At the beginning of this book, we described the context in which you will be a principal in a knowledge society in which there is a technological explosion, demographic changes, globalization, and complex work. This context is very different from the context in which veteran principals began their jobs and learned their roles. The traditional understanding of the context of schools and of the way leaders enact their roles emphasizes certainty, rationality, linear thinking, and dependence on past practices. Although these worked in part for principals of an earlier period, they no longer are effective in a complex, knowledge society. However, they are comfortable and many principals are inclined to hold on to these skills and approaches in their managerial work. For example, finding the one best way to manage a problem, relying on "tried and true" methods of professional development, or expecting things to remain the same are certainly secure ways of managing. When you become a principal, instead of the expected, you will find yourself "managing the unexpected" (Weick & Sutcliffe, 2007). Managing a PLC demands a different way of thinking and acting in an age of uncertainty in which the unexpected is more often the norm than the expected.

Several authors have provided some excellent advice, based on their research, for managing the unexpected. Two of these approaches—integrative thinking and mindfulness—seem particularly useful in the context of a PLC, where inquiry and collaboration are central.

INTEGRATIVE THINKING　Martin (2007) described effective leaders as those who are able and disposed "to hold in their heads two opposing ideas at once" (p. 62). He referred to this ability as integrative thinking. This type of thinking is distinguished from conventional thinking in which managers attempt to find one best choice. Martin admitted that "putting it (integrative thinking) to work makes us anxious. Most of us avoid complexity and ambiguity and seek out the comfort of simplicity and clarity" (p. 64). He identified four stages of decision making based on integrative thinking. The first stage is determining salience, in which the integrative thinking manager seeks "less obvious but potentially relevant factors" (p. 65). Second, the manager analyzes causality by considering multidirectional and nonlinear relationships rather than one-way relationships. In other words, the integrative thinking manager recognizes that often dilemmas, problems, and challenges have more than one cause and that acknowledging the complexity of causality is more likely to open up possibilities. Third, the manager envisions the "decision architecture" by viewing problems as a whole and decisions as affecting one another rather than taking apart the problem. Finally, the integrative thinking manager achieves resolution by imaginatively resolving tensions and generating innovative outcomes rather than making either-or choices (p. 65). As a principal in a PLC, integrative thinking is a powerful tool for you to use and for you to teach others to use. For example, asking questions that encourage expansive thinking about student learning gaps rather than linear, either-or approaches can build learning capacity in the PLC and help avoid simplistic, one-dimensional blaming regarding achievement gaps.

MINDFULNESS   The second idea—mindfulness—is found in the extensive work of Weick and his colleagues in examining failures and disasters that could have been prevented. Weick and Sutliffe (2007) defined mindfulness as "'a rich awareness of discriminatory detail.' By that we mean that when people act, they are aware of context, of ways in which details differ (in other words, they discriminate among details), and of deviations from their expectations" (p. 32). These authors warned leaders that always assuming the expected can cause blind spots in management. "Expectations act like an invisible hand that guides you toward soothing perceptions that confirm your hunches and away from more troublesome ones that don't" (p. 32). Assuming that the past is always the best indicator of the present or the future is dangerous in a world where the unexpected is the rule. For example, relating to parents based on previous approaches may ignore the changes in how contemporary parents view their roles, for example, the so-called helicopter parent. Weick and Sutliffe identified five components of mindfulness that provide critical guidance for managing the unexpected.

- track small failures,
- resist oversimplification,
- remain sensitive to operation,
- maintain capabilities for resilience,
- take advantage of shifting locations of expertise. (p. 2)

Applying these components of mindfulness to managing the unexpected in a PLC provides some useful advice for you as a new principal. In an age of high-stakes accountability, it is easy to hide errors so that the school's achievements stand out more. But ignoring small failures, for example a small group of students who are disengaged from schooling, can lead to larger problems down the road. In the fast-paced context of urban schools, for example, it is easy to look for simple causes and solutions such as the newest reading program or approach. Yet, student learning is more complex than focusing on a deficit in one content area. Although current leadership standards and training tend to emphasize the larger issues of instructional leadership, if you do not pay attention to the daily operations of the school, for example, safety, scheduling, planning, and resource allocations, you will have a hard time providing the type of environment that will support a PLC. Furthermore, contemporary schools are constantly bombarded by events, mandates, and changes that create anxiety and perplexity among staff. As a principal, you must find ways to increase the PLC's ability to be flexible and resilient. Highly resilient organizations are able to respond to changes because they do not create rigid structures that take too much time and effort to respond to change.

As an example of this principle of mindfulness, a middle school was in its third year of developing into a PLC by establishing collaborative instructional teams that were engaged in studying student data when a neighboring elementary school caught fire and was mostly destroyed. The displaced students and faculty had to move into the only existing structure and that was the middle school. A completely new schedule had to be developed for both schools to meet in the same building until the elementary school could be rebuilt. The resiliency of the middle school was impressive as they not only accommodated the elementary school students and faculty, but also included them in the building decision making. The middle school principal actually felt that her faculty had become closer and a more established PLC because of the experience.

Finally, instead of looking at one individual or group as expert, a PLC must recognize that expertise can be located in multiple areas and with multiple roles. Because the unexpected is the rule, it is frequently hard to predict who and where the necessary expertise to respond to change will occur. As a principal, you must be on the lookout for multiple sources of expertise.

PRINCIPAL'S DIRECT ROLE IN MANAGING THE UNEXPECTED

Today a variety of ideas exists regarding how to manage the unexpected. You should spend some time on the Internet or in your local bookstore checking out authors and ideas, such as Malcolm Gladwell's *Blink: The Power of Thinking Without Thinking* that argues persuasively, using new cognitive science, for the advantages and disadvantages of developing your intuitive skills. You might also consider Dr. Jerome Groopman's book, *How Doctors Think* that examines the successes and mistakes of doctors and the importance of learning to ask the right questions and listen to the right people. As a principal in a PLC, your managerial role involves complex work and unexpected contexts. Managing in these contexts no longer involves following a checklist or memorizing the policy manual; it necessitates your critical, creative, and collaborative skills. In the following sections, we identify some of the major areas of the managerial role for principals in a PLC in a context of the unexpected.

Supporting

A not so obvious factor in managing a PLC is to encourage efforts to implement and maintain this type of community. Often the school culture prevents a PLC from developing, or if the learning community does develop, it is soon abandoned. Principals and assistant principals are critical in creating a nonthreatening school culture where a learning community and change are endorsed. Hall (1986) claimed, "Throughout our years of research and experience, we have never seen a situation in which the principal was not a significant factor in the efforts of schools to improve" (p. 1). Spillane and Louis (2002) found in their research that "social conditions are the most important precondition for creating professional learning community, structural features of the school (e.g., scheduling, meeting time) are not far behind, and opportunity to develop professional communities is always the most important issue" (p. 98). Principals need to facilitate the PLC efforts by supporting inquiry, collaboration, and a focus on student learning. For example, if teachers propose a peer mentoring program within the school (as outlined in Chapter 8), the principal either facilitates or obstructs the effort by the support that is given either implicitly or explicitly. The teachers either move the idea forward or are reluctant to continue. Subsequent ideas by the teachers for other improvement efforts will be affected if they perceive that their ideas are not supported enthusiastically. Morrissey (2000) found that providing conditions and resources to support staff in continuous learning is one of the principal's roles in a PLC. In the following subsections, we discuss the principal's responsibility in supporting a PLC through four areas: money, personnel, time, and information.

MONEY   Too often PLCs never get started because of an ongoing myth that developing any reform is impossible because the budget will never allow it. However, few schools anywhere will ever complain about an overabundance of financial resources, and yet many schools are making changes and improvements. Often schools within the same district that have similar budget allocations are quite different in their approach to creating richer instructional programs. Although this is not a chapter on school finance and budgeting, principals need to ask, how can some schools operate successfully in a PLC environment and do so under the same budget restraints as do others who reject these learning community reforms.

To answer this question, a school leader should consider three areas pertaining to managing money for the PLC. First, many learning communities do not require more money but can survive with support from other areas such as personnel, time, and information—topics we discuss later. Second, many learning community efforts may need only a budget reallocation. Principals often display financial wizardry with their budgets to create ways in which worthy programs are funded. Effective principals find a way. Third, some efforts may be too grand at a particular time and therefore may need to be scaled back. This is a tough position to be in, but the principal may have to be the bearer of bad news or, at the least, steer the efforts into more reasonable directions to reflect the financial resources available.

Principals are also concerned with three acronyms and their application to the budget: ADA, ADM, and FTE. ADA refers to students' average daily attendance, and ADM refers to the average daily membership. Usually the district office uses either ADA or ADM to determine the school's budget for such items as textbooks and supplies. Full-time equivalency (FTE) refers, among other things, to the number of teachers allocated to a building. FTE is determined by the ADA or ADM, depending on the state code. For example, in many districts, one FTE is allocated for a certain number of ADM, such as twenty students. Using this formula, a school of five hundred students would have twenty-five FTEs. Classified staff also can be determined by the ADM or ADA. Managing the ADA, ADM, and FTEs effectively is vitally important to receive correct funding. In fact, problems can occur if a principal reports an ADM that is either higher or lower than the actual numbers. Unfortunately, it is more complicated than what we indicate here because schools can receive variable credit for part-time students, special-needs students, and English language learning students. You will learn more about your school budget in a finance class and in your internship, but it is important to realize that your management of these formulas will go a long way toward determining your school's budget and providing valuable resources to support a culture of inquiry.

Many schools, especially those in school-based management, can manipulate their FTE numbers for other things than teaching positions. For example, instead of using all twenty-five FTEs for twenty-five teachers, a site council could elect to use one of the FTEs for additional monies paid to the faculty for professional development, such as observation of other classrooms, attendance at workshops, and hiring of literacy coaches. Such rules and regulations depend totally on the state and local codes.

Policymakers often hesitate at increasing school funding because of various educator opinions on funding priorities. For example, many reformers want money for program development, teacher organizations lobby for salary increases, and administrators often want capital outlay for new buildings or additions. The school community, if divided on school reform efforts, may lose needed financial resources. As a school leader, you will want to manage funding toward the school's shared vision of a PLC.

One budget area that has caused principals many headaches is the activity and student body funds. These accounts are often problematic because many other people are involved with them. Teachers and coaches often are given responsibility to manage activity budgets without any training or help. A music teacher, for example, is understandably more concerned with teaching than with the accuracy of the music activity budget. Managing budgets is important not only for the principal but also for faculty and staff. As the principal or assistant principal, you have to be aware of teachers' needs so that you can support their programs, their teaching, and their collaboration with other teachers. Often it may be better to have a secretary or another person handle activity budgets to allow teachers time to perform their more important instructional duties.

With any public funding comes accountability. Because schooling is so expensive, the taxpayers' money must be spent legally and equitably. As a principal, you can assume that whatever money flows to your school, a system of accountability also will flow, often in the form of an audit. Although others in the school may be involved in the budget process, when it comes to accountability, the old axiom "the buck stops here" applies directly to the principal. When you know an audit is near, alert all involved so that no one is surprised. Consider the audit as a learning experience and seek help in understanding how to manage the accounts more efficiently. After all, you do not want the reform efforts to go astray because of accounting problems.

PERSONNEL The very nature of schools means that different people are involved in the school's everyday management. If principals dealt only with students and teachers, the role would be complex enough. However, it is not unusual on a daily basis for principals also to interact with classified personnel, district office officials, Parent Teacher

Association (PTA) members and community members, business people, social service and health professionals, and school board members. Sometimes these interactions take place within a short period. For example, in an hour's time an assistant principal may have talked to a truant student, phoned the student's parents, arranged a field-trip bus with the district transportation director, coordinated the gym schedule with two coaches, dictated a letter to the secretary, and then chatted with the lunchroom director about long lunch lines. These interactions are a big part of managing a school, and yet the vision of improving teaching and learning is still the prime mission. Administrators need to keep in mind that these interactions are necessary, important, and a part of the student learning process.

Supporting school reform for the improvement of teaching and learning and dealing with these various groups are aligned with the development and maintenance of a PLC. All people in a school are learning all the time. The principal's role becomes one of managing the environment so that an optimal learning community can develop and function. One of the more recent aspects of a learning community is the existence of interprofessional practice, that is, the interaction of multiple professional roles, for example, nurses, social workers, mental health agency personnel as well as educators, focused on ensuring student learning and engagement (Forbes & Watson, in press). As we mentioned in Chapter 1, one of the changes in the nature of the principal's role in a complex knowledge society is facilitating interaction among these multiple roles—some from outside the school organization. Riehl (2000) found that one of the three main administrative tasks of principals in responding to the needs of diverse students is building relationships between schools and communities. Principals must "negotiate interpersonal and inter-organizational dynamics that arise when separate organizations try to work together" (p. 67). These professionals outside the school bring their own unique and valuable knowledge, expertise, and perspectives to bear on supporting student learning and engagement. Your role as a principal will include ensuring these voices are heard by educators, ensuring educators' voices are heard by these other professionals, connecting the conversations to the culture and shared values of the school, and maintaining the focus on student learning. When you perform these activities, you provide a critical role in managing a rich PLC.

Another critical aspect of your role in managing personnel relates to professional development. Hargreaves (1997) reported from his studies that a fundamental mismatch exists between the demands of educational reform and the professional development opportunities afforded teachers and administrators. The principal's role in promoting, facilitating, and participating in professional development is integral to developing a learning community where all educators are continual learners. In considering the school vision, the professional development of all educators in the school turns less to the bandwagon and dog-and-pony shows and more to a sustained and developmental approach, one that is linked to building and maintaining a PLC. Past attempts at school reform often have neglected professional development. Reform packages have been implemented with the assumption that everyone is expected to follow along. Even if personnel development was included, often one-day workshops or single in-service classes were all that were offered, having little impact on developing or sustaining a PLC. Barth (2006) supported the idea that people in a learning community are not in-serviced. Instead, they engage in continuous inquiry: reflecting, discussing, reading, and learning about improving instruction.

Often neglected in professional development are the classified staff members. Administrators mistakenly think that professional development for secretaries means only improving technical skills, such as word processing. It is not uncommon to find school secretaries who have no idea what the school's vision is, what role they play in this vision, and what other roles in the school are involved with the vision. Yet these secretaries are often the first-line communicators for the school to the rest of the community. Likewise, seldom are custodians, lunch workers, and teacher aides brought into reform efforts and professional development. Yet, for a rich PLC to develop, all these individuals need to be included in continuous inquiry and learning.

TIME   Few beginning principals are more surprised by any other issue than that of managing their schedules. In fact, many principals will admit that their schedules are out-of-control monsters. Time management is quite different for school administrators than it is for business leaders. For one, a school is not an organization in which a chief executive officer can set appointments and assume that everything will take place as planned. Schools, instead, are organizations that are similar to a flock of geese heading south for the winter. The flock is headed in the right direction, but many distractions come along the way to get them off course. Because of unpredictable schedules, it is imperative for school leaders to keep their eyes on the school's shared vision and what is necessary to maintain a PLC. A learning community does not occur without the principal's and assistant principal's involvement and time is a critical element of this involvement.

In addition to the principal's own time management, Spillane and Louis's (2002) finding that time was a critical element in the principal's contribution to an effective learning community, Morrissey (2000) found several ways that principals used time as a resource in a PLC. She found that principals supported the collaboration of teachers by providing time for them to meet. This included arranging schedules so that teacher teams could meet and talk, providing release time negotiated with the district to allow whole-school meetings, and rearranging classroom locations to move teams of teachers closer to one another, all of which would increase the opportunities to talk.

Likewise, school leaders need to support others in the building in their time management, a topic we discuss later in this chapter. Suffice it to say here, however, that the faculty and staff are especially prone to reform burnout because of the many previous unsuccessful reform efforts. Time is as precious as financial resources for busy teachers and staff members.

Information

Information is usually considered to be something needed in making good decisions. Information is also important in helping others become professionally involved in decision making and the school improvement process. Thus, information is central to the effective functioning of a PLC. A good example would be in establishing a professional relationship with teacher teams. If teachers feel that they only get a one-sided report, then they can easily acquire the opinion that they are being manipulated. However, trusting in teachers' good judgment will require giving them all the information so that they can develop their own opinions. As a school leader, you must be careful about withholding information from others—doing so could jeopardize trust in your leadership and sabotage the PLC.

The sharing of information with others in the school community is an opportunity not only to gain support for the school's vision but also to discover resources and identify potential problems. When school leaders keep others informed, a stronger sense of trust is established, which is critical to a learning community. As a general rule, the hotter the issue, the more information and communication are needed.

However, not all information is of equal value. In fact, with the onslaught of the information era, principals can get access to the wrong information. For example, it is entirely possible for anyone to find Web sites that claim that the Holocaust never happened, regardless of the overwhelming evidence. Using the Internet for information is a tremendous source for all educators, but it is also an area that requires caution and discernment. You and others can find anything you want to find on the Internet—whether it is factual, realistic, or practical is another matter.

A common mistake that educators make is to claim that something is research based. For example, in supporting a block schedule for high schools, an educator may claim that longer class periods have been shown by research to be more effective for adolescent learners. Often the source is never cited. The study may have limitations as to how generalizable it is to other school settings. Likewise, educators read a lot of literature from journals that is only based on opinion and not necessarily researched empirically. As a school leader, you need to understand the existing literature and be able to analyze these sources. You also will need to explain to others what good research is and is not.

One of the most important responsibilities of principals and assistant principals in reaching the goals of higher learning achievement for all students and an enriched PLC is the use of data for decision making (Goldring & Berends, 2009). Developing your skills at gathering and analyzing information is a critical management skill that has leadership implications. Knowing how to get trustworthy, timely, and appropriate information and understanding what this information means for improving teaching and learning are among the most important things you will do.

In a PLC, data are vital, but data are only one part of the inquiry process you use. Hargreaves (2008) made the distinction between evidence-informed and data-driven and argued that educators, not data, need to drive the decision making. Some principals have responded to the current accountability environment by focusing primarily on data—especially achievement test score data. They and their teachers live and breathe data, they anxiously await data results, and they formulate plans based solely on these narrow sources of data. In a PLC, however, data come from a variety of sources and are one tool, in addition to professional judgment and experience that are used to identify evidence to make decisions.

Although we sometimes think of collecting data solely for understanding and improving student learning, data can also be useful in assessing the PLC itself, for example, in determining whether teachers are actually interacting with one another around teaching and learning. Surveys and observations provide evidence of the quality of the PLC efforts and areas for professional development to enrich the community (Goldring & Berends, 2009).

As principal, you need to analyze the methods by which you disseminate information to the faculty and staff. The weekly faculty meeting has been the method of choice for most school principals for many years. Faculty meetings, although important, are not necessarily the best method, especially with electronic methods now available. Many information-type items can be transmitted electronically through an e-mail list-serve to all faculty and staff. Consequently, each faculty and staff member can have the opportunity for individual input. In fact, some schools have established chat rooms for faculty and staff to discuss and share ideas on a particular topic. Not only do these methods ensure more individual involvement, but they also provide a written record.

DIRECT ROLE IN IMPLEMENTING THE PLC

Planning

To help make PLC a reality, you, as the school leader, have to plan for success. Nothing is more frustrating to a group that is working diligently on an improvement effort than to see it fail because of poor planning. Developing an action plan is a necessary step to give the vision a working blueprint for continuation. Action plans identify the what, how, when, who, and how much. Where the shared vision is the direction of improvement efforts, the action plan is the map to follow. However, the action plan is only meant to be a temporary map because it will need to be revised along the journey. The very nature of taking action means that the status quo no longer exists and that change has taken place. This alters how the rest of the plan may have to be implemented. Often action plans are too rigid in adapting to the changing needs of reform efforts. Creating and maintaining a PLC, in particular, involves continual assessment, inquiry, and revision of action plans. A static plan of action is anathema to a PLC.

Managing a PLC involves a new way of thinking about planning. Strategic planning is typically based on a traditional model of management that does not fit well in an era of complexity and managing the unexpected. Sergiovanni (2009) demonstrates this problem with strategic planning when he contrasts the traditional and alternative models. In the traditional model, strategic planning includes

- stating measurable outcomes,
- providing behavioral expectations,
- practicing monitoring,
- measuring outcomes. (p. 93)

The alternative way of viewing strategic planning includes the following:

- being clear about basic direction,
- providing purpose and building shared covenant,
- practicing tight and loose management,
- evaluating processes and outcomes. (p. 94)

In the traditional model of planning, the assumption is that the principal is trying to reduce complexity and uncertainty and increase control. But in a PLC, a culture of inquiry seeks out the complexities and subtleties of student learning and teaching practices and acknowledges the dynamic qualities of continual change and innovation. Planning, then, has to reflect this more fluid and complex environment. Johnson (2004) found in his study of five Australian school leadership teams in reform settings that these successful teams "mostly rejected strategic planning approaches to goal setting, preferring instead to follow nonlinear, evolutionary, and developmental pathways that were negotiated closely with participants.

Planning in a PLC involves at least two factors you should keep in mind (Lane, 2001). First, as a principal, you should recognize that planning is political and, thus, not a value-neutral endeavor. Rather it includes sometimes contested values among participants. That means that the planning process of goal setting may not include goals that are universally accepted, but rather are negotiated among stakeholders. Bargaining is not a bad thing, but the natural process when individuals have different interests. Second, planning is distributional. Teachers and other stakeholders in the planning process bring their expertise and perspectives that inform the process in richer, more complex ways than one person doing all the planning. As a principal, planning will involve your skills at consensus building (Innes, 1996).

We do not want to suggest that strategic plans do not work in schools. On the contrary, there are many good examples. The point we are making is that developing an action plan is fluid, contested, and distributed among individuals. Effective planning, especially in a PLC, is dynamic and continuous. It occurs not as a step in the process but as an integral part of the whole process. Once the plan is established, it should be continually improved as it is implemented and results are determined. Talbot (1997) reported that principals, even in reforming schools, found that long-range plans frequently were not helpful because of such events as faculty turnover or legislative and district mandates.

Taking Action

Many good reform efforts had great plans that were never implemented. It is often much easier to discuss and plan reform than it is to take action on it. During implementation, the stark realization hits that things are about to change, and although many people could have been involved in the planning stage, the realities of the change could be too threatening. Kimbrough and Burkett (1990) claimed, "During the implementation stage, the principal seems much less of a Prince Charming, but instead seems downright threatening and like an enemy" (p. 149). The implementation stage may be the most trying part of a PLC for the principal's role.

Although implementing a PLC involves everyone and therefore requires the principal to facilitate others in the process, certain aspects of taking action are important for principals and assistant principals to perform. For instance, to implement a plan developed by a teacher team, the principal and the assistant principals either need to have been involved in the planning and have ownership of it or have complete trust in those who were involved in the planning and implementing. If the planning was entrusted to others, then the principals must be aware of the progress of the planning. If the plan is not feasible, then the principal needs to help in replanning and strategizing. This does not mean that the principal acts autocratically but rather cooperatively and collaboratively, suggesting and offering comments regarding the plan's implementation.

Implementing a PLC also requires individual insight and change as well as group action. You should constantly evaluate and reflect on your own practices. Certain behaviors, especially those steeped in tradition, may need to be evaluated and possibly changed. You should model change and be willing to transform aspects of your behaviors and activities for the learning community process. Crow, Matthews, and McCleary

(1996) described a principal of a school implementing a continuous learning model. The principal reinforced the shared decision making and learning model by submitting his own proposal for a school store to the site council, rather than arbitrarily approving his own idea.

As we discussed in Chapter 5, an important responsibility for school leaders is to understand and communicate the school culture and how that culture will affect the implementation of a PLC. Reform that has been implemented successfully in one school may not necessarily be implemented with the same success in another school. In fact, it probably cannot. As principal, you must help determine the best way that the learning community plans can be implemented within the context of the school's culture.

Evaluating and Assessing

The main purpose of evaluating and assessing reform efforts, such as a PLC, is to gain an understanding of the progress, direction, and modifications that may be needed. A formal evaluation report also may be necessary for a grant, the district office, or the board of education. Although the two terms *evaluation* and *assessment* often are used interchangeably, there are some subtle differences. Usually, *evaluation* is the process of collecting data to make a decision, for example, to continue or discontinue a program. *Assessment,* on the other hand, often is associated with determining if goals and objectives are being achieved. To understand the process of various learning community plans and efforts, both evaluation and assessment may be necessary. Furthermore, evaluation and assessment are used in both formative and summative ways. *Formative evaluation* can be defined as evaluating a program or process as it is in operation or in progress. *Summative evaluation* is more limiting in that it is an evaluation at the end of a program or process, such as a formal evaluation report of a reading program or professional development initiative.

As a principal, one of your main tasks in evaluation and assessment will be overseeing the collection and analysis of data. Data can be collected by several means, such as observing, testing, questioning, surveying, and anecdotal record keeping (Goldring & Berends, 2009). Generating the data actually may be the easy part. Generating the right data and analyzing that data are more complicated, especially in education. For example, a particular instructional program may be judged effective by teachers, but student learning may not have improved. The principal may have to help others understand which data are more important to consider in the assessment of the program. In this particular instance, data on short versus long-term gains will be important.

As we discussed in Chapter 4, your role as learner in a PLC permeates all the other roles you will take. Learning is at the essence of evaluation. Rallis and Goldring (2000) suggested that principal leadership, management, and evaluation are tightly linked. Leadership and management may help shape events, but evaluation can change the shape of those events. Evaluation information helps principals learn so that they can understand and shape events. Rallis and Goldring's view of evaluation aims to establish an inquiry ethic—an inherent element of a PLC. Principals and assistant principals should use assessment results for instructional improvement. This requires that you know how to analyze and interpret school assessment information accurately. As part of your preparation program, you would be wise to pay close attention to the research and statistics courses that will help you to become a better evaluator and assessor.

Managing through Technology

Technology is a critical part of the complex, knowledge society in which principals learn and lead. It certainly is important for students in accessing knowledge and preparing for a highly-skilled job. The rapid explosion of knowledge makes technology skills critical for all students in being able to access appropriate knowledge. Despite the increasing availability of computers and the Internet, some students in our schools have been left behind in regard to the availability of technology in their homes and schools and, therefore, disadvantaged in obtaining the types of jobs that are necessary in a knowledge society.

Technology is also important for teachers and principals in accessing knowledge, using data, conducting inquiry, and facilitating collaboration. In a PLC, the use of technology is a valuable tool that enriches the culture of inquiry. The principal as manager must make technology available to students and adults in the building, encourage by example the continuous and substantive use of technology for inquiry and practice, and provide resources for professional development to support the use of technology for improving teaching and learning and enriching the PLC (Picciano, 2006).

As a principal, you should pay special attention to at least five issues. First, technology is a valuable resource, which may not be currently available to all students in your school. The lack of access to technology creates a digital divide between those advantaged students and those students, frequently from poverty, who do not have the resources. As a principal, you need to ensure that this digital divide does not further complicate the achievement gap by providing adequate technological resources to students and families. Second, technology is a tool not an end in itself. Sometimes schools focus on the latest technology without connecting it to the core mission and culture of the school. As a principal, your own example of how you use technology as a tool will be critical for your staff. The third issue is closely related to the second. You must emphasize technology as a tool primarily to enrich the learning community. Ask the question whenever a new piece of equipment is made available or a new software program is touted: How does this enrich learning in this school? Fourth, as a principal, a significant task is to ensure that all educators have the professional development sufficient to use technology in an effective and learner-centered way. The speed at which technology has advanced has left some teachers behind. In fact, teachers often lament that their students know more about the technology than they. Supporting especially veteran teachers who are anxious about technology and its use in their classrooms will be an important part of your job in managing a learning community.

Finally, you should acknowledge the importance of the principal's leadership for technology. The acknowledgement of the importance of principal leadership for technology is reflected in the development of the National Educational Technology Standards for Administrators (NETS-A) (International Society for Technology in Education [ISTE], 2002), which include six sections:

1. leadership and vision,
2. learning and teaching,
3. productivity and professional practice,
4. support, management, and operations,
5. assessment and evaluation,
6. social, legal, and ethical issues.

All these areas are critical to your management of a PLC. Anderson and Dexter (2005) found in a survey of eight hundred schools that technology leadership by the principal had a significant and positive effect on three technology outcomes: extent to which teachers used e-mail and the World Wide Web, "the degree of integration of technology into the curriculum and into teaching practices," and the degree to which students used technology in academic work (p. 60). They also found that technology leadership varied by school size, governance, and socio-economic status (SES). "Larger schools, public schools, and those with higher SES had structural advantages in terms of technology leadership" (p. 69).

In a PLC, your management role takes on several characteristic activities. Lee (2000) in a study of principals in high-technology schools found eight characteristics of these principals:

1. equitable providing (ensured access for all students and staff),
2. learner-focused envisioning (keeping student learning at the center),
3. adventurous learning (through their example, principals develop personal competence and experiment with innovative technologies),
4. patient teaching (being nonjudgmental about teacher learning technology),
5. protective enabling (removing obstacles to the use of technologies),
6. constant monitoring (ensuring technology use fits the school's vision/culture),
7. entrepreneurial networking (forming partnerships to get necessary resources),
8. careful challenging (challenging assumptions and breaking barriers).
   (pp. 292–297)

Technology is a critical and valuable resource in a PLC. But this resource depends on your example, creativity, patience, support, and focus.

THE PRINCIPAL AS FACILITATOR OF OTHERS IN MANAGEMENT OF A PLC

As school leaders build leadership capacity, they also build management capacity among others. As the school culture evolves into a PLC, principals and assistant principals are not only supporting, planning, taking action, and evaluating, but they also are helping others to manage in these areas as well. In this section, we discuss how the principal facilitates others in managing the school for the creation and enrichment of the PLC.

In an early study on principal responsibility in instructional leadership, Stokes (1984) confirmed that instructional improvement is a shared responsibility and that efforts to evaluate this function by looking only at the activities of the principal were misguided. Stokes concluded that critical functions in improving instruction were shared by many people in the school. One role that can be overlooked but shares in the improvement of instruction is that of the assistant principal. Patton (1987) examined the role of assistant principals and found that their contributions were critical to the instructional quality in effective schools. We have discussed the role of assistant principal throughout this book as a role that needs to be reconceptualized, especially for supporting a PLC. Perhaps no other area of the assistant principal's responsibility is more important to be reconceptualized than management. Too often assistant principals are slotted into narrow management roles and either neglect or are neglected in instructional reform. The principal's first responsibility in facilitating others in managing a PLC is to reconceptualize the assistant principal's role to make it an active, involved, and integral part of the learning community. Indeed, principals and assistant principals should act as a team in managing all the affairs of the school.

Another role that is often overlooked in school improvement efforts is department or grade-level chairpersons. In a study of secondary schools, Worner and Brown (1993) concluded that principals wanted department chairs to assume more responsibility in improving the instructional climate of the school and, furthermore, that the department chairs were interested in taking on more responsibility. Both the Patton (1987) and the Worner and Brown studies indicated that principals do have opportunities to distribute the management tasks among other leaders in the school to accomplish school improvement efforts. Indeed, more often than not assistant principals and department chairs are not as involved as much as they could and want to be.

Previously we discussed the roles of the principal and assistant principal in supporting, planning, taking action, and evaluating. In the next section, we continue discussing these areas and how school leaders can facilitate others' actions in these four areas.

Facilitating Support

The principal and assistant principal need to support a nonthreatening environment in order for a PLC to be established and thrive, and they likewise need to help others to be supportive. Risk taking and experimentation by teachers, which are critical conditions for a PLC, are as easily and as commonly thwarted by peers as they are by administrators. When previous norms have emphasized a status quo mentality, often teachers will perceive others who want to implement reform movements either as threats or as troublemakers. For example, implementing the peer mentoring program, as outlined in Chapter 9, would involve the cooperation of most of the faculty. Some may perceive the program as too costly in both time and money. Others may feel that beginning teachers need to find their own best way of teaching without the interference of others. These types of change efforts are tricky for principals and assistant principals who want to support the effort, want others to support it, but find that doing so polarizes members of the faculty. In this section, we discuss how you can help others in the school community be supportive of a PLC to improve instructional programs. We do this by organizing the support around the four areas mentioned previously, namely, money, personnel, time, and information.

MONEY When resources are thin, and they usually are in schools, money often becomes an issue in terms of balancing resources with competing needs. Usually the traditional school budget allocates funds for line-item categories that do not reflect a school's goals and needs. Many school districts now allow building principals and site committees to participate in the process of formulating the budget, often known as school-based budgeting. One of the principal's roles is that of helping others in the school understand the budgeting process and reflect on how resources affect the school's priorities. These priorities should be linked to the school's vision of a PLC that administrators, teachers, and others in the school community share. Individual priorities must be evaluated within the more global view of the school's priorities. The site council has to give special consideration to how the financial resources are allocated to reach the school's collective vision for establishing, maintaining, and enriching the learning community.

Part of the school-based budgeting process involves communication. As Nanus (1992) suggested (Chapter 7), principals and assistant principals become "spokespersons" for the budget and how it connects to the PLC's vision. As spokespersons, principals communicate the needs of the school and the vision of the school and how fulfilling the needs will help accomplish the vision. Likewise, as spokespersons, the principal and assistant principals are advocates of the site council's budgeting process and decisions, understanding that everyone in the school should have a voice in the process. This is critical for PLCs, because if budgeting is left out of the inquiry process a necessary element for taking action will be eliminated.

We should not assume, however, that principals are solely responsible for obtaining the money for the school budget. Administrators are not the only agents of revenue building. For instance, teachers also can and should participate in grant writing. In facilitating support, others join in the cause of generating revenue for implementing innovative strategies identified through the collective inquiry process of the learning community. Because one person cannot possibly do it all, allowing and encouraging others to find sources of funds can help the reform efforts.

PERSONNEL   Although in recent times educators have paid more attention to their role of facilitating learning through professional development, many of the approaches actually have caused more problems or have added to existing problems. Fullan and Hargreaves (1996) suggested that many professional development strategies have been as fragmented and oblivious to the needs of the teachers and the school as the reform efforts they were meant to supplement. For example, training in teaching methods and strategies often is undertaken separately from the development of peer mentoring programs. Mentoring programs, in turn, often are separated from the supervision model used by principals. Such fragmentation isolates reform efforts into separate initiatives that ignore the wider PLC. When fragmented, these reform efforts are criticized more easily, especially by those who want to maintain the status quo.

As we discussed in Chapter 4, many professional development initiatives take the form of something that is done to teachers rather than with them. Top-down approaches to professional development embody a deficit view of teachers and teaching— something must be wrong, and it needs to be fixed by experts. If professional development is used as a means of fixing something or somebody, then it only adds to the existing problems. Instead, professional development must be related to the needs of school personnel to fulfill the collective vision of the learning community. Individual needs must be considered as much—if not more—than institutional needs. Teachers and support staff members differ in their years of experience, gender, stage of career and life, and expertise in certain areas. Teachers can and will support development when they can choose the type of learning that is best for them. Seldom, if ever, should you as a principal or assistant principal enforce professional development programs on others. If it is not voluntary, then little learning will take place.

However, in a PLC, faculty and staff do need to have opportunities in learning and may need some motivation to become involved. You need to assist others to embrace learning opportunities that help them develop personally and that build on the school's vision. As Fullan and Hargreaves (1996) described it, "The greatest problem in teaching is not how to get rid of the 'deadwood,' but how to create, sustain, and motivate good teachers throughout their careers" (p. 63). Fullan and Hargreaves coined the term *interactive professionalism* as a solution to this type of development problem. The elements of interactive professionalism are

- discretionary judgment as the heart of professionalism,
- collaborative work cultures,
- norms of continuous improvement where new ideas are sought inside and outside one's setting,
- reflection in, on, and about practice in which individual and personal development is honored, along with collective development and assessment,
- greater mastery, efficacy, and satisfaction in the profession of teaching. (p. 63)

Interactive professionalism will require some needed changes in the way teachers go about their work. Principals need to help facilitate these changes in order for teachers and other personnel to develop an interactive culture. Scribner, Sawyer, Watson, and Myers (2007) found that in teacher teams, formal leaders and teachers must develop capacities in the areas of facilitation, interaction, and communication. The development and use of these capacities require a change in how we use the element of time.

TIME Facilitating others to manage in PLCs involves helping others understand the element that time plays in change efforts. Time has two important functions in learning communities:

1. the length of time for reform to work,
2. the necessary management of time by those involved.

Many reform efforts have failed before they have been given a chance to succeed. When results are not positive immediately, many reform efforts have been abandoned. Hargreaves and Fullan (1998) claimed, "Most change strategies that make a difference in the classroom take five years or more to yield results" (p. 122). Fullan and Miles (1992) also suggested, "Even in cases where reform eventually succeeds, things often go wrong before they go right" (p. 749). Reform should be considered in the context of longevity. Principals and assistant principals need to play cheerleader—keeping hopes and interest high in the change efforts and trying to keep discouragement at bay.

The second area that time affects in a PLC is the management of time by those involved in the process. Teachers can burn out easily and become discouraged if they believe that their efforts are nonefficacious. Most teachers entered the profession wanting to be involved with children and teaching. They often miss seeing the bigger picture because of their isolation in their classrooms. However, effective reform is systemic. "Improvements inside the classroom depend on improvements outside it" (Fullan & Hargreaves, 1996, p. 77). Principals need to support teachers with interactive opportunities and collaborative efforts that are viewed not as add-ons to an already busy schedule but as an integral part of their teaching role within a PLC. However, a word of caution: Workaholic teachers are not always the most productive teachers. Long hours over long periods of time probably will lead to burnout and other emotional problems. Too often principals ask the same teachers to take on more responsibilities because these teachers have a way of getting things done. As principal in a PLC, you will want to facilitate all faculty in using time, not only a few of the hard workers.

TABLE 10.1 Strategies for Working with the Daily Rush

Although there are no simple ways to change principals' daily work, there are several strategies for dealing with it. Principals should do the following:

1. *Learn to change gears quickly and smoothly.* Like new drivers with stick-shift automobiles, learn to shift from first to second and back without grinding the gears. Principals need to move from task to task with ease.

2. *Learn to go with the flow.* It's important to have priorities and "to do" lists, but some days it's not possible to get all the work done. Remember, there's always tomorrow.

3. *Look at the big picture and take a long-term view.* Understand how solving immediate problems serves larger purposes. Understand how answering a question about curriculum at 6 P.M. is part of the larger reform effort. Take the long view. See how brief interactions and problem solving with staff build long-term relationships and cement the culture.

4. *Become a historian and an anthropologist of the culture* (Deal & Peterson, 1999). Hone your skills as a historian by listening to stories of past events, exhuming old planning documents, and reviewing past efforts to understand where the school has come from. However, also develop the skills of an anthropologist by digging into existing norms and values, examining artifacts and symbols, and asking about the deeper meanings of staff traditions and rituals.

5. *Develop a deep understanding of the school's purpose and values.* Every school has a deep set of values. In toxic cultures, these values are negative and hostile. In positive cultures, these values hold deep meaning for staff. Learn to identify and interpret what these values are as they relate to curriculum, instruction, approaches to assessment, and learning. See if the current values match the community's values and your own.

6. *Become a bifocal leader.* Bifocal leadership means knowing deep down that managerial tasks communicate values and build culture and that symbolic actions help staff and students internalize the actions and routines needed to run schools (Deal & Peterson, 1999). Intuitively, bifocal leaders manage by leading and lead by managing. Every action reinforces core values and purpose. It is harder than it sounds, but it is key to being a successful principal.

7. *Enjoy the rush.* A principal's daily work is exciting, surprising, and mysterious. It will never be boring or routine. By celebrating and learning to enjoy the rush of activity through networking, stories, and collegiality, principals will gain new energy to cope with work's challenges.

Source: Adapted from K. Peterson (2001). The roar of complexity, *Journal of Staff Development* (Winter 2001), 18–21.

INFORMATION   Isolated teachers also contribute to another cultural problem—that of information hoarding. When one-room schools were the norm, who was there for teachers to share and discuss their practice with? Today's schools, although structured differently, still can maintain a one-room school atmosphere in a building with other one-room schools. Often a teacher with a good idea protects that idea with fortified and sacred buttresses. For moral and ethical reasons, information on effective instructional practices should not be hoarded. Information hoarding also contradicts both the spirit and practice of PLC. Information sharing is essential to its success.

Another way for principals and assistant principals to support teachers with information is to ensure that data-based, decision-making skills are distributed throughout the school. These skills are not the sole possession of the principal or of a few teachers.

All teachers in a PLC must have the skills to base their instructional decisions on accurate, appropriate, clear, and timely information.

Facilitating information dissemination involves providing opportunities for faculty and staff to engage in interactive professionalism (Fullan & Hargreaves, 1996). One example of increasing faculty involvement with information sharing was used by Hillside Elementary School where small group sessions replaced regular faculty meetings. During these sessions, teachers were invited to join in small groups to discuss various issues. These sessions were voluntary, and scheduling allowed teachers to share ideas with others and explore problems and solutions. These groups later added another learning bonus. As they became more involved with one another, the faculty organized book clubs. This voluntary activity involved a group of teachers reading a book and then sharing ideas about the book in their group meetings. Not only was a collaborative culture established at Hillside, but an increased learning atmosphere also developed.

In this subsection, we discussed how you facilitate others to be supportive in managing reform efforts around the areas of money, personnel, time, and information. In this next subsection, we continue exploring ways principals and assistant principals facilitate others in management by looking at how they are involved in planning and taking action.

Facilitating Others in Planning and Taking Action

Professional learning communities do not develop by chance. Behind each change effort are people using time and energy in planning the strategies that are needed to establish and maintain a PLC. As principal or assistant principal, you facilitate others involved in the process to carry out effective planning through at least three actions:

1. ensuring that information and data are available for everyone in the planning process,
2. arranging for the time and compensation of faculty and staff to be involved,
3. encouraging planning sessions that meet often and regularly before and after implementation

Your role in planning and taking action in a PLC requires the development of a collaborative culture. As principal, you cannot get bogged down in the details. You must allow others to carry out their responsibilities. This type of leadership and management is more an act of sharing than of delegating. Delegating involves the principal giving someone a task and then following up with that individual. Sharing, on the other hand, involves more of a cooperative, trusting venture in which the principal shares the task with others, accepting a lesser role at times, and trusting that professionals will work through the proper decisions. In a sense, here is where the principal has to let go and trust teachers and others in the school. You cannot be everywhere doing everything. More importantly, a sustainable PLC requires that all individuals share in the process.

A study by Short and Greer (1997) found that a principal's trust of teachers resulted from many factors that varied from principal to principal. In one case study of a high school in Murray, Utah, the principal, Richard Tranter, spoke of the shaky decisions that faculty members made. In the end, however, he acknowledged that things had worked out all right and that he had come to believe that the planning and action taken were better than he would have done himself. As Short and Greer suggested, in Richard's case, even though he had believed for many years that the faculty should be actively involved, it was the actual positive experiences that cemented his belief in the process. Thus, having had success, he was encouraged to use the process again with other change efforts. His trust in the faculty was strengthened significantly through the experience of letting go and allowing planning and action to take place.

Facilitating Others in Evaluating and Assessing

The principal as facilitator must establish accountability for the progress of students, teachers, and instructional practices through ongoing assessment within the school. However, this is not a one- or two-person responsibility. Evaluating and assessing school improvement are the responsibilities of all stakeholders in a PLC. It is the principal, however, who must facilitate others to be involved in the effort.

Different stakeholders in education use accountability differently. Policymakers often insist on strict accountability through indications such as student test scores. District office administrators want accountability with budget and resource allocation. Parents are more interested in individual assessments of their children. Several theorists have advocated other forms of accountability. For example, Stiggins (1994) and Wiggins (1993) argued for "authentic" or performance-based testing—testing not only for what students know but also for what they can do. Regardless of the accountability measures that exist within a district or a school, the principal must facilitate the process. Most important, however, is facilitating the correct approach that will yield the information needed for continual learning and improvement. As your school becomes a PLC, you need to work with teachers and other administrators to select those assessment measures that will render the results of the improvement efforts. For example, standardized testing, although required by the state, will not evaluate new teacher morale as to their professional development. Therefore, as a principal, you need to match an appropriate assessment for the new teacher development plan.

A caution for principals is to be careful about giving mixed messages, especially with pet projects. Often schools can have goals for instructional programs and then another set of goals for assessment of learning. For example, a school goal could be to improve instruction of reading by implementing a reading one-on-one program. Another goal could be to raise aggregate reading scores by one grade level. The principal's and teachers' goal may involve more interest in the one-on-one reading program than on its results, thus giving the mixed message that the success of a particular program is more important than is the learning goal. Programs may be successful with teachers but not successful for student learning.

One area of evaluation and assessment that principals should emphasize with other educators in a PLC is reflection on practice. Continual reflection on practice by teachers involves both individual inquiry and meaningful dialogue with others, especially teachers, parents, and students. Principals can facilitate this process by providing time and encouraging reflective inquiry. As colleagues in a learning community, teachers and principals should discuss questions about the why, what, and how of curriculum, instruction, and assessment.

A PLC must be accountable for student learning and assessment practices. Principals and assistant principals must lead and facilitate discussion among others about assessment practices so that the school focuses on working toward the collective vision and achieving the school goals.

INSTITUTIONALIZING A PLC

For a PLC to become institutionalized, it is necessary for it to be seen in the context of the school's culture. School culture exists at a very deep level and has resulted from the values, norms, and beliefs of those involved with the school over a number of years. Changing anything in that culture requires considerable effort over a period of time. Many scholars (e.g., Schein, 1992) believe that it is impossible to operate directly on culture. Rather, culture changes gradually as the people in the organization change in the way they go about doing their work and relating to others in their work. Management is a critical part of changing this work.

Because change is holistic, every aspect of the school has the potential to be affected. This underscores the importance of systems thinking; that is, changes in one part of the system have an impact on others. For example, implementing teacher teams affects everyone in the building, not just teachers and students. Custodians may have to help with arranging meeting locations, secretaries could be asked to schedule team meetings, and an assistant principal may communicate the justification for letting students out early to parents. Teaming also can affect other elements in the system, such as instructional time. Because finding time for teams to meet affects instructional time, the schedule will have to accommodate the new approach. Likewise, other school activities may have to be postponed or temporarily cancelled while teaming is initially established. Thus, the change in one improvement strategy usually has a managerial impact on other elements in the school.

Based on the work of Senge (1990) and Senge, Cambron-McCabe, Lucas, Smith, Dutton, and Kleiner (2000), we have adapted several features of systems thinking that are critical in facilitating a PLC from a management standpoint. First, seeing interrelationships and processes is necessary. Instead of viewing PLC as a series of change projects, viewing it as integration of changes is critical. Instead of understanding PLC from a snapshot perspective, it is important to understand it as an ongoing system-wide process involving different people, tasks, times, places, and ideas.

Second, principals and assistant principals need to influence others to move beyond blame. Instead of accusing others of preventing or hindering the PLC, look at system-wide, managerial structures and processes that discourage attitudes of change, norms of learning, and values of community. Furthermore, "avoid symptomatic solutions" (Senge et al., 2000, p. 15). The urgency of schooling sometimes encourages individuals to short-cut inquiry and focus on the symptoms rather than on the problems and opportunities of school improvement. Engaging in problem finding and problem solving is critical in creating a PLC that supports substantive, transformative change in schools.

Third, principals need to develop in themselves and others the skill of focusing on areas of high leverage. Rather than attempt to change all areas of instructional practice, the principal as facilitator should influence school constituents to focus on those areas where change is most possible and where change will make the most difference for school improvement. This will vary with each school. Nevertheless, it is the principal's responsibility to know the system and to communicate and develop that understanding with followers so that the professional learning community can have the most effect.

Conclusion

In this chapter, we discussed the role that principals and assistant principals play in the management of schools as PLCs. The role of the principal as manager is key in the daily planning, organizing, operating, executing, budgeting, maintaining, and scheduling of numerous processes, activities, and tasks that permit a school to accomplish its goals as a learning community. However, the manager role also should emphasize building a strong school culture and establishing a shared vision that encompasses school improvement and promotes learning for *all* students.

Abe Rosenblatz, in the introductory vignette, was disillusioned by the heavy managerial aspects of his administrative internship. However, these managerial responsibilities are important for developing a culture and vision that support a PLC. Moreover, knowing how politics affects the role will determine a great deal of how you will practice being a principal or assistant principal. In Chapter 11, we discuss the important role of principal as politician.

Activities

SELF-REFLECTION ACTIVITIES

1. If you are an intern, critically reflect on your own experiences in learning the management area. If you are not an intern, talk to someone who is an intern about his or her experiences. Does the management experience match Abe's in the opening vignette?
2. Get a copy of your school's budget. What are the obvious and subtle things that are being emphasized in the budget?
3. In what ways might a school's budget reflect the priorities of establishing and maintaining a PLC?

PEER REFLECTION ACTIVITIES

1. With a colleague, reflect on your experiences of how current and former principals balanced management and leadership.

2. Critically reflect on a recent school change initiative. What management tasks were critical for the principal or assistant principal to perform? In what ways were these administrators effective and ineffective in performing these tasks?

COURSE ACTIVITIES

1. If school-based budgeting is used in your area, invite a principal to class to discuss how this affects the role and how it affects a PLC.
2. Invite a principal or assistant principal to discuss student scheduling. How does the administrator relate this task to student learning and PLC?
3. Analyze a school improvement plan and reflect on the management processes and resources necessary to develop and implement that plan.

Websites

Strategic Management of Human Capital (SMHC)—education-focused site with resources and recent developments in organizational management *http://ddis.wceruw.org/*

Better Management—section of the site has resources, articles, and research on how to manage government and educational organizations www.bettermanagement.com/topic/default.aspx?f=44

U.S. Census Bureau—Federal, State, and Local Governments, Public Elementary-Secondary Education Finance Data
www.census.gov/govs/www/school.html

Center for Applied Research in Educational Technology (CARET)
http://caret.iste.org/

National Educational Technology Standards from ISTE
www.iste.org/AM/Template.cfm?Section=NETS

CHAPTER 11

Principal as Politician

Vignette

As a large urban school in an eastern U.S. city, Jefferson Elementary had two big challenges. The first challenge was a vocal and demanding faculty that had the principal, Carla Patterson, constantly responding to multiple and conflicting pressures. The second challenge was Jefferson's poor showing on test scores. Because of the low student test scores, the school had not met adequate yearly progress (AYP) with *No Child Left Behind* (NCLB) for the last two years. Thus, last spring Carla and a faculty team had proposed to the community and the school board to have an early out Wednesday to allow for instructional teams to meet and collaborate about improving student learning. The time lost with instructional time on Wednesday would be added to the other four days, making those days longer. The district was reluctant with its support because the plan would interfere with bus schedules. Several teachers at Jefferson were adamantly opposed to the idea, thinking the instructional teams or anything else would not improve student scores because of the conditions the students had in their homes and community. However, the school board was anxious that the school and its faculty do something to help with meeting AYP, so all board members had voted to approve the plan.

It was now early September, and the first Wednesday of collaborative teacher teams had been relatively successful. For the first few Wednesdays, Carla wanted all the teams in the library so that she could facilitate all of the teams' development more easily. Now she sat in her office and sighed with relief that all had gone reasonably well. She knew that the sixth-grade instructional team had the most challenges, but the others actually did quite well. Little did Carla know what was brewing outside her office.

As she sat in her office, Halley Cantor and Troy Martin knocked on her door and asked to visit with her. Most of the faculty members were in mid-career stages with ten or more years of experience, but both of these teachers were the most veteran at Jefferson Elementary, having come to the school at the same time—twenty-eight years ago. Halley and Troy both taught sixth grade for as long as anyone could remember. Carla remembered one situation that occurred three years ago when she had asked Halley if she would consider teaching in the fourth grade, and Halley vehemently protested. Carla knew that these two teachers had been against the collaborative teams and, in general, were not into change. They were also not involved in any of the professional development activities that were available. Carla knew that they both were satisfied with their instructional practices, and they often told her that they got the best they could from the children in their classes. As far as not meeting AYP, these teachers simply blamed the family and community rather than their instructional practices.

After they sat down, Halley and Troy told Carla that they wanted to discontinue meeting as an instructional team during the common collaboration time on Wednesday afternoons. Instead, they would use the extra time in preparation for their classes. After all, they claimed, sixth-grade teachers needed more time to prepare than did the other teachers. They said the collaborative time was wasted, and there was no reason for them to meet because they were collaborating all of the time.

Before responding to the teachers, Carla told them that she knew they worked hard and she appreciated their efforts. She told Halley and Troy that their efforts meant a lot to her but that student learning meant even more. Carla then pulled out some fact sheets that she had prepared over the summer. She shared some statistics with the two teachers as to their classroom test scores compared to two other sixth-grade class scores. She showed them several years' worth of scores. In each year, Halley's and Troy's classes had scored lower than the other two classes. Carla then asked the two teachers, "Do you want to improve your classes' scores?" Both of the teachers looked at each other and reluctantly consented that, indeed, they wanted their students to perform better. Carla then asked them, "If you continue with the collaboration teaming, and if in the future, you see improved student learning, will you continue with the collaborative teams?" Both of the teachers shrugged their shoulders and said they would. It was obvious that they were a bit surprised that Carla had the data showing their classes' achievement levels.

As Carla ended the conversation with the teachers, she promised them that she would meet with the team next Wednesday and help with their collaboration on ways to improve student learning. No sooner had they left her office than the receptionist told her that Superintendent Sampson was on line 2. Carla picked up the telephone. The superintendent told her that he had several parents call him within the hour. The parents were upset that the collaboration time at Jefferson Elementary meant that their children were coming home early from school and were, therefore, unsupervised because no one else was at home. Carla assured the superintendent that she would call the parents and work out a solution for these children, perhaps suggesting that their children go to the Boys and Girls Club down the street. As the conversation progressed, Carla felt as if the superintendent was keeping a list of what was wrong with the early-out day at Jefferson Elementary School.

As she put down the telephone, Carla's secretary came into her office and told her that a police officer wanted to talk to her about an incident with sixth graders burglarizing some neighborhood homes after they left school. She invited the officer into her office and cordially listened to him as he told her about the reported incidents. She could tell that he was a little perplexed with the reason these children had been allowed to leave school early.

The next morning, Carla was reading the local newspaper when she came across an article in the city section. The headline read "School Let Out Early—Students Burglarize Homes." Although the newspaper reporter could not name the juveniles involved, it did name Jefferson Elementary School as letting school out early on Wednesdays when the burglaries occurred.

As Carla got ready for work that day, she decided that she needed to go to the district office and talk to Superintendent Sampson. She knew that she was going to need his, other district office administrators', and the school board's support in the next few weeks to weather out this tempest. She also thought that she should call the newspaper reporter and see if he would talk to her so that he knew what was occurring during the early-out time on Wednesdays. In order for this collaboration plan to succeed, she knew she was going to have to play a stronger political role and become more proactive.

INTRODUCTION

Carla's experience with finding common time for teacher collaboration in developing a professional learning community (PLC) illustrates the political nature of the principal's role. Public schools are societal institutions that are influenced by the larger society and community in which they exist. Their funding, governance, curricula, and administration cannot escape the pressures and demands of these larger societal and community structures.

The principal's role fits into this larger system. We take the position in this chapter that this political role is not only necessary because schools are public institutions but also because it can be valuable in understanding and promoting learning for students and teachers in a PLC. The learning conception of the principal's role exists in a political arena. If schools are to be learning communities, principals must acknowledge and respond to the political qualities and nature of schools both internally and in their community contexts. Furthermore, the culture- and vision-building elements of the leadership conception and the supportive functions of the managerial conception exist in a highly political context. Values and resources, for example, those related to teaching and learning, are two areas where conflict is frequent and intense in schools. These conflicts are clearly political and demand a political role of the principal and assistant principal.

The traditional political view of the role of the school principal has tended to emphasize three approaches. In one approach, principals are expected to be apolitical or even nonpolitical. One era of the history of education could be described as an attempt to rid education of politics. During the 1920s, the move away from the ward politics of urban areas, such as New York and Chicago, to separately elected boards of education with nonpartisan members was an attempt to avoid the political maneuvering in which schools and administrative positions were used as paybacks for political contributions (Tyack & Hansot, 1982). To avoid this type of political role, educators historically were cautioned to stay out of politics. They were encouraged to take no stands that might be opposed by some political constituency. This conception has encouraged the notion—typically among new administrators—that they should take no politically controversial positions. More recently, this fear of politics in the schools has subsided. Crowson (1998) suggested that "memories of machine politics run amuck have faded, as today's new realization is that the public schools may be too important to the city's welfare not to be politicized" (p. 57). This memory has faded to such a degree that in several urban areas, for example, Chicago and New York City, the mayor now has a direct and close involvement in the management of schools.

The second approach conceives of the principal's political role as based on politics as manipulation. In this conception, principals gain political clout among powerful constituencies in order to manipulate resources, including people, to satisfy their own self-interests. Traditionally, this takes the form of paternalistic principals who encourage dependency relationships and perpetuate the principal's power in ways unrelated to the school's shared vision. At others times, principals become Machiavellian. Whatever tactics are necessary to maintain the principal's power and achieve the principal's vision of success are considered appropriate. This conception reflects what McClelland (1975) referred to as the *negative face* of power as exploitation rather than the positive means for creating change.

Third, a subtler traditional political role of the principalship is one that emphasizes buffering the school from parents and the community. Veteran principals frequently advised this conception of the role to new administrators, and this view was taught in some educational administration courses. Although, at times, the principal needs to buffer school faculty and staff from interruptions and inappropriate pressures, if buffering becomes the primary political role of the principal, the school loses the rich contributions of diverse constituencies that may contribute to the learning organization. We suggest that bridging is a more appropriate political role for contemporary principals in a PLC than buffering. For example, instead of buffering a new elementary teacher from parents concerned about her classroom management, perhaps it would be more beneficial to offer a bridging technique. First, as principal, you could mentor the teacher into better management practices and then ask for parental volunteer help with reading or math groups while the teacher learns how to manage his or her classroom better.

As Carla realized in the opening vignette, the principal has a critical role to play as politician that is more appropriate and valuable to schools than these three traditional conceptions. Before moving to the specifics of the principal's role as politician, we first identify and discuss elements of a political perspective.

THINKING POLITICALLY

In developing a conception of the principal's and assistant principal's roles that take seriously the political dimension, several elements of a political perspective are important to consider. Bolman and Deal (1993) identified five propositions that constitute a political perspective:

1. Organizations are *coalitions* composed of varied individuals and interest groups (e.g., hierarchical levels, departments, professional groups, gender and ethnic subgroups).
2. There are *enduring differences* among individuals and groups in their values, preferences, beliefs, information, and perceptions of reality. Such differences change slowly, if at all.
3. Most of the important decisions in organizations involve the *allocation of scarce resources*; they are decisions about who gets what.
4. Because of scarce resources and enduring differences, *conflict* is central to organizational dynamics, and *power* is the most important resource.
5. Organizational goals and decisions emerge from bargaining, negotiation, and jockeying for position among members of different coalitions.

In the opening vignette, the potential coalitions that could have developed beyond the two teachers, as well as the district office's lukewarm support for the collaboration time could destroy Jefferson Elementary's efforts for a PLC. Coalitions among teachers, community forces, political maneuvering in the district office, and the influence of media could be used to bargain and negotiate positions and resources with decision makers in developing a PLC. Carla's skill in proactive political involvement in the escalating conflict will be a powerful tool in settling disputes and obtaining resources.

Two factors previously identified are central to thinking politically: conflict and power. We typically think of conflict as something to avoid. Yet conflict in a political system is a necessary process to allow individual interests to be heard. Diverse interests and groups are becoming an increasingly apparent feature of contemporary schools. This diversity is not only racial and ethnic but also ideological. The principal who sees conflict as something always to avoid runs the risk of trying (ultimately unsuccessfully) to silence groups whose voices traditionally have not been heard but whose perspective is important. Conflict can be beneficial in developing alternative ways to address differences of values and scarcity of resources.

A tranquil, harmonious organization may very well be an apathetic, uncreative, stagnant, inflexible, and unresponsive organization. Conflict challenges the status quo and stimulates interest and curiosity. It is the root of personal and social change, creativity, and innovation. Conflict encourages new ideas and approaches to problems, stimulating innovation (Bolman & Deal, 1991, p. 185; Heffron, 1989). In a PLC, where diversity is a central feature, principals and assistant principals must be able to acknowledge not only the inevitability of conflict but also its value.

Power is also central to thinking politically. Traditionally, we think of power in negative terms, for example, coercing or forcing people to do what we want them to do. Yet power is more diverse. French and Raven (1959) identified five types of power:

- Reward (based on the ability to provide rewards)
- Coercive (based on the ability to punish or remove rewards)
- Legitimate (based on a legitimate right to prescribe behavior, e.g., position or authority)
- Referent (based on an identification or relationship with the person with power)
- Expertise (based on special knowledge)

Leaders and followers use rewards to influence one another to do something. Administrators use their position of authority to influence decisions. In the opening vignette, Carla used referent and expertise power to convince the two veteran teachers to receive training in collaboration and to give it some time to help students learn. Educators can also use teaching expertise to influence decisions. Bolman and Deal (2008), based on their review of the literature, identified three other forms of power: alliances and networks, access to and control of agendas, and control of meaning and symbols. *Thinking politically* means recognizing the multiple forms of power and when they are appropriate. Principals who confine their power to position (authority) will rapidly discover the limited potency of this form of power. Teachers, parents, students, and community members also possess power that frequently is stronger than the principal's authority for making changes and negotiating conflict. Kotter (1985) used the term *power gap* to describe this discrepancy between the authority of the manager and the power necessary to get things done or make changes. Most veteran principals will tell you that relying on your own authority as a principal will not suffice to make changes, mediate conflicts, or influence others to improve instruction. Thinking politically means expanding your understanding not only of the power you have but also of the power that others have.

Professional Dilemma 11.1

At a Rotary Club meeting, a leading businessman approaches you. He mentions to you that his sister's son, who is a seventh grader in your school, is bored by his history teacher. You have observed frequently in this teacher's classroom and find the teacher's lessons to be well organized and relevant to seventh graders. Do you tell the teacher what the businessman told you?

Thinking politically also means recognizing the spheres in which political activity occurs. Traditionally, school administrators have been trained to concentrate attention only on what is occurring within the school. In political terms, this means addressing the conflict among teachers, students, administrators, and possibly parents. But, as Carla came to realize in the opening vignette, this narrow political role is not enough. Parsons (1951) identified two problems that all organizations, and thus their administrators, must address: internal integration (e.g., morale) and external adaptation (e.g., responding to environmental demands). Principals must think politically not only in terms of how conflict within the school is negotiated and power is used but also in terms of the environmental spheres in which schools exist and within which principals are politicians. Bolman and Deal (2008) referred to organizations like schools as both political arenas and political tools. Schools are nested within districts, communities, and the larger society, and thus these spheres influence the political nature of schools.

In previous chapters, we have treated PLC and the principal's role in the community in somewhat politically neutral ways. In this chapter, however, we will emphasize that as a principal your role in a PLC involves political processes. You will find differences among members of the learning community regarding the interpretation of school data, appropriate strategies for responding to student needs, and priorities for team efforts. You will encounter conflicts over how resources are and should be distributed. These are not wrong or unsuitable events for a PLC. Rather, they are common and appropriate ways in which committed individuals in a learning community negotiate what is important to them about learning for all students. Your role as a principal is to be sensitive to these political processes, to value differences, to provide support for decisions, and to promote other individuals' work in a caring, political, PLC.

In the remainder of this chapter we address the principal's political role in terms of societal, community, district, and school contexts. As we address the principal's role as politician and as facilitator of other politicians, we acknowledge a broader role than the one traditionally identified as existing only within the school. We maintain that you as principal have a political role to play in the larger society, community, and district, as well as in the school, that promotes the learning of *all* students.

PRINCIPAL AS POLITICIAN IN THE SOCIETY

As we have mentioned, educators tend to see the principal's political role as limited to the internal context of the school. Yet the principal plays a political role that is influenced by and occurs within the society. We base our understanding of the principal as politician in the society on an understanding of schools as political institutions.

Slater and Boyd (1999) identified three ways in which schools can be considered polities, or political institutions: political systems; civil societies; and the rule of the many in the interest of the whole, or democratic institutions. We will use these distinctions to organize both our understanding of schools as political institutions in the society and our understanding of the principal's and assistant principal's roles.

Schools as Political Systems

Understanding schools as political systems seems to emphasize the internal political nature of schools, that is, how schools act as political systems using power to respond to conflicts about scarce resources. However, schools can also be seen as political systems that occur within the larger political environment of the society. One way to understand this larger political environment that influences the school as a political system is in terms of ideological differences and how individuals and groups holding these differences address social and economic changes.

Various ideological perspectives confront schools and principals with different demands and approaches to addressing the social and economic changes that contemporary schools now face. Cibulka (1999) identified three major societal changes confronting schools that are addressed by various ideological perspectives. First, there is a decreasing faith in institutions such as schools. Cibulka used the annual Gallop Poll data to illustrate this. Public support for education, as evidenced in the Gallop Poll, had declined 20 percent from 1970, from 58 percent to 38 percent. Second, we are seeing the mobilization of powerful interest groups and movements that in some instances are opposed to public schools and administrators. Among the most potent movements influencing schools are, according to Cibulka, business activism; growth of the religious right; and elected public officials, such as governors and mayors, who take a more active role in school reforms. Third, the transformation of the American economy to a globalized and nonindustrial economy is another change that influences schools and the ideological pressures being placed on schools and principals.

> All these changes made less probable and even obsolete the traditional ideology of school administration as an autonomous, apolitical, professional, technically neutral enterprise. Indeed the greater demographic diversity of the country has merely reinforced the trend toward more overt "politicization" of school affairs. (Cibulka, 1999, p. 170)

These societal changes confront principals with often conflicting demands and pressures.

Conservatives see the performance decline in public schools as the predictable result of liberal philosophies and dominance by liberal special interests (elites). Liberal analyses accept that there is a legitimate basis for public concern and seek programs and policies to restore confidence, while at the same time seeking to protect the institution against the mobilization of the political right (but not necessarily business interests). Radical interpretations, by contrast, stress that the performance problems of public schools are rooted in the structural inequities of the larger social and economic order (Cibulka, 1999).

Principals frequently face conflict among two or more ideological perspectives. The growth of the conservative religious right and the demands of those seeking radical reform of the inequalities they experience put the principal in the middle where compromise is not obvious. Schools and their principals exist in a political system where conflicts over values, beliefs, and resources are increasing.

Schools as Civil Societies

Slater and Boyd (1999) identified a second way in which schools are polities that have implications for the principal's political role: schools as civil societies. In this way, schools not only are influenced by the political system but also can contribute to the larger society by helping to create a civil society. Slater and Boyd described the characteristics of a civil society based on Lasswell's (1936) earlier work. These characteristics include:

1. an open ego, by which he [Lasswell] meant a warm and inclusive attitude toward other human beings;
2. a capacity for sharing values with others;
3. a multivalued rather than a single-valued orientation;
4. trust and confidence in the human environment;
5. relative freedom from anxiety. (p. 328)

The contemporary emphasis in school reform on student achievement, often defined by standardized test scores, fails to recognize a fundamental quality that historically we have expected schools to engender in students, that is, the willingness to contribute to society. Writers have noted recently the American emphasis on individuality and the growing disregard for community. Bellah and colleagues (1985) identified this historical tendency toward individualism in American society, recorded as far back as de Tocqueville, and the need for developing an understanding and sensitivity to community. Putnam (2000), in his work *Bowling Alone*, demonstrated evidence that individualism is increasing and communal efforts are decreasing.

Schools are one of the first and primary institutions where students encounter nonfamily members and confront the need to learn how to live, work, and play with others. Yet, as Slater and Boyd (1999) argued, the traditional curriculum and forms of instruction in schools reinforce individualism rather than community; three exceptions to this are character education, service learning, and cooperative learning. Principals play a critical political role in helping to make schools into civil societies that prepare students to contribute to their communities.

Schools as Democratic Institutions

The third form of schools as polities involves the school as a democratic institution (Slater & Boyd, 1999). The view that schools have the responsibility to teach democracy is not new. Thomas Jefferson viewed education as a key determinant for the success of a democracy. In the 1940s during World War II, schools were seen as a critical social institution for perpetuating democracy. More recently, several reforms encourage not only teaching democracy but also modeling democracy in the school. We might argue that reforms such as decentralization and site-based management could be attempts to make schools more democratic. More radical reformers have argued that schools must do a better job of modeling democracy in ways that not only respect faculty members but also value students' voices.

Maxcy (1995) identified three democratic values that contemporary schools not only must acknowledge but also must base their educational practice on:

1. A dedicated belief in the worth of the individual and the importance of the individual in participation and discussion regarding school life;
2. A belief in freedom, intelligence, and inquiry;
3. A conviction that projected designs, plans, and solutions be results of individuals pooling their intelligent efforts within communities. (p. 73)

Maxcy argued that

> School restructuring is failing, not because it is inefficient or lacks proper means for accounting for "school effects"; the problem is deeper than this. We must refocus and turn away from modernist assumptions regarding the way organizations and persons flourish. Postmodern schools as new forms of educational space should be built on the twin values of democracy and educational value. (p. 180)

Apple and Beane (1995), in a discussion of democratic schools, identified several conditions on which a democracy depends:

1. The open flow of ideas, regardless of their popularity, that enables people to be as fully informed as possible;
2. Faith in the individual and collective capacity of people to create possibilities for resolving problems;
3. The use of critical reflection and analysis to evaluate ideas, problems, and policies;
4. Concern for the welfare of others and the "common good";
5. Concern for the dignity and rights of individuals and minorities;
6. An understanding that democracy is not so much an "ideal" to be pursued as an "idealized" set of values that we must live and that must guide our life as a people;
7. The organization of social institutions to promote and extend the democratic way of life (pp. 6–7).

According to these authors, democratic schools have two major characteristics: democratic structures and processes and democratic curriculum. Among the democratic structures is the widespread participation in governance and decision making. School decisions are not just made by administrators, but teachers, students, and parents also contribute to the problem solving and decision making. In democratic schools, diversity is valued because all voices need to be heard, and the diversity of these voices adds richness to the decision making and practice of the schools. Also, in democratic schools, adults and students see themselves as part of a larger community. "Democratic educators seek not simply to lessen the harshness of social inequities in school, but to change the conditions that create them. For this reason, they tie their understanding of undemocratic practices inside the school to larger conditions on the outside" (Apple & Beane, 1995, pp. 11–12). A properly functioning PLC functions as a democratic school. Such PLC practices as shared decision making, collaborative culture, distributive leadership, collective inquiry, and shared mission, vision, values, and goals are all elements of a democratic school.

Apple and Beane (1995) also found that curricula in democratic schools are distinctive. Students are provided access to a wider range of information and a right to hear those with varied opinions. Instead of the "official knowledge" present in many schools, democratic schools reach beyond the traditional and bring in the voices of those typically silenced. Democratic curricula also encourage students and adults to be critical readers of their society. The authors provided an illustration of a class discussion of media reports on "natural events." Their teacher led them to consider whose definition of *natural* was being used. One example of a natural event reported in the media was of massive mudslides in South America. As the students thought more critically about the example, they discovered that the wealthy individuals lived in the fertile valleys, whereas the poor could only find housing on the hillsides where floods caused mudslides. "A democratic curriculum invites young people to shed the passive role of knowledge consumers and assume the active role of 'meaning makers.' It recognizes that people acquire knowledge by both studying external sources and engaging in complex activities that require them to construct their own knowledge" (Apple & Beane, 1995, p. 16).

Historically, we have expected schools to prepare students to live, work, and contribute to a democracy. "Surely it is an obligation of education in a democracy to empower the young to become members of the public, to participate, and play articulate roles in the public space" (Greene, 1985, p. 4). Principals, in their role as politician, must lead schools to fulfill this purpose.

Role of Principal as Politician in Society

These three views of schools as political systems, civil societies, and democratic institutions lead to three conceptions of the political role of principals and assistant principals.

UNDERSTANDING CURRENT IDEOLOGIES   First, principals must understand the current ideologies that influence school reform and practice. To ignore the fact that ideologies play a role in reforms, such as PLC, is to run the risk of being blindsided by controversy. Whether you agree with a particular ideology, individuals deserve a voice. Principals must be sensitive to those voices that are not being heard as well as those voices that gain media attention. Although not all the problems you face can be solved by giving people a listening ear, refusing to hear or ignoring individuals and groups that want to be heard is likely to aggravate the situation and intensify the negative aspects of the conflict. As an illustration, several years ago a rural high school received a substantial donation of concrete from the local Red Devil Cement Company for construction of curbing around the football field. In appreciation for the donation, the principal convinced the student council to adopt the mascot of Red Devils. Now several decades later, many evangelical religious groups want the name changed because of its satanic reference. The principal ignored the vocal groups' request until the groups went to the media, which escalated the conflict.

In responding to these ideological differences, as principal you must acknowledge the changes that these differences are addressing, for example, demographic differences. Some of the criticism of public schools has been aimed at the ways some schools ignore problems and needs until ideological sides have developed around them. During the early 1970s, the public school's lack of response to students with disabilities spurred the development of political lobbying groups that forced schools and districts to take decisive action. Perhaps an earlier, more proactive response to an obvious problem would have resulted in more intentional strategies and less governmental and judicial involvement. Likewise, the NCLB Act of 2001 was spurred by those who thought that schools were not teaching to standards and were not being held account-able. A lack of response by educators led to the congressional act.

ENCOURAGING AND FOSTERING DEVELOPMENT OF SCHOOLS AS CIVIL SOCIETIES   Second, as principals and assistant principals, you have a critical role to play in encouraging and fostering the development of schools as civil societies. An obvious basis for the deadly violence experienced in schools in recent years has been the bullying behavior that ostracized and humiliated some students. Creating a more civil society can go a long way toward addressing the causes of school violence. Programs such as character education, service learning programs, and cooperative learning are ways principals can encourage schools to be civil societies. These types of programs encourage students to develop skills in contributing to a society instead of merely pursuing their self-interests.

As we discussed in Chapter 7, as a principal, you will have the opportunity to influence a vision of the school. The priorities that you encourage will contribute to that vision. What you pay attention to will be noticed by others. Given this critical political role of fostering schools as civil societies, it seems clear that those priorities should include sensitivity and respect for differences. This sensitivity and respect are critical for developing the kind of trust necessary for a PLC. Schools, as effective PLCs, take seriously their role as civil societies. As a principal, your leadership is critical in promot-ing this civil society perspective.

DEVELOPING SCHOOLS AS DEMOCRATIC INSTITUTIONS   Third, principals and assistant principals can play a critical political role in developing schools as democratic institutions. Crow and Slater (1996) described the type of school leadership necessary for educating democracy as systemic leadership. This leadership occurs at classroom, school, and com-munity levels. Principals can play a political role in fostering schools as democratic institutions in three ways: articulating purpose, striking balances, and educating for democracy. First, principals can articulate purpose by empowering individuals to be learn-ers in a learning community. We will return to this idea in the last section of this chapter on facilitating others as politicians. At this point, however, we should say that the role for principals identified here involves including representatives from all school constituencies in conversations, inquiry processes, and decisions, facilitating group discussions in such a way that all voices are heard, and emphasizing individual growth in and through a PLC.

Second, principals foster schools as democratic institutions by striking balances (Crow & Slater, 1996). New principals in particular have to learn to strike a balance be-tween extremes. Encouraging traditionally silenced groups to voice their views does not mean putting the school up for the highest—loudest—bidder. Principals can play a critical role in helping constituents understand each other's perspectives and keep the focus on students and their needs within the larger society.

Third, principals play a critical role in educating teachers, students, parents, and the community about the value and processes of democracy. One of the best ways to do this is to help the school be a model of democracy in the way voices are heard, inquiry is conducted, and decisions are made. Also, principals can be key to providing training in consensus building, living with conflict, team building, and other areas of education that are critical to individuals knowing how to be part of a democracy. "In a democracy and democratic organizations, leadership is, ultimately, everyone's business and everyone has a moral obligation to exercise it" (Crow & Slater, 1996, p. 5).

PRINCIPAL AS POLITICIAN IN THE COMMUNITY

In addition to the larger societal contexts in which principals enact their roles, principals also have a political role to play in their local communities. Not long ago it was assumed that only superintendents played a community role. However, now principals clearly have a community role to play. Several political issues create the need for principals to think politically in the context of their communities.

First, the homogeneity of interests once reflected in school communities has given way to diverse interests based on racial, ethnic, and ideological differences. Post (1992) described a California suburban community that changed from a homogeneous population with similar liberal interests to a community torn apart after more conservative elements moved in. These conservative parents left larger urban areas in an attempt to escape more progressive and multicultural perspectives and approaches to education. The political conflict resulted in long-time school board members being voted out of office and a climate of turmoil that involved principals and teachers. Principals, in communities like these, daily face the political dilemmas created by diverse interests that seek resources for their particular values and beliefs.

Second, although parents typically rate their community schools higher than schools in general (according to recent Gallop Polls), a strong distrust of public education and its professionals creates political conflicts in schools. Principals encounter parents and other community members who reject what they see as the public education monopoly and the professional expertise of teachers in making decisions regarding what is best educationally for their children. In this case, principals are required to build coalitions of support for the PLC.

Third, at times media portrayals of schools reinforce negative and insensitive images of schools and educators. These images frequently support attempts to privatize education and diminish the influence and power of educators. As you gain experience in the principalship, you will find it necessary to develop relationships with the local media to diminish the effects of the negative images.

Fourth, although school funding is typically a districtwide effort, principals frequently are pulled into this political arena to highlight school successes that would influence citizens to support tax increases and bonding measures. These often pit principals and district administrators against other community groups who see these funding decisions as attempts to reduce resources for other community needs. In addition, these funding initiatives may pit administrators against those who want to decrease taxes.

Professional Dilemma 11.2

A middle school principal found herself in the middle of a conflict between a group of students who espoused vegan policies and a fast-food chain that provided tutoring and computers to the school. The fast-food chain requested that the school fly a flag with the company's logo. When the flag was raised, the vegan student group protested. What should this principal do?

Views of School–Community Relationships

In conceiving the principal's role as politician in the community, we base our understanding on two views of school–community relationships that reflect political concerns. Driscoll and Kerchner (1999) identified two perspectives of schools.

SCHOOLS AS BENEFICIARIES OF COMMUNITY SUPPORT The first perspective views schools as beneficiaries of community support. This is the view principals and other educators use most frequently in discussing the school–community relationship. This perspective identifies the human and financial resources that community members make to support the schools. The two most obvious are parental involvement in providing services to schools and business partnerships. These relationships, in many cases, provide needed volunteer and financial services that would be difficult to obtain otherwise. The example of parents who accompany teachers on field trips with third graders illustrates how this affects the teaching and learning core of the school. In addition, business partnerships provide technology that would be impossible for some schools to buy on their own.

However, these relationships are not without their political costs. For example, businesses are not always wholly altruistic in their contributions to schools. Along with their gifts come expectations and demands that schools will respond to their needs, for example, high school graduates trained in particular technologies that decrease the company's cost in training new employees. In addition, some businesses expect schools to display their logos on school property. These business and community interests sometimes conflict with other school responsibilities, for example, developing critical thinking skills and more open and diverse skills that prepare students for larger citizenship roles. New principals, while seeking these needed resources, need to be acutely aware of the potential political costs.

SCHOOLS AS AGENTS OF SOCIAL CAPITAL The second perspective, which Driscoll and Kerchner (1999) identified, views schools as agents of social capital. This perspective, although not new, has received more recent attention. These authors argued that "education in a democracy is supported in part because schools help to create a public good from which the whole society benefits" (p. 385). Instead of schools only being recipients of what the community offers, this perspective maintains that schools need to emphasize what they contribute to the community.

> It is our contention that although schools benefit from the social capital that results from extra-organizational ties among students and their families, they need not be merely passive receptacles of or thoroughfares for the accrued social capital of their student and family constituencies. Schools can also play an important role in building the social capital of the community at large and have a vital part in creating and maintaining social capital in modern cities. (pp. 385–386)

This perspective could be useful to you in your political role. Principals can demonstrate the contribution that schools make to increase the quality of life in their communities.

Crowson (1998) clarified this perspective of schools as agents of social capital by identifying two ways that schools have or can contribute. The first way is to reach out "to families and the community with assistance and supports designed to strengthen the learning and development (and thereby the opportunities) of children" (p. 59). This approach primarily has involved interagency collaborations or school-linked integrated services in which schools work with, for example, social and mental health agencies to provide holistic services to children and their families (Smrekar & Mawhinney, 1999). The second approach is to reach out in ways "to strengthen the self help capacities of individual families and their children (through empowerment) by simultaneously developing and strengthening local supports and institutions" (p. 59). This empowerment approach views schools as contributing to the capacity of communities to meet the needs of their citizens, especially in ways that reverse urban degeneration (Crowson, 2001). Crowson argued that, to date, schools have been less inclined to be involved in these empowerment attempts. He suggested that this is due to school professionals' distrust of a market orientation and their fear that their power as professionals would be weakened.

These two approaches create political issues, especially for new principals. Both service and empowerment approaches link educators with other community professionals and citizens. In so doing, they create the possibility of conflict between diverse expectations and approaches. As we mentioned in Chapter 1, the nature of work in postindustrial society involves more frequent and intense interactions with other roles, thus creating the likelihood of increased conflict. Principals must help educators and their partners negotiate these role conflicts in ways that not only sustain the school's interests but also maintain productive and effective relationships with other community individuals and groups.

These interactions and partnerships with community organizations likely will increase in the future. These approaches make sense in terms of providing more realistic and effective services to students and their families and acknowledging the embedded nature of schools in their communities. Although these relationships are valuable, they will necessitate that principals develop greater political sensitivity and expertise.

Role of Principal as Politician in the Community

The most obvious feature of the principal's political role in the community is that principals have to interact not only with the internal school setting but also with the community in which the school exists. Various writers have described this role as one of *boundary spanner*. The principal as politician in the community is situated between school and community boundaries. This necessitates political expertise in addressing the conflicts inherent in the interests of the school and the community.

Goldring and Rallis (1993), in their study of "principals-in-charge," suggested that this boundary spanning responsibility involves several different roles:

> They [principals] take on the roles of negotiator and communicator, explicitly explaining and publicizing the school's mission and relevant programs to community constituencies while developing and nourishing external support. They build bridges between the school and the surrounding worlds and then bear the school's flag across those bridges. They transmit what the school stands for, and they maneuver for strength, independence, and resources in a competitive world. (p. 72)

Negotiator, communicator, flag-bearer, and bridger are political roles. They involve many of the political elements identified earlier in this chapter in the work of Bolman and Deal (2008). These roles involve building coalitions; responding to diverse interests in values, preferences, and beliefs; allocating scarce resources; and addressing conflict.

Earlier we mentioned that the political role of the principal typically has involved buffering teachers and the larger school setting from community pressures and demands. We acknowledge that there are times when principals and assistant principals must buffer. For example, pressures that disrupt the core technology of teaching and learning or weaken the development of the PLC need to be diminished and buffered. However, buffering is inherently a distancing and isolating strategy. The valuable and appropriate voices and resources that could enrich the teaching and learning of schools and classrooms are lost when buffering is the sole political strategy.

Instead of buffering, principals need to bridge the school and community. Bridging involves acknowledging valuable voices and resources and encouraging those who can contribute to teaching and learning. Obviously, there is some selection that will occur in terms of what the principal and the school community believe contributes to their collective vision. But bridging also involves developing that collective vision with the community so that community organizations and individuals feel a sense of ownership of what the school is doing. Such bridging diminishes the likelihood that these community members will make undue demands on the school. As an illustration of the importance of bridging, one new principal learned how important the local newspaper reporter was to the school. The previous principal had strong public and media relations, and thus school personnel, students, and activities often were published in the paper. When the new principal arrived, she did not immediately see this bridge to the community through the reporter. Instead of positive media reports, the newspaper reporter, feeling somewhat slighted by the new principal, began writing articles on the problems at the school. Although the problems had existed prior to the new principal's arrival, the relationship between the previous principal and the reporter had kept the newspaper articles positive. Rallis and Goldring (2000) identified two major types of strategies that principals use in this political role of bridging. These authors claimed that principals respond to the environment and manage the relationship with the environment. First, in responding to the environment, principals lead the school to restructure in ways that address environmental contingencies or broaden the mission of the school to address new elements of the community environment. Responding to the changing demographics of the community by providing bilingual education programs is one example of this type of strategy.

Principals' roles also involve managing the relationship with the community. Rallis and Goldring (2000) identified two strategies used by principals in managing this relationship: reducing the community's environment's influence on the school and cooperative strategies. Reducing the community's influence on the school includes such actions as buffering, which, as we mentioned earlier, involves trying to isolate the school from the community. This type of strategy involves public relations as well. Working with the media and with parents to develop a community image of the school communicates what the school stands for and the successes of the school. This builds coalitions of support that can reduce undue pressure and influence on the school. A principal who inherited bad public relations when she entered the school began to cultivate positive relationships with the media. She invited journalists to special events that celebrated the school's successes, and when crises arose, she openly provided the school's perspective rather than trying to block journalists' access to the school.

Managing the relationship with the community can also involve cooperative strategies aimed at joint action between the school and its community. The reforms mentioned earlier that included integrated services and community empowerment are good examples of this. Goldring and Hausman (2001) argued for the importance of the principal's role in helping the school build civic capacity.

> As decades of research on effective schools and school reform has [*sic*] indicated, it is unlikely that substantial change can occur in the nature of-school-community partnerships unless school principals embrace a more community-oriented perspective, that is, unless school principals view the development of civic capacity and community building as part of their roles. (p. 10)

This role can include actions such as engaging government systems, building local institutions, investing in outreach, involving the corporate sector, and developing new structures. However, Goldring and Hausman (2001) found that urban principals spend very little time in this type of political role.

> The infrequency with which these principals work with social/community agencies and businesses and the lack of importance attributed to this role are alarming given the high number of students at risk in this urban sample, the low level of resources characteristic of so many schools today, and the lack of community building activities in the neighborhood at large. (pp. 18–19)

The principal has an increasingly significant political role to play in communities. Ignoring the role of principal as politician in the community harms the school's ability to respond to student and family needs in a changing context.

PRINCIPAL AS POLITICIAN IN THE DISTRICT

Public schools are embedded in 14,320 districts or similar political arrangements in the United States. The school district is a unique historical arrangement that produces numerous political issues for assistant principals and principals. These issues occur because principals are hired and evaluated by the district, most of the human and financial resources that principals acquire come through the district, and district administrators are often the medium through which community demands and concerns are transmitted to the school.

In most situations, principals are hired and evaluated by district administrators and board members. Because of this, these groups have influence, especially over new principals and assistant principals. Peterson (1984) identified several mechanisms that districts use to control principals, including supervision, input control (e.g., resources), behavior control (e.g., policies and procedures), output control (e.g., monitoring and evaluation of performance), selection-socialization, and environmental control (e.g., public reaction). These mechanisms may create conflicts between the principal's emphasis on the school context and the district administrators' emphasis on the larger district context.

District administrators also affect principals' political role in terms of the resources they provide or withhold. Gamoran and Dreeben (1986) emphasized the role that the district can play in the instructional decisions made in schools. For example, the way district administrators draw attendance boundaries has significant effects on schools. Attendance areas can affect the types of programs, the types of disciplinary problems teachers confront, and a host of other issues. The resources that principals have to enable the work of teachers can have an influence on the principal's political relationship with teachers (Crow, 1990). In the opening vignette, the district's influence was apparent in the situation with Jefferson Elementary School when district office administrators allowed changes to the bus schedules to accommodate the early-out day. The allocation of scarce resources is the source of a great deal of political conflict between the principal and the district office.

District administrators also influence schools and the political role of principals when they transmit community concerns and demands to the school. District officials can also buffer schools and principals. However, owing to the politically vulnerable nature of superintendents and boards, new principals should not be surprised to find district administrators less willing to buffer or support them when the principals are involved in politically sensitive situations.

Role of Principal as Politician in the District

The political role of principals is defined in part by the traditional middle-management nature of the job. "Principals, as middle managers, must simultaneously manage at least four sets of relationships: upward with their superiors, downward with subordinates, laterally with other principals, and externally with parents and other community and business groups" (Goldring, 1993, p. 95). The opening vignette illustrates these four sets of relationships: Carla as the principal had to deal with the superintendent, the teachers, other administrators, and the concerned parents. As the first weeks of the new school year rolled out, Carla had to work with many relationships in which she was involved as the middle manager. The specific relationship we are emphasizing in this section is the principal's relationship with administrative superiors in the district, but it is important to understand, as we will emphasize later, that this middle-management relationship interacts with other relationships.

Being in a middle-management relationship with the district creates various political demands on the principal. However, there are multiple ways of responding to these political demands. Crow (1990) found that principals tend to conceive of these roles in relation to the district office in one of two ways: as agents of the central office or as school leaders. Principals who conceive of their role as agents of central office emphasize their responsibility for enforcing district policies and procedures. In contrast, principals who see themselves as school leaders emphasize their relationship with the district as one of advocate for the school. Obviously, as middle managers, principals are involved in both types of responsibilities. However, what principals emphasize in their role influences behaviors and political relationships with other groups, for example, parents and teachers. We will discuss the relationships with teachers in the next section.

District administrators influence the political role that principals play with parents. Goldring (1993) found that administrative superiors influence principals' response to involving parents in school policies, and this influence tends to be affected by district socioeconomic status (SES). In high-SES districts, principals were more likely to involve parents in policymaking if administrative superiors used parental involvement as a criterion for evaluating the principal. This was not true for principals in low-SES districts.

The district presents another political arena for principals and assistant principals. Resources are negotiated, coalitions with parents are formed, and conflicts regarding school–district differences are encountered. Principals may enact their political role in the district by emphasizing their district role or their school role, but regardless, they play a political role that influences their practice and their leadership of the PLC.

PRINCIPAL AS POLITICIAN IN THE SCHOOL

Schools are political arenas. Everyday life in schools involves conflicts among teachers, between teachers and students, and between teachers and administrators. These conflicts involve differences in values, beliefs, and preferences. Students, teachers, and administrators struggle over scarce resources.

In order to accomplish their aims and garner scarce resources, teachers, students, and administrators form alliances and coalitions. The two teachers in the opening vignette were eager to develop their own plans for the early release time instead of working on the instructional team. Carla had to help them understand the importance of the collaboration time and its potential impact on student learning. Needless to say, if Carla had allowed these two teachers to avoid the collaboration time, other coalitions of teachers could also have developed their own plans for the teaming time. Although schools are more than political arenas, to ignore the political qualities of the school is to be blindsided by the politics that can affect teaching and learning as well as the everyday work life of students, teachers, and administrators. The politics of the society, community, and district, while real, do not have the immediacy and closeness that politics within the school have. Various writers have referred to this level of politics as *micropolitics*. Blase (1991) maintained that micropolitics involves the "strategic use of power in organizations for two purposes, influence and protection" (p. 356). School constituents attempt to persuade others that their preferences, values, and beliefs are appropriate and should be supported, and they try to protect their interests against those who wish to deny them resources or devalue their beliefs.

Role of Principal as Politician in the School

In examining the principal's political role in the school, we will focus on the two primary groups: teachers and students. Principals and teachers form an implicit political partnership in schools that influence their professional lives together and how they will function as a learning community. Although this partnership is more than political, as we have demonstrated throughout this book thus far, the political nature of the partnership is evident and critical to acknowledge. In the traditional perspective, this political partnership involves an exchange relationship in which principals agree to leave teachers alone and to respect their autonomy, and teachers agree to keep students under control and diminish any embarrassment to the principal and the school at large. Such a political arrangement has existed in some schools for years and negatively affects the ability of the school to change and the culture of the school to foster innovation and experimentation in teaching and learning. In a PLC, a more innovative partnership between principals and teachers could involve the principal providing resources, encouragement, and mentoring and the teachers contributing their expertise, commitment, cooperation, and willingness to improve teaching and learning. The principal's political role in these two perspectives is very different.

Blase (1991), in a significant study of the micropolitics of schools, investigated the style of effective and ineffective principals and the political tactics used by teachers with these two types of principals. He found that ineffective principals, whom he called *closed* principals, tended to promote "the development of relatively closed political orientations in teachers, orientations characterized by the use of protection, reactive and indirect (covert) strategies" (p. 359). The exchange relationships between teachers and closed principals "were characterized by a strong concern on the teachers' part with minimizing costs—achieving protective goals" (p. 361).

The closed principals in Blase's (1991) study tended to be characterized as authoritarian, inaccessible, unsupportive, inequitable, inflexible, and inconsistent and were known to avoid conflict. In response, teachers used the following political strategies that emphasized protection:

- Avoidance
- Rationality
- Ingratiation
- Confrontation
- Coalitions
- Intermediaries
- Noncompliance
- Documentation

We have maintained that the principal's political role affects the other role conceptions presented earlier in this book. Blase (1991) argued that "a leadership orientation characterized by control and/or distance tends to limit significantly the possibility of developing collaborative and mutually supportive working relationships with teachers" (p. 373).

In contrast, effective, or *open*, principals have different characteristics, and the teachers who work with these principals use different sets of political strategies. Blase (1989) found that teachers perceived open principals as having high expectations; being honest and nonmanipulative; being communicative; using participation in their decision making; and being collegial, informal, supportive, and accessible. In response, teachers used political strategies such as the following:

- Diplomacy
- Conformity
- Extra work
- Visibility
- Avoidance
- Ingratiation

Although some strategies were the same with the two groups, the major strategies were different: diplomacy, conformity, and extra work for teachers with open principals and avoidance, rationality, ingratiation, and confrontation for teachers with closed principals. Moreover, teachers "engaged in more two-way (i.e., bilateral influence) and more complex interaction with open versus closed principals" (Blase, 1989, p. 398).

The principal's political relationship with teachers is also influenced by the district office. Crow (1990) found that district administrators influenced principals' relationships with teachers by refusing to consider the school as unique, by placing principals in untenable positions, by creating chaos with district decisions, and by reducing principal's autonomy. Obviously, districts can contribute to a principal's relationship with teachers by providing resources, encouraging and supporting the school's shared vision, and treating the school as a unique professional learning environment.

Bolman and Deal (1991) identified three political skills of leaders that may be useful to you as a principal or assistant principal in your political role with teachers. First, these authors maintained that leaders need to be able to set an agenda. Agenda setting involves working with teachers in developing a vision and the strategies for achieving that vision. We have discussed in Chapter 6 the importance of vision for the principal's role as leader. Having a vision that is developed collectively is a powerful political strategy as well. Its effect on influencing change and persuading others to commit their efforts is an effective political tool.

Second, Bolman and Deal (1991) suggested networking and coalition building as effective political tools. This involves first finding out who needs to have ownership in the decision, plan, or vision and which interests of these individuals or groups are important to them. The principal plays a critical role in developing networks among teachers, parents, and other community groups that support learning for *all* students. Obviously, these networks are critical to a lively PLC and to its effectiveness in achieving learning for all students.

Third, these authors suggested bargaining and negotiation skills that are critical to leaders. *Bargaining*, or "horse trading," involves, first of all, knowing what is important to the teacher or group of teachers, and acknowledging it to reach consensus or develop commitment to an idea. Negotiating is a routine part of the principal's political role. Bolman and Deal (1991) suggested that a major problem with negotiating is that many leaders engage in "positional bargaining." This involves staking out a position and then making concessions to reach agreement. These authors recommend a different strategy involving "principled bargaining," based on the work of Fisher and Ury (1981). Fisher and Ury identified four strategies in principled bargaining:

1. Separate the people from the problem.
2. Focus on interests, not positions.
3. Invent alternatives that are mutually advantageous.
4. Insist on objective criteria. (pp. 3–11)

In addition to teachers, students are primary constituents within the school's political arena. Because there is an implicit political partnership among teachers and principals, there is an arrangement among teachers, administrators, and students. The traditional arrangement is based on control, where teachers and administrators provide a certain degree of autonomy to student groups, and students agree to respond to the control of teachers and administrators, especially in classroom environments. When this implicit exchange relationship breaks down, chaos ensues. In a PLC, students are viewed as partners in the teaching and learning process.

Principals play a political role with students not just in exercising reward and coercive power to control student behavior but also in encouraging and supporting the contribution of students in their own learning. Opotow (1991) suggested that one of the places that this learning can take place is in students' learning to deal with political conflict among themselves. "With adult control diminishing, adolescents actively explore interpersonal influence, deal with threat, negotiate power balances, and learn to cope with social success and disappointment. Their conflict experiences constitute a compelling moral education that absorbs much of their attention" (p. 417). She argued that the typical way administrators respond to student-peer conflict is by overreacting, for example, suspensions, or underreacting, for example, "privatizing the conflict." Instead, she suggested that school administrators and teachers should help students learn to deal with their conflict by bringing it out in the open as a learning experience. The principal and assistant principal play an important political role by helping students become successful political actors in their peer struggles and by becoming active partners in the PLC.

ASSISTANT PRINCIPALS AS POLITICIANS

Although much of what we have said applies to assistant principals as well as principals, the assistant principalship is situated in a frequently difficult and unique political position. Based on interviews with assistant principals, Marshall and Mitchell (1991) identified the features of the "assumptive world" or political culture in which assistant principals work.

In the cognitive map of the administrative culture, there are roles, statuses, tasks, loyalties, appropriate values, appropriate risk taking, and uses of power. If assistant principals violate these expectations, they can suffer sanctions that are understood by all members of that culture. Some result in a mere smack on the hand with no wider implications, and some challenges result in harm to their careers.

According to Marshall and Mitchell (1991), assistant principals work in a political environment that constrains initiative and values. Assistant principals learn that while they can initiate policy, they must limit their policymaking to areas that are approved by the district and by the principal. They also learn that "their personal and professional ethics and morality must be modified to conform to the dominant values in the culture of school administration" (p. 411).

Marshall and Mitchell (1991) identified several rules of the political arena of the school that assistant principals learn:

Rule 1: Limit risk taking.

Rule 2: Remake policy quietly.

Rule 3: Avoid moral dilemmas.

Rule 4: Don't display divergent values.

Rule 5: Commitment is required.

Rule 6: Don't get labeled a troublemaker.

Rule 7: Keep disputes private.

Rule 8: Cover all your bases.

Rule 9: Build administrator team trust.

Rule 10: Align your turf.

The rules and descriptions of assistant principals' political world depict a traditional role for these individuals. We provide this as an excellent example of political life for assistant principals as it currently exists in many schools. However, both principals and assistant principals in schools that are PLCs need to conceive of the political role of the assistant principal in ways that are not protective and reactive but innovative and proactive. Assistant principals need to develop a political role that, like that of the principals, is conducive to facilitating the work of teaching and learning in the school. There is a legitimate political role for you as an assistant principal to play, and it contributes to an inviting and innovative PLC.

THE PRINCIPAL AS FACILITATOR OF OTHERS AS POLITICIANS

Principals and assistant principals not only play a direct political role, but they also facilitate the political role played by others. Schools, districts, communities, and societies are in part political entities. Within these various levels, principals and assistant principals are not the only politicians. Others are playing political roles as well. Some of these have a negative impact on the school as individuals and groups attempt to promote their own self-interest without the consideration of the larger purpose of learning for all students. Others have a positive impact on the school toward some collective purpose that involves individual student growth in and for the learning community (Crow & Slater, 1996).

As a principal or assistant principal, you can play a significant role in facilitating the political role of others to support a PLC. This role, which can be described as "systemic leadership" (Crow & Slater, 1996), helps to empower others in their political contributions toward a learning community. As we did in the preceding section, we will organize our discussion of the principal's facilitative or systemic leadership role in terms of the four levels: society, community, district, and school.

In the Society

We have indicated that the principal plays a profound role beyond the school in the larger society. Principals can play an even more significant role by encouraging and supporting teachers, students, and parents to play a political role in the society. This facilitative role can involve viewing schools in the three ways we identified before: as political systems, as civil societies, and as democratic institutions.

Facilitating the political role of teachers, parents, and students in society involves helping them understand schools as political systems. As we mentioned earlier, this involves understanding the political ideologies that influence schools and the societal transitions that are changing schools. In order to make positive contributions to schools in our society, teachers, parents, and students need to understand how various ideologies view schools and what the practical consequences of these ideologies are for the purposes of schools. The principal can expose teachers, parents, and even students to these ideologies and guide them in critical inquiry and reflection of what these ideologies mean for school practices. The principal can also help others understand the social and economic changes that are occurring in our society and how these changes affect schools. Sometimes parents and teachers try to deny the reality of demographic and technological changes. Such a denial not only can make schools inflexible to change but also ultimately weakens the political contribution of those who deny these societal changes.

Principals can also facilitate the political role of others in the society by encouraging them to view schools as civil societies. This may be one of the most profound political actions principals can take as they help teachers, parents, and students to identify, through an inquiry process, the inequities and understand how the school can act as a learning community. The indictment of Bellah and colleagues (1985) of the extreme individualism that pervades our society calls for all those involved in educating to work to develop ways to make schools civil. Our children learn to be uncivil to each other by watching the lack of civility of their teachers, parents, peers, legislators, and other political leaders. Principals can remind these constituents that schools can and should become civil societies that support individual growth in and for a learning community.

Finally, principals can facilitate the political role of others by helping teachers, students, and parents to model democracy. Both the content of the curriculum and the structure of the school as a PLC can empower others to help build the school as a democratic institution. Supporting the open flow of information about the curriculum and how schools are organized and providing time and resources for teachers and students to critically reflect on this information empowers them politically.

These activities may seem monumental as you enter your first administrative position. However, viewing your role beyond the internal school context will allow you ultimately to make a powerful political impact that affects the lives of students and their families.

In the Community

The principal also facilitates the political role of teachers, students, and parents in the community. This facilitative role has at least two parts. First, principals can help to sensitize others in the school to the politics of the community. This sensitizing may begin by helping teachers understand that teaching and learning take place in a community with various political agendas and potential conflicts. This is most obvious in the case of community beliefs and values regarding curriculum. The case of Joshua Gap, discussed earlier and found in Post's (1992) article, centered around the use of a multicultural curriculum that some parents found offensive. Frequent community battles over sex education are another case of this type of political conflict. Often principals try to shield teachers from these political conflicts by either handling them "out of sight" or by demanding that teachers not use certain objectionable curriculum. However, facilitating the political role of teachers involves sensitizing them to these power conflicts over beliefs and values. A paternalistic orientation aimed at shielding teachers does not enable the kind of systemic leadership necessary to make teachers stakeholders in the political process. Frequently, principals have relied on the teachers' union to be the only political vehicle for teachers. However, the public frequently views the union as having a vested interest in maintaining membership. Teachers need to become strong political constituents in their own right.

Second, principals can help educate teachers to be active political partners. Understanding and developing skills such as networking, building coalitions, and negotiating are necessary political skills for teachers working in communities. In school–community partnerships, such as interagency collaboration and community development (Crowson, 2001; Smrekar & Mawhinney, 1999), teachers discover quickly that they need the skills to be strong political partners with other community agencies. Many of these agency personnel already have these political skills that strengthen their bargaining positions. Principals can provide professional development to help build these types of skills for teachers in working with community groups.

By sensitizing teachers to community politics and by supporting the development of political skills, principals help teachers to be part of the bridging process. Instead of principals orienting their approach to teachers and community conflict solely in terms of buffering, principals can help teachers to become bridges that will strengthen school–community partnerships in ways that support teaching and learning.

In the District

Teachers are increasingly becoming a part of the political process in districts. They serve on district committees with parents and other community members. They serve as interpreters of the district agenda. At the beginning of a $200-million bond campaign, district administrators educated the teachers to become strong interpreters of district needs and the details of the campaign. The teachers' efforts resulted in one of the largest successful bond elections in the country.

Principals can facilitate the political role of teachers in the district by encouraging teachers to take on committee assignments and by finding substitutes for them to attend meetings. Principals can also facilitate this political role for both teachers and parents by helping them understand the resource-allocation process in districts. Although this is not without risk, for example, with district administrators, ultimately it provides teachers and administrators with more educated partners in the political process. When teachers and parents do not have the necessary budgetary and legal information to be active political partners, they are more inclined toward distrust and opposition.

In the School

Many of the most recent educational reforms at the school level involve political processes. Strategies such as site-based management and shared decision making typically have been described in morale and instructional terms. Yet they involve political processes that frequently are ignored. Site-based management and shared decision making depend on teachers, parents, students, and administrators being able to build consensus and work as teams. These processes involve political skills such as agenda setting, networking, coalition building, and negotiating. Yet few teachers are taught these skills in their preservice education, and many do not receive additional professional development in these areas. PLCs assume that teachers have the skills to resolve value conflicts in an environment where diversity is welcomed. Although diversity among faculty can contribute to richness in the school context, it also invariably leads to conflict as teachers with different ideologies of teaching, understandings of learning, and approaches to classroom conduct come together.

Principals can facilitate the development of the political skills necessary to make these reforms successful by providing professional development and helping teachers and parents to recognize the political process inherent in these strategies. Providing

Professional Dilemma 11.3

An assistant principal observes a security guard deliberately provoking a student whose behavior had improved due to counseling with the assistant principal. When the guard reported the incident as an assault, the assistant principal explained what had happened to the principal and told him that she was going to write a negative report on the guard. Her principal, a friend of the guard and a believer in military-style discipline, responded that if she wrote such a report, he would write a negative evaluation of her. What should she do? (This is based on an actual case in Marshall & Mitchell, 1991.)

professional development in areas such as collaborative teaming, conflict mediation, consensus building, positive use of power, agenda setting, networking, coalition building, and effective negotiation is a powerful tool for principals to give to teachers in a PLC.

In addition, principals can facilitate the political role of teachers and parents by the principal's own political style. As Blase's work (1989, 1991) attests, the principal's orientation—whether closed or open—influences the types of political tactics that teachers use. Principals with closed and ineffective orientations tend to influence teachers to use protective, reactive, and covert strategies, whereas principals with more open orientations influence teachers to use more collegial political tactics. One of the strongest ways principals can facilitate teachers as politicians is by modeling orientations that emphasize more effective, open, and collegial approaches.

In addition to teachers and parents, principals and assistant principals can facilitate the political role of students. Helping students understand conflict as a democratic process teaches a powerful lesson about living in a democratic society. As Opotow (1991) suggested, principals, by bringing conflict to the surface instead of underreacting or overreacting to it, can help students develop the necessary skills to function effectively in a democratic society and to contribute to a PLC. Assistant principals, who frequently carry the majority of responsibility for resolving student conflict, can help students understand the positive side of conflict. They can also teach students political skills, such as negotiating, compromising, and diplomacy, that encourage open and productive forms of response to conflict. Such skills will help to provide a profound understanding of how to contribute productively to a civil society.

Principals play a crucial role for teachers, parents, and students in facilitating their political role. Instead of ignoring or trying to diminish the importance of the political role, principals can help others develop critical political skills that contribute to a civil society and to schools as democratic institutions. By understanding teaching and learning as occurring in a political context, principals can make a profound contribution at societal, community, district, and school levels.

BUILDING SOCIAL CAPITAL IN PROFESSIONAL LEARNING COMMUNITIES

Social capital is a critical resource and goal for the principal's role as politician. By treating social relationships as a form of capital, these relationships can become a resource on which people draw to achieve certain purposes. Assuring that students and teachers are a valued part of the school community is an important element in the political role of the principal and assistant principal. In the following section, we discuss the importance of the principal's role as politician in establishing social capital opportunities for students and teachers.

Students

Several studies have reported that a general sense of belonging at school is important for students' success. In analyzing several studies, Mulford (2007) concluded that this sense of belonging by students is so important that it should be identified as an equal indicator for future success with academic results. Mulford claimed that student–peer relations, locus of control, and self-concept were related to later life successes such as employment and earnings. Within schools, social capital is also linked to student academic results. For example, Field, J., (2005) found that student's social relationships play an important and vital role in their capacity for learning. Further, Mulford (2007) concluded that social capital among students does more than just improve a student's feeling of self-worth and their enjoyment of school, but it increases their academic capacity in such ways that the two together— academic success and social capital—increase substantially the success of students later in life.

Principals involved in developing PLCs must be involved in the political processes of establishing democratic schools to assure that all students have an equal chance at participating in the social activities of schools, and therefore creating social capital. Likewise, principals must help teachers understand the role of social capital within classrooms. Students must feel a sense of belongingness in school and in classes if they are to have a part of the learning community.

Teachers

Because of the political demands on schools to be more accountable and market competitive, some teachers are either isolated or become disenfranchised from the school community. Sweetland and Hoy (2000) concluded that to succeed in a rapidly changing and increasingly complex educational world, it is important for educators to develop, adapt, and take charge so that they can control their own futures. As discussed in Chapter 7, the principal's involvement in teacher empowerment not only increases the quality of decisions but also improves the morale of teachers. Goddard (2002) also found that where teachers have the opportunity to influence important school decisions, they also tend to have stronger beliefs in the capability of the entire faculty. In this sense, the collective inquiry and decision making of all teachers is vital to the operation of a PLC in the school. In fact, this type of social capital might be a precursor to a PLC.

The principal's engagement in the political processes is to assure that all teachers feel part of the entire faculty. It is too easy for some teachers to become isolated and marginalized from the rest of the faculty, especially in larger high schools. The principal has an important role in helping every teacher become part of the faculty's involvement. Principals need to assess teachers' social capital by helping them in the political arena to develop, adapt, and take charge of their profession.

Conclusion

Politics may not be a four-letter word, but it certainly is a topic many principals wish to avoid. However, Carla Patterson, the principal of Jefferson Elementary School in the opening vignette, found, it cannot be ignored. We have chosen to include the principal as politician as a major innovative role conception because we believe that politics is not only necessary but also valuable for leadership in a PLC. Your

political role, as a principal or assistant principal, takes place at all four levels: society, community, district, and school. Understanding and communicating how these levels affect the learning of all students is a necessary part of creating learning communities. Rather than being a necessary evil, politics can become a valuable tool for focusing your attention and the attention of others on learning as power.

Activities

SELF-REFLECTION ACTIVITIES

1. Of the three approaches to the political role presented early in this chapter, which most represents how a principal you have known conceived his or her role? What have been the consequences?
2. Talk to a retired principal regarding his or her relationship with the district office. How did district administrators affect the principal's relationships with teachers and parents? How did this principal respond to district influence?

PEER REFLECTION ACTIVITIES

1. Discuss with your colleagues the first professional dilemma in the chapter regarding whether to give community criticism to a teacher. Role-play how you would respond to the businessman.
2. Reflect with a colleague on the political strategies you both use in relating to your principal. Analyze your reflections in terms of Blase's findings regarding teachers' political strategies with open and closed principals.

3. Reflect on the professional dilemma presented in this chapter of the principal faced with a student vegan group protest over the involvement of a fast-food chain in the school. What would you do as the principal?

COURSE ACTIVITIES

1. Have each student develop a case that focuses on some specific political incident or issue at a local school or district. Use Bolman and Deal's (1991) five propositions of a political perspective to analyze the politics of the case. Also use French and Raven's (1959) five types of power to identify the kinds of power used in this situation.
2. Invite a panel of community members, including businesspeople, journalists, and government officials, to discuss their view of the schools and their expectations.
3. Invite a local principal to discuss the nature of school-community relations.

Websites

Everyday Democracy—issue site on education and how to create more democratic educational institutions and build bridges between schools and communities
http://www.everyday-democracy.org/en/Issue.2.aspx

Coalition for Community Schools—includes resources for principals and research on community school initiatives
http://www.communityschools.org/

National School Boards Association
http://www.nsba.org/

American Youth Policy Forum
http://www.aypf.org/programs/education/index.htm

CHAPTER 12

Becoming an Innovative Principal in a Professional Learning Community

Vignette

The waitress appeared for the fifth time asking if there was anything she could get Beth and Debbie. Obviously, she was wondering why they were still there after two hours. Beth ordered another cup of coffee, her third. Beth and Debbie met each Wednesday morning for breakfast in part so that Beth could ask Debbie, her mentor, for help. Gradually, Debbie had also used Beth as a sounding board for some reforms she was considering. This Wednesday morning was during winter holiday break, and they both had more time to talk. This gave Beth time to reflect on her first few months in the job as principal of Brookside High School.

Debbie had been a mentor to Beth for several years, beginning when Beth interned with Debbie at another high school in the district. The two remained close during Beth's assistant principalship and especially now that they were the only female high school principals in the district. Debbie had been a high school principal for ten years and had a great reputation with the district and with her school faculty and parents. She had been able to turn her high school around from having the worst reputation to being one of the best.

Beth had completed the administrator preparation program at State University and had received strong letters of endorsement from her professors and from Debbie, her internship supervisor. The program had a full-time internship program with a great deal of collaboration between the university and the school. Debbie had provided ongoing feedback to Beth but also had gradually given her more responsibility. Beth felt that her internship experience had prepared her well for administration. Her course work also had helped her develop extensive knowledge and skills related to best practices and reform strategies, such as professional learning communities (PLCs).

However, nothing could have prepared her for her first administrative position as an assistant principal. The principal with whom she worked found it difficult to delegate responsibilities, except the uncomfortable ones. Primarily, he gave Beth student management assignments, which were extensive. The school had no schoolwide discipline policy, and the principal encouraged the teachers to send their problems to Beth. By the third day of school, Beth always had a line of students outside her office by 9:30 A.M. Gradually, she worked with the teachers to develop some alternative classroom methods that were successful and earned her the respect of most of the faculty. However, she received little praise or support from the principal. If it had not been for Debbie, Beth was not sure that she could have made it through that first year.

Beth had been appointed as principal to Brookside High School during the summer only a month before the school year began. She had the strong support of the superintendent, who was impressed with how she had turned around the disciplinary referrals. However, a large group of parents and some of the older teachers in the school preferred another person and were disappointed when Beth was appointed.

As Beth reflected with Debbie about her last four months as a principal, she identified two major problems that she figured would follow her during the remainder of the school year: a coach with poor teaching skills and a group of parents who were working behind the scenes to undermine her. The football coach was a veteran of the school who had support from the parents of the football players. However, other parents whose children were in his history classes were not so impressed. Before school started, Beth had heard from a committee of irate parents who wanted their kids removed from his class. As Beth observed in his classroom, she found his teaching methods archaic and his classroom management methods dictatorial. However, the coach let her know very quickly that he did not respect her and that as a woman she knew nothing about football, which was all that counted.

Beth's second problem involved a group of vocal and powerful parents who had preferred the other candidate for the principalship at Brookside. The leader of this group was the sister of a board member. She let Beth know from the beginning that she had preferred the other candidate. As the semester progressed, Beth was getting calls from the district office about rumors that Beth was convinced were started by this parent.

Debbie asked Beth how her relationship with teachers was going and whether any of these problems had influenced that relationship. Beth felt that she was beginning to establish a good rapport with the teachers and was gaining support for developing a PLC. She smiled when she recalled how some of the teachers had tested her in the first month by creating little "nonproblems" and then waiting to see how she would respond, for example, teacher dress code and student referrals. Beth felt that she had won these teachers over with humor and humility. However, she knew that most teachers were waiting to see how she handled the problem with the football coach. She felt that it might be the defining moment for clarifying for the faculty and staff her vision for the school as a learning community.

As Debbie shared some memories of her first year as a principal, Beth thought how much she had learned already this first year. But there were still five months until the end of the school year.

INTRODUCTION

As Beth learned, becoming a principal is not a simple or easy transition. Even with adequate university preparation, a successful internship, and extensive prior administrative experience, becoming a principal involves surprises and frustrations. As we demonstrated in Chapter 4, the principal must be a learner, and this learning occurs throughout the career.

In previous chapters, we identified eight conceptions of the principal's and assistant principal's roles that involve innovative ways to view these roles in a PLC. In this chapter, we focus on how an individual learns to enact these role conceptions. Like the view of learning we espoused in Chapter 4, this type of learning is an active process by the individual involved. In other words, becoming an innovative principal or assistant principal is not a passive process in which others are solely in charge of your learning. Rather, it is a process in which you contribute significantly to your own learning. Another way of describing this learning process is that you and the organizations in which you will work will be part of a learning community in which you will co-construct innovative images of the principalship. Part of the process of co-constructing involves understanding how learning to become a principal or assistant principal happens. This chapter will help you understand the learning process of becoming an innovative principal.

In order to help you understand this learning process, we begin with a general introduction to socialization—how learning a new role occurs. We identify and discuss the sources, methods, stages, and outcomes of this learning and apply it to school leadership in a PLC. After this general introduction to socialization, we discuss the specific process of learning to become a new innovative assistant principal. Although the two roles of principal and assistant principal have many similarities as school leadership roles, there are unique features of both that relate to the eight innovative role conceptions we have identified. Thus, becoming an innovative assistant principal has certain specific characteristics that are worth exploring.

Following our discussion of the socialization of assistant principals, we turn to how to become an innovative principal. Again, we focus on the distinctive elements of the principal's socialization and how to learn the eight role conceptions for building and maintaining a PLC. We end the chapter with a discussion of how principals at midcareer become innovative. Although this book has been written primarily from the point of view of a new principal, many of the issues surrounding creating and improving a PLC are pertinent to someone who has been in the principalship for several years but is confronting change—either in position or in role conception. Building and maintaining a PLC challenges veteran principals with dramatic changes in their role.

SOCIALIZATION: LEARNING A NEW ROLE

Any time someone enters a new stage of life or accepts a new position, learning is necessary. When you entered kindergarten, you had to learn how to behave in a group of strangers, how to find your way around a new building, and how to follow directions from someone who was not your parent. As you enter school administration, learning is also necessary. Much of this learning will be second nature to you because of your long experience as a student and teacher. However, some of the learning will involve a new way of seeing things that you have been experiencing for years. For example, as a teacher, you saw the principal conducting faculty meetings, observing in your classroom, disciplining students, and monitoring the hall. However, as a principal or assistant principal, these responsibilities will have deeper meanings as you learn how district administrators, parents, and government entities affect these responsibilities and how a vision of the school as a PLC guides how, when, and why you enact your role.

Nature of Socialization

The typical way of describing and understanding how someone learns a new role emphasizes what the organization—usually through the supervisor—does *to* the novice. This passive process may include formal training or subtler manipulations to get the novice to do and believe what the organization and the supervisor want. Research on learning and socialization suggests that the novice is not a blank tablet waiting to be instructed but an active participant who brings experience, values, and tools for learning (Wentworth, 1980). Rather than a pawn in the organization's hands, you are a partner in this learning process.

Being a learning partner means that you are involved in two types of socialization—role taking and role making (Hart, 1993), which we discussed in Chapter 1. Role taking, which is a more passive process, involves accepting the responsibilities and mission of a role that are defined primarily by the way things have been done in the past. As an administrative intern, you are learning how principals, teachers, district supervisors, and even students define the role and how they expect you to enact it. Role making, in contrast, is a more active process that emphasizes molding the job to fit your perspectives, values, and expectations, as well as the school's needs. Beth's experience as an assistant principal demonstrates that rather than simply taking the role as the principal defined it for her in terms of student management, she molded the role in a more proactive way. Role taking and role making are seldom completely discrete activities. Both are usually present in learning any new role. As a new principal or assistant principal, you will need to learn the expectations that others have of you in leading a PLC. However, you will also have the opportunity to develop your own vision of a learning community based on your values and perspectives of the role. In becoming an innovative principal or assistant principal, your socialization "not only presents a world, it constructs one" (Wentworth, 1980). In the increasingly complex setting in which you will lead, you will face accountability, limited resources, knowledge-explosion, and other powerful influences that will make role making even more important (Stevenson, 2006).

Role taking and role making draw attention to two perspectives for understanding socialization, which are important for you to consider. First, socialization can be understood from the school or the district's perspective as "mechanisms through which members learn the values, norms, knowledge, beliefs, and interpersonal and other skills that facilitate role performance and further group goals" (Mortimer & Simmons, 1978, p. 422). The faculty, staff, students, and parents in your first school, as well as your district supervisors, will greet you with expectations about how they expect you to enact the role of principal or assistant principal. Your predecessor in the role, years of tradition at the school, or recent crises that generate the need for change may influence these expectations. These groups will use various tools—some overt and some subtle—to influence you to enact your role in ways that meet their expectations.

A second perspective emphasizes an individual way of understanding socialization. "From the perspective of the individual, socialization is a process of learning to participate in social life" (Mortimer & Simmons, 1978, p. 422). As you enter this first school, you bring with you previous experiences as a student and teacher, perspectives from your university preparation, experience from your internship, your own values and beliefs about how schools should be learning communities, and other personal goals and needs. These elements create your own expectations for the role. You also bring to this socialization process learning tools that have worked for you in the past. For example, Beth used her experience with her mentor, Debbie, as a way to reflect on her experiences and to learn how to enact the role. Your own learning style and your previous experience with learning will affect the tools you use to learn the job.

We define socialization as "a reciprocal process in which both organization and individual are active participants in professional learning" (Crow & Matthews, 1998, p. 19). To maximize your learning to become an innovative school leader, you must acknowledge this reciprocal process that involves not only your influence but also the influence of those around you (Hall, 2002). Understanding the perspective and tools that the organization uses to influence your enactment of the role is as important as understanding your own perspective and learning tools.

Learning to become an innovative school leader in a PLC involves three elements (Feldman, 1976). First, you must develop the technical knowledge and skills to be an innovative principal or assistant principal. This includes everything from the simplest skills necessary to negotiate a contract with a soft drink company to establishing a culture of inquiry. Some of these you have learned in your university preparation. Others are more specific to the school context. For example, while there are common elements to budgeting, districts use different models, and your district supervisors will expect you to learn and use the preferred one. Likewise, creating a culture of inquiry in the school is very context-specific.

Second, learning to become an innovative school leader in a PLC necessitates adjusting to the work environment. Many administrators believe that this aspect of socialization is much more difficult to learn than developing technical skills. In the opening vignette, Beth had developed excellent skills, for example, in student management, but when she became a principal, she had to learn how things were done in a new environment. She may have developed excellent interpersonal skills in earlier settings, but she had to endure new testing in a different environment. Learning to adjust to a new work environment included understanding personalities, relationships, and subcultures present in the new setting. Failure to learn this aspect of socialization can thwart attempts to be an innovative school leader in a PLC by demonstrating insensitivity to the traditions and culture of the new school. Being innovative does not mean being callous to the current values and norms of the setting. In fact, being innovative depends in part on a recognition and sensitivity to these cultural elements.

Third, learning to become an innovative principal or assistant principal involves learning new values and identities. Some of these values arise from the study and reflection in which you are currently engaged or from subsequent mentors. However, these values may also include new values that arise in your first school. Some new administrators make the critical mistake of assuming that nothing innovative or valuable can come from their new context. Such cavalier behavior results in numerous conflicts and misguided attempts to change behavior that ultimately delay or thwart the development of a PLC. Openness to new values from numerous sources can result in dynamic learning experiences that benefit the new school leader as well as the learning community. In addition to these new values, you will be developing identities or images of the role (Browne-Ferrigno, 2003; Crow, 2008). These identities relate to your perception of yourself as a principal and others' perception of you. For example, learning to become an innovative principal in a PLC involves developing identities related to you as a learner and an advocate. These identities will be based on the values, norms, and behaviors you enact.

Sources of Socialization

Learning to become an innovative school leader in a PLC also involves recognizing that there are multiple sources of socialization. In this subsection, we will identify three types of sources: professional, organizational, and personal.

PROFESSIONAL SOCIALIZATION   Becoming a principal or assistant principal is influenced by the expectations that the larger society in general and university training in particular communicate regarding how to enact the role. These influences emphasize the patterns of values, beliefs, and assumptions that have grown up around a role. They help the individual develop an administrative perspective or identity—a way of thinking that includes relationships with teachers, community members, and supervisors and the development of sensitivity to schoolwide issues and organizational stability (Browne-Ferrigno, 2003; Greenfield, W. D., 1985a).

The society holds certain views of what any principal should be and do. As Chapter 2 details, these societal views frequently have been influenced by business conceptions of the role that emphasize efficiency (Callahan, 1962). With the move to a postindustrial society, all work roles, including those of principal or assistant principal, emphasize more complexity (Bell, D., 1973; Crow, 2006a, 2006b; Hage & Powers, 1992). Society, as a source of socialization, presents ways of viewing the role that may conflict with expectations of the role from other sources, for example, university or district.

University training is another source of professional socialization and frequently is referred to as the "first wave" of socialization. This source includes course work and internship experiences that present certain conceptions or images of the role (Browne-Ferrigno, 2003). Frequently, new administrators question the relevance of their university training in terms of specific work tasks that must be learned after they arrive in their first assignment. Others have pointed out that what effective university training has done for them is to provide the big picture and the innovative conceptions that sometimes get lost in the harried rhythm of the new administrator's work. Your socialization from this source hopefully will provide the important generic skills, for example, problem solving, decision making, and culture building that are fundamental to leadership for a PLC. For example, developing your ability to critically reflect on your actions and those of others is essential for effective learning communities (Osterman & Kottkamp, 2004).

Another aspect of a successful university training program and an excellent source of socialization is a sustained, supervised, and quality internship experience. This experience provides a hands-on way of learning the tasks of administration and the pace and rhythm of the administrator's day—the brevity, variety, and fragmentation of the job (Peterson, 1977–1978). Effective internships include tiered learning opportunities for you to *observe* the leadership of others, *participate* in leadership activities, and actually *lead* groups toward some learning community goal (Southern Regional Education Board, 2006). In addition to learning the specific tasks and rhythm of the role, effective internship experiences help interns to learn the specific culture of the school in which they are placed. This provides an opportunity to develop skills for understanding and adjusting to the work environment that will be crucial in their first regular administrative assignment, especially for supporting a PLC. Probably the most important thing that an effective internship with a trained mentor helps the intern to learn is how to reflect on what the intern sees and does. This socialization content emphasizes skills for learning to learn. As Chapter 4 emphasized, the principal as learner is a critical role conception essential for school leaders in an increasingly complex school and societal environment.

ORGANIZATIONAL SOCIALIZATION   Becoming an innovative school leader is also influenced by sources that occur when you enter your first school as an assistant principal or principal. At this stage, the generic skills and administrative perspective learned during university training are reinforced, modified, and expanded as principals and assistant principals learn how things are done here. Several sources play a major role in the socialization of new school leaders, including, teachers, staff, students, parents, community leaders, other school administrators, and district administrators.

Within the school, teachers, staff, students, and parents hold strong expectations about how the roles of principal and assistant principal should be enacted. Teachers and classified staff are the primary source of influence on new principals (Daresh, J., 2006; Duke, D. L., Isaacson, Sagor, & Schmuck, 1984). They not only have expectations about what tasks new administrators should do, but they also influence the type of information to which principals and assistant principals can gain access in order to make decisions (Long, 1988). A typical early mistake of new administrators is to view teachers as a unitary group, when in fact there are frequently various subcultures and groups of teachers that sometimes hold conflicting expectations for the principal.

Students influence the socialization of new principals and assistant principals by reinforcing certain images of the role. As we will discuss later, this influence is especially potent for assistant principals in a student management role (Reed & Himmler, 1985). New administrators sometimes surprisingly forget that students have an incredible influence on the culture and climate of the learning community and thus can strongly influence the learning of new school leaders.

Parents also have strong expectations of what administrators are to do and how they are to act. In a PLC, parents play a critical role not only in expanding the culture of inquiry but also in the socialization of new principals and assistant principals (Daresh, J., 2006). Parents, like teachers and students, are also not always a homogeneous group but frequently present the new administrator with contrasting and conflicting expectations and demands.

Community members and noneducation professionals (e.g., social service, health, and mental health professionals) influence principal's learning by their expectations of the school leader and by their particular perspectives on what learning communities can be and do through interprofessional practice. They also provide resources—both economic and informational—that influence possibilities and options for innovative role enactment and identity (Crow, 2008).

Other administrators, both inside and outside the school, influence the process of becoming a new innovative principal or assistant principal. As we will discuss and as evidenced in the opening vignette, principals are a critical source of socialization for new assistant principals through the tasks they assign and the images they portray. Administrators outside the school are also major sources of influence on new administrators' learning. Networks of fellow administrators can provide valuable support and encouragement for new principals and assistant principals, but they can also reinforce status quo images of the role.

District superiors are a major source of socialization for new principals and assistant principals. This socialization can occur through the selection process, evaluation, and supervision (Peterson, 1984). These superiors have clear expectations about the role conception they expect principals and assistant principals to hold. In the opening vignette, Beth's superintendent supported her image of the assistant principal's role that went beyond viewing student management as removing students from the classroom. In so doing, this superintendent influenced Beth's socialization by promoting an innovative role conception that encouraged Beth's inventive spirit and a focus on PLC. A different superintendent could have reinforced a status quo image that would have discouraged experimentation and learning of more innovative role images.

PERSONAL SOCIALIZATION In addition to the professional and organizational socialization sources that we have identified, friends and families influence new principals and assistant principals. Although these groups may be less influential in helping the new school leader learn the technical skills or how to adjust to the work environment, they can be extremely powerful socialization agents for supporting images of the role. Family members and friends can be critical sources of support for encouraging role conceptions that involve more innovative images. Sometimes these images require more risk taking or more time that may be viewed as interfering with family obligations. If family members or friends view these images as inappropriate or in conflict with family concerns, they may put pressure on new principals and assistant principals to reconsider these role conceptions.

Stages of Socialization

Becoming an innovative principal or assistant principal does not occur overnight. It will not and should not occur simply when you get your master's degree or state administrative license. Rather, this learning or socialization process is an evolutionary process.

One way to view this evolution emphasizes information processing and the different types and sources of information that are available to new school leaders at different stages. "Newcomers' ability to acquire information is affected by the type of organization and/or occupation entered, previous organizational experience, channels available for acquiring information, and availability of peers" (Stout, 2000, p. 23). As you will discover, learning the skills, adjusting to the work environment, and acquiring values all involve information. Moreover, becoming an innovative school leader who is a learner, culture builder, advocate, mentor, supervisor, leader, manager, and politician—especially in a PLC—requires obtaining and using information.

Socialization has been conceptualized as occurring in three stages with different names for the stages. One of the most frequently used schemes includes anticipatory, encounter, and adjustment stages (Hart, 1993). These socialization stages include different views of how the individual is perceived by the organization and a variety of characteristics (Table 12.1). Typically, in the *anticipatory socialization stage*, the individual is a stranger to the occupation. However, aspiring school administrators like you are not total strangers to the occupation. You have witnessed the work of principals and assistant principals since the time you were a kindergartner. However, this experience

TABLE 12.1 Socialization Stages

Socialization Stage	View of Individual	Characteristics
Anticipatory	Stranger	Choosing the occupation; acquiring information about how others view the role; developing role expectations
Encounter	Stranger to newcomer	Reality shock: Earlier experiences collide with new experiences; making sense of role
Adjustment	Newcomer to insider	Encounter stage issues largely resolved; role making emphasized; self-confidence grows

provided a limited, "on stage" view of the role. As we mentioned before, even as a teacher there were aspects of the role that were not evident to you. Moreover, depending on your experience, the innovative role conceptions we have explored in this book may be strange and unusual to you. You may never have experienced a PLC or imagined yourself as a leader in this type of context. During the anticipatory stage, you are meeting new administrators or new sources of socialization that may have different views of the role than what you have experienced thus far. At this stage, you are acquiring information about how the larger society, your university professors, and your internship mentors view the role.

As you move into your first administrative assignment as a principal or assistant principal, you enter the encounter socialization stage. You move from being a stranger to becoming a newcomer. As you acquire new information about the school, its learning community, and the expectations of its constituencies, you are likely to experience "reality shock" as the expectations you developed earlier during teaching and the internship conflict with the expectations you encounter in this first school (Hughes, 1959). Even if you had an exceptionally good and relevant internship experience, you are likely to encounter surprise as a newcomer. This does not mean that the information you acquired during the anticipatory stage was bad information but rather that expectations are likely to vary in different settings. Among the typical mistakes administrators make is to assume that expectations derived from prior work experience are likely to be those of the new organization. This is why making sense of the information provided by organizational members is so important (Blenkinsopp & Zdunczyk, 2005). You may have expected as an assistant principal to be given wide latitude in working with teachers in a PLC. However, you may encounter administrators, teachers, and parents who expect you to focus totally on student discipline issues. Your internship experience, far from providing inaccurate information, provided a way to view the roles that are worth considering rather than abandoning.

The information you acquire to respond to the surprises you encounter will depend on your previous experiences, your personality characteristics, and the availability of others around you (Louis, 1980a). Acquiring information about the school and using the interpretations of others constitute an appropriate socialization strategy for you to use during this stage. However, you should be cautious in accepting others' interpretations of the expectations, events, and norms of this new environment. First, it is very likely that school faculty members' interpretations will vary. Thus, you will be faced with the question of which interpretation to choose. Second, interpretations from some school veterans may or may not help you to develop an innovative conception of your role in a PLC. Some of these veterans may have an interest in convincing you to perpetuate the status quo even if change is needed.

The third stage, the adjustment socialization stage, involves acquiring the information to move from newcomer to insider. Frequently this is "privileged information" that only a few people in the organization possess but which permits learning the tasks, interpersonal relationships, and values of the new setting. In this stage, the principal or assistant principal resolves the issues of the encounter stage and becomes an inside member of the organization.

Frequently, new principals find that they never really are considered insiders by the veteran power block of the school. Sometimes a group of veterans conceals privileged information in order to protect their turf, maintain dysfunctional organizational stability, and obstruct the development of the PLC. New principals or assistant principals are deprived of this information until they can be trusted not to rock the boat. This may inhibit change and discourage more innovative role conceptions.

New school leaders may also encounter an environment in which a former administrator hoarded the privileged information and even veterans in the organization never became real insiders. What constitutes insider and outsider status in an organization is a fundamental quality of the culture of the school and can have amazing influence on developing a PLC. Role making, in part, involves working with others in the organization to redefine and expand the "insider" status so that all organization members can experience the privileges—a must for an effective learning community. This is the political role we discussed in Chapter 11 and that you may need to develop early in the socialization process.

Methods of Socialization

Learning to be an innovative principal or assistant principal in a PLC involves a variety of methods. Some of the methods are obvious, such as coursework or mentoring. Other methods are subtler, such as teachers testing the authority of a new principal. The methods themselves communicate the content and goals of socialization. Some, for example, maintain the status quo of the role, whereas others encourage innovation, change, collaboration, and inquiry.

Both the organization and the individual influence the methods of learning how to become an innovative school leader (Hall, 2002). Organizational methods reflect the cultural values and norms of the school or university. For example, schools that value risk taking and inquiry are more likely to use socialization methods that celebrate and reward innovation and learning. However, you as a new principal or assistant principal also have socialization methods at your disposal that can encourage innovation or maintain the status quo. We will discuss many of these individual methods later in this chapter when we discuss the unique socialization processes for assistant principals, principals, or veteran principals. In this subsection, we will identify two types of socialization methods: organizational methods and individual influences.

ORGANIZATIONAL METHODS   Often schools are not aware of the methods or the hidden consequences of those methods they use to socialize newcomers, including assistant principals and principals. It is critical, however, for you as a newcomer to be sensitive to the socialization methods that school veterans use. These methods can contribute to your conception of the role in innovative ways that support leadership for a PLC, or they can encourage you to maintain the status quo when change is needed.

Van Maanen and Schein (1979), two researchers at the Massachusetts Institute of Technology who explored how individuals learn to become organizational members, developed the classic identification of organizational socialization methods. Their scheme involved identifying methods by posing opposites:

- collective versus individual,
- formal versus informal,
- sequential versus random,
- fixed versus variable,
- serial versus disjunctive, and
- investiture versus divestiture.

Collective versus individual   refers to whether the socialization occurs in a group or alone. If you were part of a cohort in your university training, you were part of a collective socialization method. When you become a principal or assistant principal, much of your socialization will be individual; that is, you probably will be learning the role by yourself instead of with a group of new administrators.

Formal versus informal   methods relate to whether your socialization involves being segregated from the work setting or not. Although much of your university training is formal, little of your organization socialization will be formal. Some districts provide regular, formal professional development for new administrators, but most of the training is informal.

Sequential versus random   refers to whether there is a sequence of steps leading to the role. For example, learning to be a doctor involves medical courses, internship, and residency. Learning to be a principal, however, involves courses, usually an internship, and immersion in the actual role. As veterans and newcomers will tell you, you will get all the responsibilities when you are first appointed. Gradual induction seldom occurs for new school leaders.

Fixed versus variable   involves whether or not the learning process is defined in terms of a fixed timetable. Although courses and internship come before the actual role appointment, after you become a principal or assistant principal, no other timetable is apparent. Some administrators have suggested that there are informal district timetables such that if you have not been appointed to a principalship after a certain time since you received your license, you are unlikely to be appointed in that district.

The final two methods that Van Maanen and Schein (1979) identified are especially critical to learning to become an innovative school leader in a PLC.

Serial versus disjunctive   refers to whether or not veteran administrators are available to prepare newcomers. Superintendents, for example, rarely have incumbents still around to train them in the role; thus, their socialization is more disjunctive. Principals, however, may have veteran administrator mentors who help them learn the tasks, relationships, and values of the role. Mentors can be very effective in learning role images related to transformation and innovation (Browne-Ferrigno &

Muth, 2004). However, they can also perpetuate a status quo image of the role. Serial socialization methods, such as mentoring, tend to discourage innovative role conceptions. However, there are ways you can identify mentors and work with veterans in ways that encourage rather than discourage innovation.

Divestiture versus investiture   refers to the ways organizations use the prior experiences, values, and characteristics of newcomers in helping them to learn the role. If new principals or administrators are encouraged by districts to devalue their teaching experiences and skills, divestiture is being used. In contrast, if district administrators value the use of administrators' prior teaching experience in becoming instructional leaders in their schools, they are using investiture. Depending on the quality, type, and conception of the prior experience, this type of socialization method can encourage or discourage innovation. In a PLC, your experience, along with that of the teachers in your school, becomes part of the learning capacity that enriches the learning community.

In addition to these methods, other authors focus on learning cultural values, norms, and beliefs. Trice (1993) discussed socialization methods that influence the passage through occupational roles. He suggested that rites, ceremonies, rituals, and stories can be powerful tools for learning the norms and values of a role. For example, when veteran teachers tell new principals stories about former principals, they are doing more than simply presenting interesting tales; they are also emphasizing administrator characteristics that are valued or discounted. These stories can be useful to you not only as ways the school uses to help you learn acceptable norms and values, but they can also be useful sources of information for you to use in understanding the school and its values as you develop a conception of your role in leading a PLC.

Crow and Pounders (1996) found various socialization methods that schools used to socialize administrative interns to the values and norms of the role. These methods included cultural forms such as artifacts (e.g., keys to the building, office space), rituals (e.g., early bombardment of responsibilities and shadowing), rites (e.g., selection process and testing by faculty), and ceremonies (e.g., introduction to faculty).

Individual Influences

In addition to the socialization methods that schools and districts use to shape the way you learn the administrative role, you use various methods to influence the role. Some of these methods are described more accurately as characteristics that influence the socialization process rather than methods you choose.

Your own personal characteristics, such as gender, may influence the learning or socialization process. Men and women may approach learning the job and attaching to individuals in the organization in different ways (Hall, 1987). In addition to your characteristics, your values, identity, attitudes, and vision affect how you learn the job. Various attitudes, such as desire for control, tolerance for organizational influence, sense of self-efficacy, and tolerance for ambiguity, can influence the socialization process, especially in a PLC (Jones, G. R., 1986; Nicholson, N., 1984; Schein & Ott, 1962).

Previous experience also influences the socialization process. The ways or styles you developed in learning previous roles or expectations can create "cultures of orientation" that influence the ways you learn to become an innovative school leader who supports a learning community (Van Maanen, 1984). As we discussed in Chapter 4, the constructivist view of learning involves in part the use of previous experiences and learning to serve as scaffolding for new learning. In addition, if your previous experience is aligned with the school's expectations or orientations, the types of socialization tactics used by the school are likely to emphasize investiture. In contrast, if your previous experience is out of alignment with the school's values, a "destructive or unfreezing phase" of socialization may be used (Schein, 1988).

A more specific socialization method used by aspiring administrators has been identified by Greenfield (1977a) as *GASing*, that is, "getting the attention of superiors." GASing is a socialization method that interns use to promote their candidacy and to learn the administrative perspective. Greenfield found that more assertive interns, that is, those who tested the limits and exploited resources, tended to develop broader administrative perspectives that involved the whole school. These findings suggest that rather than being a passive recipient of the socialization process, you have the opportunity to actively participate in your own learning to become an innovative school leader.

OUTCOMES OF SOCIALIZATION

Socialization obviously involves outcomes. In your case, the outcome of learning this new role should result in an innovative role orientation that focuses on leading a PLC. The major portion of this book has emphasized the nature of this outcome in terms of eight role conceptions of the principalship. However, this role is complex; it involves maintaining organizational stability as well as improving teaching and learning. The balance in the role depends on the district, the community, the school, and you. The process of learning the role that we have thus far described in this chapter leads toward different ways to balance the role and different outcomes.

Focus of Socialization Outcomes

We tend to think of professional learning as what happens to the individual during the socialization process. However, socialization can focus on two other areas that typically are ignored but are critical for change: role and organization. The outcome of socialization for you as a school principal or assistant principal involves learning new knowledge and skills, developing new identities, values and norms, and relating to a new environment. As we described earlier, you will encounter a variety of expectations that district administrators, parents, teachers, and students have for you involving what you do, whom you listen to, what you believe, what you value, and who you are as a principal. The outcomes of socialization from an individual point of view focus on these knowledge, skills, values, beliefs, and identities. As we will discuss later, this does not mean that you have been socialized successfully when you acquire everyone else's skills, beliefs, values, and identities. The socialization outcomes for you involve the reciprocal process we discussed earlier.

Socialization also involves changes in the role. In earlier chapters, we identified eight innovative role conceptions or different ways to imagine the roles of principal and assistant principal in a PLC. Socialization to these role conceptions does not only mean that you should enact your role in these different ways but also that you should influence the way others see the role. Roles can change in terms of the knowledge base that informs practice, the strategies typically used to enact the role, and the purpose or mission of the role, for example, leading a learning community (Van Maanen & Schein, 1979). Roles change because of societal pressures, your style in comparison with your predecessor's, and deliberate attempts by such groups as universities, professional associations, governmental entities, and national accrediting bodies. Thus, the socialization process of learning to become an innovative principal or assistant principal can result not only in changing your beliefs but also in influencing the way others view the role.

Socialization also involves changes in the organization. Anyone who has witnessed the arrival of a large group of newcomers to a school understands how these types of groups can change the organizational culture and climate. "Educational organizations make room for newcomers they value by adding new structures (e.g., courses or course levels), adapting procedures (e.g., giving reduced teaching loads to newcomers), and adjusting reward systems (e.g., giving extracurricular assignments to adjust the pay of newcomers)" (Crow & Matthews, 1998, p. 28). Without dismissing the powerful influence that the school will have on your learning, you have significant influence on the school. As a new principal or assistant principal, if you are sensitive to the school's culture, you can have a powerful influence during this socialization process on the image that others in the school have of the role. Thus, in a PLC, you will work to establish norms of collaboration, inquiry, and learner-centered leadership.

Types of Outcomes

Because this chapter is concerned primarily with how the innovative role conceptions we discussed earlier in this book are learned, we will concentrate on two types of socialization outcomes: individual adaptation and role adaptation. These are closely aligned with role taking and role making. In terms of individual adaptation, several outcomes are possible as you take on the role of principal or assistant principal in a PLC and as you respond to the expectations that others have of you. A useful scheme for identifying these is Schein's (1988) three types of responses that depend on whether you accept or reject the pivotal, relevant, and peripheral values and norms of the organization. Conformity involves the acceptance of all organizational or professional values regardless of whether they are pivotal, relevant, or peripheral. Rebellion, in contrast, involves the rejection of all these values. A *creative individualism* response to socialization involves the acceptance only of the pivotal values and norms and rejection of the others. An assistant principal who accepts the importance of student discipline but rejects the necessity of an autocratic approach has assumed a creative individualist response to socialization. A principal who accepts the values of and focus on schools as PLCs but rejects a one-size fits all approach is taking a creative individualist orientation to implementing change. Obviously, some values, norms, and expectations in your first school setting are worth conforming to and, in fact, must be accepted in order for you to fulfill your responsibilities, for example, being a good steward of the public's money. However, to assume that all values must be accepted uncritically is to contradict your role as a change agent. There is a place for conformity, a place for rebellion, and certainly a place for creative individualism in your response to the socialization process.

Learning to become an innovative principal or assistant principal in a PLC also results in role adaptation. Again, there are three possible role orientations: custodianship, content innovation, and role innovation (Schein, 1971). A custodial orientation to the role involves accepting the current knowledge base, strategy, and mission of the role as practiced by most principals or assistant principals. This orientation is what we have described in earlier sections as the traditional conception of the role. For example, a custodial orientation of the principal's supervisory responsibility assumes a deficit model of the teacher, a top-down snoopervision strategy, and the centrality of a control mission.

The second role orientation that is a possible outcome of socialization is content innovation. This orientation could be reflected in an assistant principal who accepts the student management mission of the role but rejects the knowledge and strategies typically used in enacting this mission. An assistant principal who is molding the role in a content-innovative orientation would acknowledge the new understanding, for example, of early adolescent development and search for strategies that engender self-discipline.

A third orientation is role innovation, which is a more radical response to socialization. This orientation involves the rejection not only of the customary strategies for enacting the role but also of the traditional mission or purpose of the role. A principal who conceives the mission of the role in terms of mentor in a learning community rejects the traditional control mission. Likewise, a principal who conceives the political role as contributing to a civil society has responded to socialization by rejecting an apolitical purpose or a manipulative mission of the role.

As with the preceding three responses to individual adaptation, these role orientations are more complex than simply opting for a role-innovation perspective. As a school leader, some of your response to the role will necessitate a custodial orientation when it is important to maintain organizational stability and integrity. At other times, a more innovative orientation will be necessary to move the school toward a shared vision of a PLC.

The traditional perspective on socialization outcomes identifies underconformity as a central problem when newcomers do not acquire the skills, values, and beliefs required by their organizations. Several researchers, however, have suggested that overconformity may be a much bigger problem (Feldman, 1981; Fisher, C.,1986; Long, 1988). Although conformity may be desirable in some occupational roles or organizational settings, for example, bank tellers and members of marching bands, it can be dysfunctional for other roles and organizations. We have argued in this book that for principals and assistant principals to be leaders of leaders and leaders of learners in a PLC, they must imagine innovative role conceptions—based on collaboration, inquiry, and critical reflection. In this instance, conformity is likely to be dysfunctional for schools to become learning communities for all students.

In the remainder of this chapter we will examine the unique socialization features of becoming an assistant principal and principal and those features of changing role conceptions at midcareer. In each instance we will identify some socialization methods that can contribute toward you becoming an innovative school leader within a PLC in each of the eight role conceptions identified earlier in this book.

BECOMING A NEW ASSISTANT PRINCIPAL

In the opening vignette, Beth's experience as an assistant principal was a shock from what she had expected in her administrative preparation and internship experiences. She encountered a principal and a group of teachers whose image of the role of assistant principal was one of student controller. Beth's experience is not unusual for many new assistant principals. The role of assistant principal is ambiguous, limited, and stressful in many settings (Hausman, Nebeker, McCreary, & Donaldson, 2001; Marshall, 1992; Weller & Weller, 2002). Yet, as an assistant principal, you can make a significant contribution to the PLC of the school. Learning to become an innovative assistant principal who contributes to student learning, teacher collaboration, and a culture of inquiry, however, takes place in a context of socialization that is important for you to know. In this section, we will identify the distinctive features of the socialization of assistant principals. Some of these features reinforce traditional roles. We describe them in order for you to understand the socialization processes and methods that some individuals may use to encourage you to maintain the status quo. However, also woven into our discussion will be suggestions to help you in your socialization as an innovative assistant principal in terms of the eight role conceptions for leaders of PLCs that we discussed previously in this book.

Distinctive Features of the Socialization of Assistant Principals

Numerous images of the assistant principal's role can be found, including hatchet man, activity coordinator, handy man, and fire fighter (Reed & Himmler, 1985). Such ambiguity and confusion create difficulty for socialization. In a PLC, however, the role images influenced by the principal should emphasize a collaborative relationship with teachers and a culture of inquiry. Several distinctive features of the assistant principal's socialization can be identified and should be helpful to you if you move into this significant leadership position.

CONTENT OF SOCIALIZATION   Becoming a new assistant principal will involve two images of the role. One image is a limited vision of the role that emphasizes primarily student management and maintenance of order (Greenfield, Marshall, & Reed, 1986; Hausman et al., 2001; Weller & Weller, 2002). The tasks involved in this view of the role include monitoring, supporting, and remediating (Reed & Himmler, 1985). Learning to be an assistant principal in this view involves both technical and cultural content. The technical content of socialization includes developing the skills to assess unstable situations and then to remedy them. Knowing how to monitor and to acquire the information necessary to prevent disorder or to uncover problems is a critical component of the assistant principal's socialization. You may have developed some of these skills as a teacher, but it is unlikely that you experienced the extensive and schoolwide nature of the stability issue in your prior experience.

In addition to the technical skills to monitor, support, and remedy unstable situations, you will have to learn cultural sensitivity to community values and standards regarding disorder and discipline. In some schools, issues such as noise in the classroom, wearing caps, or congregating in the hall are considered inappropriate and are dealt with harshly by some administrators. In other schools, these are not issues at all, and noise in the classroom is considered important to instructional engagement. Your ability to discover these community values, which may be contradictory to your previous teaching or internship experiences, is critical.

The second image of the assistant principal's role is a more expanded one for PLCs in which the role is enlarged to support instruction for all students (Hausman et al., 2001;

Marshall, 1992; Weller & Weller, 2002). This image does not ignore the student management role but views it in the larger school context of a learning community. Learning to be an assistant principal in this image necessitates developing skills to work with teachers in improving instructional effectiveness and to contribute to a PLC that encourages inquiry and collaboration. This includes technical, interpersonal, and cultural skills, such as observation, collaboration, active listening, conferencing, and action research. Many of these you bring with you from your previous experience as a teacher or from your preparation. Some of these skills you will learn as you become an assistant principal in a specific setting with values, norms, and beliefs similar to or different from your experience.

SOURCES OF SOCIALIZATION Although your socialization as an assistant principal involves some of the same sources as for principals, three are specifically distinctive for you as a new assistant principal. One of these distinctive elements is the influence of the principal as a source of socialization. Beth's experience in the opening vignette demonstrates the significance of the principal's influence as a source of socialization for new assistant principals. Your principal will influence your socialization in three major ways: assigning tasks, encouraging role images, and providing support. The principal almost certainly will determine the tasks that you are assigned. Some assistant principals have found that principals often take the more interesting tasks for themselves and assign the remainder to the assistant principal (Hess, 1985).

Principals also influence the assistant principal's socialization in a more subtle but profound way—by encouraging specific role images. These images include what receives attention in the school environment; the nature of the relationships with teachers, students, and parents; issues of control and authority; and what gets rewarded and punished. For some principals, the image of the role of administrator involves an autocratic and distant relationship with teachers and students. In a PLC, however, the role images influenced by principals should emphasize school administrators as facilitators and learners rather than autocrats and controllers. New assistant principals "learn very quickly that to be successful in the organization, they must buy into the system, learn the rules, and think like their boss" (Long, 1988, pp. 113–114).

Your principal can also influence your socialization as a new assistant principal by providing support, encouragement, and advice. In many instances, the principal becomes a mentor to the new assistant principal. Whether a mentoring relationship occurs, other principals can be influential in your socialization by what they praise and encourage about your performance and by their support and sponsorship of your future career.

A second major source of influence for assistant principals is teachers. The relationship with teachers can be both a positive influence and a perplexing dilemma. Teachers can reinforce or balance the role images of a leader in a PLC presented by the principal. They can respond positively or negatively to an expanded view of the assistant principal's role. The relationship with teachers also presents a dilemma for new administrators. In some conceptions of the role, assistant principals are expected to divest themselves of the teacher role and develop distancing relationships with teachers, thus emphasizing their loyalty to the administrative team (Marshall, 1985, 1992). Marshall (1985) called this one of the critical tasks in the enculturation of assistant principals: "separating from and defining relationships with teachers" (p. 45). It is not unusual for new assistant principals, especially if they are assigned to the same school where they taught, to realize that they are no longer welcomed in the faculty lounge. Some find that previous friends stop talking with them or inviting them out. The distancing that occurs is influenced not only by administrators themselves but also by teachers who regard the new assistant principal as a member of the "them" group.

Some new assistant principals fall into a trap by assuming that this distancing relationship is necessary. In fact, the folklore of school administration frequently supports the view. However, such a view is contradictory to more innovative and expanded images of the role in which you contribute to the PLC. This is not to say that if you choose these more innovative images, you will not experience teachers who want to distance themselves from you. Nor do we suggest that choosing this image will shield you from making hard decisions or conducting evaluations that may alienate some teachers. However, becoming an innovative assistant principal does not require you to purposely distance yourself from teachers.

A rarely acknowledged source of socialization for assistant principals is students. Although much of the job has focused traditionally on relationships with students, the literature seldom acknowledges the powerful socializing role played by students. Assistant principals are expected by teachers, parents, and principals to develop an image with students that emphasizes authority. This image can be one of drill sergeant, mother superior, or bully (Reed & Himmler, 1985). Students influence assistant principals' socialization by reinforcing the images of authority. This reinforcement may be influenced by the image held by predecessors. Some new assistant principals who try to develop a role image with students that is different from that of their predecessors are dismayed to discover that the students reject the image. In a PLC, students are a valued part of the learning community and should be seen as partners in their learning. The expanded view of the assistant principal role acknowledges and values this partnership.

Assistant principals are also sources of their own socialization in terms of their personal characteristics and previous experience. Your gender, for example, may encourage certain images of the role. "Perhaps women's socialization and the organizational expectations regarding women's roles enable them to [more easily than men] infuse an element of caring, nonaggression, and support into the task of maintaining control in schools" (Marshall, 1985, p. 53). The typically longer teaching experience of women also contributes to more instructional expertise and images of the role that encourage instructional effectiveness (Hausman et al., 2001; Shakeshaft, 1989).

In addition, your previous experience, especially as a teacher, influences the socialization process. The level of teaching, the social class of students and parents, and the administrative setting can influence the kinds of skills and sensitivities you bring or need to acquire as a new assistant principal. Moving from teaching middle-class suburban students to an assistant principalship in an inner city can require you to develop many new skills that will especially aid you in being an advocate and facilitating others' advocacy. Hausman and colleagues (2001) also found that assistant principals with five years or less of teaching experience tended to spend less time than their more experienced colleagues in instructional leadership activities.

STAGES OF SOCIALIZATION Becoming a new assistant principal involves three critical issues of time. First, the assistant principalship is a period of testing. "As they separate from the old reference group, seek entry and pass through career and organizational boundaries, they undergo a period of testing while the new group checks to see whether the aspirant can conform and adhere to their norms and meet performance expectations" (Marshall, 1985, p. 30). Administrators, teachers, parents, and students conduct this testing to determine the assistant principal's competence, loyalty, authority, and support. "Administrators evaluate the assistant principal's competency and loyalty. Teachers evaluate the assistant principal's competency, authority, and support. Students and parents assess authority and relationships" (Crow & Matthews, 1998, p. 75).

Another temporal element is what we have referred to as the *encounter stage*, where the expectations of the assistant principal meet the reality of the school context. The reality shock (Hughes, 1959) that occurs when expectations and reality are incongruent can be a difficult experience for the new assistant principal. Beth's reality shock (in the opening vignette) occurred when she encountered a principal who discouraged her more expanded view of the assistant principalship role. Early in the process of becoming an assistant principal, you will encounter different expectations and demands— some of which do not fit or encourage the development of a PLC. Part of the response to these reality shocks is to acknowledge what others expect of you and decide what is important to you in terms of the image of the assistant principalship in a PLC.

A third distinctive temporal element in becoming an assistant principal is experiencing a sense of loss. "The first year administrators seemed to experience a sense of loss regarding their old roles and their previous close relationship with peers" (Akerlund, 1988, p. 181). Although not all new assistant principals experience loss, those who do talk about how they miss the intensive instructional contact with students and the social relationships with fellow teachers. Viewing your role through the lens of a PLC, suggest that this loss may be more dysfunctional than originally thought. As we discussed earlier in this chapter, there may be some discomfort in the evaluative role that administrators play in the school, but there is no necessity of intentionally creating hierarchical distancing that hinders professional community to support learning.

METHODS OF SOCIALIZATION Becoming an assistant principal involves a variety of methods. Some are tools used by principals, teachers, staff, district administrators, parents, and students to shape the new recruit and reinforce values, norms, and beliefs held by the organization. We maintain that there are other methods that assistant principals can use not only to respond to the expectations of school constituents but also to help shape an image of the role that is innovative, expanded, and supportive of the PLC.

Although school organizations use many methods in socializing the new assistant principal, three seem especially distinctive to this role. First, learning to become a new assistant principal is typically a trial-and-error process. This means that instead of the formal, collective, and fixed process that you probably encountered in the internship, your new learning is informal, individual, and variable. Although some districts are moving toward more formal arrangements that involve assigning veterans to new administrators, the large majority of new assistant principals find that they are on their own. The trial-and-error process, however, does not mean that the organization is not aware of your actions, successes, and failures. This process tends to be influenced by such things as the style of your predecessor and the criticality of specific needs, such as student management.

Second, as we have noted, administrators, teachers, parents, and students routinely test the new assistant principal to determine competence, loyalty, authority, and support. Although some testing may have occurred during the internship, the stakes are higher for assistant principals. The testing is often subtle, and the individual assistant principal is only aware after the fact. A former graduate student described a less subtle testing that occurred in her first assistant principal position. Her previous teaching experience had been in suburban schools, but her first administrative position was in an inner-city school. One of the teachers asked her to proctor a spelling exam for second graders while the teacher made a call to a parent. The students responded to the "new" teacher by cheating and other disruptive behaviors. When the teacher returned, the new assistant principal acknowledged that she had lost control of the class. However, she asked if she could return in a week and "try again." The teacher agreed, and when the assistant principal returned to teach the class during the next week, a line of teachers was standing in the back of the room to witness her "second try." Her humility and humor—and success at the second try—won her respect from the teachers. She passed the test!

A third distinctive method used by organizations to socialize new assistant principals is divestiture. Divestiture processes regarding movement toward the assistant principal role appear to be gradual and subtle. As the candidate begins to do some of the organizational scut work (that many teachers may refuse to do) associated with monitoring children—helping to "set up" for parent and other meetings, being a "go-for," and helping the administrator with an endless stream of minor (and sometimes major) projects—the "teacher" self is gradually shed and the "administrator" self evolves (Greenfield, W. D., 1985b, pp. 22–23). Both teachers and administrators use divestiture to establish certain norms regarding what is expected of new assistant principals. Some teachers, in order to maintain the teacher subculture, try to keep the division of authority and lines of communication clear. Administrators, sometimes in response to this subculture, attempt to close ranks and create an "us and them" perspective in new assistant principals.

As we have argued before, this insider/outsider perspective does not foster a PLC. Thus, divestiture is dysfunctional for socializing new assistant principals to an innovative image of the role that views both teachers and administrators as collaborative learners and leaders.

We have maintained throughout this chapter that socialization involves both role taking and role making and that the individual is an active partner in the learning process. Thus, there are methods that you can use as a new assistant principal to learn this role and help to mold the role in terms of the eight conceptions we discussed earlier in this book that focus on supporting a PLC. First, you can use a variety of methods to enhance your role as a learner. In addition to the obvious methods, such as reading books and journals, attending professional conferences, and continuing conversations with university faculty and administrative mentors, you can also form associations with other assistant principals that you believe have adopted more expanded and innovative conceptions of the role. Visiting one another's schools, forming book clubs, and other forms of networking can help reinforce more innovative conceptions of the role of assistant principal as learner.

You can also learn and enhance your role as culture builder. This learning is particularly important in supporting PLCs. You can ask teachers and staff to tell you stories about the school, which will provide ways to learn about the cultural norms and values on which the PLC is built or could be built.

Learning to become an innovative assistant principal involves the critical area of learning to be an advocate in order to respond to the diverse needs of students and families in your school community and to support a culture of inquiry that provides learning for all students regardless of background or characteristics. Even in situations where new assistant principals are constrained to a more limited student management role, learning about the diversity of your school community can have a powerful influence on your effectiveness. Getting to know district special education, English as a second language (ESL), and bilingual administrators can help you develop an understanding of needs, programs, and procedures to respond to diversity. Attending events sponsored by ethnic community organizations in your area will provide valuable information regarding the concerns and values of diverse groups in your school and help you to develop the sensitivity, skills, and understanding to become an innovative school leader who advocates for diverse students and their families.

In terms of a mentoring role, you can develop your own mentoring relationship with students and teachers and reflect on this experience to determine how it works. Reflecting on your own experience as a mentor also opens your experience as a protégé. Peer mentoring arrangements with other former interns and veteran assistant principals can reinforce more innovative and transformative role images (Browne-Ferrigno & Muth, 2004).

Learning to be a supervisor can be difficult in situations where teachers and administrators emphasize only student management as your role. Although it may take a while to convince veteran teachers of your contribution in this area, you might start with new teachers as you reinforce the idea of student management as an instructional rather than control role. In developing your skills in this area, you can invite veteran administrators or district office specialists who have reputations as excellent instructional coaches to witness your observations or conferences and give you feedback. You also might use your networking group of former university classmates to discuss frustrations, ideas, successes, and failures.

Becoming an innovative assistant principal, we have argued, involves a more expanded role than, for example, student management, building maintenance, or activity coordination. Identifying and communicating with assistant principals or principals who view the assistant principal's role in this way can help reinforce the image. Another tool to use in this regard is to become part of a school–university partnership that conducts action research. Not only does this reinforce your image as a learner, but it also helps emphasize your instructional role as you work with teachers on instructional problems.

Frequently the assistant principal's role is restricted in terms of learning managerial tasks that will be necessary if the individual becomes a principal. Restricting the assistant principal to student management roles ignores the need to learn such critical managerial tasks as budgeting and facilities management. Getting to know the custodian and the cafeteria workers has multiple benefits including learning how the building and the lunch program function. By asking these staff members to give you a tour of the facilities, not only will you impress them with your interest in their areas, but also you will probably see more of the building than you saw on your formal introduction to the facility.

Becoming an assistant principal involves learning the micropolitics of the school and district. Developing and using your sensitivity to the conflicts among different school groups over resources and values are important learning issues. Becoming an innovative assistant principal also involves getting to know the larger political system and structure that influences community, district, and school decisions. Attending school board and city council meetings can give you enormous information about who wields power over what resources in your community.

OUTCOMES OF SOCIALIZATION   There are two ways to think about the socialization outcomes for assistant principals. First, we can identify the career outcomes of socialization. The assistant principalship traditionally has often been viewed as an apprenticeship position for the purpose of grooming new principals. However, more recently, the role has become focused on student management (Weller & Weller, 2002). There is some concern that this more limited role has decreased the qualifications of assistant principals to become principals (Hausman et al., 2001; Pounder & Merrill, 2001) and thus contributed to perceptions of a shortage in qualified candidates for the principalship.

As Beth in the opening vignette found, becoming an innovative assistant principal contributed toward her visibility in the district and her eventual move to the principalship. One of the socialization outcomes of the assistant principalship is the successful move to a principal position.

Another career outcome may be developing an innovative conception of the assistant principal's role and remaining in that role. Some assistant principals find that they prefer this position because it allows them to stay closer to students. You should not assume that remaining in the assistant principal position is a failure of socialization. As we have argued in this book, the assistant principalship is a critical leadership role in the school and deserves innovative leaders.

The second way to view socialization outcomes is in terms of role image. Earlier we identified three outcomes: conformity, rebellion, and creative individualism (Schein, 1988). In terms of becoming an assistant principal, enacting the limited view of the role as student management is clearly a more conformist outcome. However, new assistant principals must respond to the expectations of those around them as well as try to mold the role in a more instructionally focused way. In the beginning, it is not unusual for new assistant principals to focus on conforming to this limited role. However, in order to provide the type of innovative role as learner, culture builder, advocate, mentor, supervisor, leader, manager, and politician that is needed to make schools dynamic PLCs, you should keep in mind how the role of assistant principal can be changed. Creative individualism provides the opportunity to both understand and respond to the role as given and mold the role in more innovative ways.

In the context of a PLC confronting the demands of a knowledge society, assistant principals need to develop adaptability that responds to complexity in schools. Hall (2002) identifies key learnings that support the type of adaptability necessary in complex work settings, including "flexibility, exploration, openness to new and diverse people and ideas, dialogue skills and eagerness to accept new challenges in unexplored territory, and comfort with turbulent change" (p. 161).

The assistant principalship is a critical leadership role that can help change schools to become rich PLCs. We encourage you to imagine your role as assistant principal in innovative ways. Schools can be more effective learning communities for all students if more innovative images can be fostered and mentored.

BECOMING A NEW PRINCIPAL

Many, if not most, elementary school principals enter the role without assistant principal experience. Secondary school principals are more likely to have had this prior administrative experience. If you are a new principal who has never been an assistant principal, you may want to read the preceding section on becoming an assistant principal. Many of the features are similar between a new assistant principal and a new principal who has not had prior administrative experience. In this section, we identify those elements of socialization that are distinctive to a new principal. As we did with assistant principals, some of our discussion focuses on traditional socialization processes that encourage maintaining the status quo. We describe this traditional socialization so that you know what methods others may be using to influence you. However, we also identify more innovative strategies that you can use to learn and implement the eight role conceptions that support a PLC.

Content of Socialization

One of the most distinctive elements of the principal's socialization is the importance of tasks involving external constituents, including district administrators and the community. Assistant principals are obviously involved to some degree with these external groups, but the role of principal in a PLC could be described as balancing internal and external demands. The role complexity described in Chapter 1 that has become so apparent in the work of principals in contemporary society can be thought of as having both internal and external parts (Crow, 2006a, 2006b; Crow, Hausman, & Scribner, 2002). We will discuss the content of socialization in terms of internal, external, and personal spheres.

INTERNAL SPHERE   Learning to become a new principal clearly includes learning the tasks, work environment, and culture of the PLC. The tasks have been described in the earlier chapters of this book in terms of the different role conceptions of the principalship in a learning community. Learning the work environment is probably more complex as you learn the names, job responsibilities, sources of information, and personalities of the individuals with whom you work. When you enter your new school, you will encounter a large amount of chaotic, equivocal information from which you will develop "cause maps" that allow you to predict behavior (Weick, 1979). Learning what information you need, which sources of information to trust, and what to do with the information you receive is an extremely important part of your learning as a new principal in a PLC.

Learning to become a new principal also involves learning the norms, values, and beliefs of the specific learning community. Whether you have had prior administrative experience, you will need to learn the unique culture of this school. Learning the culture—how things are done here—is critical to becoming an innovative principal in the eight areas we identified earlier. For example, you cannot be a change agent in a PLC if you are insensitive to the norms and values of the context (Daresh, 2006). Another part of this cultural learning is recognizing that the culture has been there much longer than you and that cultural values and norms are much harder to change than you might assume (Schein, 2004).

EXTERNAL SPHERE   The complexity of the principalship has increased recently primarily because of external demands, such as accountability, markets, and civic capacity requirements or trends (Crow, Hausman, & Scribner, 2002). Schools are embedded in their social settings, and principals' roles for a PLC are likewise embedded.

Learning to become a new principal involves confronting new tasks, political relationships and dilemmas, and a culture that may have values in conflict with the school's vision for a learning community. Your first day on the job will no doubt include district reports, responses, and requests. Whether you imagine your role as a leader of the school or agent of central office (Crow, 1987), you still must respond to district administrators who hired you, will evaluate you, and from whom many of your resources come.

In addition to the new sets of tasks involving the district office, you must learn the cultural norms and values of the district and the larger community. These groups have their own sets of cultural values and mores that may conflict with yours or with those of the school. Principals discover, sometimes very early, that the values of the community are not necessarily the values of the learning community of teachers and administrators (Post, 1992). Frequently, these value differences occur over curriculum and student management styles. Learning what these value differences are will not resolve them, but you cannot work to resolve them unless you are aware of what areas of conflict exist.

One of the major types of learning that new principals face and that is frequently ignored in preparation programs is political skill (Bolman & Deal, 2003). We advocated in Chapter 11 that the political role is not simply a necessary evil but rather a valuable conception of the principal's role. Learning to negotiate, compromise, and bargain is a necessary and critical part of the role in a learning community. Although these skills do not develop overnight, they are as critical as learning how to change culture to your becoming an innovative principal in a learning community.

PERSONAL SPHERE   In addition to learning the technical and cultural components of the internal and external parts of the job, new principals are developing personal learning. As you begin your experience in a new job and new context, you will develop a self-image or identity as a principal (Browne-Ferrigno, 2003; Crow, 2008). Discovering new strengths and talents of which you were unaware and learning new skills not held previously will contribute toward seeing yourself in new ways. The move from teacher to principal identity is critical but can be a source of confusion and conflict if the expectations of others are that you divest yourself of your teacher identity rather than investing your principal identity with a teaching mission and emphasis (Loder & Spillane, 2005; Marshall, 1992). Developing new identities can, however, provide confidence and encouragement to take on initiatives and resolve old conflicts. It can also raise new conflicts among work, family, and other significant elements of your life. Realizing that professional identities are multiple and fluid is important as you explore these new self-images. Reflecting on how your self-images are changing and using a mentor to help with this reflection can be powerful learning tools.

Sources of Socialization

In the same way that the content of your socialization involves internal and external spheres, so there are internal and external sources of your socialization. In addition, you are also a source of your own socialization.

INTERNAL SOURCES   Your learning as a new principal will include three distinctive internal sources: teachers, your predecessor, and other school staff members. Although teachers certainly influence assistant principals, they are the primary source of socialization for new principals (Duke, et al., 1984). Teachers hold expectations for the new principal that influence the learning that occurs. They assume certain tasks that the principal will do. A traditional view of this assumption is that teachers expect principals to keep things running smoothly and buffer them from interruptions and irate parents. However, they also expect to have a voice in those decisions that they care about (Ortiz, 1982). The role conception in a PLC that we have encouraged in Chapter 11, which involves bridging rather than buffering teachers from parents, may run head on into expectations that some teachers have of you when you first arrive. Understanding the norms and values that teachers hold will help you understand what you face and how to use teachers as a valuable source to support a PLC.

Teachers also influence the learning of new principals in terms of the information they provide. Identifying credible and trustworthy sources of information will be a major learning in your early days as a principal.

The second internal source of socialization is your predecessor as principal. A large body of literature emphasizes the importance of the predecessor for a new leader's socialization (Hart, 1993; Weindling, 1992; Weindling & Earley, 1987). In her study of new principals' socialization, Shackelford (1992) found that "when a new principal arrives on the scene, the school culture responds to everything about that person that is different from the predecessor" (p. 142). As Shackelford found, this can include gender, race, worldview, and leadership style. Your vision of the school as a PLC may also vary from that of your predecessor. If your predecessor did not value PLCs, teachers and others in the school may see you as different—in both negative and positive ways.

Your predecessor may be another principal in the same district or a neighboring district, in which case you may have the opportunity to discuss norms, values, personalities, and change attempts. Regardless of whether your predecessor is close or has moved far away, the predecessor's influence can be great. The expectations that teachers, parents, and students have of your leadership style, the tasks you do, the norms and values you hold, and the degree of interest in change will be affected by this person. Even if the faculty and staff disliked your predecessor, this person will be a major influence on expectations of you in your new role.

In addition to teachers and predecessors, other school staff act as socialization sources. Daresh (2006) calls these the "invisible heroes" of the school—secretaries, professional teaching aides, custodians, cafeteria staff, and security officers. He pointed out that it is impossible to lead a learning community by ignoring these "invisible heroes." These staff members have perspectives, values, and significant information to share that will inform your view not only of the school but also of the images of the role of principal that others expect. Spending time doing school walk-throughs with the custodians or security officers, for example, will provide critical information not only about the physical plant but also about views of students and learning opportunities that exist outside the classroom.

EXTERNAL SOURCES Learning to become a principal is also influenced by individuals outside the school, including district administrators, other principals, and the community. Because the external sphere of the principal's work has become so critical for a PLC, these individuals become powerful sources of socialization.

District administrators are a major source of socialization for new principals in part because they hire, evaluate, and provide resources. The relationship between principals and district administrators is typically close but not necessarily positive. Districts have a stake in how new principals learn their jobs. Not only have they invested time and money in the selection process, but their own political vulnerability in the community is also affected strongly by the successes and failures of principals. District administrators use a variety of methods including selection, evaluation, and supervision to influence principals to learn to enact their roles in ways that protect district interests and maintain smooth and "silent" operations of the school (Peterson, 1984).

District administrators also influence new principals in two other ways: the autonomy they allow new principals to have and the ways they influence principals' relationships with teachers. Principals need autonomy to be able to respond to the unique circumstances of their schools that influence the substance and style of the PLC. In addition, district administrators can affect the principal's relationship with teachers by ignoring the school's uniqueness, pitting the principal against the faculty, enacting unpopular policies, and limiting the principal's autonomy (Crow, 1990).

A second source of new principal socialization is the influence of other principals (Akerlund, 1988). New principals turn to veteran principals for information about district-school issues when they feel uncomfortable displaying their ignorance about policies or when information is not available from the district office. Other principals use humor and oral tradition to teach new principals. Using stories about principals who succeeded and those who failed provides powerful socializing messages to new principals.

Because the principal is a "boundary spanner" (Rallis & Goldring, 2000) between the school and the external community, powerful parents and community leaders have a strong socializing force on the new principal. These individuals bring expectations regarding appropriate role images, values, norms, and beliefs that are communicated to the principal overtly and covertly in terms of support for the principal's initiatives related to the learning community.

INDIVIDUAL PRINCIPAL CHARACTERISTICS   Shackelford (1992) cautioned new principals, "Principals should take control of the socialization process, set their vision, refine their reflective skills, and develop the strategic sense needed to dodge the bullets and when to brace for support" (p. 163). Part of taking control of the socialization process is to acknowledge your individual characteristics that have an impact on the socialization experience. Among these individual sources of socialization are gender, ethnicity, and prior experience.

Your gender affects socialization in a variety of ways. Crow and Pounders (1995) found that new female urban principals tended to be placed in larger schools. Such an initial context can affect the types of tasks, expectations, and resources you encounter and thus the kinds of learning necessary and available. Gender also affects role image. Loder and Spillane (2005) found that new female principals experience role conflict in the move from the classroom to the school, with its more managerial and political responsibilities. In their study, women developed coping strategies to deal with this role conflict by retaining their identity as teachers. For example, actions such as teaching a class every week, instituting "lunch with the principal," and using popular slang with the students helped these new principals make the identity transition. In the context of a PLC, this identity continuity may be eased for both women and men by the community's focus on teaching and learning.

Professional Dilemma 12.1

In a large school district that included both inner-city and suburban schools, the assistant principals of color traditionally were placed in the most ethnically diverse schools. As role models for many students of color, these assistant principals served well in the urban schools. However, the suburban schools often had no administrators of color, limiting their perspective to mostly Caucasian models. Should the ethnicity of administrators be considered in their placement at schools?

Ethnicity can also affect socialization in terms of the types of settings of the first appointment. Several researchers have found that principals of color tend to be placed in "troubled schools" (Crow & Pounders, 1995; Ortiz, 1982). Crow and Pounders found that African American principals tended to be initially appointed to schools with high Title I populations, high student poverty, high teacher absences, low student attendance, low teacher salaries, and fewer certified teachers. This type of initial appointment presents challenges, resources, and expectations from districts and the community that strongly affect the content and methods of socialization for new principals.

Ethnicity may also affect role image. For example, several researchers have pointed to the community involvement and leadership that African American principals emphasize (Lomotey, 1989; Monteiro, 1977). Ortiz (1982) suggested a subtler but negative socialization vignette. Because principals of color are placed in troubled schools, they are expected "to contain the student unrest and community complaints, but are not readily allowed to make changes regarding the physical plant, personnel, or curriculum" (p. 104). Focusing on building a PLC when most of your learning and influence are on containing student unrest is a huge endeavor.

This discussion of individual characteristics is not intended to suggest that if you are a woman or principal of color your role conception will be determined because of these socialization sources. Rather, if, as Shackelford (1992) urged, new principals need to control their socialization, it is important for you to recognize how others may perceive you and how you can use these perceptions and these characteristics as ways to create more innovative role images in support of a PLC.

Stages of Socialization

When you become a new principal, you do not suddenly move from being a total novice to being an all-knowing expert in the job. Research suggests that learning to become a principal is a gradual and evolving process that began before you were appointed and lasts for several years (Parkay & Hall, 1992). In fact, learning to become an innovative principal in a PLC does not end even after several years as a veteran principal. Being part of a learning community means that you too are a continual learner.

There are several underlying assumptions about your development as a principal that are important to recognize. First, the influences on your learning begin before you are appointed. Your professional socialization during the administrative preparation program and your previous experience as a student and teacher both influence your learning. Another more subtle but powerful influence on your learning is the "shadows of principals past" (Weindling, 1992, p. 334). Weindling used this provocative phrase to

emphasize that you enter the principalship with the previous principal's style and relationship with teachers influencing the expectations that others have of you. He quoted
a new British headteacher (principal) who described this influence of the previous
administrator: "One of the biggest problems for a new head is not what you do or do
not do, but rather something which is out of your hands, namely, what sort of relationship existed between your predecessor and the faculty. It's annoying because there is
nothing that you can do about it" (p. 335).

Four other assumptions underlie the stages of socialization for new principals
(Parkay & Hall, 1992):

- Principals begin their careers at different stages of development.
- Principals develop within their careers at different rates.
- No single factor determines a principal's stage of development.
- Principals may operate at more than one stage simultaneously. (pp. 354–355)

These assumptions emphasize that the stages of your socialization may be similar to
others but that there are unique features to each new principal's socialization timeline.

Two factors that can influence the uniqueness of the development are previous
administrative experience and prior organizational location. Previous experience, especially as a school administrator, can affect the school where you are appointed and may
affect individual factors. Crow and Pounders (1995) found that new urban principals'
first appointments tended to be affected by whether or not they had had assistant principal experience. Those with previous administrative experience tended to be placed in
schools with lower teacher absences and fewer Title I and special-education students.
These organizational characteristics may present different socialization experiences and
challenges for new principals. Previous administrative experience may provide opportunities for new principals to have expectations that are more realistic, to gain experience in identifying credible sources of information for decision making, and to develop
skills for responding to uncertainties in the school environment.

Prior organizational location also affects the unique character of the socialization
process. Various researchers have found that whether a new administrator comes from
outside or inside the school or district can affect socialization (Carlson, 1972; Crow &
Pounder, 1994). Crow and Pounder found that principals who come from inside the district tend to focus on maintaining smooth operation and seek support from internal
school constituents. Outsiders, in contrast, seek support from individuals outside the
school, such as the superintendent. Where a principal finds support is likely to influence sources of socialization.

Research on socialization stages of new principals suggests three features of development: learning and uncertainty, gradual adjustment during which outcomes emerge,
and stabilization (Hart, 1993). These features are translated into three stages. First, new
principals begin with encounter, anticipation, and confrontation. This first stage involves
confronting the differences between what you expected the principalship to be and reality. The degree of difference depends on the amount of change between the old and the
new—contrast and surprise. In response to these differences, new principals engage in
sense making (Louis, 1980a), that is, using past experiences and others' interpretations to
understand and respond to these differences between expectations and reality. For some
new principals, this stage can be difficult if these differences are extreme. Some principals come with a "Mr. Chips" conception of the role, assuming that they will become

"head teachers" inspiring and mentoring their teacher protégés to excellent instruction. When they encounter the managerial complexities and demands of the role, these principals are shocked that the instructional image seems impossible. The response may be one of giving up the ideal conception and assuming a managerial role conception that emphasizes maintaining the status quo. Such a response is neither necessary nor effective for building learning communities for all students and educators.

The second stage for a new principal emphasizes adjustment to "the work role, the people with whom [he or] she interacts and the culture of the new school" (Hart, 1993, p. 29). At this stage, the shock that confronted the principal at the first stage of socialization subsides, and the new administrator develops ways to respond to these demands. However, sometimes these responses are inappropriate or misunderstood by school constituencies. "The new principal is like a high school freshman at the first prom—ignorant of etiquette and at times a step or two behind the band" (Cabrera & Stout, 1989, quoted in Shackelford, 1992, p. 23). This second stage is the point at which various outcomes emerge. As our example at the end of the preceding paragraph suggests, these outcomes may emphasize the status quo or role conceptions that are not conducive to effective learning communities.

The third stage of socialization emphasizes stabilization, where the new principal fits into the role. This period involves the negotiation between two spheres: internally with students, faculty, and staff and externally with superiors and the community (Duke, D. L., et al., 1984; Hart, 1993). However, this stage is not the end of development. In fact, N. Nicholson and West (1988) suggested that this is likely to be preparation for the next cycle of change and development. Because of the change inherent in work, the cycle of socialization does not end. As we emphasized in Chapter 1, work in postindustrial schools involves rapid change in response to more complex environments and technological advances. This type of change means that principals and other educators must be constantly redefining and thus relearning their roles—activities that are inherent in a PLC.

Other researchers have provided more detail to the socialization stages of new principals. In a major study of principals, Parkay and Hall (1992) identified five stages: survival, control, stability, educational leadership, and professional actualization. Instead of ending with stability, these authors suggested ongoing learning and growth. In the fourth stage, educational leadership, the focus is on curriculum and instruction, and the fifth stage emphasizes creating a culture for empowerment, growth, and authenticity. With an emphasis on creating a learning community for *all* students, the focus on instruction may occur earlier.

Another way to understand new principal socialization emphasizes how these new administrators learn to "take charge" and respond to the need for change. Weindling and Earley (1987) conducted an informative study related to socialization and change with British headteachers (principals). These researchers identified six stages that cover the first eight years of a new administrator's career:

Stage 0: *Preparation prior to appointment.*

Stage 1: *Entry and encounter (first month).* The new administrator "attempts to develop a cognitive map of the complexities of the situation, the people, the problems, and the school culture" (Weindling, 1992, p. 12).

Stage 2:   *Taking hold (approximately three to twelve months).* The new administrator begins to challenge the taken-for-granted nature of the school and introduces some organizational changes. There is frequently a "honeymoon period" in which faculty are more open to change.

Stage 3:   *Reshaping (second year).* Having gone through a full cycle of the school year, the administrator is ready to take on major changes. Faculty and staff members are also more aware of the administrator's strengths and weaknesses.

Stage 4:   *Refinement (third to fourth year).* Administrators feel that they are "hitting their stride" by refining previous innovations and introducing other curriculum changes.

Stage 5:   *Consolidation (fifth to seventh year).* Because changes are firmly in place, administrators begin to consolidate. New legislative and external changes result in the need to reexamine some changes.

Stage 6:   *Plateau (eighth year and onward).* If they stay in the same school, administrators begin to feel disenchantment.

These authors found that the types of changes these new administrators learned to make were different for various stages of the career. For example, organizational changes, involving communication, consultation, and positive school image, were made in the first year. In contrast, curricular changes began in the second year. These kinds of changes entail different socialization methods and sources.

Methods of Socialization

The methods or tactics that the organization and you will use in your development as a new principal are varied and individual. "New principals essentially design their own socialization process with specifics unique to each principal" (Crow & Matthews, 1998, p. 106). Although district administrators and school faculty and staff contribute to your socialization, the tactics they use are seldom formal. Although some districts have recently established mentoring programs for new principals, you have the primary responsibility for your learning.

In addition to being individual and informal, your socialization tends to be serial and include both divestiture and investiture (Van Maanen & Schein, 1979). Your primary socialization sources other than yourself are those currently or formerly in the role—school and district administrators. As we noted earlier, the subtle tactics of serial socialization encourage the maintenance of the status quo rather than an innovative role that focuses on creating and maintaining a PLC. In addition to serial socialization tactics, new principals' socialization involves both divestiture and investiture. District administrators and other principals may expect you to abandon your identity as a teacher and may even encourage an "us or them" type of view. At the same time, your previous experience may be valued in terms of becoming an instructional leader within a learning community, as it was with Beth in the opening vignette. This conflict between divestiture and investiture may present dilemmas for you in learning to become an innovative principal in a PLC.

In addition to the general socialization tactics described earlier, you can use specific methods to help you learn to be an innovative principal with the eight role conceptions we introduced earlier in this book. Because all these role conceptions are based on the importance of instructional improvement, your learning should be focused on making schools more effective learning communities for all students.

Becoming a principal who is a learner is probably the most important thing you can do as a new principal. Using methods that help you to become a learner not only benefits you but also facilitates the larger PLC. Storytelling is a common method used by principals in their socialization. Shackelford (1992) described four types of stories she experienced in her own socialization as a new principal: historical, organizational, humorous, and inspirational. Historical stories provided information about the school before the new principal arrived. Organizational stories described the traditions and norms of the school. Humorous stories were therapeutic in responding to the differences between expectations and reality. Inspirational stories were sources of information and support. Although storytelling is not a new method, it can be useful to you in developing your learning about this new school and its history. What are the past school improvement efforts? Are they viewed as successful? Seeking out stories also communicates to teachers, students, and parents that you care about what has happened in the school and that learning is an important part of your leadership style.

Becoming a principal who is a culture builder also involves learning about the school—its norms and values that inhibit or facilitate a learning community. One method is to conduct your own school culture diagnosis, for example, the culture inventory described in Chapter 5 (Daresh, 2006; Deal & Peterson, 1999). In specific, look for the cultural artifacts of the school, for example, celebrations, rituals, stories, and language that convey the existing culture of the school. Understanding the cultural context in which you lead is a critical first step in learning to be an innovative leader. Remember that changing culture is very difficult, especially for the new principal.

Learning to be an advocate who cares about and promotes the value of diversity in the school also involves methods you can use. Taking the time to meet ethnic leaders in the community and attending local churches in minority areas of the school community provide opportunities for you to learn the issues and concerns of diverse constituents. Although making these visits has public relations values to the school, the primary reason is for you to develop your own sensitivity to community diversity. In addition, meeting with district special education, ESL, and bilingual teachers and staff and visiting with parents of at-risk students are other learning opportunities for developing your skills and attitudes regarding diverse populations in the school. These methods help you develop the type of sensitivity that will enable you to be innovative and transformative in leading a PLC.

Becoming a principal who is a mentor involves similar methods as we described with assistant principals, for example, identifying and seeking the help of a mentor and reflecting on your own mentoring. As a new principal, you probably will have more experience being mentored and thus more variety of mentoring styles on which to reflect. You also will have more experience mentoring others, for example, assistant principals. Reflecting on what worked and did not work will help you refine your skills. In addition, mentoring workshops through universities, districts, and professional associations can help you refine your skills for mentoring in a PLC.

In learning to become a principal as supervisor, you need to understand the norms and history of the school regarding supervision. Is supervision seen as snoopervision? Is there widespread mistrust of the principal as supervisor? Listening to stories, watching reactions from teachers when you visit classrooms, observing teacher team meetings, and having conversations with teachers about teaching and learning will help you learn the context in which you will be developing your supervisory style. Furthermore, asking a veteran administrator whom you trust to observe classrooms with you and give you feedback on your conferencing behaviors will help you to learn to refine your skills and knowledge as an innovative supervisor who enriches the PLC.

Becoming an innovative leader also involves socialization methods you can use. Before you can lead others to change and to contribute to a PLC, you must take the time to understand the context in which change might occur. You can conduct a vision audit (Nanus, 1995) of your school. Doing this audit with teachers, staff, and parents also provides an opportunity for you to learn their vision of the school and to facilitate a collective vision of a PLC.

Learning to be an innovative manager is critical for the new principal. Although we have emphasized the importance of being a leader, if you do not develop managerial skills, your leadership of a PLC will be handicapped. Your first few months as a new principal will no doubt focus primarily on learning the managerial aspects of the job (Oplatka, 2004). You can use a variety of methods to help you learn these managerial skills and at the same time acknowledge the importance of leadership. For example, touring the building with custodians, lunchroom staff, counselors, librarians, and teachers will give you a sense of the physical environment and how it fosters or hinders learning. An added benefit of touring with custodians and other staff is that you communicate to these essential school constituents that creating a learning community for all students is important to you and that their work is critical in developing this community. Walking the building with an older student or with a parent may stimulate your thinking about issues that need to be confronted and new ways to think about solving old managerial dilemmas.

Learning to be a principal who is a politician involves understanding and developing coalitions in both internal and external spheres. O'Brien (1988) found that new principals discovered the interpersonal and political features of their jobs in conversations, school district literature, and nonverbal feedback. Conversations with various individuals both inside and outside the school, for example, at the local Kiwanis, Rotary, or Lions Clubs, not only provides you with information about how the school is viewed by the community but also initiates dialogue that eventually can result in bridges between community and school—thus expanding and enriching the learning community. The role of principal in building civic capacity (Goldring & Hausman, 2001), which we described in Chapter 11, can be learned through your conversations with community leaders. Visiting a local café early in the morning may provide a wealth of information in learning your political role, and it certainly does not hurt the public image of the school.

Outcomes of Socialization

In addition to the three types of socialization outcomes we discussed in the assistant principal section—conformist, rebellion, and creative individualism (Schein, 1988)—new principals' socialization may result in both personal and role development (Nicholson, 1984). Personal development involves changes in professional identity. Role development, in contrast, involves changing the conception of the job itself. Both of these are possible as you move into the principalship in a PLC.

Nicholson (1984) identified four possible outcomes that result from various socialization methods. First, replication results when neither your self-image nor the role changes. Second, absorption occurs when your self-image changes but the role does not change. Both of these are custodial outcomes. Third, determination occurs when you as a new principal change very little, but the role changes extensively. Fourth, exploration occurs when both personal and role development occur. As Hart (1993) pointed out, any of these four outcomes can be functional or dysfunctional. For example, changing the role but not your professional identity may stifle your learning.

One of the most important points in the previous discussion is the importance of developing your personal and professional identity (Crow, 2008). Hart (1993) pointed out that typically socialization for new principals emphasizes the technical aspects of the job, for example, learning how to develop a budget; however, affective and emotional growth is just as important and possibly more important. Learning to become an innovative principal in a PLC involves more than learning how to do the tasks of the job. The learning we encourage in this book involves your identity as a learner, culture builder, advocate, mentor, supervisor, leader, manager, and politician. Such learning involves the values, attitudes, and identity you develop that enable you to move beyond the traditional to more innovative role conceptions that affect schools as learning communities for all students.

If job change has the power to effect changes in identity as well as in organizational performance, then how the transition process is managed has a vital bearing on the well-being and effectiveness of organizations. It would appear that few organizations recognize this (Nicholson & West, 1988, p. 212).

Not only should organizations realize the importance of how learning influences their effectiveness, but new principals also must recognize that how they learn the job influences the role conceptions they develop.

BECOMING AN INNOVATIVE MIDCAREER PRINCIPAL

Although this book focuses on being and becoming a new assistant principal or principal, learning to be an innovative school leader is a continuing process. Thus we end this chapter by examining socialization at midcareer. Because learning to be innovative will be an ongoing process in your career as a leader of a PLC, it is important for you to understand how your socialization continues after you are established in the position. The pattern of learning you develop now is likely to be the pattern you rely on later in your career.

Focusing on socialization at midcareer is also important because, as we discussed in Chapter 1, work in postindustrial society requires you to constantly redefine work roles and conceptions. Because of the complexity created by changing demographics and technology, work roles in schools, like other occupational contexts, will require you and the school to constantly reexamine, redefine, and renew how work in a PLC is organized, conducted, and learned (Oplatka, Bargal, & Inbar, 2001; Stevenson, 2006).

Midcareer is a confusing concept because it does not necessarily mean the same as midlife. A traditional definition of midcareer is the period occurring "during one's work in an occupational (career) role after one feels established and has achieved perceived mastery and prior to the commencement of the disengagement process" (Hall, 1986, p. 127). For principals, this typically meant any time after the major tasks of the role are mastered; there is no set time (Parkay & Hall, 1992). Weindling (1992) found that between the third and fourth years, new British headteachers were "hitting their stride," ready to redefine their work in school change.

Due, however, to the rapid change in technology, knowledge explosion, and longer work life, a different understanding of midcareer has developed. Instead of the static progression from exploration—trial—mastery—exit (Hall, 1986), midcareer involves a series of "learning cycles" (Hall, 2002) or self-renewal (Oplatka et al., 2001). In this new model, individuals are continually learning and mastering new areas of work during mid and late career. For midcareer principals this may mean taking on challenges in different schools (charter, reconstituted, failing), new roles within the same school (consulting leader, mentor), or new conceptions of the role (e.g., leading professional development communities).

Unique Features of Midcareer Socialization

Instead of discussing the content, sources, stages, methods, and outcomes of socialization, as we have done in the discussions of assistant principal and principal socialization, we will identify several unique features of midcareer socialization before discussing methods that midcareer principals can use in becoming innovative principals in a learning community. These features are identified in the literature on midcareer socialization, most notably in the work of Hall (1980, 1986, 2002).

First, midcareer socialization tends to have fewer institutionalized status passages. Instead of university graduation and administrative licensure as formal events that recognize the passage to a new role, midcareer socialization involves more subtle changes. For example, recognition by the principal of gradual demographic changes in the school may initiate a different way of conceptualizing the principal's role in integrating diverse populations in the school and creating a learning community where all students learn. No formal ceremony is likely to acknowledge this change. However, the change is no less important.

Second, the socialization process at midcareer tends to emphasize individual rather than collective methods. Although the district may provide formal training in new methods for midcareer principals, for example, ESL training, it is more likely that role conception changes will occur by the individual principal's efforts to learn more about linguistic differences. This does not mean that districts have no role to play in midcareer socialization to more innovative role conceptions. Rather, individual efforts tend to be more likely at this stage. Veteran principals who strive to be innovative use peer mentoring; conversations with colleagues, university faculty, and teachers; and a variety of other individual methods.

Third, the sources of socialization tend to be different at midcareer than at the beginning of the career. Peers, family members, and friends take on a more pronounced role in influencing midcareer changes. Rather than more experienced principals being the source of socialization, peers at similar career stages—both inside and outside education—may be more influential. Furthermore, because family and life stages become more important, family members have an increasing influence on the socialization process to new role conceptions. This can work toward either custodial or innovative outcomes. If family members believe that the redefined role conception takes away from family obligations, they may try to discourage the change. However, if family members see the principal as frustrated in the role, they may encourage innovations that would bring excitement and challenge to the role.

Fourth, midcareer socialization involves a heightened awareness of longer-term dimensions of career effectiveness. Various models of adult and teacher development point to the move from concerns with survival and mastery to concerns of effectiveness and impact (Fuller, 1969). In midcareer, after the initial tasks of the role are mastered, principals should focus more on effectiveness. Questions of whether or not they are having an impact on the lives of students and the work of teachers should become more critical. Thus, the outcomes of midcareer socialization are not just redefining the role but doing so in a way that enables the principal to have an impact on learning for students, families, teachers, and the larger community. As mentioned before, this may involve taking on new role or role conceptions that are viewed as impacting greater student learning.

Fifth, midcareer socialization may involve more of the process of undoing earlier career socialization and separating from an old role. Frequently, midcareer principals who are committed to innovation realize that the images they developed earlier in their careers must be abandoned in order to view their roles differently. For example, the traditional image of the role of teacher as deficient that many principals acquired early in their careers must be undone in order to think about a conception of supervisor that affirms teachers' voice and expertise and focuses on building a PLC. Abandoning a safe image of the role is, in many respects, much more difficult than acquiring a new image at the beginning of the career because it means moving from an image of oneself as master to one of novice. As Hall (2002) explains, this moving back to the novice or exploration stage may occur multiple times in mid and late career.

Sixth, one of the major methods of midcareer socialization is exploration (Hall, 1986). Exploration is necessary to identify what options are available to redefine a role. Sometimes this means trying on new images of the role to determine whether or not they fit the context and the individual. Exploration does not mean abandoning everything that one has learned, but rather it frequently involves a more incremental process of determining whether a new image fits with a previous image. Exploration, then, can occur multiple times during midcareer. Learning in midcareer becomes a process of self-renewal. Oplatka and colleagues (2001) identified five elements of this self-renewal process.

- internal reflection,
- reframing of existing perspectives,
- searching for new opportunities and tasks,
- enthusiasm and replenishing of internal energy,
- professional updating through learning. (p. 79)

Learning to Be an Innovative Principal at Midcareer

We have emphasized that much of the socialization at midcareer is individual rather than collective. You can use a variety of methods at the midcareer stage to become an innovative principal who develops the kinds of role conceptions we discussed earlier in this book to enrich a PLC.

In order to become an innovative principal who emphasizes learning community, it is important to recognize that your learning does not end with mastery of the initial tasks of the principalship. The context in which your school is located, the technology of teaching and learning, and a host of other factors require constant learning. Finding ways to keep abreast of the latest research on student learning differences, on effective teaching practices, on changes in your school and community, and on leadership will help you to become the kind of principal who not only is a learner but also facilitates the learning community. As we have mentioned several times, your example as a learner encourages teachers, students, parents, and others to view themselves as learners and to see the school as a learning community.

In order to be an innovative midcareer principal as a culture builder, the principal will need to acknowledge how the external environment of schools have changed and are constantly changing. As environmental changes occur, it will be necessary for veteran principals to help faculty and parents rethink the school's cultural norms and beliefs. Inviting a colleague either inside education or outside to help inventory the school culture can be a valuable socialization method for learning and redefining this critical leadership role and keeping the PLC rich and effective.

Mentors can also be useful in helping to learn new ways to conceive of the role of principal as advocate that recognizes the value of diversity. Changing demographics and more heterogeneous communities require veteran principals to learn new ways to respond to diversity. Mentoring by ethnic community leaders, conversations with ministers from ethnic churches, travel, and reading literature that describes the experiences of diverse populations broaden the veteran principal's sense of the nature and value of diversity and the role of advocate.

Becoming an innovative principal as mentor at midcareer can involve a new resource—peer mentoring. Although new principals certainly can use their peers as a method of socialization, peer mentoring is an invaluable resource for midcareer colleagues who have developed a wealth of expertise. In exploring more innovative role conceptions, veteran principals can use conversations and reflections with peers. Sharing, reflecting, and collaborating regarding the change and learning processes are important elements of peer mentoring (Crow & Matthews, 1998). This peer mentoring experience can be an excellent source for developing new conceptions of mentoring that contribute to the creation and enrichment of the learning community in the school. In addition to peers within education, midcareer principals may find mentors from outside education to be a rich source for their socialization.

Redefining the role of principal as supervisor can occur as the veteran principal engages in discussions with university professors, administrative colleagues, and teachers on the latest research on teaching and learning and on new innovative strategies for working with teachers to improve instruction for all students and to create a PLC. More and more universities are expanding their roles beyond preservice to assist administrators and teachers in improving teaching and learning through, for example, professional development schools. The veteran principal's concern for long-term effectiveness allows the principal to move beyond simple mastery to work with teachers in ways that facilitate peer supervision.

As demographic and technological changes continue to occur, veteran principals will need to think in new ways about how leadership is enacted and how leaders influence changing visions within the school. New research on distributed leadership (Elmore, 2000), encourages the need for veteran principals to conceive of their roles in new ways. Keeping up with the new leadership literature and having conversations with colleagues on new ways to conceive of the leadership role in a learning community are excellent methods for learning to be an innovative veteran school leader.

At midcareer, most principals have mastered managerial tasks. However, rather than use the same old, tried and true managerial methods, an innovative school leader needs to watch for more efficient managerial techniques that will permit more time for leadership activities. Conversations with managers in other fields may provide information regarding these new techniques.

With more complex environmental settings and demands, the veteran principal must redefine the political role. Finding mentors and other administrators who are sensitive to these societal changes can provide socialization methods for learning this redefinition. Mentors that work outside school or district organizations, for example, doctors with interns, ministers, and directors of nonprofit agencies, can be valuable resources in learning innovative ways to respond to external communities. For midcareer principals, expanding the political role to take on responsibilities in larger societal and community arenas is one way to redefine the role in order to have significant impact on the learning community.

Conclusion

The importance of learning has been foundational throughout this book, and your own learning to become an innovative principal is not something to leave to chance. Beth, the principal in the opening vignette, found that her relationship with her mentor, Debbie, was a valuable tool to help her intentionally reflect on her learning. Hopefully, you are already developing resources in your university program and your relationships with peers that will serve as tools for your own development as an innovative principal.

To aid you in this development, we have described the nature, sources, stages, methods, and outcomes of socialization for new principals and assistant principals. These are presented in this book to help you intentionally reflect on and enrich your own development in order to lead a PLC.

We also have emphasized that learning to become an innovative principal or assistant principal is not a one-time event but a career-long endeavor. In Chapter 1, we stressed that one of the features of work roles in postindustrial society is the ongoing redefining of the role. In the final chapter we present some considerations for the future of the role. Just as the principalship is changing to meet postindustrial realities, you can expect that new realities will confront you as you continue in the role. Becoming a lifelong learner who can proactively respond to these future realities is essential to creating and maintaining learning communities that ensure the learning of all students.

Activities

SELF-REFLECTION ACTIVITY

1. Reflect on your prior work experience. In what ways does it influence your current learning to be a principal or assistant principal? For example, what are you likely to emphasize? What tools or styles of learning are you likely to use?

How do your family and friends influence your socialization?

2. Refer to your state's education department's Web site on administrative licensure. What are the requirements for initial license and subsequent endorsements?

PEER REFLECTION ACTIVITIES

1. With a colleague, interview an assistant principal in her or his second year. What were the sources of socialization in this assistant principal's school? Who influenced her or his learning, and what socialization methods were used?
2. Consider principals with whom you have worked. How would you characterize the outcome of their socialization using Schein's (1971) three orientations of custodial, content innovation, and role innovation? What is your evidence for this characterization?

COURSE ACTIVITIES

1. Invite a panel of new principals to class. Interview them in terms of what they had to learn in their first few days/weeks on the job. How did they learn these things? Organize your questions and analysis in terms of the three areas of work: knowledge/skills, adjustment to the work environment, and learning values.
2. Collect job descriptions for a variety of principal vacancies. Analyze the job content. What kinds of learning would be necessary? Brainstorm methods for learning these things.
3. As a class, interview a mid or late career principal who has the reputation of being innovative. Ask her/him what things were important in being able to take on new ideas and responsibilities of school leadership.

Websites

SEDL Web site on PLCs
www.sedl.org/pubs/change34/welcome.html

The Principal's Partnership
www.principalspartnership.com/

Annenberg Institute for School Reform
www.annenberginstitute.org/

Looking to the Future as a Principal

Angela sat at her office desk as the new principal of the new Barack Obama K-8 School. The teachers and students would arrive in one week. She was excited and terrified! She felt good about her university training and the assistant principal experience she had at the middle school across the valley. Elaine, her mentor and the principal of the middle school where she had served as assistant principal, had given her many opportunities to develop skills in working with students, teachers, parents, and the larger community. The superintendent and the board had expressed enormous support for her and obviously had great expectations.

One of Angela's major concerns was how to instill a sense of professional learning community (PLC) in the school and a strong school–community connection. The community was in need of a new identity, and she hoped that the school could become a community center. The school was located in a California working-class area that had been on an economic roller coaster. Although never an affluent community, it had once been thriving because of local industry. But, most of those industries had moved to foreign countries. Then a few new, smaller industries had moved in and revitalized the area only to see economic problems, forced massive layoffs, and closings. Angela knew that parents, more than ever, had higher expectations for the school that centered around preparing their children for challenging but uncertain futures.

The new school was a K—8 plan developed after the district decided to focus on smaller schools and more parental involvement in middle-level education. No longer would grades 6–8 be bused to the middle school across the valley. Instead, they would remain in their neighborhood school so that parents would be closer and hopefully more involved in their children's education.

The building that housed the new Obama K—8 School was not new. It had been used as the Mountain Valley Elementary School for the last four decades. The board of education had decided to remodel, rename, and revitalize the school to fit the new concept of a K—8 structure.

It would be a school that housed students from kindergarten through eighth grade, keeping families together longer and promoting more parental involvement with their children's education. Students could remain in their neighborhood school with a seamless transition between their primary, intermediate, and middle-grade programs. Some grades would also be combined: third and fourth grades and fifth and sixth grades would stay together with the same teacher, with younger students being tutored by older students. High-achieving, intermediate students would have access to advanced courses such as algebra and science. With this structure, teachers and parents could strengthen their connections. The school board and district administrators were hoping that the upper-level elementary and middle-level students would be less inclined to skip school, drop out, and engage in risky social behaviors.

Although Angela felt support, she also definitely felt pressure because she knew that the teachers, board members, and community would be looking over her shoulder to see if this K—8 education concept really worked and whether this new principal could succeed in developing community pride in the school. The district administrators had given Angela a six-month leave from her previous assistant principal position in the middle school so that she could get the school up and running.

To make the school smaller, a part of the original attendance area that was bused into the school was assigned to another elementary school. Many students and teachers had to move, leaving a smaller school that consisted of only those living in the neighborhood. Teachers from the previous elementary school had been given a choice to stay in the new K—8 school or transfer to another, more traditional elementary school. With the remaining faculty, Angela had the opportunity to realign teacher assignments according to their strengths and interests. She also had the opportunity to select new teachers to help balance out particular needs.

As Angela pondered the year that lay ahead, she considered what skills she would need to define her role in ways, perhaps, that were very different from what her mentor or others who had prepared her had assumed. She couldn't help think what a year from now would look like. How would the year define her role as principal? How different would it be from her original conceptualization of the role? How would other administrators consider her new role? How would the community accept her attempt to develop this K—8 school? Angela sighed, knowing that there were a lot of unanswered questions that were swirling in her mind. Nevertheless, she was excited to think of the great potential that this new school could bring to this community.

INTRODUCTION

In this book, we have identified eight role conceptions of the principalship. Our attempt has been to identify innovative ways to imagine the principalship. One of our arguments throughout this book has been the importance of understanding and redefining the role. Any attempt to identify the role conceptions of the principalship suffers from one major difficulty. The society in which schools exist and the schools themselves are in a state of constant change. It is not surprising, then, that the role of principals also must change. In this concluding chapter, we speculate about how the principalship might change in the coming years. Your experience as an assistant principal or principal also will change as you progress through your career.

In this chapter, we will identify several possible scenarios for the future of the principalship. We do not claim that the scenarios are accurate descriptions of the future. We hope, however, that these scenarios provide an opportunity to reflect on your future as an assistant principal or principal.

SOCIETAL TRENDS

As Angela contemplated her new role in the opening vignette, you will also see societal trends that will require several changes that will affect schools, principals, and assistant principals. One of the most obvious trends that schools and their leaders are experiencing and will continue to experience is changing demographics. The students of the schools of the future will not be like the students of the 1950s or even the 1990s, which were the times when much of the current curricula were developed and buildings were built. Principals, assistant principals, and teachers must recognize that many of the programs that were established to meet the needs of former students will no longer work to meet the changing demographics and technological needs of future students.

These societal trends also suggest that education will be even more important in the future. Knowledge will be the coin of the realm (Marx, 2000). But education in the future may take forms that are very different from what we expect now. Instead of the school building being the only or even primary place for creating knowledge, the Internet and other technologies will enable students and adults to access information, act on the information, and solve problems that did not exist several years ago.

Social justice, instead of being a minor interest of the school, will be a major focus. The changing demographics, the gap between the rich and the poor, and the millennial generation's concern with solving problems of injustice will influence responsibilities for educators. Instead of the insulated form of schools of the past, schools now and in the future must become intimately connected with their neighborhoods and with the larger societies in which injustices thrive.

At the time this book went to press, the *No Child Left Behind* (NCLB) Act was being reconsidered by Congress. A new administration and a different political control of Congress brought in new ideas as to how this legislation should work in schools, including the name itself. There was promise of change to NCLB, but one area that we predict will not likely change is the current concern with accountability. As Angela contemplated her role as principal, she knew that there would be a demand that her school and others would need to demonstrate improvement rather than simply assume their continued existence. Although there is much to criticize in the current emphasis on accountability and standardization, the societal expectation that schools improve and that they demonstrate this improvement is not likely to disappear in the future.

Only someone who has lived on a desert island for the last twenty years would ignore the role of technology in our society and education. Technology will become an even more important resource for schools to use in improving learning and opening access to all students. For this to occur, the digital gap between the rich and the poor must be bridged. Schools are one of the most likely places for this to occur.

Contemporary and future schools must see their role as knowledge creation, not just information acquisition. This means that principals and teachers must create learning communities that build understanding and learning capacity. These communities, as we have described in this book, must be cultures of inquiry where teaching and learning practices are observed, critiqued, and challenged, where action research is a consistent pattern rather than a special occurrence, and where all participants—students, teachers, administrators, parents—are lifelong learners.

The societal trends also suggest major ethical choices for students and the schools that will serve them in the future. Access to technology, medical advances, income disparities, disenfranchisement of large segments of the population, and the disillusionment of segments of the society present major ethical dilemmas from which schools are not immune. Not only will these become topics for the curriculum, but they will also become challenges for the school to address.

The importance of education, especially from the social, political, and economic points of view, increases the competition for controlling and providing that education. Public schools no longer have a monopoly on providing education. Even within school districts, the emergence of charter schools, private schools, and home schooling has increased competition among schools, especially in recruiting and retaining teachers and students.

Another social trend has been the migration from rural America to urban. For example, in 1900, America comprised five thousand more communities than in the year 2000 (Glass, 2008). This required a number of schools to be closed in some areas and built in other areas. Often those urban areas did not have the money to build new schools, so overcrowding of already poor school buildings occurred. This trend of the U.S. population from farms and ranches to cities continues into the twenty-first century with the increasing impact on urban schools.

Another phenomenon occurred with urbanization. According to Glass (2008), in rural societies more children meant a higher living standard because they helped make the farms and ranches productive. However, in urban societies, more children often meant a lower living standard because of the economic stress associated with raising children. Children then became more of a burden on the family and often on society. To make it financially, many of these families had to have two incomes, thus limiting parents' supervision of their children after school hours and not allowing parents' time to help with homework and schooling. The stresses of family life also led to more divorces and fewer two-parent families, putting yet more stress on children and schooling. Many schools have responded by developing before- and after-school programs, pre-kindergarten programs, and so on. Likewise, community agencies such as health care and counseling centers have become part of the school outreach program. Often these agencies have offices and clinics located inside the school building. Many of these schools have sought to develop closer ties to the communities they serve, not unlike the example given in the opening vignette. These trends reinforce the need for interprofessional practice, where teachers are working alongside health professionals, social workers, and other experts to meet the needs of the whole student.

These societal trends and others that cannot yet be identified have critical implications for the changing role of principals and assistant principals. First, these trends suggest the importance of the internal environment in which principals and assistant principals do their jobs. The major implication of these trends for this internal role is the importance of building a PLC that promotes the learning of all students. No longer can educators look only at averages and percentages. For example, high school educators cannot be proud that 83 percent of their students graduated. Instead they must look at the 17 percent who did not and reflect on what is needed to get all students to complete high school successfully. Likewise, elementary educators can no longer be satisfied that 60 percent of their students are reading at grade level. All educators everywhere must look at individuals and how each student is succeeding or failing. As we suggested in earlier chapters, the principal's role as learner is fundamental for creating innovative

Professional Dilemma 13.1

In a large school district that included both inner-city and suburban schools, the assistant principals of color traditionally were placed in the most ethnically diverse schools. As role models for many students of color, these assistant principals served well in the urban schools. However, the suburban schools often had no administrators of color, limiting their perspective to mostly Caucasian models. Should the ethnicity of administrators be considered in their placement at schools?

leadership for the future. The principal's roles as learner, culture builder, advocate, mentor, and supervisor are critical in creating an environment where knowledge is created, where both adults and students have access, and where the expertise for teaching and learning is distributed.

Second, the roles of principals and assistant principals have community implications as was illustrated in the opening vignette. No longer can administrative roles be focused solely on what happens inside the walls of the school. Principals and assistant principals have fundamental responsibilities for communicating the importance of social justice, implementing programs and structures that give voice to the disenfranchised, and monitoring school activities to make sure that social justice initiatives become reality. However, these school leaders have an even more fundamental responsibility to facilitate the sensitivity and commitment of school constituencies toward these social justice initiatives. This community role of principals and assistant principals also necessitates that bridges with external populations be built in the years to come. The day of buffering as the primary strategy for dealing with external communities is over.

Third, the societal trends require a new kind of leadership. This leadership, rather than being based on the positional authority of one person, resides in the distributed leadership of the whole school. Facilitating the leadership of both internal and external communities becomes critical to responding to the societal trends. In addition, this leadership is an ever-evolving and dynamic role. In postindustrial society, leadership roles as well as all other roles must be redefined constantly based on changing environments. Finding a comfortable style and sticking with it for your career is neither effective nor possible in schools of tomorrow.

FUTURE SCENARIOS FOR THE PRINCIPALSHIP AND SCHOOLS

The Organization for Education Cooperation and Development (OECD), an international forum of the governments of thirty democracies, has identified six scenarios for the future of schools (OECD, 2001). These scenarios present intriguing implications for the future of the principal's role, which you should consider as you define and ultimately redefine your role as a principal or assistant principal.

The first scenario, "Back to the Future Bureaucratic Systems," views the future of schools as essentially business as usual in which the traditional role of the principalship remains. The leadership role of the principal would be based on the influence and actions of one person and involve a top-down administrative approach. The focus would be on maintaining the status quo in schools. A managerial orientation would consume the attention of principals and assistant principals. Obviously, from the perspective taken in this book, we do not believe that this is likely to be a viable alternative. Maintaining the status quo in the face of the societal trends we have identified is neither likely nor effective.

The second OECD scenario, "Schools as Focused Learning Organizations," would focus on creating learning communities that take seriously the demands of the global, knowledge society and the need for working conditions for teachers that emphasize experimentation, diversity, and innovation. The principal's role in this scenario would look much like what we have described in this textbook, in which the principal is the lead learner of the school and responsible for directly and indirectly creating the type of community in which learning for all students, teachers, administrators, and parents is realized.

A third scenario, "Schools as Core Social Centres," recognizes that learning is an effort that goes beyond the work of the single school organization and must include intergenerational, interprofessional, and life-long conditions. The principal's role in this scenario becomes focused not only on the internal conditions of the school but on the external connections with social service, mental health, and health organizations and community agencies. This enlarged role still involves seeing the principal as a learner but expands the learning sphere of the principal's work.

These second and third scenarios have other interesting implications for the role of principal. First, several writers argue for distributed leadership in schools (Elmore, 2000; Spillane, Halverson, & Diamond, 2001). Rather than seeing the principal as the only leader, this approach argues for multiple leadership roles that can be fulfilled by a variety of individuals. Second, this scenario could be seen as balancing internal and external complexities (Crow, Hausman, & Scribner, 2002). Principals would be responsible internally for facilitating the development of a PLC committed to the learning of all students. Externally, principals' primary role would involve building bridges for accountability, markets, and civic capacity. In this view, principals are also not seen as the sole leaders but rather as the facilitators of leadership that balance external and internal complexity. Schools of the future, like schools of the present, involve the balance of continuity and change. Thomas Friedman (1999), in his work on globalization titled *The Lexus and the Olive Tree*, suggested that we live in an age of continuity and change. This is an age in which modern technology has changed our patterns of living and interacting. However, it is also an age where we yearn for stability, continuity, and home. Traditionally, the school has been the center of the community. In postindustrial society, the question of whether the school can be both a place of technological advancement and a community center is certainly an important issue for debate. However, the reality for principals and assistant principals of balancing continuity and change is more than a topic for debate; it is a fundamental dilemma of the role.

The fourth scenario, "Extended Market Model," expands the market approaches regarding who provides education and how it is delivered. The use of charter schools, private schools, and systems such as vouchers, diminish or eliminate the need for government-sponsored or run schools. The principal's role becomes much more entrepreneurial, selling the school to various publics and using more corporate models of leadership. Obviously, from the discussion of this text, this is not a role that we find viable for increasing the instructional success of all students. While some of the market models may increase innovation, others may increase exclusion.

A fifth scenario, "Learning in Networks Replacing Schools," "imagines the disappearance of schools per se, replaced by learning networks operating within a highly developed 'network society.'" (OECD, 2008, p. 21). In this scenario, a varied system of formal, informal, and nonformal delivery models would replace traditional schools. The role of principal could disappear, although more systemic leadership would be needed to ensure that there are not significant learning gaps within the society.

The final scenario, "Teacher Exodus and System Meltdown," would occur when significant numbers of quality teachers, unattracted or demoralized by the working conditions of schools, leave and the system ceases to exist in any credible way. Obviously, the role of principal except for residing over the dismal remnants of a failed system would disappear.

The second and third scenarios, which we hope will describe schools of the future, involve a complex role for the principal, which can be seen in terms of three metaphors. Murphy (2002) identified these three metaphors as moral steward, educator, and community builder. The moral-steward metaphor suggests that the role of principal should be focused on values and value judgments. Principals and assistant principals, as we have argued, have a social-justice role to play. This moral-steward role involves a concern with defining purpose and vision. However, in this role conception, vision is a means, not an end. The metaphor of educator means that the principal's role will be based in the culture of teaching. As we discussed in Chapter 2, teaching is the historical basis for the principal role. In Murphy's formulation, the principalship would return to its roots. The principal as educator would move from leadership as management to leadership as learning. Finally, the metaphor of community building focuses the principal role on facilitating access and voice for parents and community members. In addition, this metaphor calls attention to the need for principals to build communities of learning and personalized learning environments for all students.

Conclusion

Just as Angela, the new principal at Barack Obama K—8 School in the opening vignette, contemplated the future, you are standing at that threshold now. This is an exciting time to become an assistant principal or principal. The societal trends and possible scenarios previously identified make it clear that things will not be as they have been for school leaders. Over the next several years you will see fundamental changes in the way schooling is provided, in the way teaching is enacted, in the way learning occurs, and in the way school leadership is conceived.

Rather than being a passive spectator watching these changes occur around you, you can and should play an active role in helping to shape the way schools and school leaders respond to the societal trends. Learning to be an innovative principal or assistant principal for the next generation requires you to be an active participant in this process. Principals and assistant principals must not play the same roles they have played in the past. The future of our students—and the larger global society—depends on your active participation.

Activities

SELF-REFLECTION ACTIVITIES

1. Visualize a school without a principal. What would it look like in terms of leadership?
2. Reflect on each of the three forms of the final scenario. Which appeals to you and why?

PEER REFLECTION ACTIVITIES

1. Reflect on the K—8 school setting in the opening vignette. What would be its advantages and disadvantages?

2. Reflect on the issues regarding balancing continuity and change in schools. What does the principal's role become in the balancing process?

COURSE ACTIVITIES

1. Debate the three forms of the final scenario.
2. Divide the class into three groups. Assign each group one of Murphy's (2002) three metaphors: moral steward, educator, and community builder. Have each group elaborate on what these might mean for how principals enact their roles.

REFERENCES

Akerlund, P. M. (1988). *The socialization of first-year principals and vice-principals.* Unpublished doctoral dissertation, Seattle University.

Alfred, M. V. (2004). Immigration as a context for learning: What do we know about immigrant students in adult education? In E. E. Clover (Ed.), *Proceedings of the joint international conference of the 45th Annual Adult Education Research Conference and the Canadian Association for the study of Adult Education* (pp. 13–18). Victoria, Canada: University of Victoria.

Anderson, B., MacDonald, D. S., et al. (2004). Can measurement of results help improve the performance of schools? *Phi Delta Kappan, 85*(10), 735–739.

Anderson, J. R. (2005). *Cognitive psychology and its implications* (6th ed.). New York: Freeman.

Anderson, K. (2004). The nature of teacher leadership in schools as reciprocal influences between teacher leaders and principals. *School Effectiveness and School Improvement, 15*(1), 97–113.

Anderson, R. E., & Dexter, S. (2005). School technology leadership: An empirical investigation of prevalence and effect. *Educational Administration Quarterly, 41*(1), 49–82.

Apple, M. W. (2004). *Ideology and curriculum* (3rd ed.). New York: Routledge.

Apple, M. W., & Beane, J. A. (Eds.). (1995). *Democratic schools.* Alexandria, VA: Association for Supervision and Curriculum Development.

Archer, J. (2004). Tackling an impossible job. *Education Week, 24*(3) (September 15, 2004), S3–S6.

Arendt, H. (1958). *The human condition.* Chicago: University of Chicago Press.

Argyris, C., & Schon, D. A. (1974). *Theory in practice: Increasing professional effectiveness.* San Francisco, CA: Jossey-Bass.

Bailey, F., & Pransky, K. (2005). Are "Other people's children" constructivist learners too? *Theory into Practice, 44*(1), 19–26.

Banks, J. A. (1992). Multicultural education: For freedom's sake. *Educational Leadership, 49*(4), 32–36.

Banks, J. A. (1994). *Multiethnic education* (3rd ed.). Boston, MA: Allyn & Bacon.

Banks, J. A. (1999). *An introduction to multicultural education* (2nd ed.). Boston, MA: Allyn & Bacon.

Barkley, S. G. (2005). *Quality teaching in a culture of coaching.* Lanham, MD: Scarecrow Education.

Barnard, C. (1948). *Organizations and management.* Cambridge, MA: Harvard University Press.

Barth, R. S. (1990). *Improving schools from within: Teachers, parents, and principals can make a difference.* San Franciso, CA: Jossey-Bass.

Barth, R. S. (2006). Improving relationships inside the schoolhouse. *Educational Leadership, 63*(6), 8–13.

Beach, D., & Reinhartz, J. (2000). *Supervisory leadership: Focus on instruction.* Boston, MA: Allyn & Bacon.

Beck, L. G., & Murphy, J. (1993). *Understanding the principalship: Metaphorical Themes, 1920s–1990s.* New York: Teachers College Press.

Bell, C., & Chase, S. (1993). The underrepresentation of women in school leadership. In C. Marshall (Ed.), *The new politics of race and gender* (pp. 141–154). Washington, DC: Falmer Press.

Bell, D. (1973). *The coming of post-industrial society.* New York: Basic Books.

Bellah, R. N., Madsen, R., Sullivan, W., Swidler, A., & Tipton, S. (1985). *Habits of the heart: Individualism and commitment in America.* New York: Harper & Row.

Beyer, B., Engelking, J., & Boshee, M. (1997). *Special and compensatory programs: The administrator's role.* Lancaster, MI: Technomic Publishing.

Bills, D. B. (2004). *The sociology of education and work.* Malden, MA: Blackwell.

Blackmore, J. (1991). *Images of educational administration.* Study Guide 3. Geelong, Australia: Deakin University Press.

Blake, R. R., & Mouton, J. S. (1978). *The new managerial grid.* Houston, TX: Gulf Press.

Blank, M. A., Kershaw, C., & Sparks, B. S. (1999). How to supervise the marginal teacher. *NASSP Tips for Principals,* (January 1999), 2–5.

Blankstein, A. M. (2004). *Failure is not an option: Six principles that guide student achievement in high-performing schools.* Thousand Oaks, CA: Corwin Press.

Blase, J. J. (1989). The micropolitics of the school: The everyday political orientation of teachers toward open school principals. *Educational Administration Quarterly, 25*(4), 377–407.

Blase, J. J. (1991). The micropolitical orientation of teachers toward closed school principals. *Education and Urban Society, 23*(4), 356–378.

Blase, J., & Blase, J. (1994). *Empowering teachers: What successful principals do.* Thousand Oaks, CA: Corwin Press.

Blase, J., & Blase, J. (1998). *Handbook of instructional leadership: How really good principals promote teaching and learning.* Thousand Oaks, CA: Corwin Press.

Blase, J., & Blase, J. (2004). *Handbook of instructional leadership: How successful principals promote teaching and learning* (2nd ed.). Thousand Oaks, CA: Corwin Press.

Blase, J., Blase, J., Anderson, G., & Dungan, S. (1995). *Democratic principals in action: Eight pioneers.* Thousand Oaks, CA: Corwin Press.

Blase, J., & Kirby, P. C. (2000). *Bringing out the best in teachers: What effective principals do* (2nd ed.). Thousand Oaks, CA: Corwin Press.

Blenkinsopp, J., & Zdunczyk, K. (2005). Making sense of mistakes in managerial careers. *Career Development International, 10*(5), 359–374.

Block, P. (1987). *The empowered manager.* San Francisco, CA: Jossey-Bass.

Block, P. (1993). Stewardship: Choosing service over self-interest. San Francisco: Berrett-Koehler Publishers.

Brass, D. J. (1984). Being in the Right Place: A Structural Analysis of Individual Influence in an Organization. *Administrative Science Quarterly, 29*(4), 518–539.

Bolman, L. G., & Deal, T. E. (1991). *Reframing organizations.* San Francisco, CA: Jossey-Bass.

Bolman, L. G., & Deal, T. E. (2003). *Reframing organizations: Artistry, choice, and leadership* (3rd ed.). San Francisco, CA: Jossey-Bass.

Bolman, L. G., & Deal, T. E. (2008). *Reframing organizations: Artistry, choice, and leadership* (4th ed.). San Francisco, CA: Jossey-Bass.

Borko, H. (2004). Professional development and teacher learning: Mapping the terrain. *Educational Researcher, 33*(8), 3–15.

Bower, M. (1996). *Will to manage*. New York: McGraw-Hill.

Bowers, G. R., & Eberhart, N. (1988). Mentoring and the entry year program. *Theory into Practice, 27*(3), 226–230.

Boyd, D., Grossman, P., Lankford, H., Loeb, S., & Wycloff, J. (2007). *Who leaves? Teacher attrition and student achievement*. New York: Teacher Pathway Project.

Boyd, D., Lankford, H., Loeb, S., & Wyckoff, J. (2005). Explaining the short careers of high achieving teachers in schools with low performance. *American Economic Review, 95*(2), 166–171.

Bridges, E. M. (1986). *The incompetent teacher*. Philadelphia: Falmer Press.

Bridgman, A. (1986, February 19). Better elementary leaders called for. *Education Week*.

Brighton, C. M. (1999). Keeping good teachers: Lessons from novices. In M. Scherer (Ed.), *A better beginning: Supporting and mentoring new teachers* (pp. 197–201). Alexandria, VA: Association for Supervision and Curriculum Development.

Brookfield, S. (1986). *Understanding and facilitating adult learning*. San Francisco, CA: Jossey-Bass.

Browne-Ferrigno, T. (2003). Becoming a principal: Role conception, initial socialization, role identity transformation, purposeful engagement. *Educational Administration Quarterly, 39*(4), 468–503.

Browne-Ferrigno, T., & Muth, R. (2004). Leadership mentoring in clinical practice: Role socialization, professional development, and capacity building. *Educational Administration Quarterly, 40*(4), 468–494.

Brubacher, J. S. (1966). *A history of the problems of education*. New York: McGraw-Hill.

Bryk, A., & Schneider, B. (2002). *Trust in schools: A core resource for improvement*. New York: Russell Sage Foundation.

Bryk, A., & Schneider, B. (2003). Trust in schools: A core resource for school reform. *Educational Leadership, 60*(6), 40–50.

Bryk, A., Camburn, E., & Louis, K. S. (1999). Professional community in Chicago elementary schools: Facilitating factors and organizational consequences. *Educational Administration Quarterly, 35*(Suppl.), 751–781.

Bryk, A., Sebring, P., Kerbow, D., Rollow, S., & Easton, J. (1998). *Charting chicago school reform*. Boulder, CO: Westview Press.

Bulach, C., Bothe, D., & Michael, P. (1999, April 19–23). *Supervisory behaviors that affect school climate*. Paper presented at the American Educational Research Association, Montreal, Canada.

Burden, L., & Whitt, R. L. (1973). *The community school principal: New horizons*. Midland, MI: Pendell.

Burnett, G. (1995). Alternatives to ability grouping: Still unanswered questions. *ERIC Clearinghouse on Urban Education ED390947* (111).

Burns, J. M. (1978). *Leadership*. New York: Harper & Row.

Cabrera, R., & Stout, K. (1989). Helpful hints for first-year principals. *Principal, 68*, 22–24.

Callahan, R. (1962). *Education and the cult of efficiency: A study of the social forces that have shaped the administration of the public schools*. Chicago: University of Chicago Press.

Callister, R. B., Kramer, M. W., & Turban, D. B. (1999). Feedback seeking following career transitions. *Academy of Management Journal, 42*(4), 429–438.

Campbell, R. F., Fleming, R., Newell, L. J., & Bennion, J. W. (1987). *A history of thought and *practice in educational administration.* New York: Teachers College Press.

Canales, P., & Stark, S. L. (2004). Professional development models: Impact on school leadership competencies as identified by superintendents in education service center, Region 20, Texas. *NCPEA Education Leadership Review, 5*(2), 37–45.

Caplow, T. (1954). *The sociology of work.* New York: McGraw-Hill.

Carlson, R. O. (1972). *School superintendents: Careers and performance.* Columbus, OH: Charles E. Merrill.

Carter, K., & Richardson, V. (1989). A curriculum for an initial year of teaching program. *Elementary School Journal, 89,* 405–419.

Cheng, Y. C. (1993). Profiles of organizational culture and effective schools. *School Effectiveness and School Improvement, 4*(2), 85–110.

Cherniss, C., & Goleman, D. (Eds.). (2001). *The emotionally intelligent workplace.* San Francisco, CA: Jossey-Bass.

Chrispeels, J. H., & Martin, K. J. (2002). Four school leadership teams define their roles within organizational and political structures to improve student learning. *School Effectiveness and School Improvement, 13*(3), 327–365.

Cibulka, J. G. (1999). Ideological lenses for interpreting political and economic changes affecting schooling. In J. Murphy & K. S. Louis (Eds.), *Handbook of research on educational administration* (2nd ed., pp. 163–182). San Francisco, CA: Jossey-Bass.

Claudet, J. G., & Ellett, C. D. (1999). Conceptualization and measurement of supervision as a school organization climate construct. *Journal of Curriculum and Supervision, 14*(4), 318–351.

Cochran-Smith, M., & Lytle, S. L. (1992). *Inside/Outside: Teacher research and knowledge.* New York: Teachers College Press.

Coleman, J. S., Campbell, E., et al. (1966). *Equality of educational opportunity.* Washington, DC: U.S. Government Printing Office.

Copland, M. A. (2003). Leadership of inquiry: Building and sustaining capacity for school improvement. *Educational Evaluation and Policy Analysis, 25*(4), 375–395.

Covey, S. R. (1989). *The seven habits of highly effective people: Restoring the character ethic.* New York: Simon & Schuster.

Covey, S. (2004). The 8th habit. New York: Simon & Schuster.

Crehan, E. P., & Grimmett, P. P. (1989, March 27–31). *Teachers' perspective on dyadic supervisory interaction.* Paper presented at the American Educational Research Association, San Francisco, CA.

Creighton, T. B. (2005). *Leading from below the surface: A non-traditional approach to school leadership.* Thousand Oaks, CA: Corwin Press.

Creighton, T. R. (1997). *Teachers as leaders: Is the principal really needed?* Oklahoma City, OK: National Conference on Creating Quality School.

Crow, G. M. (1987). Career mobility of elementary school principals and conflict with the central office. *Urban Review, 19*(3), 139–150.

Crow, G. M. (1990). Central office influence on the principal's relationships with teachers. *Administrators Notebook, 34*(1), 1–4.

Crow, G. M. (1993). Reconceptualizing the school administrator's role: Socialization at mid-career. *School Effectiveness and School Improvement, 4*(2), 131–152.

Crow, G. M. (2006a). Democracy and educational work in an age of complexity. *UCEA Review, 48*(1), 1–5.

Crow, G. M. (2006b). Complexity and the beginning principal in the United States: Perspectives on socialization. *Journal of Educational Administration, 44*(4), 310–325.

Crow, G. M. (2007). The professional and organizational socialization of new English headteachers in school reform contexts. *Educational Management Administration, 35*(1), 51–71.

Crow, G. M. (2008, May 30). *The development of school leaders' professional identities: Challenges and implications for interprofessional practice.* Keynote presentation for Seminar Series: Research into professional identities: Theorizing social and institutional identities, at University of Aberdeen (Scotland), King's College, School of Education.

Crow, G. M., & Matthews, L. J. (1998). *Finding one's way: How mentoring can lead to dynamic leadership.* Thousand Oaks, CA: Corwin Press.

Crow, G. M., & Pounder, D. G. (2000). Teacher work groups: Context, design, and process. *Educational Administration Quarterly, 36*(2), 216–254.

Crow, G. M., & Pounders, M. L. (1994, October). *The symbolic nature of the administrative internship: Building a sense of occupational community.* Paper presented at the University Council for Educational Administration, Philadelphia.

Crow, G. M., & Pounders, M. L. (1995). *Organizational socialization of new urban principals: Variations of race and gender.* Paper presented at the American Educational Research Association, San Francisco, CA.

Crow, G. M., & Pounders, M. L. (1996, April). *The administrative internship: "Learning the ropes" of an occupational culture.* Paper presented

at the American Educational Research Association, New York.

Crow, G. M., & Slater, R. O. (1996). *Educating democracy: The role of systemic leadership.* Fairfax, VA: National Policy Board for Educational Administration.

Crow, G. M., Hausman, C. S., & Scribner, J. P. (2002). Reshaping the role of the school principal. In J. Murphy (Ed.), *The leadership challenge: Redefining leadership for the 21st century* (pp. 189–210). Chicago: National Society for the Study of Education.

Crow, G. M., Matthews, L. J., & McCleary, L. E. (1996). *Leadership: A relevant and realistic role for principals.* Princeton, NJ: Eye on Education.

Crowson, R. L. (1998). Community empowerment and the public schools: Can educational professionalism survive? *Peabody Journal of Education, 73*(1), 56–68.

Crowson, R. L. (2001). *Community development and school reform.* Oxford, England: Elsevier.

Crowson, R. L., & McPherson, R. B. (1987). The legacy of the theory movement: Learning from the new tradition. In J. Murphy & P. Hallinger (Eds.), *Approaches to administrative training in education* (pp. 45–66). Albany, NY: State University of New York Press.

Cuban, L. (1984). *How teachers taught. Constancy and change in American Classrooms 1890-1980.* New York, NY: Longman.

Cuban, L. (1988). Why do some reforms persist? *Educational Administration Quarterly, 24*(3), 329–335.

Cuban, L. (1990). Reforming again, again, and again. *Educational Researcher, 19*(1), 3–13.

Cubberley, E. P. (1909). *Changing conceptions of education.* Boston, MA: Houghton Mifflin.

Cubberley, E. P. (1916). *Public school administration.* Boston, MA: Houghton Mifflin.

Cubberley, E. P. (1923). *The principal and his school*. Boston, MA: Houghton Mifflin.

Culbertson, J. A. (1988). A century's quest for a knowledge base. In N. J. Boyan (Ed.), *Handbook of research on educational administration*. New York: Longmans.

Daft, R. L. (1999). *Leadership theory and practice*. Fort Worth, TX: Dryden Press.

Daft, R. L. (2006). *Leadership theory and practice*. Fort Worth, TX: The Dryden Press.

Daloz, L. A. (1983). Mentors: Teachers who make a difference. *Change, 5*(6), 24–27.

Dantley, M. E., & Tillman, L. C. (2006). Social justice and moral transformative leadership. In C. Marshall & M. Oliva (Eds.), *Leadership for social justice. Making revolutions in education* (pp.16–30). Boston, MA: Pearson.

Daresh, J. (2006). *Beginning the principalship: A practical guide for new leaders* (3rd ed.). Thousand Oaks, CA: Corwin Press.

Daresh, J. C., & Playko, M. A. (1993). *Leaders helping leaders: A practical guide to administrative mentoring*. New York: Scholastic.

Darling-Hammond, L. (1983). Teacher evaluation in the organizational context: A review of the literature. *Review of Educational Research, 53*(3), 285–328.

Darling-Hammond, L. (1996). The quiet revolution: Rethinking teacher development. *Educational Leadership, 53*(6), 4–10.

Darling-Hammond, L., & Bransford, J. (Eds.). (2005). *Preparing teachers for a changing world: What teachers should learn and be able to do*. San Francisco, CA: Jossey-Bass.

Darling-Hammond, L., Wise, A. E., & Klein, S. P. (1995). *A license to teach: Building a profession for 21st century schools*. Boulder, CO: Westview Press.

Davis, S. (1998). Superintendents' perspectives on the involuntary departure of public school principals: The most frequent reasons why principals lose their jobs. *Educational Administration Quarterly, 34*(1), 58–90.

Deal, T. E., & Kennedy, A. A. (1982). *Corporate cultures: The rites and rituals of corporate life*. Reading, MA: Addison-Wesley.

Deal, T. E., & Peterson, K. D. (1990). *The principal's role in shaping school culture*. Washington, DC: U.S. Department of Education.

Deal, T. E., & Peterson, K. D. (1999). *Shaping school culture: The heart of leadership*. San Francisco, CA: Jossey-Bass.

Deal, T. E., & Peterson, K. D. (2000). Eight roles of symbolic leaders. In M. Fullan (Ed.), *The Jossey-Bass reader on educational leadership* (pp. 202–214). San Francisco, CA: Jossey-Bass.

Deal, T. E., & Peterson, K. D. (2003). *Shaping school culture: The heart of leadership*. San Francisco, CA: Jossey-Bass.

Deal, T. E & Peterson, K. D (2009). *Shaping school cultures: Pitfalls, paradoxes, and promises* (2nd edition). San Francisco: Jossey-Bass

DeBevoise, W. (1984). Synthesis of research on the principal as instructional leader. *Educational Leadership, 41*(5), 14–20.

DeJong, D. H. (1990). *Friend or foe? Education and the American Indian*. Unpublished M.A. thesis, University of Arizona.

Delpit, L. (1996). *Other people's children: Cultural conflict in the classroom*. New York: The New Press.

Dembele, M. (1996). *Mentors and mentoring: Frames for action, ways of acting, and consequences for novice teachers' learning (Professional development)*. Ph.D. Dissertation, Michigan State University.

Dewey, J. (1900). *The school and society*. Chicago: The University of Chicago Press.

Dewey, J. (1958). *Experience and education*. New York: McMillan.

Dixon, N. M. (1997). The hallways of learning. *Organizational Dynamics, 25*(4), 23–34.

Doud, J. L., & Keller, E. P. (1998). The K-8 principal in 1998. *Principal, 78*(1), 5–6.

Douglas, H. R. (1932). *Organization and administration of secondary schools.* Boston, MA: Ginn & Co.

Downey, C., English, F., Frase, L., Poston, W., & Steffy, B. (2004). *The three-minute classroom walk-through: Changing school supervision practice one teacher at a time.* Thousand Oaks, CA: Corwin Press.

Doyle, W. (1988). *Learning to teach: Directions from the current research base.* Paper presented at the meeting of the Association of Teacher Educators, San Diego, CA.

Drake, T. L., & Roe, W. H. (1999). *The Principalship* (5th ed.). Upper Saddle River, NJ: Merrill.

Driscoll, M. E., & Kerchner, C. T. (1999). The implications of social capital for schools, communities, and cities: Educational administration as if a sense of place mattered. In J. Murphy & K. S. Louis (Eds.), *Handbook of research in educational administration* (pp. 385–404). San Francisco, CA: Jossey-Bass.

Duffy, F. M. (2003). *Courage, passion, and vision.* Lanham, MD: Scarecrow Press.

DuFour, R. (2004). What is a professional learning community? *Educational Leadership, 61*(8), 6–11.

DuFour, R., & Burnette, B. (2002). Pull out negativity by its roots. *Journal of Staff Development, 23*(3), 27–30.

DuFour, R., & Eaker, R. (1992). *Creating the new American school: A principal's guide to school improvement.* Bloomington, IN: National Educational Service.

DuFour, R., & Eaker, R. (1998). *Professional learning communities at work: Best practices for enhancing student achievement.* Bloomington, IN: National Educational Service.

DuFour, R., DuFour, R., & Eaker, R. (2008). *Revisiting professional learning communities.* Bloomington, IN: Solution Tree.

DuFour, R., DuFour, R., Eaker, R., & Many, T. (2006). *Learning by doing: A handbook for professional learning communities at work.* Bloomington, IN: Solution Tree.

DuFour, R., Eaker, R., & DuFour, R. (Eds.). (2005). *On common ground: The power of professional learning communities.* Bloomington, IN: Solution Tree.

Duke, D. (2008). Diagnosing school decline. *Phi Delta Kappan, 6*(30), 667–671.

Duke, D. L., Isaacson, N. S., Sagor, R., & Schmuck, P. A. (1984). *Transition to leadership: An investigation of the first year of the principal* (Transition to Leadership Project). Portland, OR: Lewis and Clark College.

Dupper, D. R., & Meyer-Adams, N. (2002). Low-level violence: A neglected aspect of school culture. *Urban Education, 37*(3), 350–364.

Dwyer, D., Barnett, B., & Lee, G. (1987). The school principal: Scapegoat or the last great hope? In L. Sheive & M. Schoenheit (Eds.), *Leadership: Examining the elusive* (pp. 30–46). Alexandria, VA: Association and Supervision and Curriculum Development.

Ebmeier, H. (1999). The impact of peer and principal collaborative supervision on teachers' trust, commitment, desire for collaboration, and efficacy. *Journal of Curriculum and Supervision, 14*(4), 351–378.

Edmunds, R. (1979). Effective schools for the urban poor. *Educational Leadership, 37*(12), 15–24.

Education Research Society. (2000). *The principal keystone of a high-achieving school: Attracting and keeping the leaders we need.* Arlington, VA: Education Research Society.

Educator Evaluation. (1990). *Utah Code* (Subsection 53A-10-108).

Ehrich, L. C., Hansford, B., & Tennent, L. (2004). Formal mentoring programs in education and other professions: A review of literature. *Educational Administration Quarterly, 40*(4), 518–540.

Eisner, E. W. (1985). *The educational imagination: On the design and evaluation of school programs* (2nd ed.). New York: Macmillan.

Elbow, P. (1986). *Embracing contraries: Explorations in learning and teaching.* Oxford, UK: Oxford University Press.

Elmore, R. F. (2000). Building a new structure for school leadership. *American Educator, 23*(4), 6–13.

Elmore, R. F. (2003). Accountability and Capacity. In M. Carnoy, R. Elmore, & L. S. Siskin (Eds.), *The new accountability: High schools and high-stakes testing* (pp.195–209). New York: Routledge Falmer.

Elmore, R. F. (2004). *School reform from the inside out.* Cambridge, MA: Harvard Education Press.

Ensign, F. C. (1923). Evolution of the high school principalship. *School Review* (March), 179–190.

Erikson, E. H. (1963). *Childhood and society* (2nd ed.). New York: Norton.

Estler, S. (1975). Women as Leaders in Public Education. *Journal of Women in Culture and Society, 1*(2), 363–386.

Feiman-Nemser, S., Carver, C., Schwille, S., & Yusko, B. (1999). Beyond support: Taking new teachers seriously as learners. In M. Scherer (Ed.), *A better beginning: Supporting and mentoring new teachers* (pp. 3–12). Alexandria, VA: Association for Supervision and Curriculum Development.

Feldman, D. C. (1976). A contingency theory of socialization. *Administrative Science Quarterly, 21,* 433–452.

Feldman, D. C. (1981). The multiple socialization of organization members. *Academy of Management Review, 6,* 309–318.

Fenwick, T. (2003). *Learning through experience: Troubling orthodoxies and intersecting questions.* Malabar, FL: Krieger.

Fenner, M. S., & Fishburn, E. C. (1944). *Pioneer american educators.* Washington, D.C.: Hugh Birch-Horace Mann Fund National Education Association.

Ferrance, E. (2000). *Action research.* Providence, RI: Northeast and Islands Regional Educational Laboratory at Brown University.

Fiedler, F. E. (1967). *A theory of leadership effectiveness.* New York: McGraw-Hill.

Field, J. (2005). *Social capital and lifelong learning.* Bristol: The Policy Press.

Fisher, B. A. (1986). Leadership: When does the difference make a difference? In R. Hirokawa & M. Poole (Eds.), *Communication and group decision making* (pp. 197–215). Beverly Hills, CA: Sage.

Fisher, C. (1986). Organizational socialization: An integrative review. *Research in Personnel and Human Resources Management, 4,* 101–145.

Fisher, R., & Ury, W. (1981). *Getting to yes.* Boston, MA: Houghton Mifflin.

Fleishman, E. A., & Harris, E. F. (1962). Patterns of leadership behavior related to employee grievances and turnover. *Personnel Psychology, 15,* 43–56.

Forbes, J., & Watson, C. (in press). *Service integration in schools: Research and policy discourses, practices and future prospects.* Rotterdam, Netherlands: Sense Publications.

Foster, W. (1986). *Paradigms and promises: New approaches to educational administration.* Buffalo, NY: Prometheus Books.

Freire, P. (1970). *Pedagogy of the oppressed*. New York: Herder and Herder.

French, J. R. P., Jr., & Raven, B. H. (1959). The bases of social power. In D. Cartwright (Ed.), *Studies in social power* (pp. 150–167). Ann Arbor, MI: Institute for Social Research, University of Michigan.

French, J. R. P., & Raven, B. (2001). The bases of social power. In I. G. Asherman & S. V. Asherman (Eds.), *The negotiation sourcebook* (2nd ed., pp. 61–73). Amherst, MA: Human Resource Development Press.

Friedman, T. L. (2005). *The world is flat: A brief history of the twenty-first century*. New York: Farrar, Straus, & Giroux.

Friedman, T.L. (1999). *The lexus and the olive tree*. New York: Farrar, Strauss, & Giroux.

Friend, M., & Cook, C. (1992). *Interactions: Collaboration skills for school professionals*. New York: Longman.

Friedkin, N. E. (1983). Horizons of observability and limits of informal control in organizations. Social Forces, 62(1), 54–77

Friedkin, N. E., & Slater, M. R. (1994). School leadership and performance: A social network approach. *Sociology of Education, 67*(2), 139–157.

Fullan, M. (1993). *Change forces: Probing the depths of educational reform*. London: Falmer Press.

Fullan, M. (1999). *Change forces: The sequel*. Philadelphia: Falmer Press.

Fullan, M. (2002). The change leader: Beyond instructional leadership. *Educational Leadership, 59*(8), 16–21.

Fullan, M. (2005). *Leadership and sustainability: System thinkers in action*. Thousand Oaks, CA: Corwin Press.

Fullan, M. (2007). *The NEW meaning of educational change* (4th ed.). New York: Teachers College Press.

Fullan, M., & Hargreaves, A. (1996). *What's worth fighting for in your school?* New York: Teachers College Press.

Fullan, M., & Miles, M. B. (1992). Getting reform right: What works and what doesn't. *Phi Delta Kappan, 73,* 745–752.

Fullan, M. (2001). Leading in a culture of change. San Francisco: Jossey-Bass.

Fuller, E. (1998). *Do properly certified teachers matter? A comparison of elementary school performance on the TAAS in 1997 between schools with high and low percentages of properly certified regular education teachers*. Austin, TX: The Charles A. Dana Center, University of Texas at Austin.

Fuller, E. (2000). *Do properly certified teachers matter? Properly certified Algebra teachers and Algebra I achievement in Texas*. New Orleans, LA: American Educational Research Association.

Fuller, F. (1969). Concerns of teachers: A developmental conceptualization. *American Educational Research Journal, 6*(2), 207–266.

Fulton, K., Yoon, I., & Lee, C. (2005). *Induction into learning communities*. Washington, DC: National Commission on Teaching and America's Future.

Furman, G. C. (1998). Postmodernism and community in schools: Unraveling the paradox. *Educational Administration Quarterly, 34*(3), 298–328.

Futernick, K. (2007). *A possible dream: Retaining California teachers so all students learn*. Sacramento, CA: Center for Teacher Quality, California State University.

Gabarro, J. J. (1974). *Robert F. Kennedy high school*. Cambridge, MA: Harvard Business School.

Gamoran, A., & Dreeben, R. (1986). Coupling and control in educational organizations. *Administrative Science Quarterly, 31*(4), 612–632.

Ganser, T. (1996). Preparing mentors of beginning teachers: An overview for staff developers. *Journal of Staff Development, 17*(4), 8–11.

Ganser, T., Marchione, M. J., & Fleischmann, A. K. (1999). Baltimore takes mentoring to the next level. In M. Scherer (Ed.), *A better beginning: Supporting and mentoring new teachers* (pp. 69–76). Alexandria, VA: Association for Supervision and Curriculum Development.

Gardiner, M. E., Grogan, M., & Enomoto, E. (2000). *Coloring outside the lines: Mentoring women into school leadership.* Albany, NY: SUNY Press.

Gardner, H. (1983). *Frames of mind.* New York: Basic Books.

Gardner, H. (2006). *Multiple intelligences: New horizons.* New York: Basic Books.

Gardner, J. W. (1987). *Leadership development: Leadership papers.* Washington: Independent Sector.

Garrod, A. (1988). *Psychological skills of adolescent leaders.* Unpublished manuscript, Dartmouth College, Hanover, NH.

Garton, S. C. (2004). *Teacher leadership: New applications for distributive leadership theory in administrator preparation programs.* Unpublished manuscript, Kansas City, Mo.

Gehrke, N. (1988). Toward a definition of mentoring. *Theory into Practice, 27*(3), 190–194.

Gehrke, N. J., & Kay, R. S. (1984). The socialization of beginning teachers through mentor-protege relationships. *Journal of Teacher Education, 35*(3), 21–24.

Gilligan, C. (1982). *In a different voice.* Cambridge, MA: Harvard University Press.

Gladwell, M. (2005). *Blink: The power of thinking without thinking.* New York: Little, Brown & Co.

Glanz, J. (1994). Where did the assistant principalship begin? Where is it headed? *NASSP Bulletin, 78*(564), 35–40.

Glasman, N. S. (1994). *Making better decisions about school problems: How administrators use evaluation to find solutions.* Thousand Oaks, CA: Corwin Press.

Glass, G. V. (2008). Are demographics the nation's destiny? *School Administrator, 65*(6), 38–39.

Glickman, C. D. (1985). The supervisor's challenge: Changing the work environment. *Educational Leadership, 42*(4), 38–40.

Glickman, C. D. (2002). *Leadership for learning: How to help teachers succeed.* Alexandria, VA: Association for Supervision and Curriculum Development.

Glickman, C. D., Gordon, S. P., & Ross-Gordon, J. M. (2001). *SuperVision und instructional leadership: A developmental approach* (5th ed.). Needham Heights, MA: Allyn & Bacon.

Glickman, C. D., Gordon, S. P., & Ross-Gordon, J. M. (2004). *Supervision of instruction: A developmental approach* (6th ed.). Boston, MA: Allyn & Bacon.

Glickman, C. D., Gordon, S. P., & Ross-Gordan, J. M. (2007). *Supervision of instruction: A developmental approach* (7th ed.). Boston, MA: Allyn & Bacon.

Glickman, C. D., Gordon, S.P., & Ross-Gordon, J. M. (2009). Supervision and instructional leadership. A developmental approach (8th ed.). Boston: Pearson.

Glickman, C. D., Gordon, S. P., & Ross-Gordon, J. M. (2008). *The basic guide to supervision and instructional leadership* (2nd ed.). Boston, MA: Pearson.

Glickman, C. D., Allen, L. R., et al. (1994). Voices of principals from democratically transformed schools. In J. Murphy & K. S. Louis (Eds.), *Reshaping the principalship: Insights from transformational reform efforts* (pp. 44–79). Thousand Oaks, CA: Corwin Press.

Goddard, R. (2002). Collective efficacy and school organization: A multilevel analysis of teacher influence in schools. *Theory and Research in Educational Administration, 1,* 169–184.

Gold, Y. (1996). Beginning teacher support: Attrition, mentoring and induction. In J. Sikula, T. J. Buttery, & E. Guyton (Eds.), *Handbook on research on teacher education* (pp. 548–616). New York: Macmillan.

Goldhaber, D. D., & Brewer, D. J. (1998). When should we reward degrees for teachers? *Phi Delta Kappan, 80*(2), 134, 136–138.

Goldring, E. B. (1993). Principals, parents, and administrative superiors. *Educational Administration Quarterly, 29*(1), 93–117.

Goldring, E., & Berends, M. (2009). *Leading with data: Pathways to school improvement.* Thousand Oaks, CA: Corwin Press.

Goldring, E. B., & Hausman, C. (2001). Civic capacity and school principals: The missing links for community development. In R. Crowson (Ed.), *Community development and school reform* (pp. 193–2099. Oxford, England: Elsevier.

Goldring, E. B., & Rallis, S. F. (1993). *Principals of dynamic schools: Taking charge of change.* Newbury Park, CA: Corwin Press.

Goldring, E., Huff, J., May, H., & Camburn, E. (2008). School context and individual characteristics: What influences principal practice? *Journal of Educational Administration, 46*(3), 332–352.

Goldring, E., Porter, A., Murphy, J., & Elliott, S. (2007). *Leadership for learning: Assessing behaviors that matter most.* Report to the Midwest Regional Educational Laboratory. Naperville, IL: REL Midwest at Learning Point Associates.

Goleman, D. (1995). *Emotional intelligence.* New York: Bantam Books.

Goleman, D. (1998). What makes a leader? *Harvard Business Review, 76*(6), 93–102.

Goleman, D. (2005). *Emotional intelligence.* New York: Bantam.

Gordon, B. G., Stockard, J. W. J., & Williford, H. (1992). The principal's role as school leader. *Educational Research Quarterly, 15*(4), 29–38.

Greene, M. (1985). The role of education in democracy. *Educational Horizons, 63*(Special Issue), 3–9.

Greenfield, W. (1987). Moral imagination and interpersonal competence: Antecedents to instructional leadership. In W. Greenfield (Ed.), *Instructional leadership: Concepts, issues, and controversies* (pp. 56–75). Newton, MA: Allyn & Bacon.

Greenfield, W. D. (1977a). Administrative candidacy: A process of new role learning, part I. *Journal of Educational Administration, 15*(1), 30–48.

Greenfield, W. D. (1977b). Administrative candidacy: A process of new role learning, Part I. *Journal of Educational Administration Quarterly, 19*(2), 5–26.

Greenfield, W. D. (1985a, April). *Being and becoming a principal: Responses to work contexts and socialization processes.* Paper presented at the American Educational Research Association, Chicago.

Greenfield, W. D. (1985b). Studies of the assistant principalship: Toward new avenues of inquiry. *Education and Urban Society, 18*(1), 7–27.

Greenfield, W. D. (1985c). The moral socialization of school administrators: Informal role learning outcomes. *Educational Administration Quarterly, 21*(4), 99–119.

Greenfield, W. D., Marshall, C., & Reed, D. B. (1986). Experience in the vice principalship: Preparation for leading schools. *Journal of Educational Administration, 24*(1), 107–121.

Greenleaf, R. (1970). *The servant as leader.* Indianapolis: The Robert K. Greenleaf Center.

Gregg, R. T. (1943). The principal and his school in wartime. *Bulletin of the National Association of Secondary School Principals, 27*(112), 7–19.

Gronn, P. (1983). Talk as work: The accomplishment of school administration. *Administrative Science Quarterly, 28*(1), 1–21.

Groopman, J. (2007). *How doctors think.* Boston, MA: Houghton Mifflin.

Gross, B. (1994). The scientific approach to administration. In D. E. Griffiths (Ed.), *Behavioral science and educational administration, 63rd yearbook of the National Society for the Study of Education* (pp. 33–72). Chicago: University of Chicago Press.

Gross, S. (2006). *Leadership mentoring: Maintaining school improvement in turbulent times.* Lanham, MD: Rowman & Littlefield Education.

Grubb, W. N., & Flessa, J. J. (2006). "A job too big for one": Multiple principals and other nontraditional approaches to school leadership. *Educational Administration Quarterly, 42*(4), 518–550.

Guarino, C., Santibanez, L., & Daley, G. (2006). Teacher recruitment and retention: A review of the recent empirical literature. *Review of Educational Research, 76*(2), 173–208.

Gulick, L. (1937). Notes on the theory of organization. In L. Gulick & L. Urwick (Eds.), *Papers on the science of administration* (pp. 1–45). New York: Institute of Public Administration, Columbia University.

Gurr, D., Drysdale, L., & Mulford, B. (2006). Models of successful principal leadership. *School Leadership and Management, 26*(4), 371–395.

Hage, J., & Powers, C. H. (1992). *Post-industrial lives. Roles and relationships in the 21st century.* Newbury Park, CA: Sage.

Hall, D. T. (1980). Socialization processes in later career years: Can there be growth at terminal level? In C. B. Derr (Ed.), *Work, family, and the career* (pp. 219–236). New York: Praeger.

Hall, D. T. (1986). Breaking career routines: Mid-career choice and identity development. In D. T. Hall (Ed.), *Career development in organizations* (pp. 120–159). San Francisco, CA: Jossey-Bass.

Hall, D. T. (1987). Careers and socialization. *Journal of Management, 13*(2), 302–321.

Hall, D. T. (2002). *Careers in and out of organizations.* Thousand Oaks, CA: Sage.

Hallinger, P., & Heck, R. H. (1996). Reassessing the principal's role in school effectiveness: A review of empirical research. *Education Administration Quarterly, 32*(1), 5–44.

Hallinger, P., & Heck, R. H. (1998). Exploring the principal's contribution to school effectiveness: 1980–1995. *School Effectiveness and School Improvement, 9*(2), 157–191.

Hallinger, P., & Murphy, J. (1987). Instructional leadership in the school context. In W. Greenfield (Ed.), *Instructional leadership: Concepts, issues, and controversies* (pp. 179–203). Newton, MA: Allyn & Bacon.

Hammerness, K., Darling-Hammond, L., et al. (2005). How teachers learn and develop. In L. Darling-Hammond & J. Bransford (Eds.), *Preparing teachers for a changing world:*

What teachers should learn and be able to do (pp. 358–389). San Francisco, CA, Jossey-Bass.

Hansford, B., & Ehrich, L. (2006). The principalship: How significant is mentoring? *Journal of Educational Administration, 44*(1), 36–52.

Hanushek, E. A., Kain, J. F., O'Brien, D. M., & Rivkin, S. G. (2005). *The market for teacher quality.* Working Paper 11154 (http://www.nber.org/papers/w11154). Cambridge, MA: National Bureau of Economic Research.

Hargreaves, A. (1990). *Contrived collegiality: The micropolitics of teacher collaboration.* Toronto, Canada: Ontario Institute for Studies in Education.

Hargreaves, A. (1995). Renewal in the age of paradox. *Educational Leadership, 52*(7), 14–19.

Hargreaves, A. (1997). *Rethinking educational change with heart and mind.* Alexandria, VA: Association for Supervision and Curriculum Development.

Hargreaves, A. (2003). *Teaching in the knowledge society. Education in the age of insecurity.* New York: Teachers College.

Hargreaves, A. (2008, September). *Keynote address at conference of the Commonwealth Council for Educational Administration and Management.* Durban, South Africa.

Hargreaves, A., & Dawe, R. (1990). Paths of professional development: Contrived collegiality, collaborative cultures, and the case of peer coaching. *Teaching and Teacher Education, 6*(3), 227–241.

Hargreaves, A., & Fink, D. (2003). Sustaining leadership. *Phi Delta Kappan, 84*(9), 693–700.

Hargreaves, A., & Fink, D. (2004). The seven principles of sustainable leadership. *Educational Leadership, 61*(7), 8–13.

Hargreaves, A., & Fullan, M. (1998). *What's worth fighting for out there.* New York: Teachers College Press.

Hart, A. W. (1991). Leader succession and socialization: A synthesis. *Review of educational research, 61*(4), 451–474.

Hart, A. W. (1993). *Principal succession: Establishing leadership in schools.* Albany: State University of New York.

Hart, A. W., & Bredeson, P. V. (1996). *The principalship: A theory of professional learning and practice.* New York: McGraw-Hill.

Hartzell, G. N., Williams, R. C., & Nelson, K. T. (1995). *New voices in the field: The work lives of first-year assistant principals.* Thousand Oaks, CA: Corwin Press.

Hausman, C., Nebeker, A., McCreary, J., & Donaldson, G., Jr. (2001). The worklife of the assistant principal. *Journal of Educational Administration, 40*(2), 136–157.

Hawley, W. D. (Ed.). (2007). *The keys to effective schools. Educational reform as continuous improvement.* Thousand Oaks, CA: Corwin Press.

Hay, J. (1995). *Transformational mentoring: Creating developmental alliances for changing organizational cultures.* London: McGraw-Hill.

Heffron, F. (1989). *Organization theory and public organizations: The political connection.* Englewood Cliffs, NJ: Prentice-Hall.

Heifetz, R. (1994). *Leadership without easy answers.* Cambridge, MA: Harvard University Press.

Heifetz, R. A., & Laurie, D. L. (1996). The work of leadership. *Harvard Business Review* (January–February), 124–134.

Hersey, P., & Blanchard, K. H. (1977). *Management of organizational behavior: Utilizing human resources* (3rd ed.). Englewood Cliffs, NJ: Prentice-Hall.

Heller, M. F. & Firestone, W. A. (1995). Who's in Charge Here: Sources of Leadership and Change in Eight Schools. *The Elementary Principals Journal 96*(1) 65–86.

Hess, F. (1985). The socialization of the assistant principal: From the perspective of the local school district. *Education and Urban Society, 18*(1), 93–106.

Higgins, M. C., & Kram, K. E. (2001). Reconceptualizing mentoring at work: A developmental network perspective. *Academy of Management Review, 26*(2), 264–288.

Hord, S. M. (1997). *Professional learning communities: Communities of continuous inquiry and improvement.* Austin, TX: Southwest Educational Development Laboratory.

Hord, S. M. (2004). Professional learning communities: An overview. In S. M. Hord (Ed.), *Learning together, leading together: Changing schools through professional learning communities.* Oxford, OH: Teachers College Press.

Hord, S. M., & Sommers, W. A. (2008). *Leading professional learning communities: Voices from research and practice.* Thousand Oaks, CA: Corwin Press.

House, R. J. (1974). A path-goal theory of leadership effectiveness. *Administrative Science Quarterly,* (Autumn), 81–97.

Hoy, W. K., & Miskel, C. G. (2000). *Educational administration: Theory, research, and practice* (6th ed.). New York: McGraw-Hill.

Hoy, W. K., Tarter, C. J., & Witkoskie, L. (1992). Faculty trust in colleagues: Linking the principal with school effectiveness. *Journal of Research and Development in Education, 26*(1), 38–45.

Hoyle, J. R. (1995). *Leadership and futuring: Making visions happen.* Thousand Oaks, CA: Corwin Press.

Huff, S. (2008). Digging deep into data. In R. DuFour, R. DuFour, & R. Eaker (Eds.), *The collaborative administrator: Working together as a professional learning community* (pp. 196–215). Bloomington, IN: Solution Tree.

Huffman, J. B., & Hipp, K. K. (2003). *Reculturing schools as professional learning communities.* Lanham: Scarecrow Education.

Hughes, E. C. (1959). The study of occupations. In R. K. Merton, L. Broom, & L. Cottrell (Eds.), *Sociology today* (pp. 442–458). New York: Basic Books.

Hunt, D. E. (1966). A conceptual systems change model and its application to education. In O. J. Harvey (Ed.), *Experience, structure, and adaptability* (pp. 277–302). New York: Springer-Verlag.

Hunter, M. (1984). Knowing, teaching, and supervision. In P. Hosford (Ed.), *Using what we know about teaching* (pp. 169–203). Alexandria, VA: Association for Supervision and Curriculum Development.

Ingersoll, R. (2001). Teacher turnover and teacher shortages: An organizational analysis. *American Educational Research Journal, 38*(3), 499–534.

Ingersoll, R. M., & Alsalam, N. (1997). *Teacher professionalization and teacher commitment: A multilevel analysis.* Statistical Analysis Report (0 16 048975 x NCES 97 069). Washington, DC: National Center for Education Statistics U.S. Department of Education.

Innes, J. E. (1996). Planning through consensus building. A new view of the comprehensive planning ideal. *Journal of the American Planning Association, 62*(4), 460–472.

Institute for Educational Leadership. (2000). *Leadership for student learning: Reinventing the principalship.* Washington, DC: Institute for Educational Leadership, Task Force on the Principalship.

International Society for Technology in Education (ISTE). (2002). *National educational technology standards for administrators*. Eugene, OR: Author.

Johnson, B. (2004). Local school micropolitical agency: An antidote to new managerialism. *School Leadership and Management, 24*(3), 267–286.

Johnson, S. M. (1990). Teachers at work: Achieving succes in our schools. New York: Basic Books.

Johnson, S. M. (2004). *Finders and keepers: Helping new teachers survive and thrive in our schools*. San Francisco, CA: Jossey-Bass.

Johnson, S. M., Kardos, S. M., Kauffman, D., Liu, Ed., & Donaldson, M. L. (2004). The support gap: New teachers' early experiences in high-income and low-income schools. *Education Policy Analysis Archives, 12*(61). Retrieved June 26, 2009, from http://epaa.asu.edu/epaa/v12n61/)

Jones, B. D., & Egley, R. J. (2006). Looking through different lenses: Teachers' and administrators' views of accountability. *Phi Delta Kappan, 87*(10), 767–771.

Jones, G. R. (1986). Socialization tactics, self-efficacy, and newcomers' adjustments to organizations. *Academy of Management Journal, 29*(2), 262–279.

Joyce, B. (2004). How are professional learning communities created? *Phi Delta Kappan, 86*(1), 76–83.

Kain, D. L. (1996). Looking beneath the surface: Teacher collaboration through the lens of grading practices. *Teachers College Record, 97*(4), 569–581.

Kalvelage, J. (1978). *The decline in female elementary principals since 1928: Riddles and clues.* Eugene, OR: University of Oregon.

Katz, D., & Kahn, R. L. (1978). *The social psychology of organizations.* New York: Wiley.

Katz, D., Maccoby, N., & Morse, N. (1950). *Productivity, supervision, and morale in an office situation.* Ann Arbor, MI: Institute for Social Research.

Katzenbach, J. R., & Smith, B. K. (1993). *The wisdom of teams.* New York: Harper Business.

Kearns, D. (1988). An educational recovery plan for America. *Phi Delta Kappan, 69*(8), 565–570.

Kellmayer, J. (1995). *How to establish an alternative school.* Thousand Oaks, CA: Corwin Press.

Kelly, D. M. (1993). *Last chance high school: How girls and boys drop in and out of alternative schools.* New Haven: Yale University Press.

Kelly, G. (1987). The assistant principalship as a training ground for the principalship. *NASSP, 7*(501), 13–20.

Kerr, D. H. (1987). Authority and responsibility in public schooling. In J. I. Goodlad (Ed.), *The ecology of school renewal, 86th Yearbook (Part I) of the National Society for the Study of Education.* Chicago: University of Chicago Press.

Kimbrough, R. B., & Burkett, C. W. (1990). *The principalship: Concepts and practices.* Boston, MA: Allyn & Bacon.

Kirkpatrick, S. A., & Locke, E. A. (1991). Leadership: Do traits matter? *Academy of Management Executives, 5*(2), 48–60.

Kohlberg, L., & Armon, C. (1984). Three types of stage models used in the study of adult development. In M. Commons, F. A. Richards, & C. A. Armon (Eds.), *Beyond formal operations: Late adolescent and adult cognitive development* (pp. 383–394. New York: Praeger.

Kohn, M. L., & Schooler, C. (1978). The reciprocal effects of the substantive complexity of work and intellectual flexibility: A longitudinal assessment. *American Journal of Sociology, 84,* 24–52.

Koplow, L. (2002). *Creating schools that heal: Real-life solutions.* New York: Teachers College Press.

Kotter, J. P. (1985). *Power and influence: Beyond formal authority.* New York: Free Press.

Kowalski, T. J., & Reitzug, U. C. (1993). *Contemporary school administration: An introduction.* New York: Longmans.

Kram, K. E. (1985). *Mentoring at work.* Glenview, IL: Scott, Foresman.

Kram, K. E. (1986). Mentoring in the workplace. In D. T. Hall (Ed.), *Career development in organizations* (pp. 160–210). San Francisco, CA: Jossey-Bass.

Kruse, S. D., & Louis, K. S. (1995). An emerging framework for analyzing school-based professional community. In K. S. Louis & S. D. Kruse (Eds.), *Professionalism and community* (pp. 23–42). Thousand Oaks, CA: Corwin Press.

Lambert, L. (2002). A framework for shared leadership. *Educational Leadership, 59*(8), 37–40.

Lambert, L. (2003). *Leadership capacity for lasting school improvement.* Alexandria, VA: Association for Supervision and Curriculum Development.

Lane, M. B. (2001). Affirming new directions in planning theory: Comanagement of protected areas. *Society and Natural Resources, 14,* 657–671.

Langer, G. M., Colton, A. B., & Goff, L. S. (2003). *Collaborative analysis of student work: Improving teaching and learning.* Alexandria, VA: Association for Supervision and Curriculum Development.

Lasswell, H. (1936). *Politics: Who gets what, when, how.* New York: McGraw-Hill.

Lave, J., & Wenger, E. (1991). *Situated learning. Legitimate peripheral participation.* Cambridge, England: Cambridge University Press.

Lee, V. E., Bryk, A., & Smith, J. B. (1993). The organization of effective high schools. In L. Darling-Hammond (Ed.), *Review of research in education, 19* (pp. 171–267). Washington, DC: American Educational Research Association.

Lee, V. E., Smith, J. B., & Croninger, R. G. (1995). Another look at high school restructuring: More evidence that it improves student achievement and more insight into why. *Issues in Restructuring Schools, 9,* 1–10.

Leithwood, K. (2007). Organizational conditions that enhance teaching and learning. In W. D. Hawley (Ed.), *The keys to effective schools. Educational reform as continuous improvement* (pp. 139–152). Thousand Oaks, CA: Corwin Press.

Leithwood, K., & Jantzi, D. (2006). Transformational school leadership for large-scale reform: Effects on students, teachers, and their classroom practices. *School Effectiveness and School Improvement, 17*(2), 201–227.

Leithwood, K., & Stager, M. (1989). Expertise in principals' problem solving. *Educational Administration Quarterly, 25*(2), 126–161.

Levin, H. M. (1987). New schools for the disadvantaged. *Teacher Education Quarterly, 14*(4), 60–83.

Levinson, D. J., Darrow, C. N., Klein, E. B., Levinson, M. H., & McKee, B. (1978). *Seasons of a man's life.* New York: Ballantine Books.

Lewin, K., & Lippet, R. (1938). An experimental approach to the study of autocracy and democracy: A preliminary note. *Sociometry, 1,* 292–300.

Lieberman, A., & Miller, L. (1991). *Staff development for education in '90s: New demands, New realities, New perspectives.* New York: Teachers College Press.

Likert, R. (1961). *New patterns of management.* New York: McGraw-Hill.

Lindsey, R. B., Roberts, L. M., & Campbell Jones, F. (2005). *The culturally proficient school. An implementation guide for school leaders.* Thousand Oaks, CA: Corwin Press.

Little, J. W. (1982). Norms of collegiality and experimentation: Workplace conditions of school success. *American Educational Research Journal, 19*(3), 325–340.

Little, J. W. (1990). The persistence of privacy: Autonomy and initiative in teachers' professional relations. Teachers College Record, 91(4), 509–536.

Little, J. W. (2002). Professional communication and collaboration. In W. D. Hawley & D. L. Rollie (Eds.), *The keys to effective schools. Educational reform as continuous improvement* (pp. 43–55). National Education Association.

Little, J. W. (2007). Professional communication and collaboration. In W.D. Hawley (Ed.), *The keys to effective schools. Educational reform as continuous improvement* (2nd ed., pp. 51–65). Thousand Oaks, CA: Corwin Press.

Loder, T. L. (2005). African American women principals' reflections on social change, Community, other mothering, and Chicago Public School Reform. *Urban Education, 40*(3), 298–320.

Loder, T. L., & Spillane, J. P. (2005). Is a principal still a teacher? US women administrator's accounts of role conflict and role discontinuity. *School Leadership and Management, 25*(3), 263–279.

Lomotey, K. (1989). *African-American principals: School leadership and success.* New York: Greenwood.

Lomotey, K. (1993). African American principals: Bureaucrat/administrators and Ethnohumanists. *Urban Education, 27*(4), 395–412.

Long, D. H. (1988). *A study of the socialization process of beginning public school administrators.* Unpublished doctoral dissertation, Vanderbilt University, Nashville, TN.

Lortie, D. C. (1975). *Schoolteacher: A sociological study.* Chicago: University of Chicago Press.

Louis, K. S. (2006). Changing the culture of schools: Professional community, organizational learning, and trust. *Journal of School Leadership, 16*(5), 477–489.

Louis, K., & Kruse, S. (1995). *Professionalism and community: Perspectives on reforming urban schools.* Thousand Oaks, CA: Corwin Press.

Louis, K. S., & Marks, H. M. (1998). Does professional community affect the classroom? Teachers' work and student experiences in restructuring schools. *American Journal of Education, 106*(4), 532–575.

Louis, K. S., Marks, H. M., & Kruse, S. (1996). Teachers' professional community in restructuring schools. *American Educational Research Journal, 33*(4), 757–798.

Louis, K. S., & Murphy, J. (1994). The evolving role of the principal: Some concluding thoughts. In J. Murphy & K. S. Louis (Eds.), *Reshaping the principalship: Insights from transformational reform efforts* (pp. 242–254). Thousand Oaks, CA: Corwin Press.

Luehe, B. (1989). *The principal and supervision.* Bloomington, IN: Phi Delta Kappan Educational Foundation.

Luft, J. (1970). *Group processes: An introduction to group dynamics.* New York: National Press.

Lyman, L. L., & Villani, C. J. (2004). *Best leadership practices for high-poverty schools.* Lanham, MD: Scarecrow Press.

Madison, J. (1788). The federalist no. 51. In G. Wills (Ed.), *The federalist papers* New York: Bantam Books.

Maeroff, G. I. (1993). *Team building for school change: Equipping teachers for new roles.* New York: Teachers College Press.

Mann, H. (1842). *Fifth annual report of the secretary of the board.* Boston, MA: Dutton and Wentworth, State Printers.

Markman, L. B. (2002). The impact of school culture on adolescents' prosocial motivation. *Dissertation Abstracts International: Section B— The Sciences and Engineering, 62*(12-B), 6024.

Marks, H. M., & Printy, S. M. (2003). Principal leadership and school performance: An integration of transformational and instructional leadership. *Educational Administration Quarterly, 39*(3), 370–397.

Marland, S. (1972). *Education of the gifted and talented: Report to congress.* Washington, DC: U.S. Government Printing Office.

Marquardt, M. J., & Loan, P. (2006). *The manager as mentor.* Westport, CT: Praeger.

Marsh, J. A., McCombs, J. S., Lockwood, J. R., Martorell, F., Gershwin, D., Naftel, S., et al. (2008). *Supporting literacy across the sunshine state: A study of Florida middle school reading coaches.* Santa Monica, CA: Rand Corp.

Marshall, C. (1985). Professional shock: The enculturation of the assistant principal. *Education and Urban Society, 18*(1), 28–58.

Marshall, C. (1992). *The assistant principal. Leadership choices and challenges.* Newbury Park, CA: Corwin Press.

Marshall, C., & Hooley, R. M. (2006). *The assistant principal: Leadership choices and challenges.* Thousand Oaks, CA: Corwin Press.

Marshall, C., & Mitchell, B. A. (1991). The assumptive worlds of fledgling administrators. *Education and Urban Society, 23*(4), 396–415.

Marshall, C., & Ward, M. (2004). "Yes, but . . .": Education leaders discuss social justice. *Journal of School Leadership, 14*, 530–563.

Marsick, V. J., & Watkins, K. E. (2005). Learning organizations. In L. M. English (Ed.), *International encyclopedia of adult education* (pp. 355–360). New York: Palgrave Macmillan.

Martin, R. (2007). How successful leaders think. *Harvard Business Review,* (June, 2007), 60–67.

Martin, T. L. (2008). Professional learning in a professional learning community. In S. Tree (Ed.), *The collaborative administrator: Working together as a professional learning community* (pp. 49–68). Bloomington, IN: Solution Tree.

Marvel, J., Lyter, D. M., Peltola, P., Strizek, G. A., & Morton, B. A. (2006). *Teacher attrition and mobility: Results from the 2004–2005 teacher follow-up survey* (NCES 2007-307). U.S. Department of Education, National Center for Education Statistics. Washington, DC: U.S. Government Printing Office.

Marx, G. (2000). *Ten trends: Educating children for a profoundly different future.* Arlington, VA: Educational Research Service.

Matthews, L. J., & Crow, G. M. (2003). *Being and becoming a principal: Role conceptions for contemporary principals and assistant principals.* Boston, MA: Allyn & Bacon.

Matthews, L. J., William, E. J., & Stewart, C. D. (2007). Defining the elements of a learning community: A search of the existing literature. *Impact.*

Maxcy, S. J. (1995). *Democracy, chaos, and the new school order.* Thousand Oaks, CA: Corwin Press.

McCaul, R. L. (1959). Dewey's Chicago. *The School Review, 67*(2), 258–280.

McClelland, D. C. (1975). *Power: The inner experience.* New York: Irvington.

McCreary, J. (2001). Getting clubbed over a club. *Journal of Cases in Educational Leadership, 4*(1). Retrieved from *www.ucea.org/cases.*

McIntyre, D., & Hagger, H. (1996). Mentoring: Challenges for the future. In D. McIntyre &

H. Hagger (Eds.), *Mentors in schools: Developing the profession of teaching* (pp. 144–164). London: David Fulton.

McLaughlin, M. W., & Talbert, J. E. (2006). *Building school-based teacher learning communities professional strategies to improve student achievement.* New York: Teachers College Press.

McMillan, D. W., & Chavis, D. M. (1986). Sense of community: A definition and theory. *Journal of Community Psychology, 14*(January), 6–23.

McPartland, C. (1985). The myth of the mentor. *Campus Voice, 2*(1), 8–11.

McPherson, R. B., Crowson, R. L., & Pitner, N. (1986). *Managing uncertainty.* Columbus, OH: Charles E. Merrill.

Megginson, D., & Clutterbuck, D. (1995). *Mentoring in action.* London: Kogan Page.

Mendez-Morse, S. (2004). Constructing mentors: Latina educational leaders' role models and mentors. *Educational Administration Quarterly, 60*(4), 561–590.

Merriam, S. B., Caffarela, R. S., & Baumgartner, L. M. (2007). *Learning in adulthood. A comprenhensive guide.* San Francisco, CA: John Wiley & Sons.

Mertz, N. T. (2004). What's a mentor, anyway? *Educational Administration Quarterly, 60*(4), 541–560.

Mezirow, J., & Associates. (2000). *Learning as transformation: Critical perspectives on a theory in progress.* San Francisco, CA: Jossey-Bass.

Michaletz, J. E. (1984). The preparation and training of the catholic school administrator. In J. J. Lane (Ed.), *The making of a principal* (pp. 116–128). Springfield, IL: Charles C. Thomas.

Micklethwhait, J., & Wooldridge, A. (1996). *The witch doctors: Making sense of the management gurus.* New York: Times Books.

Mitchell, C., & Sackney, L. (2006). Building schools, building people: The school principal's role in leading a learning community. *Journal of School Leadership, 16*(5), 627–640.

Monteiro, T. (1977). Ethnicity and the perceptions of principals. *Integrated Education, 15*(3), 15–16.

Moore-Johnson, S. (2006). *The workplace matters: Teacher quality, retention, and effectiveness.* Washington, DC: National Education Association.

Morris, V. C., Crowson, R. L., Porter-Gehrie, C., & Hurwitz, J. E. (1984). *Principals in action: The reality of managing schools.* Columbus, OH: Charles E. Merrill.

Morrissey, M. S. (2000). *Professional learning communities: An ongoing exploration.* Austin, TX: Southwest Educational Development Laboratory.

Mortimer, J. T., & Simmons, R. G. (1978). Adult socialization. *Annual Review of Sociology, 4,* 421–454.

Mulford, B. (2007). Building social capital in professional learning communities: Importance, challenges, and a way forward. In L. Stolle & K. S. Louis (Eds.), *Professional learning communities: Divergence, depth, and dilemmas* (pp. 166–180). New York: McGraw-Hill.

Mulford, B., & Silins, H. (2003). Leadership for organizational learning and improved student outcomes. *Cambridge Journal of Education, 33*(2), 175–195.

Mulford, B., & Silins, H. (2005). Developing leadership for organizational learning. In M. J. Coles & G. Southworth (Eds.), *Developing leadership. Creating the schools of tomorrow* (pp. 139–157). Maidenhead, England: Open University Press.

Mullen, C. A., & Cox, M. D. (1997). Breaking the circle of one through mentorship. In

C. A. Mullen, M. D. Cox, C. K. Boettcher, & D. S. Adoue (Eds.), *Breaking the circle of one: Redefining mentorship in the lives and writings of educators* (pp. xv–xxiii). New York: Peter Lang.

Mullen, C. A., & Kealy, W. A. (1999). Breaking the circle of one: Developing professional cohorts to address challenges of mentoring for teacher educators. *Teacher Educators Journal, 9*(1), 35–50.

Muller, C. (1998). Gender differences in parental involvement and adolescents' mathematics achievement. *Sociology of Education, 71*(4), 336–356.

Murphy, J. (2002). Reculturing the profession of educational leadership: New blueprints. In J. Murphy (Ed.), *The leadership challenge: Redefining leadership for the 21st century* (pp. 65–82). Chicago: National Society for the Study of Education.

Muse, I. D., Wasden, F. D., & Thomas, G. J. (1988). *The mentor principal: A handbook.* Provo, UT: Brigham Young University.

Nanus, B. (1992). *Visionary leadership: Creating a compelling sense of direction for your organization.* San Francisco, CA: Jossey-Bass.

Nanus, B. (1995). *Visionary leadership: Creating a compelling sense of direction for your organization* (2nd ed.). San Francisco, CA: Jossey-Bass.

National Center for Education Statistics. (1992). *The digest of education statistics 1992: Schools and staffing survey, 1987–1988.* Washington, DC: U.S. Department of Education, National Center for Education Statistics.

National Center for Education Statistics. (1994). *The digest of education statistics 1994: Schools and staffing survey, 1990–1991.* Washington, DC: U.S. Department of Education, National Center for Education Statistics.

National Center for Education Statistics. (1998). *The digest of education statistics 1998: Schools and staffing survey, 1993–1994.* Washington, DC: U.S. Department of Education, National Center for Education Statistics.

Natriella, G., McDill, E. L., & Pallas, A. M. (1990). *Schooling disadvantaged children: Racing against catastrophe.* New York: Teachers College Press.

NCEE. (1983). *A nation at risk: The imperative for educational reform.* National Commission on Excellence in Education. Washington, DC: U.S. Government Printing Office.

Nelson, B. S., & Sassi, A. (2000). Shifting approaches to supervision: The case of mathematics supervision. *Educational Administration Quarterly, 36*(4), 553–584.

Newman, F. M. (2007). Improving achievement of all students. In W. D. Hawley (Ed.), *The keys to effective schools. Educational reform as continuous improvement* (pp. 33–49). Thousand Oaks, CA: Corwin Press.

Newman, F. M., & Associates. (1996). *Authentic instruction: Restructuring schools for intellectual quality.* San Francisco, CA: Jossey-Bass.

Nicholson, N. (1984). A theory of work role transitions. *Administrative Science Quarterly, 29*(2), 172–191.

Nicholson, N., & West, M. A. (1988). *Managerial job change: Men and women in transition.* Cambridge, England: Cambridge University Press.

Nicholson, P. (1996). *Gender, power and organization: A psychological perspective.* London: Routledge.

Noddings, N. (1984). *Caring: A feminine approach to ethics and moral education.* Berkeley: University of California Press.

Noguera, P. (2003). *City schools and the American dream. Reclaiming the promise of public education.* New York: Teachers College Press.

O'Brien, D. E. (1988). *Taking the role of principal: A qualitative investigation of the socialization during the first year*. Unpublished doctoral dissertation, Kent State University.

O'Neill, J. (1996). On emotional intelligence: A conversation with Daniel Goleman. *Educational Leadership, 54*(1), 6–11.

Oaks, J. (1986). Tracking, inequality, and the rhetoric of reform: Why schools don't change. *Journal of Education, 168*(1), 60–80.

Odden, A. R. (1995). *Educational leadership for America's schools*. New York: McGraw-Hill.

Odell, S. J. (1990a). *Mentor teacher programs*. Washington: National Education Association.

Odell, S. J. (1990b). Support of new teachers. In T. M. Bey & C. T. Holmes (Eds.), *Mentoring: Developing successful new teachers* (pp. 3–23). Reston, VA: Virginia Association of Teacher Educators.

OECD (2001). *What schools for the future?* Paris: Organization for Education Cooperation and Development.

Ogawa, R. T., & Bossert, S. T. (1995). Leadership as an organizational quality. *Educational Administration Quarterly, 31*(2), 224–243.

Oja, S. N., & Reiman, A. J. (1998). Supervision for teacher development across the career span. In G. R. Firth & E. F. Pajak (Eds.), *Handbook of research on school supervision* (pp. 463–487). New York: Simon & Schuster McMillan.

Oplatka, I. (2004). The principal's career stage: An absent element in leadership perspectives. *International Journal of Leadership in Education, 7*(1), 43–55.

Oplatka, I., Bargal, D., & Inbar, D. (2001). The process of self-renewal among women head-teachers in mid-career. *Journal of Educational Administration, 39*(1), 77–94.

Opotow, S. (1991). Adolescent peer conflicts: Implications for students and for schools. *Education and Urban Society, 23*(4), 416–441.

Orfield, G. (2004). *Dropouts in America: Confronting the graduation rate crisis*. Cambridge, MA: Harvard Education Press.

Orland, M. E. (1994). Demographics of disadvantage: Intensity of childhood poverty and its relationship to educational achievement. In J. I. Goodlad & P. Keating (Eds.), *Access to knowledge* (pp. 00–00 126–149). New York: College Entrance Examination Board.

Orlich, D. C. (2000). Education reform and limits to student achievement. *Phi Delta Kappan, 81*(6), 468–473.

Ortiz, F. I. (1982). *Career patterns in education: Women, men, and minorities in public school administration*. New York: Praeger.

Ortiz, F. I., & Marshall, C. (1988). Women in educational administration. In N. J. Boyan (Ed.), *Handbook of research on educational administration* (pp. 123–141. New York: Longmans.

Osterman, K. F. (2000). Students' need for belonging in the school community. *Review of Educational Research, 70*(3), 323–367.

Osterman, K. F., & Kottkamp, R. B. (1993). *Reflective practice for educators: Improving schooling through professional development*. Newbury Park, CA: Corwin Press.

Osterman, K. F., & Kottkamp, R. B. (2004). *Reflective practice for educators: Professional development to improve student learning* (2nd ed.). Thousand Oaks, CA: Corwin Press.

Pai, Y., & Adler, S. A. (2001). *Cultural foundations of education* (3rd ed.). Upper Saddle River, NJ: Merrill, Prentice-Hall.

Pankake, A., & Moller, G. (2007). What the teacher leader needs from the principal. *Journal of Staff Development, 28*(1), 32–34.

Parkay, F. W., & Hall, G. E. (1992). *Becoming a principal. The challenges of beginning leadership.* Boston, MA: Allyn & Bacon.

Parsons, T. (1951). *The social system.* Glencoe, IL: Free Press.

Patton, J. (1987). *The role and function of assistant principals in Virginia's public schools.* Blacksburg, VA: Virginia Tech.

Peters, D. A. (1989). *How to get the most from teacher observations: Tips for principals.* Reston, VA: NASSP.

Peters, T., & Waterman, J. R. H. (1982). *In search of excellence: Lessons from America's best-run companies.* New York: Warner Books.

Peters, T., & Waterman, J. R. H. (2004). *In search of excellence: Lessons from America's best-run companies.* New York: Harper Collins.

Peterson, K. D. (1977–78). The principal's tasks. *Administrator's Notebook, 26,* 1–4.

Peterson, K. D. (1984). Mechanisms of administrative control over managers in educational organizations. *Administrative Science Quarterly, 29,* 573–597.

Peterson, K. D. (2002). Positive or negative. *Journal of Staff Development, 23*(3), 10–15.

Peterson, K. D., & Deal, T. (1998). How leaders influence the culture of schools. *Educational Leadership, 56*(1), 28–30.

Pfeffer, J. (1978). The micropolitics of organizations. In M. W. Meyer (Ed.), *Environments and organizations* (pp. 29–50). San Francisco, CA: Jossey-Bass.

Phillips-Jones, L. (1982). *Mentors and protégés.* New York: Arbor House.

Picciano, A. G. (2006). *Educational leadership and planning for technology.* Upper Saddle River, NJ: Pearson Prentice Hall.

Pierce, P. R. (1935). *The origin and development of the public school principalship.* Chicago: University of Chicago Press.

Podgursky, M., Monroe, R., & Watson, D. (2004). The academic quality of public school teachers: An analysis of entry and exit behavior. *Economics of Education Review, 23,* 507–518.

Post, D. (1992). Through Joshua gap: Curricular control and the constructed community. *Teachers College Record, 93*(4), 673–696.

Pounder, D. G. (Ed.). (1998). *Restructuring schools for collaboration.* Albany, NY: State University of New York Press.

Pounder, D. G., & Merrill, R. J. (2001). Job desirability of the high school principalship: A job choice theory perspective. *Educational Administration Quarterly, 37*(1), 27–57.

Prawat, R. S., & Peterson, P. L. (1999). Social constructivist views of learning. In J. Murphy & K. S. Louis (Eds.), *Handbook of research on educational administration* (pp. 203–226). San Francisco, CA: Jossey-Bass.

Putnam, R. (2000). *Bowling alone: The collapse and revival of American community.* New York: Simon & Schuster.

Rallis, S., & Goldring, E. (2000). *Principals of dynamic schools. Taking charge of change.* Thousand Oaks, CA: Corwin Press.

Raywid, M. A. (1994). Alternative schools: The state of the art. *Educational Leadership, 52*(1), 26–31.

Reed, D. B., & Himmler, A. H. (1985). The work of the secondary assistant principal. *Education and Urban Society, 18*(1), 59–84.

Reeves, D. B. (2004). *Accountability for learning: How teachers and school leaders take charge.* Alexandria, VA: Association of Supervision and Curriculum Development.

Reeves, D. B. (2006). *The learning leader: How to focus school improvement for better results.* Alexandria, VA: Association for Supervision and Curriculum Development.

Reitzug, U. C. (1997). Images of principal instructional leadership: From supervision to collaborative inquiry. *Journal of Curriculum and Supervision, 12*(4), 324–343.

Reyes, P., Scribner, J. D., & Paredes-Scribner, A. (1999). *Lessons from high performing Hispanic schools: Creating learning communities*. New York: Teachers College Press.

Richmond-Abbott, M. (1992). *Masculine and feminine: Gender roles over the life cycle* (2nd ed.). New York: McGraw-Hill.

Riehl, C. J. (2000). The principal's role in creating inclusive schools for diverse students: A review of normative, empirical, and critical literature on the practice of educational administration. *Review of Educational Research, 70*(1), 55–81.

Roberts, R. (2000). *Principals' responses to perceived teacher incompetence*. Unpublished Ed.D. dissertation, University of Utah, Salt Lake City, UT.

Roberts, S. M., & Pruitt, E. Z. (2003). *Schools as professional learning communities: Collaborative strategies for professional development*. Thousand Oaks, CA: Corwin Press.

Rosenholtz, S. J. (1985). Political myths about education reform: Lessons from research in teaching. *Phi Delta Kappa, 66*(5), 349–355.

Rosenholtz, S. (1989). Workplace conditions that affect teacher quality and commitment: Implications for teacher. *The Elementary School Journal, 89*(4), 421–439.

Rosenthal, R., & Jacobsen, L. (1968). *Pygmalion in the classroom*. New York: Holt, Rinehart, & Winston.

Rost, J. C. (1991). *Leadership in the Twenty-first century*. New York: Praeger.

Rowan, B. (1995). The organizational design of schools. In S. B. Bacharach & B. Mundell (Eds.), *Images of schools: Structures and roles in organizational behavior* (pp. 11–42). Thousand Oaks, CA: Sage Publications.

Rowe, M. (1981). Building mentorship frameworks as part of an effective equal opportunity ecology. In J. Farley (Ed.), *Sex discrimination in higher education: Strategies for equality* (pp. 23–87). Ithaca, NY: Cornell University Press.

Roy, P., & Hord, S. M. (2006). It's everywhere, but what is it? Professional learning communities. *Journal of School Leadership, 16*(5), 490–501.

Ruff, W. G., & Shoho, A. R. (2005). Understanding instructional leadership through the mental models of three elementary school principals. *Educational Administration Quarterly, 41*(3), 554–577.

Sagor, R. (1993). *At-Risk students: Reaching and teaching them*. Swampscott, MA: Watersun Publishing.

Saphier, J., & King, M. (1985). Good seeds grow in strong cultures. *Educational Leadership, 42*(6), 67–74.

Sapon-Shevin, M. (1994). *Playing favorites: Gifted education and the disruption of community*. Albany, NY: State University of New York Press.

Scandura, T. A., & Williams, E. A. (2002). Formal mentoring: The promise and the precipice. In C. L. Cooper & R. J. Burke (Eds.), *The new world of work. Challenges and opportunities* (pp. 241–257). Oxford, England: Blackwell.

Schein, E. H. (1971). Occupational socialization in the professions: The case of the role innovator. *Journal of Psychiatric Research, 8*, 521–530.

Schein, E. H. (1978). *Career dynamics: Matching individual and organizational needs*. Reading, MA: Addison-Wesley.

Schein, E. H. (1988). Organizational socialization and the profession of management. *Sloan Management Review*, February, 53–65.

Schein, E. H. (1992). *Organizational culture and leadership* (2nd ed.). San Francisco, CA: Jossey-Bass.

Schein, E. H. (2004). *Organizational culture and leadership* (3rd ed.). San Francisco, CA: Jossey-Bass.

Schein, E. H., & Ott, J. S. (1962). The legitimacy of organizational influence. *American Journal of Sociology, 67,* 682–689.

Scheurich, J. J., & Skrla, L. (2003). *Leadership for equity and excellence.* Thousand Oaks, CA: Corwin Press.

Schlechty, P. (1984, November). *Restructuring the teaching occupation: A proposal.* Paper presented at the American Educational Research Association, Washington, DC.

Schlechty, P. C. (2002). Leading a school system through change: Key steps for moving reform forward. In M. S. Tucker & J. B. Codding, (Eds.), *The principal challenge: Leading and managing schools in an era of accountability* (pp. 182–201). San Francisco, CA: Jossey-Bass.

Schmoker, M. (1999). *Results: The key to continuous school improvement.* Alexandria, VA: Association for Supervision and Curriculum Development.

Schmoker, M. (2006). *Results now.* Alexandria, VA: Association for Supervision and Curriculum Development.

Schnur, J., & Gerson, K. (2005). Reforming the principalship. In F. M. Hess (Ed.), *Urban school reform: Lessons from San Diego* (pp. 93–114). Cambridge, MA: Harvard Education Press.

Schön, D. A. (1983). *The reflective practitioner: How professionals think in action.* San Francisco, CA: Jossey-Bass.

Schooler, C. (1989, April 27–30). *A sociological perspective in intellectual development.* Paper presented at the Biennial Meeting of the Society for Research in Child Development (ERIC ED 308 932). Kansas City, MO.

Scribner, J. P., Cockrell, K. S., Cockrell, D. H., & Valentine, J. W. (1999). Creating professional communities in schools through organizational learning: An evaluation of a school improvement process. *Educational Administration Quarterly, 35*(1), 130–160.

Scribner, J. P., Sawyer, R. K., Watson, S. T., & Myers, V. L. (2007). Teacher teams and distributive leadership: A study of group discourse and collaboration. *Educational Administration Quarterly, 43*(1), 67–100.

Senge, P. (1990). *The fifth discipline: The art and practice of the learning organization.* New York: Doubleday.

Senge, P., Cambron-McCabe, N., Lucas, T., Smith, B., Dutton, J., & Kleiner, A. (2000). *Schools that learn.* New York: Doubleday.

Senge, P., Cambron-McCabe, N., Lucas, T., Smith, B., Dutton, J., & Kleiner, A. (2000). *Schools that learn: A fifth discipline fieldbook for educators, parents, and everyone who cares about education.* New York: Doubleday.

Sergiovanni, T. J. (1992). *Moral leadership: Getting to the heart of school improvement.* San Francisco, CA: Jossey-Bass.

Sergiovanni, T. J. (1994). Organizations or communities? Changing the metaphor changes the theory. *Educational Administration Quarterly, 30*(2), 214–226.

Sergiovanni, T. J. (1995). *The principalship: A reflective practice.* Boston, MA: Allyn & Bacon.

Sergiovanni, T. J. (1996). *Leadership for the schoolhouse: How is it different? Why is it important?* San Francisco, CA: Jossey-Bass.

Sergiovanni, T. J. (2009). *The principalship: A reflective practice perspective* (6th ed.). Boston: Allyn & Bacon.

Sergiovanni, T. J., & Starratt, R. J. (1998). *Supervision: A redefinition* (6th ed.). New York: McGraw-Hill.

Sergiovanni, T., & Starrat, R. J. (2007). *Supervision: A redefinition* (8th ed.). New York: McGraw Hill.

Shackelford, J. A. (1992). *An uphill battle: Socialization of a novice female elementary principal*. Unpublished doctoral dissertation, Oklahoma State University, Stillwater, OK.

Shakeshaft, C. (1987). *Women in educational administration*. Newbury Park, CA: Sage.

Shakeshaft, C. (1989). *Women in educational administration* (2nd ed.). Newbury Park, CA: Sage.

Shakeshaft, C. (1999). The struggle to create a more gender-inclusive profession. In J. Murphy & K. Louis (Eds.), *Handbook of research on educational administration* (2nd ed., pp. 99–118). San Francisco, CA: Jossey-Bass.

Shellard, E. (2003). *Using professional learning communities to support teaching and learning*. Arlington, VA: Educational Research Service.

Sheppard, B. (1996). Exploring the transformational nature of instructional leadership. *Alberta Journal of Educational Research, 42*(4), 325–344.

Short, P. M., & Greer, J. T. (1997). *Leadership in empowered schools: Themes from innovative efforts*. Englewood Cliffs, NJ: Prentice-Hall.

Silins, H., Mulford, B., & Zarins, S. (2002). Organizational learning and school change. *Educational Administration Quarterly, 38*(5), 613–642.

Sirotnik, K. A. (1990). Society, schooling, teaching, and preparing to teach. In J. I. Goodlad, R. Soder, & K. A. Sirotnik (Eds.), *The moral dimensions of teaching* 190–216. San Francisco, CA: Jossey-Bass.

Sirotnik, K. A. (1994). Equal access to quality in public schooling: Issues in the assessment of equity and excellence. In J. I. Goodlad & P. Keating (Eds.), *Access to knowledge* (pp. 159–185). New York: College Entrance Examination Board.

Slater, R. O., & Boyd, W. L. (1999). School as polities. In J. Murphy & K. S. Louis (Eds.), *Handbook of research on educational administration* (2nd ed., pp. 323–335). San Francisco, CA: Jossey-Bass.

Smith, B. L., MacGregor, J., Matthews, R. S., & Gabelnick, F. (2004). *Learning communities: Reforming undergraduate education*. San Francisco, CA: Jossey-Bass.

Smrekar, C. E., & Mawhinney, H. B. (1999). Integrated services: Challenges in linking schools, families, and communities. In J. Murphy & K. S. Louis (Eds.), *Handbook of research on educational administration* (2nd ed., pp. 443–462). San Francisco, CA: Jossey-Bass.

Smylie, M. A., & Hart, A. W. (1999). School leadership for teacher learning and change: A human and social capital development perspective. In J. Murphy & K. S. Louis (Eds.), *Handbook of research on educational administration* (2nd ed., pp. 421–442). San Francisco, CA: Jossey-Bass.

Smyth, J. (1997). Is supervision more than the surveillance of instruction? In J. Glanz & R. F. Neville (Eds.), *Educational supervision: Perspectives, issues, and controversies* (pp. 286–295). Norwood, MA: Christopher-Gordon.

Snowden, P. E., & Gorton, R. A. (2001). *School leadership and administration: Important concepts, case studies and simulations* (7th ed.). New York: McGraw-Hill.

Snyder, T., & Hoffman, C. (2003). *Digests of educational statistics 2002*. Washington, DC: National Center for Educational Statistics, U.S. Department of Education.

Soloman, D., Watson, M., Battistich, V., Schaps, E., & Delucchi, K. (1996). Creating classrooms that students experience as communities. *American Journal of Community Psychology, 24*(6), 719–748.

Sommers, C. H. (2000). *The war against boys: How misguided feminism is harming our young men.* New York: Simon & Schuster.

Southern Regional Education Board. (2006). *Developing internship programs for school leaders. A how-to guide for university and school district partners.* Atlanta, GA: Author.

Southworth, G. (2004). *Primary school leadership in context. Leading small, medium, and large sized schools.* London: Routledge-Falmer.

Sparks, D. (2005a). *Leading for results: Transforming teaching, learning, and relationships in schools.* Thousand Oaks, CA: Corwin Press.

Sparks, D. (2005b). Leading for transformation in teaching, learning, and relationships. In R. DuFour, R. Eaker, & R. DuFour (Eds.), *On common ground* (pp. 154–175). Bloomington, IN: National Educational Service.

Sparks, D. (2005c). What it takes to create profound change in leaders. *National Staff Development Council, 26*(2), 8–15.

Speck, M. (1999). *The principalship: Building a learning community.* Englewood Cliffs, NJ: Prentice-Hall.

Spillane, J. P. (2006). *Distributed leadership.* San Francisco, CA: Jossey-Bass.

Spillane, J. P., & Louis, K. S. (2002). School improvement processes and practices: Professional learning for building instructional capacity. In J. Murphy (Ed.), *The educational leadership challenge: Redefining leadership for the 21st century* (pp. 83–104. Chicago, IL: National Society for the Study of Education Yearbook.

Spillane, J.P., Halverson, R., & Diamond, J.B. (2001). Investigating school leadership

practice: A distributed perspective. *Educational Researcher, 30*, 23–28.

Spring, J. (2002). *American education* (10th ed.). New York: McGraw-Hill.

Starratt, R. J. (1993). *The drama of leadership.* London: Falmer Press.

Starratt, R. J. (1994). *Building an ethical school: A practical response to the moral crisis in schools.* Washington, DC: Falmer Press.

Starratt, R. J. (1996). *Transforming educational administration: Meaning, community, and excellence.* New York: McGraw-Hill.

Sternberg, R. J., & Wagner, R. K. (1986). *Practical intelligence: Nature and origins of competence in the everyday world.* Cambridge, England: Cambridge University Press.

Stevenson, H. (2006). Moving towards, into, and through principalship: Developing a framework for researching career trajectories of school leaders. *Journal of Educational Administration, 44*(4), 408–420.

Stiggins, R. J. (1994). *Student-centered classroom assessment.* Upper Saddle River, NJ: Merrill/ Prentice Hall.

Stiggins, R. J. (2004). New assessment beliefs for a new school mission. *Phi Delta Kappan, 86*(1), 22–27.

Stodolsky, S. (1988). *The subject matters: Classroom activity in math and social studies.* Chicago: University of Chicago Press.

Stokes, L. (2001). Lessons from an inquiring school: Forms of inquiry and conditions for teacher learning. In A. Lieberman & L. Miller (Eds.), *Teachers caught in the action: Professional development that matters* (pp. 141–158). New York: Teachers College Press.

Stokes, R. L. (1984). *Instructional leadership activities in senior high schools in Virginia.* Blacksburg, VA: Virginia Tech.

Stoll, L., & Bolam, R. (2005). Developing leadership for learning communities. In M. J. Coles & G. Southworth (Eds.), *Developing leadership. Creating the school of tomorrow* (pp.50–64). Maidenhead, England: Open University Press.

Stoll, L., Bolam, R., McMahon, A., Walace, M., & Thomas, S. (2006). Professional learning communities: A review of the literature. *Journal of Educational Change, 7*(4), 221–258.

Stoll, L., McMahon, A., & Thomas, S. (2006). Identifying and leading effective professional learning communities. *Journal of School Leadership, 16*(5), 611–623.

Stolp, S. (1994). Leadership for school culture. *ERIC Digest, 91*(June), 1–4.

Stout, K. R. (2000). *The re-conceptualization of organizational socialization: The multiple levels of inclusion and exclusion in sorority membership.* Unpublished doctoral dissertation, University of Utah, Salt Lake City, UT.

Strahan, D. (2003). Promoting a collaborative professional culture in three elementary schools that have beaten the odds. *The Elementary School Journal, 104*(2), 127–146.

Supovitz, J. A. (2002). Developing communities of instructional practice. *Teachers College Record, 104*(8), 1591–1626.

Sweetland, S., & Hoy, W. K. (2000). Social characteristics and educational outcomes: Towards an organizational model of student achievement in Middle Schools. *Educational Administration Quarterly, 36*(5), 703–729.

Talbot, D. (1997). *Looking for tomorrow through yesterday's eyes: A study of training, experience, and role conceptions of principals in restructuring schools.* Unpublished doctoral dissertation, University of Utah, Salt Lake City, UT.

Tannenbaum, A. S. (1962). Control in organizations: Individual adjustment and organizational performance. *Administrative Science Quarterly, 7,* 236–257.

Taylor, Frederick, W. (1911). *The Principles of Scientific Management.* New York: Harper Bros.

Terman, D. L., Larner, M. B., Stevenson, C. S., & Behrman, R. E. (1996). Special education for students with disabilities: Analysis and recommendations. *The Future of Children, 6*(1), 4–24.

Testerman, J. (1996). Holding at-risk students: The secret is one-to-one. *Phi Delta Kappan, 77*(5), 364–365.

Theobold, P., & Nachtigal, P. (1995). Culture, community, and the promise of rural education. *Phi Delta Kappan, 76*(2), 132–135.

Thomas, D. (2001). The truth about mentoring minorities. Race matters. *Harvard Business Review, 79*(4), 98–107, 168.

Thomas, K. (1976). Conflict and conflict management. In M. D. Dunnette (Ed.), *Handbook of industrial and organizational psychology, Vol 1* (pp. 889–935). Chicago: Rand McNally.

Thompson, J. D. (1967). *Organizations in action.* New York: McGraw-Hill.

Thompson, J. (1995). The renaissance of learning in business. In S. Chawala & J. Renesch (Eds.), *Learning organizations: Developing cultures for tomorrow's workplace* (pp. 85–100). New York: Productivity.

Tighe, E., Wang, A., & Foley, E. (2002). *An analysis of the effect of children achieving on student achievement in Philadelphia elementary schools.* Philadelphia: Consortium for Policy Research in Education.

Tillman, L. (2002). The impact of diversity in educational administration. In G. Perreault & F. Lunenberg (Eds.), *The changing world of school administration* (pp. 144–156). Lanham, MA: Scarecrow Press.

Tillman, L. C. (2005). Mentoring new teachers: Implications for leadership practice in an urban school. *Educational Administration Quarterly, 41*(4), 609–629.

Tingley, S. (1996). Pooling our resources: Why are there so few candidates for superintendent? Maybe we're looking in the wrong places. *Education Week, 38,* 48.

Tocci, C. M., & Engelhard, G. E., Jr. (1991). Achievement, parental support, and gender differences in attitudes toward mathematics. *Journal of Educational Research, 84*(5), 280–306.

Tomlinson, P. (1995). *Understanding mentoring: Reflective strategies for school-based teacher preparation.* Buckingham, UK: Open University Press.

Tracy, S. J. (1998). Models and approaches. In G. R. Firth & E. F. Pajak (Eds.), *Handbook of research on school supervision* (pp. 463–487). New York: Simon & Schuster McMillan.

Trice, H. M. (1993). *Occupational subcultures in the workplace.* Ithaca, NY: ILR Press.

Tsang, E. W. K. (1997). Organizational learning and the learning organization: A dichotomy between descriptive and prescriptive research. *Human Relations, 50*(1), 73–90.

Tschannen-Moran, M. (2004). *Trust matters: Leadership for successful schools.* San Francisco, CA: Jossey-Bass.

Tucker, P. D., & Stronge, J. H. (2005). *Linking teacher evaluation and student learning.* Alexandria, VA: Association of Supervision and Curriculum Development.

Tyack, D., & Hansot, E. (1982). *Managers of virtue: Public school leadership in America, 1820–1980.* Boston, MA: Basic Books.

U.S. Bureau of the Census. (2006). National population estimates by characteristics. Retrieved June 1, 2007, from http://www.census.gov/popest/national/asrh/NC-EST2006/NC-EST2006-04-WANH.xls.

Grissmer, D.W. & Ross, J.M. (Eds.). (2000). *Analytic issues in the assessment of student achievement, NCES 2000–050.* Washingon, DC.: U.S. Department of Education.

Valentine, J., Clark, D., Hackmann, D., & Petzko, V. (2003). *A national study of leadership in middle-level schools.* Arlington, VA: National Association of Secondary School Principals.

Van Linden, J. A., & Fertman, C. I. (1998). *Youth leadership: A guide to understanding leadership development in adolescents.* San Francisco, CA: Jossey-Bass.

Van Maanen, J. (1984). Doing new things in old ways: The chains of socialization. In J. L. Bess (Ed.), *College and university organization* (pp. 211–247). New York: New York University Press.

Van Maanen, J., & Schein, E. H. (1979). Toward a theory of organizational socialization. In B. M. Staw & L. L. Cummings (Eds.), *Research in organizational behavior* (Vol. 1, pp. 209–264). Greenwich, CT: JAI Press.

Van Mannen, J., & Barley, S. (1984). Occupational communities: Culture and control in organizations. In B. Staw & L. Cummings (Eds.), *Research in organizational behavior* (Vol. 6, pp. 287–365). Greenwich, CT: JAI Press.

Vroom, V. H., & Jago, A. G. (1988). *The new leadership: Managing participation in organizations.* Englewood Cliffs, NJ: Prentice-Hall.

Vygotsky, L. (1986). *Thought and language* (A. Kozulin, trans.). Cambridge, MA: MIT Press.

Wagner, C. R. (2006). The school leader's tool for assessing and improving school culture. *Principal Leadership, 7*(4), 41–44.

Walker, C., & Dimmock, A. (2005). *Educational leadership: Culture and diversity.* London: Sage Publications Ltd.

Walker, D., & Lambert, L. (1995). Learning and leading theory: A century in the making.

In L. Lambert, D. Walker, D. P. Zimmerman, J. E. Cooper, M. D. Lambert, M. E. Gardner, & P. J. F. Slack (Eds.), *The constructivist leader* (pp. 1–27). New York: Teachers College Press.

Wall, R., & Rinehart, J. S. (1998). School-based decision making and the empowerment of secondary school teachers. *Journal of School Leadership, 8*(1), 49–64.

Waterhouse, L. (2006). Multiple intelligences, the Mozart effect, and emotional intelligence: A critical review. *Educational Psychologist, 41*(4), 207–225.

Watkins, P. (1986). *A critical view of leadership concepts and research: The implications for educational administration.* Geelong: Deakin University.

Webb, L. D., Montello, P. A., & Norton, M. S. (1994). *Human resources administration: Personnel issues and needs in education* (2nd ed.). New York: Macmillan.

Webb, L. D., Montello, P. A., et al. (2004). *Human resources administration: Personnel issues and needs in education.* New York: Macmillan.

Weick, K. (1969). *The social psychology of organizing.* Reading, MA: Addison-Wesley.

Weick, K. (1978). The spines of leaders. In M. W. McCall, Jr., & M. M. Lombardo (Eds.), *Leadership: Where else can we go?* (pp. 37–61). Durham, NC: Duke University Press.

Weick, K. E. (1979). *The social psychology of organizing* (2nd ed.). Reading, MA: Addison-Wesley.

Weick, K. E. (1982). Administering education in loosely coupled schools. *Phi Delta Kappan, 63*(10), 673–676.

Weick, K. (1995, October 25). *Fighting fires in educational administration.* Paper presented at the University Council for Educational Administration, Salt Lake City, UT.

Weick, K. E., & Sutcliffe, K. M. (2007). *Managing the unexpected: Resilient performance in an age of uncertainty.* San Francisco, CA: John Wiley & Sons.

Weindling, D. (1992). New heads for old: Beginning principals in the United Kingdom. In F. W. Parkay & G. E. Hall (Eds.), *Becoming a principal: The challenges of beginning leadership* (pp. 329–348). Boston, MA: Allyn & Bacon.

Weindling, D., & Earley, P. (1987). *Secondary headship: The first years.* Philadelphia: NFER-Nelson.

Weller, L. D., & Weller, S. J. (2002). *The assistant principal. Essentials for effective school leadership.* Thousand Oaks, CA: Corwin Press.

Wenger, E. (1999). *Communities of practice: Learning, meaning, and identity.* Cambridge, MA: Cambridge University Press.

Wenger, E., McDermott, R., & Snyder, W. (2002). *Cultivating communities of practice.* Boston, MA: Harvard Business School Press.

Wenglinsky, H. (2002). How schools matter: The link between teacher classroom practices and student academic performance. *Education Policy Analysis Archives, 2*(12). Retrieved from http://epaa.asu.edu/epaa/v10n12/.

Wentworth, W. M. (1980). *Context and understanding: An inquiry into socialization theory.* New York: Elsevier.

Westheimer, J. (1999). Communities and consequences: An inquiry into ideology and practice in teachers' professional work. *Educational Administration Quarterly, 35*(1), 71–105.

Wheelan, S. A. (2005). *Faculty groups: From frustration to collaboration.* Thousand Oaks, CA: Corwin Press.

Whitaker, K. S. (1995). Principal burnout: Implications for professional development. *Journal of Personnel Evaluation in Education, 9*(3), 287–296.

Wiggins, G. (1993). *Assessing student performance.* San Francisco, CA: Jossey-Bass.

Wiggins, G. (1994). None of the above. *The Executive Educator, 16*(7), 14–18.

Williams, E., Matthews, J., Stewart, C., & Hilton, S. (2007, November). *The learning community culture indicator: The development and validation of an instrument to measure multi-dimensional application of learning communities in schools.* Paper presented at the University Council for Education Administration, Washington, DC.

Wilson, A. L. (2005). Activity theory. In L. M. English (Ed.), *International encyclopedia of adult education* (pp. 25–30). London: Palgrave Macmillan.

Withers, M. (2003). *The quality of state mandated mentoring and the impact on teacher performance.* Unpublished doctoral dissertation, Salt Lake City: University of Utah.

Wolf, A. (1977). *Poverty and achievement.* Washington, DC: National Institute of Education.

Wong, K. K., & Nicotera, A. (2007). *Successful schools and educational accountability: Concepts and skills to meet leadership challenges.* Boston, MA: Pearson Education.

Worner, W., & Brown, G. (1993). The instructional leadership team: A new role for the department head. *NASSP Bulletin, 77*(553), 37–45.

Yee, D. L. (2000). Images of school principals' information and communication technology leadership. *Journal of Information Technology for Teacher Education, 9*(3), 287–302.

York-Barr, J., & Duke, K. (2004). What do we know about teacher leadership? Findings from two decades of scholarship. *Review of Educational Research, 74*(3), 255–316.

York-Barr, J., Sommers, W. A., Ghere, G. S., & Montie, J. (2001). *Reflective practice to improve schools: An action guide for educators.* Thousand Oaks, CA: Corwin Press.

Youngs, P. (2007). How elementary principals' beliefs and actions influence new teachers' experiences. *Educational Administration Quarterly, 43*(1), 101–137.

Yukl, G. (2005). *Leadership in organizations.* Englewood Cliffs, NJ: Prentice Hall.

Zachary, L. (2000). *The mentor's guide.* San Francisco, CA: Jossey-Bass.

Zepeda, S. J., & Langenbach, M. (1999). *Special programs in regular schools: Historical foundations, standards, and contemporary issues.* Boston, MA: Allyn & Bacon.

Zera, D. (1992). Coming of age in a heterosexist world: The development of gay and lesbian adolescents. *Adolescence, 27*(108), 849–854.

Zmuda, A., Kuklis, R., & Line, E. (2004). *Transforming schools: Creating a culture of continuous improvement.* Alexandria, VA: Association of Supervision and Curriculum Development.

INDEX

('b' indicates boxed material; 't' indicates a table)

Academic qualifications, principal, 27
Accelertaion, 133
Accountability, 215–216, 234
Action research, 82
Activity theory, 62, 64
Actor, principal as, 97
Adequate yearly progress (AYP), 2, 38b,
    42b, 53, 215
Adjustment socialization stage, 300t, 301
Adler, S. A. 118, 120, 123
Administrators, school leadership
    influence, 144
Adult learning, 63–65
Advisory decision making, 169f, 170
Advocacy
    community, 136–137
    definition, 111
    facilitation, 137–139
    legal criterion, 113
    moral criterion, 111–113
    school, 129–136
    students, 117–129
    thoughtfulness criterion, 114–115
    transformative, 110
Advocate, principal as, 14–15, 106–108,
    117–120
African American school leaders,
    23t, 25
Agenda setting, 284
Allocation of scarce resources, 268
Alsalam, N., 193
Alternative education, 135–136
American Association of School Administrators
    (AASA), 28
American public school, history, 19–20
Anderson, K., 82, 83
Anderson, R. E., 256
Anticipatory socialization stage,
    299, 300t

Apple, M. W., 273, 274
Argyris, C., 71, 72
Assessment, reform efforts, 254
Assistant principal
    average salaries 2004, 39t
    history, 21–22
    political role, 285–286
    in professional learning community, 80–81
    socialization, 306–313
    supervisor role, 213–214
    future trends, 334
Association for Supervision and Curriculum
    Development (ASCD), 19b, 28
At-risk students
    alternative programs, 135–136
    identification, 128–129
    success as PLC element, 48
Attribution theory, leadership
    study, 156
Average daily attendance
    (ADA), 247
Average daily membership (ADM), 247, 248

"Back to the Future Bureaucratic Systems,"
    OECD scenario, 334–335
Balkanization, collaboration, 173
Banks, J. A., 121, 129, 130
Barkley, S. G., 197
Barnard, Henry, 19
Barth, R. S., 14, 51
Basic assumptions, school culture, 88–89
Beach, D., 211
Beane, J. A., 273, 274
Beck, L. G., 31, 33
Behavior approaches, leadership, 150–152
Beliefs, school culture, 88
Bellah, R. N., 272, 287
Best Mode for Opening Institutions of Learning,
    The (Sturm), 21

Beyer, B., 121
Bilingual education, 130–131
Blake, R. R., 151
Blankstein, A. M., 46
Blase, J., 153, 202, 211, 225, 282, 283, 289
Blink: The Power of Thinking Without Thinking
    (Gladwell), 70, 246
Block, P., 154
Bolman and Deal Leadership Frameworks
    model, 74t
Bolman, L. G., 47, 73, 115, 268, 269, 270,
    279, 284
Boshee, M., 121
Bossert, S. T., 154
Bothe, D., 223
Boundary spanner, principal as, 278, 317
Bowling Alone (Putnam), 272
Boyd, W. L., 270, 272
Bredeson, P. V., 79
Bridges, E. M., 230
Brighton, C. M., 192
Brown, G., 257
Brown v. Board of Education of Topeka (1954),
    113, 120
Bryk, A., 9–10, 45, 54, 152, 226, 227
Buffered model, leadership reciprocity, 82
Builder, principal as, 55
Bulach, C., 223
Burden, L., 32
Burkett, C. W., 33, 253
Burnette, B., 102
Burns, J. M., 32

Callahan, Raymond, 27, 28, 243, 297
Cambron-McCabe, N., 263
Camburn, E., 9–10, 54, 209
Campbell, E., 20, 32
Capacity, constructivist learning, 62
Career development, mentoring, 194–196
Caring, moral responsibility, 112–113
Carnegie Forum's report, 36
Carter, K., 201
Catholic Church, education
    influence, 31
Celebrations, mentoring, 195–196

Center, principal as, 55
Centrality, 51
Centralization, 36, 37
Certification, principal, 27–28
Change agent, principal as, 160
Change, and leadership, 5, 8
Charter schools, 37
Chavis, D. M., 45
Child-centered approach, 36
Chrispeels, J. H., 82
Christian ideal, education
    influence, 30
Churchill, Winston, 7
Cibulka, J. G., 271
Civil Rights Act of 1964, 36
Civil societies, schools as, 272, 275
Claudet, J. G., 225, 236
Closed principals, political role,
    283, 284
Closure, mentoring, 191
Co-constructing, 294
Co-mentoring, 179–180
Coach, principal as, 160
Coalitions, 268, 284
Coleman, J. S., 36
Collaboration
    conflict mediation, 171–173
    decision-making, 168, 169f, 170
    facilitating, 167–168
    problems, 173–174
    teaming, 170–171
Collaborative problem solving, 243
Collaborative teaming, 47, 50
    and student success, 49
Collective vision, 158–160
Collective vs. individual, socialization
    method, 302
Collegial mentoring, 198
Comfortable collaboration, 173–174
Commitment
    in collaboration, 168
    vs. control, 8
Committee of Ten, 1993 report, 35
Common mission, PLC element, 47
Common school movement, 19–20

Common School Teacher's Association
(1839), 20
Commonly held values and beliefs, school
culture, 88
Community advocacy, 136–137
Community
building as school responsibility, 33
characteristics of, 9
principal's political role in, 287–288
schools as, 8–10
term, 45–46
Community constructivist learning, 62–63
Community-school relationships, 277–280
Competence, moral responsibility, 112
Complexity, principal as learner, 72–73
Conceptual influences, 30–32
Conferencing, mentoring, 190
Conflict
benefits, 269
collaborative teams, 171–172
management, 172–173
organizational dynamics, 268
Conformity, 305
Consideration, leader behavior, 150
Constituents, school leadership influence,
144–145
Constructivist learning, 61–63
capacity, 62
community, 62–63
criticality, 63
Consulting decision making, 169f, 170
Content innovation, 306
Contested model, leadership reciprocity, 83
Context, 62, 64
Contingency approaches,
leadership, 152
Continuous assessment, PLC
element, 48
Contrived collegiality, 174, 219
Control, in schools, 8
Cook, C., 172
Copland, M. A., 68
Corporate model schools, 24
Counseling, mentoring, 196
"Country-club management," 151

"Country club" sports, 119
Covey, S. R., 32
Cox, M. D., 179
Creative individualism, 305
Criterion referenced tests (CRT), 42b
Criticality, constructivist learning, 63
Criticism, in mentoring, 202
Crow, G. M., 50, 244, 253–254, 275, 281, 296,
298, 327
Crowson, R. L., 267, 278
Cuban, L., 36, 44, 156
Cubberley, Ellwood P., 20, 29–30, 30–31, 32,
107, 120
Culbertson, J. A., 27
Cultural diversity, 65, 107, 120–121
Cultural shifts, in PLC, 96t
Culturally proficiency continuum, 119
Culture building, 14, 86. *See also* School
culture
Culture change facilitation, 101–102
Culture reinforcement mechanisms, 93
Culture shifting, 44–45
Curriculum compacting, 133
Custodial orientation, 306

Daft, R. L., 7, 11, 88, 151, 152, 158
Daily activities, and school culture, 99
Dantley, M. E., 110
Daresh, J. C., 184, 314, 316
Data and research based decision making, PLC
element, 47–48, 69
Data-directed dialogue, 92
Dawe, R., 174
Deal, T. E., 14, 47, 71, 87, 89, 90, 92,
95, 97, 99, 101, 115, 268, 269, 270,
279, 284
Debevoise, W., 34
Decentralization, 36, 37
Deficit perspective, 60
Dembele, M., 183
Democratic institutions, schools as,
272–274, 275
Democratic schooling, 34
Demographics, changes, 65–66,
106–108, 332

Deprivatization of practice, 9
Dewey, John, 8, 24b, 35, 45, 62, 70
Dexter, S., 256
Dimmock, A., 117
Direct supervision, 214–216
Direction-setter, principal as, 160
Distributed leadership, 78, 164
Diversity, teacher selection, 218–219
Divestiture vs. investiture, socialization
　　method, 303, 321
Double-loop learning, 71
Douglas, H. R., 32
Doyle, W., 199
Dreeban, R., 281
Driscoll, M. E., 277
Duffy, F. M., 50
DuFour, Richard, 43, 46, 50, 53, 96, 102, 238
Duke, K., 81
Dutton, J., 263
Dyadic approach, leadership, 153

Eakcr, Robert, 43, 46, 50, 96, 238
Ebmeier, H., 233
Ebonics, 123
Economic development, school
　　responsibility, 33
*Education and the Cult of Efficiency: A Study of
　　the Social Forces That Have Shaped the
　　Administration of the Public Schools*
　　(Callahan), 243
Education for All Handicapped Children Act
　　(EAHC, 1975), 126, 127, 131
Education Research Service, leadership
　　shortages report, 38
Educational Leadership, 86b
Educational reform, 43
　　federal and state requirements, 49
　　in learning communities, 43–45
Educational underclass, 65
Educator growth promotion, 220–226, 236
Egley, R. J., 234
Ehrich, L., 184, 185
Elementary and Secondary Education Act
　　(ESEA, 1965), 36, 43
　　Title I, 134–135

Ellett, C. D., 225, 236
Elmore, R. F., 44
Embedding culture, 92–93
Emotional intelligence, 67
Empowerment, 164, 165
Emulation, 7
Encounter socialization stage, 300t,
　　300–301
Enduring differences, 268
Engelking, J., 121
English as a second language (ESL), 130, 131
English Language Learners (ELL), 130
Enomoto, E., 199
Enrichment in regular classroom, 133
Enrollments, future, 39
Equity, and excellence, 114
Espoused theories, 72
Estler, S., 24
Ethic diversity, 65, 107, 120–121
Ethical leadership, 31–32
Evaluation
　　educational results, 227–230, 237–238
　　instructional capacity building, 227–230
　　performance data collection and analysis,
　　　231–232
　　reform efforts, 254
　　supervision as, 210
Excellence, and equity, 114
Expertise
　　in collaboration, 168
　　teacher selection, 217–218
"Extended Market Model," OECD scenario,
　　335–336
External constituents, and school
　　culture, 101
External sources, leadership, 143–145
Extra-school activities, 133

Facilitation, 64, 65
　　advocacy, 137–139
　　evaluation and assessment, 262–263
　　leadership, 164–174
　　mentoring, 196–204
　　PLC management, 256–261
　　PLC planning, 261–262

political role, 286–289
school culture change, 101–102
supervision, 232–238
teacher leader, 82–83
Facilitator, principal as, 74–80
Fairness, 31
Fayol, Henri, 242
Feiman-Nemser, S., 196, 201
Fertman, C. I., 206
Fink, D., 137
First-order change, 156–157, 157t
Fisher, R., 284
Fit, teacher selection, 217
Fixed vs. variable, socialization method, 302
Followers, and leadership, 8
Forbes, Esther, 52
Formal mentors, 198–199
Formal position, 6
Formal vs. informal, socialization
    method, 302
Formative evaluation, 254
Fragmented school culture, 90, 91
Frameworks for leadership, 73, 74t
Freedom, and social justice, 113
French, J. R. P., 153, 269
Friedman, Thomas, 335
Friend, M., 172
Full Communication model, peer
    mentoring, 197
Full-collaboration decision making,
    169f, 170
Full-time equivalency (FTE), 247, 248
Fullan, Michael, 77, 80, 86b, 91, 96, 161, 173,
    174, 258, 259

Gamoran, A., 281
Ganser, T., 196,197, 200
Gardiner, H., 182
Gardiner, M. E., 199
Gardner, Howard, 61
Gardner, J. W., 205
Garrod, A., 205
GASing socialization method, 304
Gay, lesbian, bisexual and transgendered
    individuals (GLBT), 116, 126

Gehrke, N. J., 178, 179
Gender, educational impact, 125
General supervisor, 32
Gerson, K., 215
Ghere, G. S., 70
Gifted and talented (GT) education, 127–128
    programs, 133–134
Gladwell, Malcolm, 70, 246
Glanz, J., 21, 22
Glass, G. V., 333
Glickman, C. D., 188, 222, 223, 224
Global knowledge society, 10
Globalization, and learning, 66
Goal statements, 158, 159t
Goddard, R., 290
Goldring, E., 254, 278, 279, 280, 281, 317
Goleman, Daniel, 67, 68
Gordon, S. P., 223
Gorton, R. A., 163
"Great man theory," 6–7, 149
Greene, M., 274
Greenfield, W. D., 13, 34, 304, 304, 311
Greenleaf, R., 32, 155
Greer, J. T., 164, 165, 261, 262
Gregg, R. T., 32
Grogan, M., 199
Groopman, Jerome, 246
Gross, B., 243
Group think, 219
Gulick, Luther, 242–243

Hage, J., 10, 66
Hagger, H., 183, 184
Hall, D, T., 4, 247, 301, 303, 313, 324, 326
Hallinger, , 34
Hansford, B., 184, 185
Hansot, E., 20, 24, 25, 27
Hargreaves, A., 78, 96, 137, 173, 174, 192, 249,
    251, 258, 259
Harper, William Rainey, 35
Hart, A. W., 79, 295, 299, 324
Hart and Bredeson's leadership roles, 79–80
Hausman, C., 309
Headmaster, term, 21
Healer, principal as, 97

Higgins, M. C., 179
Hipp, K. K., 43
Hispanic school leaders, 23t, 25
Historical and current artifacts, school
    culture, 88
Holder of the vision, principal as, 55
Hord, S. M., 43, 45, 46
How Doctors Think (Groopman), 246
Hoy, W., K., 167, 237
Hoyle, J. R., 162
Huff, S., 204
Huffman, J. B., 43
Human resource framework, 73, 74t

Identity, and social justice, 115–116
Ideologies, understanding current, 274–275
Immigrant population, 66
Implementation, reform efforts, 253–254
"Impoverished management," 151
Improving America's School Act (IASA,
    1994), 37
Individual education plan (IEP), 126
Individual role conception, 3
Individuals with Disabilities Education Act
    (IDEA, 1990), 126, 131, 132
Individuals with Disabilities Education
    Improvement Act (IDEIA, 2004), 108, 126
Industrial age assumptions, 60
Influence, in leadership, 7
Influences, principal's role, 4, 13, 26–30
Information collecting, 69
Information management, 260–261
Ingersoll, R. M., 193
Initiating structure, leader behavior, 150
Innovation
    mid-career, 324–328
    in professional learning community, 296
    in supervision, 214–215
Inquiry
    moral responsibility, 111–112
    principal as learner, 67–69
Inspector, vs. mentor, 30
Instructional capacity building, 215
    accountability, 215–216
    evaluation, 227–230

growth promotion, 220–226
recruitment, 216–217
selection, 216–219, 234–235
trust, 226–227
Instructional leadership,34–35
Integration, of knowledge, 61
Integrity, 31
Interactive model, leadership reciprocity, 82
Interactive professionalism, 259
Interdependence, PLC element, 47
Internal sources, leadership, 145–146
Interstate School Leaders Licensure
    Consortium Standards (ISLCC), 28,
    31–31
Interstate School Leadership Consortium
    Council (ISLLC), 86
Isolation, 51

Jacobsen, L., 118
Jeanes, Anna T., 25
Jefferson, Thomas, 19
Johari window, 68
Johnson, B., 252
Johnson, Susan Moore, 185, 188, 199,
    217, 219
Jones, B. D., 234

Kalvelage, J., 23, 24
Kealy, W. A., 179
Kelly, D. M., 135
Kelly, G., 22
Kennedy, A. A., 99
Kerchner, C. T., 277
Kerr, D. H., 115
Kimbrough, R. B., 33, 253
King James Bible, 31
King, M., 99
Kirby, P. C., 202
Kleiner, A., 263
Knowledge
    explosion and learning, 66–67
    future importance, 332
    moral responsibility, 112
Knowledge society, 10–11
Kohn, M. L., 182

Kotter, J. P., 269
Kottkamp, R. B., 72
Kowalski, T. J., 28
Kram, K. E., 179, 181, 190, 202
Kruse, S. D., 46, 117

Lambert, Linda, 81
Langenbach, M., 123
Language diversity, 122–123
Language-plural world, 124
Leader Behavior Description Questionnaire
    (LBDQ), 150
Leadership
    competence acquisition, 11–12
    definitions, 5–7
    ethical, 31–32
    experiential learning, 6–7
    external sources, 143–145
    frameworks for, 73, 74t
    instructional, 34–35
    internal sources, 145–146
    of learning, 5
    literature, 146–149
    moral, 30–31
    person and system view, 13
    principal, 143, 146
    reciprocity, 82–83
    research, 149–156
    Rost's definition, 7–8
Leadership for Organizational Learning and
    Student Outcomes (LOLSO) study, 78
Leadership teams, school culture, 102
Learner, principal as, 14, 59–60, 65–73
Learning
    adult , 63–65
    constructivist 61–63
    knowledge society, 65–67
    and leadership, 5
    primacy of, 59
    traditional conception of, 60–61
Learning cycles, 325
"Learning in Networks Replacing Schools,"
    OECD scenario, 336
Learning organizations, 75
    assistant principal's role, 80–81

characteristics, 77–78
core ideas, 76
Hart and Bredeson's leadership roles, 79–80
principal's facilitating role, 78–79, 82–83
Senge's disciplines, 76t, 76–77
teacher leader's role, 81–82
Learning partner, 295
Least-restrictive environment (LRE), 126,
    127, 132
Leithwood, F., 69
Lenses, and social justice, 115
Lexus and the Olive Tree, The (Friedman), 335
Licensure, principal, 27–28
Limited English proficiency (LEP), 123, 130,
    131, 215
Lindsey, R. B., 119
Literature, leadership, 146–149, 148t
Little, J. W., 51, 53, 98
Local education agency (LEA), 126, 134
Local reform initiatives, 44
Loder, T. L., 317
Lomotey, K., 182
Loosely coupled systems, 44
Lortie, D. C., 231
Louis, K. S., 9–10, 46, 49, 52, 54, 117, 247, 250
Lucas, T., 263
Luehe, B., 211

Madeline Hunter teaching effectiveness
    model, 41b, 43
Madison, James, 113
Maeroff, G. I., 171
Magnet schools, 133–134, 135
Management, 241–242
    contemporary conditions, 37
    facilitation, 261–263
    information, 260–261
    and leadership, 6
    money, 257–258
    personnel, 258–259
    strategies, 260t
    technology, 255–256
    time, 259
    the unexpected, 244–252
Manager, principal as, 15

Mann, Horace, 19, 20, 43
Many, T., 96, 238
Markman, L. B., 92
Marks, H. M., 49, 52
Marland, S., 127
Marshall, C., 22, 285, 308
Marsick, V. J., 77
Martin, K. J., 82, 244–245
Martin, T. L., 203
Marvel, J., 219
Mathews, J., 46
Matthews, L. J., 253–254, 296, 327
Maxcy, S. J., 273
McCleary, L. E., 253–254
McIntyre, D., 183, 184
McMillan, D. W., 45
Mediation, collaborative team conflict,
    171–173
Melting pot conformity, 120
Mendez-Morse, S., 179
Mental models, Senge discipline, 76t, 76–77
Mentor
    in *Odyssey*, 178
    vs. inspector, 30
Mentoring, 137–138, 178–180
    benefits, 184
    career development, 194–196
    and coaching, 180
    content, 182–183
    functions, 181
    new teachers, 196–199
    participants, 181–182
    peer, 200–201
    pitfalls, 184–185
    processes, 183–184
    profession development, 186–190
    psychosocial development, 192–194
    reflective, 190–191
    roles, 180
    students, 204–205
    teaching teams, 203–204
    training, 199–200
    veteran teachers, 201–203, 204–205
Merriam, S. B., 65
Merrill, R. J., 38

Mertz, N. T., 180
Mezirow, J., 64
Micropolitics, 282
Mid-career innovation, 324–328
Miles, M. B., 259
Minorities, as principals, 23t, 25–26
Miskel, C. G., 167
Mission statements, 158, 159t
Mitchell, B. A., 285
Mitchell, C., 55
Moller, G., 83
Money management, 257–258
Mono-ethnic courses, 129
Montello, P. A., 228
Montie, J., 70
Moral leadership, 30–31
Morrissey, M. S., 247, 250
Mortimer, J. T., 295
Moulding, students, 108
Mulford, B., 290
Mullen, C. A., 179
Multicultural curriculum development, 121
Multicultural education, 130
    programs, 129–130
Multiethnic education, 130
Multiethnic studies, 129-130
Multiple intelligences, 61
Murphy, J., 31, 34, 35, 210, 336
Murry v. Curlett (1963), 122
Myers, V. L., 259

Nachtigal, P., 33
Nanus, B., 160, 166, 258
*Nation at Risk, A: The Imperative for Educational
    Reform* (NCEE, 1983), 35, 36
National Association of Elementary School
    Principals (NAESP), 28
National Association of Secondary School
    Principals (NASSP), 28
National Center for Education Statistics
    (NCES), 22
National Commission of Excellence in
    Education (NCEE), 35
National Education Administration (NEA), 23,
    28, 29

National Educational Technology Standards
for Administrators (NETS-A), 255
National Staff Development Council
(NSDC), 29
Native American school leaders, 23t, 25
"Natural" leader, 6
Negative face of power, 268
Negative roles, toxic school culture, 91
Network centrality, principal's 52
Networking, 196, 284
New teachers
mentoring, 196–199
sources of anxiety, 193
Newcomers, and school culture, 100
Newmann, F. M., 102
Nicotera, A., 228
No Child Left Behind Act (NCLP, 2001), 16,
34, 35, 37, 43, 44, 53, 85b, 107, 130, 134,
215, 332
Noddings, N., 113
Nonteaching principal, 24
Normal schools, 27
Norton, M. S., 228

O'Brien, D. E., 323
Obey-Porter Comprehensive Reform
Demonstration Program (1997), 36–37
Observation skills, 70
Ogawa, R. T., 154
Open principals, political role, 283, 284
Oplatka, I., 325, 326
Opotow, S., 285, 289
Opportunities, school culture, 98
Opposition, and vision, 162
Organization for Education Cooperation and
Development (OECD), future school
scenarios, 334–336
Organizational feature, leadership as, 153–154
Organizational learning, 75
Organizational socialization, 298–299, 301–303
Ortiz, F. I., 22, 26
Outcomes clarity, 50

Pai, Y., 118, 120, 123
Pankake, A., 83

Parkay, F. W., 318, 319, 320
Parsons, T., 270
Participate leadership, 47
Patton, J., 256, 257
Peer collaboration, 9
Peer mentoring, 200–201, 327
Performance-based testing, 262
Person and system view, 13
Person-orientation, leader behavior, 150
Personal mastery, Senge discipline, 76, 76t
Personal socialization, 299, 303–304
Personnel management,258–259
Peters, D. A., 94, 224
Peterson, K. D., 14, 87, 89, 90, 92, 95, 97, 101,
102, 280, 299
Piaget, Jean, 62
Pierce, P. R., 20, 21, 26, 30, 242
"Playing politics," 33
Playko, M. A., 184
Plessy v. Ferguson, 113
Poet, principal as, 97
Policymakers, school leadership
influence, 144
Political framework, 73, 74t
Political systems, schools, as 271–272
Political thinking, 268–270
ideologies, 274–275
Politician, principal as, 15, 139, 267–271
Popular literature, leadership literature,
146–147
POSDCoRB, scientific management list, 243
Positional leadership, 78
Positive Reinforcement model, peer
mentoring, 197
Post, D., 276, 287
Potter, principal as, 97
Pounder, D. G., 38, 50, 319
Pounders, M. L., 303, 317
Poverty, educational impact, 124–125
Power gap, 269
Power resources, 7, 268
Powers, C. H., 10, 66
Practice influence, 29–30
Praxis, 64, 65
Prevention and intervention, PLC element, 48

Primary mentor, 181
Principal
    advocate role, 106–108
    average salaries 2004, 39t
    and culture building, 92–93, 97–102
    current demands on, 37–39
    as facilitator, 74–80
    future trends, 334
    and district, 281–282
    historical role, 19–22
    and leadership, 5–8
    leadership facilitation, 164–174
    leadership purpose, 156–157
    as learner, 14, 59–60, 65–73, 293–294
    managing the unexpected, 246–252
    mentoring role, 185–190
    minorities as, 22–26
    political role, 138–139, 274–285
    professional learning community functions,
        54–55
    professional learning community role, 51–53
    role conceptions, 3–5, 13–16
    role misconceptions, 6–7
    role perceptions, 1b–2b, 2–3
    socialization, 314–324
    student learning focus, 53–54
    supervisor role, 209–213
    term, 21
    vision building, 158–164
    women as, 22–26
Principal teacher, duties of 20–21
Problem finding, 69
Profession development, mentoring, 186–190
Professional associations, 28–29, 34
Professional community, 46
    core practices, 9
Professional development, 48
Professional journals, school leadership, 147t
Professional learning community (PLC), 8–10
    cultural shifts in, 44–45, 96t, 108
    development barriers, 50–51
    and educational reform, 43–45
    elements, 46–48
    institutionalizing, 263
    leadership, 143–146

    management, 252–256
    management facilitation, 256–261
    models, 46
    movement, 34, 42b
    perception, 1b–2b
    principal's functions, 54–55
    principal's role in, 51–53
    social capital building, 289–290
    and social justice, 110
    supervision facilitation, 232–238
    supporting research, 48–50
    leadership literature, 147
Professional socialization, 297–298
Programmatic vision, 159
Protestantism, education influence, 30–31
Psychosocial development, mentoring,
    192-194
Public Law 94-142. *See* Education for All
    Handicapped Children Act
Public self, 68
Pullout programs
    enrichment 133
    Title I, 135
Putnam, R., 272

Qualitative method, 69
Quantitative method, 69

Racial diversity, 120–121
Rallis, S., 254, 278, 279, 317
Raven, B., 153, 269
Raywid, M. A., 136
Reciprocal leadership, 7
Recommendation decision making,
    169f, 170
Recruitment, 216–219, 234–235
"Reculturing," 62
Reeves, D. B., 221
Reflective dialogue, 9
Reflective mentoring, 190–191
Reflectivity, principal as learner, 70–72
Reinhartz, J., 211
Reitzug, U. C., 28, 212, 213, 214, 221, 222, 224
Relationship, leadership as, 153
Relevance, in collaboration, 167–168

Religion, education influence, 30–31
Religious diversity, 122
Resistance to change, 50–51
Resources
    school culture, 98
    and vision, 162
Response to intervention (RTI), 126
Retention, 219–220, 235
Richardson, V., 201
Riehl, C. J., 116, 117, 240
Roberts, R., 230
Roberts, S. M., 79
Role conception, 3
Role conflict, 4–5
    and ambiguity in teaching, 182–183
Role definition, 4
Role innovation, 306
Role making, 4, 301
Role model, principal as, 55
Role taking, 4
Rosenthal, R., 118
Ross-Gordon, J. M., 223
Rost, J. C.,7-8, 11, 156, 157
Ruff, W. G., 77

Sackney, L., 55
Saphier, J., 99
Sawyer, R. K., 259
Scaffolding knowledge, 62
Schein, E. H., 87, 92, 101, 155, 302, 305, 321
Schein's cultural elements, 87–89
Scheurich, J. J., 117
Schlechty, P., 201, 228
Schmoker, M., 231
Schneider, B., 45, 152, 226, 227
Schnur, J., 215
Scholarly literature, leadership literature,
    147–149, 148t
Schön, Donald A., 70, 71, 72, 190
School administration, 2
School advocacy, 129
    alternative education, 135–136
    bilingual education, 130–131
    gifted and talented (GT) programs, 133–134
    multicultural education programs, 129–130

special education, 131–133
Title 1 ESEA program, 134–135
School-based management, 243
School-community relationships, 277–280
School culture, 86–87
    developing, 97–98
    elements, 87–89
    existing, 89–90
    external constituents, 101
    facilitating change, 101–102
    leadership teams, 102
    maintenance, 93–96
    newcomers, 100
    principal leadership, 14, 92–93
    strong, 91–92
    toxic, 90–91
    veteran teachers, 98–100
School district, political influence,
    280–282, 288
School District of Abington Township v. Schempp
    (1963), 122
School population changes, 26–27
School reforms, 35–37
Schooler, C., 182
Schools
    as community, 8, 45–46
    as learning organizations, 75–78
    as political arena, 282–285, 288–289
"Schools as Core Social Centres," OECD
    scenario, 335
"Schools as Focused Learning Organizations,"
    OECD scenario, 335
Schools That Learn (Senge), 46
Scientific management, 29, 59, 242–243
Scribner, J. P., 54, 259
Second Vatican Council, 31
Second-order change, 156, 157, 157t
Secondary mentor, 181
Selection criteria, new teachers, 217
Self-awareness, principal as
    learner, 67
Senge, Peter, 8, 46, 58b, 60, 61, 70, 71
Senge's five disciplines, 76t, 76–77
Sequential vs. random, socialization
    method, 302

Sergiovanni, T. J., 8, 32, 33, 155, 165, 228, 229, 252, 263
Serial vs. disjunctive, socialization method, 302
Servant leader, 32, 79
Sexual orientation, discrimination, 116, 125–126
Shackelford, J. A., 316, 318, 320, 322
Shared beliefs, in community, 9
Shared decision-making, 243
Shared interests and purposes, school culture, 98
Shared norms, of learning, 9
Shared purposes, in leadership, 7, 8
Shared vision, Senge discipline, 76, 76t
Shoho, A. R., 77
Short, P. M., 164, 165, 261, 262
Significant change, in leadership, 7–8
Silent Mentor model, peer mentoring, 197
Simmons, R. G., 295
Single-loop learning, 71
Sirotnik, K. Λ., 111, 112, 114
Situated cognition, 62, 64
Skrla, L., 117
Slater, R. O., 270, 272, 275
Smith, B., 263
Smith, Marshall, 36
Snowden, P. E., 163
Social capital, 277–278
Social class, educational impact, 124–125
Social construction, 62, 87
Social demographics, schools impact, 26–27, 106–108
Social justice, 33, 34, 108–109, 332
    barriers to, 116
    components, 108
    and freedom, 113
    and principals, 115–117
Social learning, of leadership, 12–13
Socialization
    assistant principal, 306–313
    content, 295–297, 307–308, 314–315
    definition, 296
    methods, 301–303, 310–313, 321–323
    mid-career innovation, 324–328

    new roles, 294–297
    outcomes, 304–306, 313, 323–324
    principal, 314–325
    sources, 297–299, 308–309, 315–318
    stages, 299–301, 300t, 309–310, 318–321
Societal trends, 332–324
Society, principal's political role in, 286–287
Socioeconomic status (SES), districts, 282
Sommers, W. A., 45, 70
Southworth, G., 78, 79
Special education, 131–133
Special supervisors, 31
Spillane, J. P., 247, 250, 317
Spokesperson, principal as, 160
Stager, M., 69
Standard English, 123
Starratt, R. J., 159, 228, 229
Status quo, and leadership, 5
Stewart, C., 46
Stewartship theory (Block), 154–155
Stiggins, R. J., 262
Stokes, R. L., 256
Stories, mentoring, 191
Storytelling, socialization, 322
Strategic planning, 252, 253
Stronge, J. H., 232
Structural framework, 73, 74t
Student learning focus, principal leadership, 47, 53–54
Student performance data collection and analysis, 231–232
Students, mentoring, 204–205
Students with special needs, 126–127
Sturm, Johann, 21
Subculture understanding, 99
Summative evaluation, 254
Supervision
    conceptions of, 224–226
    direct, 214–216
    elements, 211–213
    facilitation, 232–233
    history, 211
    innovation, 214–215
    instructional capacity building, 215–230

practice, 212t
shared, 233
term, 30, 209, 210
Sutliffe, K. M., 245
Symbolic framework, 73, 74t
Symbols, principal as, 97
Systems thinking, Senge discipline,
76t, 77

Talbot, D., 253
Tarter, C. J., 237
Task orientation, leader behavior, 150
Taylor, Frederick W., 29, 242
"Teacher Exodus and System Meltdown,"
OECD scenario, 336
Teacher expectations/student achievement,
118–119
Teacher leader
principal's facilitation of, 82–83
in professional learning community, 81–82
Teachers College of Columbia, 27
Teaching and learning focus, PLC element, 47
Team collaboration, 170–171
decision making, 169f, 170
Team learning, Senge discipline, 76t, 77
"Team management," 151
Teams, mentoring, 203–204
Technology
future schools, 332
and learning, 66
management, 255–256
Theobold, P., 33
Theories in use, 72
Theory movement, 27
Thomas, D., 182
Thompson, J. D., 238
TiGeR model, supervision, 225
Tillman, L. C., 110
Time, in collaboration, 168
Time management, 259
Title 1 ESEA programs, 134–135
Tomlinson, P., 189–190
Toxic school culture, 90–91
Tracking, 109
Tracy, S. J., 236

Trait approaches, leadership, 149
Transactional leadership, 154
Transformational leadership, 154
Transformational learning
theory, 64
Transformative advocacy, 110
Trice, H. M., 303
Trust
building, 226–227, 236–237
in school culture, 47, 91
Tschannen-Moran, M., 226
Tucker, P. D., 232
Two-way Communication model, peer
mentoring, 197
Tyack, D., 20, 24, 25, 27

Understanding levels, school
culture, 89
Unexpected, managing the, 244–246
Unilateral decision making, 169f, 170
University of Chicago, 35
Unknown self, 68
Urban school systems, 26–27
Urbanization, 333
Urv, W., 284

Values and goals setting, 33
Values, school culture, 88
Van Linden, J. A., 206
Van Maanen, J., 302, 321
Veteran teachers
mentoring, 201–203, 204–205
mentoring as advocates, 138
school culture, 98–99
Vision
building, 158–160
challenges of building, 162
communicating, 162–164
dark side, 161
facilitating teachers, 166—167
PLC element, 47
principal's role, 55, 97, 160–161
programmatic, 159
shared, 76, 76t
teacher, student and parent roles, 166

Vision statements, 158, 159t
Visionary, principal as, 97
Vouchers, 37
Vygotsky, L., 62

Wagner, C. R., 90
Walker, C., 117
Waterman, J. R. H., 94
Watkins, K. E., 77
Watson, S. T., 259
Webb, L. D., 228
Weick, Karl E., 44, 72, 73, 245, 314
Weindling, D., 318, 320
Well-being, and social justice, 113
Westheimer, J., 9

Whitaker, K. S., 37
Whitt, R. L., 32
Wiggins, G., 231, 262
Williams, E., 46
Witkoskie, L., 237
Wolf, A., 124
Women, as principals, 22–25, 23t
Wong, K. K., 228
Worner, W., 257

York-Barr, J., 70, 81
Young, Ella Flagg, 23, 24b

Zachary, L., 191
Zepeda, S. J., 123, 136